FOUNDED BY BURNS MANTLE

THE BEST PLAYS THEATER YEARBOOK 2004–2005

JEFFREY ERIC JENKINS
Editor

EDITORIAL BOARD
ROBERT BRUSTEIN
TISH DACE
CHRISTINE DOLEN
ROBERT HURWITT
JOHN ISTEL
CHRIS JONES
JULIUS NOVICK
MICHAEL PHILLIPS
CHRISTOPHER RAWSON
ALISA SOLOMON
JEFFREY SWEET
LINDA WINER
CHARLES WRIGHT

PAST EDITORS
(1919-2000)
BURNS MANTLE
JOHN CHAPMAN
LOUIS KRONENBERGER
HENRY HEWES
OTIS L. GUERNSEY JR.

CONSULTING EDITOR
HENRY HEWES

PHOTO EDITOR
ROBERT KAMP

ASSISTANT EDITORS
RUE E. CANVIN, PAUL HARDT, VIVIAN CARY JENKINS

○ ○ ○ ○ ○
○ ○ ○ ○ ○ THE BEST PLAYS
○ ○ ○ ○ ○ THEATER YEARBOOK
○ ○ ○ ○ ○
○ ○ ○ ○ ○

Editorial research and data compilation
for *The Best Plays Theater Yearbook 2004–2005*
has been partly underwritten by a generous grant from
the Harold and Mimi Steinberg Charitable Trust.

Carole A. Krumland, James D. Steinberg, Michael A. Steinberg,
Seth M. Weingarten, William D. Zabel
Directors

THE BEST PLAYS THEATER YEARBOOK 2004–2005

EDITED BY

JEFFREY ERIC JENKINS

Illustrated with production photographs

LIMELIGHT EDITIONS

Published in 2006 by
Limelight Editions
512 Newark Pompton Turnpike
Pompton Plains, New Jersey 07444, USA
www.limelighteditions.com

The Best Plays Theater Yearbook 2004–2005
is dedicated to the memory of Mel Gussow.

A passionate contributor to the *Best Plays Theater Yearbook* for 23 editions, Mel was a tireless advocate for the finest in theater—both in the mainstream and at the margins. Although he was best known for his work in *The New York Times*, he was extremely generous with his time and energy, seeing many productions that lay far beyond his cultural beat in order to explore the possibilities of art and to report those considerations here and elsewhere.

INTRODUCTION

IN EACH OF the past five years, as the current editorial team has made final preparations for sending *The Best Plays Theater Yearbook* to press, we have spent weeks examining the index for correct spelling of personal names, play titles and theater companies. Each time we engage in this extensive process, we are inspired—awestruck, really—by the commitment of the thousands of persons who work in the professional theater in the United States. Playwright Robert Anderson famously remarked that "you can't make a living in the theater, but you can make a killing"—he was speaking of Broadway, of course, where it is still possible to make that killing. It is clear, however, from our surveys of Broadway, Off Broadway, Off Off Broadway and across the USA, that many persons concern themselves with making neither a living nor a killing. These committed theater workers, particularly Off Off Broadway and in smaller resident theaters around the country, focus on making *lives* in the theater—even if the only remuneration is sometimes carfare.

Filling 80 or so pages with more than 12,000 individual citations, the index to this book is an accurate gauge of the artistic ferment in our national theater. We include all Broadway productions, exclusive of benefit performances or the occasional unreviewed concert, and all Off Broadway productions operating eight performances per week in theaters of sufficient size—usually more than 100 seats. Under the Off Off Broadway rubric, we include hundreds of productions ranging from well-known institutional theaters that operate seven (or fewer) performances per week to a broad sampling of professional theatrical productions that thrive beyond the mainstream. In the USA section we try to capture a sense what is happening beyond the provincial confines of New York City: what is new in US playwriting, which classics are being re-thought, who is working in our national theater (and where).

Despite our enthusiasm for our work, errors inevitably occur and they are the bane of a book editor's existence. Unlike daily newspapers, which are instant fodder for recyclers, or websites, which can correct errors but have their own kind of impermanence, millions of books sit on library shelves awaiting reference—and it's a safe bet that there are small errors in each of them. Part of our standard practice is to include among our awards' listings the Theatre Library Association's annual George Freedley Memorial Award for best book about live theater. When Ted Chapin, president of the Rodgers and Hammerstein Organization, received a special jury prize for *Everything Was Possible: The Birth of the Musical Follies* from the association's Awards committee, we thought Chapin's accomplishment should be memorialized. We included the special jury prize with the Freedley award. Unfortunately, the title of Chapin's book was mistyped and a glitch in the indexing program cut off the final word of the (incorrect) title. (The errors occurred on pages 396 and 467, please feel free to correct your copy of the 2003–2004 edition.)

The foregoing reiterates what we have said in this space before: this book is but the second draft of theater history in the US—presuming, of course, that theater journalism is always the first.

II

WHEN THE BEST PLAYS of each season are chosen, little thought is given to an essential theme—until it's time to create this Introduction. Whenever the 10 Best Plays are considered, though, there are always trends that arise to construct a kind of throughline.

In the 2003–2004 edition, last year, it was a pleasant surprise to discover that women were well represented among that season's authors—9 of the 12 authors and co-authors in that season. For the current edition, women are again strongly represented as 5 of the 11 authors or co-authors. Although last season it was easy to discern issues concerning female subjectivity in our cultural life—in *Anna in the Tropics, Caroline, or Change, Intimate Apparel, Living Out* and others—several of this year's plays focus more broadly on the intersections of the public and the private. In each of the 10 plays celebrated in this volume, journeys are undertaken by characters who explore what it means to be human in a world where borderlines between public and private have become increasingly blurred.

In the case of *Guantánamo: Honor Bound to Defend Freedom*—the most openly political of the plays under consideration—that journey is a hellscape of bureaucratic bafflegab accompanied by a litany of abuses committed against incarcerated persons of Arab extraction who are suspected of terrorist leanings. Victoria Brittain and Gillian Slovo's play, which also raises concerns about the long-term global ramifications of US detention policies, was constructed artfully from public documents and private interviews—but it was not the only play with a political bent this season. Michael Frayn's *Democracy*, a hit in London that seemed to get lost in "translation" with its New York cast, examines the intricate bonds between a modern West German leader, Willy Brandt, and his trusted aide who spies for the East Germans. A compelling take on the interpersonal stakes at play in politics—private and public—Frayn's drama (and his fifth Best Play) plumbs the nature of charisma and its impact on those who have it, as well as on those who do not.

David Mamet's work returns to these pages for a seventh time with the quirky farce *Romance*, which takes as its ostensible topics Big Themes of Justice, Peace and Love as they relate to both public and private spheres. Along the way, Mamet manages also to skewer (at times, uncomfortably) the dark biases that inform anti-Semitism and homophobia, among other contemporary prejudices that continue to haunt human relationships. Even Martin McDonagh's typically gruesome *The Pillowman* (his second Best Play) explores the collision of public and private with his dismal vision of a totalitarian state where a writer's grim tales of the deaths of children begin to come true. *The Pillowman* also encourages its audience to question how state-inspired anxiety may become a motivating factor (or its opposite) in the creation of art.

Caryl Churchill's fourth Best Play, *A Number*, likewise centers on a topic of concern that resonates in politics and personal lives. At a time when politicians (and their surrogates) employ ideology to battle scientific progress—even "settled" science—Churchill's play raises ethical issues about the impact of experimentation in genetics as well as the nature of nurture in human development. Beyond the political and the scientific, though, *A Number*'s consideration of cloning also sounds the depths of that quintessential question in modern drama: Who am I? It's the same question faced by Eric Weiss, the title character in Donald Margulies's fourth Best Play, *Brooklyn Boy*. For Weiss, success as a man of letters has come at a cost: a profound alienation from the person he was as a boy and young man—and from the people he loved. As he sorts (literally and figuratively) through his past and present, he grows gradually more comfortable in his own skin.

In Gina Gionfriddo's *After Ashley*, public and private conflate when the tragic death of a young man's mother leads to her becoming an iconic image of the suffering of women everywhere—all in pursuit of tabloid television ratings for the young man's father. The boy, Justin, is forced to confront his demons (including his father) and to take control of their power over him. Along the way, playwright Gionfriddo lampoons the tragedy-based reality television business, an industry that shows no signs of abating. Family dynamics and tragedy also play a role in Paula Vogel's *Hot 'n' Throbbing*, the story of a woman who writes soft-core pornography to support her children and who attempts to make peace with her estranged husband. Throughout *Hot 'n' Throbbing* (Vogel's third Best Play), literature takes on a life of its own as masterworks are interwoven with the playtext while noirish voiceovers unspool the doomed mother's thought-narrative. As the layers of Vogel's play reach the final scene, the audience discovers that much of what has happened may have existed only in the mind of a literature professor reliving the domestic violence of her past as she attempts—in the present—to teach and to balance her evolving identity.

In John Patrick Shanley's *Doubt, a Parable* (his first Best Play), a nun in the 1960s confronts a crisis of conscience when a young priest seems to engage in overly chummy relationships with his younger male charges. Sister Aloysius's journey through the play is one that is easily recognized by anyone who has suffered the ignominious reversals that often accompany certitude. Finally, the public and the private conflate in August Wilson's *Gem of the Ocean* (his ninth Best Play). Although *Gem* ran a mere 72 performances, it is sure to become a classic narrative—and celebration—of the lives of black freemen (and freewomen) struggling to break the oppressive hold of the South. The community created in Aunt Ester's 1903 home brings a sense of peace to African Americans escaping life at the margins of southern society—only to find a similar experience in the burgeoning industrial cities of the North.

Of the Best Plays this year, productions hailing from London and environs have had an impact on our choices: *Democracy*, *The Pillowman*, *Guantánamo* and *A Number* all originated "across the pond." The former two enjoyed Broadway runs while the latter appeared Off Broadway. But the American resident theater circuit was also responsible for supporting and originating four plays (*Brooklyn Boy*, *Gem of the Ocean*, *After Ashley* and *Hot 'n' Throbbing*). Again, the former two appeared on Broadway, but the latter two were produced in OOB runs. After receiving less than stellar reviews—including a particularly shallow and coarse critique in *The New York Times*—*Hot 'n' Throbbing* was closed by the Signature Theatre Company two weeks ahead of time, bringing a celebratory year for playwright Vogel to a rather anticlimactic end. The other two plays of the 10 Best both began Off Broadway (*Doubt* and *Romance*); *Doubt* managed a Broadway run when *Gem of the Ocean*'s producer, Carole Shorenstein Hays—who also produced *Doubt*—pulled *Gem* from the Walter Kerr Theatre and replaced it with the more accessible play by Shanley. (See the Plays Produced on Broadway, Plays Produced Off Broadway and Plays Produced Off Off Broadway sections in this volume for listings and historical reference.)

In addition to the plays celebrated in these essays, we also hope that readers enjoy the volume's expanded statistics and index. Whenever possible we track all Broadway and Off Broadway revivals back to their original presentations in New York, around the country and abroad. In the case of William Shakespeare and others of his ilk, we employ George C.D. Odell's *Annals of the New York Stage*—which links with the *Best Plays Theater Yearbook* series to chronicle New York theater back to the 18th century. We also use the archives of *The New York Times* and other major publications as we attempt to locate plays in their original contexts.

With our colleagues in the American Theatre Critics Association, we also keep close tabs on new plays developing in theaters across the US. Through the Harold and Mimi Steinberg Charitable Trust, we recognize the honorees of the American Theatre Critics/Steinberg New Play Award and Citations. The Steinberg Charitable Trust, which has supported the *Best Plays Theater Yearbook* series since 2001, recently demonstrated its support of our mission by refocusing its commitment to our work. We extend our deepest thanks to the Trust and its board (William D. Zabel, Carole A. Krumland, James D. Steinberg, Michael A. Steinberg and Seth M. Weingarten) for making *Best Plays Theater Yearbook* a priority for their support.

Honorees for the 2005 American Theatre Critics/Steinberg New Play Award and Citations include Craig Lucas's *Singing Forest*, which won the Steinberg top prize ($15,000). Lucas's play is discussed by Misha Berson. The 2005 American Theatre Critics/Steinberg New Play Citations (along with $5,000 each) went to Gina Gionfriddo's Best Play *After Ashley* (detailed here by Elizabeth Maupin), and to Sarah Ruhl for *The Clean House* (essay by Michele Volansky).

III

AS WE MOVE FORWARD with the 86th volume of this chronicle of theater in the United States, we celebrate our ongoing partnership with Limelight Editions, now under the aegis of John Cerullo.

The collection of data for a volume such as this relies on the labors of many people. Our thanks to Paul Hardt for his efforts on the Cast Replacements and Touring Productions section, and to John Istel for his essay on Off Off Broadway theater. After the death of our valued contributor and friend Mel Gussow, to whom this volume is dedicated, Istel has begun a long-term process of rethinking OOB and how this series covers it. Rue

E. Canvin, who has worked on the *Best Plays* series for more than 40 years, continues to make the USA section a "must-read" for those interested in theater around the country. Jonathan Dodd, the longtime publisher of the *Best Plays* series, continues to provide important background information and good advice. Our good friend Henry Hewes, himself a former editor of this series and our invaluable consulting editor, never stops thinking of ways to help improve the series.

We are also deeply indebted to all of the press representatives who assisted in the gathering of information for this volume, but we particularly acknowledge Adrian Bryan-Brown and Chris Boneau of Boneau/Bryan-Brown for their unflagging support of the series and its editors.

Thanks also are due to the members of the *Best Plays Theater Yearbook*'s editorial board, who give their imprimatur to our work by their presence on the masthead. Thanks as well to those who have offered and provided extra support and assistance to this edition: Charles Wright, John Istel, Christopher Rawson, Caldwell Titcomb (Elliot Norton Awards), David A. Rosenberg (Connecticut Critics' Circle Awards), Elizabeth Maupin (American Theatre Critics/Steinberg New Play Award and Citations), Edwin Wilson and Mimi Kilgore (Susan Smith Blackburn Prize), Michael Kuchwara (New York Drama Critics' Circle Awards), Henry Hewes (Theater Hall of Fame Awards) and Allen Hubby of the Drama Book Shop (New Plays and Publications).

We congratulate and thank all of the Best Plays honorees who made the 2004–2005 season so invigorating to contemplate. Victoria Brittain, Caryl Churchill, Michael Frayn, Gina Gionfriddo, David Mamet, Martin McDonagh, Donald Margulies, John Patrick Shanley, Gillian Slovo, Paula Vogel and August Wilson all enriched our lives during the season under review. The photographers who capture theatrical images on film and help keep those ephemeral moments alive for historical perspective are also due thanks for their generous contributions to the greater body of theatrical work. Building on our work from past years, we have included credits with each photograph and indexed the photographers' names for easier reference. Similarly, we continue offering biographical information about each of this volume's essayists and editors in a brief section at the back of the book.

A personal note: In addition to serving as editor of this book, I teach full-time in the Drama Department at New York University's Tisch School of the Arts. In addition to the superb students who inspire me to strive for excellence in my teaching, research, editing and writing, I have the support and friendship of as fine a faculty as I have known. Each member of the senior faculty has, in ways large and small, provided the kind of encouragement one needs to do an annual compendium of critical perspective and historical reference that runs nearly 500 pages. My thanks to Awam Amkpa, Una Chaudhuri, Jan Cohen-Cruz, Laura Levine, Carol Martin and Robert Vorlicky. For the season under review, I especially thank our department chair, Kevin Kuhlke, and our director of theater studies, Edward Ziter, for their continuing support of my work as a teacher, researcher and writer. Thanks also to Amma Ghartey-Tagoe, my excellent teaching assistant during the season under review, for helping to make my work more manageable.

My wife, Vivian Cary Jenkins, continues to serve the theater and *Best Plays Theater Yearbook* as a tracker of what's happening in the New York theater. Although I repeat these thanks each year, one thing remains true: It is largely through her consistent efforts, and her love and support, that the series continues to appear.

JEFFREY ERIC JENKINS
NEW YORK

Contents

THE SEASON
ON AND OFF
BROADWAY

THE SEASON:
BROADWAY AND OFF BROADWAY

○ ○ ○ ○ ○ *By Jeffrey Eric Jenkins* ○ ○ ○ ○ ○

IT WAS ONLY A FEW days after the 2004 Tony Awards when one of the big stories of the 2004–2005 Broadway season emerged. After waging a David versus Goliath election-style campaign for Tony Awards, during which the producers suggested that members of the electorate vote with their "hearts," *Avenue Q* won Tony Awards for best musical, best book and best score. Thus wooed and won, the road presenters—who comprise a substantial bloc of Tony voters and eagerly await Tony Award-winning shows in their theaters around the country—were stunned by an announcement a few days later that the *Avenue Q* producers had signed an exclusive agreement to present the musical in an open-ended run in Las Vegas. As Chris Jones reported in the June 11 edition of *Variety*:

> Producers Kevin McCollum, Robyn Goodman and Jeffrey Seller Fed-Exed hundreds of letters to interested parties that were timed to arrive the same day as the [New York] *Times* story. In the letter, the producers argued they had an obligation to make the best possible deal for their investors. [. . .] By mid-morning, words like "bait and switch" were flowing. As many people saw it, the Vegas deal was carefully kept under wraps until after the Tony Awards so the musical could present itself as the sweet little show that could.

For many Broadway observers, the contretemps signaled the emergence of new concerns about Tony Award lobbying, advertising campaigns aimed at winning awards and the burgeoning Las Vegas theater scene. How those concerns evolve will be tracked in these pages as *Best Plays Theater Yearbook* constructs its year-by-year narrative on theater in this country. For this season, though, the fruits of *Avenue Q*'s 2004 Tony Award victory bore a bitter taste to some producers around the United States.

As the new season got underway, the usual spate of summer closings—some planned, others market-driven—caused several shows to go dark between Memorial Day and Labor Day. One of those productions, Roundabout Theatre Company's *Twentieth Century* (84 performances) closed

BROADWAY SEASON 2004–2005

Productions in a continuing run on May 31, 2005 in bold

Plays honored as Best Plays selections in italics

Best Plays from prior seasons are noted with a date in parentheses

NEW PLAYS (6)
Twelve Angry Men
  (Roundabout Theatre Company)
Democracy
Gem of the Ocean
Brooklyn Boy
  (Manhattan Theatre Club)
Doubt
The Pillowman

NEW MUSICALS (11)
The Frogs
  (Lincoln Center Theater)
Dracula: The Musical
Brooklyn: The Musical
Little Women
Good Vibrations
Dirty Rotten Scoundrels
Spamalot
All Shook Up
The Light in the Piazza
  (Lincoln Center Theater)
Chitty Chitty Bang Bang
The 25th Annual Putnam
  County Spelling Bee

PLAY REVIVALS (11)
After the Fall (63–64)
  (Roundabout Theatre Company)
Reckless
  (MTC and Second Stage Theatre)

PLAY REVIVALS *(cont'd)*
'night, Mother (82–83)
The Rivals
  (Lincoln Center Theater)
Who's Afraid of
  Virginia Woolf? *(62–63)*
The Glass Menagerie *(44–45)*
Julius Caesar
Steel Magnolias *(87–88)*
On Golden Pond *(78–79)*
A Streetcar Named Desire *(47–48)*
Glengarry Glen Ross *(83–84)*

MUSICAL REVIVALS (3)
Pacific Overtures (75-76)
  (Roundabout Theatre Company)
La Cage aux Folles *(83–84)*
Sweet Charity

SOLO PERFORMANCES (6)
Laugh Whore
The Good Body
Whoopi: The 20th Anniversary Show
700 Sundays
Jackie Mason: Freshly Squeezed
Love/Life: A Life in Song
  (Lincoln Center Theater)

SPECIALTIES (2)
Forever Tango
Dame Edna: Back With a Vengeance!

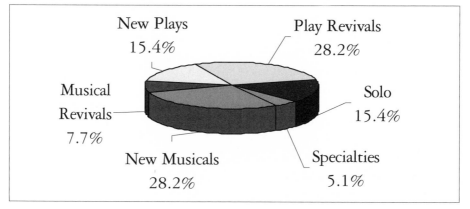

New Plays 15.4%

Play Revivals 28.2%

Musical Revivals 7.7%

Solo 15.4%

New Musicals 28.2%

Specialties 5.1%

June 6—the date of the Tonys—to make room at the American Airlines Theatre for the eagerly anticipated revival of Arthur Miller's *After the Fall* (July 29–September 12; 53 performances). Starring Peter Krause as a man ensnared in a web of women—including a certain needy starlet believed to be based on Miller's ex-wife, Marilyn Monroe—the production failed to match critical expectations. Michael Feingold in *The Village Voice*, called it "a patchy, misguided rendering [. . .] nakedly cynical and artistically irresponsible [. . .] a gesture of contempt toward theater, audience, and play alike." Brendan Lemon in *The Financial Times* (London) was more positive, if tepidly so, when he wrote that director Michael Mayer had "removed almost all the preachiness [. . .] from each of the 1964 drama's three versions and stitched them into a coherent evening." *The Washington Post*'s Peter Marks argued that Mayer's "latest encounter with Miller reveals a slipshod dependence on slickness at the expense of anything close to psychological nuance." Partly due to Krause's fame on the HBO cable television phenomenon, *Six Feet Under*, the production did respectable business during its 12-week run. It is also possible that the premiere of Miller's *Finishing the Picture* at Chicago's Goodman Theatre scheduled for early October—a play loosely based on the author's experiences when Monroe was working on *The Misfits* in 1961 and Miller was the screenwriter—may have contributed to interest in the revival. Miller, who became a significant national figure with the production of *Death of a Salesman* in 1949, died of heart failure February 10, 2005 at age 89. Productive to the end of his life, he had two short stories about to be published when he died. The moralizing tone of Miller's socially committed work lost traction in the shallows of postwar American optimism, but the impact of his *oeuvre*—including eight Best Plays—will long outlast his detractors. He was, as Edward Albee said, "A writer who mattered. A lot." Indeed, he still matters.

Following *Twentieth Century*'s planned closing, nine other productions made Broadway's summer lights a bit dimmer as they closed during the high season for tourists. The long-running *Thoroughly Modern Millie* (903 performances) darkened the Marquis Theatre June 20, and both *A Raisin in the Sun* (88 performances) and *Jumpers* (89) ended their planned runs July 11. As the Republican National Convention loomed on the late-summer horizon, Roundabout Theatre Company also pulled the plug on its electric production of *Assassins* (July 18; 101 performances), the Tony Award-winning revival of the John Weidman and Stephen Sondheim musical about presidential assassins and "wannabes." Weidman told the audience at an American Theatre Wing panel that he had been assured by artistic director

Todd Haimes there were no political implications to the early shuttering of the musical. Given that the show was averaging approximately 95 percent capacity during the final nine weeks of its run—which includes at least two weeks before the revival's Tony Award—that reassurance must have rung a bit hollow to some members of the production's cast and crew.

Manhattan Theatre Club's production of *Sight Unseen* at the Biltmore Theatre—has anyone noticed an acoustical problem in the theater's new, more intimate configuration?—closed July 25 after 70 performances. *Little Shop of Horrors* (372 performances) and *Frozen* (128) made it almost to Labor Day, but closed August 22. Other closings before the Labor Day holiday included the August 29 endings of *Caroline, or Change* (136 performances) and *Sly Fox* (173). The long-running Disney musical, *Aida* (September 5; 1,852 performances), was the final closing of summer. Taken together, the 11 summer closings represent more than a third of all Broadway productions playing when the summer of 2004 began. This was no cause for acute alarm, though, because five of the shows were scheduled as limited runs (*Twentieth Century, A Raisin in the Sun, Jumpers, Assassins* and *Sight Unseen*) and summer has historically been a time for closings—despite the influx of cash-bearing tourists to the theater district. Some of those seasonal tourists must have dropped into the Imperial Theatre to see 2004 Tony Award-winner Hugh Jackman in *The Boy From Oz*, which performed for capacity crowds throughout the dog days of summer and up to the September 12 closing (364 perfomances).

Before the Fall

A WEEK BEFORE *After the Fall* opened, another much-anticipated show broke ground in Lincoln Center's Vivian Beaumont Theater. The first Broadway show of the 2004–2005 season was Nathan Lane's updated version of the Burt Shevelove and Stephen Sondheim musical *The Frogs*—itself an adaptation of Aristophanes—which bore an interesting history. It was first presented, long before Lane was involved in the project, in a swimming pool at Yale University by the Yale Repertory Theatre in May 1974. In the original play, Aristophanes sends Dionysus—Dionysos, in the Shevelove spelling—into Hades to fetch Euripides, until Aeschylus proves himself the greater thinker in an ancient version of a poetry slam. In the Shevelove-Lane version, the Greek god of wine and theater crosses the River Styx to retrieve a more modern poet such as William Shakespeare or George Bernard Shaw (the Bard wins the battle). The production ran into a snag when former *Saturday Night Live* star Chris Kattan, who was to play Dionysos's wise-cracking slave Xanthias, left the show after three weeks of previews "by mutual consent." Kattan was replaced by Roger Bart who had worked with Lane and director Susan Stroman on their hugely successful production of *The Producers* in 2001. Updated with topical references to war and failed political leadership, the hyperactive production—a reflection, perhaps, of Lane's iconic stage persona—had a measure of amusing moments but not enough to keep the usually charitable Elysa Gardner of *USA Today* from observing, "the central conceit is beaten over your head so thoroughly you may need an ice pack afterward." Marilyn Stasio in *Variety* noted that

Nonprofit theaters (and Britons) appear to set the New York theater agenda.

the "political throughline never becomes integral to the book. [. . .] Consequently, Lane and Bart are under the constraint of being funny just for the sake of being funny." *The Frogs* closed October 10 after 92 performances.

Although the past two seasons saw breakout musical hits open in the summer—and some thought *The Frogs* might be next—there was no *Hairspray* (2002–2003) or *Avenue Q* (2003–2004) using the slow months of summer to build a following. (It must be noted that both *Hairspray* and *Avenue Q* had successful tryouts, respectively, in Seattle and at New York's Vineyard Theatre before trying the Main Stem. *The Frogs* opened beneath the white-hot lights of the Broadway media.) Indeed, it would be spring before musicals opened that could qualify as hits, there were four in all, which will be covered below. As the season got rolling, however, Luis Bravo returned to New York with a revival of his celebration of the tango, *Forever Tango*, which first opened on Broadway in the 1997–1998 season. Despite dance critic Jennifer Dunning's claim in *The New York Times* that "sex and danger still shimmer like a summer heat wave beneath the surface of the most traditional dancing" in the show, the heated passions (and physical virtuosity) with which one usually associates the raw language of tango were notably absent from the production. After opening July 24, the production went on hiatus for the month of September and finally closed November 28 after 114 performances.

The final Broadway opening of summer was another of those curiosities known as the "vampire musical." More peculiarly, there are still investors willing to bankroll musicals by composer Frank Wildhorn, even though he has yet to write something that turns a profit on Broadway—not even *Jekyll and Hyde*, which ran 1,543 performances, made money. According to Charlie Suisman in *The New York Times*, though, Wildhorn's lack of critical respect and financial success on Broadway does not deter backers because his "devoted fans" can help the shows "earn money in international, regional, stock and amateur productions, as well as through recordings." With *Dracula: The Musical*, which opened August 19, Wildhorn and his collaborators (Don Black and Christopher Hampton wrote the book) served their audiences a somnambulent machine of a show that Michael Kuchwara of The Associated Press wrote was "an anemic, inert attempt to make the world's most famous vampire sing." But the result was, Kuchwara concluded, "enough to send the poor guy flying back to Transylvania, bat wings flapping." Nevertheless, with $8 million or so invested in the Des McAnuff production, the producers kept the show running for 157 performances before driving a stake through its heart January 2, 2005.

It seemed, in fact, as if the entire Theater District was barely alive for much of the season—at least when it came to opening new productions. Of the 39 productions to open on Broadway this season, 18 of them premiered in the last three months of the season, which made the pickings pretty lean for the middle six months of the season. There were no openings in September, but two plays, a musical and a solo show brightened the lights in October. Of the four October openings, the strongest was the Roundabout Theatre Company's extraordinarily well-acted production of *Twelve Angry Men* (opened October 28), which received extension after extension on its limited run. Featuring Boyd Gaines, Philip Bosco, Larry Bryggman and a host of other veterans actors, the piece was a timely reminder that patience, persistence and careful thought can make a difference in public discourse. Although the 1954 television drama—later made into a theatrical film—easily might have gone the way of a tired civics lesson, New York audiences were impressed with its message of hope for justice in a society often too ready to overlook details and just get on with life. When the production closed May 15, 2005, before a planned national tour, it had completed an impressive 228 performances. The other play to open in October was Craig Lucas's quirky comedy, *Reckless* (October 14), at Manhattan Theatre Club's Biltmore Theatre. Starring Mary-Louise Parker as Rachel, the play focuses on a woman whose husband has hired a killer to murder her on Christmas Eve, which sets in motion a chain of dark adventures and odd happenings that lead Rachel to become a therapist—triggering an even stranger situation. Combining the talents of at least three critical darlings—Lucas, Parker and director Mark Brokaw—the production received largely positive reviews despite the play's insistence on the essential good nature of people, which flies giddily in the face of all evidence to the contrary these days (onstage and off). Parker's natural charm went a long way toward overcoming the play's world view, which several critics noted was better suited to the more intimate surroundings of its 1988 Off Broadway premiere at Circle Repertory Company.

Of the other two October premieres, Mario Cantone's *Laugh Whore* (opened October 24), which chronicled the comedian's life growing up in an Italian family in Massachusetts, was the more satisfying. Cantone's was the first of a handful of high-profile solo shows this season—the others were Eve Ensler, Whoopi Goldberg, Billy Crystal and the perennial Jackie Mason (Dame Edna fits into the specialty category for *Best Plays*'s purposes, surely she would approve). David Rooney in *Variety* perhaps put it best when he wrote that Cantone was "profane and pugnacious," and that he was "supplying more laughs [. . .] than anything else on a New York stage right now." The raw anger that percolates just beneath the surface of Cantone's stage psyche resembles a geyser about to blow at any moment. A collection of tales about his Italian family along with bits from his comedy act, *Laugh Whore* lacked what Rooney called "narrative shape." The show often veered into camp with Cantone's impressions of divas such as Cher, Liza Minnelli and Judy Garland. But the darkly funny stories about his sometimes shady Italian family, Nicki Gostin wrote in *Newsweek*, would make television's Mafia doyenne, Carmela Soprano, "feel right at home." After 66 performances, some of which were recorded for broadcast on the Showtime cable television network, *Laugh Whore* closed January 2, 2005.

Brooklyn: The Musical opened October 21 and became the final show to premiere in the Plymouth Theatre, which was renamed for Shubert executive Gerald Schoenfeld later in the season. Opening to largely negative notices, the production chronicled the difficult lives of street people who have the same kinds of fame-fueled dreams as the thousands of people who audition for *American Idol*, Fox television's reality program that searches for the Next Big Thing in pop music. *Brooklyn*, however, relying on schmaltz ladled by co-creators Mark Schoenfeld (no apparent relation to the Shubert executive) and Barri McPherson sank artistically under its own gooey weight. The background to the musical's creation—collaborator Schoenfeld had himself lived on the streets for a time before a chance reconnection with McPherson—was more interesting than the show's street battles for diva primacy engaged by leading characters. In addition, the characters "made" their "performance" costumes from "found" materials, making the production seem to be done on the cheap—if $7 million can be considered cheap (it can, these days). Ben Brantley in *The New York Times* probably spoke for many theatergoers when he likened *Brooklyn* to a "soot-and-sugar revue bound for Vegas, where it might fit comfortably amid the simulated big-city authenticity of the New York-New York Hotel."

With 10 openings in the final two months of the calendar, audiences could have been forgiven for anticipating some theatrical sparks as the holiday season lay before them. Some sparks came, but not before a disappointing November: there was the bland, Michael Mayer-directed revival of Marsha Norman's taut relationship play, *'night, Mother* (November 14), starring Edie Falco (who plays the aforementioned Carmela Soprano with much more verve); Eve Ensler's sequel (of sorts) to *The Vagina Monologues* titled *The Good Body* (November 15), which took a more global perspective that, oddly, lacked the range and depth of her earlier study of women's bodies in a culture dominated by the male gaze; the 20th anniversary revival of Whoopi Goldberg's explosion into American consciousness, *Whoopie* (November 17); a curiously ineffectual production—some blamed the American cast—of Michael Frayn's fascinating Best Play on the politics of personal destruction, *Democracy* (November 18); and the return of Barry Humphries's amusing performance-art creation, Dame Edna Everage, in *Dame Edna: Back With a Vengeance!* (November 21).

The Broadway picture improved slightly in December with a chilly Roundabout Theatre Company revival of John Weidman and Stephen Sondheim's *Pacific Overtures* (December 2), directed by the talented Japanese director Amon Miyamoto with B.D. Wong in the role of the narrator. Miyamoto had directed a Japanese-language version of the play for Tokyo's New National Theatre in 2000, which was later celebrated for its run at the 2002 Lincoln Center Festival. Ben Brantley in *The New York Times* drew a sharp distinction between the two, writing that the earlier Miyamoto production was "remarkable for its conviction and cohesiveness," but that the new production had "the bleary, disoriented quality of someone suffering from jet lag after a sleepless trans-Pacific flight." Although it's fairly typical Brantley for its too-clever turn of phrase, there was—as there sometimes is—a more serious point embedded. While the production had a certain physical beauty, it ultimately was a lumbering giant with the delicate spirit of a hummingbird. Beyond the production's drawbacks—among other things, it was probably best viewed from the balcony where the audience could better appreciate the scenic effect—*Pacific Overtures* remains an odd exploration of colonial discourse that itself colonizes a certain "Asian" experience.

Billy Crystal's crowd-pleasing nostalgia trip, *700 Sundays* (December 5), delved into the comic actor's personal biography as filtered through the experience of losing his father at a young age. The title of the solo show, which enjoyed a $10 million advance before it opened, refers to the number of Sundays during Crystal's life that his father was alive. In *700 Sundays*, the comedian celebrates all families, which he claims "have the same five relatives. They just jump from [photo] album to [photo] album." For anyone who has followed Crystal's performance career more than casually, there was not a lot of new material in the show. Many of the stories have been told in Crystal's characterizations in television and film or on talk shows when he was interviewed. Clearly, though, audiences were in the mood to have the cockles of their hearts warmed by tales of Crystal's uncle, Milt Gabler, who was a significant producer of African-American jazz musicians, and of little Billy's popularity with artists such as Billie Holiday, who took him to see his first movie. Indeed, Crystal's warm persona and the overwhelmingly positive reviews he received led to a $600,000 single-ticket sales record the day after the opening, according to a December 28 press release from the League of American Theatres and Producers. Extensions kept the limited-run operating through the end of the season, with a closing planned for June 12 in the 2005–2006 season. Crystal received a 2005 Tony Award for best special theatrical event.

The first truly remarkable event of the 2004–2005 season was the opening of August Wilson's latest Best Play, *Gem of the Ocean* (December 6), after a gestational process at theaters such as Chicago's Goodman, Los Angeles's Mark Taper Forum and Boston's Huntington. The process was not without bumps in the road that included a major cast change when the extraordinarily elegant Phylicia Rashad became 285-year-old Aunt Ester—a figure who recurs (offstage) throughout Wilson's 10-play cycle. (Wilson pinned the date of Ester's birth to the 1619 landing of the first African slaves in Virginia—though he suggests in *Gem* that her name is a title handed from one generation to the next.) When director Marion McClinton was taken ill before the Boston opening of the play, Kenny Leon—who had performed the pivotal role of Citizen Barlow, a man with a guilty conscience who hopes for a new beginning in the North—took over the production and guided it to Broadway. Leon is the former artistic director of Atlanta's Alliance Theatre who also directed the 2003–2004 Broadway revival of *A Raisin in the Sun* with Rashad and Sean Combs, a financial, if not critical success. Not long after Leon took the helm, film star Delroy Lindo (*Crooklyn*, *Get Shorty*, *The Cider House Rules*) left the production just before the first Boston performance over "creative differences" and was replaced by gravel-voiced Anthony Chisholm, who had originated the role of Solly Two Kings in Chicago. As the end of the Boston run neared the Broadway financing began to unravel, leaving Wilson's longtime producer, Benjamin Mordecai, scrambling to raise as much as $2 million. Mordecai, a lead producer on the struggling *Brooklyn: The Musical* who had helped to produce eight Wilson productions on Broadway, ultimately dropped out of the production and was replaced by Carole Shorenstein Hays. (Mordecai also may have been suffering from the effects of cancer, of which he died a few months later, May 8, at age 60.) It may be that the true miracle of *Gem* was that it appeared at all on Broadway, given the challenges it faced before opening. But the spiritual power of the play, set in 1904 Pittsburgh, never translated into large enough audiences that would allow the production to run. During its all-too-brief Broadway stand of 72 performances, *Gem* did not reach 80 percent of capacity until the final week of performances, by which time the closing had been announced. For most of the run, the play performed to nearly half-empty houses.

As an opening frame for Wilson's 20th-century cycle (his ninth Best Play), in which the playwright attempts to reclaim historical narrative through the lens of African-American experience, *Gem of the Ocean* recalls Eugene O'Neill's *The Emperor Jones* (1920) in its construction of a mythic collective consciousness. Where O'Neill employed characterization and dialect that reflected the wildly popular minstrel stereotypes of his day, Wilson imagines instead a consciously ritualized revival of spirit aimed at freeing African Americans from the burden of their progenitors' struggle through the "middle passage" in the holds of slave ships. All of this conjuring happens as a gesture of remembrance and honor for the lost souls, and of forgiveness for the living. Surrounding this "soul revival" are scenes in which Wilson reminds his audiences that the white majority historically has used power to drive wedges between members of disenfranchised groups. The playwright calls on African Americans to follow the example of Solly Two Kings and to work within the community to help the community. That one of Solly's acts is to burn a mill, where black workers are unfairly treated, signals the revolutionary impulse that courses throughout Wilson's work—and sometimes alienates (consciously or otherwise) white audiences. But the raw spirituality of *Gem of the Ocean* and the richly textured characters on display ensure the play's legacy as literature. What remains of the ill-fated production at the Walter Kerr Theatre is a lingering suspicion that more aggressive marketing might have helped to turn the production around. Producer Hays moved the proven Off Broadway success, *Doubt, a Parable*, into the Kerr immediately following *Gem*'s closure—*Doubt*'s previews began four weeks after *Gem* went dark. The move drew Hays's pre-closing-announcement comments to *Variety*, reported by Robert Hofler, into sharp relief: "I am a theatrical owner and a producer. I understand the economics. I can look at it from both sides, passionately and dispassionately. There is always a life for a show. We'll see." Sure enough: we saw.

Into the Winter

AS POLITICIANS OF various persuasions squared off in the fall of 2004 to determine who among them was the most militantly anti-gay marriage, Harvey Fierstein and Jerry Herman prepared their musical *La Cage aux Folles* (December 9) for a revival at the Marquis Theatre. By the time *La Cage* opened under Jerry Zaks's direction, the nation had been made "safe" from sanctioned homosexual unions by the presidential election and by anti-gay-marriage amendments that were added to 11 state constitutions around the country (the amendments won in every state where they were proposed, including Oregon). In that environment, would Fierstein and Herman's musical adaptation of a French play about two gay men who run a popular nightclub featuring men in drag—and who have a son about to marry into the family of a moralizing politican—be terribly controversial? Of course not. This is blue-state New York City, a small island off the coast of the United States, where gay men with children have become much more commonplace since the musical first opened in 1983. As Michael Kuchwara of The Associated Press wrote, *La Cage* is "Broadway's favorite family values musical." In fact, though, the musical at times trades on worn stereotypes of gay men that probably aren't very titillating even in Kansas. Whatever voyeuristic edge the show may once have had is diminished now—although Jerry Mitchell's athletic Tony Award-winning choreography was a wonder to behold. Daniel Davis, as the more alpha male, and Gary Beach, as the more feminine of the pair, are each fine performers, but there was a spark missing from the heart of their relationship—Beach had played a similar role, and won a Tony Award, as director Roger De Bris in *The Producers*. The lack of chemistry purportedly extended backstage where there was "friction" between "Davis and other members of the production." After the matinee performance of March 27, 2005, Davis left the show—without comment—and was replaced by his understudy (John Hillner) until Robert Goulet could complete rehearsals for the role. That the production company had Goulet's name ready to announce the morning after Davis's departure indicated that Davis was fired and the producers had Goulet waiting in the wings. (As all of the backstage drama was

OFF BROADWAY SEASON 2004–2005

Productions in a continuing run on May 31, 2005 in bold
Productions honored as Best Plays selections in italics
Best Plays from prior seasons are noted with a date in parentheses

NEW PLAYS (37)
Address Unknown
Fabulation or, the Re-Education of
   Undine (Playwrights)
Comedy 101
The Man Who Would Be King
   (Aquila)
Fiction (Roundabout)
*Guantánamo: Honor Bound to
   Defend Freedom* (Culture Project)
Pugilist Specialist
People Be Heard (Playwrights)
White Chocolate (Culture Project)
Triptych (Irish Rep)
Spatter Pattern (Or, How I Got
   Away With It) (Playwrights)
Trying
Eve-olution
Jewtopia
Two Brothers Who Are Not Brothers
Five by Tenn (MTC)
A Second Hand Memory (Atlantic)
Doubt (MTC)
Rodney's Wife (Playwrights)
Souvenir (York)
Modern Orthodox
A Number (NYTW)
Picon Pie
McReele (Roundabout)
On the Mountain (Playwrights)
The Controversy of Valladolid
   (Public)
Romance (Atlantic)
The Last Days of Judas Iscariot
   (Public/Labyrinth)
Orson's Shadow
Eyewitness Blues (NYTW)
This Is How It Goes (Public)
Moonlight and Magnolias (MTC)
A Picasso (MTC)
Privilege (Second Stage)

NEW PLAYS (*cont'd*)
Beast on the Moon
Memory House (Playwrights)
BFE (Playwrights)

PLAY REVIVALS (14)
The Imaginary Invalid
   (BAM/Comédie-Française)
Comedy of Errors (Aquila)
Othello (Aquila)
Much Ado About Nothing (Public)
Hedda Gabler (NYTW)
Othello (BAM/Cheek by Jowl)
Lysistrata
   (National Theatre of Greece)
Richard III (Public)
The Playboy of the Western World
   (Abbey)
The Foreigner (84–85) (Roundabout)
Danny and the Deep Blue Sea
   (Second Stage)
As You Like It
   (BAM/Theatre Royal Bath)
Happy Days
   (Classic Stage/Worth Street)
Endgame (Irish Rep)

NEW MUSICALS (9)
From My Hometown
The Immigrant
Under the Bridge
The 25th Annual Putnam County
   Spelling Bee (Second Stage)
We're Still Hot!
Altar Boyz
Dessa Rose (LCT)
Captain Louie (York)
Trolls

MUSICAL REVIVALS (4)
The Gospel at Colonus
Cinderella (NYC Opera)

The Pirates of Penzance
 (G&S Players)
Shockheaded Peter

REVUES (6)
Forbidden Broadway Summer Shock!
Let's Put on a Show (Irish Rep)
Absolutely Fascinating
Sondheim: Opening Doors
 (Carnegie Hall)
Newsical
Forbidden Broadway:
 Special Victims Unit

SOLO (14)
Squeeze Box
Plums in New York
The Loves of Shakespeare's Women
Mandy Patinkin in Concert
Nine Parts of Desire (MET)
Dirty Tricks (Public)
Uncle Jacques' Symphony

Who Is Floyd Stearn?
Belfast Blues (Culture Project)
Thom Pain (based on nothing)
The End of the Moon (BAM)
**Woman Before a Glass
Score** (NYTW)
Songs From an Unmade Bed
 (NYTW)

SPECIALTIES (9)
Afterbirth: Kathy and Mo's Greatest
 Hits (Second Stage)
Patriot Act: A Public Meditation
 (NYTW)
Slava's Snowshow
Symphonie Fantastique
Belle Epoque (LCT)
A Tree Grows in Brooklyn (Encores!)
Play Without Words
 (BAM/Center Theatre Group)
Purlie (Encores!)
The Apple Tree (Encores!)

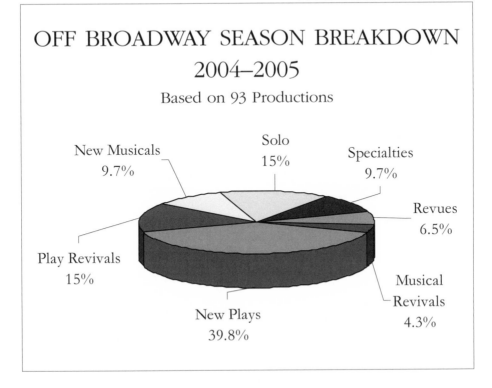

OFF BROADWAY SEASON BREAKDOWN
2004–2005
Based on 93 Productions

New Musicals
9.7%

Solo
15%

Specialties
9.7%

Revues
6.5%

Play Revivals
15%

Musical
Revivals
4.3%

New Plays
39.8%

happening, book writer Harvey Fierstein was down the block, working as the replacement Tevye—for Alfred Molina—in *Fiddler on the Roof,* which he began in January to respectful reviews.)

With the calendar headed for the New Year, one of the brightest lights on Broadway this season began to glow 15 blocks north of the Theater District at Lincoln Center's Vivian Beaumont Theater. Mark Lamos's production of *The Rivals* (December 16), a 1775 comedy by Richard Brinsley Sheridan that sparkled with wit and elegance, demonstrated the timeless quality of the human foibles on display. Although some critics complained that Lamos's staging prevented a wilder production from emerging—Michael Feingold wrote in *The Village Voice* that the audience never gets "the play's full, freewheeling spirit" and David Rooney wrote in *Variety* that Lamos kept "the play's engine at a steady hum where some wild revving might not have been amiss"—it seemed from this corner that Lamos's steady hand allowed Sheridan's text to work its magic. The director's work proved that attention to detail can overcome an audience's much reduced attention spans without resorting to hyperactive antics. The show closed January 23 after a mere 45 performances to make way for the musical version of *The Light in the Piazza,* which would open in April.

The new year ushered a new musical onto the stage in the form of an adaptation of Louisa May Alcott's *Little Women* (January 23) with a book by Allan Knee, music by Jason Howland and lyrics by Mindi Dickstein. Although Knee wrote the book for the short-lived *Late Nite Comic* at the Ritz Theatre (now the Walter Kerr) in 1987 and Howland is an experienced Broadway musical-director, it was Dickstein's first outing on Broadway and the results were not beloved by the critics. There was, however, passing interest from mothers with 10-year-old girls. With the extraordinary Sutton Foster in the central role of Jo, *Little Women* might have been expected to overcome deficiencies in the material. Unfortunately, the estimable director Susan H. Schulman—perhaps best remembered for her innovative 1989 Broadway revival of *Sweeney Todd*—leaned a bit too heavily on Foster, resulting in song after song delivered as defining-moment anthems. As a result, each moment seemed to carry the same weight as every other and the sometimes confusing book did not help matters. When a story's most tragic moment is kept from the stage, it becomes clear that the musical is aimed at young people—and not-very-bright young people, at that. The production closed May 22 after 137 performances without recovering its nearly $6 million capitalization, but the fault does not lie at the feet of the (mostly) male critics who panned the production. A five-month run is arguably long enough for word-of-mouth to affect a show. By mid-April the word was out on the show, which was playing to half-empty houses and could not manage to do better than 42 percent of capacity in the week that ended with Mother's Day.

As the big guns lined up for the March to May push, one of the certifiable disasters of the season opened: *Good Vibrations* (February 2). The production was another in an ongoing trend of so-called jukebox musicals, which mine the catalogs of popular recording artists, string together songs with the flimsiest of plot lines and pray for the financial success of ABBA's *Mamma Mia!* In the case of *Good Vibrations*, producers seem to have rushed a show into production as an option on the music of Brian Wilson and the Beach Boys was about to expire. However it happened, it was a huge mistake with a slipshod book by the often-clever playwright Richard Dresser. Despite the presence of a talented cast, a trip to *Good Vibrations* had the effect of making Brian Wilson fans want to avoid his music until the memory of the musical had faded. The day after the *Good Vibrations* premiere, Donald Margulies's play about a writer who returns home to make peace with his dying father, *Brooklyn Boy* (February 3), opened at Manhattan Theatre Club's Biltmore Theatre. A 2004–2005 Best Play, the piece focuses on the personal costs of success and the ways identities are shed as new ones are developed. Far from being schematic as some have argued, *Brooklyn Boy*'s individual scenes often end quite differently from the way audiences might expect. That Eric Weiss may find his way back to himself, to an integrated sense of identity, may come as no surprise, but it is Margulies's construction of the character's journey that makes the experience worthwhile—and Daniel Sullivan's expert direction of the fine Adam Arkin and terrific company certainly did not hurt.

Like a Lion

THE BROADWAY SEASON roared into full swing with seven openings in March including two musical adaptations of movies (*Dirty Rotten Scoundrels* and *Spamalot*), two play revivals (*Who's Afraid of Virginia Woolf?* and *The Glass Menagerie*), another solo show (*Jackie Mason: Freshly Squeezed*), another jukebox musical (*All Shook Up*) and the transfer of a new play from Off Broadway (*Doubt, a Parable*). In *Dirty Rotten Scoundrels* (March 3), John Lithgow teamed with Norbert Leo Butz to fleece Sherie René Scott of her character's reputed fortune while the men competed for her affection. Most critics compared it unfavorably to that other caper musical made from a film, *The Producers*, finding *Scoundrels* lacking in finesse and execution. More than one critic used a line from the play's final scene, "What you lack in grace, you certainly make up for in vulgarity," to frame arguments about the coarseness of the musical. Anyone reading this type of criticism, might think the critics are completely unaware of contemporary culture, but even competing theater producers could be heard commenting on the show's vulgar nature—apparently thinking Broadway the ultimate in refinement. The truth, from this corner, is that David Yazbek's music was eminently hummable, his lyrics consistently clever. Jeffrey Lane's book made the most of the film from which it was adapted—in fact the 1988 film was based on a 1964 David Niven, Marlon Brando and Shirley Jones comedy, *Bedtime Story*—and director Jack O'Brien kept the action lively so there was no time to think about vulgarity (until critics got back to their writing cubicles). Butz received the Tony Award for best actor in a musical, beating his co-star Lithgow—Butz played the vulgar one, Lithgow the more refined.

Two weeks later, with the opening of *Spamalot* (March 17), some of those same critics seemed to have forgotten their objections to coarseness in the Broadway musical when they typically wrote, as David Rooney did in *Variety*, of the "boisterous energy that appropriately evokes the idea of naughty schoolboys running riot with a budget." Based on the sketch comedy of (and films by) Monty Python's Flying Circus, *Spamalot* not only lampooned the Broadway musical by repeatedly skewering Andrew Lloyd Webber's songwriting—in an ironic twist, Lloyd Webber receives royalties from *Spamalot* because he invested in an underlying film—but it also suggests, as Ben Brantley wrote in *The New York Times*, "what the satiric revue *Forbidden Broadway* might be like if it had an $11 million budget." Yet one is hard pressed to figure out why a song titled "You Won't Succeed on Broadway (If You Don't Have Any Jews)" is any less objectionable than an excitable conman rapping of his desire for a home "where the centerfolds roam." Why are the farting Frenchmen in *Spamalot* classier than the scatological humor of "All About Ruprecht"? It's not that the Monty Python musical wasn't a load of fun, it was (and is), but the critical objections to *Scoundrels* raise issues of a fairly typical New York loathing of the homegrown in favor of almost anything with its roots across the pond. It's a tradition that has been in play in this country at least since the 18th century, when theater managers such as William Dunlap were happier staging European plays than work that celebrated American life. Indeed, those early American plays, such as John Daly Burk's *Bunker Hill*, often were extremely popular with the masses—but early theater managers sought a more elite clientele. It's hard to imagine that the identical issue is in play today, but it is interesting to note the indulgence by critics of British vulgarity over the American brand.

There was little time to consider Anglophilia in the press, though, because Edward Albee's *Who's Afraid of Virginia Woolf?* (March 20) opened at the Longacre Theatre just three days after *Spamalot*. Although Bill Irwin had been tested on Broadway as a replacement for Bill Paxton in Albee's *The Goat, or Who Is Sylvia?*, many wondered if he would be up to the challenge of playing George to Kathleen Turner's Martha. Turner, who is known for her smoldering sexuality and powerful presence, was believed to be too much for Irwin's nice-guy demeanor. As it happened, though, Irwin was a superb balance to Turner and the pair made the duels of a middle-age marriage at a small New England college deeply human, affecting and funny. Irwin was honored with a Tony Award for best actor in a play. David Harbour and Mireille Enos were exceptionally fine as Nick and Honey, the younger faculty couple chasing demons of their own. The direction by Anthony Page was perfectly modulated and served to remind audiences just how small were the minds that comprised the Pulitzer Prize board when it rejected the play in 1963 after it was proposed by the drama jury.

Two days after the *Virginia Woolf* opening, another great American play, Tennessee Williams's *The Glass Menagerie* (March 22), opened at the Ethel Barrymore. Presented by British producer Bill Kenwright, the production featured Jessica Lange as Amanda Wingfield and Christian Slater as Tom. Slater was hired for the production just a few days before the show began previews when Dallas Roberts, the original choice for Tom, was fired. Roberts—a well-respected New York actor who had recently completed a run with Lange's husband, Sam Shepard, in the New York Theatre Workshop production of Caryl Churchill's *A Number*—was ousted for creative differences that included "pursuing a radically different approach," according to *Variety*. By the time critics finished with the production, director David Leveaux may have wished that he too had pursued another angle. Slater's macho take on Tom Wingfield, which vitiated the poetic longing at the core of Williams's acknowledged doppelgänger, might have been more appropriate for a stage production of *On the Waterfront*. But there is no way anyone could lay this production's problems at the feet of the man who stepped into a role and began performing about 10 days later. Seeing the great talent of Jessica Lange derailed by a role that is certainly within her grasp was at times painful to watch. And then there was the "shower curtain." Scene designer Tom Pye hung a large opaque curtain that ran on racket-raising rails. It was used to divide the onstage room, for projections of the absent father's picture on its front and for backlit silhouettes. To all appearances, it was indeed Leveaux who was pursuing a "radically different approach" that proved too alienating for most audience members.

The final three openings in March including the latest evening of solo comedy from Jackie Mason titled *Jackie Mason: Freshly Squeezed* (March 23), the Elvis Presley-inflected jukebox musical *All Shook Up* (March 24) and the transfer from Off Broadway of *Doubt, a Parable* (March 31). Mason's performance of what was billed as all-new material played to 65 percent capacity in its first week of previews and never did that well again during the run; it was his 10th Broadway stand since 1969 when his ill-fated play, *A Teaspoon Every Four Hours*, opened and closed the same night. As for *All Shook Up*, Elysa Gardner of *USA Today* hit the mark when she wrote,

> There are some pretty and potent voices here, to be sure; but their approach to the material tends to range from painfully self-conscious to outright clueless. [. . .] The calculated growls and mannered sneers that sometimes embellish golden oldies such as "Hound Dog," "Don't Be Cruel" and "That's All Right" only add to the false, sterile feel of the numbers.

Others were kinder in their assessments of this pallid imitation of a musical—which delivered the restless energy of Elvis Presley with the force of a limp noodle. Still, it managed to sell respectably well and kept running into the next season. A few days after John Patrick Shanley's gripping Best Play, *Doubt, a Parable*, opened March 31, it received a well-deserved Pulitzer Prize. The 90-minute production's tale of a charismatic young priest who is suspected by a worldly, older nun of taking liberties with the boys in his charge proved to be as potent on the stage of the Walter Kerr Theatre as it was at the Manhattan Theatre Club's more intimate Off Broadway space. The production won Tony Awards for best play, best director of a play, best actress and best featured actress in a play.

April kept pace with the previous month in the number of new productions, if not quite the quality. The month began with a rough-edged production of William Shakespeare's *Julius Caesar* (April 3) featuring film star Denzel Washington as a stiffly brooding Brutus. Director Daniel Sullivan wisely gave Washington his own entrance in a wordless prologue that allowed the actor's whooping fans to express themselves. *Steel Magnolias* (April 4), Robert Harling's play about a group of southern women who socialize in a beauty shop and offer each other support, opened on Broadway more that 15 years after its Off Broadway run, which had overlapped with the release of a 1989 film version starring Julia Roberts, Sally Field, Dolly Parton and others. Besides providing work for the fine cast of Delta Burke, Christine Ebersole, Lily Rabe, Rebecca Gayheart, Marsha Mason and Frances Sternhagen, there is no reason for doing this creaky, retrogressive play.

When news came that James Earl Jones and Leslie Uggams were starring in a revival of Ernest Thompson's *On Golden Pond* (April 7), the first thought that came to mind was "Here we go again, another bit of stunt casting to sell tickets." In fact, though, Jones, Uggams and their fine supporting cast shined a light on a play that, far from being a chestnut, was a poignant reminder of the difficulties involved in being a member of a family. Uggams and Jones made a fine couple, but it was Jones who breathed humorous, vivid life into the crotchety character of Norman Thayer Jr. A few days after *On Golden Pond* opened, Martin McDonagh returned to Broadway with his latest exercise in grotesquerie (and a Best Play), *The Pillowman* (April 10). The title of the play refers to a character in a story written by the play's central character, a writer named Katurian. The writer has been detained by police in a totalitarian state because his horror tales of the deaths of children match a pattern of crimes they are currently investigating. Starring Billy Crudup, Jeff Goldblum, Zeljko Ivanek and Michael Stuhlbarg, the production was a favorite of younger audiences who seemed thrilled by the excess of it all. But the play's larger theme wrenchingly addresses the role of the writer in culture and how much freedom exists now even to imagine the horrifying.

Of the final three plays to open in April, Craig Lucas and Adam Guettel's *The Light in the Piazza* (April 18) became one of the most celebrated of the season, winning six Tony Awards in the musical categories of score, actress, scene design, lighting, costumes and orchestrations. An adaptation of Elizabeth Spencer's novella, the story centers on a wealthy woman, Margaret, touring early 1950s Italy with her brain-damaged daughter, Clara, who falls in love with an Italian boy, Fabrizio. In her relationship with Fabrizio, Clara appears to find the marital happiness that has eluded her frustrated mother—and seems also to elude members of Fabrizio's family. Developed at the Intiman Theatre Company in Seattle, the musical is notable as history for the Broadway bow of composer Adam Guettel, son of Mary Rodgers and grandson of Richard Rodgers, which gave the production bloodlines of theatrical royalty. Although critics and audiences were enthusiastic about the humanity of the subject matter—to some extent a reaction against the jukebox shows and self-referential parodies—they were divided over *Piazza*'s shortcomings: Which was better, the book or the score? The bulk of Tony Awards voters clearly voted that the score was worthy of honor, but as Michael Feingold argued in *The Village Voice*, "the music doesn't define either events or characters strongly, [and] the overall effect is more nebulous than gripping." In *Variety*, David Rooney concurred, "It's the music that seems ill-conceived and unsatisfying. [. . .] Too often, also, Guettel's lyrics seem to run out of steam, either drowning in the lush orchestrations or dissolving into light operatic vocalise, which furthers the sense of underscore masquerading as score." The book also had drawbacks, though, that made audiences wonder how any of the situations occurring onstage might have happened. Who would let her at-risk daughter get into a relationship like this one, particularly in 1953? Bookwriter Lucas would have us believe that because of her own miserable romantic life, the mother would be willing to take such a big chance on her own daughter's happiness—and that a bourgeois Italian family would go along with it. There are, ultimately, too many gaps in the tale, too many instances in which the audience reasonably must ask itself, "Why?" As a result, certain overheated musical passages seem designed to bridge the gaps without answering the questions. With those questions on the table, though, it's worth noting that some naysayers have revisited and revised their opinions—as often happens with award-winning, hit shows. Never in dispute, however, was the remarkable melding of actor and character in casting the superb Victoria Clark in the role of Margaret Johnson. Clark received the Tony Award for best actress in a musical for her portrayal.

The other two April openings were *A Streetcar Named Desire* (April 26) and *Chitty Chitty Bang Bang* (April 28). Roundabout Theatre Company's *Streetcar* featured the luminous Natasha Richardson as Blanche Dubois and independent-film star John C. Reilly as Stanley Kowalski in the second production of a Tennessee Williams play directed by a Briton this season. Edward Hall, son of legendary director Peter Hall, seemed unable to channel the anger that lies beneath the surface of Reilly's usual Joe Lunchbucket characters into Stanley's untamed, earthy sensuality. The talented Chris Bauer was a sturdy Mitch, but it was impossible not to think that it was a role better suited to Reilly. Lovely Amy Ryan struck just the right notes as sensual, knowing Stella. Richardson, a vision in white on her first entrance, could have used an actor more versatile than Reilly to help her performance soar—her husband Liam Neeson, for instance. *Chitty* was a dark musical import from London that featured Jan Maxwell as a sexy, scene-stealing Baroness opposite bigger-than-life Marc Kudisch as the Baron. The story about a wacky, widowed inventor (Raúl Esparza) with children is ultimately an excuse for a flying car to whiz out over the heads of folks in the first rows of the audience. Kevin Cahoon's creepy childcatcher was a character that seemed far too weird for a family musical and parents all around cringed when the proto-pedophile appeared.

As the Tony Awards deadline approached, the final four shows of the Broadway season opened. Brian Stokes Mitchell's *Love/Life* (May 1) was a

90-minute cabaret show that performed only eight times when *Piazza* was dark at Lincoln Center. David Mamet's *Glengarry Glen Ross* (May 1), which received the 1984 Pulitzer Prize but lost the Tony Award that year to Tom Stoppard's *The Real Thing*, was a crackling presentation of the male animal as he struggles for survival in competition with others. It offered some of the best acting on Broadway in years, though it also brought to mind the superb ensemble in *Twelve Angry Men*. Alan Alda brought a new depth to the characterization of pathetic Shelly Levene, but it was Liev Schreiber as Richard Roma who made the drama sizzle. When the dust settled the production won Tony Awards for best play revival and for Schreiber as best actor in a play. When Second Stage Theatre mounted a Rachel Sheinkin and William Finn musical about a spelling bee earlier this season, few people could have thought that it would end up on Broadway. *The 25th Annual Putnam County Spelling Bee* (May 2) turned out to be a pleasant little musical with relatively low overhead—no stars, a fairly simple set—and a wide appeal. Focusing on the alienated, gently geeky lives of the young people who fall under the thrall of correct spelling, the musical struck a chord with critics and audiences alike.

The final production of the Broadway season was the revival of *Sweet Charity* (May 4) that had been on-again/off-again for several years. Jenna Elfman was first mentioned to play the dance-hostess-with-a-heart-of-gold before Marisa Tomei landed the part for a New York workshop. Director Walter Bobbie dropped out of the workshop and was replaced by Timothy Sheader, but Bobbie later returned. Tomei was in turn replaced by Tony Award-winner Jane Krakowski, who feuded with book writer Neil Simon. After Krakowski departed, producers Fran and Barry Weissler—who apparently weren't reading the warning sings from the theater gods—hired Christina Applegate. Known for her work on the television program *Married With Children*, Applegate had limited theater experience but underwent an audition process and had begun a series of out-of-town tryouts when she broke her ankle in Chicago. Her standby, Charlotte d'Amboise, went on for her and played in Boston to decent notices, but the producers decided to close the show. Then, *The New York Times* reported, Applegate spent a weekend on the telephone with producer Barry Weissler making a "passionate and compelling case for moving forward with the Broadway plans." Weissler was impressed enough by her persistence to open on Broadway with the still-healing Applegate. The audience seemed to hold its breath when she danced—in specially crafted boots that provided support—but she handled the footwork with aplomb and received a lot of credit for her "show must go on" attitude. Unfortunately, *Sweet Charity* was already old-fashioned when it premiered in 1966 and time hasn't been kind to it. Despite some updating of Neil Simon's book and changes made to the score by Cy Coleman before his sudden death November 19, 2004, at age 75, the musical had little of the sparkle needed to help it succeed. Applegate, on the other hand, showed herself to be a real trouper. She even made fun of herself at the 2005 Tony Awards by strutting onto the stage to perform and then "falling" into a pit before going on with the show.

By the Numbers

WHEN THE SEASON came to an end this year, Broadway attendance had once again broken the 11 million mark (11,527,767)—ranking 2004–2005 as the fourth highest attendance in the past 20 years. (It is worth noting that *Best Plays Theater Yearbook* relies on figures provided by the League of American Theatres and Producers and on those published in *Variety*'s seasonal totals. The League's figures, as published in *The Demographics of the Broadway Audience 2004–2005*, take into account a 13-month season based on June to June, which does not match the June-to-May rubric of *Best Plays*. Whenever there is a discrepancy, *Best Plays* uses figures provided by individual production companies, which must report accurately to investors.) In fact, were it not for the 53-week season in 2003–2004, a calendrical anomaly that occurs every seven years, this season would have ranked third. In terms of box-office income, this season's second-place ranking at $768,555,109 would have likewise moved up a place to first except for the seventh-year anomaly that preceded it. In their end of the season overview, *Variety*'s Robert Hofler and David Rooney noted that average ticket prices rose only $.20 over the previous season. This increase is a dramatic slowdown from the price increases of the previous five seasons, which averaged $3.16 per year. Hofler and Rooney also noted that the increased sales for "premium" tickets—those double- and triple-price orchestra tickets that are often available on the day of the show—seemed to have little impact overall on increased average prices. Although total attendance as a percentage of capacity declined for the season by 1.4 percent—from 80.5 to 79.1—Broadway theater attendance is still greater than the combined home attendance for the six New York-area professional baseball, basketball and football teams (whose average ticket prices would, of course, be much higher).

Of more interest here than dollars and cents, are the trends in new production on Broadway and off. (The Broadway season breakdown and chart is located on page 4; Off Broadway information is located on pages

14 and 15.) Of the 39 new Broadway productions this season—marking a steady increase over the past five seasons—6 were new plays. Although this represents a decline in quantity from the previous season when 10 new plays premiered, it is certainly an improvement in quality. The previous season included such plays as *Six Dance Lessons in Six Weeks* and *Prymate*, among other ignominious entries. Five of the new plays were named Best Plays, while the sixth, *Twelve Angry Men*, was "new" only in the narrowest of definitions—its lack of a New York professional run is what allows *Twelve Angry Men* onto our new list. Over the past five seasons, the average number of new plays each season was 7.6—these numbers and those to follow are all figured solely under the rubric of the *Best Plays Theater Yearbook*, except as otherwise noted—an average skewed somewhat by the 2003–2004 season's unusually high number of new plays. The number of play revivals on Broadway increased by one, from 10 to 11, bringing the five-year average to 9.8 per season. Of the 11 play revivals this season, 8 were former Best Plays and 2 were classics (*The Rivals* and *Julius Caesar*). As a result, it can be seen that Broadway play production overall this season (17 plays) was just under the five-year average of 17.4. Given the growing proportion of solo productions (6 productions, or 15.4 percent) and specialties (2 productions, or 5.1 percent), neither plays nor musicals represent a statistical majority of new productions on Broadway—and there are probably those who would argue (reasonably) that jukebox musicals might be better included in the specialty figures. As a percentage of total production, plays represented 43.6 percent, a decline from last season's dominance at 52.6 percent.

There was a sharp increase in new musicals this season to 11 from 7 in the previous year. Two of those 11 were of the jukebox variety, *Good Vibrations* and *All Shook Up*. For all of the concern over the proliferation of the jukebox genre—three are scheduled for the 2005–2006 season—they comprise a relatively small number of the total for the past five seasons (although, admittedly, they seem to be on the rise). Of the 36 new Broadway musicals over the past five seasons, only 9 were jukeboxes and that's if we include shows such as *Taboo, Never Gonna Dance, Movin' Out* and *A Class Act*. Although these four shows to greater and lesser extents mine the catalogs of Boy George, Jerome Kern, Billy Joel and Edward Kleban, only *Movin' Out* seems straightforwardly from the jukebox model—due to Twyla Tharp's ingenuity, however, it is another thing altogether. The jukebox issue aside, Broadway musicals—according to figures based on breakdowns provided by the League—account for approximately 82 percent of total Broadway attendance over the past five seasons. Even if new-play production on Broadway has a slightly higher five-year average than new-musical production, more intimate venues, smaller audiences (unless the cast includes a film star) and limited runs keep plays—new and revived—at the margins of the Broadway business.

In a *New York Times* article after the 2004–2005 season, Jesse McKinley noted the decline of success among musical revivals, "the list of recent money-losers reads like a syllabus for a college musical theater survey: *Gypsy* (2003), *Little Shop of Horrors* (2003), *Man of La Mancha* (2002), *Oklahoma!* (2002), *Into the Woods* (2002), *Bells Are Ringing* (2001), *42nd Street* (2001)." McKinley found that producers increasingly believe musical revivals to be too risky. Producer Barry Weissler told McKinley, "The first tier" of well-known musicals, "you can keep doing over and over again, if you cast [. . .] properly. You really shouldn't mess with the secondary or the tertiary." There have been only 21 musical revivals over the past five seasons, which are barely enough to have a contested Tony Award category: all three musical revivals were nominated this season. In the last season to have only three musical revivals, 2001–2002, two of the three were nominated (which really must have stung the production team of *One Mo' Time*).

It isn't only Broadway having a diffcult time with musical revivals. Over the past five years, there have been merely 10 Off Broadway musical revivals. (City Center Encores! performances are considered in the Off Broadway specialty category.) In the 2001–2002 and 2002–2003 seasons, there were none. Of the 10 over the past five seasons, four have been Gilbert and Sullivan operettas, and two were New York City Opera stagings of legitimate musicals (*Cinderella* and *Sweeney Todd*). The other four were *The Gospel at Colonus*, *Shockheaded Peter*, *Godspell* and a 2003 revival of a 2002 production of *The Prince and the Pauper*. This season's revival of *Shockheaded Peter* (February 22), which is based on an gruesome 19th century children's book, titillated the critics again on its way to playing 112 performances at the Little Shubert Theatre. The unimpressive statistics on Off Broadway musical revivals over the past several seasons, however, belie the generative energy coming from Off Broadway where 9 new musicals and 37 new plays had their New York premieres during the 2004–2005 season.

Although the total of new Off Broadway productions declined by two this season to 93 from 95, Off Broadway production on the whole seems to have rebounded from the five-year low of 78 productions in the post-terrorist attack season of 2001–2002. Despite the challenges faced by the Off Broadway community during the 2001–2002 season, there still were 44 productions of new plays, marking a high point for the past five seasons.

The 2002–2003 season, which followed the September 11 season, saw a precipitous drop in Off Broadway new-play production to 30 new plays, a 32 percent decrease. Due to plucky producers such as Scott Morfee and others, however, the new-play producing category is working its way back. Morfee's production of Tracy Letts's *Bug*, it was noted here last year, battled the odds to stay afloat during the last half of the difficult 2003–2004 season and managed to keep operating into the season under review. When the show closed January 30, 2005, after 384 performances, it had recovered its costs, but as Morfee told *The New York Times*'s Jesse McKinley, "It took us pretty much the whole ride to recoup." This season, Morfee shepherded a production of the Austin Pendleton play, *Orson's Shadow* (March 13), into the Barrow Street Theatre, where *Bug* also ran. With 90 performances to its credit at the end of the season, the production was a lively telling of artistic encounters between Orson Welles, Kenneth Tynan, Laurence Olivier, Vivien Leigh and Joan Plowright. Critic John Heilpern of *The New York Observer*, a Tynan acolyte, complained in print about the (mis)characterization of Tynan, but others were amused. The capable cast included *Bug* playwright Tracy Letts as Tynan.

Real estate continues to be a concern for producers at every level of theater production, but it has always been a special problem for Off Broadway. These days, however, several new venues have arisen even as venerable old spaces have fallen to the wrecking ball. During the 2004–2005 season, the Variety Arts Theatre on Third Avenue between 13th and 14th Streets was closed and scheduled for demolition, as were the John Houseman and Douglas Fairbanks Theatres on 42nd Street between 9th and 10th Avenues. The new Off Broadway spaces to open in recent years include the Little Shubert Theatre on West 42nd Street, the Acorn Theatre at the Theatre Row Theatres on West 42nd Street, the "A" space at 59E59 Theaters on East 59th Street, three new theaters in a $28 million complex called 37 Arts on West 37th Street and Dodger Stages, a five-theater complex on West 50th Street. Besides these theaters, there are numerous other, smaller new theaters in the Off Off Broadway range of 99 and fewer seats. What remains to be seen is whether these fine new spaces can be kept operating with high overheads typical of renovated (or new) spaces in New York.

Off Broadway Commerce

NINE IS A NUMBER that figures prominently in the tally of Off Broadway commercial productions this season. There were nine holdovers from previous Off Broadway seasons still running when the 2004–2005 season ended May 31, 2005. Of those holdovers, *The Musical of Musicals—The Musical* had the shortest run by the season's end (321 performances) due to production hiatus on two separate occasions. The other way that "nine" figures into the mix is in the number of new 2004–2005 productions still running at the end of the season, which means that there were 18 commercial Off Broadway productions running as of May 31, 2005. There were also four nonprofit productions running at season's end, all of which were in limited runs and scheduled to close within weeks of the new season's beginning June 1, 2005. (See Plays Produced Off Broadway section of this volume for details.)

Although this strong showing at the end of the season—of 22 productions running Off Broadway at the end of the season, 18 were commercial entities—might seem as if it were positive news for commercial Off Broadway producers, it is the same number of commercial holdovers from the beginning of the season. With openings and closings along the way, new commercial production is essentially flat. This season, commercial production accounted for only 38 percent of total Off Broadway production. None of the commercial productions were play revivals: The most recent commercial play revivals Off Broadway were *Passion Play* and *Uncle Bob* in the 2000–2001 season.

In addition to *Orson's Shadow*, mentioned above, other new commercial plays—a term used advisedly for many of these shows, *Orson's Shadow* first played at Chicago's Steppenwolf Theatre Company in 2000—that managed to continue their runs at the end of the season included *Jewtopia*, *Picon Pie* and *Beast on the Moon*. Each of these plays center on issues of ethnic identity and how those identities intersect with American culture. In *Jewtopia* (October 21), a comedy by Bryan Fogel and Sam Wolfson, a gentile wants to marry a Jewish girl so he won't need to make decisions for himself, causing him to undergo a makeover to help him "pass" as a Jew. Awash in stereotypes that would be offensive if they were indulged by an actual gentile, the show opened a few weeks before another play about Jewish marriages, Daniel Goldfarb's *Modern Orthodox* (December 6). The Goldfarb comedy dealt only somewhat more sensitively with love and marriage issues of concern to Orthodox Jewish couples and to Jews who are more reform-minded. Featuring a talented cast in Craig Bierko, Molly Ringwald, Jason Biggs and Jenn Harris, *Modern Orthodox* was withdrawn after a respectable 205 performances. The more joke-laden *Jewtopia* had 254 performances as of May 31, 2005, and continued into the next season. In *Picon Pie* (February 17), a biographical play with music about the legendary Yiddish theater star Molly Picon, Rose Leiman

Goldemberg constructs a sentimental tale that follows the contours of the well-known fantasia of attaining the American Dream on the stage (or screen). Barbara Minkus originated the role in California and played it Off Off Broadway in New York for several months until June Gable replaced her before the commercial transfer to the Lamb's Theatre. Richard Kalinoski's *Beast on the Moon* (April 27) was honored by the American Theatre Critics Association in 1996 as a work by an emerging writer. Addressing the fallout of the Armenian genocide on new Americans attempting to build new lives, the drama demonstrates (at least as sentimentally as *Picon Pie*) the need to let go of the past in order to move toward the future.

If these commercial plays appear unchallenging, it is fairly understandable given the risks of Off Broadway production this season. Of the other six new plays in commercial production, only two (*Pugilist Specialist* and *Eve-olution*) seem to evince the world in which we live today. Adriano Shaplin's *Pugilist Specialist* (September 17), created in collaboration with the Riot Group, was a taut drama on a bare stage about a military team out to kill a leader in the Mideast at a time when American adventures in that region were under a great deal of scrutiny. *Eve-olution* (October 20), by Hilary Illick and Jennifer Krier, addressed the concerns of ambitious, educated middle-class women who are torn over being relegated to the Mommy Track. Although the play focuses on the angst of the privileged, as directed and designed by the talented wife and husband team of Carolyn Cantor and David Korins, the production managed to entertain and make its audiences ponder the progress of women over the past several decades. Other commercial productions offered certain satisfactions, such as *Address Unknown* (June 10), Frank Dunlop's adaptation of a 1938 novella about business partners whose relationship is ruptured when one becomes enamored of Nazism (the other is Jewish). Jim Dale played Max Eisenstein, the German-Jewish partner in a San Francisco art gallery who remains in the US when Martin Schulse (William Atherton) returns to Germany to make sure his sons get a German education. Told in rather static, epistolary form—which is difficult to sustain even for fine actors such as these two—*Address Unknown* closed August 22 after 85 performances uptown at the Promenade Theatre. Another commercial production at the Promenade that provided a demonstration of acting talent was Joanna McClelland Glass's *Trying* (October 13). First presented at Chicago's Victory Gardens Theater in the previous spring, *Trying* was a slight detailing of the relationship between a young woman (based on the author) and the celebrated jurist Francis Biddle near the end of the latter's life. What gave the sentimental piece currency was to see the superb Fritz

Weaver on the stage once again—he was 78 years old when the play opened in New York. The production played 94 performances before closing January 2.

Of the 9 new musicals to open Off Broadway this season, 6 were produced commercially (*From My Hometown, The Immigrant, Under the Bridge, We're Still Hot!, Altar Boyz* and *Trolls*). Different versions of *From My Hometown* (July 22) have bounced around New York and the US since 1998, when it was first presented at Milwaukee Repertory Theater. Three African-American men who represent the musical traditions of their hometowns—Memphis, Detroit and Philly—combine forces to form a singing group. The production played 36 performances at the Gramercy Theatre before closing August 21. Based on Mark Harelik's similarly titled 1985 play, *The Immigrant* (November 4), with music by Steven M. Alper and lyrics by Sarah Knapp charted the struggles of a Russian Jew in 1909 Texas who balances assimilation with the need to retain his identity. The earnestness of the musical's theme failed to strike a chord with New York audiences and the piece was withdrawn November 28 after 29 performances at Dodger Stages. Kathie Lee Gifford wrote the book and lyrics to *Under the Bridge* (January 6), which opened at the Zipper Theatre with music by David Pomeranz. Based on the children's book *The Family Under the Bridge*, the musical's focus on the homeless prompted barbs from critics who had seen enough of the dispossessed on the stage this season (see *Brooklyn: The Musical*). The main complaints against Gifford's project, though, were its lack of focus and overweening cuteness. *Under the Bridge* closed February 20 after 54 performances. Although *We're Still Hot!* (February 15) seemed as if it might have been "inspired" by the long-running *Menopause: The Musical*—which opened Off Broadway in 2002 and had performed 1,336 performances as of May 31, 2005—the earliest presentation of record for the latter was in an August 2001 run in West Palm Beach. *We're Still Hot!* had its first performance in Vancouver in 1998, when it was still known as *Menopositive! The Musical*. Featuring an original book and lyrics by JJ McColl, with music by McColl and Rueben Gurr, *We're Still Hot!* was an entity distinct from *Menopause: The Musical*. There was, alas, room for only one Off Broadway musical about the challenges of women in middle age. *We're Still Hot!* closed May 8 after 96 performances at the Theater at St. Luke's. *Altar Boyz* (March 1) transferred to a commercial run at Dodger Stages after a successful outing in September 2004 at the New York Musical Theatre Festival. More of a concert than a musical, the piece tells the story of a boy band whose members have gospel names such as Matthew, Mark, Luke and Juan; there is also a Jewish member named Abraham. With a book by

Kevin Del Aguila, music and lyrics by Gary Adler and Michael Patrick Walker, the piece gently spoofs the rising tide of Christianity in the US even as it capitalizes on it. By the end of the season, *Altar Boyz* had amassed 105 performances as it continued into the next season. Bill Dyer and Dick DeBenedictis's musical, *Trolls* (May 19), focuses on the difficult love lives of gay men over 40, the "trolls" of the title. As of May 31, it had performed 15 times at Actors Playhouse and continued into the summer.

Off Broadway Art

SPEAKING TO A GROUP of producers from Broadway and nonprofit theater institutions in 1974, the year he retired from overseeing the arts-granting activities of the Ford Foundation, W. McNeil Lowry said, "There is not necessarily a dichotomy between Broadway and art, but there is a dichotomy between commerce and art." What Lowry said about commerce and art still rings true more than 30 years later, partly because of the exigencies present whenever the profit motive comes into play when making theater. The drive to return a profit often prevents investment in theater works that exist at the margins—and even mainstream theater is at the margin of our society, which prizes instant electronic access: film, television, internet.

The "new media universe," in fact, was part of the reason that *The New York Times* undertook a controversial makeover of its arts section this season. According an e-mail from one senior *Times* editorial staffer involved in the process, the old format, which included fairly comprehensive (and free) theater listings in the Sunday paper, was now "redundant" and the space "might be better used for actual coverage of the arts." The dropping of free listings, however, was just one part of changes such as the elimination of the Friday theater column—which seemed to acknowledge Michael Riedel's dominance at the *New York Post*—the addition of reviews of shorter lengths (with few or no production details) and the inclusion of Sunday features that became perceptibly more flippant and personality-oriented. Protests by theater professionals, who sent petitions, held town-hall meetings and complained bitterly in public at every opportunity, seemed to have some small influence when a modified version of the listings returned. Overall, though, the changes demonstrate the rub between art and commerce. Media outlets are shrinking their coverage of the arts and the *Times*—with the most expensive theater-advertising space on the planet—is following suit while insisting that less is more.

Some argue that the nonprofit theater—in New York and across the country—has merely become the development arm of the commercial theater. While that may have been one of the things that Lowry was hoping to forestall, of the 18 new plays or musicals appearing on Broadway this season all except four had their first appearance in a nonprofit theater. The same trend holds true for new plays and musicals Off Broadway. In the season under review, nearly 68 percent of new plays Off Broadway were produced by nonprofit theaters. The brief survey of nonprofit Off Broadway companies that follows, however, shows very few works that might be considered to have commercial prospects.

The nonprofit Off Broadway season started with the opening of Lynn Nottage's *Fabulation or, the Re-Education of Undine* (June 13). It opened at Playwrights Horizons on the same day that her critically hailed *Intimate Apparel*, from the 2003–2004 season, closed at the Roundabout Theatre Company's Harold and Miriam Steinberg Center for Theatre. It could hardly be argued that a comedy about an African-American woman who loses everything and must face life at the margins of society was developed for a commercial run. In Kate Whoriskey's production, Charlayne Woodard let the audience peer into the experience of a black woman in modern urban America. Although not as poignant as *Intimate Apparel*, *Fabulation* provided a telling comic glimpse at how the notion of "expectations" in life can change in a heartbeat. As the Playwrights Horizons season unfolded, six more productions opened to greater and lesser degrees of artistic success. In *People Be Heard* (September 23), a "comedy with songs" by Quincy Long and Michael Roth, a single mother (and stripper) finds herself dealing with a son who is withdrawn from reality. Oddly, she is appointed to her semi-rural school board where she becomes a voice of reason in favor of the teaching of evolution. The comic possibilities seemed promising, but the production condescended to nearly every character, making it difficult to root for anyone. Neal Bell's *Spatter Pattern (Or, How I Got Away With It)* (October 10), a murder mystery of sorts, demonstrated the writer's skillful use of dialogue. As *The Village Voice*'s Michael Feingold wrote, "there are no handy moral tags in the dialogue to explain the play, and the more you unpack its events, the more troubling they become." *Rodney's Wife* (December 1) was the latest work from the gifted Richard Nelson, who also directed the piece. Set in 1962 Rome, where an American actor (played by David Strathairn) attempts to revive his shriveling career, the play deals with betrayals large and small that come to a family focused on one person. Unfortunately, it's fairly easy to tell where the big betrayal will manifest itself long before it happens. Christopher Shinn's *On the Mountain* (February 24) featured the lovely Amy Ryan as a mother with a hidden rock and roll past. A younger man (Ebon Moss-Bachrach) who has taken an interest in the woman ultimately reveals himself to be a rock fan in search of an artifact. Dianne Wiest starred in Kathleen Tolan's *Memory House* (May 17), in which a mother bakes a blueberry pie while her adopted daughter carps about being taken from her home country—all of this as the daughter is supposed to be writing a college-entrance essay. Wiest's charming way with the text (and the pie) could not overcome the singular bitterness of the daughter's character. Julia Cho's *BFE* (May 31) has as its title initials that stand for Bum Fuck Egypt, which implies a location beyond nowhere. In the play, a 14-year-old girl named Panny yearns to break free of the stultifying life she experiences in a suburban desert.

Roundabout Theatre Company began its Off Broadway season at the Harold and Miriam Steinberg Center for Theatre with Steven Dietz's *Fiction* (July 25) in which two writers, a married couple, spar over the details of their relationship, their careers and the nature of reality. A recognizable stroll through marriage in middle age, the play was filled with witty lines—ably handled by Julie White and Tom Irwin—but ultimately showed the writer's intent a bit too soon. It was, however, a pleasant ride. Next up was a serviceable revival of Larry Shue's *The Foreigner* (November 7), which provided an amusing vehicle for Matthew Broderick's patented nerdy guy who rises to the challenge. Without this cast—Broderick, Frances Sternhagen, Neal Huff, Byron Jennings, Mary Catherine Garrison, Kevin Cahoon and Lee Tergeson—the rather thin play is probably not worth doing. Stephen Belber's *McReele* (February 24) centered on a convicted killer who convinces a journalist to help obtain his release. The convict, an African American, becomes well known for his political views before going on to become a candidate for office. Over the course of the play, McReele changes himself to suit his situation, which shows him to be a natural politician.

This was the season for change at the artistic helm of the Public Theater. In November 2004, Oskar Eustis was named to replace George C. Wolfe and a rather smooth transition seems to have taken place. The Public's season started as it does every year in Central Park when the company's New York Shakespeare Festival presented *Much Ado About Nothing* (July 13) starring Jimmy Smits, Kristen Johnston, Sam Waterston and other notable actors. Despite the seeming perfection in casting Johnston as sharp-tongued Beatrice, there was little spark between her character and Smits's Benedick. The fall brought another Shakespeare production that warned of stunt casting when it was announced that Peter Dinklage, a dwarf actor, would play the title role in *Richard III* (October 11). Dinklage, however, was more than up to the task in the role. Peter Dubois's somewhat overheated (and underrealized) production, on the other hand, was not. A few days after

Richard III opened, the estimable Judith Ivey opened a solo show in the Public's Anspacher Theater, *Dirty Tricks* (October 20). The monologue by John Jeter replicates the loose-lipped madness of Martha Mitchell when her husband, John Mitchell, and his boss, Richard Nixon, were sweating out Watergate. The monologue is a thin bit of theater; Ivey was her marvelously versatile self. *The Controversy of Valladolid* (February 27) was a timely piece about the ultimate futility of colonial projects. Translated by Richard Nelson and based on a teleplay by Jean-Claude Carrière, the play is staged as a papal debate regarding the relative humanity of native peoples. Stephen Adly Guirgis's *The Last Days of Judas Iscariot* (March 2) was a compelling joint presentation of the Public and the Labyrinth Theater Company. Directed by Philip Seymour Hoffman, the play centers on a re-trial of Judas to see if it is possible to release him from damnation. Unfortunately, Eric Bogosian had the best lines as Satan—the bad kids are always the cool ones, aren't they?—and the play could have used a trimming. Neil LaBute's *This Is How It Goes* (March 27) marked the season's final production with a stellar cast of Amanda Peet, Ben Stiller and Jeffrey Wright performing the playwright's typically disconcerting study of men in all their shades of ugliness.

The Culture Project, under the direction of Allan Buchman, continued producing Off Off Broadway theater but also presented three Off Broadway productions this season: *Guantánamo: Honor Bound to Defend Freedom*, *White Chocolate, Belfast Blues*. Victoria Brittain and Gillian Slovo's *Guantánamo* (August 26) was named a Best Play for its riveting tale of geopolitical gamesmanship set against the suffering of ordinary people. William Hamilton's *White Chocolate* (October 6) was an uncharacteristically frothy piece for the Culture Project that addressed the tired notion of what might happen to a white couple who awaken one morning to find that they are black. Geraldine Hughes's *Belfast Blues* (January 20) was a world-touring solo memoir of the bleak existence of Catholics in Northern Ireland.

The Irish Repertory Theatre, as is the case with companies such as Atlantic Theater Company, Classic Stage Company, Signature Theatre Company and others, often does not present shows on a eight performance per week basis, which is the dividing line for Off and Off Off Broadway. This season, however, the company launched its Off Broadway season with a revue featuring Mickey Rooney and his wife, Jan, *Let's Put on a Show* (August 10). The production focused on Rooney's legendary career and life, logging 40 performances before closing September 12. Edna O'Brien's *Triptych* (October 7) featured Margaret Colin, Ally Sheedy and Carrie Specksgoor in a drama about three women who love, from different perspectives, the same man. Artistic director Charlotte Moore staged a revival of Samuel Beckett's *Endgame* (February 24) with Tony Roberts and Alvin Epstein. Epstein, of course, was in the first New York production of the play in 1958.

Manhattan Theatre Club seemed to shed its "cursed" season of 2003–2004 when the new Off Broadway season got underway. The company presented an evening of delicate one-acts titled *Five by Tenn* (November 11) that were culled from recently discovered works by Tennessee Williams. Most of the work was interesting from a purely academic perspective, but Michael Kahn's conventional staging did little to heighten the theatricality of the work, always a major concern of Williams's. John Patrick Shanley's *Doubt, a Parable* (November 23) enjoyed much acclaim, a Broadway transfer and piles of deserved awards—all for a 90-minute play that asks its audience to consider the costs of certitude. Ron Hutchinson's *Moonlight and Magnolias* (March 29) was a madcap comedy about the rewriting of the script for *Gone With the Wind*. Working from a thin premise, director Lynne Meadow wrung more comedy from the play than it was reasonable to believe possible—with ample assistance from the cast of Matthew Arkin, David Rasche, Douglas Sills and Margo Skinner (who died, sadly, two weeks after the opening). Jeffrey Hatcher's *A Picasso* (April 19), with Dennis Boutsikaris and Jill Eikenberry, examined the loyalty of the artist to certain political perspective when his art is threatened.

With *A Second Hand Memory* (November 22), Atlantic Theater Company premiered another Woody Allen play. Unlike the company and Allen's 2002–2003 collaboration on two one-acts titled *Writer's Block*, this latest play was a full-length piece in which three men in one family make bad choices (and bad marriages) while a woman in their family provides a ghostly commentary for the proceedings. The brilliant Elizabeth Marvel was the narrator, and director Allen cast Michael McKean, Dominic Chianese and Kate Blumberg in other key roles. Allen's stage directorial strengths are slight and he would do well to find a director he could trust so that his stage plays might find more felicitous shapes. David Mamet, a co-founder of the company, returned with a Best Play, *Romance* (March 1). As directed by company artistic director Neil Pepe, *Romance* was a fast-paced farce that meditated—not too deeply or for too long—on themes such as peace, justice, anti-Semitism, homophobia and love. Along the way, Mamet shocked his audience—a good trick at this point in his career—with outrageous slurs that perhaps only he could write with relative impunity.

As York Theatre Company's holdover production of *The Musical of Musicals—The Musical* took the occasional production hiatus before settling into a run at Dodger Stages (February 10), the group prepared two productions for the 2004–2005 Off Broadway season. Stephen Temperley's *Souvenir* (December 1), a play with music, lampooned the "singing" career of Florence Foster Jenkins (no relation). Jenkins (Judy Kaye) was a wealthy woman who "heard" music beautifully in her head, but when it came from her mouth it was painful for her audiences to hear. Ultimately, audiences attended her performances and encouraged her to sing—according to her accompanist, Cosme McMoon (Jack F. Lee)—in order to laugh at her. It's a sad story probably better forgotten, but it is undoubtedly destined for a future life. With Anthony Stein and Stephen Schwartz's *Captain Louie* (May 8), the company revived a children's musical first presented in 1983 by the First All Children's Theatre—a group that included the 2004–2005 creative team.

New York Theatre Workshop jumpstarted its season with an evening of political commentary accompanied by feats of prestidigitation. Media critic Mark Crispin Miller was joined by magician Steve Cuiffo to discuss the current state of affairs in pre-election 2004. *Patriot Act: A Public Meditation* (June 22) probed around the edges of George W. Bush's psyche, explained why Miller is terrified of the Christian Right (and why everyone else should be) and illustrated how the president's press conferences might work better with background music by The Who. Ivo van Hove returned to the theater with a stunning production of *Hedda Gabler* (September 21). Located in a huge, bright-white minimalist room, Elizabeth Marvel's Hedda was a font of sexy, unrestrained id. When her Hedda committed mayhem, it was clear from whence it came. Caryl Churchill's meditation on what constitutes identity, *A Number* (December 7), saw the conversion of the theater from a large white cube (*Hedda Gabler*) into a semicircular operating theater—complete with large overhead searchlight—where the audience could watch a man and his son(s) attempt to unwind genes from consciousness. Sam Shepard and Dallas Roberts were the fascinating father and son. Roberts played the three sons and managed to make each one distinct. *Eyewitness Blues* (March 21) was a tale by Mildred Ruiz and Steven Sapp using vignettes, poetry and music. The theater's season ended with two solo shows that operated in a type of repertory. The first, *Score* (May 1), was a SITI Company production that offered a reconstructed look at the genius of Leonard Bernstein. Performed by Tom Nelis, who also played opposite Peter Dinklage in *Richard III*, the piece was a typically energetic work directed by Anne Bogart. In *Songs From an Unmade Bed* (May 24), Michael Winther performed songs about love and loss as experienced by a gay man living in the city.

It was a mixture of programming for Second Stage Theatre in 2004–2005. The company began the season by offering the latest version of Mo Gaffney and Kathy Najimy's perspective on the world, *Afterbirth: Kathy and Mo's Greatest Hits* (June 17). The duo of comic actors had presented an earlier version of their good-natured satires of American gender roles at Second Stage in 1986. Even before *Doubt, a Parable* opened at Manhattan Theatre Club (November 23), it was already a John Patrick Shanley season in New York. Earlier that month Labyrinth Theater Company presented Shanley's *Sailor's Song* (November 7) in an Off Off Broadway production at the Public Theater. A few days after *Sailor's Song*, Second Stage presented a revival of *Danny and the Deep Blue Sea* (November 10), Shanley's dark exploration of a couple who are emotionally damaged goods. Despite the warning signs, they get involved in what appears to be an explosive relationship—we never know for sure because Shanley stops the play at the end of their beginning. Second Stage also premiered one of the most successful musicals of the season *The 25th Annual Putnam County Spelling Bee* (February 7), which charmed the critics and transferred to Broadway (see above). In the new-play department, Second Stage presented Paul Weitz's *Privilege* (April 25), a poignant story of two brothers whose father (played by television star Bob Saget) is indicted for insider trading causing the boys to lose everything—except each other.

With four productions on its Broadway stage this season, Lincoln Center Theater managed only two productions Off Broadway. In *Belle Epoque* (November 21), Martha Clarke and Charles L. Mee collaborated to create a dance-theater piece along the lines of their *Vienna: Lusthaus*. The latter production was a Lynn Ahrens and Stephen Flaherty musical, *Dessa Rose* (March 21). The musical focuses on two southern women—one white, the other black—who never meet, but each deal with the consequences of slavery in the antebellum South.

Still Breathing

OF THE 14 Off Broadway play revivals this season, 6 have been mentioned as parts of various companies' seasons. But it is worth reiterating that all of the play revivals were presented by nonprofit organizations. The 2004–2005 season marks a high point in the number of play revivals Off Broadway over the past five seasons. It also represents the highest percentage of the total Off Broadway output (15 percent) for any of those five years. These figures might be cause for concern, if the companies presenting the revivals ordinarily had done new plays. In fact, though, all of the companies represented in the play revivals category have a history of that type of work. There were five Shakespeare plays represented, although *Othello* was presented twice this season: once by Aquila Theatre Company (June 10), which also produced *Comedy of Errors* (June 1); and once by the English troupe Cheek by Jowl at the Brooklyn Academy of Music (October 5). BAM also offered the Theatre Royal Bath production of *As You Like It* (January 18), directed by Peter Hall. Indeed, BAM had started the season of play revivals with the summer opening of the Comédie-Française's production of *The Imaginary Invalid* (June 9). Other revivals included touring productions of *Lysistrata* (October 6) from the National Theatre of Greece and *The Playboy of the Western World* (October 26) from the Abbey Theatre. Finally, Classic Stage Company co-produced Samuel Beckett's *Happy Days* (February 15) with Worth Street Theater Company.

In addition to the Off Broadway solo productions mentioned above, Susannah York brought her touring production of *The Loves of Shakespeare's Women* (August 18) to town, Mandy Patinkin (September 20) returned with another of his concert, and Laurie Anderson performed a piece at the Brooklyn Academy of Music based on her tenure as artist-in-residence at NASA, the space agency, titled *The End of the Moon* (February 22). The total number of solo productions to open Off Broadway this season declined by a third from the previous season, but three in particular—not covered by the companies mentioned above—stood out. Heather Raffo's *Nine Parts of Desire* (October 9) took as its inspiration Geraldine Brooks's 1994 book of the same name. After performing the piece at the 2003 Edinburgh Fringe Festival, Raffo presented it at the Bush Theatre in London. In the solo piece, Raffo, an American whose father is Iraqi, portrays nine different Iraqi women seeking respite from the oppression of war, privation and Muslim men. Raffo received Lortel and Drama League Awards for her work. The show was presented 246 times by the Manhattan Ensemble Theater before closing May 22. Will Eno's *Thom Pain (based on nothing)* (February 1) was first workshopped at the Soho Theatre in London before a successful run at the 2004 Edinburgh Fringe Festival. Eno, a protégé of Edward Albee's, had earlier received plaudits for *The Flu Season*. During *Thom Pain's* Edinburgh run, the British press was deeply impressed with the existential angst of his solo piece about a man who, steeped in his own misery, cannot quite see his own problems as worthy of concern. The normally reserved Charles Isherwood, writing in the *The New York Times*, dubbed Eno "a Samuel Beckett for the Jon Stewart generation." Echoing the playwright's own rhythms, Isherwood insisted that theater patrons, "Run, don't walk. Four stars. Plus an extra. If you care about theater, blah blah blah. If you only see one show Off Broadway this season, etc." Although the critic was signaling his approval, he also engaged in the self-ironizing negation that makes Eno's character by turns charming and a bore. Charlotte Stoudt thoughtfully objected, in *The Village Voice*, to the play's studied quirks when she noted, "smirky asides appear lazy—and all too often. The first barely amuses; by the fifth, we're way ahead and wondering what time it is." At one performance, nearly two months into the run, an audience mostly comprised of presumed *New York Times* readers—late in middle age, chic, moneyed—sat nonplussed for 70 minutes and then, annoyed, grilled each other about what in the hell it meant as they departed. As Isherwood suggested, it was a scene that may well have played when Parisians in 1953 departed *Waiting for Godot*. Or not.

Mercedes Ruehl's performance in *Woman Before a Glass* (March 10) well might have been included in the commercial Off Broadway section. Although produced by commercial partners at the Promenade Theatre, the Lanie Robertson solo performance piece was commissioned by Primary Stages, the Off Off Broadway company led by Casey Childs and Andrew Leynse. Ruehl's powerhouse performance of wealthy art (and artist) collector Peggy Guggenheim managed to capture as Marilyn Stasio wrote in *Variety*, "what a cruel looking glass never could: [. . .] her inner beauty." The play details her sexual escapades but, as Michael Feingold noted in *The Village Voice*, "it becomes something more than the usual biographical solo show with its and-then-I-screwed recitation of a parade of gossipy facts." As a result of the felicitous pairing of actor and play, the piece had accumulated 94 performances by May 31; it continued into the next season.

Revues and specialty acts have been essentially flat in terms of new Off Broadway productions over the past five years. There were 6 revues and 9 specialties that opened this season; both of those numbers are identical to the previous season's tally. In addition to the Mickey and Jan Rooney revue at Irish Repertory Theatre, the Forbidden Broadway production company opened two new shows this season: *Forbidden Broadway Summer Shock!* (July 5) and *Forbidden Broadway: Special Victims Unit* (December 16). The topical revue featuring the women of Fascinating Aïda returned to Off Broadway with *Absolutely Fascinating* (September 26). Carnegie Hall presented a revue of Stephen Sondheim's work titled *Sondheim: Opening Doors* (October 5) that was first presented in London under the title *Moving On* (2000). *Newsical* (October 7), a revue based on current events, capitalized on the popularity of Jon Stewart's *The Daily Show* and the coming 2004 election—not to mention considerable New York frustration over its outcome—to manage a 254-performance run at Upstairs at Studio 54.

Specialty acts are those theatrical experiences that do not fit comfortably into the play, musical or solo categories. As mentioned above, the City Center Encores! concerts are considered specialties. Basil Twist returned with his water-tank puppetry in *Symphonie Fantastique* (September 6) at Dodger Stages, running through the holidays on the way to 126 performances. Matthew Bourne brought his *Play Without Words* (March 15) to the Brooklyn Academy of Music. A dance-theater piece focusing on 1960s decadence in London, Bourne's work first premiered at London's National Theatre in 2002. The specialty production that made the biggest splash, however, was a hit at the 1996 Edinburgh Fringe Festival before touring to the US and Canada. *Slava's Snowshow* (September 8) opened at the Union Square Theatre six or seven years after it had been mentioned for a 1998 New York engagement by Dodger Productions. The brainchild of master clown Slava Polunin, *Snowshow* employed a small cadre of clowns to explore the magic, majesty and darkness at the core of human life. A former member of Cirque du Soleil, Polunin is less likely to embody sad-eyed Emmett Kelly than Charlie Chaplin. Some thought it a Beckettian experience: Vladimir and Estragon in *Waiting for Godot* might well agree. By the end of the season, *Slava's Snowshow* had played 304 performances and continued into the next. And so, from here, shall we.

THE BEST PLAYS
OF 2003–2004

2004–2005 Best Play
2005 ATCA/Steinberg Citation

AFTER ASHLEY
By Gina Gionfriddo

○ ○ ○ ○ ○

Essay by Elizabeth Maupin

ASHLEY: Don't get married until you're thirty. Thirty-five. You don't know who you are in your twenties. Try not to get a girl pregnant, but if you do, have an abortion. It's not the end of the world. You'll be traumatized for like two days but then you'll get over it.

JUSTIN: Did you have an abortion?

ASHLEY: No, but I could have and . . . Look, I love you more than anything. You're the only good thing in my life. But I was twenty-one and I didn't know myself and I didn't know your dad at all; we'd been dating like a couple of months—a little longer . . .

JUSTIN: So I'm an accident?

ASHLEY: Yeah, should I not have told you that?

JUSTIN: I'm not sure.

ASHLEY: Am I screwing you up by telling you this?

JUSTIN: I don't know yet.

"TORN FROM THE HEADLINES" has a transitory feel, like an easy dismissal. Here today, gone tomorrow. Easy come, easy go. But there's more to Gina Gionfriddo's dark comedy *After Ashley* than her incisive satire of America's infatuation with victims, true-crime stories and Court TV. Gionfriddo understands the delicate push-and-pull between parent and progeny, the unhappy circumstance in which a child must play father to the people who gave him birth. If she continues to marry her sardonic lampoons of modern culture with her compassion for such characters as the muddled Ashley and her preternaturally grown-up teenage son, Gionfriddo's plays should have long and happy lives.

In *After Ashley,* the shrewd, troubled Justin Hammond finds himself the sole voice of sanity in a suburban world that is thrown off-kilter when

Too much information: Dana Eskelson and Kieran Culkin in the New York production of Gina Gionfriddo's After Ashley. *Photo: Carol Rosegg*

his unhappily married mother, Ashley, is murdered and his father becomes the host of a television true-crime show. While his father, the self-righteous Alden, uses Ashley's death to further his own career, Justin becomes famous as the "911 Kid," the boy whose recorded phone call to an emergency operator is sampled in a rap song and makes him the flavor of the month—the celebrity victim of his mother's death.

Gionfriddo's play was the runaway hit of the 2004 Humana Festival of New American Plays at Actors Theatre of Louisville, and it came to New York in early 2005 in a celebrity-laden Off Broadway production at the Vineyard Theatre, featuring glamour-kids Kieran Culkin and Anna Paquin directed by Steppenwolf Theatre's Terry Kinney. *After Ashley* won a $5,000 ATCA/Steinberg New Play Citation that same spring, and Gionfriddo collected a Guggenheim Fellowship and an Obie Award grant as "distinguished emerging playwright" for the 2004–2005 theater season.

Like most youngish playwrights in the contemporary theater scene, Gionfriddo, who is in her mid-30s has been "emerging" for quite a while. By the time she received an MFA from Brown University in 1997 as a student of Paula Vogel's, she already had been a finalist in Actors Theatre of Louisville's National Ten-Minute Play Contest and the winner (in 1996) of the first Lucille Lortel Playwriting Fellowship.

In 2002 her play *U.S. Drag* won the prestigious Susan Smith Blackburn Award, presented annually to a woman playwright, and the Helen Merrill Award for emerging playwrights. But *U.S. Drag,* a comedy about Gen-X materialism and competitiveness, has had only two productions—one Off Off Broadway by Clubbed Thumb and the other at the Connecticut Repertory Theatre. *Guinevere,* which received a staged reading at the O'Neill Playwrights Conference in 2001, has had none.

Let's honor the (female) victim by memorializing her to death.

IT WAS THE EVENTS of September 11, 2001, that first gave rise to her breakout play, *After Ashley*, a commission from the Philadelphia Theatre Company. Gionfriddo has said that her plays begin with a moral or ethical dilemma "and from there characters present themselves." In this case, she was moved to write after witnessing the media's take on the September 11 attacks and their aftermath—after noticing that media coverage began restrained and respectful but quickly turned exploitative.

"Would we—God forbid—become jaded to 9/11 due to overexposure and over-immersion?" she said to a Vineyard Theatre interviewer in early 2005. But Gionfriddo reacted to September 11 in a way similar to other contemporary playwrights who treat horror with humor—notably Vogel, her former teacher, who used the same technique in her 1992 dark comedy about AIDS, *The Baltimore Waltz.*

As Gionfriddo has said, her views of the political became personal—that is, they became part of one very specific story about a teenage boy and his world. *After Ashley* begins quietly, but hilariously, with 14-year-old Justin sick with mononucleosis and his 35-year-old mother Ashley bored and out of sorts. They're watching the worst kind of television talk show, a fatuous psychologist named Dr. Bob, and their desultory conversation is right on target, just the kind of talk you'd expect from a bright, testy 14-year-old and his sad, self-indulgent mother.

> DR. BOB: (*Voiceover*) . . . and I will say to you . . . what I say to patients in my private practice. There are five things you need to

know to get yourself a life license. You ignore these rules and you are living without a license and you will be pulled over, you will find yourself stalled on the expressway while the other drivers speed ahead. [. . .]

Justin sees right through the guy: "This man is an idiot," he says flatly. But Ashley buys into it.

ASHLEY: That's not helpful, Justin. These people have incompatible sex drives and they are asking for help. What should they do?

JUSTIN: They should stay home. They should have some dignity.

Dignity, though, is foreign to the restless Ashley, and she presses her son to entertain her—to tell her who he's "messing around" with, to have a sex talk or a drug talk or . . . *something*.

ASHLEY: . . . I just have been feeling like something's got to change, you know? OK, I know you hate Dr. Bob, but he talks about, you know, traveling without a map and I feel like that's exactly what I did. I—I didn't use a map and now here I am and it's all wrong and the choice is keep going or exit and—

JUSTIN: Can you talk about this without road metaphors?

Youthful disaffection: Kieran Culkin and Anna Paquin in the New York production of Gina Gionfriddo's After Ashley. *Photo: Carol Rosegg*

It turns out that Ashley thinks that Justin's father, a bleeding-heart newspaper reporter, has turned out to be a phony, and she needs something else in her life. When Alden enters, we see why: He's earnest, humorless and oblivious to his family's needs. Alden has met a schizophrenic homeless man at a Starbucks and has offered him a job doing yardwork. That offer sends Ashley fleeing from the house.

Then both the stage and the mood turn very, very dark. In voiceovers, we hear Justin talking to a 911 operator. His mother is in the basement, he says. Someone "did something to her." There's blood everywhere.

> OPERATOR: (V.O.) OK, if you believe this person may still be in the house, you need to leave—
>
> JUSTIN: (V.O.) I'm not leaving her! She's my mother!

WHEN THE LIGHTS come up, three years have passed. Alden has written a best-selling true-crime book called *After Ashley*. Justin, now 17, has become an angry young man.

Father and son appear on a talk show that focuses on the survivors of violent crimes, and Justin is out of control. He makes fun of the title of the sanctimonious host's own book, *A Crime Against Hope*. He disagrees vehemently with his father's whitewashed memories of Ashley. And, in his disingenuous way, he claims to the host—a self-important man named David Gavin—that he doesn't mind Alden's dedicating the book to the murderer's mother.

> JUSTIN: Not at all, David. I understand that my drug and alcohol abuse and, of course, my hospitalization and arrests impeded the completion of the book. Arlene, on the other hand, contributed childhood stories about the man who hammered my mother's head in. Arlene provided that extra special something that elevated the book from true crime pulp to American epic. So, in answer to your question about the dedication, I'm fine with it.

Alden banishes Justin to the car and, in turn, finds himself the recipient of a job offer—to host a sex crime program on a television network for women. The idea, David says, is to reenact the crimes—tastefully, of course.

This is JonBenet Ramsey territory, Laci Peterson territory: Let's honor the (female) victim by memorializing her to death. Alden is all for it, and he doesn't mind the move to Central Florida, where the show will be shot. Justin says he'll go along with the move—provided he gets his own apartment, a car and an ample allowance. His self-serving father agrees to the plan.

THE SCENE SHIFTS to a Central Florida bar, where Eminem's song "Stan" is playing in the background and Justin is nursing a beer. Gionfriddo has spoken of her own fascination with the song, about celebrity worship gone sour, in which the fan of a rock-star turns violent when the star doesn't acknowledge his existence.

In the bar Justin meets a girl named Julie, who seems determined to have what he calls a "bonding experience." She's a college student, an English major, and Justin sizes her up instantly:

> JUSTIN: You . . . cut gym class to smoke cigarettes and read . . . Sylvia Plath. The lesbian gym teacher—we'll call her Jean—she's like, "Julie put down *The Bell Jar* and go play kickball." So you go. You get out there in your little black shorts and your Nine Inch Nails babydoll tee and you . . . you wince as boy after boy kicks the ball at you. You stand . . . still, but not indifferent, pummeled by the kickball . . . taunted and jeered at . . . too alienated and lethargic to just kick the fucking ball—
>
> JULIE: Wow.
>
> JUSTIN: I'm dead on. Right?
>
> JULIE: No.
>
> JUSTIN: Did you cut gym to smoke?
>
> JULIE: Yeah, but—
>
> JUSTIN: BINGO.

It turns out both that Julie has what Justin calls "like, a functioning brain in her head" and that she knows he's the 911 Kid—that she's coming on to him because he's a celebrity victim. Justin calls her the "c" word. And then he takes her home.

ACT II BEGINS with the fictional rap song "Down to Mother," the one that samples Justin's 911 call. Justin and Julie are sharing a hostile morning after: He's still combative, and she's feeling persecuted. But when they put in a videotape of Alden's show—with its neo-Gothic reenactment of a rape, prettified into a *Dark Shadows*-style seduction—they find a kind of common ground, or at least a way to talk.

Americans don't know how to grieve, Justin says. Rather than revere the people they have lost, rather than be quiet, they turn their loved ones into media celebrities.

So is Justin's solution, Julie asks, silence?

> JUSTIN: I don't have a solution. But shutting the fuck up would be a start.

Daddy dearest: Grant Shaud and Kieran Culkin
in the New York production of Gina Gionfriddo's
After Ashley. *Photo: Carol Rosegg*

When Alden drops in, the two youngsters can unite, in a way, against a common foe. At first Julie is impressed by Alden's television-host status. But Alden has news—that a local philanthropist wants to put Ashley's name on a spa-like shelter for battered women, the "Canyon Ranch of women's shelters." Justin goes off once again.

> JUSTIN: My mother was killed by a homeless person! Putting her
> name on a SHELTER is not an appropriate tribute!

After Alden leaves, Justin confides in Julie. He has a journal of Ashley's, and in it she reveals that she participated in orgies with strangers, orgies that were videotaped. Justin thinks it's his fault: He told her to find something to do with her time, and what she found was a sex cult.

But he knows what to do with the information—to use it to stop the shelter scheme. He and Julie decide to get in touch with Roderick, the guy who directed the sex videos, and to use him to dynamite the plan.

> JULIE: You really think your mom having freaky group sex would
> bring down Ashley House?

JUSTIN: I think the only way to save her is to trash her. Do you think that's crazy?

JULIE: No, I don't.

As the scene changes, we hear the fictional rap "Down to Mother" again—and Gionfriddo suggests, in the stage directions, that our growing sick of hearing the 911 call might not be a bad thing.

A few days later, the sex-cult guy, Roderick Lord, comes to call. Gionfriddo has fun with Roderick, who is both smug and slimy, the kind of self-impressed lowlife who turns up with his face partially blacked out on the cover of *The New York Times Magazine*. He's like a bad Mickey Rourke movie, Justin tells him—a "Marquis de Sade from the suburbs."

Roderick has the tape Justin wants, but he'll hand it over only if Justin and Julie let him direct them—and videotape them—having sex. Justin balks, but eventually, in a sequence that's both creepy and comical, the two of them agree to it.

The scene jumps to dedication day at Ashley House. *60 Minutes* is there for a story, and the situation clearly is all about the glorification of the center's donor, and not Ashley's memory. Justin pretends to Alden that the videotape he's about to show is one of Ashley at his fifth birthday party. He shows the sex tape. Pandemonium ensues.

The scene shifts one last time to Justin and Julie, settling down on folding chairs beside a lake. Justin asks Julie if they're breaking up. It seems he got drunk, insulted her friends and got them thrown out of a bar.

JUSTIN: You and your fucking friends just come at me with all these expectations of who I am—

JULIE: Yeah, you're absolutely right. We do. We expect you to, like, make small talk without being abrasive and insulting . . . (*Pause*) Look. If you don't want to date me, no hard feelings. But say that. Stop hiding behind what happened to your mom.

Justin admits he's been approached by MTV to be part of a reality show of his own—"in a house with five other contrasting personalities and have me be the one who kicks the TV in and gets voted out of the house."

JULIE: But you said no?

JUSTIN: Of course I said no. I just ruined my father's life because he wanted to be a TV star. It'd be pretty fucked up if I started taking meetings, don't you think?

He apologizes for his behavior: Since Ashley died, he has taken on all of her worst qualities, from smoking pot to picking fights. Julie understands.

JULIE: It isn't you. (*Pause.*) Look, your dad's book is dishonest and all those things you say it is, but the title is . . . (*Pause.*) There has to be an after Ashley, you know? You do have to let her die.

(*Pause.*)

JUSTIN: OK. Now would be one of those times when I choose silence.

JULIE: Great. Silence is great.

IN THE ACTORS THEATRE of Louisville production, designer Paul Owen kept the production spare, as Gionfriddo's script directs, and artistic director Marc Masterson—a last-minute fill-in for associate artistic director Timothy Douglas, who pulled out 10 days before opening because of "artistic differences" with the playwright—found the fluidity and easy humor in the play.

The stylized minor characters seemed only barely larger than real life—especially the unctuous, John Walsh-like television producer (Frank X) and the smarmy Roderick (a clever Jason Pugatch). Stephen Barker Turner and Sabrina Veroczi did what they could with Alden and Julie, roles that came across merely as foils to Justin. But Carla Harting was a riot as the careless Ashley, and a charismatic acting apprentice named Jesse Hooker found in Justin all the necessary sweetness behind the rage.

The critics were mostly tickled by the smart production of a smart, pointed script. The *Chicago Tribune's* Michael Phillips called the play "a supple black comedy" and described Gionfriddo as "purveyor of some of the most stageworthy comic dialogue—glib, but not dopey—heard in several moons."

That kind of enthusiasm wasn't quite so plentiful 10 months later with the New York production. In *The Village Voice*, Michael Feingold said of Kinney's direction that it "catches the feeling Gionfriddo evokes, but doesn't do much to deepen or enhance it." Mark Rosenthal's Roderick and Dana Eskelson's Ashley came on too strong, Feingold wrote. But he and other critics praised Paquin's Julie and especially Culkin's empathetic Justin.

And, like those who reviewed the Louisville production, the New York critics found plenty to like in Gionfriddo's script. Despite some reviewers' qualms—a tendency to fall back into "tedious satire," an imbalance stemming from "having one foot in intimate realism and the other in borderline parody"—both the play's cleverness and its insights came across. American audiences may have been desensitized to such horrors as violence, disease and war. But the way through our deadened feelings, Gionfriddo seems to say, is through wit sharp as a knife. *After Ashley* cuts right through.

2004–2005 Best Play

BROOKLYN BOY

By Donald Margulies

○ ○ ○ ○ ○

Essay by Michael Feingold

ERIC: I've come to see that Houdini and I actually have more in common than our names.

ALISON: Yeah?

ERIC: We're both escape artists.

ALISON: What did you ever escape from?

ERIC: (*matter-of-factly*) Brooklyn.

IN THE HOSPITAL-ROOM scene that opens Donald Margulies's *Brooklyn Boy*, the old movie playing on the television set is the 1947 classic, *A Double Life*. The choice of film is a playful gesture that, like so many of the subtly chosen details in Margulies's work, both sums up and mocks the complex and conflicting emotions poured into this seemingly simple story. A double life, in a sense, is precisely what Margulies's hero, Eric Weiss, has been living. He's a Brooklyn Jewish boy, raised in an old-style, ethnically homogeneous urban neighborhood only a few generations removed from the Eastern European shtetl. From the old neighborhood he has gone on to an Ivy League college and entered the cultural melting pot of the educated middle class. When the play begins, he has become that ultimate mainstream figure, a national celebrity—which he's done, ironically, by writing a best-selling autobiographical novel, titled *Brooklyn Boy*.

Eric's tale is quintessentially American, the dilemma of every ethnic-minority member who has struggled to break out of the separatist enclaves of the past. Eric's father, Manny, seemingly asleep when Eric enters in the play's opening moment, says he has been "looking at" the movie but not watching it; he left it on, he says, because it was "black and white." Manny Weiss sees life, too, as a set of black and white issues, a mode of perception that disorients his son. The frail and dying Manny, still mentally alert enough to press his son on every point, grumbles at Eric for not wearing a tie on the *Today* show, for dedicating his novel "To my mother and to my father" without mentioning their names, for not bringing his wife

53

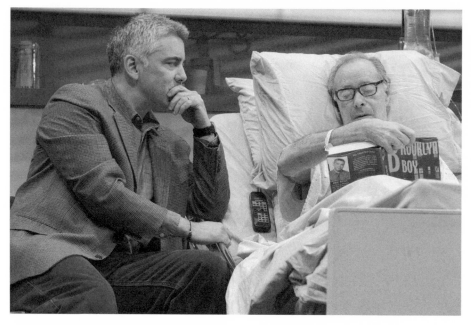

Daddy's boy? Adam Arkin and Allan Miller in Donald Margulies's Brooklyn Boy. *Photo: Joan Marcus*

on the hospital visit. Told that Eric's book will be number 11 on the bestseller list in the upcoming Sunday *Times*, he wonders how Eric can know the news before it's printed, and how there can be 11 items on a 10-best list. Though full of efforts at conciliation, the scene is a harrowing exercise in the mutual fraying of nerves.

The past that Eric confronts so awkwardly in life is also the reality that he has successfully captured in art. This isn't the first play in which Margulies has wrestled with the troubling dialectic between art and the real-life experience from which it grows: *The Loman Family Picnic, Sight Unseen,* and *Collected Stories* all explore aspects of the topic. But in *Brooklyn Boy,* it occupies center stage. In each scene, Eric is confronted from a different angle by questions about the ethics of his using his own life—and the lives of others—as material for his novel. His father, to whom Eric presents the book in the opening scene, is concerned that he and Eric's deceased mother have been treated fairly. In the hospital cafeteria (Scene 2), where Eric goes to wind down from the harrowing visit with his father, he meets his best friend from elementary school, Ira Zimmer, who bought and read the novel instantly on its appearance. It turns out that Ira, who was bar mitzvahed together with Eric, has fixated on Eric with a mixture of loving idolatry and hostile resentment. Recognizing himself as a character in *Brooklyn Boy*, Ira is half proud to have been immortalized and half indignant at the details that Eric has gotten "wrong."

IN TERMS OF ethnic identity, Ira is Eric's antithesis. At the hospital because his mother, like Eric's father, is dying, he not only still lives in the Brooklyn house where he grew up, but has inherited the nearby deli that his father and uncle used to operate. While proud to be carrying on the family tradition, Ira is also disconcerted to find himself becoming so like his father.

Significantly, his marriage has made him rediscover his religious roots. He invites Eric to the hospital's chapel, where they can say a traditional

---

Eric confronts questions about the ethics of his using his own life as material.

Jewish prayer for their dying parents, an invitation that Eric sloughs off, on the plea that he must get home to his wife, another of the evasions we see him practicing all through the first act's three scenes.

In no scene is Eric ever seen "at home," in either the geographical or the psychological sense. The first two scenes take place in the disorienting technological sterility of the hospital; in the third, when Eric stops in to see his wife, Nina, in what was formerly "their" East Village apartment, we learn much of what he evaded, uncomfortably, in the scenes with his father and Ira. Rival writers, married since graduate school, Eric and Nina are divorcing; the apartment is now wholly Nina's, and Eric has nominally stopped by only to pick up a last parcel of odds and ends that have accumulated while he was away on the first leg of his book tour. As Nina acidly notes, the volume of his mail has increased greatly since the success of *Brooklyn Boy*. Her own writing career, in contrast, has plainly stalled: galleys of a computer textbook she is proofreading for income lie on the table.

As in his relations with his father and with Ira, Eric tries to dodge the discomfort of his situation with Nina, practicing evasion and denial. He has arrived later than he said he would, and has brought a bagful of takeout Chinese food, expecting that they could sit down and talk together quietly over a meal. Nina is blunt about the facts of their comparative lives, and about the degree to which her career has been sidetracked, and the stability of their marriage harmed, by their repeated and unsuccessful efforts, to have a child (a subject on which both Manny and Ira have questioned Eric); we see plainly the extent to which Eric has failed to perceive the emotional effect that the repeated miscarriages and failed hopes have had on Nina.

The pain of the scene is reinforced by our recollection, from the two previous scenes, of the glimpses we've gotten of marital stability within the ethnic enclave of the "old neighborhood." In this as in other aspects of the play, Margulies works by Chekhovian indirection. We see that Eric has tried to make his marriage to Nina a housewife-and-breadwinner arrangement like his parents'—or Ira's—and a sharing, two-career meeting of minds of a more modern and assimilated kind. One cannot have both, and Eric's marriage is an inevitable failure. The crowning irony, though, is our realization that Nina is not only proud of his book's success, but genuinely glad of it for his sake. Her recognition that their marriage is impossible has not blunted her regard for him as a person or as a writer. The stark closing moment of Act I, in which she relieves him of his key to their apartment, is made more anguished by our awareness of their innate understanding of each other.

Divorce dialogue: Polly Draper and Adam Arkin in Donald Margulies's Brooklyn Boy. *Photo: Joan Marcus*

THE FOURTH SCENE, which opens the second act, takes place in the middle of the night. Eric's companion is Alison, a young woman whom he has picked up at his bookstore reading that evening. She displays attitudes and opinions as startling to Eric as his are to his father. Though plainly an intelligent person with a degree of sensitivity that equals Eric's, Alison is completely immersed in her desire to become famous by writing and producing films. A voracious reader herself, she believes that "fiction is like so over." Novelists who "devote themselves so completely to a dying craft" are "touching" to her, "like watchmakers or violinmakers or something."

Alison has written a screenplay, which she hopes to make into an independent film, a science-fiction story full of violence that is revealed to be an allegory with some relevance to Eric's plight: On "a space colony," the life of which is endangered, the first generation born there rises in revolt, massacring their parents, whom they hold responsible for the situation. But at the end, when "all the grown-ups are dead," the youngsters realize that "They're still doomed! They're just as clueless as their parents!" Despite her story's casual use of extremism and violence, it's plain that Alison is in her way as uncomfortable as Eric with our culture's failure of tradition, its failure to pass stability along in any convincing way. While displaying no discomfort at the idea of having sex with Eric, a man old enough to be her father, she points out firmly that she is not a groupie and has never before gone back to a hotel room with someone famous.

Just as she has no illusions about the future of reading or about Eric's intentions in inviting her back to his room, Alison has no patience with his half-denials of his novel's source in his own experience. "You're Kenny, right?" she declares, having read only the opening chapters. But though he finds Alison fascinating and is attracted to her sexually, Eric's discomfort wins out. Phoning the hotel desk to get a cab for Alison, he sends her on her way, rather than either consummating what began as a pickup or forging some kind of collegial bond with her. As Alison leaves, she asks him to inscribe her copy of *Brooklyn Boy*. When she thanks him, he says, "My pleasure." In a sense, it may be the only one he has.

Certainly, Eric finds little pleasure in Scene 5, which takes place in a producer's office at the movie studio that has purchased the rights to *Brooklyn Boy*. While seeming merely to satirize Hollywood manners and mores (an American playwriting tradition that goes back to *Merton of the Movies* and *Once in a Lifetime*), the scene also displays a more complex vision of Hollywood reality than is usual in spoofs of the film industry. Eric's producer, Melanie, is both shrewd in her requests for revision of the screenplay he has adapted from his novel, and utterly frank about the commercial reasons for them. When she suggests toning down the Jewishness of the Fleischman family, she does so on grounds that, however appalling they may seem, are not at all factitious as a box-office practicality:

> MELANIE: [I]t's one thing to be Jewish in a book, and another to be Jewish in a movie. [. . .] In a movie you're seeing them. [. . .] They're right there in front of you, there's nothing imaginary about them. Imagining Jews is much easier than seeing them.
>
> ERIC: Easier for whom?
>
> MELANIE: For most of the world. [. . .] You're talking about putting a relatively small segment of the population out there as mass entertainment. Let's face it, Jews are exotic to most of the planet, and frankly some people could care less about Jews.
>
> ERIC: What about *Schindler's List?*
>
> MELANIE: Righteous Gentile. Jew as victim. You can get away with that. [. . .] Look, the studio didn't buy your book because it's a wonderful novel about a Jewish family. Let's get real. They bought it because it's a great coming of age story they think they can market and generate substantial profits from.

While Melanie's demands are both ludicrous and offensive to Eric, they are also matters of good sense in terms of the challenges she must deal with in making the movie. Eric's discomfort with this situation is ratcheted up another notch when Melanie produces the trump card that she feels will guarantee the movie version's box-office success: a "hot" young television actor named Tyler Shaw. Tyler appears to be the living antithesis of the novel's hero and the worst possible choice for the role. Good-looking, obviously Gentile and a nonstop babbler, he seems in his first few moments after bouncing into Melanie's office to be scatterbrained, foolish and laughably narcissistic. Though Tyler confesses that he has not yet read the novel, he gushes over Eric, addressing him deferentially as "sir." He mispronounces Kenny's last name "Fleeshman," chatters about altering his hairdo and his body mass to fit the role, and gives indications of being helplessly dependent on his entourage. Eric's monosyllabic responses, combined with the agony that the audience can read on his face while Tyler jabbers, are a study in pain.

But Tyler has read the screenplay. Underneath his Hollywood babble, his observations are both practical and astute, whatever the limitations of his ethnic understanding. Describing his plans for research, and expressing his desire to "hang out" with Eric so that he can absorb his mannerisms, he impresses us as a capable and determined young man, as serious and professional in his approach to the work as Melanie is in hers.

"Pitch" perfect: Adam Arkin, Kevin Isola and Mimi Lieber in Donald Margulies's Brooklyn Boy. Photo: Joan Marcus

> TYLER: Maybe I'm not what you saw in your head when you wrote
> your book. But I "get" this kid. I can play him. I can become him.

The good sense and honest self-knowledge in this statement are confirmed when he begins to read a pivotal scene from Eric's screenplay. Margulies's text gives no indication of how good we should find Tyler's reading, but in the Broadway production, the choice was made to have him read convincingly and movingly, so that the audience believes Tyler to be a fine actor, and understands why Eric breaks down in tears, to the consternation of both Melanie and Tyler.

Eric may be weeping at the thought of his dying father; at the intensity of the painful memory the scene brings back; at his joy that he has captured it so well; at his guilty sense of having exploited his family's private tensions. He may weep from frustration, knowing that the movie will inevitably become a pale shadow of his book, or from an awareness that he must remove himself from any further work on the film. He may be weeping from any one or all of these things, from his suddenly tangible realization that it is the nature of our lives to cause us tears.

BUT LIFE HAS not yet finished teaching Eric. The play's final scene finds him again "at home," on Ocean Avenue in Brooklyn. His father has died. We discover in this scene that he has actually gotten the news before the two previous scenes took place, so that we are now obliged to look back at them with a new awareness. While Eric sorts through the accumulation of things his father has piled up, he receives two visitors in succession, one real and one imaginary, both Brooklyn figures we have met in Act I: Ira and Manny.

The first to arrive is Ira. He has learned the news of Manny's death, in a way that is a typical combination of tradition's hold and the anonymity of contemporary life. On his way from a visit to his own hospitalized mother, he has stopped in to see Eric's father and found a stranger in the bed that Manny had occupied. Eric describes his father's mercifully quick decease, explaining that he was in California and that he came back only in time for the funeral. Searching for something consoling to say about the deceased, Ira declares, "Your dad was a real character"—an unintentionally ironic phrase, on which the novelist who has just used his father as a fictional character judiciously declines to comment.

Among the things Eric has unearthed in the house is a vast accumulation of unopened liquor bottles, which his father has received as seasonal gifts over the years. He opens a bottle and offers Ira a drink. Although asserting that he is not a drinker, Ira accepts. Eric bemoans the amount of stuff he is obliged to clean out. "I've been at it for hours and I haven't made a dent." Ira remonstrates, urging him to follow the mourning ritual and let the dismantling of the household goods wait. "I don't know what to do with myself," Eric explains, adding that mourning with his family would have been "a different kind of hell," as would "the prospect of going home to an empty apartment." "Why empty?" asks Ira, causing Eric to confess that he and Nina are divorcing, and that he has gotten his own place. "So," says Ira, "on top of everything you're alone."

After another exchange, understanding develops between the two: there is an apology from Ira for being contentious at the hospital, some shared memories of childhood, Eric's admission that he has asked to be taken off the screenwriting assignment and that in LA he has picked up a girl young enough to be his daughter. The sudden vulnerability on Eric's part spurs Ira to press the writer into saying Kaddish (the mourner's prayer) with him. Eric angrily refuses, pushing away the yarmulke that Ira proffers, and the slip of paper on which he has written out the prayer phonetically. "Jesus," Eric exclaims, "stop trying to convert me!" "What's the big deal?" Ira asks. "You say a prayer for the dead. [. . .] It might actually make you feel better." "Judaism," Eric retorts, "has never made me feel better." Asked what he does believe, he responds: "I believe in survival. I believe organisms make choices in order to survive. I chose to escape from all this. You chose to stay."

Persistent Ira, after one last attempt, gives up and starts to leave. As he departs, Eric, perhaps feeling guilty about his harsh words, abruptly makes one last confession, on a point he evaded in Scene 2. "You were right," he tells Ira. "Seth Bernstein is you." "I knew it," says Ira, genuinely pleased. Their parting is quiet and friendly.

As Eric resumes his packing and discarding, Manny appears. The apparition immediately begins badgering Eric about his final admission to Ira and his previous evasions over the source of his novel's characters.

> MANNY: Did it kill you to tell him he was Seth Bernstein? [. . .] What did you think it would do to you, huh? Did you think it would take away from what you wrote? So defensive, Ricky. Why so defensive?
>
> ERIC: I don't know. Do you think it might have something to do with having you as a father?

Obviously, the dialogue takes place in Eric's mind. Yet, at the same time, it is full of information—and of wisdom brought by hindsight—that could only be available to Manny himself. This daring game, the culmination of Margulies's tale-within-a-tale strategy, is a tribute to the power of fiction (including dramatic fiction) to articulate truths, to embody what people cannot express for themselves, and ultimately to heal. Though the scene is brief, everything that we have seen as an unresolved issue in Eric's life comes back for reexamination: his Jewishness, Brooklyn, his father's seeming lack of affection for him, their Oedipal rivalry for his mother's love, his guilt over using real-life material in his art, his difficulties with Nina.

"I gave you something to write about," Manny tells him, adding that, in the day before his death, he stayed up all night to finish reading *Brooklyn Boy*. "It's a good book you wrote, Ricky," he says, to Eric's surprise. "You sure were paying attention all those years." And he confesses his awe of Eric's ability as a writer: "Must be a great thing to be able to do." "Dad," Eric responds plaintively, "why couldn't we talk like this when you were alive?" And Manny, shrugging, replies, "Life isn't like this"—another gently distancing joke on Margulies's part. As Eric laughs, Manny disappears. Left alone, Eric notices on the floor the yarmulke and prayer left behind by Ira. He puts the cap on and, as the lights fade, haltingly begins to recite the prayer for the dead. His emotional turmoil over the past resolved, at least temporarily, he is at last able to mourn. The art that he took up to escape from home has enabled him, however briefly, to come home again.

2004–2005 Best Play

DEMOCRACY

By Michael Frayn

○ ○ ○ ○ ○

Essay by Chris Jones

GUILLAUME: How thin that single voice sounds once your ears have got attuned to the complexity of the counterpoint.

"THE ONLY PART of German history that seems to arouse much interest in the British," the playwright Michael Frayn has complained, "is the Nazi era." That's surely true of Americans, for whom dramatic encounters with German political discourse of the 20th century invariably has involved fascists, their victims and a small but persistently diabolic fellow with a moustache.

This is understandable. Hitler was hellbent on turning the world upside down. And the Nazi era fits very easily into the melodramatic structure upon which Hollywood, Broadway and mass dramatic culture on both sides of the Atlantic have long relied for popularity and profit.

But when Michael Frayn's strikingly successful *Democracy* showed up at the National Theatre of Great Britain in September 1993, here suddenly was the first major English-language play to make the case that Germany's extraordinary postwar metamorphosis from weak and vanquished aggressor to leading force in European democracy was also worthy of theatrical inquiry.

It might seem like a tough sell. Germany transformed from a morally and structurally bankrupt nation into an enviable industrial powerhouse in no more than a quarter of a century. But the transition has usually been portrayed by historians and writers alike as a Teutonic plod towards dull respectability made with teeth gritted and back to the wall. The era doesn't exactly scream for a commercial play.

Frayn saw it differently, though, in part because he viewed the late Willy Brandt, the gregarious German chancellor from 1969 to 1974, as a fascinating and underexposed political personality whose achievements (beginning in the 1950s) were both without obvious parallel and typically overlooked. But while *Democracy* is a biographical drama about Brandt's time in power that closely follows the historical record, it's also far more.

Puppet and master: Richard Thomas and Michael Cumpsty in Michael Frayn's Democracy. *Photo: Don Perdue*

AT ITS CORE, this remarkable play is a study in the attractions of duality, and in the perpetually complex relationship between the personal and political, the global and the intimate. Simply put, Frayn saw Brandt and his rule as a compelling dramatic study in contradiction—with Shakespearean implications.

After all, during the time of that extraordinary West German capitalist reinvention—the nation also lived with a powerful and paranoid enemy located right next door. On the one hand, Brandt was free to build a self-contained, market-driven democracy from the ashes of National Socialism. On the other, he had to watch out for spies behind every closet door. Adjoining Brandt's nascent West Germany was its East German doppelgänger. Therein, 15 million fellow Germans spoke the same language but worshipped a different, Soviet god. Or so it seemed at the time.

Furthermore, the West German seat of government in Bonn was positively teeming with East Germans. Many millions of them were already in and around Bonn. But were they political refugees or spies? It was hard to tell. In some cases, it was both at once.

Frayn focuses his study of Brandt on one pivotal relationship from the historical record—that between the chancellor and one Günter Guillaume, initially a governmental functionary of East German extraction but longtime West German residence. In both *Democracy* and reality, Guillaume rose through the government's notably treacherous offices during the early 1970s to become Brandt's personal assistant—the man responsible for his schedule, his paper flow, his logistics.

Like George W. Bush and Karl Rove, the two men developed a close personal relationship. But in fact, Guillaume was a spy functioning under the command of his East German paymasters. Eventually, that disclosure brought Brandt down, contributing (at least in part) to his resignation.

The era doesn't exactly scream for a commercial play.

So on one level, *Democracy* is a spy-thriller—a conventional tale of communist infiltration in a Western government, replete with hidden cameras, merciless Stasi agents, cloak-and-dagger meetings and the rest of the generic detritus.

But audiences at the National Theatre—and, a year or so later, the Brooks Atkinson Theatre on Broadway—were quick to sense that Frayn really hadn't hung his hat on the James Bond stuff. That was merely the window-dressing.

Rather, Frayn had written a play about how the two faces of Janus-like postwar Germany were, in fact, the closest of kin. In actuality, each side of the Berlin Wall was fascinated and defined by the other—and loyalties were made of weaker materials than stone.

The play is about far more than German politics. *Democracy* is about a spy who falls in love with his victim and about a brilliant, warmhearted political leader perpetually seduced by danger—be it a string of damaging sexual affairs or too many late-night chats with a guy who could not be trusted. Incredibly, Brandt (both in life and this play) was warned against Guillaume's possible duplicity. But like the moth to the proverbial flame, that just made the man more interesting among a coterie of sycophants. Brandt subsequently withheld none of his intimacies from his dodgy aide-de-camp; in fact, he became inclined to reveal more of them.

> BRANDT: The merest possibility that Guillaume's not what he seems makes him infinitely more tolerable.

So was Brandt's recklessness his tragic flaw? Perhaps. But Frayn's argument goes deeper. Without that fondness for human failing, he argues, Brandt could never have been so popular, nor could he have put into place the reforms that ultimately proved so vital to Germany's eventual triumph over communism and the renewal of the nation's collective dream.

By now, this political story will sound familiar. Frayn could easily have been writing about another famously dreamy and self-destructive politician—one William Jefferson Clinton.

Guillaume as Monica Lewinsky minus the thong? Not exactly. But you would have had to have been sound asleep in your Broadway seat to miss the allegory.

DEMOCRACY OPENS WITH Brandt's 1969 election to the Chancellorship of the Federal Republic of Germany. It is, we discover, a flashback and part of a story told by Guillaume to Arno Kretschmann, an East German spy-controller and paymaster. Kretschmann sits at the peripherary of this drama, but nonetheless pulls most of its strings. Brandt is loquacious in victory:

Deutsche mark: Richard Thomas and James Naughton in Michael Frayn's Democracy. *Photo: Don Perdue*

> BRANDT: [O]n this day, the war that Hitler waged, against the peoples
> of Europe and against so many of our own people has finally been
> lost. We have a chance at last to create the Germany glimpsed by
> that ordinary Leipzig working-man a hundred years ago—a fatherland
> of love and justice.

The East German émigré Guillaume, we learn, has been offered a job
by Brandt's chief of staff, Horst Ehmke, as the Brandt administration's liaison
with trade unions. Although they ask a few pointed questions about his
East German past, Brandt's people are unaware Guillaume is a spy. And
they badly want a regular man-of-the-street (an "ordinary voter") in their
liberal midst. Guillaume's East German bosses are delighted: they now
have their own man in the heart of the Federal Chancellor's office.

> KRETSCHMANN: What Mischa really wants from you, though, is all
> the things that politicians and civil servants *don't* write down. The
> gossip. The background. The smell of things. The way they think.
> Who's in, who's out. Who's got their knife into whom.

Slowly but surely, Guillaume ingratiates himself with the staff, getting
to a place where he can spy directly on Brandt and learn his plans for
future relations with the East. Despite the ongoing uneasiness of the tough
and bitter Dr. Reinhard Wilke ("the dragon guarding Willy's door"), Guillaume
becomes the in-house voice of the people. Eventually, he ends up as Brandt's
personal assistant—the Sancho Panza to his Don Quixote.

Guillaume makes Brandt's copies, fixes his sandwiches and sends his
own reports to East Berlin. His spying duties notwithstanding, Guillaume
falls—emotionally, although not romantically—for his mark:

> GUILLAUME: You can't help trusting him. When you're there in the
> audience. You look up at him—and there he is looking straight back
> at you. You personally. Talking to you alone. One human being to
> another.

Increasingly, Guillaume sees himself through Brandt's eyes. Both men
have sons. Both have an acute awareness of the ambiguities and complexities
in political life and the hypocrises of the general populace. Most importantly,
Guillaume comes to understand that Brandt, like himself, is a romantic:

> GUILLAUME: He listens! That's his trick. He listens to what other
> people say. Anyway, how can you see into someone's heart if you
> don't fall a little in love with them?

Brandt, it becomes clear, is in the thrall of a variety of secretaries and
other transitory women. And like the rest of Brandt's staff, Guillaume
becomes involved in a variety of inappropriate liaisons that have the capacity

to bring about Brandt's political ruin. Brandt, who has come to trust Guillaume, makes no attempt to hide his love of these trysts. Indeed, they function as a kind of essential escape valve for a man with expansive appetites and a restless spirit:

> GUILLAUME: What is it about women, chief?
>
> BRANDT: The way they look at you . . . the way they look straight into your eyes and you look straight into theirs. The way you can't understand them. The way you can.
>
> GUILLAUME: The way they smile.
>
> BRANDT: The way they look seriously at you. The way they make fun of you.
>
> GUILLAUME: The way they're not like men.
>
> BRANDT: The way they are. The way they touch your hand. The way they touch your face. The softness of their touch on your skin. The softness of your own on theirs . . . All the different people you can be with them. All the different ways your life might go.

BY ACT II, Brand is facing a mounting array of political problems: inflation, worker unrest, industrial unease. His minders suggest a search for the "New Middle" (something akin to the Clintonian declaration of the need for newly pragmatic Democrats).

Ehmke, Guillaume's protector in Brandt's inner-circle, already has been removed (his new job is re-organizing the post office). And suspicions are mounting that Guillaume may be more than he seems:

> NOLLAU: The name keeps jumping out of files at us. Three separate espionage cases where Herr Guillaume seems to have known the defendants . . .

Guillaume asks Krestchmann to let him quit—so that he can leave before Brandt finds out about him. But the East German boss refuses, insisting that Guillaume remain a spy and in place at Brandt's side. And ironically, Brandt not only refuses to believe the rumors about his aide, he ratchets up their personal relationship to a different level, inviting Guillaume to bring his wife and son on a trip, so the two families can spend time together. They do—and all enjoy themselves on a vacation in the woods.

Boundaries blur further in the rural haze. Perhaps Brandt knows Guillaume's true identity, perhaps not.

> GUILLAUME: We sit there through the long Norwegian evenings, and in that unfamiliar Northern light everything begins to seem strange and uncertain. I've become transparent to him, and he's playing with me, just as I am with him. Or is it only the possibility that he's

Brandt's Boys: Terry Beaver, Lee Wilkof, Richard Masur, John Christopher Jones, Robert Prosky, John Dossett and Julian Gamble in Michael Frayn's Democracy. *Photo: Don Perdue*

playing with? Or is that what I'm doing? Is it him I'm seeing in the half-light? Or is it a reflection of myself?

Upon their return, the West German economy and political matters deteriorate further. Brandt's popularity collapses. Guillaume has many chances to flee back to the Eastern Bloc, but he takes none of them. Finally, he is arrested.

He confesses at once. His betrayal public, Guillaume becomes famous. And Brandt's minders belated realize that Guillaume knew of the boss's proclivities with women on trains and they become agitated. The West German newspapers know too. Inevitably, Brandt is forced to resign.

Immediately thereafter, the former premier finds himself in a contemplative mood, pondering the deeper meaning of his own political demise:

BRANDT: The journalists rang me in the middle of the night to get my reaction. The event we'd waited so long for has actually begun to happen. The state whose existence I recognized is passing out of existence before our eyes. The point of all that suffering and struggle and deception is crumbling into dust. . . . And at last what belongs together is coming together. Our divided self has become one self.

And Guillaume has his own contemplations and regrets:

> GUILLAUME: Does he ever miss me organizing the timetables and laying out his suit? Does he ever consider that I played my own small part in this? The little man who looked at the great man and saw he could be trusted.

Such, of course, is the stuff of democracy.

UNDER THE EXCEPTIONALLY taut and savvy direction of Michael Blakemore, the longtime Frayn collaborator, the London production of *Democracy*, opened at the National Theatre on September 9, 2003. It featured two actors who looked uncommonly like the actual historical figures they were playing. Roger Allam played Willy Brandt as somewhere between a messy backbencher and a Clinton clone.

It was a performance both in sync with the script and inherently sympathetic to the Brandt legacy. All at once, Allam interpreted Brandt as a political poet, a dreamer, intellectual and ironist. In other words, he forged a character that was the kind of guy one doubtless would like to see in charge of the country. Any country.

Meanwhile, Conleth Hill's Guillaume probed both the political realities of the relationship and the sexual tension—or, at least, the inevitable complications of any relationship of male intimacy, that lay hidden between Frayn's lines.

British critics admired the play's complexities and palpable humanity. "In *Copenhagen*," wrote Michael Billington in *The Guardian*, "Frayn dealt with the unknowability of the past. Here he is primarily concerned with the elusiveness of human personality."

Billington went on to praise the production, especially the way it melded with the play's themes: "Roger Allam's Brandt is one of the best portrayals of a politician I have ever seen in that it shows how total public command coexists with depressive private uncertainty." In other words, Billington saw a play that grasped the dirtiness of the government job. "What makes Frayn's play essential viewing," Billington wrote, "is its Schiller-like grasp of practical politics."

Billington's view were echoed widely (in the *Daily Telegraph*, Charles Spencer called the play " the most intelligent and gripping new English drama since, well, since Frayn's last stage outing with *Copenhagen* in 1998"). Predictably, a West End transfer followed shortly afterwards and *Democracy* moved to the Wyndham's Theatre, opening April 20, 2004. The cast and the production elements both remained largely the same.

By the summer of 2004, critics in London were hailing a bold new wave of issue-based, political theater, noting that *Democracy* had showed up in the same season as the likes of *Guantánamo: Honor Bound to Defend Freedom* and David Hare's *Stuff Happens*. By fall, the play was set for the Brooks Atkinson Theatre on Broadway. There was to be a new American cast.

Most of the people who saw both the London and the New York productions found the latter to be notably inferior. Although the original British production team was in place (and casting was the main distinction between the two productions), James Naughton was widely thought to offer a more bombastic kind of presence and to lack the physical resemblance to Brandt. More problematic still, Naughton emphasized the hubris of the grand leader, not the cheerful, ambivalent muddle that Allam had suggested.

Similarly, Richard Thomas's Guillaume also was neither as authentic nor as clearly associated with ambivalence. And the relationship between the two men did not seem taut.

All that said, the play was still greeted with enthusiastic reviews and major critics extolled the work's complexity, craft and seriousness of purpose.

"You can start salivating now," wrote Ben Brantley in *The New York Times*. "After many months of serving the theatrical equivalent of half-thawed TV dinners, Broadway has finally delivered a juicy gourmet's banquet of a play."

But the play did not end up a commercial success. In typically reductive fashion the following April, Michael Riedel of the *New York Post* dubbed the play "too boring for Broadway."

It was doubtless true that the Broadway production had not crackled with political and personal tensions in the fashion of the London original. But the problem probably had more to do with American disinterest in Brandt's era—the very reason Frayn wanted to write the play.

The British, after all, had watched Germany enviously in the years after World War II, wondering who had won after all. For those audiences (especially of a certain age), *Democracy* belatedly made some sense of an era that was always on the British radar, if never at its center.

But Americans had become increasing remote from European politics and issues—the chattering classes were preoccupied with the war in Iraq and President George W. Bush's tax cuts for the rich. In such an environment, *Democracy* seemed remote, esoteric and needlessly intellectual. Always a danger with prestigious British imports, such preconceptions harmed the show at the box office and hastened its demise.

Democracy collapsed after four months on Broadway, losing almost all its $2.5 million investment. Although it was generally agreed that Blakemore and Frayn should have brought over the British actors, it had been widely reported that the decision to use American actors on Broadway reflected the playwright and director's desire to make the play seem more relevant to American audiences.

Had Bill Clinton still been in the White House, that might just have worked.

2004–2005 Best Play

DOUBT, A PARABLE

By John Patrick Shanley

○ ○ ○ ○ ○

Essay by Jeremy McCarter

FATHER FLYNN: You have not the slightest proof of anything.

SISTER ALOYSIUS: But I have my certainty. [. . .]

FATHER FLYNN: You have no right to step outside the Church!

SISTER ALOYSIUS: I will step outside the Church if that's what needs to be done, though the door should shut behind me! I will do what needs to be done, Father, if it means I'm damned to Hell!

TWO DAYS AFTER the Broadway opening of *Doubt, a Parable*, Pope John Paul II died. The coincidence generated an uncanny harmony in New York, where theater audiences had just begun sorting out the implications of John Patrick Shanley's provocative drama.

That weekend, mourners around the world celebrated the late pope for helping to defeat Soviet Communism, and for stabilizing the Church amid the modernizing reforms of the Second Vatican Council; detractors rebuked him for aggregating power in Rome, and for turning a deaf ear to the victims of pedophile priests. The force of will required to carry out these diverging acts, it was recalled, could be traced to a single source of certainty. In 1978, in his first homily as pope, John Paul had addressed suffering modern man, who is "uncertain about the meaning of his life on this earth" and "assailed by doubt, a doubt which turns to despair." He declared that the remedy lay in absolute faith, a refrain he would sound again and again over the 27 years of his global ministry: "Do not be afraid. Open wide the doors to Christ."

In this he could have been speaking on behalf of an era. American life, in the early years of the 21st century, has been marked by a fierce commitment to orthodoxies, sacred and secular. They are expressed sometimes in the transcendent fashion of the Holy Father, sometimes in less delicate terms. ("I know what I believe," said President George W. Bush on the eve of a meeting with John Paul in 2001, "and I believe what I believe is right.")

Padre parable: Brían F. O'Bryne in John Patrick Shanley's Doubt, a Parable. *Photo: Joan Marcus*

But when is certainty misleading? When does doubt lead not to despair, but to wisdom? These are the questions Shanley addresses. He crafted a story about a nun, the principal of a school, who believes that a popular young priest has abused one of the boys; her subsequent pursuit may be judged a heroic defense of children or a hysterical act of vigilantism. Shanley was inspired by the headlines of the pedophilia scandals, but *Doubt* is no mere problem play. Its subtitle—*a Parable*—is a tribute to the unfettered mind, an exploration of healthy skepticism, which the playwright calls a "passionate exercise."

To make such a case at a time like this is contrarian almost to the point of perversity. Unlike the era's political and religious leaders, Shanley maintains that doubt is not a weakness, but a strength; not a failure, but a triumph. Though the play abounds with old-fashioned theatrical virtues, the real key to its power may lie in the eerie synchronicity of that weekend. To watch a New York audience captivated at once by two such disparate events is to gain new admiration for how fully the play echoes—and how boldly it challenges—the temper of its time.

SHANLEY WASN'T THE first writer to see dramatic potential in the stories of abuse and betrayal that arose from the pedophilia scandals of 2002. Still, nothing in the previous treatments of the subject could have predicted the power of *Doubt*. Nor, for that matter, could Shanley's prior career. Never having seen one of his plays reach Broadway, he watched this one sweep through awards season. It was the consensus play of the year, winning the Tony Award, Pulitzer Prize, and the New York Drama Critics' Circle Award.

If it's true that Shanley's track record couldn't have anticipated the play's triumph, it's also true that only a playwright of such long seasoning could have achieved it. The virtues of *Doubt* are the virtues of hard-won experience: economy, balance, command of the material. With just four actors and nine scenes, running only 90 minutes, the play shifts the audience's

Shanley's masterpiece has no expiration date.

loyalties with dizzying frequency, sometimes on successive lines. Shanley's compact method is to use small details to signal larger truths, truths that possess great resonance.

This potent efficiency begins with the play's first line. "What do you do when you're not sure?" says Father Flynn. The question provokes not least because he asks it directly of the audience. It's an ingenious theatrical stroke, forcing us at once to contemplate the play's ideas for ourselves, and, by enlisting us as the congregation for Father Flynn's homily, involving us in the play's action. (As played by the diabolically compelling actor Brían F. O'Byrne, we are more than involved—we are implicated.) Father Flynn tells the parable of a man lost at sea. After one glimpse of the stars, which allow him to point his craft towards home, clouds roll in, obscuring his view.

> FATHER FLYNN: The message of the constellations—had he imagined it because of his desperate circumstance? Or had he seen Truth once, and now had to hold on to it without further reassurance? That was his dilemma on a voyage without apparent end.

That is also very near to being a metaphor for Shanley's entire play, or at least for the predicament of its protagonist, who now appears.

Sister Aloysius is a stern disciplinarian of the old school. She wears a black habit, severe black bonnet, and horn-rimmed glasses. (In creating the role, Cherry Jones added a wonderfully evocative detail: she can only see what's to either side of her by making an effort, by turning her whole body.) She disapproves of ballpoint pens and finds art and dance classes a waste of time. When Sister James visits her office, she criticizes the young teacher for favoring history over other subjects, lectures her on "the chain of discipline" that runs through her all the way to Rome, and chides her for performing before her classes "as if on a Broadway stage."

Sister Aloysius suspects that Father Flynn has taken, or is about to take, liberties with the students: that is the real beginning of the action of the play. Since Shanley never reveals what Father Flynn did or didn't do, the play is a battle for our sympathies, with the priest defending his innocence, Sister Aloysius claiming his guilt. The figure in the middle is Sister James, who desperately wishes she were not. (Young Heather Goldenhersh made her discomfort at standing between two strong-willed figures painfully clear.) She is our surrogate, asking the questions we would ask, raising the objections we would raise. When, during the next scene, we see Father Flynn in the school's locker room with the boys—here, the audience represents the class—it's easy to see why Sister James likes him. He's jocular and funny, telling them it's okay to keep their fingernails long like his, but important to keep them clean: "You try to talk to a girl with

Fire and ice: Brían F. O'Bryne and Cherry Jones in John Patrick Shanley's Doubt, a Parable. *Photo: Joan Marcus*

those filthy paws, Mr. Conroy, she's gonna take off like she's being chased by the Red Chinese!" Yet it's also uncomfortably easy to see what she finds suspicious in his invitation that they join him in the rectory for "Kool-Aid and cookies, we'll have a bull session."

Sister James tells Sister Aloysius that Donald Muller, the school's first black student, once returned from a meeting with Father Flynn acting strangely, with alcohol on his breath. This is all the evidence Sister Aloysius needs. She determines to drive him out of the school, and demands that Sister James help her. They lure Father Flynn to the principal's office by claiming that they must discuss the upcoming Christmas pageant. (O'Byrne immediately claimed Sister Aloysius's desk. It was, he said in interviews, the sort of liberty a priest would have taken in his native Ireland, where the old church customs lingered.) Father Flynn says he'd like to add secular songs to the pageant; Sister James agrees, proposing "Frosty the Snowman." But Sister Aloysius refuses. She wants the song banned from the airwaves. It "espouses a pagan belief in magic."

Shanley wants to complicate our sympathies in this scene, and he succeeds. Here and elsewhere, Father Flynn presents himself as an open-minded man who says all the right things, taking positions that will endear him to the liberal audience likely to see the play. The message of Jesus, he maintains, is "love—not suspicion, disapproval, and judgment." It's the sort of argument made by many left-leaning Catholics today, particularly those seeking broader acceptance of gays and lesbians. Yet this lively, progressive man also appears to be a child molester. The dour Sister Aloysius, who claims most of our attention and sympathy, sounds like a modern conservative. Her explanation for why she wraps the school's rose bushes before the first frost arrives—"When it comes, it's too late,"—may be a subtle echo of the Bush Doctrine of preemptive warfare. Shanley proves himself a master not least of confuting his audience's biases.

It doesn't take long for Father Flynn to grasp the true reason for their meeting. Confronted by Sister Aloysius, he reveals that Donald had been caught drinking altar wine, and that the child had pleaded with him not to be discharged as an altar boy. Father Flynn had said nothing of the incident because it would have meant Donald's removal. As "he is the only Negro in the school [. . .] a certain ignorant element in the parish would be confirmed in their beliefs." Unmoved, Sister Aloysius says the boy will have to be dismissed. The explanation convinces Sister James that the priest is innocent, but Sister Aloysius's conviction remains intact. "I'll bring him down, with or without your help," she declares.

Only now do we begin to see the full implications of her earlier declaration to Sister James,

> SISTER ALOYSIUS: When you take a step to address wrongdoing, you are taking a step away from God, but in his service.

Certainly it is the most harrowing line of the play; probably of the theatrical year. It is a formula for untold wickedness, allowing a zealot to justify any action, no matter how extreme, while feeling none of the constraints that religion might provide: the most dangerous of both worlds.

Sister Aloysius's fervor, her complete lack of misgiving, was not lost on the play's critics. Overwhelmingly, they received the show with praise. Linda Winer of *Newsday* called it "important and engrossing," and Howard Kissel of the *Daily News* deemed it "the richest piece of theater we've had in years." The closest thing to a pan came from *The New York Observer*'s John Heilpern, who called Sister Aloysius "blind bigotry wrapped in a nun's habit." Of her stated willingness to step away from God, Heilpern wrote, "That is what all religious fanatics do." Shanley, deftly equivocal as ever, declines to foreclose the possibility that he's right. At a time when the American president says God speaks to him, Islamic fundamentalists enthusiastically spill blood on behalf of the prophet and fringe Jewish settlers preach violence against Ariel Sharon for closing the Gaza settlements, Sister Aloysius's statement might be the credo of the frighteningly theistic age in which it was written.

SHANLEY HAS SAID in interviews that he was not molested by priests. Other elements of the story, however, were drawn from his experiences. The play's St. Nicholas School is based on St. Anthony's, which he attended in the 1950s: director Doug Hughes and scenic designer John Lee Beatty even visited the Bronx school as part of their research. He was taught by priests and nuns who resemble the teachers in his play; he even had one named Sister James, who came to see the original Off Broadway run at Manhattan Theatre Club.

Her onstage counterpart's pivotal scene transpires in the courtyard. Father Flynn has reacted to his confrontation with Sister Aloysius by delivering a stinging homily on gossip, likening it to feathers torn from a pillow and set aloft on the breeze: they travel great distances and can never be taken back. Now he discovers Sister James on a bench, alone and unable to sleep. He warns her to avoid Sister Aloysius, a "block of ice" with "a poisoned mind" who seeks only to kill the kindness in others. Like so much else in the play, the exchange is thoroughly enigmatic. Audaciously,

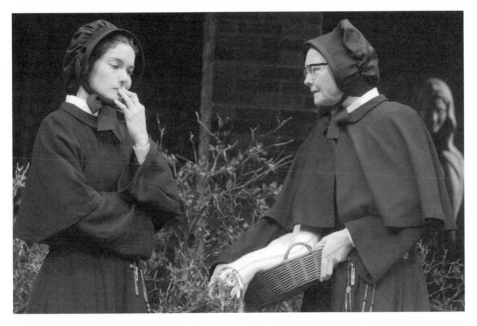

Soul searchers: Heather Goldenhersh and Cherry Jones in John Patrick Shanley's Doubt, a Parable. *Photo: Joan Marcus*

Father Flynn takes the young nun's hand. Is it meant as a sign of friendship, or callow manipulation?

   With the arrival of Mrs. Muller, Donald's mother, Shanley gives the plot one last twist. He nimbly folds in the issues of race and sexuality. Instead of raging against Father Flynn, as we might expect, Mrs. Muller—played with stoic fire by Adriane Lenox—says all that matters is that her son graduate and get out. More shocking is her revelation that Donald is "that way," an implication of homosexuality, which is why his father beats him. Though Shanley's dialogue strains here under the weight of his thematic concerns, the scene adds another layer of complexity to the play. Navigating this show requires the audience to think critically, weigh evidence and consider a mounting array of ethical and moral quandaries.

   No sooner does Mrs. Muller storm out of Sister Aloysius's office than Father Flynn barges in, setting the stage for the play's climactic showdown. Shanley does his most powerful writing here, as Sister Aloysius keeps up a constant prosecutorial tone, and Father Flynn switches from angry counterattack to vain pleading. Director Hughes and stars Jones and O'Byrne turned it into the most riveting scene in recent memory. The decisive moment comes when Sister Aloysius tells him she called his old parish and learned of his past record of misconduct. It's a lie—she made no such call—but he doesn't know that, and cracks. "Have you never done anything wrong?" he says. His desperation seems to confirm that her suspicions were right.

Yet the victory is short-lived, as Shanley has saved his greatest surprise for the finale. Father Flynn has been reassigned, but not dismissed. No one has believed Sister Aloysius, not even Sister James. The move was actually a promotion for Father Flynn, to become pastor of a church and school. For the devastated nun's final line, Jones dropped to an altogether new voice, one that came from someplace deep and anguished, unlike any she'd used before. "Oh, Sister James!" she moaned, "I have doubts! I have such doubts!"

It is a breathtaking curtain line, coloring everything that has preceded it. Only at the end do we realize the play has less to do with Father Flynn's guilt or innocence than with the progress of Sister Aloysius's soul. Only now do we see how the parable that started the play must end. Like the man stranded on the raft, Sister Aloysius saw a glimpse of what seemed to be a certain truth. She moved toward it as best she could, without any other stars to guide her. But when her pursuit brought her at last to where she expected to find home, she discovered that it was no longer there, or that it never existed in the first place.

The heartbreaking finale suggests a final layer of metaphor, verging on allegory. We never see the ultimate authority figure of St. Nicholas School, Monsignor Benedict. We know little of him beyond the fact that he is, as Sister Aloysius puts it, "otherworldly in the extreme." The language is suggestive. One way to read the sad tale of Sister Aloysius is that she is a lonely soul in need of guidance from above—from God—and, not finding it, needing to seek out the truth as best she can on her own. Catholic theology lends some credence to this interpretation. St. Augustine's *Confessions* culminates in an epiphany, as the chastened sinner rejects his wicked ways, adopting a life of righteousness. "For where I found Truth, there found I my God, who is the Truth," wrote Augustine. "Thou art the Truth, and every man a liar." In the end, Sister Aloysius, that staunch believer in facts and order, has been left bereft of truth—and of Truth. She lives in a universe of liars; everything in shades of gray. How does she live now? How does anyone?

A FEW DAYS after John Paul's death, Cardinal Joseph Ratzinger, the late pontiff's friend and conservative ally, delivered a sermon in which he condemned "the dictatorship of relativism." Though many found the tone strident, the College of Cardinals did not. Shortly after the address, they elected him Pope Benedict XVI.

The world's fever for certainty—in its religious and secular guises—shows no signs of breaking. In Iraq, as I write this, American diplomats are trying to prevent the country from adopting a constitution that would enshrine a stringent form of Islam as the basis of the nation's laws. There is a growing base of support for teaching creation in science classes of American public schools. At such a moment, *Doubt* seems a lonely defense of Enlightenment values.

Without question, these circumstances have added to the play's potency. Still, Shanley's masterpiece has no expiration date. He has dramatized a debate that will always be part of the modern condition, particularly here in America. At the height of World War II, Judge Learned Hand addressed a large crowd of listeners in Central Park, many of whom were new American citizens. The American quest for liberty, he told them, will not succeed or fail on the basis of national institutions, of laws and courts: "These are false hopes." Liberty, he said, will triumph or collapse according to what lies in the hearts and minds of individual Americans. "The spirit of liberty," he said, "is the spirit which is not too sure that it is right." In this country—and not just this country—the lesson of Shanley's play will always be worth heeding: No matter how painful and terrifying the sensation might be, it is doubt that makes us free.

2004–2005 Best Play

GEM OF THE OCEAN

By August Wilson

○ ○ ○ ○ ○

Essay by Christopher Rawson

SOLLY: You got to fight to make it mean something. [. . .] What good
is freedom if you can't do nothing with it?

THE 20TH CENTURY begins with a thunderous nighttime knocking on a
stout wooden door at 1839 Wylie Avenue in the Hill District of Pittsburgh.
With this reverberating plea for succor and call to action, August Wilson
begins the century of the Pittsburgh Cycle with which he dramatizes the
anger, aspirations and spiritual trials of black Americans in plays set in
every decade of the 20th century.

That pounding opens *Gem of the Ocean*, the ninth play in the cycle
but the first in chronology. Set in 1904 when human slavery was a living
memory, *Gem* is a robust, rich melodramatic struggle amid changing times.
Forty years after the Emancipation Proclamation, as Solly Two Kings says,
its promise remains unfulfilled. And in Wilson's 1904 Pittsburgh, revolution
looms—blacks against whites, new arrivals against those already there,
workers against mill owners and greed against the common good.

But in the midst of turmoil, *Gem* offers hope. That the play had a
troubled, delayed arrival on Broadway in December 2004, and a precipitous
departure after only 87 performances is a shame, but it oddly fits the painful
story it tells. And in its assured mix of comedy, tragedy and spiritual discovery,
Gem has the heft of an American classic.

That heft is individual: *Gem* is sufficient unto itself. That's one of
Wilson's distinctive achievements, the ability of each play in the Pittsburgh
Cycle to stand on its own. In his *Village Voice* review, Michael Feingold
quoted Gertrude Stein, another Pittsburgh-born playwright: "Everything being
the same, everything is always different." Just so. From one Wilson play to
another there are occasional links of family relationship and even a couple
of specific characters, but those provide an extra dimension for the
aficionado, nothing essential to plot. The greatest continuity is the Hill
District, where all but one of the ten plays are set, but even that is transformed

Magical spirits: Phylicia Rashad and LisaGay Hamilton in August Wilson's Gem of the Ocean. *Photo: Carol Rosegg*

into an archetypal urban crossroads—August Wilson country, home of a great national epic.

As in the other plays, *Gem* looks back to slavery and forward to a full equality that keeps glimmering in the distance. Like the cycle's following play, *Joe Turner's Come and Gone*, set in 1911, *Gem* also looks further back to the middle passage of the slave ships and the mid-Atlantic City of Bones, testimony to the human cost of slavery and the spiritual burden and inspiration that is its heritage. As in *Ma Rainey's Black Bottom* and *The Piano Lesson*, *Gem* also deals with black migration from agrarian South to industrial North. And it rings another variant on Wilson's recurring theme of the quest for an individual "song" that embodies a spiritual relationship to a troubled heritage.

GEM MOVES QUICKER than most Wilson plays, establishing its high stakes right off, with less meandering through inset stories. In its turmoil, Pittsburgh is not alone. In a new version of slavery, Southern states are terrorizing their field hands to keep them from migrating northward. Solly, a 67-year-old veteran of the pre-Civil War Underground Railway, receives a letter from his sister in Alabama:

BLACK MARY: [*reading letter to Solly*] [. . .] The white peoples is gone crazy and won't let anybody leave. They beat one fellow on the road so bad his mama say "Who is he?" They killed some more and say the colored can't buy any tickets on the train to get away.

One person who has escaped northward from Alabama is Citizen Barlow, another of Wilson's fresh-faced innocents trying to find his way in a difficult world—an image of Wilson himself, perhaps, when he left his own mother's house at age 20 for the streets of the Hill District in order, as he memorably put it, "to learn from the community how to be a man." But

Gem of the Ocean has the heft of an American classic.

Barlow, the mud still fresh on his country clodhoppers, finds a hard welcome: low pay, kickbacks to employers, cheating boarding houses, indebtedness to the mill and police who work for the owners. Meanwhile, Rutherford Selig, a sympathetic white peddler, reports people in the Monongahela Valley steel towns near Pittsburgh say they'd go to war to bring back slavery.

It is Barlow whose frantic knocking starts the play. Amid the 1904 turmoil, 1839 Wylie is "a house of peace," as Eli, the careful doorkeeper, announces. Barlow comes to this sanctuary not out of socio-economic dislocation but bent under the guilt of unintentional murder. He seeks to have his soul washed by the semi-mythical Aunt Ester, the most important of the tribal elders of the Pittsburgh Cycle who transmit inherited wisdom. We've never seen Aunt Ester before, but we've heard of her as the mysterious offstage healer in *Two Trains Running* (set in 1969) who then dies in *King Hedley II* (set in 1985). *Gem* makes her real and installs her in the spiritual center of the cycle.

Three others in *Gem* have passed through Aunt Ester's stout doors on troubled quests. Black Mary is a strong, angry young woman who arrived three years earlier as a laundress and now serves as housekeeper. In the sacramental structure of the play, she and Barlow are the initiates who learn from their elders what roles they must play.

The most fiery quester is Solly, born Albert Jackson, aka Uncle Albert and Two Kings – both David and Solomon, warrior and judge. In 1857, age 20, he escaped slavery via the Underground Railroad to Canada, then went back to save 62 others before turning his hand to guiding Union troops through the backwoods he knew so well. He lives off the land, which in

1904 Pittsburgh means collecting "pure"—dog manure—and selling it to tanners and canny gardeners. But just as the Underground Railway freed human beings from being chattal property, so Solly now carries the fight to the slavery of the mills.

The most troublesome quester is Caesar Wilks, Black Mary's half-brother. He's moved from the shady side of the law to become the sheriff who keeps the black folks in line for the mill owners and white bosses. ("Caesar's the kind of people I would want working for me," says Solly. "If I ever get me a plantation, I'm gonna hire him to keep my niggers in line.") Caesar makes plenty himself from flop houses and a dubious bakery. In his quest for money and power, Caesar expresses a raw Darwinian contempt for his fellows, but beneath that he knows that he has lost something important in his estrangement from his sister.

Aunt Ester has a quest as well, to find her successor. Just who and how old she is have been a mystery since we heard Holloway advise Sterling to have her wash his soul in *Two Trains*. Holloway says there she's 322 years-old, but she tells Sterling she's 349. When she later dies in *King Hedley*, she is said to be 366 years-old. Here, she is 285. All of this establishes that she dates herself from 1619—the year the first shipment of black African

Toast freedom: Eugene Lee, Anthony Chisholm and John Earl Jelks in August Wilson's Gem of the Ocean. *Photo: Carol Rosegg*

slaves arrived in Virginia. But near the end of Act I we learn that hers is actually an hereditary function. She tells Black Mary:

> AUNT ESTER: [. . .] Miss Tyler passed it on to me. If you ever make up your mind I'm gonna pass it on to you. People say it's too much to carry. But I told myself somebody got to carry it. [. . .] I got memories go way back. I'm carrying them for a lot of folk. All the old timey folks. I'm carrying their memories and I'm carrying my own. If you don't want it I got to find someone else. I'm getting old. Going on three hundred years now. That's what Miss Tyler told me. Two hundred eighty-five by my count.

Notice the legerdemain in Aunt Ester's speech. Initially, the "it" of "Miss Tyler passed it on to me" seems to refer to the name she adopted and proposes to pass on to Black Mary. But with "it's too much to carry," the "it" becomes something more. By association, this "it" is now the whole story of the people, recorded in their accumulated memories. And through the sometimes irascible, sometimes patient schooling we see Aunt Ester give Black Mary, "it" becomes her whole function as tribal memory and healer. Aunt Ester is clearly in a long line of folk priestesses, each training a successor. When Black Mary accepts the charge, it becomes she (then nearing 110), who dies in 1985—unless she had a younger successor. *Radio Golf*, the 1990s play, will tell us if the line continues.

Aunt Ester has made 1839 Wylie into a sanctuary in opposition to the new economic slavery of owners and racist unions. Eli, once an Underground Railroader alongside Solly, serves as her caretaker. Guarding her door, he has quasi-priestly duties; out back, he is building a stone wall against the Caesars of the world. And the peddler, the first sympathetic white man in Wilson's whole cycle (just as Caesar is the first black villain), is Rutherford Selig, whom we know much less positively as the "people finder" and descendant of slavers in *Joe Turner*.

AT TWO AND A HALF hours, *Gem* moves briskly. Much happens: A man dies evading capture for a crime he didn't commit, there's a riot, the mill burns, there are mass arrests, guns are drawn. All of this roils the waters at Aunt Ester's. But the signature scene is early in Act II when Ester, Solly, Eli and Black Mary conduct Citizen Barlow on a terrifying, soul-filling journey to the City of Bones, repository of those who died on the middle passage. It's a shining city, gruesome and grand, as described in the folk song, "12 Gates to the City." Barlow relives the slave crossing and washes himself of guilt, emerging with his soul fresh. "I ain't lonely now," he tells Black Mary as they discuss love. And Solly and Eli welcome him into "the band."

Then *Gem* turns frankly melodramatic, complete with a villain to boo. Solly has burned the mill down in protest. Caesar tries to arrest Solly, who assaults him and escapes on Selig's wagon, heading south to help his sister. When Caesar arrests Aunt Ester for aiding and abetting, Black Mary finally breaks with him:

> BLACK MARY: I remember you when you was on the other side of the law. [. . .] The one who believed everybody had the same right to life . . . the same right to whatever there was in life they could find useful. That's my brother. I don't know who you are.

Suddenly, Solly returns to burn down the jail to free the protestors. Caesar shoots him and he's brought back to die at Aunt Ester's. As the play ends, Barlow puts on Solly's cape and takes up his staff, enlisting as a warrior for freedom, just as Black Mary will adopt Aunt Ester's robes as a healer.

Throughout the play, Wilson's symbolism is rich in such Christian references as the bucket of nails Barlow steals, in pervasive water imagery and in the talismanic use made of Ester's slave bill of sale. Constanza Romero's Broadway costumes included Biblical details like Solly's cape and staff and Ester's shawl and beads. David Gallo's blue-green set, especially as washed by Donald Holder's lights—and with Dan Moses Schreier's ship sounds—easily turned into the pitiless but healing ocean on which there once sailed a ship called *Gem of the Ocean.*

As Aunt Ester describes that ship, it's not always clearly a slaver; sometimes its crew is heroic. It may or may not have been a real ship; her visions can be as tangled as some of Wilson's Pittsburgh geography. She is shrewdly wise but rambling, and she has occasional doubts. It takes a wind to drive the ship, she tells Barlow, but, "What god drives the wind?" That a god can power slave ships shakes your faith; so does the harmless rope put to evil use in lynching (as she implies) her son, Junebug. But elsewhere, in talking about Jesus and Peter, she makes it clear her Christianity is neither sentimental nor doctrinaire. And out of all this comes succor. The rock on which Aunt Ester founds her teaching is love. As part of her ongoing instruction, she tells Black Mary:

> AUNT ESTER: The people will come and tell you anything. [. . .] You'll come to find most of the time they looking for love. [. . .] You got to show them how to find it for themselves.

Aunt Ester is not the only one with wisdom to impart. Wilson gives all his people a share of oracular truth, even Caesar, who leans toward the pragmatic: "Money ain't got nobody's name on it," he tells Solly. "It's floating out there go on and grab you some." In the first of the two longest speeches

Brotherly advice: Ruben Santiago-Hudson and LisaGay Hamilton in August Wilson's Gem
of the Ocean. *Photo: Carol Rosegg*

in the play, Caesar spells out his philosophy of social control, prophesying
what will happen if rioters close down the mill:

> CAESAR: A hundred niggers is going to jail for trying to steal
> something. That's what's gonna happen. A hundred niggers is going
> to jail for loitering. A hundred niggers is going to jail for disturbing
> the peace after they get mad and start fighting each other. Five
> hundred babies is gonna go hungry. You gonna have a hundred
> new prostitutes. [. . .] It's Abraham Lincoln's fault. [. . .] Some of
> those niggers was better off in slavery.

Then in Caesar's longer, more sympathetic speech, he tells his life's story,
explaining how he fought his way up to attain his plantation overseer
morality. Eventually the mayor of Pittsburgh gave him his gun and badge
of office and said, "you fry the little fish and send the big fish to me," and
he does.

NO ONE WHO saw the Broadway production can separate Caesar's searing
speeches from Ruben Santiago-Hudson, who gave him a deadpan force
that brought the antagonistic outside world right onstage. This is what was
lost in the early Broadway closing—not the play, which will go on to an

active life in the nationwide theater that is Wilson's true home, but this vibrant cast, which we can never expect to see matched. It's easy to blame the producers, who declined to keep *Gem* running through the slow winter months, and one of whom, Carole Shorenstein Hays, surely wanted the Walter Kerr Theatre available to stage *Doubt*. But some blame goes to Broadway, both audience and Zeitgeist. The prospective audience never discovered the rousing experience *Gem* offers.

At the center of that brilliant cast was Phylicia Rashad, the soul of director Kenny Leon's production just as Aunt Ester is the soul of the play. The glamorous Rashad, who surprised Broadway the previous season by aging into the grandmother in *A Raisin in the Sun*, here aged amazingly into the ageless Ester. Palsied, with a twinkle or passionate tears as needed, she initiated Barlow, Mary and a willing audience into the heart of the play's mysteries.

Along with Rashad and Santiago-Hudson, the other performance that I cannot imagine matched was LisaGay Hamilton's erect and feisty Mary, terse when needed, furious on cue, a woman to desire and a priestess in the making. Each of the four performances I saw, the biggest audience response came when Aunt Ester's incessant carping finally pushed Black Mary to protest—"I can't do nothing to satisfy you [. . .] If I stay around here I'm doing it my own way"—to be met by Ester's smiling rejoinder, "What took you so long?" The storm of laughter and cheers showed how strongly the audience cared about both and how relieved it was to find them reconciled.

As Solly, Anthony Chisholm was a craggy, garrulous force, the most idiosyncratic presence in the play. Making his Broadway debut as Barlow, John Earl Jelks proved a find, touching in his bewilderment and inspiring in his discovery of vocation. Eugene Lee's Eli was an appealing aide-de-camp and Raynor Scheine was a gritty Selig, reprising his Broadway performance as the same character in *Joe Turner* in 1988.

Gem arrived on Broadway directed by Leon, but it was piloted by Marion McClinton both in its early 2003 premiere at Chicago's Goodman Theatre (where Leon played Barlow) and when re-cast that summer at Los Angeles's Mark Taper Forum. A year later, McClinton was hospitalized during rehearsals for the pre-Broadway staging at Boston's Huntington Theatre, and Leon replaced him. But before *Gem* could move directly to Broadway, one of the major investors backed out, putting the move in jeopardy. The savior—ironically, given the speedy closing—was Hays, who had produced Wilson's most profitable work, *Fences*.

As usual with Wilson, *Gem* improved greatly since honored last year with an ATCA/Steinberg New Play Citation, based on the Goodman premiere. For this improvement, Wilson especially credited the casting. But the delay in Boston played a part. Near the end of that run, knowing there would be a pause before moving to Broadway, Wilson decided to cut 20 minutes off the running time. He said he expected he would want to restore the cuts, but he discovered, "I didn't miss them. [. . . I]t's like a diamond: You cut away and get to the light."

"O Columbia! the gem of the ocean," goes the hymn: "The home of the brave and the free." Wilson's title is ironic, of course; America's promise of freedom has not been equally fulfilled; bravery has nothing to do with it. But bravery can bestow grace. The City of Bones is also a gem of the ocean, a talisman of a tragic history polished into a gem by remembrance. That's Wilson's constant theme: You honor the past to refresh the future. Of the plays of the Pittsburgh Cycle, he has said, "They're all about the same things: love, honor, duty, betrayal."

2004–2005 Best Play

GUANTÁNAMO:
HONOR BOUND TO DEFEND FREEDOM

By Victoria Brittain and Gillian Slovo

○ ○ ○ ○ ○

Essay by Charles Wright

GARETH PEIRCE: [. . .] Guantánamo is an experiment in how you obtain information from people and [. . .] an experiment in whether anyone is going to protest about that.

THE PLAYWRIGHT'S MANDATE is to be compelling. To fulfill that mandate, writers recreating events on stage, from Aeschylus to the present, have been drawn to tales with definitive climaxes and denouements. *Guantánamo: Honor Bound to Defend Freedom* by Victoria Brittain and Gillian Slovo is an exception to this rule. Premiering in the midst of the political episode it chronicles, *Guantánamo* proved theatrically gripping yet, at the same time, unsatisfying in the manner of a musical composition that concludes on a dissonant chord.

A chronicle of British Muslims detained at the United States outpost in Cuba, *Guantánamo* was commissioned by Nicolas Kent, artistic director of the nonprofit Tricycle Theatre in northwest London. The authors, Slovo and Brittain, interviewed families of detainees, their lawyers and others, then sliced the interviews into pieces and interspersed the pieces with material from letters and the public record. The result isn't a play in the usual sense but, rather, a two-hour series of monologues arranged in fugal sequence. Directed in New York by Kent and Sacha Wares, *Guantánamo* was noteworthy for the aplomb with which an 11-member cast handled the text's bursts of rhetorical brilliance and the way design inspirations by Miriam Buether (sets and costumes), Johanna Town (lighting) and Bill Grady (sound) camouflaged the drier, didactic moments of the text.

Characterized by its authors as "taken from spoken evidence," *Guantánamo* commences with a statement by the Lord of Appeal in Ordinary (played by Robert Langdon Lloyd):

LORD JUSTICE STEYN: The most powerful democracy is detaining hundreds of suspected foot soldiers of the Taliban in a legal black

Ruptured lives: Harsh Nayyar, Maulik Pancholy, Ramsey Faragallah in Victoria Brittain and Gillian Slovo's Guantánamo: Honor Bound to Defend Freedom. *Photo: Brian Michael Thomas*

hole at the United States naval base at Guantánamo Bay, where they await trial on capital charges by military tribunals.

This and the exhortation that follows are drawn from the controversial 27th F.A. Mann Lecture, "Guantánamo Bay: The Legal Black Hole," which Steyn—a member of Britain's highest court—delivered at Lincoln's Inn, London, November 25, 2003. Steyn's speech sounds a "recurring theme in history":

> LORD JUSTICE STEYN: [. . . I]n times of war, armed conflict, or perceived national danger, even liberal democracies adopt measures infringing human rights in ways that are wholly disproportionate to the crisis. Ill-conceived, rushed legislation is passed granting excessive powers to executive governments which compromise the rights and liberties of individuals beyond the exigencies of the situation.

It's an audacious beginning—a British Institute of International and Comparative Law lecture as the curtain speech for an evening of theater. Steyn's prologue contains an unambiguous admonition that becomes a theme of the play: the "loss of liberty," rationalized in the heat of crisis, is likely to prove "permanent."

The playwrights use Steyn to establish the Kafka-esque upshot of President George W. Bush's post-September 11, 2001, executive orders: hundreds of detainees from around the globe, with alleged but unproved connections to terrorist activities, languish in cramped, off-shore facilities, without being charged, without benefit of counsel and without the right to file writs of habeas corpus. In this nightmare world, the United States military serves not only as the detainees' interrogator and prosecutor but also as their defense counsel, their judge and, in the event of a capital sentence, their executioner.

"I still don't know what crime I am supposed to have committed."

LORD JUSTICE STEYN: [The procedure] is [. . .] in all respects subject to decisions of the President as Commander-in-Chief even in respect of guilt and innocence in individual cases as well as appropriate sentences. It is an awesome responsibility. The President has made public in advance his personal view of the prisoners as a group: he has described them as killers . . .

DIVIDED INTO THREE acts (performed in New York with a single intermission), *Guantánamo* features a panoply of faces and voices, cinematically intercut, which expound the predicament of British Muslims (played by Ramsey Faragallah, Aasif Mandvi, Maulik Pancholy, Andrew Stewart-Jones and Waleed Zuaiter) caught in places such as Afghanistan, Pakistan and West Africa at the moment the American military began implementing President Bush's global war on terror. Moazzam Begg (Mandvi) is the closest Brittain and Slovo come to creating a protagonist; and he's illustrative of all the play's detainees.

A native of Birmingham, where he operated an Islamic bookshop, Moazzam is a family man and devout Muslim. He traveled to Afghanistan to found a school but, faced with Taliban resistance to his plans, transferred his altruistic impulse to building water-pumping systems for five villages. When the post-September 11 bombardment began, Moazzam and his family fled. Captured by Americans in Kandahar, he was taken to Bagram, then to Guantánamo Bay (widely known as "Gitmo"). After a year in US custody, chained and caged in an eight-by-eight cell and "treated like an animal," Moazzam reports to his father (Harsh Nayyar):

MOAZZAM: [. . .] I still don't know what crime I am supposed to
have committed for which not only I, but my wife and children
should continually suffer[. . . .] I am in a state of desperation and am
beginning to lose the fight against depression and hopelessness.
Whilst I do not at all complain about my personal treatments,
conditions are such that I have not seen the sun, sky, moon etc for
nearly a year!

Gareth Peirce (Kathleen Chalfant), a London solicitor, tells the audience
that those monitoring the fate of prisoners have ascertained that Moazzam
has been designated an enemy combatant and is in solitary confinement.
"We have very good reason to think he's been driven into mental illness
[and is] in a very bad way," she says. Another lawyer, Clive Stafford Smith
(Joris Stuyck), whose professional life is devoted to matters *pro bono publico*,
reports that Moazzam "confessed" to involvement with Al-Qaeda and to
playing a role in a plot to use an unmanned drone aircraft to infect that
House of Commons with anthrax.

CLIVE STAFFORD SMITH: [I say] if you believe that, you believe in
the tooth fairy . . . [. . .] the only people who have drone aircraft in
the world are the Americans, they cost $50 million each, they don't
ever hit the target anyway and if you want to drop anthrax on

*Freedom fighter: Kathleen Chalfant with Waleed
Zuaiter (behind) in Victoria Brittain and Gillian
Slovo's* Guantánamo: Honor Bound to Defend
Freedom. *Photo: Brian Michael Thomas*

someone, you just stick it in the damn air-conditioning system, and
the whole thing is ludicrous.

The playwrights use the character of a young Englishman (Jeffrey
Brick) whose sister died during the terrorist attack on the World Trade
Center as dramaturgical ballast. "Let's say for the sake of argument," remarks
this Englishman, "that among those detained at Guantánamo Bay are some
of the people who led to [my sister's] death—who murdered her
essentially—that's a little difficult for me to, you know, it's difficult for me
to say it was a bad thing that they were there." But even this grieving man
recoils from the reported excesses of Gitmo.

In contrast to the poignance and desolation of the detainees' case
histories, the clash between their advocates and the Bush administration is
Theatre of the Absurd. Secretary of Defense Donald Rumsfeld (Robert
Langdon Lloyd in an adroit piece of doubling) wields fractured logic and
extravagant rhetoric (but shies away from factual justification), dismissing
the detainees—all of them—as "among the most dangerous, best trained
vicious killers on the face of the earth" and as satellites of Al Qaeda who
"learned [. . .] how [to] kill innocent people" in Middle Eastern training
camps. Brittain and Slovo don't utilize Rumsfeld's "stuff happens" response
to news of looting in post-invasion Baghdad; but that remark furnishes the
title for another documentary drama critical of the Bush administration,
David Hare's *Stuff Happens*, which premiered in London during the New
York run of *Guantánamo*.

Rumsfeld defends Gitmo with flights of Newspeak; he skirts the
jurisdiction of the Geneva Conventions by dubbing the prisoners "unlawful
combatants."

> RUMSFELD: We call them detainees, not prisoners of war. [. . .] We
> have said that, you know, being the kind of a country we are, it's
> our intention to recognise that there are certain standards that are
> generally appropriate for treating people who were—are prisoners
> of war, which these people are not, and—in our view—but there—and
> you know to the extent that it's reasonable, we will end up using
> roughly that standard. [. . .] I don't—I wouldn't want to say that I
> know in any instance where we would deviate from that or where
> we might exceed it.

Another example of the administration's semantic sleight of hand is
"Manipulative Self-Injurious Behavior," a seemingly anodyne phrase which
is actually as preposterous as any of the linguistic tricks George Orwell
fabricated in *1984*. Stafford Smith recalls a moment when statistics seemed
to indicate that suicide attempts in Gitmo had ceased.

> CLIVE STAFFORD SMITH: There was an effort on behalf of the powers that be down there to act as if, ah, everyone's calmed down now, they're taking their Prozac, there's no problem. But then we discover that far from suicide efforts stopping, they'd just been reclassified.

The human-rights lawyers, Peirce and Stafford Smith, are effective foils to Rumsfeld's bluster and doublethink. Peirce (interpreted magisterially by Chalfant) is the most lucid among the drama's voices.

> GARETH PEIRCE: [T]he American administration [. . .] seized people for purposes that are clearly the obtaining of information, [. . .] it transferred them to a place which it believed would be beyond the reach of courts in America. It claimed that it had seized people on the battlefield [. . .] and [. . .] found itself stuck with the immediate response [that] they deserve to be treated as the Geneva Convention dictates [. . .]. So having at first flush grabbed the nearest label [. . .] the regime very quickly had to redefine what it had, and therefore it said these were unlawful combatants who were not wearing uniform and were not conforming to the norms of warfare.

While *Guantánamo* is nominally about US atrocities, the London-based authors draw an analogy between US policy and the UK detainment of foreign nationals at Belmarsh Prison in southeast London under Parliament's post-September 11 anti-terrorism legislation. (Of Belmarsh, Amnesty International has commented, "The conditions are cruel, inhuman and degrading. The parallels with Guantánamo Bay are stark.") At many points, Slovo and Brittain equate Tony Blair's Britain, Bush's US and Iraq under Saddam Hussein. One detainee, an Iraqi-born Briton (Faragallah), declares he can't discern any moral distinctions among Hussein, Bush and Blair:

> WAHAB AL-RAWI: Saddam Hussein did exactly the same thing to my country and that is why we came [to the UK] and we end up with the same misery—ten times over—because this is supposed to be a land of freedom and laws.

In the view of another, the Bush and Blair administrations are waging "a war on Muslims, a war on Islam." The play dramatizes the western view—outmoded and never defensible—that the Muslim is, as Edward W. Said phrased it almost three decades ago, "the very epitome of an outsider against which the whole of European civilization from the Middle Ages on [has been] founded." This "Orientalist perspective" (Said's phrase) sees "Semites (or subdivisions thereof) as by nature lacking the desirable qualities of Occidentals." Stafford Smith, the pro bono lawyer, laments that, with a billion Muslims around the world, the institutionalized hatred represented

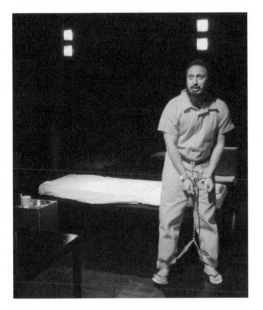

Trying souls: Aasif Mandvi in Victoria Brittain and Gillian Slovo's Guantánamo: Honor Bound to Defend Freedom. *Photo: Brian Michael Thomas*

by Gitmo contributes to "a world which is a very, very dangerous and unpleasant place."

The dramatists give Lord Justice Steyn the final words. He laments the "arbitrariness of what is happening at Guantánamo Bay" and predicts that this mockery of justice will make martyrs of the prison population, exacerbating the division between West and East, imperiling the hope that Europe and North America may achieve a peaceful coexistence with the Muslim world. Steyn poses the rhetorical question, "ought [the British] government to make plain publicly and unambiguously our condemnation of the utter lawlessness at Guantánamo Bay?" Then, as in the actual Mann lecture, he yields to the eloquence of John Donne:

> LORD JUSTICE STEYN: No man is an Island, entire of itself; [. . .] any man's death diminishes me [. . .]; never send to know for whom the bell tolls; it tolls for thee.

FOR A QUARTER century, the Tricycle Theatre has staged politically trenchant works such as Marie Jones's *Stones in His Pockets* and the South African musical *Kat and the Kings* (both of which transferred to Broadway) and the London premieres of dramas by August Wilson. In its so-called Tribunal Plays, the Tricycle has dramatized investigations of the 1993 murder of a young, black Londoner; the 1995 Srebrenica massacre in the former Yugoslavia; and the 2003 suicide of a governmental weapons expert after public disclosure that he had engaged in unauthorized colloquy with the BBC prior to the invasion of Iraq. *Guantánamo* is consistent with the previous Tribunal plays, though unquestionably of greater interest to US audiences.

To Kent, commissioning *Guantánamo* for the Tricycle in January 2004, Slovo must have seemed a natural choice for the project. Daughter of political martyr Ruth First and anti-apartheid activist Joe Slovo, she is a Londoner (and has been since 1964 when, at age 12, she took refuge in England along with the rest of her family). Slovo's *Red Dust* (2000), a psychologically complex portrayal of men and women gathered in a small desert town in the mid-1990s for amnesty hearings conducted by the South African Truth Commission, had recently elevated her to the company of novelists such as Alan Paton and Nadine Gordimer. Her subsequent book, *Ice Road*, is an ambitious depiction of a Russian family amid the sweep and agony of Stalin's purges, the show trials, and the siege of Leningrad. *Red Dust*, *Ice Road* and *Guantánamo* all address the political expedience of torture, the speciousness of official versions of "truth," and the manner in which the social status quo trends toward moral bankruptcy.

After Kent tapped her for *Guantánamo*, Slovo recruited Brittain, a long-time *Guardian* journalist (now a research associate at the London School of Economics), to collaborate. The authors conducted their interviews in late March and early April, then worked with alacrity, preparing the script for a May 24 opening. The premiere coincided with breaking news about how US Military Police and Military Intelligence soldiers had mistreated Iraqi prisoners at the Abu Ghraib Detention Facility the previous year. Those headlines made Brittain and Slovo's theme of governmental abuse of power resonate all the more with audiences. The production moved from the Tricycle to the West End in mid-June.

Produced by The Culture Project (celebrated for the previous year's *The Exonerated*), *Guantánamo* arrived in New York at the same moment as the 2004 Republican Party Convention. Members of the creative team, most of whom participated in the Tricycle production, replicated the aesthetic of the original—cold light, harsh sounds, chains, cages, narrow cots and orange prison jump suits. In his all-important *New York Times* review, Ben Brantley praised *Guantánamo* as a "deeply moving documentary play" exerting "an icy visceral charge that is never achieved by flashier agitprop satire like Tim Robbins's Bush-bashing *Embedded*." Michael Feingold, in *The Village Voice*, characterized the play as "a way of opening a door that our theater has foolishly kept shut, for the most part, since the mid '70s: Visible beyond the door," said Feingold, "is a conversation we should be having, nationally, about issues, principles, human rights, and human lives, that is itself a vista of freedom—one of the reasons that people love, or used to love, America."

However solemn the playwrights' aims, *Guantánamo* offered inherently funny lines, as well as speeches rendered with humorous irony. The richest irony, though, was (and is) the play's subtitle—*Honor Bound to Defend Freedom*. That phrase sounds like a tribute to the outraged voices of Moazzam Begg and his defenders. It is, rather, a legend displayed prominently outside the prison at Guantánamo Bay. In an interview, Brittain has compared that phrase to "work makes men free," which appeared at Auschwitz. In five words, the subtitle establishes the extent to which the Bush administration's assaults on humanitarian safeguards and the due process of law in the "global war on terror" are degrading the values of democracy.

As Republican delegates and other conventioneers invaded this famously liberal city, Brittain and Slovo offered playgoers a booster shot against right-wing contagion. Word-of-mouth, as well as reviews, made *Guantánamo*, along with *Embedded*, the most conspicuous cultural drawing card below 14th Street. The play ran from August 20 to December 19, 2004 (with the official opening on August 26). Late in the run, the producers raised the show's profile by inviting prominent figures involved in the public debate about the morality and legality of Guantánamo Bay—Archbishop Desmond Tutu, retired Chief Judge John Gibbons of the US Third Circuit Court of Appeals, historian Howard Zinn, and lawyer Barry Scheck—to appear as Lord Justice Steyn and participate in post-performance discussions.

Well before *Guantánamo* closed, an election sealed the nation's fate: four years more of federal policy comparable to that depicted by Slovo and Brittain. In another theater season, a nonprofit production like *Guantánamo*, with modest running costs and huzzahs from the influential critics, might have transferred readily to a commercial engagement. For *Guantánamo*, in this election year, such was not to be. The reasons are clear only to the would-be presenters who walked away from the prospect. It's tempting, though, to speculate that, by December, those producers, like their potential audiences, had run out of hope that the conflict of *Guantánamo* will reach a climax and denouement any time soon.

2004–2005 Best Play

HOT 'N' THROBBING

By Paula Vogel

○ ○ ○ ○ ○

Essay by David Savran

CHARLENE: When I really get going, it's like a trance—it's not me writing at all. It's as if I just listen to voices and I'm taking dictation.

THE VOICE: Sometimes when I'm waiting for the body bags, I think—she's young enough to be my daughter, or maybe she's someone's mother—and they talk to me. Frankly it scares the shit out of me.

CLYDE: Doesn't that spook you? I mean, whose voices are these? Who's in control?

VOICE-OVER: But she was in control.

ALTHOUGH PAULA VOGEL is known for writing plays that get under your skin, none is as disturbing as *Hot 'n' Throbbing.* The mixture of sexual fantasy, pornography, domestic violence and (yes!) literary history that are the subjects of the play is guaranteed to make some audiences—and critics—very uncomfortable. Indeed, none of her plays confronts spectators with such explosive subject matter and a structure that is as deliberately fragmented and disjointed. None of her plays mixes real characters with fantasy characters with such abandon. None of her plays focuses so explicitly on the fears of the writer, listening to voices and taking dictation from them while trying to retain control of her narrative. It is little wonder that every production has received decidedly mixed reviews or that some theatergoers in New York seemed not to know what to make of such a challenging play.

Hot 'n' Throbbing was the final presentation of Signature Theatre's season devoted to the works of Paula Vogel, its 12th playwright-in-residence. It was preceded by the New York premiere of *The Oldest Profession* and a revival of *The Baltimore Waltz*, the play that put Vogel on the map when first performed at Circle Rep in 1992. As with *The Oldest Profession, Hot 'n' Throbbing* has a long, pre-New York stage history. It was first produced in 1994 by American Repertory Theatre in Cambridge, directed by Anne Bogart. A revised version was mounted at Arena Stage in Washington in 1999, directed by Molly Smith. For its New York debut, Vogel again revised the

Desire and danger: Lisa Emery and Elias Koteas in Paula Vogel's Hot 'n' Throbbing. *Photo: Joan Marcus*

script and teamed with director Les Waters, set designer Mark Wendland, costume designer Ilona Somogyi, lighting designer Robert Wierzel and sound designer Darron L. West to create one of the most innovative, uncompromising, and lucid productions Vogel's work has received in New York. Blessed with rich, vibrant and nuanced performances, Waters and Vogel rethought the play, multiplied its resonances and solved its daunting theatrical problems.

THE PLOT OF *Hot 'n' Throbbing* is easily and quickly summarized. Yet doing so barely begins to describe the real action of the play. The play centers on Charlene (Lisa Emery), a divorced, working-class mother with two children: Calvin (Matthew Stadelmann) and Leslie Ann (Suli Holum). Leslie Ann, in the throes of adolescent rebellion, wants to trade in her "dumb-shit name" for Layla. Charlene also has an ex-husband, Clyde (Elias Koteas), prone to alcohol and violence. To make ends meet, Charlene writes what she calls "adult entertainment" for a feminist movie company named Gyno Productions that makes erotic films (a.k.a. pornography) for women.

One Friday night, after the children have decided to vacate the premises rather than read *Ulysses* and *Moby-Dick* for high-school English, Clyde breaks into Charlene's apartment to retaliate for the restraining order she has obtained against him. Alarmed yet poised, Charlene grabs her gun and shoots him in the behind—it's only "a flesh wound." She then dresses his injury and, softened by his compliance, offers him brandy and sympathy. Calvin suddenly bursts in to rescue Charlene from his father, with whom he has a competitive and antagonistic relationship. After a brief confrontation and Calvin's outraged exit, it's Leslie Ann's turn to enter the scene and offer her father a much warmer greeting. But Charlene, with whom Leslie Ann

---

Vogel's ambition is to interrogate, explore, seduce, frighten, insinuate—and repair.

---

has a relationship as charged as Calvin's is with his father, convinces her to return to her friend Lisa's for a sleepover. With the children out of the way for the evening, the unemployed Clyde confesses his deep personal and sexual frustrations. One thing leads to another until Charlene finally agrees to bestow one last sexual favor on her ex-husband. But Clyde, still angered at her defiance, strangles her in the heat of the moment and then, dazed and horrified at what he has done, turns her gun upon himself. Leslie Ann returns home to discover the bodies as the action abruptly leaps ahead 10 years to the conclusion of a college freshman seminar she is teaching on *Lolita*. Despite her self-assurance and command of the classroom, Leslie Ann still hears Charlene's voice expressing her enthusiasm for the next week's reading assignment, *Moby-Dick*. The play ends with a spooked Leslie Ann trying to regain her composure as her mother's words ring in her ears.

Perhaps the most innovative aspect of *Hot 'n' Throbbing*, and the reason a plot summary barely scratches the play's surface, is its simultaneous depiction of two orders of reality. One, described above, is situated in a small, cookie-cutter, suburban apartment while the other is a dangerous dream world (often bathed in red light) inhabited by the characters that populate Charlene's screenplay and her fantasies: a seductive female Voice-Over (Rebecca Wisocky) and a cool male Voice (Tom Nelis) who are constantly changing identities. The former "narrates the script that the Woman [Charlene] is writing"; she is Charlene's "inner voice"; Leslie Ann's friend, Lisa; a sex-worker; and Charlene's alter-ego. The Voice is the more authoritative figure: a hard-boiled detective in Charlene's screenplay who from time to time reads aloud from Charlene's books; a client in a "strip joint"; the "director of a Gyno film gone bad"; and Clyde's alter-ego. In the earliest version of the play, the two orders of reality were represented by two distinct spaces: the living room and a nude dance hall that was the jurisdiction of the Voice-Over and the Voice.

For Arena Stage, Vogel reconceived the spatial relation so that under red light, the living room becomes the "film set," a "strip joint," and "dance hall." In Les Waters's production, the two orders of reality and the two spaces were completely superimposed so that the fantasy characters and alter-egos drifted unseen among the real characters, ghosts among the living. The production team, moreover, designed the living room—with its stark white walls, tacky furnishings, and fold-out couch—so that the walls came apart to transform the domestic interior step by step into a movie set on which the final snuff film (i.e., Charlene's murder) is enacted. The dismembered set was both a shrewdly appropriate container for the two levels of action and an analogue for the dismembered narrative.

Oedipal struggle? Elias Koteas, Matthew Stadelmann and Lisa Emery in Paula Vogel's Hot 'n' Throbbing. *Photo: Joan Marcus*

DESPITE THEIR FREQUENT transformations, the Voice-Over and Voice consistently represent the unspoken sentiments and thoughts of the characters. They articulate and embody the desires and fears of Charlene and Clyde; they act out fantasies about what Leslie Ann does on Friday nights; and they play the characters in the snuff film. The two characters also represent certain emblematic qualities attributed to women and to men in American culture—but with a difference. The Voice-Over, for example, costumed in black bustier, stockings, and dog collar, seems to epitomize woman as sex object. But, in keeping with the tenets of Gyno Productions, which makes movies that "try to create women as protagonists in their own dramas," she is more dominatrix than simple object of desire. The Voice, in contrast, plays the part of a customer at a strip club and the director of the snuff film. But during most of the play he takes on the role of a character in Charlene's screenplay, a Dashiell Hammett-style private eye, complete with trench coat and fedora. Most troubling, he is also the detective who comes to Charlene's house to investigate the murder-suicide. The multiple roles taken by the Voice suggest that there are at least two time-schemes in play in *Hot 'n' Throbbing*. The slowly unfolding action that leads to the murder proceeds simultaneously with the detective's ex post facto investigation of the crime scene.

Among the Voice's many activities, none is more curious than his reading aloud from the books in Charlene's house which are, after all, evidence at the crime scene. For Charlene is a well-educated and ambitious writer who put herself through school and has a particular weakness for certain canonical male authors and works, especially *Moby-Dick* ("I loved that book," she says in words repeated at the end of the play), the most frequently cited text in the play. Leslie Ann is reading the same book for English class, while Calvin studied it the year before. And the Voice, investigating the murder scene, several times picks up the novel and reads aloud from it as well as from *Ulysses* and *Lolita*. Even the horn of Lisa's car imitates Humbert Humbert's famous incantation: "Lo. Lee. Ta." Preferring sex to violence and books to trashy films, Charlene warns her daughter, "I'd rather have you read Henry Miller or D.H. Lawrence than watch *Texas Chain Saw Massacre*."

Most intriguingly, the characters' repeated invocations of passages from landmark novels functions to blur the distinction between literary classics and so-called pornography. When Clyde and Calvin envision Leslie Ann dancing in the strip club, their reverie is accompanied by the Voice reading some muscular, purple prose from *Moby-Dick* that, the stage directions point out, "really does read like a triple-X flick." And all the fiction cited in the play could be described as evidence of a patriarchal tradition that tends to objectify, eroticize and sometimes even administer violence against women. (In former times, the writings of Lawrence, Miller, Joyce and Nabokov have been repeatedly pronounced pornographic. Since the rebirth of feminism in the 1960s, they have more often been decried as misogynist.) Charlene herself is a victim of domestic violence, yet the screenplay she is writing has unmistakable sadomasochistic overtones. The opening reads:

> VOICE-OVER: He was hot. He was throbbing. And out of control. He needed to be restrained. Tied down. And taught a lesson.
>
> But not hurt. Not too much. Just . . . enough. She would make his flesh red all over. She would raise the blood with her loving discipline.

It is clear that both the female and male characters in the play eroticize differences in power, whether those differences inhere in their personal relationships or in the fiction they read (and write). Sometimes this eroticization seems benign and thrilling, especially when a woman is cast as dominatrix. But more ominously, the extreme power differential between women and men is also portrayed as dangerous and alarming. (In any sadomasochistic relationship danger and sexual excitement are inextricably linked.) Thus Leslie Ann confesses to her friend Lisa:

> LESLIE ANN: Do you think of [boys], like, "hurting" you? Well, I don't mean like hurting you, but like, you're tied down and you can't stop them and they do things to you that hurt you, that make you scream but you can't and you wouldn't really want it to happen in real life, you would really get hurt, but when you close your eyes, you see it and it makes you get hot only it's 'cause it's not for real?

In other words, for Leslie Ann—and apparently for Charlene as well—sadomasochism is exciting as long as it remains fantasy or fiction. Once it happens for real, it is terrifying and potentially fatal. But the central problem that the play confronts is the near impossibility of separating fact from fiction, reality from fantasy. Who, after all, fashions the snuff film fantasy at the end of the play? Clyde? The Voice? Herman Melville? Or is it Charlene herself? Have the Voice-Over and Voice wrested control of the scene from Charlene? Are the fantasy characters more true than the real ones? Is fiction more real than real life?

THE LINK THAT *Hot 'n' Throbbing* draws between eroticism and danger is very disturbing for many people. But the most chilling thing about the play, the *truth* of the play lies in the reality of fiction, that is, in the fact that the novels *Moby-Dick* and *Lolita* (unlike the characters Charlene and Clyde) really exist. These cornerstones of modernist fiction have inspired generations of fervent readers and generations of college students—such as the ones Leslie Ann teaches in the play's last scene—to wax lyrical about them, and to believe that fanatical, murderous men are charismatic and heroic. This is not to suggest that *Lolita* has inspired generations of pedophiles (although it may have) but that the elite literary tradition is far less benign and far less distant from the politics of sexual violence than one might imagine. A corollary of this observation is the suggestion that Charlene's "adult entertainment" is very much a branch of literature. Although Clyde thinks that Charlene is only a pornographer, she clearly has more serious and legitimate ambitions for her writing than putting food on the table. She is genuinely delighted when Calvin tells her, "I really like the detective."

> CHARLENE: I'm kinda proud of the detective.
>
> CALVIN: Mama, I think you can really write.
>
> CHARLENE: Oh, honey—not really. Not yet. Someday, maybe, when you kids are all taken care of—someday. I'd like to think I have one good book in me.

But what if Charlene has already written that book? What if her one good book is the play itself? What if she has managed to join the ranks of the great (male) authors by writing a work in which she becomes the victim of sexual violence?

Above all, *Hot 'n' Throbbing* seems intent on exploring the role that fantasy (and literature as a mode of fantasy) plays in our lives, its power to soothe and unsettle, to excite and terrify, and its uncanny ability to seem more real than life. I would expect that many well-read people have experienced the peculiar sensation of the fictional character who seems more vital than many people with blood in their veins. Don't some of us feel we know and understand Emma Bovary or Holden Caulfield or Hedda Gabler better than many of the people who pass through our lives? For Charlene, and for the other characters, fantasy is more powerful and seductive than their humdrum suburban lives. It is a mode of escape and transfiguration. Charlene, after all, was once stuck in a violent, dead-end marriage. But she has rewritten the story of her life by taking control of her desires (and vice versa).

> CHARLENE: Now I close my eyes and see beautiful, strong bodies touching each other.
>
> VOICE-OVER: Coupling with each other. And we write down these words. And the words become flesh.

Fantasy is also a way the characters enrich their lives materially. Charlene has transformed herself from a nurse's aide, earning minimum wage and "cleaning up" other people's messes, into an author. And both Leslie Ann and Calvin follow in their mother's footsteps. In the final scene, we discover that Leslie Ann has become a graduate student in English literature and a teacher of writing while her brother "is becoming a screenwriter." An adept literary critic, Leslie Ann discerns in the works of Melville et al. precisely the same techniques that Vogel uses so skillfully throughout the play: "juxtaposition of high and low culture," "wild and erratic mixture of genres," "ambiguity, doubleness, the unreliability of the narrator, and stream of consciousness." Moreover, the transformation she undergoes before the last scene as well as the title of her class, Literature of Obsession, suggest that she has chosen her vocation in part to analyze the seductive power of fantasy and of being "hurt," to understand the reasons why her mother was killed. For Leslie Ann remains haunted by her mother. As she speaks to her class, she is suddenly interrupted by one disembodied voice we have not yet heard, Charlene's Voice-Over, telling her (and repeating her earlier lines), "You want to go far away from here? Read the goddamn book that's due on Monday. *Moby-Dick*." In the final lines of the play, the stage directions emphasize the invasive and inexorable power of Charlene's ghost:

> (*Leslie Ann can't shut it out. For a moment it appears as if Leslie Ann will lose control in front of her class. She closes her eyes and tries to gain composure.*)
>
> LESLIE ANN: —Excuse me. I can get very emotional when I talk about *Moby-Dick*.
>
> (*Beat. She takes a breath and then moves to dismiss her class:*)
>
> LESLIE ANN: Your papers on *Moby-Dick* will be due four weeks from today. As always, I expect you to be in control of your arguments, in control of your words, and in control of your—
>
> (*But Charlene again breaks into her daughter's stream of consciousness:*)
>
> CHARLENE'S VOICE-OVER: (*whispered*)—thoughts.

THE ENDING OF *Hot 'n' Throbbing* suggests an additional interpretation of the play. Isn't it possible that the action has, Ambrose Bierce-like, been a flashback staged in Leslie Ann's imagination during the split-second after she finishes her lecture? Perhaps for a moment her mind has wandered and she has replayed everything that happened the night of her mother's murder—or at the least, some combination of her memories and fantasies.

For all the while the play insists on the importance of retaining control of one's thoughts, it suggests the impossibility of doing so. Can one ever be sure where a thought, a word or an action has come from? From one's parents? One's teachers? The novels one reads? The movies one goes to? The plays one sees?

Paula Vogel does not and cannot answer the many questions that *Hot 'n' Throbbing* poses. For her ambition is not to hammer home a political point but to interrogate, explore, seduce, frighten, insinuate—and repair. The heady mixture of sex and violence, pleasure and pain, and the "wild and erratic mixture of genres" make for a challenging evening of theatre, one that urges audiences to confront their own fantasies and fears. But not all theatergoers—or critics—have been willing to do so. When the play was first produced at ART, the *Boston Globe* critic noted presciently that it was "likely to be the most controversial play of the year." And it has continued to divide audiences.

Unfortunately, several New York critics opted to close their eyes to its interrogation of fantasy and fact. The *New York Times* critic, Jason Zinoman (for one), having decided that the play was focused narrowly on pornography and domestic violence, chose to dismiss it as "too busy, an academic exercise" without "any trace of humanity." His sneering review is symptomatic (alas!) of precisely the kind of cultural myopia, narrow-minded moralism and discomfort with fantasy that *Hot 'n' Throbbing* critiques. But until our society rethinks its ideas about fiction and real life, pornography and literature, and the insinuating pervasiveness of sexual violence, *Hot 'n' Throbbing* is likely to remain a lightening rod for controversy.

2004–2005 Best Play

A NUMBER

By Caryl Churchill

○ ○ ○ ○ ○

Essay by Robert Hurwitt

SALTER: tell me something about yourself that's really specific to you, something really important

MICHAEL: what sort of?

SALTER: anything

MICHAEL: it's hard to

SALTER: yes.

'**P**LAYWRIGHTS DON'T GIVE answers, they ask questions," Caryl Churchill wrote in a 1960 essay. "We need to find new questions, which may help us answer the old ones or make them unimportant, and this means new subjects and new form."

True to her words, Churchill has been asking hard questions in new dramatic forms for 45 years. The forms have been as varied as comedy, tragedy, radio plays, opera, docudrama, dance-theater, agitprop, history plays, large ensemble works and avant-garde chamber pieces, and the subjects have ranged from intensely topical to metaphysical. But the questions are almost always as evocative as they are provocative. Taking on an issue as current as genetic cloning, as she does in *A Number*, Churchill turns contemporary controversy on its head to probe timeless questions lurking within the timely.

The ostensible central issues are among the hottest of today's buttons. Politicians, religious leaders and scientists debate the legality, morality and long-range impacts of genetic experiments with plants and animals. The topic of cloning—of any animals, but increasingly of humans—has moved from the pages of science fiction and headlines in tabloids to serious consideration in scientific journals and mainstream media. *A Number* wastes no time reiterating the public arguments or dramatizing the most obvious social-melodrama aspects of the problem. Writing with ruthlessly pared precision, Churchill probes beneath the surface social, political, scientific

Existential angst: Dallas Roberts and Sam Shepard in Caryl Churchill's A Number. *Photo: Joan Marcus*

and religious issues to raise unsettling questions about paternity, parenthood and the essence of what it means to be human.

The immediacy of the play's impact—emotional as well as intellectual—and the extent to which its disturbing ideas linger are not surprising coming from Churchill. Nor is the remarkable economy of *A Number*. Only an hour in length, as staged at the New York Theatre Workshop, it's a one-set (and an extremely stripped-down set, at that) two-hander. Two actors play four characters, one portraying a father; the other, three different versions of his son—the original and two of an indeterminate number of clones. The play's radically spartan dramaturgy, penetrating imagery, impatience with conventional ideas and refusal to be confined within the norms of time and space are typical of Churchill's restless originality.

CHURCHILL HAS PLAYED fast and creatively with realistic constructs for four decades, perhaps most famously in *Cloud Nine*—with its radical 100-year gap between the settings of its two acts, during which the characters have aged 25 years—and *Top Girls*, with its opening dinner at which fictional and historical women from many different eras (Pope Joan, Chaucer's Patient Griselda, Brueghel's Dull Gret) celebrate the promotion of a contemporary business manager. The least famous of the three great playwrights whose careers date from circa 1960—with Harold Pinter and Edward Albee—she arguably has been equally influential on succeeding generations of dramatists in Europe and throughout the English-speaking world.

Born in 1938 in London, and partly raised (for about a decade) in Canada, Churchill's first plays were staged while she was still a student at

If not our genetic makeup, what is it that makes each of us unique?

Cambridge University in the late 1950s. She spent much of the 1960s writing radio plays, and giving birth to three sons—the same number, though probably coincidentally, as in *A Number*. She rose to prominence in the 1970s, beginning a long relationship with the Royal Court Theatre (which lasts to this day) in 1972 with *Owners*, a radical look at property rights, and creating new works with the collectives Monstrous Regiment (*Vinegar Tom*) and Joint Stock Theatre Group (*Light Shining in Buckinghamshire, Cloud Nine*).

A degree of commercial success came in the 1980s, particularly with *Cloud Nine, Top Girls* and her remarkably raucous look at stock-exchange mania, *Serious Money*, her first play to move to Broadway (in 1988). Unlike Pinter and Albee, Churchill doesn't seem at home on Broadway, in the West End or at most major regional theater companies. *Number*, which has been announced for the 2005–2006 season at San Francisco's American Conservatory Theater, may be her first new play to achieve such mainstage acceptance since *Serious Money* and her penetrating docudrama about Romania after the fall of Ceauçescu, *Mad Forest* (1990). Few playwrights of Churchill's years and international stature, let alone wide-ranging influence, are more likely to continue to have their new works staged, not by mainstream theaters, but by cutting-edge experimental companies.

THE OPENING SETUP is both familiar and rigorously cryptic. *A Number* opens on a troubled father, Salter, in conversation with his deeply distressed, but equally reserved, grown son in a resolutely minimal representation of a living room. At the New York Theatre Workshop, Eugene Lee's eloquently simple set consisted of a black leather couch and a standing lamp, set off against a distressed brick wall with a wooden door in the middle. Lee and director James Macdonald (of the Royal Court) enhanced the play's almost clinical detachment by arranging the house seats in steeply raked, semicircular tiers, as in an operating room theater or science lecture hall.

> B2: A number
>
> SALTER: you mean
>
> B2: a number of them, of us, a considerable
>
> SALTER: say
>
> B2: ten, twenty
>
> SALTER: didn't you ask?
>
> B2: I got the impression

Celebrity casting certainly helped draw audiences in both London and New York. *A Number* opened at the Royal Court in 2002, directed by Stephen Daldry, with Michael Gambon as Salter (and Daniel Craig as the sons). The NYTW production, which opened in November 2004, featured playwright and film star Sam Shepard as Salter. Whatever the initial draw, though, Churchill's inexorably compelling stagecraft takes over immediately.

Topsy-turvy: Dallas Roberts and Sam Shepard in Caryl Churchill's A Number. *Photo: Joan Marcus*

SALTER: it is, I am, the shocking thing is that there are these, not
how many but at all

B2: even one

SALTER: exactly, even one, a twin would be a shock

B2: a twin would be a surprise but a number

SALTER: a number any number is a shock.

The dialogue is fragmented, a realistic—if artistically heightened—representation of the confusion of two men faced with an extraordinary turn of events. The basic idea is quickly established, however. B2, Churchill's script shorthand for Bernard the second, has just learned that there are perhaps 20 exact genetic clones of himself and has come home to confront his father with this fact—and seek an explanation. Salter's response, which comes gradually and in contradictory statements, both clarifies the facts and deepens the thematic mysteries.

Churchill uses exposition as a plot device—half the story may be said to consist of unearthing the past, while the key events in the present take place offstage (and become exposition in the following scene)—and as a thematic mechanism. She reveals details sparingly in each of the play's five scenes. An ambiguous initial setup is clarified only to become more provocatively puzzling as each fact is unearthed. The clearer the relationships between the characters become, the greater is our unease with their situation. Each revelation raises more questions. Why did the father have his first son cloned? Who created the other clones and why? What explains the marked personality differences between the sons (portrayed with stunningly versatile realism by Dallas Roberts in New York)? Churchill doesn't provide answers. She raises more thought-provoking questions instead.

THE FIRST SCENE is essentially a standoff between B2 and Salter in which a few key facts emerge from a web of evasions and lies. Shepard and Roberts established a compelling sense of uneasy closeness between father and son, compounded by Shepard's downcast or shifting gaze. Salter at first expresses complete ignorance and outrage at the existence of the clones. He tries to reassure B2 that he's the real original, born naturally ("You think I wouldn't know if I wasn't your father?") of a woman who died in childbirth. He tries to divert the conversation into a potential lawsuit against the "mad scientist" responsible for this personal trespass. His argument introduces the theme of cloning as a threat to the cloned person's (and the clones') sense of individuality, an idea that is already beginning to trouble his son.

SALTER: a million is the least you should take, I think it's more like
half a million each person because what they've done they've

damaged your uniqueness, weakened your identity, so we're looking at five million for a start.

B2 isn't convinced. Gradually he gets Salter to admit that the truth is more complicated. There was an earlier son. B2's mother didn't die in childbirth but in an accident, four years later, and the first son died with her. Salter had the son cloned because "I wanted one just the same because that seemed to me the most perfect." B2, he says, is that son.

B2: I'm just a copy. I'm not the real one.

SALTER: You're the only one.

B2: What do you mean only, there's all the others, there's

SALTER: but I didn't know that, that wasn't part of the deal. They were meant to make one of you not a whole number, they stole that, we'll deal with, it's something for lawyers. But you're what I wanted, you're the one.

The second scene peels back another layer of reality and introduces some of the play's more troubling themes. It opens with a mirror image of the initial twosome, but this time Salter is being confronted by B1—the original son, though the audience by this time is not about to accept any son as the original. It soon will, as the story takes a tragic turn. Churchill, who inventively used the widespread custom of one actor playing multiple roles to comment on gender-identity conventions in *Cloud Nine*, employs the same device to more disturbing effect here. In Roberts's increasingly impressive portrayal, B1 both looks identical to and very different from B2, the subtle physical shifts in tone, stance and facial expressions proving even more unsettling than the more obvious differences in attitude and behavior. Later, when Salter claims that he could never confuse one Bernard for the other, we know exactly what he means.

The scene begins with another lie. Salter is telling B1 that "they stole your genetic material." The truth, as it emerges, is that Salter's wife committed suicide. "She was one of those people when they say there has been a person under a train and the trains are delayed she was a person under a train." Salter tried to raise his son on his own, but he was depressed, angry and neglectful. B1 talks about screaming for a father who would never answer his calls and about the dust under his bed, where he took refuge. Salter admits having finally sent the difficult, unhappy B1 away after having him cloned, in an attempt to make a new start.

SALTER: Nobody regrets more than me the completely unforeseen unforeseeable which isn't my fault and does make it more upsetting but what I did did seem at the time the only and also it's a tribute, I

Identity crisis: Dallas Roberts in Caryl Churchill's A Number. *Photo: Joan Marcus*

could have had a different one, a new child altogether that's what most people but I wanted you again because I thought you were the best.

B1: It wasn't me again.

SALTER: No but the same basic the same raw materials because they were perfect. You were the most beautiful baby everyone said. As a child too you were very pretty, very pretty child.

The issue of the essential arrogance of cloning grows increasingly more apparent, painfully expressed in B1's sarcastic retort: "they take this painless scrape this specky little cells of me and kept that and you threw the rest of me away." Churchill interweaves that idea with problems in parenting, tying her narrative to the essential age-old conflict between nature and nurture. B1 is a frightening example of the results of parental abuse, whether solely from Salter's treatment or from a combination of that with whatever foster or adoptive care he'd received since. He's unremittingly angry, unhappy and prone to violence. By the end of the scene, he's threatened to get rid of the clones that have replaced him as a son and as a unique individual.

The difference in Salter's treatment of his sons becomes even clearer in the third scene. Between scenes, B1 has found and confronted B2. A shaken B2 returns in Scene 3 to demand more answers from Salter and to tell him that he's leaving the city, perhaps the country, for fear of his genetic prototype. Salter reveals more of the true story of what happened to his wife and how he tried to make amends for being a bad father by being the best parent he could be to B2. In an extraordinary speech that raises the nature vs. nurture stakes, B2 accuses and tries to excuse his father with a confused argument about genetic determinism.

"Maybe it was genetic," he begins, his thoughts in such a rushed jumble that they keep outstripping his ability to put them into words as he jumps from the idea that his father had a genetic predisposition to alcoholism, or perhaps to addiction to which another person wouldn't have been as vulnerable. Or perhaps a person "with the same genetic exactly the same but at a different time a different cultural and of course all the personal all kinds of what happened in your own life your childhood"—a genetically identical person raised differently might have had more capacity to be a loving father to B1. But then, B2 admits, Salter was a loving father to him. "So it's a combination of very complicated and that's who you were so probably I shouldn't blame you."

The scene closes with one of the play's very few outright expressions of affection—one that's thrown back in the speaker's face, with startling cruelty however understandable and dispassionate:

SALTER: I love you.

B2: That's something else you can't help.

Two acts of violence occur between each of the final scenes—offstage, in the best classical Greek tradition. Scene 4 brings back B1, essentially to tell Salter that he's successfully tracked down the fleeing B2 and killed him. He taunts his father with a refusal to reveal the details of what happened, while Salter desperately tries to establish a connection with his original son, confessing more specifics of his neglect of the child. B1 leaves him with the teasing hint of a possible revelation.

BY THE BEGINNING of the final scene, B1 has killed himself as well. Salter is meeting Michael, a clone the same age (35) as B2 but a completely different person. Michael is a comparatively happy, average citizen, a math teacher, married with three children. Salter tries everything he can to elicit some information that will explain Michael to him, what defines his personality or makes him unique.

Michael can only reply with unhelpful generalities. He offers a parable, about an ancient tribe that lived in tunnels underground, burying their dead in sealed up chambers in the walls. He provides the play's only overt political statement, a generic antiwar sentiment that would scarcely differentiate him from most members of the audience. He speaks of his loving admiration for his wife's ears.

Michael, of course, is a person who wouldn't exist at all without the cloning experiment that has so upset, and destroyed, the two Bernards. It's still something of a shock when he professes himself delighted with the turn of events.

> MICHAEL: all these very similar people doing things like each other or a bit different or whatever we're doing, what a thrill for the mad old professor if he'd lived to see it, I do see the joy of it. I know you're not at all happy.

The play ends with Salter not only unhappy but completely dissatisfied. He's lost both of the sons he knew, the one he discarded and the one he nurtured. More than that, he's also lost a sense of identity, which is what he seeks in his attempts to have Michael define himself.

On the one hand, *A Number* is a dramatic case study in the nature-nurture argument. Churchill presents us with three genetically identical people who've grown into three completely different individuals—a confused, tender but somewhat lost, loving son; an angry psychopath; a rather happy, well-adjusted and apparently constructive citizen. Two were raised by the same father, but at different times and by a much-changed man. The third was raised in a completely different home environment. Michael makes the genetic argument specific: "We've got 99 percent the same genes as any other person. We've got 90 percent the same as a chimpanzee. We've got 30 percent the same as a lettuce. Does that cheer you up at all? I love about the lettuce. It makes me feel I belong." But Churchill has also built in enough similarities between her three son-characters not to let that settle the issue entirely.

More than that, *A Number* probes deeper, more disturbing questions about just what constitutes our treasured sense of individuality. If not our genetic makeup, what is it that makes each of us unique? Or are we?

2004–2005 Best Play

THE PILLOWMAN

By Martin McDonagh

○ ○ ○ ○ ○

Essay by John Istel

TUPOLSKI: [...] Some of your stories are very good too. I did like some of them.

KATURIAN: Which ones?

TUPOLSKI: (*pause*) There was something about "The Pillowman" that stayed with me. There was something gentle about it.

HERE'S ANOTHER GOOD STORY. Once upon a time, a young high school dropout from London began writing strange and wondrous tales set in the woolly west of Ireland. He lived with his brother and didn't read much. But he wrote stories, television scripts, and screenplays, as he told an interviewer, to "avoid having a real job." Not long after seeing David Mamet's *American Buffalo*, the young man decided to turn his stories into stage plays. Out came brutish, almost cartoon wonders, more comic and more menacing than those conjured by his aesthetic predecessor, Harold Pinter. And, as in a fairy tale, the plays, which the writer dubbed "just stories [. . .] little things," began to be produced. And they were deemed good.

Martin McDonagh's latest play to hit New York, *The Pillowman*, contains a swirl of stories-within-stories, dark Beckettian vaudeville routines and Pirandellian questions about each character's reality. The play, in fact, questions whether a story can be just a wee thing, or whether a writer's work has the potential to grow into something larger and more powerful. If a story affects behavior, whose responsibility is that?

In *The Pillowman*, the police suspect McDonagh's stage doppelgänger, Katurian, of being involved in a series of child murders because he has written some particularly vicious fables featuring the torture and murder of children. The cops, Tupolski and Ariel, have zeroed in on a handful of particularly gruesome tales. In one, a girl is literally crucified and then buried alive.

McDonagh isn't the only one to have a dramatic mirror image: Everything in this play is doubled—as if funhouse mirrors were held up to

Brother love: Michael Stuhlbarg and Billy Crudup in Martin McDonagh's The Pillowman.
Photo: Joan Marcus

each other. There are two brothers, two police officers, two murdered parents, two child murder-victims. Although there are three acts in the published script (Faber and Faber, 2003), each is divided into two parts, one existing in the "reality" of the play and the other in the surreality of the imaginative fables written by Katurian. Further, McDonagh calls for the intermission of the nearly three-hour play not between acts, but smack in the middle of the second act, effectively dividing the performance of the play into two halves. There are also two "real-life" pillowmen: Katurian, whom we see use pillows to smother all the members of his family; and Ariel, the bulldog cop who we learned suffocated his father with a pillow after being abused for years.

That's certainly the viewpoint of Katurian, who begins the play blindfolded in a foreboding gray police interrogation room. His interlocutors, Tupolski and Ariel, are grilling him about the gruesome killings of children in which the murders mirror those of victims in Katurian's stories. The terrified writer tries to assuage the cops and claims that none of the four hundred stories he's written and put in a box (only one has been published) have meaning or agendas:

> KATURIAN: [. . .] A great man once said, "The first duty of a storyteller is to tell a story," and I believe in that wholeheartedly, "The first

duty of a storyteller is to tell a story." Or was it "The *only* duty of a storyteller is to tell a story?" I can't remember, but anyway, that's what I do, I tell stories. [. . .]

The Pillowman continually questions the value of stories and storytellers in society. Do stories have any value (specifically, political or moral value) other than escape and entertainment? Ultimately, McDonagh suggests a paradox at the heart of an artist's work: it's only real power over the world is unreal—the power of imagination.

THE PILLOWMAN'S THREE acts all begin in the play's "real world": an interrogation room or a holding cell in a nameless police building,

---

Some accept the violence and gore as "works of the imagination."

---

somewhere in a vaguely Eastern European "fascist totalitarian state." Each act concludes with a fictional story created by Katurian, and each features a resurrection. The first two acts end with stories narrated by Katurian, which are acted out in dumbshow. In director John Crowley's production, based on his National Theatre staging in London, a rectangular slab of the cellblock wall slid back to reveal a diorama high above the stage floor. Although the third act doesn't have a literal Scene 2, it carries the same structure to the end when Katurian, whom we've seen summarily executed for his crimes, comes back from the dead to offer a coda to the play.

Throughout the first scene's interrogation, Katurian clearly prides himself on his stories, which he considers his life work. Although we learn he makes a living in a slaughterhouse, Katurian is careful to make a distinction: "I don't cut stuff. I just clear stuff." This just makes the cops sneer. It's tempting to see that comment as McDonagh's view of the artist's place in society: The authorities have the power to tell stories that do the real damage of slaughter; authors just entertain.

When questioned about "The Three Gibbet Crossroads," which is the only story in the play that doesn't feature a child being abused, Katurian again denies any agenda. In the story, a character wakes to find himself barely alive in an iron gibbet, a device used to display executed prisoners' bodies at a medieval crossroads. Like Katurian, he doesn't know what crime he's committed, although there's a sign explaining his sin just out of sight. Whenever anyone reads his sign, they get disgusted and horrified.

Finally, a highwayman frees other criminals in adjacent gibbets but shoots the man who dies not knowing the crime for which he was killed.

After Tupolski paraphrases this harrowingly existential fable, Katurian responds by again abjuring any comparisons or literary analysis:

> KATURIAN: That's a good story. That's something-esque. What kind of "esque" is it? I can't remember. I don't really go in for that "esque" sort of stuff anyway, but there's nothing wrong with that story. Is there?

Although Katurian refuses to let anyone read "meaning" into his stories, he nevertheless cares deeply about them and the policemen's reaction to them. He delights in his own imagination, and as Tupolski reads the gory ending of "Apple Men," which involves the swallowing of razor blades hidden in carved apple pieces, he pipes in a line, acting the voice of an appleman himself.

> TUPOLSKI: But then it goes on. The girl wakes up that night. A number of applemen are walking up her chest. They hold her mouth open. The say to her . . .
>
> KATURIAN: (*slight voice*) "You killed our little brothers . . ."

Horror, horror: Jeff Goldblum in Martin McDonagh's The Pillowman. *Photo: Joan Marcus*

> TUPOLSKI: "You killed our little brothers." They climb down her throat. She chokes to death on her own blood. The end.
>
> KATURIAN: It's a bit of a twist. You think it's a dream sequence. It isn't. (*Pause.*) What? I said it wasn't my best work.

Katurian reveals that the story he's most proud of is the only one he has ever published—"The Tale of the Town on the River"—in a magazine called *The Libertad*. It's a macabre "prequel" to the Pied Piper fairy tale, reimagining the Piper as a ghoulish man who chops off the toes of an innocent boy sitting by the side of the road and throws them to the rats he has brought to town. "It was the children he was after in the first place," says Katurian.

The literary dissection ends and the officers' purpose becomes clear when suddenly there's the sound of a prisoner being tortured. It's Katurian's learning disabled brother, Michal. Katurian picks up Michal from school every day, walking through the same Jewish quarter where the authorities found a dead boy without any toes on one foot, just as in Katurian's story. Moreover, a little girl has been found dead with razor blades wrapped in an apple stuck down her throat. Michal is being questioned offstage, in the next room, by Ariel, who had slipped out earlier. Ariel re-enters with his hand bleeding, as if he'd been banging Michal's head.

They confront Katurian with some evidence in a little tin box, which they claim they found inside Katurian and Michal's house: five toes from the dead Jewish boy. Ariel then tries to force the writer to reveal where a third child, "a mute girl," has disappeared.

> TUPOLSKI: [. . .] Along with the evidence we found in your house, your brother, spastic or not, has, under duress or not, admitted enough about the killings for us to execute him before the evening's out, but, as Ariel said, he's hardly the brains behind the operation, so we want you to confess, too. We like executing writers. Dimwits we can execute any day. And we do. But, you execute a writer, it sends out a signal, y'know?

THE NEXT SCENE is a bizarre narrated story. Katurian tells the tale—in third person—that he's apparently titled, "The Writer and the Writer's Brother." As he narrates, it's acted out in dumbshow. The story is about a young, creative boy whose model parents lovingly nurture him and teach him how to write. Then at the age of seven, he begins hearing the hideous shrieks of someone in pain behind a locked door in his room. Every night until the age of 14, the boy hears the screams until he finally breaks down the door. He finds his parents holding the notification of his having won a short story contest. But, according to the story, years later the writer returns to the house after publishing his first book only to find the actual skeleton of a torture victim and realizes the horrible price he paid for his stories to take on such dark beauty. Moreover, there's a manuscript of a story in the skeleton's hand which the writer sees is more beautiful than anything he's written. He burns it.

The audience barely has any time to ponder any questions raised by the tale because Katurian explains what he calls the "truer story": that when the young teenage writer broke down the door, the brother was a living, writhing torture victim. In the production, this moment caused audible gasps and cries as the enactment of the story featured a bloody body suddenly sitting bolt upright. Freeing his brother, the writer is so angry at his parents, that he suffocates both of them in bed with a pillow that very night. The audience is left to ponder what exactly is true and what is fictional as the lights fade to black and end the scene.

Later in the play, Katurian confesses to killing his parents and when asked why he did the deed, he refers back to the story we've just witnessed:

> KATURIAN: [. . .] I think people who only write about what they know only write about what they know because they're too fucking stupid to make anything up, however "The Writer and the Writer's Brother" is, I suppose, the only story of mine that isn't really fiction.

This epitomizes McDonagh's priorities: imagination trumps reality. As it turns out, even this confession is false; too many parts of the story can't be true.

The second act begins with a scene in which Michal hears Katurian being tortured offstage. Katurian is then pushed, battered and bloody, into the room. The two brothers are the only characters onstage during the rest of the long, pivotal scene. First, Katurian discovers that Michal wasn't really tortured earlier that day; he was just told to scream. It was Ariel's attempt to scare Katurian into confessing to the child murders. As Michal says, he might be brain-damaged, but he's not stupid: "Oh, no, the man said he was *going* to torture me, but I thought, 'No way, boy, that'd hurt,' so I just told him whatever he wanted to hear, and he was fine then."

Katurian surmises that Ariel's bloody hands were part of the same ruse and he wonders what else the authorities have made up. He realizes the cops must be good actor-storytellers, too; perhaps they even made the fake toes that they claimed to find in his house. He begins to wonder what's real and what has been concocted:

Writer's block: Billy Crudup and Zeljko Ivanek in Martin McDonagh's The Pillowman.
Photo: Joan Marcus

> KATURIAN: We don't even know that there were any children killed
> at all.
>
> MICHAL: It was in the papers.
>
> KATURIAN: Who runs the papers?
>
> MICHAL: The police. Ohh. You're quite clever.
>
> KATURIAN: Oh my God. "A writer in a totalitarian state is interrogated
> about the gruesome content of his short stories and their similarities
> to a number of child-murders that are happening in his town. A
> number of child-murders . . . that aren't actually happening at all."

Katurian's spirits are lifted by this possibility and when Michal complains
of "an itchy arse," he sets about telling his brother "The Pillowman" to take
his mind off his discomfort. Katurian's fairy tale is about a giant nine-foot-tall
man made out of pink pillows who finds people about to commit suicide
and takes them back in time to the age of five. He then arranges these kids'
suicides by making them look like tragic accidents. Thus the parents are
spared the heartache of having to understand why their innocent child
would be so unhappy as to commit suicide.

MCDONAGH IS NOT satisfied with such a simple plot twist, however. Katurian's world is turned upside down after he finishes the story. Michal offhandedly says he doesn't understand how the police found his box of toes because he thought he hid them really well. Soon, he's explaining how he also killed the little girl by forcing applemen with razors inside down her throat. The confession, coming from the naïve, mentally challenged Michal is horrifying:

> MICHAL: But the girl was a pain in the arse. Kept bawling her eyes out. And she wouldn't eat them. She wouldn't eat the applemen, and I'd spent *ages* making them. It's really hard to get the razor blades inside. You don't say how to make them in the story, do ya?

Michal thought of himself as a Pillowman, sparing these children lives of suffering. Although Katurian objects that not all children "lead horrible lives," it's clear that every character in this play does. Ariel killed his own father after being abused for years by him, and even Tupolski has a story. Tupolski reveals in a bit dialogue that perhaps a "pillowman" visited his own son:

> TUPOLSKI: [...] (*Pause.*) And the idea of, if a child died, alone, through some accident, he wasn't really alone. He had this kind, soft person with him, to hold his hand and whatnot. And that it was the child's choice, somehow. Made it somewhat, reassuring, somehow. That it wasn't just a stupid waste.
>
> KATURIAN: (*nods. Pause*) Did you lose a child?
>
> TUPOLSKI: (*pause*) Unlike old Ariel, I don't go into those sorts of things with the condemned.
>
> *Katurian nods. Sad pause.*
>
> Son drowned. (*Pause.*) Fishing on his own. (*Pause.*) Silly.

Katurian is determined to find a way to save his stories for posterity, even if he and his brother are executed. When Michal suggests he forget about them, referring to them as "just paper," Katurian loses his temper and attacks his brother, banging his head on the floor. Katurian says: "If they came to me right now and said, 'We're going to burn two out of the three of you – you, your brother, or your stories,' I'd have them burn you first, I'd have them burn me second, and I'd have it be the stories they saved."

He then asks Michal how he killed the third child, the little missing girl the police have grilled and tortured him about. Michal tells him he tried to act out a story called "The Little Jesus" and as Katurian pictures the details, he begins to weep. Eventually, he and Michal calm down after insulting each other, and Katurian tells another story: "The Little Green

Pig." It's an Aesop-like revenge fantasy about a green pig who is teased and resented by all the other pigs. One day, as a prank, the others paint him pink with indelible permanent paint. He no longer has any distinctive features. But that night, it rains green paint and all the other pigs become green and the formerly green pig again becomes a stand out.

By the end of the story, Michal has dozed off. Katurian suddenly decides to kill him and smothers his brother with the jailhouse pillow. He then pounds on the cell door for help: he's ready to confess to any and all murders—if he can work out a deal to save his stories.

THE THIRD ACT is a battle of wits between Katurian, who wants to ensure that his stories will be saved for posterity, and the pair of policemen who want to wrap up the case. The scene begins with Tupolski reading Katurian's confession to the killing of his mother and father, the three missing children and his brother Michal—a confession offered in exchange for the promise that his stories won't be burned.

When asked whether the little girl that he dressed as Jesus was alive or dead when he buried her, Katurian hesitates. He's not sure becauses his brother didn't offer that detail. He remembers that Michal said she was entombed near his parents next to the wishing well in their backyard. Ariel rushes out to see if they can save her since, in the story, the girl was given enough oxygen for three days.

McDonagh's twists now tumble in a rush: The little girl isn't dead, but alive, happy, and painted as a green pig. Clearly, Katurian didn't know Michal had acted out that story instead of "The Little Jesus." This turn means that Katurian's confession is worthless—and pointless—because Tupolski promises that his stories will burn anyway. He's also about to be executed at point-blank range but before he can say his prayers, he attempts to think of a new story. Tupolski shoots him, but Katurian rises from the dead to narrate a final twist in which Ariel, the policeman who is about to burn the stories, has a change of heart and files them away instead:

> KATURIAN: [. . .] A fact which would have ruined the writer's fashionably downbeat ending but was somehow . . . somehow . . . more in keeping with the spirit of the thing.

The final blackout occurs when Ariel blows out the fire in the wastebasket.

Critics and audience members can read the play completely differently: some accept the violence and gore as "works of the imagination"; others are literalists who are sickened by the acts described in Katurian's fairy tale stories. McDonagh uses the theater's compact with the audience to make us complicit in his Grand Guignol visions. He toys with the willingness to suspend disbelief: we're not seeing a girl crucified, we're watching a young actor in a play portray a character in a story within a story. It's ironic how many who complained about the brutality in the fictional stories rarely objected to the violence of the interrogation, torture, and execution at the hands of the State.

The playwright reminds us that artists' imaginations are rarely more dangerous to society than, say, the Patriot Act. That's the artist's paradox that Katurian articulates: stories don't really "exist" but in the minds of its teller and audiences; although they can change the world in the right (or wrong) hands.

2004–2005 Best Play

ROMANCE

By David Mamet

○ ○ ○ ○ ○

Essay by Robert Vorlicky

> JUDGE: I guess what I am trying to say is this: we get caught up in the "form," the Law, Religion, Nationality . . . uh . . . skin color. And then, and then, *miraculously*, *Miraculously*, now and then, and by the grace of God, we are free. And see, that, underneath. We love each other.

DAVID MAMET, UNDENIABLY one of our preeminent playwrights, gave the much-respected Atlantic Theater Company an impressive gift for 2004–05 season: his latest play, *Romance*. Although Mamet and actor William H. Macy founded the company in 1985, *Romance* was Atlantic's first premiere of the playwright's work.

The play is a courtroom comedy whose four scenes occur simultaneously with an offstage Middle East peace conference between two "great men"—powerful leaders of "Two Warring Peoples, Arabs and Jews, an Ancient Enmity." During the production's limited, sold-out run, the timeliness of the play's context was unavoidable. As their homelands maintained a fragile peace, Israeli and Palestinian leaders slowly moved forward in negotiations toward the historic transfer of contested land in the Gaza Strip from Israeli to Palestinian occupancy.

In the microcosm of Mamet's stage world, his characters also seek peace, albeit of various natures—from an articulated comfort level of mutual understanding within human relationships to the resolution of conflict that comes systemically (if not ideally) with a judge's verdict. But at no point does Mamet allow his characters or his audience to forget that peace is a pawn in society's power plays. And for Mamet, the all-male play remains a favorite site for the theatricalization of this firmly held belief.

Expanding upon his previous dramaturgical use of such workplace environments as a barge, a junk shop and a real estate office, the courtroom of *Romance* is anything but business as usual. In this play, Mamet's theatrical form has more in common with burlesque and vaudeville than it does with the searing judicial dramas of *To Kill a Mockingbird* or *Twelve Angry Men*.

133

Justice delayed: Steven Hawley, Larry Bryggman, Christopher Evan Welch, Bob Balaban and Steven Goldstein in David Mamet's Romance. *Photo: Gerry Goodstein*

SCENE 1 IN *Romance* opens with the prosecutor interrogating the defendant, who is later identified as George Bernstein, a chiropractor. We remain uncertain throughout as to why Bernstein is even standing trial. His charge is never revealed. Against his lawyer's wishes, he is on the witness stand being grilled by the prosecutor. The attorney's vague questions at the opening of the play yield veiled answers from the accused, often generating among everyone in the courtroom a lot of talk about the specificity, or lack thereof, of meaning. For Mamet, this metalinguistic feature—talk about talk—is a longstanding characteristic of his dialogue and its comedic potential is exploited to hilarious ends in *Romance*.

Despite the authority emanating from scene designer Robert Brill's imposing, mahogany bench that fills the entire upstage area with the obligatory portrait of George Washington, the judge who presides over the formal proceedings is a rabble-rousing anarchist at heart when it comes to adhering to the letter of the law. Danny, as the judge's name is later revealed (played with amusing mastery by Larry Bryggman), constantly disrupts the trial's procedures—which he is responsible to uphold—by talking at any time about anything that comes to mind. If he isn't expressing his delight in parades, fantasizing about potential progress at the peace conference or sharing random thoughts, the judge is ingesting inordinate amounts of medication to control his allergies. He is woozy from pills throughout the court's session and his mind is always drifting.

Early on, the judge makes it clear that he is not a fan of form, whether it is evident in the structures of "the Law, Religion, Nationality . . . uh . . . skin color." Paradoxically, as the one granted the authority to maintain (legal) form, the judge actually celebrates formlessness: a "freedom" to see that "underneath. We love each other." If in fact we truly "love each other," Danny the judge implies, all people have the capacity to understand, if not

---

True progress has the potential to arise peacefully between Home and its Other.

---

transcend, their differences—differences that, when institutionalized, aggressively work against understanding, transcendence and love. The forms taken by the Law—the courtroom, the language, the behavior, the authority—contextualize the opening and final scenes of *Romance*. But the non-conformist, self-absorbed, freedom-loving judge makes it clear from the beginning that his space exists, in most ways, outside the bounds of legal protocol.

In Scenes 2 and 3, Mamet captures characters who interact, initially, within institutional forms that are influenced from structures determined outside the self: "Religion" and, to a lesser degree, domestic partnership. George Bernstein and his lawyer confer in a small conference room in Scene 2; the bailiff sits with them, reading the newspaper. The defense attorney is trying to get his client to explain what he was doing in Hawaii November 10, an event that is central to George's case. Rather than replying directly, George reminds his lawyer about his obligation to come up with an "alternative," a different "way of 'looking'" at this potentially damaging fact. According to George, "*Why did you* go to *Law* School? If you don't want to *Lie*." George announces his intention to fire his attorney since he won't lie on his behalf, which sets the defense attorney on a tirade of pent-up, verbal abuse directed toward his client:

DEFENSE ATTORNEY: YOU'RE *GUILTY*. DO YOU UNDERSTAND? [. . .] YOU MAKE ME SICK. [. . .] I'M FILLED WITH CONTEMPT,

WITH, *FUCK* CONTEMPT, WITH LOATHING, AND YOU SIT UP
THERE, GUILTY AS SIN, CRIMINAL, SICK, PERVERTED. [. . .]

The suggestion of perversion is not challenged by George, nor does the
attorney elaborate, as he streamrolls to a more defining slur:

DEFENSE ATTORNEY: [I'm . . . f]orced to sit *next* to you, you SICK
FUCK, day-after-day, *supporting* you; nodding at your infantile,
hypocrisies. This sick Talmudic, Jewish . . . (*pause*) Ohmigod.

Caught! The truth comes out! Just beneath the surface of the men's
institutionally prescribed, professional relationship resides a deep, pervasive
animosity that is ancestral in its blood origins. Quickly, they unhinge from
their roles as defendant and defense attorney in favor of their more resonant
identities as Jew and Christian. Mamet sets up the men as "Warring People,"
albeit inferior, hypocritical, prejudiced counterparts to the offstage great
world leaders who are also determined by and rooted in their religions.
Once they voice their religious affiliations, the defendant and defense
attorney are merciless in their mutual verbal taunting. As portrayed by
Steven Goldstein and Christopher Evan Welch, respectively, the two men
seethe with palpable animosity. George snipes that the attorney, when he

*Call me Danny: Larry Bryggman in David
Mamet's* Romance. *Photo: Gerry Goodstein*

picks up his son Tommy from a church hockey game, will have "trouble getting the Priest's dick out of your son's ass," to which the defense attorney responds by shooting a litany of epithets at the Jewish defendant: "fucken kike," "Christkilling, Jew, Cocksucking *bastard*," "Rug Merchant, Greasy, Hooknosed, *no*-dick." The Christian then effortlessly releases his most sweeping, racist feelings about George, his family and his race: "I hope that the Arabs. Rise in their droves, and drive your people into the sea. Killing the children. Raping their wives and burning down all traces of your two-thousand year long sacrilege."

IN THE FIRST of many striking confessions that are blurted out in *Romance*, the defense attorney's comment and behavior perfectly capture how he is "caught up in the 'form,' the Law, Religion, Nationality . . . uh . . . skin color" that were marked earlier by the Judge as constraints that keep people from loving one another. This is also the case for George, who strikes back with his own crude assessment of the defense attorney:

> DEFENDANT: [. . .] You fucken asshole. You brain-dead, white socks, country club, plaid pants, Campbell's soup fucken *sheigetz* Goy. [. . .] We eat Christian *Children*. We bake them in *pies*, just like you have been saying these two thousand years. Your whole dolt, Catholic . . . [. . .] Go back to the Country Club. Drink, fuck each other's wives, and increase the defense budget. [. . .]

Scene 2, in effect, is the quintessence of male speech in Mamet's canon: demeaning, crude, foul, and prejudicial. However, by relying upon, ironically, a "spoken" *deus ex machina* in the final seconds of the scene, the playwright, uncharacteristically, lifts the Christian's and Jew's tongue lashings into the realm of revelation, as the defendant blurts out, "OHMIGOD. OHMIGOD! [. . .] *I KNOW HOW TO BRING PEACE TO THE MIDDLE EAST!!!*" End of scene.

Mamet juxtaposes the aggressive, unrelenting, macho racist rant between the pair of men in Scene 2 with a distinctive, sustained verbal interaction between male lovers—a first for Mamet—in a very brief Scene 3. In the domestic space of their home, the suit and tie prosecutor (a scrappy bulldog played by Bob Balaban) spats with his thong-clad boy toy, Bernard (the endearing Keith Nobbs), over the attorney's rehearsal performance of his closing remarks to the jury. "Do you have any notion how *humiliating* this is . . . [. . .] . . . to indulge in this *hypocrisy*," the older man privately pleads with his lover, as his own relationship with Bernard stands outside the acceptable "form" condoned by the Law. For the prosecutor, the very nature of his job as defender of Law comes in conflict with the reality of his home life. But the scene between the two men is further complicated:

> PROSECUTOR: [. . .] Have I "hurt your *feelings*"?
>
> BERNARD: . . . I . . .
>
> PROSECUTOR: I'm losing you. I'm losing you. I know it. Don't lie to me. Please please please, just tell me the truth. For once, as if I were man enough to hear it. (*Alarm.*)
>
> BERNARD: You are man enough to hear it.

Here, Mamet both echoes and sets apart his writings of homosexual characters: in the recent *A Boston Marriage* (his only play featuring an all-female cast), lesbians living in the Victorian era speak obliquely to one another, while his modern gay couple in *Romance* is filled with emotion that language cannot contain. But protestations of personal angst soon deteriorate into the trading of insults, such as:

> PROSECUTOR: [. . .] You little two-bit piece of fucking INTELLECTUAL FLUFF.

And:

> BERNARD: [. . .] MY FRIENDS LOOKED AT YOU LIKE I'D BROUGHT HOME SOME FUCKING *WEATHERMAN*.

Bernard bursts into tears of real "feelings," which also causes him to lose a contact lens and finally to brandish a burned roasting pan. As Bernard crawls on the floor looking fruitlessly for his lens, the prosecutor deals with yet another disrupting telephone call during the duo's intense, personal conversation (reminiscent of the same theatrical device used in *Oleanna*). The calls are from the defense attorney, ostensibly still engaged with his client back in Scene 2, who wants a continuance granted for George so that he can take part in the peace process. The prosecutor resoundingly rejects the absurd request as he comfortably slips back into the form offered by the Law: "Get your ass and your client's ass into court tomorrow at 10 a.m." The squabble in this scene's domestic playing field is now mirroring the warring powers ensconced in the courthouse.

DESPITE HIS RECURRING wish to "use correct '*form*,'" Judge Danny presides over a courtroom in which legal propriety is immediately disregarded at the opening of Scene 4. There is no peace where or when Judge Danny presides. The magistrate is confused about where he is, uncertain about what case he is hearing, and he is noticeably sluggish and flighty since he is on new medication. Consequently, the defense attorney's pleas for a

Judicial restraint: Steven Hawley, Larry Bryggman and Jim Frangione in David Mamet's Romance. *Photo: Gerry Goodstein*

continuance so that George can present his method to the Israeli and Palestinian leaders fall on half-listening ears. Cellphone rings persist throughout the mayhem, as the prosecutor receives disruptive calls from his distressed lover. As staged with split-second precision by Atlantic's artistic director Neil Pepe, the dialogue remains at cross-purposes with establishing any formal coherency in the scene. Flying through the air is language filled with puns, double entendres, innuendoes and the casual mimicry of cultural references (from the Bible and Martin Luther King's "I Had a Dream" speech, to *Boys in the Band*, *Death of a Salesman* and *A Streetcar Named Desire*). For the audience, its laughter becomes infectious as Mamet's men top one another, line by comic line.

Amid the pandemonium it becomes clear very early in the session that this court's "high" judge is as obsessed with religion and sex as were his subordinates in Scenes 2 and 3. In Danny's courtroom, focus on a continuance that may aid the Middle East peace process loses out to more immediate hot issues that concern the judge: Was Shakespeare a "Fag"? Was he a Jew or "was he a Normal Human Being"? Was Abraham Lincoln a

Jew? Was Theodore Roosevelt a "Mulatto"? After all, if these "great men" had something in their closets, then perhaps it might be okay if lesser men did too!

Before the district attorney can, with disbelief and disgust, say the word "queer," nearly every man in the courtroom "outs" himself. But he does so hoping that at least in this sanctimonious male enclave it's possible for a man to be two things, without diminishing his position as a man among men. No Mamet play has ever given this much stage time to the proclivities of gay men, albeit hyper-stereotyped, completely farcical and quite bizarre. Scene 4 blossoms into a kind of male parody of Claire Boothe Luce's *The Women*. Testimonies abound as Mamet's gang comedy evolves into the rising action of sexual and religious confessions—or Mamet's fanciful homage to the effectiveness of masterly "storytelling."

A madcap outpouring, mostly orchestrated by the judge's racist, sexist commentary and questions, spills out of the characters' mouths: The judge, who is married, intimates special private vacations with the bailiff to the gay mecca of Ibiza; he may have committed incest with his daughter; and he is presently obsessed with disgust that he, himself, may be a Jew (with a penchant for paraphrasing Shylock). The prosecutor publicly declares his homosexuality, just before his vision-impaired, Tiresian boyfriend, Bernard, bursts into the courtroom, burnt roasting pan in tow, calling for judicial retribution for the prosecutor's "lack of sensitivity." The judge then takes great pleasure in having the young lad sit on his lap, and he soon after begins to take off his own clothes. Even the divorced, card-carrying Christian defense attorney admits that he cheated on his income tax. And while it is surprising that Jewish George discloses that he is a married closeted homosexual who had an affair with Bernard in Hawaii, nothing prepares the men (or the audience) for his confession that he "had sex with a goose"—another of the play's many intertextual references to earlier dramatic classics, here echoing Edward Albee's *The Goat, or Who Is Sylvia?*

Despite the cavalcade of deeply held secrets that reveal the extent to which every man in the room stands outside the form of the Law, the courtroom renegades don't completely lose sight of the day's agenda: to entertain the motion of George's continuance so he can aid in the Middle East peace process. Chiropractor George demonstrates on a skeleton prop with a skull turban that through proper manipulation of the world leaders' necks, their subsequent physical alignment will result in their "mental balance" and the rectification of the "imbalance in their countries," since the leaders are a "reflection" of their countries. This strategy is vociferously denounced by the court's domestic honey-bunny (as well as "blind" seer):

BERNARD: OH, FUCK *YOU*. HOW CAN YOU HAVE PEACE IN THE
MIDDLE EAST WHEN YOU CAN'T HAVE PEACE IN YOUR *HOME*.

Wiser words were never spoken.

IN THE RAPID, closing moments of the play, a doctor (Jim Frangione), at
the behest of the bailiff, comes to cart away the judge for medical care. But
Mamet's fiesty Blanche du Boisian judge is not so easily disposed of because
the doctor is sidetracked by a battle with the chiropractor over the latter's
lesser professional status. This leads to the play's first act of physical violence
when George climbs over the bench to attack the doctor. Not uncommon
for Mamet's woman-less sites, the courtroom devolves into a bullish arena
that contains vengeful, fighting bad boys, which mirrors the news from
offstage that the peace talks have broken down: one of the great men
called his counterpart an unrepeatable, objectionable name. So, "the leaders
have departed in wrath."

But Mamet is keen to demonstrate that existing along side the violent,
bullying guys are good boys who know how to play nicely through
compromise and reconciliation. Upon seeing the prosecutor and Bernard
affirm what he envisions as their commitment to romance, love and peace,
the judge blissfully remarks, "This, *this* is what I live for. This is my dream."
In his courtroom, in spite of its presumed adherence to a definitive "form"
that stifles freedom, the judge actually presides over an anarchistic aberration
where punishment is obliterated in the name of truth telling.

Despite most critics' resistance to seeing romance in *Romance*, Mamet
has captured—amid raucous humor, absurd circumstances and potentially
offensive stereotypes—a resonating image for his audience: a gay couple
who comes to express freely their appreciation and affection toward one
another. The distinguished playwright accomplishes this without sacrificing
critical qualities of the play's genre or excessively sentimentalizing the
prosecutor and Bernard's unabashedly proud relationship. Notably, Mamet
has created a stage world of men among men that includes an openly
committed gay couple. This romance, however giddily presented, should
not go unacknowledged during these reactionary years of George W. Bush's
presidency, an administration aggressively opposed to marital rights for
same-sex couples to the point that it advocates amending the Constitution
of the United States to guarantee their denial.

Theatricalizing a challenge to President Bush's legal obsession, Mamet's
Judge Danny presides over a courtroom in which the Law is not blind to
the justice of Love. The peace process, as Bernard rightly claimed, starts at

home. And whether or not home is informed by such identifying powers as God, Moses, Mohammed, gay or straight, peace is possible, Mamet seems to suggest, only when people are committed to recognizing differences and working toward mutual respect and understanding. Then, true progress, as if "miraculously," has the potential to arise peacefully between Home and its Other.

PLAYS PRODUCED IN
NEW YORK

PLAYS PRODUCED ON BROADWAY

○ ○ ○ ○ ○

FIGURES IN PARENTHESES following a play's title give the number of performances. These figures do not include previews or extra nonprofit performances. In the case of a transfer, the Off Broadway run is noted but not added to the figure in parentheses.

Plays marked with an asterisk (*) were still in a projected run June 1, 2005. Their number of performances is figured through May 31, 2005.

In a listing of a show's numbers—dances, sketches, musical scenes, etc.—the titles of songs are identified wherever possible by their appearance in quotation marks (").

HOLDOVERS FROM PREVIOUS SEASONS

BROADWAY SHOWS THAT were running on June 1, 2004 are listed below. More detailed information about them appears in previous *Best Plays* volumes of the years in which they opened. Important cast changes since opening night are recorded in the Cast Replacements section in this volume.

*The Phantom of the Opera (7,231). Musical with book by Richard Stilgoe and Andrew Lloyd Webber; music by Andrew Lloyd Webber; lyrics by Charles Hart; additional lyrics by Richard Stilgoe; adapted from the novel by Gaston Leroux. Opened January 26, 1988.

*Beauty and the Beast (4,560). Musical with book by Linda Woolverton; music by Alan Menken; lyrics by Howard Ashman and Tim Rice. Opened April 18, 1994.

*Rent (3,787). Transfer from Off Broadway of the musical with book, music and lyrics by Jonathan Larson. Opened Off Off Broadway January 26, 1996 and Off Broadway February 13, 1996 where it played 56 performances through March 31, 1996; transferred to Broadway April 29, 1996.

*Chicago (3,555). Revival of the musical based on the play by Maurine Dallas Watkins; book by Fred Ebb and Bob Fosse; music by John Kander; lyrics by Fred Ebb; original production directed and choreographed by Bob Fosse. Opened November 14, 1996.

*The Lion King (3,185). Musical adapted from the screenplay by Irene Mecchi, Jonathan Roberts and Linda Woolverton; book by Roger Allers and Irene Mecchi; music by Elton John; lyrics by Tim Rice; additional music and lyrics by Lebo M, Mark Mancina, Jay Rifkin, Julie Taymor and Hans Zimmer. Opened November 13, 1997.

Aida (1,852). Musical suggested by the Giuseppe Verdi opera; book by Linda Woolverton, Robert Falls and David Henry Hwang; music by Elton John; lyrics by Tim Rice. Opened March 23, 2000. (Closed September 5, 2004)

*The Producers (1,711). Musical with book by Mel Brooks and Thomas Meehan; music and lyrics by Mel Brooks. Opened April 19, 2001.

42nd Street (1,524). Revival of the musical based on the novel by Bradford Ropes and the 1933 movie; book by Michael Stewart and Mark Bramble; music by Harry Warren; lyrics by Al Dubin. Opened May 2, 2001. (Closed January 2, 2005)

*Mamma Mia! (1,519). Musical with book by Catherine Johnson; music and lyrics by Benny Andersson and Björn Ulvaeus, some songs with Stig Anderson. Opened October 18, 2001.

Thoroughly Modern Millie (903). Musical with book by Richard Morris and Dick Scanlan; new music by Jeanine Tesori; new lyrics by Mr. Scanlan; based on the story and screenplay by Richard Morris for the Universal Pictures film. Opened April 18, 2002. (Closed June 20, 2004)

*Hairspray (1,160). Musical with book by Mark O'Donnell and Thomas Meehan; music by Marc Shaiman; lyrics by Marc Shaiman and Scott Wittman; based on the film by John Waters. Opened August 15, 2002.

*Movin' Out (1,081). Dance musical based on the songs of Billy Joel; with music and lyrics by Mr. Joel; conceived by Twyla Tharp. Opened October 24, 2002.

*Avenue Q (765). Transfer of the Off Off Broadway musical with book by Jeff Whitty; music and lyrics by Robert Lopez and Jeff Marx. Opened July 31, 2003.

Little Shop of Horrors (372). Revival of the musical with book and lyrics by Howard Ashman; music by Alan Menken; based on the film by Roger Corman. Opened October 2, 2003. (Closed August 22, 2004)

Golda's Balcony (493). Transfer from Off Broadway of the solo performance piece by William Gibson. Opened October 15, 2003. Production hiatus March 15–21, 2004. (Closed January 2, 2005)

The Boy From Oz (364). Musical with book by Martin Sherman, original book by Nick Enright; book and lyrics by Peter Allen and others. Opened October 16, 2003. (Closed September 12, 2004)

*Wicked (661). Musical with book by Winnie Holzman; music and lyrics by Stephen Schwartz; based on a novel by Gregory Maguire. Opened October 30, 2003.

Wonderful Town (497). Revival of the musical with book by Joseph Fields and Jerome Chodorov; music by Leonard Bernstein; lyrics by Betty Comden and Adolph Green; based on the play *My Sister Eileen* by Messrs. Fields and Chodorov, and on stories by Ruth McKenney. Opened November 23, 2003. (Closed January 30, 2005)

I Am My Own Wife (360). Transfer of the Off Broadway solo performance piece by Doug Wright. Opened December 3, 2003. Production hiatus August 30–September 5, 2004. (Closed October 31, 2004)

*Fiddler on the Roof (626). Revival of the musical with book by Joseph Stein; music by Jerry Bock; lyrics by Sheldon Harnick; based on stories by Sholom Aleichem. Opened February 26, 2004.

Roundabout Theatre Company production of **Twentieth Century** (84). Revival of the play by Ben Hecht and Charles MacArthur; based on a play by Charles Bruce Millholland; adapted by Ken Ludwig. Opened March 25, 2004. (Closed June 6, 2004)

Sly Fox (173). Revival of the play by Larry Gelbart; based on *Volpone* by Ben Jonson. Opened April 1, 2004. (Closed August 29, 2004)

Roundabout Theatre Company production of **Assassins** (101). Revival of the musical with book by John Weidman; music and lyrics by Stephen Sondheim. Opened April 22, 2004. (Closed July 18, 2004)

Jumpers (89). Revival of the play by Tom Stoppard. Opened April 25, 2004. (Closed July 11, 2004)

A Raisin in the Sun (88). Revival of the play by Lorraine Hansberry. Opened April 26, 2004. (Closed July 11, 2004)

Bombay Dreams (284). Musical with book by Meera Syal and Thomas Meehan; music by A.R. Rahman; lyrics by Don Black; based on an idea by Shekhar Kapur and Andrew Lloyd Webber. Opened April 29, 2004. (Closed January 1, 2005)

Caroline, or Change (136). Transfer from Off Broadway of the musical with book and lyrics by Tony Kushner; music by Jeanine Tesori. Opened May 2, 2004. (Closed August 29, 2004)

Frozen (128). Transfer from Off Off Broadway of the play by Bryony Lavery. Opened May 4, 2004. (Closed August 22, 2004)

Marc Salem's Mind Games on Broadway (30). Opened May 24, 2004. Presented Mondays when *I Am My Own Wife* was dark, with a full schedule the week of August 30–September 5, 2004. (Closed November 22, 2004)

Manhattan Theatre Club production of **Sight Unseen** (70). Revival of the play by Donald Margulies. Opened May 25, 2004. (Closed July 25, 2004)

PLAYS PRODUCED JUNE 1, 2004–MAY 31, 2005

Lincoln Center Theater production of **The Frogs** (92). Musical with book by Burt Shevelove and Nathan Lane; music and lyrics by Stephen Sondheim; adapted from Aristophanes. André Bishop artistic director, Bernard Gersten executive producer, in association with Bob Boyett, at the Vivian Beaumont Theater. Opened July 22, 2004. (Closed October 10, 2004)

Dionysos	Nathan Lane	Three Graces .... Meg Gillentine,
Xanthias	Roger Bart	Jessica Howard,
Herakles	Burke Moses	Naomi Kakuk
Charon; Aeakos	John Byner	Handmaiden Charisma .... Bryn Dowling
Pluto	Peter Bartlett	Virilla, the Amazon .... Pia C. Glenn
George Bernard Shaw	Daniel Davis	Ariadne .... Kathy Voytko
William Shakespeare	Michael Siberry	
Fire Belly Bouncing Frogs .... Ryan L. Ball, Luke Longacre		

Pluto's Hellraisers: Bryn Dowling, Meg Gillentine, Francesca Harper, Jessica Howard, Naomi Kakuk.

Shavians: Rebecca Eichenberger, Meg Gillentine, Tyler Hanes, Francesca Harper, David Lowenstein, Jay Brian Winnick.

Ensemble: Ryan L. Ball, Bryn Dowling, Rebecca Eichenberger, Meg Gillentine, Pia C. Glenn, Tyler Hanes, Francesca Harper, Rod Harrelson, Jessica Howard, Naomi Kakuk, Kenway Hon Wai K. Kua, Luke Longacre, David Lowenstein, Kathy Voytko, Steve Wilson, Jay Brian Winnick.

Orchestra: Paul Gemignani conductor; Annbritt duChateau associate conductor, piano; Thad Wheeler assistant conductor, percussion; Marilyn Reynolds concertmistress; Mineko Yajima violin; Richard Brice viola; Deborah Sepe cello; John Beal bass; Les Scott first clarinet; Eric Weidman second clarinet; Tom Sefcovic first bassoon; Gili Sharett second bassoon; Dominic Derasse first trumpet; Phil Granger second trumpet; Richard Clark first trombone; Mike Boschen second trombone; Dean Plank bass trombone; Paul Pizzuti drums, percussion; Jennifer Hoult, harp.

Understudies: Mr. Lane—Timothy Gulan, Jay Brian Winnick; Mr. Bart—Timothy Gulan, Jay Brian Winnick; Mr. Moses—Ryan L. Ball, Steve Wilson; Mr. Byner—David Lowenstein, Jay Brian Winnick; Mr. Bartlett—Eric Michael Gillett, Timothy Gulan; Mr. Davis—Eric Michael Gillett, Steve Wilson; Mr. Siberry—Eric Michael Gillett, Steve Wilson; Ms. Voytko—Meg Gillentine, Mia Price; Ms. Glenn—Meg Gillentine, Francesca Harper; Ms. Dowling—Meg Gillentine, Mia Price.

Swings: James Brown III, Eric Michael Gillett, Timothy Gulan, Joanne Manning, Mia Price.

Directed and choreographed by Susan Stroman; scenery, Giles Cadle; costumes, William Ivey Long; lighting, Kenneth Posner; sound, Scott Lehrer; wigs and hair, Paul Huntley; puppets, Martin P. Robinson; orchestrations, Jonathan Tunick; dance arrangements, Glen Kelly; music direction, Mr. Gemignani; casting, Tara Rubin Casting; stage manager, Thom Widmann; press, Philip Rinaldi Publicity, Philip Rinaldi, Barbara Carroll.

Time: The present. Place: Ancient Greece. Presented in two parts.

Updated musical version of the Aristophanes comedy in which the Greek god of theater journeys to Hades in search of a great dramatist. First presented in a swimming pool at Yale University by the Yale Repertory Theatre, New Haven, Connecticut (5/1974).

ACT I

Prologue: Onstage at the Vivian Beaumont
Invocation and Instructions to the Audience .... First Actor, Second Actor,
Greek Chorus
Scene 1: Ancient Greece
"I Love to Travel" .... Dionysos, Xanthias, Greek Chorus
Scene 2: The House of Herakles
"Dress Big" .... Herakles, Dionysos, Xanthias
Scene 3: The Banks of the River Styx
"I Love to Travel" .... Dionysos, Xanthias
"All Aboard" .... Charon
Scene 4: On the River Styx
"Ariadne" .... Dionysos
"The Frogs .... Dionysos, A Splash of Frogs,
Fire Belly Bouncing Frogs

ACT II

Scene 1. On the River Styx
Scene 2: On the Shore of Hades
Scene 3: A Myrtle Grove in Hades
Hymn to Dionysos .... Three Graces, Dionysians,
Dionysos, Xanthias
Scene 4: Outside the Palace of Pluto
Scene 5: The Palace of Pluto
"Hades" .... Pluto, Hellraisers
"It's Only a Play" .... Greek Chorus
Scene 6: Ourside the Palace of Pluto
Scene 7: Outside the Palace of Pluto
"Shaw" .... Dionysos, Shaw, Shavians
"All Aboard" .... Charon
"Fear No More" .... Shakespeare
Scene 8: Return from Hades
Hymn to Dionysos .... Green Chorus
Final Instructions to the Audience .... Dionysos, Company

Forever Tango (114). Revival of the dance concert by Luis Bravo. Produced by Jack Ulstick /BACI Worldwide at the Shubert Theatre. Opened July 24, 2004. Production hiatus August 30–September 28, 2004. (Closed November 28, 2004)

Singer .... Miguel Velázquez

Dancers: Jorge Torres, Marcela Durán and Guillermina Quiroga, Gabriel Ortega and Sandra Bootz, Carlos Vera and Laura Marcarie, Francisco Forquera and Natalia Hills, Marcelo Bernadaz and Verónica Gardella, Claudio González and Melina Brufman, Alejandra Gutty and Juan Paulo Horvath.

Orchestra: Rodion Boshoer, Abraham Becker violin; Alexander Sechkin viola; Patricio Villarejo cello; Pablo Motta bass; Victor Lavallén, Santos Maggi, Jorge Trivisonno, Carlos Niesi bandoneón; Jorge Vernieri piano; Gustavo Casenave keyboard.

Directed by Mr. Bravo; costumes, Argemira Affonso; lighting, Mr. Bravo; sound, Mike Miller; hair and makeup, Jean Luc Don Vito; production stage manager, Jorge González; press, Richard Kornberg and Associates, Rick Miramontez, Don Summa, Tom D'Ambrosio, Carrie Friedman.

Presented in two parts.

Dance concert of stories told through the medium of tango. First presented on Broadway for 332 performances at the Walter Kerr Theatre (6/19/1997–4/5/1998) and the Marquis Theatre (4/15–8/2/1998).

ACT I

Preludio del Bandoneón y la Noche	Sandra Bootz and Gabriel Ortega
Overture	Orchestra
El Suburbio	Company
A Los Amigos	Orchestra
Derecho Viejo	Francisco Mercado and Natalia Hills
Los Mareados	Miguel Velázquez
La Mariposa	Carlos Vera and Laura Marcarie
Comme I'll Faut	Claudio González and Melina Brufman
Berretín	Orchestra
La Tablada	Marcelo Bernadaz and Verónica Gardella
Negracha	Alejandra Gutty and Juan Paulo Horvath
Responso	Orchestra
Oro y Plata: *Candombe*	Company

ACT II

Vampitango	Sandra Bootz and Gabriel Ortega
Romance entre el Bandoneón mi Alma	Jorge Torres and Guillermina Quiroga
Payadora	Orchestra
Quejas de Bandoneón	Carlos Vera and Laura Marcarie
Gallo Ciego	Francisco Forquera and Natalia Hills
Zum	Alejandra Gutty and Juan Paulo Horvath
El Día que me Quieras	Miguel Velázquez
Tanguera	Claudio González and Melina Brufman
La Cumparsita	Francisco Mercado and Natalia Hills, Alejandra Gutty and Juan Paulo Horvath, Carlos Vera and Laura Marcarie
Jealousy	Orchestra
Felicia	
Marcelo Bernadaz and Verónica Gardella	
Preludio a mi Viejo	Orchestra
Romance del Bandoneón y la Noche	Sandra Bootz and Gabriel Ortega
A Evaristo Carrìego	Jorge Torres and Marcela Durán
Finale	Company

Roundabout Theatre Company production of **After the Fall** (53). Revival of the play by Arthur Miller. Todd Haimes artistic director, Ellen Richard managing director,

Ladies' man: Peter Krause surrounded by (left to right) Vivienne Benesch, Jessica Hecht, Carla Gugino and Candy Buckley in After the Fall. *Photo: Joan Marcus*

Julia C. Levy executive director of external affairs, at the American Airlines Theatre. Opened July 29, 2004. (Closed September 12, 2004)

Quentin	Peter Krause	Maggie	Carla Gugino
Holga	Vivienne Benesch	Man in the Park	Baylen Thomas
Mother	Candy Buckley	Dan	Ken Marks
Father	Dan Ziskie	Secretary	Roxanna Hope
Elsie	Kathleen McNenny	Student	James O'Toole
Louise	Jessica Hecht	Nurse	Lisa Louttit
Lou	Mark Nelson	Lucas	Chris Bowers
Mickey	Jonathan Walker		

Understudies: Mr. Krause—Baylen Thomas; Ms. Gugino—Roxanna Hope; Mses. Hecht, Benesch, Buckley—Kathleen McNenny; Messrs. Ziskie, Nelson, Walker—Ken Marks; Mses. McNenny, Hope—Lisa Louttit; Messrs. Thomas, Marks—Chris Bowers.

Directed by Michael Mayer; scenery, Richard Hoover, costumes, Michael Krass; lighting, Donald Holder; sound, Dan Moses Schreier; projections, Elaine J. McCarthy; hair and wigs, Paul Huntley; casting, Jim Carnahan, Mele Nagler; production stage manager, James Harker; stage manager, Andrea O. Saraffian; press, Boneau/Bryan-Brown, Adrian Bryan-Brown, Matt Polk, Jessica Johnson.

Time: 1962. Place: Idlewild Airport, New York City. Presented in two parts.

A man examines his past relationships with women while waiting for a new one to begin. A 1963–64 *Best Plays* choice, the original Broadway production opened at the ANTA Washington Square Theatre (1/23/1964–5/29/1965; 208 performances).

Dracula: The Musical (157). Musical with book and lyrics by Don Black and Christopher Hampton; music by Frank Wildhorn. Produced by Dodger Stage Holding and Joop van den Ende, in association with Clear Channel Entertainment, at the Belasco Theatre. Opened August 19, 2004. (Closed January 2, 2005)

Jonathan Harker .... Darren Ritchie
Dracula .... Tom Hewitt
Mina Murray .... Melissa Errico
First Vampire .... Megan Reinking;
                                          Jenifer Foote (alt.)
Second Vampire .... Celina Carvajal;
                                      Elizabeth Loyacano (alt.)
Third Vampire .... Pamela Jordan;
                                          Melissa Fagan (alt.)

Renfield .... Don Stephenson
Jack Seward .... Shonn Wiley
Lucy Westenra .... Kelli O'Hara
Quincey Morris .... Bart Shatto
Arthur Holmwood .... Chris Hoch
Van Helsing .... Stephen McKinley Henderson
Child .... Michael Herwitz;
                                      Michael Soloway (alt.)

Ensemble: Celina Carvajal, Melissa Fagan, Jenifer Foote, Pamela Jordan, Elizabeth Loyacano, Megan Reinking, Graham Rowat.

Orchestra: Constantine Kitsopoulos conductor, keyboard; Ethyl Will associate conductor, keyboard; Chungsun Kim cello; Richard Heckman reeds; Barbara Merjan percussion; Karl Mansfield keyboard.

Standby: Messrs. Hewitt, Henderson, Shatto–Chuck Wagner.

Understudies: Mr. Hewitt—Graham Rowat; Ms. Errico—Elizabeth Loyacano, Megan Sikora; Mr. Ritchie—Anthony Holds, Shonn Wiley; Mr. Stephenson—Chris Hoch, Graham Rowat; Mr. Wiley—Anthony Holds, Bart Shatto; Ms. O'Hara—Celina Carvajal, Megan Sikora; Mr. Shatto—Anthony Holds; Mr. Hoch—Anthony Holds, Bart Shatto; Mr. Henderson—Graham Rowat.

Swings: Anthony Holds, Megan Sikora.

Directed by Des McAnuff; choreography, Mindy Cooper; scenery, Heidi Ettinger; costumes, Catherine Zuber; lighting, Howell Binkley; sound, Acme Sound Partners; flying, Foy; fight direction, Steve Rankin; orchestrations, Doug Besterman; musical direction and arrangements, Mr. Kitsopoulos; music coordination, John Miller; casting, Dave Clemmons Casting; production stage

Tragic beauty: Melissa Errico in Dracula: The Musical. *Photo: Joan Marcus*

manager, Kelly A. Martindale; press, Boneau/Bryan-Brown, Adrian Bryan-Brown, Jim Byk, Susanne Tighe, Juliana Hannett.

Time: A century ago. Place: Transylvania; England; and across Europe aboard the Orient Express. Presented in two parts.

Bloody passions unleashed in a musical treatment of a time-honored horror tale. An earlier version of this production was first presented at La Jolla Playhouse in San Diego, California (10/28/2001).

ACT I

Prelude .... Jonathan Harker
"A Quiet Life" .... Dracula
"Over Whitby Bay" .... Jonathan, Mina Murray
"Forever Young" .... First Vampire, Second Vampire, Third Vampire
"Fresh Blood" .... Dracula
"The Master's Song" .... Renfield, Jack Seward
"How Do You Choose?" .... Lucy Westenra, Mina, Quincey Morris,
 Jack, Arthur Holmwood, Company
"The Mist" .... Lucy
"Modern World" .... Company
"A Perfect Life" .... Mina
"The Weddings" .... Company
"Prayer for the Dead" .... Company
"Life After Life" .... Dracula, Lucy

ACT II

"The Heart Is Slow to Learn" .... Mina
"The Master's Song" (Reprise) .... Renfield, Dracula
"If I Could Fly" .... Mina
"There's Always a Tomorrow" .... Dracula and Mina
"Deep in the Darkest Night" .... Van Helsing, Quincey, Arthur,
 Jack, Jonathan, Mina
"Before the Summer Ends" .... Jonathan
"The Longer I Live" .... Dracula
"All Is Dark"/"Life After Life" (Reprise) .... Dracula, Mina
Finale .... Dracula, Mina

Manhattan Theatre Club and **Second Stage Theatre** production of **Reckless** (77) Revival of the play by Craig Lucas. Lynne Meadow artistic director, Barry Grove executive producer of Manhattan Theatre Club; Carole Rothman artistic director, Timothy J. McClimon executive director of Second Stage Theatre, at the Biltmore Theatre. Opened October 14, 2004. (Closed December 19, 2004)

Rachel .... Mary-Louise Parker	Roy;	
Tom;	Tim Timko;	
Man in Ski Mask;	Talk Show Host .... Jeremy Shamos	
Tom Junior .... Thomas Sadoski	Doctors One Through Six .... Debra Monk	
Lloyd .... Michael O'Keefe	Trish; Woman Patient .... Olga Merediz	
Pooty; Sue .... Rosie Perez		

Understudies: Mses. Parker, Perez—Jennifer Mudge; Messrs. Sadoski, O'Keefe, Shamos—Curtis Mark Williams.

Directed by Mark Brokaw; scenery, Allen Moyer; costumes, Michael Krass; lighting, Christopher Akerlind; sound and music, David Van Tieghem; fight direction, Rick Sordelet; casting, Nancy Piccione/David Caparelliotis, Tara Rubin; production stage manager, James FitzSimmons; stage manager, Jill Cordle; press, Boneau/Bryan-Brown, Chris Boneau, Jim Byk, Aaron Meier.

Presented in two parts.

A woman marked for death by her husband flees to a new life and meets an assortment of odd characters on her quirky journey. First presentation of record was given Off Off Broadway

Ignorant bliss: Thomas Sadoski and Mary-Louise Parker in Reckless. *Photo: Joan Marcus*

by the Production Company (5/19–6/5/1983). A revised version was presented Off Broadway by Circle Repertory Company (9/25/1988–1/1/1989; 113 performances).

*Brooklyn: The Musical (253). Musical with book, music and lyrics by Mark Schoenfeld and Barri McPherson. Produced by Producers Four (Robert G. Bartner, Brian Brolly, Michael A. Jenkins, Benjamin Mordecai, Lauren Doll), John McDaniel, Jeff Calhoun, Steven Leiter/Stan Levine and Scott Prisand, Jay and Cindy Gutterman Productions, in association with Mr. Bartner, Dallas Summer Musicals, Danny Seraphine, Rick Wolkenberg and Sibling Entertainment, at the Plymouth Theatre. Opened October 21, 2004.

A City Weed; Taylor .... Kevin Anderson
A City Weed;
  Streetsinger .... Cleavant Derricks
A City Weed; Brooklyn .... Eden Espinosa
A City Weed; Paradice .... Ramona Keller
A City Weed; Faith .... Karen Olivo

Vocalists: Manoel Felciano, Caren Lyn Manuel, Haneefah Wood.

Orchestra: James Sampliner conductor, keyboard; Daniel Weiss associate conductor, keyboard; Clay Ruede cello; John Putnam, Gary Sieger guitar; Irio O'Farrill Jr. bass; Jack Bashkow reeds; Roger Squitero percussion; Shannon Ford drums.

Understudies: Mses. Espinosa, Olivo—Caren Lyn Manuel, Julie Reiber; Ms. Keller—Haneefah Wood; Mr. Anderson—Manoel Felciano; Mr. Derricks–Horace V. Rogers.

Swings: Julie Reiber, Horace V. Rogers.

Directed by Jeff Calhoun; scenery, Ray Klausen; costumes, Tobin Ost; lighting, Michael Gilliam; sound, Jonathan Deans and Peter Hylenski; orchestrations, John McDaniel; music direction, Mr. Sampliner; music coordination, John Miller; associate director, Coy Middlebrook; associate producers, Douglas R. Feurring/Gary and Charlie Maffei/Jonathan and Cathy Pinsky, Ken Denison; casting, Dave Clemmons Casting; production stage manager, Kimberly Russell; stage manager, Jason Trubitt; press, Boneau/Bryan-Brown, Adrian Bryan-Brown, Matt Polk, Jessica Johnson.

Time: The present. Place: A street corner under the Brooklyn Bridge. Presented without intermission.

New York City's homeless celebrate life despite desperate circumstances.

Homeless "idols": Eden Espinosa belts as Ramona Keller, Kevin Anderson, Karen Olivo and Cleavant Derricks provide support in Brooklyn: The Musical. *Photo: Joan Marcus*

MUSICAL NUMBERS

"Heart Behind These Hands" .... City Weeds
"Christmas Makes Me Cry" .... Faith, Taylor
"Not a Sound" .... City Weeds
"Brooklyn Grew Up" .... Brooklyn, City Weeds
"Creating Once Upon a Time" .... Brooklyn, Faith
"Once Upon a Time" .... Brooklyn, City Weeds
"Superlover" .... Paradice, City Weeds
"Brooklyn in the Blood" .... Paradice, Brooklyn, City Weeds
"Magic Man" .... Streetsinger, City Weeds
"Love Was a Song" .... Taylor
"I Never Knew His Name" .... Brooklyn
"The Truth" .... Taylor, Brooklyn, City Weeds
"Raven" .... Paradice
"Sometimes" .... Taylor, City Weeds
"Love Me Where I Live" .... Paradice, City Weeds
"Love Fell Like Rain" .... Brooklyn
"Streetsinger" .... Brooklyn, Streetsinger, City Weeds
"Heart Behind These Hands" (Reprise) .... City Weeds

Laugh Whore (66). Solo performance piece by Mario Cantone; music by Jerry Dixon; additional music by Mr. Cantone and Harold Lubin; lyrics by Messrs. Cantone, Dixon and Lubin. Produced by Showtime Networks, in association with Jonathan Burkhart, at the Cort Theatre. Opened October 24, 2004. (Closed January 2, 2005)

Performed by Mr. Cantone.

Directed by Joe Mantello; scenery, Robert Brill; lighting, Jules Fisher and Peggy Eisenhauer; sound, Tony Meola; orchestrations and music direction, Tom Kitt; arrangements, Messrs. Dixon and Kitt; production stage manager, William Joseph Barnes; stage manager, Jon Krause; press, Pete Sanders Group, Pete Sanders, Jim Mannino, Glenna Freedman, Jeremy Shaffer, Bill Coyle.

Presented in two parts.

Mr. Cantone interweaves stories about his Italian family with tales of his career as an actor and comedian.

Roundabout Theatre Company production of **Twelve Angry Men** (228). By Reginald Rose. Todd Haimes artistic director, Ellen Richard managing director, Julia C. Levy executive director, at the American Airlines Theatre. Opened October 28, 2004. (Closed May 15, 2005)

Guard	Matte Osian	Juror Seven	John Pankow
Juror One	Mark Blum	Juror Eight	Boyd Gaines
Juror Two	Kevin Geer	Juror Nine	Tom Aldredge
Juror Three	Philip Bosco	Juror Ten	Peter Friedman
Juror Four	James Rebhorn	Juror Eleven	Larry Bryggman
Juror Five	Michael Mastro	Juror Twelve	Adam Trese
Juror Six	Robert Clohessy	Voice of the Judge	Robert Prosky

Understudies: Messrs. Blum, Gaines, Trese—Karl Kenzler; Messrs. Geer, Bosco, Aldredge—Terry Layman; Messrs. Rebhorn, Mastro, Bryggman, Osian—Guy Paul.

Directed by Scott Ellis; scenery, Allen Moyer; costumes, Michael Krass; lighting, Paul Palazzo; sound, Brian Ronan; music, John Gromada; casting, Jim Carnahan and Mele Nagler; production stage manager, Roy Harris; press, Boneau/Bryan-Brown, Adrian Bryan-Brown, Matt Polk, Jessica Johnson.

Time: Late summer, 1954. Place: A jury room of a New York City court. Presented without intermission.

Adaptation of a popular television and film drama about the power of one man to make a positive difference in a criminal case. First New York stage presentation of record was given by the Brooklyn Arts Company at the Brooklyn Academy of Music (5/16–5/27/1961).

Face off: Boyd Gaines confronts Philip Bosco as Kevin Geer observes in Twelve Angry Men. *Photo: Joan Marcus*

Enough is enough: Brenda Blethyn and Edie Falco in 'night, Mother. *Photo: Joan Marcus*

'night, Mother (65). Revival of the play by Marsha Norman. Produced by Fox Theatricals, Harbor Entertainment, East of Doheny Theatricals, The Araca Group, Terry E. Schnuck, Amanda Dubois, Ruth Hendel, Hal Goldberg, Cheryl Wiesenfeld/Jerry Meyer, at the Royale Theatre. Opened November 14, 2004. (Closed January 9, 2005)

Thelma Cates .... Brenda Blethyn   Jessie Cates .... Edie Falco

Standbys: Ms. Blethyn—Barbara Eda-Young; Ms. Falco—Julia Gibson.

Directed by Michael Mayer; scenery, Neil Patel; costumes, Michael Krass; lighting, Brian MacDevitt; sound, Dan Moses Schreier; wigs, Paul Huntley; casting, Jim Carnahan; production stage manager, James Harker; stage manager, Heather Cousens; press, Boneau/Bryan-Brown, Chris Boneau, Amy Jacobs, Juliana Hannett.

Time: Tonight. Place: The home where Mama and Jessie live. Presented without intermission.

A woman who can no longer cope with life spends an evening discussing her impending suicide with her mother. A 1982–83 *Best Plays* choice and 1983 Pulitzer Prize honoree, the original Broadway production opened at the John Golden Theatre (3/31/1983–2/26/1984; 380 performances). The first presentation of record—under the title *G'night Mother*—was given at the American Repertory Theatre in Cambridge, Massachusetts (12/15/1982; 19 performances). Following the initial Broadway run, the play transferred with its original cast to Off Broadway's Westside Arts Theatre (4/18–6/3/1984; 54 performances).

The Good Body (40). Solo performance piece by Eve Ensler. Produced by Harriet Newman Leve, The Araca Group, East of Doheny Theatricals, in association with the American Conservatory Theater, at the Booth Theatre. Opened November 15, 2004. (Closed December 19, 2004)

Performed by Ms. Ensler.

Directed by Peter Askin; scenery, Robert Brill; costumes, Susan Hilferty; lighting, Kevin Adams; sound, David Van Tieghem and Jill BC DuBoff; music, Mr. Van Tieghem; video, Wendall K.

Harrington; associate producers, Clint Bond Jr., Edward Nelson, Allison Prouty, Laura Wagner; production stage manager, Arabella Powell; stage manager, Elisa Guthertz; press, The Publicity Office, Bob Fennell, Marc Thibodeau, Michael S. Borowski.

Presented without intermission.

Author of *The Vagina Monologues* continues her ruminations on the female body as a site for cultural exploitation and commentary. First presentation of record was given in a new play workshop at Seattle Repertory Theatre (4/15/2004).

Whoopi: The 20th Anniversary Show (72). Revival of the solo performance piece by Whoopi Goldberg. Produced by Mike Nichols, Hal Luftig, Leonard Soloway, Steven M. Levy, Tom Leonardis, Eric Falkenstein, Amy Nederlander, at the Lyceum Theatre. Opened November 17, 2004. (Closed January 30, 2005)

Performed by Ms. Goldberg.

Lighting, Benjamin Pearcy; sound, Peter Fitzgerald; production stage manager, Barclay Stiff; press, Pete Sanders Group, Pete Sanders, Jeremy Shaffer, Glenna Freedman, Bill Coyle.

Presented without intermission.

Performer re-presents characters from her 1984–85 solo show, updating her comic turns to reflect current American culture. First presentation of record was given at Broadway's Lyceum Theatre (10/24/1984–3/10/1985; 156 performances).

The National Theatre of Great Britain production of **Democracy** (173). By Michael Frayn. Produced by Boyett Ostar Productions, Nederlander Presentations, Inc., Jean Doumanian, Stephanie P. McClelland, Arielle Tepper, Amy Nederlander, Eric Falkenstein,

Stop looking! Eve Ensler in The Good Body.
Photo: Joan Marcus

Roy Furman, at the Brooks Atkinson Theatre. Opened November 18, 2004. (Closed April 17, 2005)

Günter Guillaume .... Richard Thomas	Ulrich Bauhaus .... Julian Gamble
Arno Kretschmann .... Michael Cumpsty	Herbert Wehner .... Robert Prosky
Willy Brandt .... James Naughton	Helmut Schmidt .... John Dossett
Horst Ehmke .... Richard Masur	H-D Genscher .... John Christopher Jones
Reinhard Wilke .... Terry Beaver	Günther Nollau .... Lee Wilkof

Standbys: Messrs. Thomas, Gamble—Tony Carlin; Messrs. Masur, Beaver, Cumpsty—Paul O'Brien; Messrs. Prosky, Jones, Wilkof—Martin Shakar; Messrs. Naughton, Dossett—Ray Virta.

Directed by Michael Blakemore; scenery, Peter J. Davison; costumes, Sue Wilmington; lighting, Mark Henderson; sound, Neil Alexander; casting, Jim Carnahan; production stage manager, David Hyslop; stage manager, Deirdre McCrane; press, Boneau/Bryan-Brown, Adrian Bryan-Brown, Jim Byk, Juliana Hannett.

An East German spy ingratiates himself with the West German leader, bringing about the latter's downfall. First presentation of record at the National Theatre of Great Britain's Cottesloe Theatre (9/9–12/30/2003) before runs at the National's Lyttelton Theatre 2/12–3/30/2004) and Wyndham's Theatre in London's West End (4/20–10/9/2004). A 2004–05 *Best Plays* choice (see essay by Chris Jones in this volume).

Dame Edna: Back With a Vengeance! (163). Performance piece by Barry Humphries; additional material by Andrew Ross; music, Wayne Barker; lyrics, Messrs. Humphries,

Nothin' like her: Dame Edna Everage in Back With a Vengeance! *Photo: Greg Gorman*

Barker. Produced by Creative Battery, by arrangement with Harley Medcalf and Boxjellyfish LLC, at The Music Box. Opened November 21, 2004. (Closed May 1, 2005)

Dame Edna Everage .... Dame Edna	TestEdnarones .... Randy Aaron,
Ednaettes .... Teri DiGianfelice,	Gerrard Carter
Michelle Pampena	

Directed by Mr. Humphries; choreography, Jason Gilkison; scenery, Brian Thomson; costumes, Will Goodwin and Stephen Adnitt; lighting, Jane Cox; sound, Dan Scheivert; production stage manager, James W. Gibbs; stage manager, Ruth Saunders; press, Bill Evans and Associates, Jim Randolph.

Presented in two parts.

The latest incarnation, created by performance artist Barry Humphries, of a demented housewife who has climbed the ranks of pseudo-nobility and joined the fraternity (or sorority) of cultural icons. An earlier production, *Dame Edna: The Royal Tour*, played the Booth Theatre (10/17/1999–7/2/2000; 297 performances).

Roundabout Theatre Company production of **Pacific Overtures** (69). Revival of the musical with book by John Weidman; music and lyrics by Stephen Sondheim; additional material by Hugh Wheeler. Todd Haimes artistic director, Ellen Richard managing director, Julia C. Levy executive director, in association with Gorgeous Entertainment, at Studio 54. Opened December 2, 2004. (Closed January 30, 2005)

Reciter .... B.D. Wong	Manjiro .... Paolo Montalban
Observer; Officer;	Councilor; Grandmother .... Alan Muraoka
Warrior; British Admiral ...... Evan D'Angeles	Kanagawa Girl;
Samurai; Thief;	Daughter .... Mayumi Omagari
Soothsayer;	Priest; Kanagawa Girl;
Storyteller .... Joseph Anthony Foronda	French Admiral .... Daniel Jay Park
Tamate .... Yoko Fumoto	Shogun's Wife,
Shogun's Mother; Old Man .... Alvin Y.F. Ing	Kanagawa Girl .... Hazel Anne Raymundo
Noble .... Fred Isozaki	Lord Abe .... Sab Shimono
Madam; Dutch Admiral .... Francis Jue	Son; Shogun's Wife's Servant;
Officer; American Admiral;	Kanagawa Girl .... Yuka Takara
Sailor .... Darren Lee	Fisherman; Physician;
Merchant; Commodore Perry;	Older Swordsman;
Lord of South; Sailor .... Hoon Lee	Russian Admiral;
Kayama .... Michael K. Lee	Samurai Bodyguard .... Scott Watanabe
Councilor; Priest;	Townspeople; Officers;
Emperor Priest .... Ming Lee	Priests; Samurai .... Company
Observer; Shogun's Companion;	
Boy; Noble; Sailor .... Telly Leung	

Orchestra: Paul Gemignani conductor; Mark Mitchell associate conductor, keyboard 2; Suzanne Ornstein violin, viola; Deborah Assael cello; Dennis Anderson woodwinds; Paul Ford keyboard 1; Paul Pizzuti percussion 1; Thad Wheeler percussion 2.

Understudies: Mr. Wong—Joseph Anthony Foronda; Mr. Montalban—Darren Lee; Mr. Shimono—Ming Lee; Michael K. Lee—Telly Leung; Mr. D'Angeles—Hoon Lee, Rick Edinger; Mr. Foronda—Hoon Lee, Fred Isozaki; Mr. Ing—Ming Lee, Rick Edinger; Mr. Isozaki, Darren Lee, Ming Lee, Mr. Park—Eric Bondoc; Mr. Jue—Alan Muraoka; Hoon Lee—Alan Muraoka; Hoon Lee, Mr. Muraoka—Rick Edinger; Mr. Leung—Eric Bondoc; Mr. Leung (sailor)—Daniel Jay Park; Mr. Watanabe—Fred Isozaki, Rick Edinger; Mses. Fumoto, Omagari, Takara, Raymundo, Messrs. Muraoka, Watanabe—Kim Varhola.

Swings: Eric Bondoc, Rick Edinger, Kim Varhola.

Directed and choreographed by Amon Miyamoto; scenery and mask design, Rumi Matsui; costumes, Junko Koshino; lighting, Brian MacDevitt; sound, Dan Moses Schreier; orchestrations, Jonathan Tunick; music direction, Mr. Gemignani; executive producer, Sydney Beers; casting, Jim Carnahan; production stage manager, Arthur Gaffin; press, Boneau/Bryan-Brown, Adrian Bryan-Brown, Matt Polk, Jessica Johnson, Joe Perrotta.

Colonizing text: B.D. Wong and the company in Pacific Overtures. *Photo: Joan Marcus*

Time: 1853–Present. Place: Japan. Presented in two parts.

Musical tale of the seismic shifts in Japanese culture when Western countries demand an end to the island nation's insularity. A 1975–76 *Best Plays* choice, the original Broadway production opened at the Winter Garden Theatre (1/11–6/27/1976; 193 performances). The 2004–05 production was based on an earlier version directed by Mr. Miyamoto for Tokyo's New National Theatre (10/2–10/21/2000; 25 performances).

ACT I

"The Advantages of Floating in the Middle of the Sea" .... Reciter, Company
"There Is No Other Way" .... Observers
"Four Black Dragons" .... Fisherman, Thief, Reciter, Company
"Chrysanthemum Tea" .... Shogun, Shogun's Mother,
Shogun's Wife, Soothsayer, Priests,
Shogun's Companion, Physician,
Shogun's Wife's, Servant
"I Will Make a Poem" .... Kayama, Manjiro
"Welcome to Kanagawa" .... Madam, Girls
"Someone in a Tree" .... Old Man, Reciter, Boy, Warrior
"Lion Dance" .... Company

ACT II

"Please Hello!" .... Lord Abe, Reciter,
Admirals (American, British, Dutch, Russian and French)
"A Bowler Hat" .... Kayama
"Pretty Lady" .... Sailors
"Next" .... Reciter, Company

*700 Sundays (163). Solo performance piece by Billy Crystal; additional material Alan Zweibel. Produced by Janice Crystal, Larry Magid and Face Productions, in association with Clear Channel Entertainment, at the Broadhurst Theatre. Opened December 5, 2004. Production on hiatus March 14–20, 2005 and April 18–24, 2005.

Performed by Mr. Crystal.

Directed by Des McAnuff; scenery, David F. Weiner; costumes, David C. Woolard; lighting, David Lee Cuthbert; sound, Steve Canyon Kennedy and John Shivers; production stage manager, Lurie Horns Pfeffer; stage manager, Donald Fried; press, Barlow-Hartman Public Relations, John Barlow, Michael Hartman, Carol Fineman, Leslie Baden.

Presented in two parts.

The title refers to the approximate number of Sundays Mr. Crystal was able to enjoy his father's company before the older man's untimely death. This production received a 2005 Tony Award for best special theatrical event. First presented as *700 Sundays . . . Billy Crystal . . . A Life in Progress* in a workshop at La Jolla Playhouse in San Diego (4/20–5/2/2004).

Gem of the Ocean (72). By August Wilson. Produced by Carole Shorenstein Hays and Jujamcyn Theaters at the Walter Kerr Theatre. Opened December 6, 2004. (Closed February 6, 2005)

Eli	Eugene Lee	Rutherford Selig	Raynor Scheine
Citizen Barlow	John Earl Jelks	Solly Two Kings	Anthony Chisholm
Aunt Ester	Phylicia Rashad	Caesar	Ruben Santiago-Hudson
Black Mary	LisaGay Hamilton		

Standbys: Messrs. Lee, Chisholm—Ron Cephas Jones; Messrs. Jelks, Santiago-Hudson—Billy Eugene Jones; Ms. Rashad—Ebony Jo-Ann; Ms. Hamilton—Heather Alicia Simms; Mr. Scheine—Tuck Milligan.

Directed by Kenny Leon; scenery, David Gallo; costumes, Constanza Romero; lighting, Donald Holder; sound, Dan Moses Schreier; fight direction, J. Allen Suddeth; musical and vocal

Soul revival: Phylicia Rashad and John Earl Jelks in Gem of the Ocean. *Photo: Carol Rosegg*

arrangements, Kathryn Bostic; dramaturg, Todd Kreidler; associate producer, Robert G. Bartner; casting, Harriet Bass; production stage manager, Narda E. Alcorn; stage manager, Neveen Mahmoud; press, Barlow-Hartman Public Relations, Michael Hartman, John Barlow, Carol Fineman, Leslie Baden.

Time: 1904. Place: The parlor of Aunt Ester's home at 1839 Wylie Avenue in Pittsburgh's Hill District. Presented in two parts.

Aunt Ester's home in Pittsburgh's Hill District is a place of peace and respite for African Americans struggling through the first decade of the 20th century. First presented at Chicago's Goodman Theatre (4/28–5/24/2003) before runs at the Center Theatre Group's Mark Taper Forum (7/30–9/7/2003) in Los Angeles and Boston's Huntington Theatre Company (9/24–10/30/2004). A 2004–05 *Best Plays* choice (see essay by Christopher Rawson in this volume).

*La Cage aux Folles (198). Revival of the musical with book by Harvey Fierstein; music and lyrics by Jerry Herman; based on the play *La Cage aux Folles* by Jean Poiret. Produced by James L. Nederlander, Clear Channel Entertainment, Kenneth Greenblatt, Terry Allen Kramer, Martin Richards, at the Marquis Theatre. Opened December 9, 2004.

Georges .... Daniel Davis	Albin .... Gary Beach
Les Cagelles	Jean-Michael .... Gavin Creel
Chantal .... T. Oliver Reid	Anne .... Angela Gaylor
Monique .... Christopher Freeman	Jacqueline .... Ruth Williamson
Dermah .... Eric Otte	St. Tropez Townspeople
Nicole .... Nathan Peck	M. Renaud .... Merwin Foard
Hanna .... Brad Musgrove	Mme. Renaud .... Dorothy Stanley
Mercedes ....Josh Walden	Paulette .... Emma Zaks
Bitelle .... Joey Dudding	Hercule ....Joey Dudding
Lo Singh .... Jermaine R. Rembert	Etienne .... John Hillner
Odette .... Charlie Sutton	Fisherman .... Dale Hensley
Angelique; White Bird .... Andy Pellick	Colette .... Patty Goble
Phaedra .... Will Taylor	Fisherman .... Adrian Bailey
Clo-Clo .... Paul Canaan	Edouard Dindon .... Michael Mulheren
Francis .... John Shuman	Mme. Dindon .... Linda Balgord
Jacob .... Michael Benjamin Washington	

Orchestra: Patrick Vaccariello conductor; Jim Laev associate conductor, keyboard 1, accordion; Paul Woodiel concertmaster, violin; Mary Whitaker, Victor Heifets, Dana Ianculovici violin; Peter Prosser, Vivian Israel cello; Bill Sloat bass; Ted Nash, Ben Kono, David Young, Ron Jannelli reeds; Jeff Kievit lead trumpet; Trevor Neumann, Earl Gardner trumpet; Michael Seltzer, Randy Andos trombone; Roger Wendt, French horn; Ron Tierno drums; Dan McMillan percussion; Maggie Torre keyboard 2; JJ McGeehan guitar, banjo.

Standby: Bryan Batt.

Swings: Clark Johnsen, Paul McGill, Eric Stretch, Leah Horowitz.

Understudies: Mr. Beach—Bryan Batt, Dale Hensley; Mr. Davis—John Hillner; Mr. Creel—Joey Dudding, Will Taylor; Ms. Gaylor—Leah Horowitz, Emma Zaks; Ms. Williamson—Patty Goble, Dorothy Stanley; Mr. Mulheren—Merwin Foard, John Hillner; Ms. Balgord—Patty Goble, Dorothy Stanley; Mr. Shuman—Adrian Bailey, John Hillner, Mr. Washington—Adrian Bailey, T. Oliver Reid.

Directed by Jerry Zaks; choreography, Jerry Mitchell; scenery, Scott Pask; costumes, William Ivey Long; lighting, Donald Holder; sound, Peter Fitzgerald; wigs and hair, Paul Huntley; orchestrations, Jim Tyler; additional orchestrations, Larry Blank; dance arrangements, David Krane; music coordination, Michael Keller; associate producers, TGA Entertainment, Leni Sender, Bob Cuillo, Kathi Glist; casting, Jim Carnahan; production stage manager, Steven Beckler; stage manager, Michael Pule; press, Barlow-Hartman Public Relations, Michael Hartman, John Barlow, Wayne Wolfe, Andrew Snyder.

Time: Summer. Place: St. Tropez, France. Presented in two parts.

The son of two gay men who operate a glitzy nightclub featuring drag performers becomes engaged to the daughter of a conservative politician and complications ensue. A 1983–84 *Best*

Plays choice, the original Broadway production opened at the Palace Theatre (8/21/1983–11/15/1987; 1,761 performances). That first production received Tony Awards for best musical, book (Mr. Fierstein), score (Mr. Herman), actor (George Hearn), costumes (Theoni V. Aldredge) and direction (Arthur Laurents). The current production received Tony Awards for best musical revival and choreography (Mr. Mitchell).

ACT I

Overture	Orchestra
"We Are What We Are"	Les Cagelles
"A Little More Mascara"	Albin, Friends
"With Anne on My Arm"	Jean-Michel, Georges
"With You on My Arm" (Reprise)	Georges, Albin
"The Promenade"	Townspeople
"Song on the Sand"	Georges
"La Cage aux Folles"	Albin, Les Cagelles
"I Am What I Am"	Albin

ACT II

Entr'acte	Orchestra
"Song on the Sand" (Reprise)	Georges, Albin
"Masculinity"	Georges, Albin, Townspeople
"Look Over There"	Georges
"Cocktail Counterpoint"	Georges, Dindon, Mme. Dindon, Jacob, Jean-Michel, Anne
"The Best of Times"	Albin, Jacqueline, Patrons
"Look Over There" (Reprise)	Jean-Michel
Grand Finale	Company

Lincoln Center Theater production of **The Rivals** (45). Revival of the play by Richard Brinsley Sheridan. André Bishop artistic director, Bernard Gersten executive producer, at the Vivian Beaumont Theater. Opened December 16, 2004. (Closed January 23, 2005).

Fag	James Urbaniak	Faulkland	Jim True-Frost
Thomas	Herb Foster	Bob Acres	Jeremy Shamos
Lucy	Keira Naughton	Errand Boy	P.J. Verhoest
Lydia Languish	Emily Bergl	Sir Lucius O'Trigger	Brian Murray
Julia Melville	Carrie Preston	David	David Manis
Mrs. Malaprop	Dana Ivey	Footmen	David Furr, Malcolm Ingram,
Sir Anthony Absolute	Richard Easton		Jim Stanek, David Christopher Wells
Capt. Jack Absolute	Matt Letscher		

Understudies: Mr. Urbaniak—Jim Stanek, David Christopher Wells; Messrs. Easton, Verhoest—David Furr; Mses. Bergl, Naughton—Sarah Zimmerman; Mses. Preston, Naughton, Mr. Verhoest—Laura Odeh; Ms. Ivey—Barbara Caruso; Messrs. Easton, Murray, Foster—Malcolm Ingram; Mr. Murray—David Manis; Mr. True-Frost—David Christopher Wells; Messrs. Shamos, Manis—Jim Stanek; Messrs. Furr, Ingram, Stanek, Wells—David Furr, Laura Odeh, Sarah Zimmerman.

Directed by Mark Lamos; choreography, Seán Curran; scenery, John Lee Beatty; costumes, Jess Goldstein; lighting, Peter Kaczorowski; sound, Scott Stauffer; music, Robert Waldman; dramaturg, Anne Cattaneo; casting, Daniel Swee; stage manager, Michael McGoff; press, Philip Rinaldi Publicity, Philip Rinaldi, Barbara Carroll.

Time: 1775. Place: Bath, England. Presented in two parts.

Cloaked identities and romantic machinations bookend the mangled speech of Mrs. Malaprop in this comic romance. This production received the 2005 Tony Award for best costume design of a play (Mr. Goldstein). First presentation of record was at London's Covent Garden (1/17/1775). The first presentation of record in this country was given by the British military at the Theatre Royal (4/21/1778)—known as the John Street Theatre until the British capture of New York during the American Revolution.

Little Women (137) Musical with book by Allan Knee; music by Jason Howland; lyrics by Mindi Dickstein; based on the novel by Louisa May Alcott. Produced by Randall L. Wreghitt, Dani Davis, Ken Gentry, Chase Mishkin, Jack Utsick, Ruben Brache, Lisa Vioni, Jana Robbins, Addiss/Duke Associates, in association with· John and Danita Thomas, Thomas Keegan, Scott Freiman and Theatre Previews at Duke, at the Virginia Theatre. Opened January 23, 2005. (Closed May 22, 2005)

Professor Bhaer	John Hickok	Mr. Brooke	Jim Weitzer
Jo	Sutton Foster	"Operatic Tragedy" Players	
Amy	Amy McAlexander	Clarissa	Jenny Powers
Meg	Jenny Powers	Braxton	Jim Weitzer
Beth	Megan McGinnis	Rodrigo	Danny Gurwin
Marmee	Maureen McGovern	The Hag	Maureen McGovern
Mr. Laurence	Robert Stattel	The Troll	Amy McAlexander
Laurie	Danny Gurwin	The Knight	Robert Stattel
Aunt March; Mrs. Kirk	Janet Carroll	Rodrigo Too	Megan McGinnis

Orchestra: Andrew Wilder conductor; Robert Meffe associate conductor, piano; Eric DeGioia, Karl Kawahara violin; Liuh-Wen Ting viola; Ted Mook cello; Richard Sarpola bass; Lawrence Feldman, Lynne Cohen reeds; Tony Kadleck trumpet; Mark Lusk trombone; Russel Rizner horn; James F. Saporito percussion.

Standbys: Ms. Sutton—Julie Foldesi, Larissa Shukis; Mses. McGovern, Carroll—Anne Kanengeiser; Mses. McGinnis, Powers—Julie Foldesi, Larissa Shukis; Ms. McAlexander—Larissa Shukis; Mr. Weitzer—Chris Gunn, Andrew Varela; Mr. Gurwin—Chris Gunn; Messrs. Hickok, Stattel—Andrew Varela.

Directed by Susan H. Schulman; choreography, Michael Lichtefeld; scenery, Derek McLane; costumes, Catherine Zuber; lighting, Kenneth Posner; sound, Peter Hylenski; wigs and hair, Lazaro Arencibia; orchestrations, Kim Scharnberg; vocal arrangements, Lance Horne; music direction and additional arrangements, Mr. Wilder; music coordination, John Miller; casting, Barry Moss and Bob Kale; stage manager, Scott Taylor Rollison; press, Pete Sanders Group, Pete Sanders, Glenna Freedman.

Time: Christmas 1863–spring 1867. Place: Concord, Massachusetts and New York City. Presented in two parts.

Musical version of the classic tale of a 19th-century American girl's development into womanhood.

ACT I

Scene 1: Summer 1865, Mrs. Kirk's boarding house; Christmas 1863, the attic, the March parlor
"An Operatic Tragedy" .... Jo, Clarissa, Braxton,
Rodrigo, Professor Bhaer
"Better" .... Jo
"Our Finest Dreams" .... Jo, Beth, Meg, Amy
"Here Alone" .... Marmee
Scene 2: Early winter 1864, Aunt March's house
"Could You?" .... Aunt March, Jo
Scene 3: Winter 1864, Aunt March's house, Anne Moffat's ball.
"I'd Be Delighted" .... Marmee, Meg, Jo, Beth
"Take a Chance on Me" .... Laurie
"Better" (Reprise) .... Jo
Scene 4: Late winter 1864, the March parlor
"Off to Massachusetts" .... Beth, Mr. Laurence
"Five Forever" .... Jo, Laurie, Beth, Meg, Amy
Scene 5: Early spring 1865, outside the March house
"More Than I Am" .... John Brooke, Meg
Scene 6: Late spring 1865, the attic
"Astonishing" .... Jo

ACT II

Scene 1: Early summer 1866, Mrs. Kirk's boarding house
"The Weekly Volcano Press" .... Company

Scene 2: Summer 1866, the March parlor; late summer 1866, Mrs. Kirk's boarding house
"Off to Massachusetts" (Reprise) .... Beth, Mr. Laurence
"How I Am" .... Professor Bhaer
Scene 3: Fall 1866, Falmouth, Cape Cod
"Some Things Are Meant to Be" .... Beth, Jo
Scene 4: Winter 1867, the March parlor, the attic
"The Most Amazing Thing" .... Laurie, Amy
"Days of Plenty" .... Marmee
"The Fire Within Me" .... Jo
Scene 5: Spring 1867, outside the March house
"Small Umbrella in the Rain" .... Professor Bhaer, Jo

Good Vibrations (94). Musical with book by Richard Dresser; music and lyrics by
Brian Wilson and the Beach Boys. Produced by NCJ Productions/Michael Watt and
Dodger Theatricals, with SEL and GFO, TheaterDreams/Shamrock Partners, Stage
Holding/Joop van den Ende, at the Eugene O'Neill Theatre. Opened February 2, 2005.
(Closed April 24, 2005)

Surfer Guys .... Heath Calvert,		Class President;	
	John Jeffrey Martin,	Giggles Manager .... Tom Deckman	
	Jesse Nager,	Rhonda .... Milena Govich	
	Joe Paparella,	Country Dude .... John Jeffrey Martin	
	David Reiser	Cowboy .... Heath Calvert	
Bobby .... David Larsen		Jan .... Sebastian Arcelus	
Bikini Girl .... Amanda Kloots		Dean .... David Reiser	
Marcella .... Jessica-Snow Wilson		Deirdre .... Jackie Seiden	
Caroline .... Kate Reinders		Wendy .... Tracee Beazer	
Dave .... Brandon Wardell		Randy .... Joe Paparella	
Eddie .... Tituss Burgess			

Ensemble: Sebastian Arcelus, Tracee Beazer, Heath Calvert, Janet Dacal, Tom Deckman, Sarah
Glendening, Milena Govich, Amanda Kloots, John Jeffrey Martin, Jesse Nager, Joe Paparella,
David Reiser, Jackie Seiden, Allison Spratt.

D-u-u-u-u-de: Sebastian Arcelus in Good Vibrations. *Photo: Carol Rosegg*

Orchestra: Susan Draus conductor, keyboard; Henry Aronson associate conductor, keyboard, accordion; Chris Biesterfeldt, Larry Saltzman guitar; John Arbo bass; Matt Hong reeds; Frank Pagano drums; Bill Hayes percussion.

Understudies: Mr. Larsen—Sebastian Arcelus, Steve Morgan; Mr. Wardell—John Jeffrey Martin, David Reiser; Mr. Burgess—Jesse Nager, Joe Paparella; Ms. Reinders—Sarah Glendening, Krysta Rodriguez; Ms. Wilson—Tracee Beazer, Krysta Rodriguez; Mr. Arcelus—Carlos L. Encinias, Steve Morgan, David Reiser; Mr. Deckman—Carlos L. Encinias, Jesse Nager; Ms. Govich—Jackie Seiden, Allison Spratt; Ms. Kloots—Vasthy Mompoint, Krysta Rodriguez; Mr. Martin—Carlos L. Encinias, Steve Morgan; Mr. Calvert—Carlos L. Encinias, Steve Morgan; Mr. Reiser—Carlos L. Encinias, Steve Morgan; Mr. Paparella—Carlos L. Encinias, Jesse Nager.

Swings: Carlos L. Encinias, Steve Morgan, Vasthy Mompoint, Krysta Rodriguez.

Directed and choreographed by John Carrafa; scenery, Heidi Ettinger; costumes, Jess Goldstein; lighting, Brian MacDevitt and Jason Lyons; sound, Tom Morse; projections, Elaine J. McCarthy; wigs and hair, Charles LaPointe; orchestrations, Steve Margoshes; musical supervision and arrangements, David Holcenberg; music direction, Ms. Draus; music coordination, John Miller; dance arrangments, Henry Aronson and Jeff Kazee; executive producers, Dodger Management Group and Sally Campbell Morse; associate producers, William J. Kenney, Silverman Partners; casting, Tara Rubin Casting; production stage manager, Peter Wolf; stage manager, Karen Moore; press, Boneau/Bryan-Brown, Adrian Bryan-Brown, Susanne Tighe, Heath Schwartz.

Presented in two parts.

Guys, girls and a post-high school road trip to California provide the backdrop for a collection of well-known tunes by Brian Wilson and the Beach Boys. Originally presented by New York Stage and Film and the Powerhouse Theater at Vassar (7/29–8/1/2004).

ACT I

"Our Prayer" .... Surfer Guys
"Fun, Fun, Fun" .... Bobby, Company
"Karate" .... High School Kids
"Keep an Eye on Summer" .... Surfer Guys
"Wouldn't It Be Nice" .... Eddie, Marcella, Surfer Guys
"In My Room" .... Caroline, Marcella, High School Kids
"I Get Around" .... Dave, Bobby, Eddie, Surfer Guys
"When I Grow Up to Be a Man" .... Caroline, Bobby, David, Eddie, Marcella, High School Kids
"Breakaway" .... Bobby, Dave, Eddie, Surfer Guys
"Don't Worry Baby" .... Caroline, Bobby, High School Kids
"Surf City" .... Dave, Bobby, Eddie, Caroline, Surfer Guys
"Shutdown" .... Bobby, Caroline, Dave, Eddie, Surfer Guys
"Be True to Your School" .... Country Dude, Chili Dog Kids
"Car Crazy Cutie" .... Bobby, Dave, Eddie, Surfer Guys
"Warmth of the Sun" .... Marcella, Caroline, Giggles Girls
"Pet Sounds" .... Instrumental
"Surfin' USA" .... Jan, Dean, Beach Kids
"Dance, Dance, Dance" .... Caroline, Jan, Beach Kids

ACT II

"California Girls" .... Jan, Dean, Beach Kids
"Help Me, Rhonda" .... Eddie, Bobby, Dave, Beach Guys
"Stoked" .... Beach Guys
"Surfer Girl" .... Bobby, Beach Guys
"Darlin'" .... Jan, Caroline, Beach Kids
"Your Imagination" .... Caroline, Marcella
"Caroline, No" .... Bobby
"All Summer Long" .... Beach Kids
"I Just Wasn't Made for These Times" .... Dave, Bobby, Eddie
"Wouldn't It Be Nice" (Reprise) .... Eddie, Marcella, Surfer Guys
"Sail on Sailor" .... Eddie, Dean, Beach Kids
"Sloop John B" .... Jan, Dave, Beach Kids

Generation gap: Adam Arkin and Ari Graynor in Brooklyn Boy. *Photo: Joan Marcus*

"Friends" .... Surfer Guys
"Good Vibrations" .... Bobby, Company
"God Only Knows" .... Bobby, Caroline, Company
Finale .... Company

Manhattan Theatre Club production of **Brooklyn Boy** (62). By Donald Margulies. Lynne Meadow artistic director, Barry Grove executive producer, at the Biltmore Theatre. Opened February 3, 2005. (Closed March 27, 2005)

Eric Weiss .... Adam Arkin   Alison .... Ari Graynor
Manny Weiss .... Allan Miller   Melanie Fine .... Mimi Lieber
Ira Zimmer .... Arye Gross   Tyler Shaw .... Kevin Isola
Nina .... Polly Draper

Understudies: Mr. Isola—Bill Heck; Ms. Graynor—Liesel Matthews; Mses. Draper, Lieber—Charlotte Maier; Messrs. Arkin, Gross—Mark Zeisler.

Directed by Daniel Sullivan; scenery, Ralph Funicello; costumes, Jess Goldstein; lighting, Chris Parry; music and sound, Michael Roth; casting, Nancy Piccione/David Caparelliotis and Joanne Denaut; production stage manager, Roy Harris; stage manager, Denise Yaney; press, Boneau/Bryan-Brown, Chris Boneau, Jim Byk, Aaron Meier.

Time: The present. Place: Various location in Brooklyn, New York City and Los Angeles. Presented in two parts.

A writer in middle age confronts his past as he considers his future. First presented at South Coast Repertory in Costa Mesa, California (9/11/2004). A 2004–05 *Best Plays* choice (see essay by Michael Feingold in this volume).

*Dirty Rotten Scoundrels (100). Musical with book by Jeffrey Lane; music and lyrics by David Yazbek; based on the film by Dale Launer, Stanley Shapiro and Paul Henning. Produced by Marty Bell, David Brown, Aldo Scrofani, Roy Furman, Dede Harris,

Mr. Big Stuff: Norbert Leo Butz and friends in Dirty Rotten Scoundrels. *Photo: Carol Rosegg*

Amanda Lipitz, Greg Smith, Ruth Hendel, Chase Mishkin, Barry and Susan Tatelman, Debra Black, Sharon Karmazin, Joyce Schweickert, Bernie Abrams/Michael Speyer, Barbara Whitman, Weissberger Theater Group/Jay Harris, Cheryl Wiesenfeld/Jean Cheever, Clear Channel Entertainment and Harvey Weinstein, in association with MGM On Stage/Darcie Denkert and Dean Stolber, at the Imperial Theatre. Opened March 3, 2005.

Andre Thibault	Gregory Jbara	Freddy Benson	Norbert Leo Butz
Lawrence Jameson	John Lithgow	Jolene Oakes	Sara Gettelfinger
Muriel Eubanks	Joanna Gleason	Christine Colgate	Sherie René Scott

Ensemble: Timothy J. Alex, Andrew Asnes, Roxane Barlow, Stephen Campanella, Joe Cassidy, Julie Connors, Rachel De Benedet, Laura Marie Duncan, Sally Mae Dunn, Tom Galantich, Jason Gillman, Amy Heggins, Grasan Kingsberry, Michael Paternostro, Rachelle Rak.

Orchestra: Fred Lassen conductor; Jan Rosenberg associate conductor, keyboard; Howard Joines assistant conductor, percussion; Antoine Silverman concertmaster, violin; Michael Nicholas, Claire Chan violin; Anja Wood cello; Erik DellaPenna guitar; Mike DuClos bass; Andrew Sterman, Dan Willis, Mark Thrasher woodwinds; Hollis (Bud) Burridge, Jim Hynes trumpet; Mike Boschen trombone; Theresa MacDonnell horn; Dan Lipton keyboard; Dean Sharenow drums.

Standby: Mr. Lithgow—Nick Wyman.

Understudies: Mr. Jbara—Joe Cassidy, Michael Paternostro; Mr. Lithgow—Tom Galantich; Ms. Cassidy—Rachel De Benedet, Laura Marie Duncan; Mr. Butz—Joe Cassidy, Jason Gillman, Michael

Paternostro; Ms. Gettelfinger—Julie Connors, Rachelle Rak; Ms. Scott—Laura Marie Duncan, Gina Lamparella.

Swings: Jeremy Davis, Nina Goldman, Greg Graham, Gina Lamparella.

Directed by Jack O'Brien; choreography, Jerry Mitchell; scenery, David Rockwell; costumes, Gregg Barnes; lighting, Kenneth Posner; sound, Acme Sound Partners; orchestrations, Harold Wheeler; vocal arrangements, Ted Sperling and Mr. Yazbek; dance arrangements, Zane Mark; music direction, Mr. Sperling; music coordination, Howard Joines; executive producers, Marty Bell and Aldo Scrofani; casting, Bernard Telsey Casting; production stage manager, Michael Brunner; stage manager, Daniel S. Rosokoff; press, Barlow-Hartman Public Relations, Michael Hartman, John Barlow, Rick Miramontez, Jon Dimond.

Presented in two parts.

Suave ladies' man in the South of France in challenged by a low-rent newcomer who seeks the lifestyle of a cultured swindler. Mr. Butz received the 2005 Tony Award for best actor in a musical. First presented at The Old Globe in San Diego (9/22–10/31/2004). The 1988 film *Dirty Rotten Scoundrels* with Michael Caine, Steve Martin and Glenne Headley was itself based on the David Niven, Marlon Brando and Shirley Jones comedy *Bedtime Story* (1964).

ACT I

Overture	Orchestra, Ensemble
"Give Them What They Want"	Lawrence, Andre, Ensemble
"What Was a Woman to Do?"	Muriel, Women
"Great Big Stuff"	Freddy, Ensemble
"Chimp in a Suit"	Andre
"Oklahoma?"	Jolene, Lawrence, Ensemble
"All About Ruprecht"	Lawrence, Ruprecht, Jolene
"What Was a Woman to Do?" (Reprise)	Muriel
"Here I Am"	Christine, Ensemble
"Nothing Is Too Wonderful to Be True"	Christine, Freddy
"The Miracle"	Company

ACT II

Entr'acte	Orchestra, Ensemble
"Rüffousin' mit Shüffhausen"	Freddy, Christine, Dr. Shüffhausen
"Like Zis, Like Zat"	Andre, Muriel
"The More We Dance"	Lawrence, Christine, Ensemble
"Love Is My Legs"	Freddy, Christine, Ensemble
"Love Sneaks In"	Lawrence
"Son of Great Big Stuff"	Freddy, Christine
"The Reckoning"	Lawrence, Freddy, Andre
"Dirty Rotten Number"	Lawrence, Freddy
Finale	Company

*Spamalot (86). Musical with book and lyrics by Eric Idle; music by John Du Prez and Mr. Idle; based on the motion picture *Monty Python and the Holy Grail*. Produced by Boyett Ostar Productions, The Shubert Organization, Arielle Tepper, Stephanie P. McClelland/Lawrence Horowitz, Elan V. McAllister/Allan S. Gordon, Independent Presenters Network, Roy Furman, GRS Associates, Jam Theatricals, TGA Entertainment, Clear Channel Entertainment, at the Shubert Theatre. Opened March 17, 2005.

Historian; Not Dead Fred; French Guard; Minstrel; Prince Herbert	Christian Borle
Mayor; Patsy; Guard 2	Michael McGrath
King Arthur	Tim Curry
Sir Robin; Guard 1; Brother Maynard	David Hyde Pierce
Sir Lancelot; French Taunter; Knight of Ni; Tim the Enchanter	Hank Azaria
Sir Dennis Galahad; Black Knight; Herbert's Father	Christopher Sieber

Dennis's Mother;
  Sir Bedevere;
  Concorde .... Steve Rosen
The Lady of the Lake .... Sara Ramirez
Sir Not Appearing .... Kevin Covert
God ....John Cleese

French Guards .... Thomas Cannizzaro,
                                                            Greg Reuter
Minstrels .... Brad Bradley, Emily Hsu,
                                                            Greg Reuter
Sir Bors .... Brad Bradley

Ensemble: Brad Bradley, Thomas Cannizzaro, Kevin Covert, Jennifer Frankel, Lisa Gajda, Jenny Hill, Emily Hsu, Abbey O'Brien, Ariel Reid, Greg Reuter, Brian Shepard, Scott Taylor.

Orchestra: Todd Ellison conductor; Ethyl Will associate conductor, keyboard 1; Ann Labin concertmaster, violin; Maura Giannini, Ming Yeh violin; Richard Brice viola; Diane Barere cello; Scott Kuney guitar; David Kuhn bass; Ken Dybisz, Alden Banta reeds; John Chudoba lead trumpet; Anthony Gorruso trumpet; Mark Patterson trombone; Zohar Schondorf, French horn; Antony Geralis keyboard 2; Dave Mancuso percussion; Sean McDaniel drums.

Standbys: John Bolton, James Ludwig, Darlene Wilson.

Swings: Pamela Remler, Rick Spaans.

Directed by Mike Nichols; choreography, Casey Nicholaw; scenery and costumes, Tim Hatley; lighting, Hugh Vanstone; sound, Acme Sound Partners; projections, Elaine J. McCarthy; wigs and hair, David Brian Brown; orchestrations, Larry Hochman; music direction and vocal arrangements, Todd Ellison; musical arrangements, Glen Kelly; music coordination, Michael Keller; associate producers, Randi Grossman, Tisch/Avnet Financial; casting, Tara Rubin Casting; production stage manager, Peter Lawrence; stage managers, Mahlon Kruse, Jim Woolley, Rachel Wolff; press, Boneau/Bryan-Brown, Adrian Bryan-Brown, Jackie Green, Aaron Meier.

Presented in two parts.

Musical based on the sketch material of *Monty Python's Flying Circus* and the film *Monty Python and the Holy Grail*. The production received 2005 Tony Awards for best musical, direction of a musical (Mr. Nichols) and featured actress in a musical (Ms. Ramirez).

Spiced ham: David Hyde Pierce, Hank Azaria, Christopher Sieber, Steve Rosen and Tim Curry in Spamalot. *Photo: Joan Marcus*

ACT I

Overture .... Orchestra
Scene 1: The Mighty Portcullis
Scene 2: Moose Village
    "Fisch Schlapping Song" .... Historian, Mayor, Villagers
Scene 3: Mud Castle
    "King Arthur's Song" .... King Arthur, Patsy
Scene 4: Plague Village
    "I Am Not Dead Yet" .... Not Dead Fred, Lance, Robin, Bodies
Scene 5: Mud Village
Scene 6: The Lady of the Lake and the Laker Girls
    "Come With Me" .... King Arthur, Lady of the Lake, Laker Girls
    "The Song That Goes Like This" .... Sir Galahad, Lady of the Lake
Scene 7: The Knights
    "All for One" .... King Arthur, Patsy, Sir Robin, Sir Lancelot, Sir Galahad, Sir Bedevere
Scene 8: Camelot
    "Knights of the Round Table"Lady of the Lake, King Arthur, Patsy, Sir Robin, Sir Lancelot, Sir Galahad, Sir Bedevere, Camelot Dancers
    "The Song That Goes Like This" (Reprise) .... Lady of the Lake
Scene 9: The Feet of God
Scene 10: Find Your Grail
    "Find Your Grail"Lade of the Lake, King Arthur, Patsy, Sir Robin, Sir Lancelot, Sir Galahad, Sir Bedevere, Knights, Grail Girls
Scene 11: The French Castle
    "Run Away" ...... French Taunters, King Arthur, Patsy, Sir Robin, Sir Lancelot, Sir Galahad, Sir Bedevere, French Guards, French Citizens

ACT II

Scene 1: The Mighty Portcullis
Scene 2: A Very Expensive Forest
    "Always Look on the Bright Side of Life" .... Patsy, King Arthur, Knights, Knights of Ni
Scene 3: Sir Robin and His Minstrels
    "Brave Sir Robin" .... Sir Robin, Minstrels
Scene 4: The Black Knight
Scene 5: Another Part of the Very Expensive Forest
    "You Won't Succeed on Broadway" .... Sir Robin, Ensemble
Scene 6: A Hole in the Universe
    "The Diva's Lament" .... Lady of the Lake
Scene 7: Prince Herbert's Chamber
    "Where Are You?" .... Prince Herbert
    "Here Are You" .... Prince Herbert
    "His Name Is Lancelot" .... Sir Lancelot, Prince Herbert, Ensemble
Scene 8: Yet Another Part of the Very Expensive Forest
    "I'm All Alone" .... King Arthur, Patsy, Knights
    "The Song That Goes Like This" (Reprise) .... Lady of the Lake, King Arthur
Scene 9: The Killer Rabbit
    "The Holy Grail"King Arthur, Patsy, Sir Robin, Sir Lancelot, Sir Galahad, Sir Bedevere, Knights
Finale
    "Find Your Grail Finale-Medley" .... Company

Who's Afraid of Virginia Woolf? (77). Revival of the play by Edward Albee. Produced by Elizabeth Ireland McCann, Daryl Roth, Terry Allen Kramer, Scott Rudin, Roger Berlind, James L. Nederlander, Nick Simunek, at the Longacre Theatre. Opened March 20, 2005.

Martha .... Kathleen Turner   Honey .... Mireille Enos
George .... Bill Irwin   Nick .... David Harbour

    Standbys: Ms. Turner—Jennifer Regan; Mr. Irwin—Christopher Burns; Ms. Enos—Stina Nielsen; Mr. Harbour—David Furr.

Directed by Anthony Page; scenery, John Lee Beatty; costumes, Jane Greenwood; lighting, Peter Kaczorowski; sound, Mark Bennett; fight direction, Rick Sordelet; executive producer, Joey Parnes; casting, Jay Binder, Jack Bowdan, Laura Stanczyk; production stage manager, Susie Cordon; stage manager, Allison Sommers; press, Shirley Herz Associates, Shirley Herz, Sam Rudy, Kevin P. McAnarney, Dale Heller, Robert Lasko, Daniel Demello.

Time: 1960. Place: The living room of a house on the campus of a small New England college. Presented in three parts: "Fun and Games," "*Walpurgisnacht*" and "The Exorcism."

A college professor and his wife shed their marital illusions in the company of a younger couple during a night of drink, stinging comments and sexual innuendo. The text used in this production is based on the 2004 revised version. A 1962–63 *Best Plays* choice, the original Broadway production opened at the Billy Rose Theatre (10/13/1962–5/16/1964; 664 performances). Although the original production received five Tony Awards in 1963 (play, actor, actress, direction and producer), the play was denied the Pulitzer Prize in a controversial decision of the Pulitzer board—the work was deemed unseemly—that caused the resignation of drama jurors John Gassner and John Mason Brown. The current version is the third Broadway production of the play; Mr. Irwin received a 2005 Tony Award for his portrayal of George. A 1976 Broadway production, directed by the author, featured Colleen Dewhurst and Ben Gazzara.

*The Glass Menagerie (81). Revival of the play by Tennessee Williams. Produced by Bill Kenwright at the Ethel Barrymore Theatre. Opened March 22, 2005.

Amanda Wingfield	Jessica Lange	Laura Wingfield	Sarah Paulson
Tom Wingfield	Christian Slater	The Gentleman Caller	Josh Lucas

Understudies: Ms. Lange—Jennifer Harmon; Messrs. Slater, Lucas—Joey Collins; Ms. Paulson—Cheyenne Casebier.

Mama's boy: Jessica Lange and Christian Slater in The Glass Menagerie. *Photo: Paul Kolnik*

Directed by David Leveaux; scenery and costumes, Tom Pye; lighting, Natasha Katz; sound, Jon Weston; wigs and hair, David Brian Brown; music, Dan Moses Schreier; casting, Pat McCorkle, Bonnie Grisan; production stage manager, Bonnie L. Becker; stage manager, J. Philip Bassett; press, Philip Rinaldi Publicity, Philip Rinaldi, Barbara Carroll.

Time: Now and the past. Presented in two parts.

A man tortured by the memory of family left behind seeks expiation in the company of an audience. A 1944–45 *Best Plays* choice, the original Broadway production opened at the Playhouse Theatre, completing its run at the Royale Theatre (3/31/1945–8/3/1946; 563 performances). The first presentation of record was given at Chicago's Civic Theatre (12/26/1944). The current version is the sixth Broadway production of the play

*Jackie Mason: Freshly Squeezed (67). Solo performance piece by Mr. Mason. Produced by Jyll Rosenfeld, Jon Stoll, James Scibelli, at the Helen Hayes Theatre. Opened March 23, 2005.

Performed by Mr. Mason.

Directed by Mr. Mason; lighting, Paul Miller; sound, Peter Hylenski; production stage manager, Don Myers.

The latest of Mr. Mason's comedy shows and his tenth Broadway stand. The first was *A Teaspoon Every Four Hours*, presented at the ANTA Playhouse—now the Virginia Theatre—for one performance (6/14/1969) following 97 previews.

*All Shook Up (78). Musical with book by Joe DiPietro; music and lyrics by various artists, see list below; inspired by the songs of Elvis Presley. Produced by Jonathan Pollard, Bernie Kukoff, Clear Channel Entertainment, Harbor Entertainment, Miramax Films, Bob and Harvey Weinstein, Stanley Buchthal, Eric Falkenstein, Nina Essman/Nancy Nagel Gibbs, Jean Cheever, Margaret Cotter, in association with Barney Rosenzweig, Meri Kassner, FGRW Investments, Karen Jason, Phil Ciasullo Conrad, at the Palace Theatre. Opened March 24, 2005.

Natalie Haller; Ed .... Jenn Gambatese	Chad .... Cheyenne Jackson
Jim Haller .... Jonathan Hadary	Mayor Matilda Hyde .... Alix Korey
Dennis .... Mark Price	Dean Hyde .... Curtis Holbrook
Sylvia .... Sharon Wilkins	Sheriff Earl .... John Jellison
Lorraine .... Nikki M. James	Miss Sandra .... Leah Hocking

Ensemble: Brad Anderson, Justin Bohon, Justin Brill, Paul Castree, Cara Cooper, Michael Cusumano, Francesca Harper, Trisha Jeffrey, Michelle Kittrell, Anika Larsen, Michael X. Martin, Karen Murphy, John Eric Parker, Justin Patterson, Michael James Scott, Jenny-Lynn Suckling, Virginia Ann Woodruff.

Orchestra: Stephen Oremus conductor, keyboard; August Eriksmoen associate conductor, organ, keyboard 2; Ken Brescia, Chris Delis guitar; Cary Potts bass; Charles Pillow, Tim Ries, Andy Snitzer, Don McGeen reeds; Joe Giorgianni lead trumpet; Tino Gagliardi, Brian Pareschi trumpet; Mike Davis trombone; Joe Mowatt percussion, Steve Bartosik drums.

Understudies: Ms. Gambatese—Cara Cooper, Anika Larsen; Mr. Hadary—Brad Anderson, Michael X. Martin; Mr. Price—Justin Brill, Paul Castree; Ms. Wilkins—Francesca Harper, Virginia Ann Woodruff; Ms. James—Trisha Jeffrey, Jenelle Lynn Randall; Mr. Jackson—Brad Anderson, Justin Patterson; Ms. Korey—Karen Murphy, Jenny-Lynn Suckling; Mr. Holbrook—Justin Bohon, Justin Brill; Mr. Jellison—Michael X. Martin, Justin Patterson; Ms. Hocking—Michelle Kittrell, Anika Larsen, Jenny-Lynn Suckling.

Swings: Randy A. Davis, Jennie Ford, Jenelle Lynn Randall.

Directed by Christopher Ashley; choreography, Ken Roberson; additional choreography, Sergio Trujillo; scenery, David Rockwell; costumes, David C. Woolard; lighting, Donald Holder; sound, Brian Ronan; wigs and hair, David H. Lawrence; orchestrations, Michael Gibson and Stephen Oremus; dance arrangements, Zane Mark; music coordination, Michael Keller; associate producers, Marcia Goldberg, Greg Schaffert; casting, Bernard Telsey Casting; production stage manager, Lois L. Griffing; stage manager, Paul J. Smith; press, Barlow-Hartman Public Relations, Michael Hartman, John Barlow, Wayne Wolfe, Andrew Snyder.

Presented in two parts.

Story of a small town awakened by the raw, male energy of a new kid, using the songs made famous by Elvis Presley. First presented by Goodspeed Musicals (5/13/2004) before a pre-Broadway run in Chicago's Cadillac Palace Theatre (1/13/2005).

ACT I

"Love Me Tender" .... Natalie, Dennis
(Elvis Presley, Vera Matson)

"Heartbreak Hotel" .... Barflies
(Elvis Presley, Mae Boren Axton, Tommy Durden)

"Roustabout" .... Chad
(Bill Giant, Bernie Baum, Florence Kaye)

"One Night With You" .... Natalie
(Dave Bartholomew, Pearl King)

"C'mon Everybody" .... Chad, Company
(Joy Byers)

"Follow That Dream" .... Chad, Natalie
(Fred Wise, Ben Weisman)

"Teddy Bear"/"Hound Dog" .... Chad, Sandra, Dennis, Natalie
(Kal Mann, Bernie Lowe/Jerry Leiber, Mike Stoller)

"That's All Right" .... Sylvia, Lorraine, Chad, Dennis, Barflies
(Arthur Crudup)

"(You're the) Devil in Disguise" .... Matilda, Ladies Church Council
(Bill Giant, Bernie Baum, Florence Kaye)

"It's Now or Never" .... Dean, Lorraine, Company
(Aaron Schroeder, Wally Gold)

"Blue Suede Shoes" .... Ed, Chad
(Carl Perkins)

"Don't Be Cruel" .... Chad, Jim
(Otis Blackwell, Elvis Presley)

"Let Yourself Go" .... Sandra, Statues
(Joy Byers)

"Can't Help Falling in Love" .... Company
(George David Weiss, Hugo Peretti, Luigi Creatore)

ACT II

"All Shook Up" .... Company
(Otis Blackwell, Elvis Presley)

"It Hurts Me" .... Dennis, Company
(Joy Byers, Charles E. Daniels)

"A Little Less Conversation" .... Ed, Company
(Mac Davis, Billy Strange)

"The Power of My Love" .... Chad, Jim, Sandra
(Bill Giant, Bernie Baum, Florence Kaye)

"I Don't Want To" .... Chad
(Janice Torre, Fred Spielman)

"Jailhouse Rock" .... Chad, Prisoners
(Jerry Leiber, Mike Stoller)

"There's Always Me" .... Sylvia
(Don Robertson)

"If I Can Dream" .... Chad, Lorraine, Dean, Company
(W. Earl Brown)

"Can't Help Falling in Love" (Reprise) .... Earl, Jim, Sylvia, Matilda
(George David Weiss, Hugo Peretti, Luigi Creatore)

"Fools Fall in Love" .... Natalie, Company
(Jerry Leiber, Mike Stoller)

"Burning Love" .... Chad, Natalie, Company
(Dennis Linde)

*Power play: Brían F. O'Byrne and Cherry Jones
in* Doubt, a Parable. *Photo: Joan Marcus*

*Doubt, a Parable (70). Transfer of the Off Broadway play by John Patrick Shanley. Produced by Carole Shorenstein Hays, MTC Productions, Roger Berlind, Scott Rudin, at the Walter Kerr Theatre. Opened March 31, 2005.

Father Flynn .... Brían F. O'Byrne   Sister James .... Heather Goldenhersh
Sister Aloysius .... Cherry Jones   Mrs. Muller .... Adriane Lenox

Standbys: Ms. Goldenhersh—Nadia Bowers; Ms. Lenox—Caroline Stefanie Clay; Mr. O'Byrne—Chris McGarry.

Directed by Doug Hughes; scenery, John Lee Beatty; costumes, Catherine Zuber; lighting, Pat Collins; sound and music, David Van Tieghem; executive producer, Greg Holland; casting, Nancy Piccione/David Caparelliotis; production stage manager, Charles Means; stage manager, Elizabeth Moloney; press, Boneau/Bryan-Brown, Chris Boneau, Jim Byk, Aaron Meier, Erika Creagh.

Time: Autumn, 1964. Place: St. Nicholas Church School in the Bronx. Presented without intermission.

A nun grows concerned over a priest's relationships with boys in his charge. Transfer of the Manhattan Theatre Club production (Lynne Meadow artistic director, Barry Grove executive producer) Off Broadway at City Center Stage I (11/23/2004–1/30/2005; 77 performances). See Plays Produced Off Broadway section in this volume. A 2004–05 *Best Plays* choice (see essay by Jeremy McCarter in this volume). This production received 2005 Tony Awards in the play categories of best play, actress (Ms. Jones), featured actress (Ms. Lenox) and direction (Mr. Hughes). Mr. Shanley also received the 2005 Pulitzer Prize.

*Julius Caesar (66). Revival of the play by William Shakespeare. Produced by Carole Shorenstein Hays and Freddy DeMann at the Belasco Theatre. Opened April 3, 2005.

Soothsayer .... Stephen Lee Anderson   Portia .... Jessica Hecht
Marcus Brutus .... Denzel Washington   Artemidora .... Jacqueline Antaramian

Bloody murderers: Denzel Washington and conspirators in Julius Caesar. *Photo: Joan Marcus*

Flavius .... John Douglas Thompson
Marullus .... Henry Woronicz
Carpenter .... Howard W. Overshown
Cobbler .... Keith Davis
Guards to Caesar .... Mark Mineart,
Dan Moran
Mark Antony .... Eamonn Walker
Julius Caesar .... William Sadler
Calpurnia .... Tamara Tunie
Casca .... Jack Willis
Decius Brutus .... Patrick Page
Cassius .... Colm Feore
Cicero .... David Cromwell
Cinna .... Richard Topol
Metellus Cimber .... Peter Jay Fernandez
Trebonius .... Henry Woronicz
Lucius .... Maurice Jones
Servant to Caesar .... Seth Fisher

Popilius Lena .... Jason Manuel Olazábal
Servant to M. Antony .... Ed Onipede Blunt
Servant to O. Caesar .... Quentin Maré
Cinna the Poet .... David Cromwell
Octavius Caesar .... Kelly AuCoin
Lepidus .... Richard Topol
Lucilius .... Peter Jay Fernandez
Pindarus .... Keith Davis
Messala .... Patrick Page
Titinius .... Stephen Lee Anderson
Messenger .... Quentin Maré
Cato .... Ed Onipede Blunt
First Soldier .... Seth Fisher
Second Soldier .... Christopher McHale
Clitus .... Quentin Maré
Volumnius .... Dan Moran
Dardanius .... Howard W. Overshown

Ensemble: Stephen Lee Anderson, Jacqueline Antaramian, Kelly AuCoin, Ed Onipede Blunt, David Cromwell, Keith Davis, Peter Jay Fernandez, Seth Fisher, Jessica Hecht, Effie Johnson, Maurice Jones, Ty Jones, Aaron Krohn, Quentin Maré, Mark Mineart, Christopher McHale, Dan Moran, Jason Manuel Olazábal, Howard W. Overshown, Patrick Page, Kurt Rhoads, John Douglas Thompson, Richard Topol, Tamara Tunie, Henry Woronicz.

Understudies: Mr. Washington—Peter Jay Fernandez; Mr. Walker—Ty Jones; Mr. Sadler—Henry Woronicz; Mr. Feore—Patrick Page; Mses. Tunie, Hecht—Jacqueline Antaramian; Mr. Willis—Richard Topol; Messrs. Anderson, Moran—Ty Jones; Mr. Woronicz—Quentin Maré; Messrs. Blunt, Jones, Maré—Aaron Krohn; Messrs. Fernandez, Page, Topol—Christopher McHale; Ms. Antaramian—Effie Johnson; Messrs. Overshown, Moran, Olazábal, Thompson—Mark Mineart; Mr. Davis—Dan Moran; Messrs. Cromwell, Topol, Fernandez, Jones, Page, Woronicz—Kurt Rhoads.

Directed by Daniel Sullivan; scenery, Ralph Funicello; costumes, Jess Goldstein; lighting, Mimi Jordan Sherin; sound and music, Dan Moses Schreier; wigs and hair, Charles LaPointe; fight direction, Robin H. McFarquhar; executive producers, Pilar DeMann and Greg Holland; dramaturg, Dakin Matthews; casting, Daniel Swee; production stage manager, Lisa Dawn Cave; stage manager, Brian Meister; press, Boneau/Bryan-Brown, Chris Boneau, Adriana Douzos, Erika Creagh.

Presented in two parts.

Murderous aristocrats overthrow an incipient tyrant, reaping a whirlwind of societal chaos. The first presentation of record is believed also to be the first production in Southwark's newly constructed Globe Theatre (9/21/1599). The first presentation of record in this country was given at the John Street Theatre featuring Lewis Hallam II as Brutus, John Hodgkinson as Marc Antony and "Mr. Richards" (Richard Crosby or "Crosbie") in the title role (3/14/1794; 1 performance).

*Steel Magnolias (65). Revival of the play by Robert Harling. Produced by Roy Gabay, Robyn Goodman, Danzansky Partners, Ergo Entertainment, Ruth Hendel, Sharon Karmazin, Susan Dietz/Ina Meibach, Michael Galvis/Billy Huddleston, Elsa Daspin Suisman/Martha R. Gasparian, at the Lyceum Theatre. Opened April 4, 2005.

Truvy	Delta Burke	Shelby	Rebecca Gayheart
Annelle	Lily Rabe	M'Lynn	Christine Ebersole
Clairee	Frances Sternhagen	Ouiser	Marsha Mason

Standbys: Patricia Kilgarriff, Ginifer King, Sally Mayes.

Directed by Jason Moore; scenery, Anna Louizos; costumes, David Murin; lighting, Howell Binkley; sound, Ken Travis; wigs and hair, Bobby H. Grayson; associate producers, Stephen Kocis and Bill Goodman; casting, Bernard Telsey Casting; production stage manager, James FitzSimmons; stage manager, Neil Krasnow; press, Boneau/Bryan-Brown, Chris Boneau, Susanne Tighe, Heath Schwartz.

Time: April 1987–November 1989. Place: Chinquapin, Louisiana. Presented in two parts.

Denizens of a beauty parlor in the South deal with the triumphs and tragedies dispensed by life. A 1987–88 *Best Plays* choice, the original production opened Off Broadway at the Lucille

Gals' club: Rebecca Gayheart, Delta Burke, Lily Rabe and Christine Ebersole (left to right) in Steel Magnolias. *Photo: Joan Marcus*

Stormin' Norman: James Earl Jones and Leslie Uggams in On Golden Pond. *Photo: Joan Marcus*

Lortel Theatre (6/19/1987–2/25/1990; 1,126 performances). The first New York presentation of record was the WPA Theatre production (3/11/1987; 42 performances), which transferred to Off Broadway's Lortel Theatre.

*On Golden Pond (62). Revival of the play by Ernest Thompson. Produced by Jeffrey Finn, Arlene Scanlan and Stuart Thompson at the Cort Theatre. Opened April 7, 2005.

Norman Thayer Jr.	James Earl Jones	Chelsea Thayer Wayne	Linda Powell
Ethel Thayer	Leslie Uggams	Billy Ray	Alexander Mitchell
Charlie Martin	Craig Bockhorn	Bill Ray	Peter Francis James

Standbys: Mr. Jones—Charles Turner; Ms. Uggams—Petronia Paley; Ms. Powell—Opal Alladin; Messrs. James, Bockhorn—Cornell Womack; Mr. Mitchell—Rydell Rollins.

Directed by Leonard Foglia; scenery, Ray Klausen; costumes, Jane Greenwood; lighting, Brian Nason; sound and music, Dan Moses Schreier; associate producers, Magnesium.com, Inc., Neal Edelsen and Andy Sawyer; casting, Stuart Howard, Amy Schecter and Paul Hardt; production stage manager, Kelley Kirkpatrick; stage manager, Marti McIntosh; press, The Publicity Office, Marc Thibodeau, Bob Fennell, Michael S. Borowski.

Time: The present. Place: The Thayers' home on Golden Pond in Maine. Presented in two parts.

Aging couple in their longtime summer home are visited by their daughter with her new husband and stepson in tow. A 1978–79 *Best Plays* choice, the original Broadway production opened at the New Apollo Theatre (2/28/1979–6/16/1979; 126 performances). After a three-month hiatus in the summer of 1979, the Broadway production moved—with the same cast—to the Century Theatre (9/12/1979–4/20/1980; 256 performances). The first Broadway production was a transfer from Off Broadway's Hudson Guild Theatre (9/13/1978–10/22/1978; 30 performances).

*The Pillowman (58). By Martin McDonagh. Produced by Boyett Ostar Productions, Robert Fox, Arielle Tepper, Stephanie P. McClelland, Debra Black, Dede Harris/Morton

Swinsky, Roy Furman/Jon Avnet, in association with Joyce Schweickert, at the Booth Theatre. Opened April 10, 2005.

Tupolski	Jeff Goldblum	Father	Ted Koch
Katurian	Billy Crudup	Mother	Virginia Louise Smith
Ariel	Zeljko Ivanek	Boy	Jesse Shane Bronstein
Michal	Michael Stuhlbarg	Girl	Madeleine Martin

Understudies: Messrs. Goldblum, Ivanek—Ted Koch; Messrs. Crudup, Stuhlbarg, Koch—Rick Holmes; Ms. Smith—Kate Gleason; Mr. Bronstein and Ms. Martin—Colby Minifie.

Directed by John Crowley; scenery and costumes, Scott Pask; lighting, Brian MacDevitt; sound, Paul Arditti; music, Paddy Cunneen; fight direction, J. Steven White; casting, Jim Carnahan; production stage manager, James Harker; press, Barlow-Hartman Public Relations, John Barlow, Michael Hartman, Dennis Crowley, Ryan Ratelle.

Writer in an unnamed police state is persecuted and his dark, gory tales are used as evidence against him. The production received 2005 Tony Awards in the play categories of scenery (Mr. Pask) and lighting (Mr. MacDevitt). The first presentation of record was given at the National Theatre of Great Britain's Cottesloe Theatre (11/13/2003–4/17/2004). A 2004–05 *Best Plays* choice (see essay by John Istel in this volume).

*Lincoln Center Theater production of **The Light in the Piazza** (49). Musical with book by Craig Lucas; music and lyrics by Adam Guettel; based on the novella by

Just my imagination: Billy Crudup in The Pillowman. *Photo: Joan Marcus*

Three pairs: Matthew Morrison, Kelli O'Hara, Mark Harelik, Patti Cohenour, Michael Berresse and Sarah Uriarte Berry in The Light in the Piazza. *Photo: Joan Marcus*

Elizabeth Spencer. André Bishop artistic director, Bernard Gersten executive producer, at the Vivian Beaumont Theater. Opened April 18, 2005.

Margaret Johnson .... Victoria Clark	Franca Naccarelli .... Sarah Uriarte Berry
Clara Johnson .... Kelli O'Hara	Signora Naccarelli .... Patti Cohenour
Fabrizio Naccarelli .... Matthew Morrison	Roy Johnson .... Beau Gravitte
Signor Naccarelli .... Mark Harelik	Tour Guide .... Felicity LaFortune
Giuseppe Naccarelli .... Michael Berresse	Priest .... Joseph Siravo

Ensemble: David Bonanno, David Burnham, Laura Griffith, Prudence Wright Holmes, Jennifer Hughes, Felicity LaFortune, Michel Moinot, Joseph Siravo.

Orchestra: Ted Sperling conductor; Dan Riddle associate conductor, piano, celesta; Christian Hebel concertmaster, violin; Matthew Lehmann, Sylvia D'Avanzo, James Tsao, Lisa Matricardi, Katherine Livolsi-Stern violin; Peter Sachon, Ariane Lallemand cello; Andrew Schwartz guitar, mandolin; Brian Cassier bass; Richard Heckman clarinet, English horn, oboe; Gili Sharett bassoon, Willard Miller percussion; Victoria Drake harp.

Understudies: Ms. Clark—Patti Cohenour; Ms. O'Hara—Jennifer Hughes; Mr. Morrison—David Burnham; Messrs. Harelik, Gravitte—Joseph Siravo; Ms. Cohenour—Felicity LaFortune; Mr. Berresse—David Bonanno; Ms. Berry—Laura Griffith; Ms. LaFortune—Catherine LaValle; Mr. Siravo—Glenn Seven Allen.

Swings: Glenn Seven Allen, Catherine LaValle.

Directed by Bartlett Sher; choreography, Jonathan Butterell; scenery, Michael Yeargan; costumes, Catherine Zuber; lighting, Christopher Akerlind; sound, Acme Sound Partners; orchestrations, Ted Sperling and Mr. Guettel; additional orchestrations, Bruce Coughlin; music direction, Mr. Sperling; music coordination, Seymour Red Press; associate producer, Ira Weitzman; production stage manager, Thom Widmann; press, Philip Rinaldi Publicity, Philip Rinaldi, Barbara Carroll.

Synopsis: Time: Summer, 1953. Place: Florence and Rome with occasional side trips to America. Presented in two parts.

A disenchanted American wife experiences romantic Italian culture as her mentally challenged daughter—a grown woman—finds love and marriage while on a grand tour. This production received 2005 Tony Awards in the musical categories of best score (Mr. Guettel), actress (Ms. Clark), scenery (Mr. Yeargan), costumes (Ms. Zuber), lighting (Mr. Akerlind) and orchestrations (Messrs. Sperling and Guettel). First presented by Seattle's Intiman Theatre Company (6/14/2003) before a run at Chicago's Goodman Theatre (1/20/2004). The Elizabeth Spencer story was made into a 1962 MGM film with Olivia de Havilland, Yvette Mimieux, George Hamilton, Barry Sullivan and Rossano Brazzi.

ACT I

Overture .... Orchestra
"Statues and Stories" .... Margaret, Clara
"The Beauty Is" .... Clara
"Il Mondo Era Vuoto" .... Fabrizio
"Passeggiata" .... Fabrizio, Clara
"The Joy You Feel" .... Franca
"Dividing Day" .... Margaret
"Hysteria" .... Clara, Margaret
"Say It Somehow" .... Clara, Fabrizio

ACT II

"Aiutami" .... The Naccarelli Family
"The Light in the Piazza" .... Clara
"Octet" .... Company
"Tirade" .... Clara
"Octet" (Reprise) .... Company
"The Beauty Is" (Reprise) .... Margaret
"Let's Walk" .... Signor Naccarelli, Margaret
"Love to Me" .... Fabrizio
"Fable" .... Margaret

*__Roundabout Theatre Company__ production of __A Streetcar Named Desire__ (36). Revival of the play by Tennessee Williams. Todd Haimes artistic director, Ellen Richard managing director, Julia C. Levy executive director, at Studio 54. Opened April 26, 2005.

A Negro Woman	Wanda L. Houston	Steve Hubbell	Scott Sowers
Eunice Hubbell	Kristine Nielsen	Pablo Gonzales	Frank Pando
Stanley Kowalski	John C. Reilly	A Young Collector	Will Toale
Harold Mitchell (Mitch)	Chris Bauer	A Mexican Woman	Teresa Yenque
Stella Kowalski	Amy Ryan	A Doctor	John Carter
Blanche DuBois	Natasha Richardson	A Nurse	Barbara Sims

Street People: John Carter, Will Toale, Teresa Yenque, Alfredo Narciso, Starla Benford, Frank Pando.

Understudies: Mses. Richardson, Ryan—Angela Pierce; Messrs. Reilly, Bauer—Charles Borland; Mses. Nielsen, Houston, Yenque, Sims—Starla Benford; Messrs. Sowers, Carter—Robert Emmet Lunney; Messrs. Pando, Toale—Alfredo Narciso.

Directed by Edward Hall; scenery, Robert Brill; costumes, William Ivey Long; lighting, Donald Holder; sound and music, John Gromada; wigs and hair, Paul Huntley; fight direction, Rick Sordelet; casting, Jim Carnahan; production stage manager, Jane Grey; stage manager, Philip Cusack; press, Boneau/Bryan-Brown, Adrian Bryan-Brown, Matt Polk, Jessica Johnson, Joe Perrotta.

Time: 1947. Place: New Orleans. Presented in two parts.

A faded dame of Southern gentry visits her younger sister and brutish brother-in-law in search of comfort that she is never to attain. A 1947–48 *Best Plays* choice, the original Broadway production opened at the Ethel Barrymore Theatre (12/3/1947–12/17/1949; 855 performances). Jessica Tandy received the 1948 Tony Award for best actress in the original production, which made Marlon Brando a star, and featured Karl Malden and Kim Hunter. Although *A Streetcar Named Desire* won the 1948 Pulitzer Prize, the Tony Award that year went to *Mister Roberts*. The current version is the sixth Broadway production of the play.

*Chitty Chitty Bang Bang (38). Musical with book by Ian Fleming, adapted for the stage by Jeremy Sams; music and lyrics by Richard M. Sherman and Robert B. Sherman; based on the MGM/United Artists film. Produced by Dana Broccoli, Barbara Broccoli, Michael G. Wilson, Frederick Zollo, Nicholas Paleologos, Jeffrey Sine, Harvey Weinstein, East of Doheny Theatricals and Michael Rose Limited, by special arrangement with MGM On Stage, at the Hilton Theatre. Opened April 28, 2005.

Caractacus Potts .... Raúl Esparza	Jeremy Potts .... Henry Hodges
Truly Scrumptious .... Erin Dilly	Jemima Potts .... Ellen Marlow
Grandpa Potts .... Philip Bosco	Coggins; Chicken Farmer .... JB Adams
Baron Bomburst .... Marc Kudisch	Phillips .... Dirk Lumbard
Baroness Bomburst .... Jan Maxwell	Lord Scrumptious .... Kenneth Kantor
Goran .... Chip Zien	Sid .... Kurt Von Schmittou
Boris .... Robert Sella	Violet .... Robyn Hurder
Childcatcher .... Kevin Cahoon	Toby .... Michael Herwitz
Toymaker .... Frank Raiter	

Inventors: JB Adams, Robert Creighton, Rick Faugno, Dirk Lumbard, William Ryall, Kurt Von Schmittou.

Ensemble: JB Adams, Tolan Aman, Julie Barnes, Troy Edward Bowles, Jeffrey Broadhurst, Robert Creighton, Antonio D'Amato, Struan Erlenborn, Rick Faugno, Ashlee Fife, Emily Fletcher, Kearran Giovanni, Rod Harrelson, Ben Hartley, Merritt Tyler Hawkins, Michael Herwitz, Robyn Hurder, Libbie Jacobson, Matt Loehr, Dirk Lumbard, Mayumi Miguel, Malcolm Morano, Jaclyn Neidenthal, Heather Parcells, Lurie Poston, Craig Ramsay, William Ryall, Alex Sanchez, Bret Shuford, Janelle Viscomi, Kurt Von Schmittou, Emma Wahl, Brynn Williams.

Orchestra: Stan Tucker associate conductor, keyboard 2; Victor Costanzi concertmaster, violin; Suzy Perelman violin; Gary Kosloski violin, viola; Mairi Dorman-Phaneuf cello; Justin Quinn

Fallen gentry: Natasha Richardson and Amy Ryan in A Streetcar Named Desire. *Photo: Joan Marcus*

guitar, banjo, mandolin; Patrick Glynn bass, tuba; Robert DeBellis, Steven Kenyon, Salvatore Spicola reeds; Stu Satalof, Joe Burgstaller trumpet; Jeff Nelson, French horn; Marc Donatelle, Charles Gordon trombone; Milton Granger keyboard 1; Dave Roth percussion; Edward Fast drums.

Understudies: Mr. Esparza—Rick Hilsabeck, Matt Loehr, Dirk Lumbard; Ms. Dilly—Julie Barnes, Julie Tolivar; Mr. Bosco—JB Adams, Rick Hilsabeck; Mr. Kudisch—Kenneth Kantor, Kurt Von Schmittou; Ms. Maxwell—Emily Fletcher; Mr. Zien—Robert Creighton, Rick Faugno; Mr. Sella—Dirk Lumbard, Kurt Von Schmittou; Mr. Cahoon—Rick Hilsabeck, William Ryall; Mr. Raiter—JB Adams, William Ryall; Mr. Hodges—Tolan Aman, Struan Erlenborn; Ms. Marlow—Jaclyn Neidenthal, Janelle Viscomi, Emma Wahl.

Swings: Phillip Attmore, Rick Hilsabeck, Joanne Manning, Jeff Siebert, Julie Tolivar.

Directed by Adrian Noble; choreography, Gillian Lynne; scenery and costumes, Anthony Ward; lighting, Mark Henderson; sound, Andrew Bruce; fight direction, B.H. Barry; orchestrations and dance arrangements, Chris Walker; music direction, Kristen Blodgette; music coordination, Sam Lutfiyya; associate producer, Frank Gero; casting, Jim Carnahan; production stage manager, Peter von Mayrhauser; stage manager, Michael J. Passaro; press, Barlow-Hartman Public Relations, Michael Hartman, John Barlow, Carol Fineman, Leslie Baden.

Place: England and Vulgaria. Presented in two parts.

Magical car and quirky inventor protect a family from evil foreigners in a musical adaptation of Mr. Fleming's stories and the 1968 MGM/United Artists film starring Dick Van Dyke. First presented in the West End at the London Palladium (4/16/2002–9/4/2005).

ACT I

Overturre .... Orchestra
Prologue .... Company
"You Two" .... Caractacus, Jeremy, Jemima
"Them Three" .... Grandpa Potts
"Toot Sweets" .... Caractacus, Truly Scrumptious, Lord Scrumptious, Ensemble
"Act English" .... Boris, Goran
"Hushabye Mountain" .... Caractacus
"Come to the Fun Fair" .... Company
"Me Ol' Bamboo" .... Caractacus, Ensemble
"Posh" .... Grandpa Potts, Jeremy, Jemima
"Chitty Chitty Bang Bang" .... Caractacus, Truly, Jeremy, Jemima
"Truly Scrumptious" .... Jeremy, Jemima, Truly
"Chitty Chitty Bang Bang" (Nautical Reprise) .... Caractacus, Truly, Jeremy, Jemima
"Chitty Takes Flight" .... Company

ACT II

Entre'acte .... Orchestra
"Vulgarian National Anthem" .... Company
"The Roses of Success" .... Grandpa Potts, Inventors
"Kiddy-Widdy-Winkies" .... Childcatcher
"Teamwork" .... Caractacus, Toymaker, Truly, Juvenile Ensemble
"Chu-Chi Face" .... Baron, Baroness
"The Bombie Samba" .... Baroness, Baron, Ensemble
"Doll on a Music Box"/"Truly Scrumptious" (Reprise) .... Truly, Caractacus
"Us Two"/"Chitty Prayer" .... Jeremy, Jemima
"Teamwork" (Reprise) .... Toymaker, Company
"Chitty Flies Home" (Finale) .... Company

*Glengarry Glen Ross (34). Revival of the play by David Mamet. Produced by Jeffrey Richards, Jerry Frankel, Jam Theatricals, Boyett Ostar Productions, Ronald Frankel, Philip Lacerte, Stephanie P. McClelland/CIM Productions, Barry Weisbord, Zendog Productions, in association with Herbert Goldsmith Productions, by special arrangement with Roundabout Theatre Company (Todd Haimes artistic director, Ellen Richard managing director, Julia C. Levy executive director), at the Bernard B. Jacobs Theatre. Opened May 1, 2005.

Shelly Levene .... Alan Alda	Richard Roma ....Liev Schreiber
John Williamson .... Frederick Weller	James Lingk .... Tom Wopat
Dave Moss .... Gordon Clapp	Baylen ....Jordan Lage
George Aaronow .... Jeffrey Tambor	

Standbys: Messrs. Schreiber, Weller—Jordan Lage; Messrs. Alda, Tambor–Jack Davidson; Messrs. Wopat, Clapp, Lage—Jay Patterson.

Directed by Joe Mantello; scenery, Santo Loquasto; costumes, Laura Bauer; lighting, Kenneth Posner; casting, Bernard Telsey Casting; production stage manager, William Joseph Barnes; stage manager, Jill Cordle; press, Jeffrey Richards Associates, Irene Gandy, Alana Karpoff, Eric Sanders, Adam Farabee.

Presented in two parts.

An examination of the cutthroat world of business as seen through the eyes of real estate salesmen who are little more than con artists. This production received 2005 Tony Awards in the play categories of best revival and featured actor (Mr. Schreiber). A 1983–84 *Best Plays* choice, the original Broadway production opened at the John Golden Theatre (3/25/1984–2/17/1985; 378 performances). The 1992 film version featured Alec Baldwin, Al Pacino, Ed Harris, Alan Arkin and Kevin Spacey. Although Mr. Mamet received the 1984 Pulitzer Prize for this play, the 1984 Tony Award for best play went to Tom Stoppard's *The Real Thing*.

Lincoln Center Theater concert performance of **Love/Life: A Life in Song** (8). André Bishop artistic director, Bernard Gersten executive producer, at the Vivian Beaumont Theater. Opened May 1, 2005. (Closed May 23, 2005)

Performed by Brian Stokes Mitchell.

Orchestra: Gerard D'Angelo piano; Bob Cranshaw bass; Lou Marini woodwinds; Warren Smith percussion; Buddy Williams drums.

Directed by Charles Randolph-Wright; lighting, Michael J. Spadaro; music direction, Mr. D'Angelo; stage manager, Lisa Iacucci; press, Philip Rinaldi Publicity, Philip Rinaldi, Barbara Carroll.

Presented without intermission.

Ninety-minute performance of Mr. Mitchell's cabaret act in revised form. Presented on Sunday and Monday evenings when *The Light in the Piazza* was dark.

*The 25th Annual Putnam County Spelling Bee (33). Transfer of the musical with book by Rachel Sheinkin; music and lyrics by William Finn; conceived by Rebecca Feldman; additional material by Jay Reiss. Produced by David Stone, James L. Nederlander, Barbara Whitman, Patrick Catullo, Barrington Stage Company, Second Stage Theatre, at Circle in the Square. Opened May 2, 2005.

Mitch Mahoney .... Derrick Baskin	Olive Ostrovsky .... Celia Keenan-Bolger
Marcy Park .... Deborah S. Craig	Chip Tolentino .... Jose Llana
Leaf Coneybear .... Jesse Tyler Ferguson	Douglas Panch .... Jay Reiss
William Barfee .... Dan Fogler	Logainne Schwartzand-
Rona Lisa Peretti .... Lisa Howard	grubenierre .... Sarah Saltzberg

Orchestra: Vadim Feichtner conductor, piano; Carmel Dean associate conductor, synthesizer; Amy Ralske cello; Richard Heckman reeds; Glenn Rhian percussion, drums.

Understudies: Messrs. Fogler, Ferguson—Todd Buonopane; Mr. Baskin—Todd Buonopane, Willis White; Mr. Llana—Willis White; Mr. Reiss—Todd Buonopane, Willis White; Mses. Keenan-Bolger, Craig—Kate Wetherhead, Lisa Yuen; Ms. Howard—Lisa Yuen; Ms. Saltzberg—Kate Wetherhead.

Directed by James Lapine; choreography, Dan Knechtges; scenery, Beowulf Boritt; costumes, Jennifer Caprio; lighting, Natasha Katz; sound, Dan Moses Schreier; orchestrations, Michael Starobin; vocal arrangements, Carmel Dean; music direction, Mr. Feichtner; music coordination, Michael Keller; casting, Tara Rubin Casting; production stage manager, Andrea "Spook" Testani; stage manager, Kelly Hance; press, The Publicity Office, Bob Fennell, Marc Thibodeau, Michael S. Borowski.

Spelling champs: Jose Llana, Deborah S. Craig, Jesse Tyler Ferguson, Sarah Saltzberg, Dan Fogler and Celia Keenan-Bolger in The 25th Annual Putnam County Spelling Bee. *Photo: Joan Marcus*

Presented in two parts.

A young group of social misfits sing and spell their ways through a contest. This production received 2005 Tony Awards in the musical categories of best book (Ms. Sheinkin) and featured actor (Mr. Fogler). Transfer of the Off Broadway production from Second Stage Theatre (2/7/2005–3/20/2005; 48 performances). See Plays Produced Off Broadway section of this volume for details. A 2002 version produced by The Farm, an improvisational theater group, went by the title *C-R-E-P-U-S-C-U-L-E.* Under the current title, the first presentation of record was given at Barrington Stage Company, Sheffield, Massachusetts (7/7/2004). See the Directory of New United States Productions section of this volume for details.

*Sweet Charity (32). Revival of the musical with book by Neil Simon; music by Cy Coleman; lyrics by Dorothy Fields. Produced by Barry and Fran Weissler and Clear Channel Entertainment, in association with Edwin W. Schloss, at the Al Hirschfeld Theatre. Opened May 4, 2005.

Charity .... Christina Applegate	Ursula .... Shannon Lewis
Charlie .... Tyler Hanes	Vittorio Vidal .... Paul Schoeffler
Policeman; Manfred;	Frug Dancer .... Corinne McFadden
YMCA Recept. .... Timothy Edward Smith	Oscar Lindquist .... Denis O'Hare
Nickie ....Janine LaManna	Daddy J. S. Brubeck .... Rhett George
Helene .... Kyra Da Costa	Rosie .... Dylis Croman
Herman ....Ernie Sabella	

Daddy's All-Girl Rhythm Choir: Joyce Chittick, Anika Ellis, Mylinda Hull.

Quartet: Todd Anderson, Bob Gaynor, Tyler Hanes, Timothy Edward Smith.

Ensemble: Todd Anderson, Joyce Chittick, Tim Craskey, Dylis Croman, Anika Ellis, Bob Gaynor, Rhett George, Tyler Hanes, Manuel I. Herrera, Kisha Howard, Mylinda Hull, Amy Nicole Krawcek, Shannon Lewis, Corinne McFadden, Marielys Molina, Timothy Edward Smith, Seth Stewart.

Orchestra: Don York conductor; John Samorian associate conductor, keyboard; Mineko Yajima, Cecelia Hobbs Gardner, Jonathan Dinklage violin; Stephanie Cummins cello; Bill Holcomb bass;

Ed Hamilton guitar; Chuck Wilson, Walt Weiskopf, Tom Christensen, Roger Rosenberg reeds; Don Downs, Glenn Drewes trumpet; Keith O'Quinn, Jeff Nelson trombone; Brad Gemeinhardt, French horn; Charles Descarfino percussion; David Ratajczak drums.

Understudies: Ms. Applegate—Dylis Croman; Mr. O'Hare—Timothy Edward Smith; Ms. LaManna—Joyce Chittick; Ms. Da Costa—Anika Ellis; Mr. Schoeffler—Bob Gaynor; Ms. Lewis—Corinne McFadden.

Swings: Alexis Carra, Reginald Holden Jennings.

Directed by Walter Bobbie; choreography, Wayne Cilento; scenery, Scott Pask; costumes, William Ivey Long; lighting, Brian MacDevitt; sound, Peter Hylenski; hair, Paul Huntley; orchestrations, Don Sebesky; music direction, Mr. York; music coordination, John Miller; additional musical and vocal arrangements, Michael Rafter; additional dance arrangements, Jim Abbott; executive producer, Alecia Parker; associate producers, Daniel Posener and Jay Binder, Hazel and Sam Feldman, Allen Spivak, Harvey Weinstein; casting, Jay Binder and Laura Stanczyk; production stage manager, David O'Brien; stage manager, Beverly Jenkins; press, Barlow-Hartman Public Relations, Michael Hartman, John Barlow, Dennis Crowley, Ryan Ratelle.

Time: The 1960s. Place: New York City. Presented in two parts.

Dance-hall hostess looks for love in all of the wrong places. First presented at the Palace Theatre (1/29/1966–7/15/1967; 608 performances). The first production received a 1966 Tony Award for best choreography (Bob Fosse). A later Fosse production received 1986 Tony Awards in the musical categories of best featured actor (Michael Rupert) and featured actress (Bebe Neuwirth), as well as for costumes (Patricia Zipprodt) and reproduction of a play or musical.

ACT I

Overture	Orchestra
"You Should See Yourself"	Charity
"Big Spender"	Nickie, Helene, Company
"Charity's Soliloquy"	Charity
"Rich Man's Frug"	Company
"If My Friends Could See Me Now"	Charity
"Too Many Tomorrows"	Vittorio
"There's Gotta Be Something Better Than This"	Charity, Nickie, Helene
"I'm the Bravest Individual"	Charity, Oscar

ACT II

"The Rhythm of Life"	Charity, Oscar, Daddy, Daddy's All-Girl Rhythm Choir, Company
"A Good Impression"	Oscar, Quartet
"Baby Dream Your Dream"	Nickie, Helene
"Sweet Charity"	Oscar, Company
"Big Spender" (Reprise)	Company
"Where Am I Going?"	Charity
"I'm a Brass Band"	Charity, Company
"I Love to Cry at Weddings"	Herman, Company
"I'm the Bravest Individual" (Reprise)	Charity

PLAYS PRODUCED OFF BROADWAY

○ ○ ○ ○ ○

FOR THE PURPOSES of *Best Plays* listing, the term "Off Broadway" signifies a show that opened for general audiences in a Manhattan theater seating 499 or fewer and 1) employed an Equity cast, 2) planned a regular schedule of 8 performances a week in an open-ended run (7 a week for solo shows and some other exceptions) and 3) offered itself to public comment by critics after a designated opening performance.

Figures in parentheses following a play's title give number of performances. These numbers do not include previews or extra non-profit performances. Performance interruptions for cast changes and other breaks have been taken into account. Performance numbers are figured in consultation with press representatives and company managements.

Plays marked with an asterisk (*) were still in a projected run on June 1, 2005. The number of performances is figured from press opening through May 31, 2005.

In a listing of a show's numbers—dances, sketches, musical scenes, etc.—the titles of songs are identified wherever possible by their appearance in quotation marks (").

HOLDOVERS FROM PREVIOUS SEASONS

OFF BROADWAY SHOWS that were running on June 1, 2004 are listed below. More detailed information about them appears in previous *Best Plays* volumes of appropriate date. Important cast changes since opening night are recorded in the Cast Replacements section in this volume.

*Perfect Crime** (7,458). By Warren Manzi. Opened October 16, 1987.

*Blue Man Group (Tubes)** (7,004). Performance piece by and with Blue Man Group. Opened November 17, 1991.

*Stomp** (4,724). Percussion performance piece created by Luke Cresswell and Steve McNicholas. Opened February 27, 1994.

*I Love You, You're Perfect, Now Change** (3,672). Musical revue with book and lyrics by Joe DiPietro; music by Jimmy Roberts. Opened August 1, 1996.

De La Guarda (2,473). Spectacle devised by De La Guarda (Pichon Baldinu, Diqui James, Gabriel Kerpel, Fabio D'Aquila, Tomas James, Alejandro Garcia, Gabriella Baldini). Opened June 16, 1998. (Closed September 12, 2004)

*Naked Boys Singing!** (2,244). Musical revue conceived by Robert Schrock; written by various authors. Opened July 22, 1999.

*The Donkey Show (1,329±). Musical conceived and created by Randy Weiner and Diane Paulus; adapted from William Shakespeare's *A Midsummer Night's Dream*. Opened August 12, 1999. (Verified performance total unavailable at press time.)

Forbidden Broadway: 20th Anniversary Celebration (983). Musical revue created and written by Gerard Alessandrini. Opened February 25, 2002. (Closed July 4, 2004)

*Menopause: The Musical (1,336). Musical revue with book and lyrics by Jeanie Linders; music by various popular artists. Opened April 4, 2002.

Fame on 42nd Street (264). Musical with book by José Fernandez; music by Steve Margoshes; lyrics by Jacques Levy; based on the MGM Studios film developed by David De Silva. Opened November 11, 2003. (Closed June 27, 2004)

*York Theatre Company production of **The Musical of Musicals–The Musical** (321). Musical with book by Eric Rockwell and Joanne Bogart; music by Mr. Rockwell; lyrics by Ms. Bogart. Opened December 16, 2003. Production hiatus January 25–June 10, 2004 and October 2–February 10, 2005. Transferred to Dodger Stages for run beginning February 10, 2005.

Bridge and Tunnel (180). Solo performance piece by Sarah Jones. Opened February 19, 2004. (Closed August 15, 2004)

Bug (384). By Tracy Letts. Opened February 29, 2004. (Closed January 30, 2005)

*Cookin' (513). Transfer of the Off Off Broadway performance piece by Seung Whan Song. Opened March 7, 2004.

The Public Theater presentation of **The Actors' Gang** production of **Embedded** (84). By Tim Robbins; with reportage by John Simpson (BBC), Alan Feuer (*The New York Times*), Robert Fisk (*The Independent*), Martha Gellhorn. Opened March 14, 2004. (Closed June 5, 2004)

From Door to Door (110). By James Sherman. Opened March 24, 2004. (Closed June 27, 2004)

Ears on a Beatle (97). By Mark St. Germain. Opened March 28, 2004. (Closed June 20, 2004)

The Marijuana-Logues (425). By Arj Barker, Doug Benson and Tony Camin. Opened March 30, 2004. (Closed March 27, 2005)

Manhattan Theatre Club production of **Sarah, Sarah** (80). By Daniel Goldfarb. Opened March 30, 2004. (Closed June 6, 2004)

Roundabout Theatre Company production of **Intimate Apparel** (72). By Lynn Nottage. Opened April 11, 2004. (Closed June 13, 2004)

Loudmouth (225). By Toxic Audio. Opened April 18, 2004. (Closed October 31, 2004)

The Public Theater presentation of the **Worth Street Theater Company** production of **The Normal Heart** (63). Revival of the play by Larry Kramer. Opened April 21, 2004. (Closed June 29, 2004)

The Public Theater presentation of the **Labyrinth Theater Company** production of **Guinea Pig Solo** (29). By Brett C. Leonard; based on *Woyzeck* by Georg Büchner. Opened May 9, 2004. (Closed June 6, 2004)

The Joys of Sex (39). Musical with book by Melissa Levis and David Weinstein; music by Mr. Weinstein; lyrics by Ms. Levis. Opened May 12, 2004. (Closed June 13, 2004)

Atlantic Theater Company production of **The Two and Only** (110). Solo performance piece by Jay Johnson. Opened May 13, 2004. (Closed August 15, 2004)

New York Theatre Workshop production of **Light Raise the Roof** (30). By Kia Corthron. Opened May 20, 2004. (Closed June 13, 2004)

Playwrights Horizons production of **Chinese Friends** (22). By Jon Robin Baitz. Opened May 27, 2004. (Closed June 13, 2004)

PLAYS PRODUCED JUNE 1, 2004–MAY 31, 2005

Brooklyn Academy of Music presentation of the **Comédie-Française** production **The Imaginary Invalid (Le Malade Imaginaire)** (5). Revival of the play by Molière. Alan H. Fishman chairman of the board, Karen Brooks Hopkins president, Joseph V. Melillo executive producer at the BAM Harvey Theater. Opened June 9, 2004. (Closed June 13, 2004)

Argan .... Alain Pralon	Beralde .... Alain Lenglet
Toinette .... Muriel Mayette	Thomas Diafoirus .... Nicolas Lormeau
Beline .... Catherine Sauval	Monsieur Bonnefoy;
Cleante .... Eric Ruf	Monsieur Fleurat .... Christian Gonon
Monsieur Diafoirus;	Angelique .... Julie Sicard
Monsieur Purgon .... Christian Blanc	Louison .... Alma Vincey; Penelope Cellier

Directed by Claude Stratz; choreography, Sophie Mayer; scenery and costumes, Ezio Toffolutti; lighting, Jean-Philippe Roy; press, Sandy Sawotka, Fatima Kafele, Eva Chien, Tamara McCaw, Jennifer Lam.

Presented without intermission.

Hypochrondriac beset by "illness" and intrigue finally discovers who has his best interest in mind. The first presentation was given at a time of ill health for Mr. Molière, who was convulsed with a coughing spasm during the fourth performance of the play—while playing, in an ironic twist, the title role. He died in bed within a few hours of the final curtain (2/10–2/17/1673; 4 performances). The first presentation of record in this country was given at Laura Keene's Theatre in Charles Reade's adaptation titled *Physic and Fancy, or the Hypochrondriac* (10/31/1860).

Address Unknown (85). By Kathrine Kressman Taylor; adapted by Frank Dunlop from the 1938 novella. Produced by D and L Productions at the Promenade Theatre. Opened June 10, 2004. (Closed August 22, 2004)

Max Eisenstein .... Jim Dale	Martin Schulse .... William Atherton

Directed by Mr. Dunlop; scenery, James Youmans; costumes, Jim Stewart; lighting, David Lander; sound, Matthew Burton; production stage manager, Christine Catti; press, Richard Kornberg and Associates, Richard Kornberg, Tom D'Ambrosio.

Presented without intermission.

Fast friends become bitter enemies as the Nazis come to power in 1930s Germany.

Aquila Theatre Company production of **Comedy of Errors** (4). Revival of the play by William Shakespeare; adapted by Robert Richmond. Peter Meineck artistic director, Robert Richmond associate artistic director, at Baruch Performing Arts Center. Opened June 1, 2004. (Closed June 22, 2004)

Antipholus of Syracuse .... Richard Willis	Luciana .... Lindsay Rae Taylor
Antipholus of Ephesus .... "Sheridan Willis"	Solinus; others .... Andrew Schwartz
Dromio of Syracuse .... Louis Butelli	Nell; others .... Heather Murdock
Dromio of Ephesus .... "John Butelli"	Egeon; others .... Alex Webb
Adriana .... Lisa Carter	

Directed by Mr. Richmond; scenery, David Coleman and Owen Collins; costumes, Lisa Martin Stuart; lighting, Mr. Meineck; composer and musical director, Anthony Cochrane; press, Richard Kornberg and Associates, Rick Miramontez.

Presented in two parts.

Mr. Shakespeare's comedy about long-lost brothers and mistaken indentity. First presentation of record at Gray's Inn, London, December 1594. First New York presentation of record at the Park Theatre (5/25/1804). This presentation is a return engagement of an Aquila production from the 2002–03 season at the East 13th Street and Harold Clurman Theatres (7/11–11/17/2002; 150 performances). In this conception, Messrs. Willis and Butelli play their own twins, "Sheridan" and "John"; i.e., they double as both Antipholuses and both Dromios.

Aquila Theatre Company production of **Othello** (19). Revival of the play by William Shakespeare; adapted by Robert Richmond. Peter Meineck artistic director, Robert Richmond associate artistic director, at Baruch Performing Arts Center. Opened June 10, 2004. (Closed June 27, 2004)

Iago ....Anthony Cochrane	Duke ....Todd Batstone
Brabantio ....Richard Willis	Desdemona ....Kathryn Merry
Othello ....Lloyd Notice	Casio ....Tom Tate
Emilia ....Lisa Carter	Bianca ....Heather Murdock
Roderigo ....Louis Butelli	

Ensemble: Katherine Brook, Anna McHugh, Rick McKelvey, Jay Painter, Courtnie Sauls, Brandon Scott.

Directed by Mr. Richmond; design, Messrs. Meineck and Richmond; music, Mr. Cochrane; press, Richard Kornberg and Associates, Richard Kornberg.

Presented in two parts.

Mr. Shakespeare's Moor is convinced by treacherous Iago that his wife has been unfaithful and tragedy follows. The first presentation of record was given at the court of James I (11/1/1604).

Reality check: Saidah Arrika Ekulona and Charlayne Woodard in Fabulation or, the Re-Education of Undine. *Photo: Joan Marcus*

The first presentation of record in this country was given at the Theatre in Nassau Street under the management of Robert Upton (12/23/1751).

Playwrights Horizons production of **Fabulation or, the Re-Education of Undine** (33). By Lynn Nottage. Tim Sanford artistic director, Leslie Marcus managing director, William Russo general manager, in the Peter Jay Sharp Theater. Opened June 13, 2004. (Closed July 11, 2004)

Undine Barnes Calles ...... Charlayne Woodard
Stephie; Counselor;
  Rosa; Pregnant #1;
  Ensemble .... Melle Powers
Accountant; Addict #1;
  Doctor; Ensemble .... Stephen Kunken
Agent Duva; Flow;
  Dealer; Addict #2;
  Ensemble .... Daniel Breaker
Hervé; Guy;
  Ensemble .... Robert Montano

Dr. Khdair; Grandma;
  Inmate #1;
  Caseworker;
  Ensemble .... Myra Lucretia Taylor
Allison; Mother;
  Inmate #2; Devora;
  Ensemble .... Saidah Arrika Ekulona
Yoruba Priest; Father;
  Judge; Ensemble .... Keith Randolph Smith

Directed by Kate Whoriskey; choreography, Gregory Mitchell; scenery, Walt Spangler; costumes, Kaye Voyce; lighting, David Weiner; sound, Ken Travis; casting, James Calleri; production stage manager, Gillian Duncan; press, The Publicity Office, Bob Fennell, Marc Thibodeau, Michael S. Borowski.

Presented in two parts.

African-African woman learns how quickly material success can disappear.

Second Stage Theatre production of **Afterbirth: Kathy and Mo's Greatest Hits** (25). Comedy revue by Mo Gaffney and Kathy Najimy. Carole Rothman artistic director, Timothy J. McClimon executive director, at the Second Stage Theatre. Opened June 17, 2004. (Closed July 11, 2004)

Performed by Ms. Najimy and Ms. Gaffney.

Directed by Mark Brokaw; scenery, Allen Moyer; costumes, Linda Ross; lighting, Mary Louise Geiger; sound, Jon Gottlieb; production stage manager, Pam Edington; press, Richard Kornberg and Associates, Tom D'Ambrosio.

Presented in two parts.

Sketch comedy focused on the lives of ordinary people, some of whom exist in extraordinary circumstances. First presentation of record of this version of the duo's work was given at the Canon Theatre, Los Angeles (2/24–3/21/2004). Earlier versions included *The Further Adventures of Kathy and Mo* for Second Stage Theatre (5/27–7/15/1986; 35 performances) and *The Kathy and Mo Show: Parallel Lives* at Westside Arts Theatre (1/31/1989–4/29/1990; 466 performances).

New York Theatre Workshop production of **Patriot Act: A Public Meditation** (29). By Mark Crispin Miller, with Steve Cuiffo. James C. Nicola artistic director, Lynn Moffat managing director. Opened June 22, 2004. (Closed July 22, 2004)

Performed by Mr. Miller and Mr. Cuiffo.

Directed by Gregory Keller; scenery, Narelle Sissons; lighting, Jason Lyons; projections, Kimberly Reed; production stage manager, Elizabeth Miller; press, Richard Kornberg and Associates, Richard Kornberg, Don Summa.

Presented without intermission.

Political commentary with prestidigitation. Three additional performances, one by invitation only, were added during the Republican National Convention (8/30–9/1/2004).

Comedy 101 (15). By Mitch Hogue. Produced by Homemade Productions at the John Houseman Theatre. Opened June 24, 2004. (Closed July 6, 2004)

Frank Ridins .... Mitch Hogue   Miss Nomer .... Jennifer Hogue
    Directed by Kim Doi; press, Brett Singer.
    College professor lectures on the theory of comedy as his assistant attempts to inject levity
into the discourse.

Forbidden Broadway Summer Shock! (83). Musical revue by Gerard Alessandrini.
Produced by John Freedson, Harriet Yellin and Jon B. Platt, at the Douglas Fairbanks
Theater. Opened July 5, 2004. (Closed September 15, 2004)

    Performed by David Benoit, Valerie Fagan, Jennifer Simard, Michael West.
    Directed by Mr. Alessandrini, with Phillip George; scenery, Bradley Kay and Megan K. Halpern;
costumes, Alvin Colt; lighting, Marc Janowitz; press, Pete Sanders Group, Pete Sanders, Glenna
Freedman.
    Presented in two parts.
    Latest version in the *Forbidden Broadway* franchise. See Long Runs Off Broadway section of
this volume for information on earlier productions.

Aquila Theatre Company production of **The Man Who Would Be King** (32). By
Rudyard Kipling; adapted by Peter Meineck. Mr. Meineck artistic director, Robert
Richmond associate artistic director, at the Baruch Performing Arts Center. Opened
July 13, 2004. (Closed August 8, 2004)

Kipling .... Louis Butelli   Daniel Dravot .... Anthony Cochrane
Peachy Carnehan .... Richard Willis

    Directed by Robert Richmond; design, Messrs. Meineck and Richmond; music, Mr. Cochrane;
production stage manager, Francesca Russell; press, Richard Kornberg and Associates, Rick
Miramontez.
    Presented in two parts.
    Adaptation of the classic 1888 Kipling tale about the colonial impulse and its ultimate folly.

*Big squeeze: Jimmy Smits and Kristen
Johnston in* Much Ado About Nothing.
Photo: Michal Daniel

The Public Theater production of **Much Ado About Nothing** (24). Revival of the play by William Shakespeare. George C. Wolfe producer, Mara Manus executive director, at the Delacorte Theater. Opened July 13, 2004. (Closed August 8, 2004)

Leonato	Sam Waterston	Conrad	Julio Monge
Friar Francis	Steven Skybell	Don John	Christopher Evan Welch
Beatrice	Kristen Johnston	Borachio	Sean Patrick Thomas
Hero	Elisabeth Waterston	Margaret	Laura Kai Chen
Don Pedro	Peter Francis James	Ursula	Jayne Houdyshell
Benedick	Jimmy Smits	Dogberry	Brian Murray
Claudio	Lorenzo Pisoni	Verges	Dane Knell
Antonio	Dominic Chianese		

Ensemble: Frank Faucette, Manoel Felciano, Elizabeth Haselwood, Aleta Hayes, Bill Heck, Andre Holland, Kevin Kelly, Peter McCain, Emily Swallow.

Musicians: Manoel Felciano violin, guitar, mandolin, clarinet; Kevin Kelly accordion, guitar.

Directed by David Esbjornson; choreography, Jane Comfort; scenery, Christine Jones; costumes, Jess Goldstein; lighting, Michael R. Chybowski; sound, Acme Sound Partners; music, Mark Bennett; wigs and hair, Charles LaPointe; associate producers, Peter DuBois and Steven Tabakin; casting, Jordan Thaler and Heidi Griffiths; production stage manager, Charles Means; press, Carol R. Fineman, Elizabeth Wehrle.

Place: Messina, Sicily. Presented in two parts.

Confirmed bachelor spars verbally with an equally acerbic woman and a lively relationship emerges as other lovers part over charges of inconstancy and betrayal. Although the play is believed to have been presented for the first time late in 1598 or early 1599—Will Kempe, for whom the character of Dogberry was probably written, left Mr. Shakespeare's company early in 1599—there is no definitive first presentation. *Much Ado* is known to have been instantly popular and often performed in the early 1600s. The first presentation of record in this country was given at the John Street Theatre with Lewis Hallam II in the role of Benedick (3/19/1787).

From My Hometown (36). Musical with book by Lee Summers, Ty Stephens and Herbert Rawlings Jr.; music by Mr. Summers, Mr. Stephens and Will Barrow. Produced by Mr. Summers, in association with Leonard Soloway and Steven M. Levy, at the Gramercy Theatre. Opened July 22, 2004. (Closed August 21, 2004)

Memphis	Kevin R. Free	Philly	Rodney Hicks
Detroit	André Garner		

Musicians: Stacey Penson conductor; Thom Zlabinger, Jim Hershman, Kenneth Crutchfield.

Directed by Kevin Ramsey; choreography, Mr. Ramsey and Leslie Dockery; scenery and projections, Matthew Myhrum; costumes, Deborah A. Cheretun; lighting, Aaron Spivey; sound, Ryan Powers; orchestrations and music direction, Jo Lynn Burks; production stage manager, Valerie A. Peterson; press, Origlio Public Relations, Tony Origlio, Martine Sainvil, Catie Monck.

Presented without intermission.

Three guys on the road to rhythm and blues stardom. First presentation of record was given at Milwaukee Repertory Theater (4/1998). Amas Musical Theatre presented it as a developmental project (6/19/2003).

Roundabout Theatre Company production of **Fiction** (57). By Steven Dietz. Todd Haimes artistic director, Ellen Richard managing director, Julia C. Levy executive director, in the Laura Pels Theatre of the Harold and Miriam Steinberg Center for Theatre. Opened July 25, 2004. (Closed September 12, 2004)

Linda	Julie White	Abby	Emily Bergl
Michael	Tom Irwin		

Understudies: Ms. White—Natacha Roi; Mr. Irwin—Doug Wert; Ms. Bergl—Ruth Eglsaer.

Directed by David Warren; scenery, James Youmans; costumes, David C. Woolard; lighting, Jeff Croiter; sound, John Gromada; casting, Mele Nagler; production stage manager, Jay Adler;

stage manager, Elisa R. Kuhar; press, Boneau/Bryan-Brown, Adrian Bryan-Brown, Joe Perrotta, Jessica Johnson, Matt Polk.

Time: The present. Place: Various American cities; Paris. Presented in two parts.

Married couple who are writers unspool competing narratives, logged in their journals, that ultimately rupture their relationship. First commissioned and presented in a workshop at ACT Theatre, Seattle (3/1–3/3/2002). First fully staged presentation of record was given by the McCarter Theatre Company, Princeton (3/25/2003).

Squeeze Box (86). Solo performance piece by Ann Randolph. Produced by Anne Bancroft at the Acorn Theatre. Opened July 29, 2004. (Closed November 20, 2004)

Performed by Ms. Randolph.

Directed by Alan Bailey; lighting, Jonathan Spencer; music arrangements, Bill Schimmel; executive producers, Robert F.X. Sillerman, Tiffani Gavin; press, Barlow-Hartman Public Relations, John Barlow, Michael Hartman, Jeremy Shaffer, Dayle Gruet.

Presented without intermission.

Warm-hearted woman who works in a women's homeless shelter on a voyage of self-discovery and renewal. First presentation of record was given in 2002 at the Court Theatre, Los Angeles.

Irish Repertory Theatre presentation of **Let's Put on a Show** (40). Musical revue by Jan and Mickey Rooney. Charlotte Moore artistic director, Ciarán O'Reilly producing director, in association with Densmore Productions and Christopher Aber, at the Irish Repertory Theatre. Opened August 10, 2004. (Closed September 12, 2004)

Performed by Jan and Mickey Rooney.

Scenery, James Morgan; lighting, Gregory Cohen; sound, Javier Berzal; music, Mr. Rooney; music arrangements, Sam Kriger and Frank Collette; music direction, Mr. Kriger; stage manager, Andrea Sarubbi; press, Shirley Herz Associates, Shirley Herz, Kevin P. McAnarney.

Presented in two parts.

Mr. Rooney and his eighth wife review, in song and story, the legendary performer's career.

Plums in New York (49). Solo performance piece by Anna Rosa Sigurdardottir. Produced by Susan Burdian, in association with the Icelandic Connection, at the Clurman Theatre. Opened August 15, 2004. (Closed September 26, 2004)

Performed by Ms. Sigurdardottir.

Directed by Hera Olafsdottir; design, Egill Ingibergsson and Moeidur Helgadottir; music, Rosa Gudmundsdottir.

Presented without intermission.

An obsession with August Strindberg sends a woman to New York in search of answers regarding the nature of dreams and reality.

The Loves of Shakespeare's Women (16). Solo performance piece by Susannah York. Produced by the Federal Bureau of Entertainment and Joseph S. Ajilouny, in association with the Theatre Guild and Philip Langner, at the Blue Heron Arts Center. Opened August 18, 2004. (Closed August 29, 2004)

Performed by Ms. York.

Scenery, Kishan Khana; lighting, Christopher Bailey.

Presented in two parts.

Ms. York renders women of the Shakespearean canon such as Juliet, Viola, Rosalind, Isabella, Portia, Lady Macbeth, Gertrude, Emilia and Constance.

The Culture Project presentation of **Guantánamo: Honor Bound to Defend Freedom** (133). By Victoria Brittain and Gillian Slovo. Allan Buchman artistic director, at 45 Bleecker. Opened August 26, 2004. (Closed December 19, 2004)

War machinist: Robert Langdon Lloyd in Guantánamo: Honor Bound to Defend Freedom. *Photo: Brian Michael Thomas*

Lord Steyn;
　Donald Rumsfeld ...... Robert Langdon Lloyd
Mr. Begg ....Harsh Nayyar
Wahab al-Rawi .... Ramsey Faragallah
Jamal al-Harith .... Andrew Stewart-Jones
Gareth Peirce .... Kathleen Chalfant
Mark Jennings;
　Greg Powell .... Steven Crossley

Bisher al-Rawi;
　Major Dan Mori .... Waleed Zuaiter
Moazzam Begg;
　Mr. Ahmed .... Aasif Mandvi
Tom Clarke ....Jeffrey Brick
Ruhel Ahmed .... Maulik Pancholy
Clive Stafford Smith;
　Jack Straw, M.P. .... Joris Stuyck

Directed by Nicolas Kent, Sacha Wares; scenery and costumes, Miriam Buether; lighting, Johanna Town; sound, Bill Grady; casting, Judy Henderson and Associates; production stage manager, Bonnie Brady; press, Origlio Public Relations, Tony Origlio, Martine Sainvil.

Presented in two parts.

Documentary drama examining detainments at Guantánamo Bay, and their impact on prisoners, families and human rights. First presentation of record was given at London's Tricycle Theatre (5/24–6/12/2004). A 2004–05 *Best Plays* choice (see essay by Charles Wright in this volume).

*Slava's Snowshow (304). By Slava Plunin. Produced by Foster Mollison Entertainment at the Union Square Theatre. Opened September 8, 2004.

Performed by Mr. Polunin, Ivan Polunin, Elena Ushakova, Onofrio Colucci, Robert Saralp, Yury Musatov, Fyodor Makarov, Aelita Loukhaeva, Alexandre Frish, Stanislav Varkki, Derek Scott, Nikolai Terentiev, Boris Hybner.

Directed by Mr. Punin; lighting; Oleg Iline; sound, Rastyam Dubinnikov; press, The Publicity Office, Marc Thibodeau.

Presented in two parts.

East European artists present a clown show that is part Cirque du Soleil, part Samuel Beckett. The first presentation of record was given at the 1996 Edinburgh Fringe Festival before runs at the Kennedy Center (11/11–11/23/1997), Toronto's Princess of Wales Theatre (1/5–2/8/1998) and other venues.

Symphonie Fantastique (126). Revival of the puppet show by Basil Twist. Produced by Dodger Stage Holding and Tandem Otter at Dodger Stages. Opened September 16, 2004. (Closed January 2, 2005)

Performed by Mr. Twist, Matthew Acheson, Oliver Dalzell, Sophia Michahelles, Lake Simons, Kevin Taylor.

Directed by Mr. Twist; lighting, Andrew Hill; music, Hector Berlioz; stage manager, Brenna St. George Jones; press, Sam Rudy Media Relations.

Presented without intermission.

Puppetry in a 1,000 gallon water tank set to the music of Hector Berlioz. First presentation of record was given at Off Off Broadway's Here Arts Center (5/28/1998–8/22/1999; 438 performances).

Pugilist Specialist (61). By Adriano Shaplin. Produced by Chantal Arts + Theatre Ltd., in association with Oberton Books, at 59E59 Theaters. Opened September 17, 2004. Production hiatus October 11–November 2, 2004. (Closed November 28, 2004)

Lt. Emma Stein	Stephanie Viola	Lt. Travis Freud	Mr. Shaplin
Lt. Studdard	Drew Friedman	Col. Johns	Paul Schnabel

Direction and scenery, The Riot Group; sound, Mr. Shaplin; production stage manager, Maria Shaplin; press, Publicity Outfitters, Timothy Haskell.

Presented without intermission.

Soldiers on a mission to terminate a Middle Eastern leader. First presentation of record was given at the 2003 Edinburgh Fringe Festival before a tour of the UK. New York production transferred to 45 Bleecker after hiatus.

God and country: Funda Duval and Annie Golden in People Be Heard. *Photo: Joan Marcus*

Mandy Patinkin in Concert (25). Concert performance by Mr. Patinkin. Produced by Dodger Stage Holding at Dodger Stages. Opened September 20, 2004. (Closed October 28, 2004)

Performed by Mr. Patinkin, with Paul Ford (piano).

Press, Boneau/Bryan-Brown, Adriana Douzos.

Presented without intermission.

Performance of songs by Rodgers and Hammerstein, Stephen Sondheim, Harry Chapin and others.

New York Theatre Workshop production of **Hedda Gabler** (40). Revival of the play by Henrik Ibsen; translated by Christopher Hampton. James C. Nicola artistic director, Lynn Moffat managing director, at the New York Theatre Workshop. Opened September 21, 2004. (Closed October 24, 2004)

Berte	Elzbieta Czyzewska	Aunt Julia	Mary Beth Peil
Eilert Lovborg	Glenn Fitzgerald	Mrs. Elvsted	Ana Reeder
George Tesman	Jason Butler Harner	Judge Brack	John Douglas Thompson
Hedda Gabler	Elizabeth Marvel		

Directed by Ivo van Hove; scenery, Jan Versweyveld; costumes, Kevin Guyer; production stage manager, Martha Ronaldson; press, Richard Kornberg and Associates, Don Summa.

Presented in two parts.

Mr. Ibsen's tale of an unhappy housewife, who seeks vicarious thrills as she attempts to influence the destiny of others, unwinds in a gleaming white room. First New York English-language production of record was given at the Fifth Avenue Theatre (3/30/1898). Elizabeth Robins played the title role.

Playwrights Horizons production of **People Be Heard** (22). Comedy with songs by Quincy Long; music by Michael Roth. Tim Sanford artistic director, Leslie Marcus managing director, William Russo general manager, in the Mainstage Theater. Opened September 23, 2004. (Closed October 10, 2004)

Don Mesner	Conrad John Schuck	Russell Delaney; Ekaraxu (voice); Bernie Redman;	
Jim Schuler; Refik	Dashiell Eaves		
Pam; Danny Delaney; Cindy	Laura Heisler	Dr. Mueller	Brian Hutchison
Earl Frye	Guy Boyd	Margo; Ekaraxu; Melanie Gilfert; Dr. Schottenstein;	
Linda Vobiato; Candy	Kathy Santen	Helen McMichaels;	
Rita Dell Delaney	Funda Duval	Mother Wit	Annie Golden

Musicians: Steve Tarshis acoustic guitar, electric guitar; Jonathan Dinklage violin, electric bass, harmonica, guitar.

Directed by Erica Schmidt; choreography, Peter Pucci; scenery, Christine Jones; costumes, Michelle R. Phillips; lighting, Michael Lincoln; sound, Brett Jarvis; fight direction, J. Steven White; musical and vocal arrangements, Michael Roth; music direction, Messrs. Roth and Tarshis; music coordination, John Miller; casting, James Calleri and Alaine Alldaffer; production stage manager, Michael McGoff; press, The Publicity Office, Bob Fennell, Michael S. Borowski.

Time: The present. Place: Middle America. Presented in two parts.

A stripper joins a school board and becomes the progressive voice of reason.

Absolutely Fascinating (57). Musical revue by Fascinating Aïda. Produced by Edward Snape at the Acorn Theatre. Opened September 26, 2004. (Closed November 14, 2004)

Performed by Adele Anderson, Dillie Keane, Liza Pulman.

Directed by Simon Green; scenery and lighting, Chris Lee; music direction, Russell Churney; press, Miller Wright and Associates, Miller Wright, Dan Fortune.

Presented in two parts.

Political satire and social commentary accompanied by music. Following this engagement, the production played a limited run in the 99-seat Kirk Theatre (4/11/2005–5/15/2005; 40 performances). See the Plays Produced Off Off Broadway section of this volume. First New York presentation of record for Fascinating Aïda was given at the Firebird Café (3/1998). The first New York theatrical presentation of *Absolutely Fascinating* was given at the 59E59 Theater (5/18/2004–6/13/2004; 32 performances).

Carnegie Hall presentation of **Sondheim: Opening Doors** (6). Musical revue by Stephen Sondheim. Sanford I. Weill chairman, Robert J. Harth executive and artistic director, at Zankel Hall. Opened October 5, 2004. (Closed October 9, 2004)

Performed by Kate Baldwin, Victoria Clark, Gregg Edelman, Jan Maxwell, Eric Jordan Young.

Orchestra: Rob Berman piano; Mairi Dorman cello; Dick Sarpola bass.

Directed by David Kernan; choreography, James Scott Wise; costumes, Jane Greenwood; lighting, Vivien Leone; sound, Peter Hylenski; music direction, Mr. Berman; musical arrangements, Jason Carr and John Kane; casting, Jay Binder, Laura Stanczyk.

Presented in two parts.

Songs from Sondheim intercut video interviews of the composer reflecting on his life and work. First presentation of record was given at London's Bridewell Theatre under the title *Moving On* (7/25–8/19/2000).

Musical numbers included: "The Hills of Tomorrow," "Our Time," "Opening Doors," "Everybody Says Don't," "Take Me to the World," "I Know Things Now," "Who Wants to Live in New York?," "What More Do I Need?," "Uptown, Downtown," "Another Hundred People," "I Believe in You," "The Best Thing That Ever Has Happened," "Merrily We Roll Along," "A Weekend in the Country," "Barcelona," "A Parade in Town," "By the Sea," "Sunday," "Someone Is Waiting," "Multitudes of Amys," "No, Mary Ann," "Johanna," "I Do Like You," "Old Friends," "Side by Side," "Putting It Together," "Bounce," "Something's Coming," "Everything's Coming Up Roses," "Loving You," "Not a Day Goes By," "So Many People," "That Old Piano Roll," "Marry Me a Little," "The Little Things You Do Together," "The Miller's Son," "Goodbye for Now," "I Wish I Could Forget You," "Pretty Women," "There's Always a Woman," "Ah, But Underneath," "No More," "No One Is Alone," "Being Alive," "With So Little to Be Sure Of," "Our Time," "Back in Business."

Brooklyn Academy of Music presentation of the **Cheek by Jowl** production of **Othello** (7). Revival of the play by William Shakespeare. Alan H. Fishman chairman of the board, Karen Brooks Hopkins, Joseph V. Melillo executive producer at the BAM Harvey Theater. Opened October 5, 2004. (Closed October 10, 2004)

Roderigo	Matthew Douglas	Desdemona	Caroline Martin
Iago	Jonny Phillips	Emilia	Jaye Griffiths
Brabantio; Gratiano	David Hobbs	Bianca	Kirsty Besterman
Othello	Nonso Anozie	Gentlemen	Robin Pearce,
Cassio	Ryan Kiggell		Oliver Boot,
Duke of Venice;			Alex Kerr
Lodovico	Michael Gardiner		

Directed by Declan Donnellan; choreography, Jane Gibson; scenery and costumes, Nick Ormerod; lighting, Judith Greenwood; music, Catherine Jayes; stage manager, Kim Beringer; press, Sandy Sawotka, Fatima Kafele, Eva Chien, Tamara McCaw, Jennifer Lam.

Presented in two parts.

Mr. Shakespeare's Moor is convinced by treacherous Iago that his wife has been unfaithful and tragedy follows. The first presentation of record was given at the court of James I (11/1/1604). The first presentation of record in this country was given at the Theatre in Nassau Street under the management of Robert Upton (12/23/1751).

National Theatre of Greece production of **Lysistrata** (6). Revival of the play by Aristophanes; translated by Kostas Tsianos. Eleni Ahrweiler president, Nikos Kourkoulos artistic director, Mr. Tsianos deputy artistic director, at City Center. Opened October 6, 2004. (Closed October 10, 2004)

Corinthian Woman	Elena Gerodimou	Cleonice	Eleni Kastani
Boeotian Woman	Eleni Giorgi	Lysistrata	Lydia Koniordou
Myrrhine	Vasso Iatropoulou	Provoulos	Antonis Loudaros
Lambito	Maria Kantife	Herald of the Spartans	Christos Ninis
Cinesias	Nikos Karathanos	Singer	Yiannis Stollas
Dean of the Athenians	Dimitris Karaviotis	Manes	Loucas Zikos

Directed by Mr. Tsianos; choreographer, Fokas Evaggelinos; scenery and costumes, Rena Georgiadou; lighting, Spyros Kardaris; music, Christos Leontis; production stage manager, Ionnis Blazoudaki; press, Richard Kornberg and Associates, Richard Kornberg.

Presented without intermission.

Sex comedy in which women withhold attention in an attempt to end war. First presentation of record was given during the Peloponnesian War (411 BCE).

White Chocolate (130). By William Hamilton. Produced by The Culture Project and Allan Buchman, in association with Nile Rogers' We Are Family Foundation, at Century Center for the Performing Arts. Opened October 6, 2004. (Closed January 30, 2005)

Brandon Beale	Reg E. Cathay	Winston Lee	Paul H. Juhn
Vivian Beale Somerset	Julie Halston	Louise Beale	Samantha Soule
Ashley Brown	Erik LaRay Harvey	Deborah Beale	Lynn Whitfield

Directed by David Schweizer; scenery James Noone; costumes, David Zinn; lighting, David Weiner; sound, Robert Kaplowitz; production stage manager, Scott Pegg; press, Origlio Public Relations, Tony Origlio, Philip Carrubba.

Presented in two parts.

An affluent Upper East Side white couple wake one morning to find they've become black.

Newsical (215). Musical revue by Rick Crom. Produced by Fred M. Caruso, in association with Gary Maffei, Jacki Florin, Barry Fisher and Jesse Adelaar, at Upstairs at Studio 54. Opened October 7, 2004. (Closed April 17, 2005)

Performed by Kim Cea, Todd Alan Johnson, Stephanie Kurtzuba, Jeff Skowron.

Directed and choreographed by Donna Drake; scenery, Peter P. Allburn; costumes, David Kaley; lighting and sound, Michael Flink; wigs, Jason Hayes; musical direction, Ed Goldschneider; production stage mansger, Mark Harborth; press, Publicity Outfitters, Timothy Haskell.

Presented in two parts.

Musical satire on the events of the day.

Irish Repertory Theatre production of **Triptych** (45). By Edna O'Brien. Charlotte Moore artistic director, Ciarán O'Reilly producing director; in association with Jeannie Donovan, Julian Schlossberg, Weissberger Theater Group, at the Irish Repertory Theatre. Opened October 7, 2004. (Closed November 14, 2004)

The Wife (Pauline)	Margaret Colin	The Daughter (Brandy)	Carrie Specksgoor
The Mistress (Clarissa)	Ally Sheedy		

Directed by David Jones; scenery, Michael McGarty; costumes, Jane Greenwood; lighting, David Weiner; sound, Scott Myers; production stage manager, Matthew Silver; press, Shirley Herz Associates.

Presented without intermission.

Three women love the same man. First presentation of record was given at San Francisco's Magic Theatre (12/6/2004–1/4/2005).

Manhattan Ensemble Theater production of **Nine Parts of Desire** (246). Solo performance piece by Heather Raffo; inspired by Geraldine Brooks's book, *Nine Parts of Desire*. David Fishelson artistic director, James Sparnon producing director, at the Manhattan Ensemble Theater. Opened October 9, 2004. (Closed May 22, 2005)

Performed by Ms. Raffo.

Directed by Joanna Settle; scenery, Antje Ellermann; costumes, Mattie Ullrich; lighting, Peter West; sound and music, Obadiah Eaves; production stage manager, Lisa Gavaletz; press, Richard Kornberg and Associates, Rick Miramontez.

Presented without intermission.

Solo exploration of the ways oppression and war in Iraq affect individual women. First presentation of record was given at Edinburgh's Traverse Theatre (8/2003) before a run at London's Bush Theatre (9/10–10/4/2003).

Playwrights Horizons production of **Spatter Pattern (Or, How I Got Away With It)** (25). By Neal Bell. Tim Sanford artistic director, Leslie Marcus managing director, William Russo general manager, in the Peter Jay Sharp Theater. Opened October 10, 2004. (Closed October 31, 2004)

Selma; others .... Deirdre O'Connell	Tate .... Darren Pettie
Dunn .... Peter Frechette	Detective; others .... John Lavelle

Directed by Michael Greif; scenery, Mark Wendland; costumes, Miranda Hoffman; lighting, Kevin Adams; sound, Jill BC DuBoff; music, Michael Friedman; production stage manager, Judith Schoenfeld; press, The Publicity Office, Bob Fennell, Michael S. Borowski.

Presented without intermission.

Murder mystery evolves into a buddy story about a grieving gay man and a suspected murderer, who's straight and lives next door.

The Public Theater production of **Richard III** (17). Revival of the play by William Shakespeare. George C. Wolfe producer, Mara Manus executive director, in Martinson Hall. Opened October 11, 2004. (Closed October 24, 2004)

Plea or ploy? Ty Burrell and Peter Dinklage in Richard III. *Photo: Michal Daniel*

Richard .... Peter Dinklage
George; Lord Mayor .... Ron Cephas Jones
Brackenbury .... Jojo Gonzalez
Lord Hastings .... Stephen Barker Turner
Lady Anne .... Kali Rocha
Lord Rivers; Priest .... Gareth Saxe
Lord Grey;
  Richmond; Priest .... Shane McRae
Queen Elizabeth .... Mercedes Herrero
Marquess of Dorset;
  Tyrrel .... James Yaegashi
Lord Stanley .... Thomas Schall

Duke of Buckingham .... Ty Burrell
Queen Margaret .... Isa Thomas
Sir William Catesby .... Harry Barandes
John, Duke of North
  (first murderer) .... David Don Miller
Christopher
  (second murderer) .... Matthew Maher
Edward IV; Cardinal .... Tom Nelis
Duchess of York .... Roberta Maxwell
Duke of York .... Connor Paolo
Edward, Prince of Wales .... Peter Vack

Directed by Peter DuBois; choreography, David Neumann; scenery, Riccardo Hernández; costumes, Marina Draghici; lighting, Scott Zielinski; sound and music, Scott Myers; fight direction, Rick Sordelet; associate producers, Peter DuBois, Steven Tabakin and Heidi Griffiths; casting, Jordan Thaler and Ms. Griffiths; production stage manager, Megan Schneid; press, Arlene Kriv, Elizabeth Wehrle.

Presented in two parts.

Mr. Shakespeare's ill-formed plotter schemes (and murders) his way to power. First presentation believed to be in the 1590s with Richard Burbage in the title role. The first presentation of record in this country was given in New York at the Theatre in Nassau Street (3/5/1750) in an adaptation by Colley Cibber.

Trying (94). By Joanna McClelland Glass. Produced by Michael Leavitt, Maidstone Productions, Libby Adler Mages, Mari Stuart, Tony D'Angelo, Steve Dahl, Maria Cozzi, in association with Victory Gardens Theater, at the Promenade Theatre. Opened October 13, 2004. (Closed January 2, 2005)

Judge Biddle .... Fritz Weaver   Sarah Schorr .... Kati Brazda

Understudies: Mr. Weaver—William Cain; Ms. Brazda—Addie Brownlee.

Directed by Sandy Shinner; scenery, Jeff Bauer; costumes, Carolyn Cristofani; lighting, Jacqueline Reed; sound, Andrew Hopson; associate producers, Fox Theatricals, Eileen LaCario, William Pullinsi, Bob Bartner; production stage manager, Andrea "Spook" Testani; press, Richard Kornberg and Associates, Richard Kornberg, Don Summa, Tom D'Ambrosio, Carrie Friedman.

Time: November 1967–June 1968. Place: Judge Biddle's office over a garage in Georgetown. Presented in two parts.

An aging lion of the judiciary hires a new secretary to help him bring order to his life and work. First presentation of record was given at Chicago's Victory Gardens Theater (3/29–5/15/2004).

The Public Theater production of **Dirty Tricks** (20). Solo performance piece by John Jeter. George C. Wolfe producer; Mara Manus executive director, in the Anspacher Theater. Opened October 20, 2004. (Closed November 7, 2004)

Martha Mitchell .... Judith Ivey

Directed by Margaret Whitton; scenery, Neil Patel; costumes, Joseph G. Aulisi; lighting, Stephen Strawbridge; sound, Fitz Patton; video, Sage Marie Carter; wigs and hair, Paul Huntley; associate producers, Peter DuBois and Steven Tabakin; casting, Jordan Thaler and Heidi Griffiths; production stage manager, Buzz Cohen; press, Arlene Kriv, Elizabeth Wehrle.

Time: August 8, 1974, and the past. Place: Martha Mitchell's apartment in New York. Presented without intermission.

A wife's loose lips help sink her husband's (Attorney General John Mitchell) boss's (President Richard Nixon) ship of state.

Eve-olution (62). By Hilary Illick and Jennifer Krier. Produced by Mari Nakachi, Lucy D. Anda, Meg Felton Staunton at the Cherry Lane Theatre. Opened October 20, 2004. (Closed December 12, 2004)

Liza .... Sabrina Le Beauf   Alison .... Carolyn McCormick
    Understudies: Mses. Le Beauf, McCormick–Judith Lightfoot Clarke.
    Directed by Carolyn Cantor; scenery, David Korins; costumes, Jenny Mannis; lighting, Matthew Richards; sound, Eric Shim; production stage manager, Dyanne McNamara; press, Origlio Public Relations, Tony Origlio, Catie Monck.
    Presented without intermission.
    Psychological conflicts that arise between motherhood and career are explored in a contemporary setting.

*Jewtopia (254). By Bryan Fogel and Sam Wolfson. Produced by WEJ Productions and Jenkay at the Westside Theatre. Opened October 21, 2004.

Chris O'Connell .... Bryan Fogel   Dennis Lipschitz .... Lorry Goldman
Adam Lipschitz .... Sam Wolfson   Bad dates; Jill;
Rabbi Schlomo;   Nurse; Allison .... Jackie Tohn
  Irving Lipschitz .... Gerry Vichi   Marcy Cohen;
Rachel .... Inna Pantaeva   Arlene Lipschitz .... Cheryl David

    Directed by John Tillinger; scenery, Patrick Fahey; costumes, Cynthia Nordstrom; lighting, Mike Baldassari; sound, Kevin Lacy; production stage manager, Jeff Benish; press, Keith Sherman and Associates, Keith Sherman, Brett Oberman.
    Presented in two parts.
    A gentile decides that marrying a Jewish girl is the path to a life with fewer decisions he will be forced to make, so his Jewish friend teaches him how to "pass" as a Jew. First presentation of record at Los Angeles's Coast Playhouse (5/8/2003–7/8/2004).

The Gospel at Colonus (12). Revival of the musical with book and lyrics by Lee Breuer; music by Bob Telson; based on *Oedipus at Colonus* by Sophocles. Presented by Washington Mutual, in association with Dovetail Productions, at the Apollo Theatre. Opened October 25, 2004. (Closed November 7, 2004)

The Messenger .... Charles S. Dutton   Choir Director .... J.D. Steele
Oedipus .... The Blind Boys of Alabama   Balladeer .... Sam Butler
                featuring Clarence Fountain   Creon .... Jay Caldwell
Theseus .... Earl F. Miller   Polyneices .... Kevin Davis
Choragos .... The Legendary Soul Stirrers   Choir Soloist .... Carolyn Johnson-White
                Willie Rogers, Ben Odom,   The Acolyte .... Josie Johnson
                Lloyd Moore, Gene Stewart   Chorus .... The Abyssinian Baptist
Ismene .... Jevetta Steele   and Institutional Radio Choirs
Antigone .... Bernardine Mitchell

    Directed by Mr. Breuer; scenery, Alison Yerxa; costumes, Ghretta Hynd; lighting, Jason Boyd; sound, Ron Lorman; music direction, Mr. Telson; choir direction, Butch Heyward; production stage manager, Babette Roberts.
    Gospel musical based on an adaptation of Sophocles's *Oedipus at Colonus* that includes passages from *Oedipus Rex* and *Antigone*. First presentation of record was given as a work-in-progress performance by ReCherChez Studio for the Avant-Garde Performing Arts at the Washington Square United Methodist Church (12/23/1981). The New York premiere was given by the Brooklyn Academy of Music during its first Next Wave Festival with Morgan Freeman in the role of the Messenger (11/8–11/20/1983). It was later presented at Broadway's Lunt-Fontanne Theatre with Mr. Freeman continuing in the role (3/24–5/15/1988; 61 performances).

ACT I

The Welcome and Quotations .... Messenger
The Invocation
    "Live Where You Can" .... Ismene and Choir
Recapitulation From Oedipus the King .... Antigone and Theseus
Oedipus and Antigone Enter Colonus .... Antigone and Messenger

Ode to Colonus
"Fair Colonus" .... Soloist (Willie Rogers)
"Stop, Do Not Go On" .... Balladeer, Oedipus, Choragos
Choral Dialogue
"Who Is This Man?" .... Soloists (Jay Caldwell, Jimmy Carter)
Messenger, Oedipus
Ismene Comes to Colonus
"How Shall I See You Through My Tears?" .... Ismene, Oedipus
Narrative of Ismene .... Antigone
Chorus Questions Oedipus .... Soloist (Jay Caldwell),
Messenger, Blind Boys
The Prayer
"A Voice Foretold" .... Oedipus, Balladeer, Soloist (J.D. Steele)
Oedipus Is Welcomed in Colonus
Peroration .... Theseus
Jubilee
"No Never" .... Choragos, Oedipus, Choir
Creon Comes to Colonus
"Come Home" .... Creon, Ushers
Seizure of the Daughters .... Creon, Ushers
Oedipus Curses Creon
"Evil Kindness/You'd Take Him Away" .... Oedipus, Choir,
Creon, Messenger
Choral Ode
"Numberless Are the World's Wonders" .... Soloists (J.D. Steele, Jevetta Steele),
Choir

ACT II

Oedipus Laments
"Lift Me Up" .... Oedipus
Polyneices's Testimony and Supplication
"Evil" .... Balladeer
Oedipus's Curse .... Polyneices, Messenger, Oedipus
"Stand By Me/You Break My Heart" .... Heroes
Poem
"Love Unconquerable" .... Antigone
Preaching With Tuned Response .... Messenger and Oedipus
Special Effect
"Ah, Heaven's Height Has Cracked!"
The Teachings .... Messenger, Theseus
The Descent of Oedipus
"Oh Sunlight of No Light" .... Antigone, Ismene, Balladeer
"Eternal Sleep" .... Soloist (Willie Rogers) and Choragos
Mourning .... Antigone, Theseus, Ismene
Doxology, the Paean
"Lift Him Up" .... Soloist (Carolyn Johnson-White), Choir
The Sermon .... Messenger
Closing Hymn
"Now Let the Weeping Cease" .... Choragos, Choir
Benediction .... Messenger

The Abbey Theatre production of **The Playboy of the Western World** (7). Revival
of the play by J.M. Synge. Ben Barnes artistic director, Brian Jackson managing director,
at the Jack H. Skirball Center for the Performing Arts. Opened October 26, 2004.
(Closed October 31, 2004)

Bellman	Simon O'Gorman	Michael James	John Olohan
Pegeen Mike	Cathy Belton	Jimmy Farrell	David Herlihy
Shawn Keogh	Andrew Bennett	Philly Cullen	Brendan Conroy

Riot act: Tom Vaughan Lawlor and Cathy Belton in The Playboy of the Western World. *Photo: Tom Lawlor*

Christy Mahon .... Tom Vaughan Lawlor   Old Mahon .... Maeliosa Stafford
Widow Quin .... Olwen Fouéré

Directed by Mr. Barnes; scenery, Guido Tondino; choreography, Caimin Collins; costumes, Monica Frawley; lighting, Peter Mumford; sound and music, Joe Townsend; production stage manager, John McNamara; press, Boneau/Bryan-Brown, Chris Boneau, Adriana Douzos.

Time: Night and the next day. Place: Country public house. Presented in two parts.

Mr. Synge's darkly comic take on the superstitions and poverty that oppressed the Irish at the beginning of the 20th century. First presentation of record was given in Dublin at the Abbey Theatre (1/26/1907), which caused a riot over perceived criticism of the peasantry. First presentation of record in this country was given at Boston's Plymouth Theatre (10/16/1911).

Two Brothers Who Are Not Brothers (15). By Paul Rawlings. Produced by All For Two at the Players Theatre. Opened October 27, 2004. (Closed November 7, 2004)

Dix ....Joe Thompson   Jack ....John Jimerson

Directed by Sue Lawless; scenery, Michael J. Hotopp; costumes, Vanessa Leuck; lighting, Gregory A. Hirsch; sound, Michael G. Ward; production stage manager, Nick Leavens; press, Origlio Public Relations, Tony Origlio, Richard Hillman.

Presented in three parts.

Brothers-in-law cope with devastating tragedy.

Uncle Jacques' Symphony (15). Solo performance piece by Dominic Hoffman. Produced by Jon Zimmerman and Darren Lee Cole at the Soho Playhouse. Opened October 28, 2004. (Closed November 14, 2004)

Performed by Mr. Hoffman.

Lighting, Graham Kindred; music, Billy Mitchell; press, The Jacksina Company, Judy Jacksina. Presented without intermission.

Numerous characters expound on the meaning of life. First presentation of record was given at London's Hackney Empire Studio (7/1999). The production later had runs in Los Angeles and San Francisco.

Who Is Floyd Stearn? (64). Solo performance piece by Michael Raynor. Produced by Rick Waxman and Men of the Court Productions at the 47th Street Theatre. Opened November 1, 2004. (Closed December 26, 2004)

Performed by Mr. Raynor.

Directed by Larry Moss; scenery, Peter R. Feuchtwanger; lighting, Jonathan Spencer; sound and projections, Michael Matthews; executive producers, Carl D. White and Tom Smedes; production stage manager, Max Wixom; press, Publicity Outfitters, Timothy Haskell.

Presented without intermission.

A man searches for his unknown father and finds darker tales than he might have imagined. First presentation of record was given at the 2002 Edinburgh Fringe Festival.

The Immigrant (29). Musical with book by Mark Harelik; music by Steven M. Alper; lyrics by Sarah Knapp. Produced by Hello Entertainment, in association with Richard G. Weinberg for Omneity Entertainment and Jeffrey B. Hecktman, at Dodger Stages. Opened November 4, 2004. (Closed November 28, 2004)

Haskell Harelik	Adam Heller	Milton Perry	Walter Charles
Ima Perry	Cass Morgan	Leah Harelik	Jacqueline Antaramian

Mystery man: Neal Huff, Kevin Cahoon, Mary Catherine Garrison, Frances Sternhagen and Matthew Broderick in The Foreigner. *Photo: Joan Marcus*

Directed by Randal Myler; scenery, Brian Webb; costumes, Willa Kim; lighting, Don Darnutzer; sound, Peter Fitzgerald; wigs and hair, Paul Huntley; musical arrangements and orchestrations, Mr. Alper; music direction, Kimberly Grigsby; casting, Tara Rubin Casting; production stage manager, Antonia Gianino; press, Cromarty and Company, Peter Cromarty.

Presented in two parts.

A Russian Jew settles in Texas in 1909 to find himself faced with competing pressures to assimilate and to retain his religious heritage. Based on Mr. Harelik's play, *The Immigrant: A Hamilton County Album*, which premiered at the Denver Center Theatre Company in 1985.

Roundabout Theatre Company production of **The Foreigner** (81). Revival of the play by Larry Shue. Todd Haimes artistic director, Ellen Richard managing director, Julia C. Levy executive director, in the Laura Pels Theatre at the Harold and Miriam Steinberg Center for Theatre. Opened November 7, 2004. (Closed January 16, 2005)

Charlie Baker .... Matthew Broderick	Rev. David Marshall Lee .... Neal Huff
Betty Meeks .... Frances Sternhagen	Sgt. "Froggy" LeSueur .... Byron Jennings
Ellard Simms .... Kevin Cahoon	Owen Musser .... Lee Tergesen
Catherine Simms ...... Mary Catherine Garrison	

Understudies: Ms. Sternhagen—Rita Gardner; Messrs.Cahoon, Huff, Tergesen—Matthew Schmidt; Ms. Garrison—Lauren McCord; Messrs. Broderick, Jennings, Tergesen—James Hindman.

Directed by Scott Schwartz; scenery, Anna Louizos; costumes, David Murin; lighting, Pat Collins; sound, Janet Kalas; casting, Mele Nagler; production stage manager, Jay Adler; stage manager. Amy Patricia Stern; press, Boneau/Bryan-Brown, Adrian Bryan-Brown, Joe Perrotta, Erika Creagh, Matt Polk.

Time: The recent past. Place: Betty Meeks's fishing lodge resort in Georgia. Presented in two parts.

Mild-mannered proofreader seeking peace in a Georgia retreat finds back-country intrigue that leads to farcical results. A 1984–85 *Best Plays* choice, the original Off Broadway production opened at the Astor Place Theatre (11/1/1984–6/8/1986; 686 performances). First presentation of record was given at Milwaukee Repertory Theater with a cast that included Kenneth Albers, Laurence Ballard and Ellen Lauren (1/14–2/20/1983).

Second Stage Theatre production of **Danny and the Deep Blue Sea** (30). Revival of the play by John Patrick Shanley. Carole Rothman artistic director, Timothy J. McClimon executive director, at the Second Stage Theatre. Opened November 10, 2004. (Closed December 5, 2004)

Roberta .... Rosemarie DeWitt	Danny .... Adam Rothenberg

Directed by Leigh Silverman; scenery, Santo Loquasto; costumes, Jennifer von Mayrhauser; lighting, Jeff Croiter; sound and music, John Gromada; casting, Tara Rubin Casting; production stage manager, Kelly Hance; stage manager, Jennifer O'Byrne; press, Richard Kornberg and Associates, Tom D'Ambrosio.

Presented without intermission.

Emotionally scarred couple meet and fall into an instant relationship that seems doomed from the outset. First presentation of record, following development at the 1983 O'Neill Playwrights Conference, was given at the Humana Festival of New American Plays by Actors Theatre of Louisville with John Turturro in the title role (3/1984). The Louisville production was moved to Off Broadway in a co-production of Circle in the Square Theatre (Downtown) and Circle Repertory Company (6/6–9/16/1984; 117 performances).

Manhattan Theatre Club production of **Five by Tenn** (46). By Tennessee Williams. Lynne Meadow artistic director, Barry Grove executive producer, at City Center Stage II. Opened November 11, 2004. (Closed December 19, 2004)

The Writer .... Jeremy Lawrence

May–December: Robert Sella and Kathleen Chalfant in The Fat Man's Wife *from* Five by Tenn. *Photo: Joan Marcus*

Summer at the Lake (1937)
Performed under the title *Escape* at the Kennedy Center (see note).

Mrs. Fenway .... Penny Fuller   Anna .... Kathleen Chalfant
Donald Fenway .... Cameron Folmar

The Fat Man's Wife (1938)

Josie Cartwright .... David Rasche   Dennis Merriwether .... Robert Sella
Vera Cartwright .... Kathleen Chalfant

And Tell Sad Stories of the Deaths of Queens (c. 1959)

Candy Delaney .... Cameron Folmar   Alvin Krenning .... Hunter Gilmore
Karl .... Myk Watford   Jerry Johnson .... Robert Sella

Adam and Eve on a Ferry (1939)

Lawrence .... David Rasche   Visitor .... Penny Fuller
Frieda .... Kathleen Chalfant

I Can't Imagine Tomorrow (1970)

One .... Kathleen Chalfant   Two .... David Rasche

Directed by Michael Kahn; scenery, James Noone; costumes, Catherine Zuber; lighting, Traci Klainer; sound, Scott Killian; music, Adam Wernick; casting, Nancy Piccione and David Caparelliotis; production stage manager, Denise Yaney; press, Boneau/Bryan-Brown, Chris Boneau, Jim Byk, Aaron Meier.

Presented in two parts.

Collection of early one-act works by Mr. Williams. An earlier version, under the title *Eight by Tenn*, was given at Hartford Stage (10/8–11/2/2003). First presentation of record for the current version was given at the Kennedy Center with Mr. Kahn as the director (4/22/2004).

New York City Opera production of **Cinderella** (13). Revival of the musical with book and lyrics by Oscar Hammerstein II; music by Richard Rodgers. Artistic director Paul Kellogg, at the New York State Theater at Lincoln Center. Opened November 12, 2004. (Closed November 21, 2004)

Royal Herald	Scott Hogsed	King	Dick Van Patten
Stepmother	John Epperson	Royal Chef	Roland Rusinek
Joy	Lea DeLaria	Royal Steward	Eric Michael Gillett
Portia	Ana Gasteyer	Prince	Christopher Sieber
Cinderella	Sarah Uriarte Berry	Fairy Godmother	Eartha Kitt
Queen	Renée Taylor		

Directed and choreographed by Baayork Lee; scenery, Henry Bardon and David Jenkins; costumes, Gregg Barnes; lighting, Richard Winkler; sound, Abe Jacob; music direction, Gerald Steichen; press, Richard Kornberg and Associates.

Presented in two parts.

Evil stepsisters and stepmother get their comeuppances when the prince finds his princess. First presentation of record was given on CBS television network, with Julie Andrews in the title role, to a estimated audience of 107 million (3/31/1957). Two other television productions were made in 1965 and 1997. This season's production was the third by New York City Opera, the others were in 1993 and 1995. Although touring productions occasionally come to New York, there has been no Broadway production of record.

Lincoln Center Theater production of **Belle Epoque** (49). Dance-theater piece by Martha Clarke and Charles L. Mee. André Bishop artistic director, Bernard Gersten executive producer, at the Mitzi E. Newhouse Theater. Opened November 21, 2004. (Closed January 2, 2005)

Performed by Mark Povinelli, Honora Fergusson, Vivienne Benesch, Michael Stuhlbarg, Joyce Castle, Ruth Maleczech, Robert Besserer, Paola Styron, Tome Cousin, Gabrielle Malone, Robert Wersinger, Nina Goldman, Rebecca Wender, Jill Jaffe, Will De Vos, Hector "Tito" Castro, Sam Davis.

Directed by Ms. Clarke; scenery, Robert Israel; costumes, Jane Greenwood; lighting, Christopher Akerlind; sound, Scott Stauffer; orchestrations and music direction, Jill Jaffe; production stage manager, Jennifer Rae Moore; press, Philip Rinaldi Publicity, Philip Rinaldi, Barbara Carroll.

Presented without intermission.

A sequel, of sorts, to Ms. Clarke and Mr. Mee's dance-theater meditation on *fin de siècle* Vienna—titled *Vienna: Lusthaus*—this time set in Paris of the *belle époque*.

Atlantic Theater Company production of **A Second Hand Memory** (78). By Woody Allen. Neil Pepe artistic director, Andrew D. Hamingson managing director, at the Atlantic Theater Company. Opened November 22, 2004. (Closed January 23, 2005)

Alma Wolfe	Elizabeth Marvel	Bea Wolfe	Kate Blumberg
Lou Wolfe	Dominic Chianese	Phil Wellman	Michael McKean
Eddie Wolfe	Nicky Katt	Diane	Erica Leerhsen
Fay Wolfe	Beth Fowler		

Directed by Mr. Allen; scenery, Santo Loquasto; costumes, Laura Bauer; lighting, James F. Ingalls; sound, Obadiah Eaves; casting, Bernard Telsey Casting; production stage manager, Janet Takami; press, Boneau/Bryan-Brown, Chris Boneau, Susanne Tighe, Joe Perrotta.

Presented in two parts.

Bad marriages lead three men to desperation in a darkly comic view of one Brooklyn family in the 1950s.

Concerned mom: Adriane Lenox in Doubt,
a Parable. *Photo: Joan Marcus*

Manhattan Theatre Club production of **Doubt, a Parable** (77). By John Patrick Shanley.
Lynne Meadow artistic director, Barry Grove executive producer, at City Center Stage I.
Opened November 23, 2004. (Closed January 30, 2005)

Sister James	Heather Goldenhersh	Mrs. Muller	Adriane Lenox
Sister Aloysius	Cherry Jones	Father Flynn	Brían F. O'Byrne

Directed by Doug Hughes; scenery, John Lee Beatty; costumes, Catherine Zuber; lighting, Pat
Collins; sound and music, David Van Tieghem; production stage manager, Charles Means; stage
manager, Elizabeth Moloney; press, Boneau/Bryan-Brown, Chris Boneau, Jim Byk, Aaron Meier.

Time: Autumn, 1964. Place: St. Nicholas Church School in the Bronx. Presented without
intermission.

A nun grows concerned over a priest's relationships with boys in his charge. Transferred to
Broadway's Walter Kerr Theatre (3/31/2005; 70 performances as of 5/31/2005). See Plays Produced
on Broadway section in this volume. A 2004–05 *Best Plays* choice (see essay by Jeremy McCarter
in this volume).

Playwrights Horizons production of **Rodney's Wife** (23). By Richard Nelson. Tim
Sanford artistic director, Leslie Marcus managing director, William Russo general manager,
in the Mainstage Theater. Opened December 1, 2004. (Closed December 19, 2004)

Rodney	David Strathairn	Lee	Jessica Chastain
Fay	Haviland Morris	Henry	John Rothman
Eva	Maryann Plunkett	Ted	Jesse Pennington

Secret life: Haviland Morris and Jessica Chastain in Rodney's Wife. *Photo: Joan Marcus*

Directed by Mr. Nelson; scenery and costumes, Susan Hilferty; lighting, David Weiner; sound, Scott Lehrer; casting, James Calleri, Alaine Alldaffer and Cindy Tolan; production stage manager, Matthew Silver; press, The Publicity Office, Bob Fennell, Marc Thibodeau, Michael S. Borowski.

Time: 1962. Place: A small villa on the edge of Rome. Presented without intermission.

A man struggles with his waning career as an actor while his wife battles demons of her own. First presentation of record was given at Williamstown Theatre Festival (7/7–7/18/2004).

York Theatre Company production of **Souvenir** (52). Play with music by Stephen Temperley. James Morgan producing artistic director, in association with Ted Snowdon, at Theatre at Saint Peter's. Opened December 1, 2004. (Closed January 16, 2005)

Florence Foster Jenkins .... Judy Kaye   Cosme McMoon ....Jack F. Lee

Directed by Vivian Matalon; scenery, R. Michael Miller; costumes, Tracy Christiansen; lighting, Ann G. Wrightson; sound, David Budries; casting, Hughes Moss Casting, Ltd.; production stage manager, Jack Gianino; press, Helene Davis.

Presented in two parts.

Woman who has deluded herself into thinking she can sing, practices assiduously with an accompanist who needs the money.

Modern Orthodox (205). By Daniel Goldfarb. Produced by Ars Nova and Kara Medoff, in association with the Underwood Theater and Jewcy, at Dodger Stages. Opened December 6, 2004. (Closed May 8, 2005)

Ben Jacobson .... Craig Bierko   Hannah Ziggelstein .... Molly Ringwald
Hershel Klein .... Jason Biggs   Rachel Feinberger .... Jenn Harris
    Understudies: Messrs. Bierko, Biggs—Peter Smith; Mses. Ringwald, Harris—Sandy Rustin.

    Directed by James Lapine; scenery, Derek McLane; costumes, Dona Granata; lighting, David Lander; sound, Fitz Patton; associate producers, Amanda Lipitz and Greg Smith, Michael and Marjorie Stern; casting, David Caparelliotis; production stage manager, Jane Grey; stage manager, Dan Shaheen; press, Carol R. Fineman/Barlow-Hartman Public Relations, Leslie Baden.

    Time: The present. Place: New York City. Presented without intermission.

    Orthodox Jewish man seeks an Orthodox Jewish woman and finds her—but he also makes unlikely friends along the way. First presentation of record was given at New Haven's Long Wharf Theatre (10/11–11/19/2000).

New York Theatre Workshop production of **A Number** (76). By Caryl Churchill. James C. Nicola artistic director, Lynn Moffat managing director. Opened December 7, 2004. (Closed February 13, 2005)

Bernard; Michael .... Dallas Roberts   Salter .... Sam Shepard
    Understudies: Michael Chernus, Robert Lavelle.

    Directed by James Macdonald; scenery, Eugene Lee; costumes, Gabriel Berry; lighting, Edward Pierce; sound, Darron L. West; production stage manager, Martha Donaldson; press, Richard Kornberg and Associates, Richard Kornberg, Don Summa.

    Presented without intermission.

    A man is confronted by his son and his son's genetically engineered doppelgängers. First presented by the English Stage Company at London's Royal Court Theatre Downstairs (9/26–11/16/2002). A 2004–05 *Best Plays* choice (see essay by Robert Hurwitt in this volume).

Disturbed dad: Sam Shepard in A Number.
Photo: Joan Marcus

Forbidden Broadway: Special Victims Unit (190). Musical revue by Gerard Alessandrini. Produced by John Freedson, Jon B. Platt, Harriet Yellin, at the Douglas Fairbanks Theater. Opened December 16, 2004. (Closed May 29, 2005)

Performed by Ron Bohmer, Christine Pedi, Jason Mills, Jennifer Simard, David Caldwell (piano).

Directed by Mr. Alessandrini and Phillip George; choreography, Mr. George; scenery, Megan K. Halpern; costumes, Alvin Colt; lighting, Marc Janowitz; music direction, David Caldwell; associate producers, Gary Hoffman, Jerry Kravat and Masakazu Shibaoka; production stage manager, Jim Griffith; press, Pete Sanders Group, Glenna Freedman.

The latest version of the long-running musical revue. This same version is planned to re-open June 24, 2005 at the 47th Street Theatre. See Long Runs Off Broadway section of this volume for information on earlier productions.

Under the Bridge (54). Musical with book and lyrics by Kathie Lee Gifford; music by David Pomeranz; based on the book *The Family Under the Bridge* by Natalie Savage Carlson. Produced by Lambchop Productions at the Zipper Theatre. Opened January 6, 2005. (Closed February 20, 2005)

Jacques; Police Officer .... Dan Cooney	Mireli .... Florence Lacey
Armand .... Ed Dixon	Madame Calcet .... Jacquelyn Piro
Evelyne .... Alexa Ehrlich	Pierre; Monsieur Latour .... Greg Stone
Do-Gooder .... Thursday Farrar	Suzy .... Maggie Watts
Do-Gooder .... Tamra Hayden	Paul .... Andrew Blake Zutty

Ensemble: Alexa Ehrlich, Tamra Hayden, Greg Stone, Maggie Watts.

Orchestra: Paul Raiman conductor, piano; David Wolfson assistant conductor; keyboards; Eric Havorson percussion.

Understudies: Mr. Dixon—Dan Cooney; Ms. Lacey—Thursday Farrar; Ms. Piro–Tamra Hayden; Mses. Watts, Ehrlich, Mr. Zutty—Bethany Tesarck.

Directed by Eric Schaeffer; scenery, Jim Kronzer; costumes, Anne Kennedy; lighting, Chris Lee; sound, Kai Harada; orchestrations, Brian Besterman; vocal arrangements, Ms. Gifford, Messrs. Pomeranz and Raiman; music direction, Mr. Raiman; associate producer, Christine Gardner; stage manager, Marybeth Abel; press, Pete Sanders Group, Bill Coyle, Jeremy Shaffer.

Time: 1952. Place: Paris. Presented in two parts.

Family-oriented musical about the trials and tribulations of a homeless Parisian family.

ACT I

"Paris" .... Armand, Company
"You Will Meet With Adventure Today" .... Mireli
"Half a Dream" .... Armand, Children
"Under the Bridge" .... Armand, Madame Calcet
"The Marriage of Lady Tartine" .... Children
"It Was My Bridge" .... Armand
"This House Where We Live" .... Suzy
"Do-Gooders Lament" .... The Do-Gooders
"What Might Have Been" .... Armand, Mireli
"This Is the Gypsy Life!" .... Mireli, Gypsies
"What Kind of a Mother Am I?" .... Madame Calcet, Do-Gooders, Armand

ACT II

"This Is the Gypsy Life" (Reprise) .... Company
"He Is With You" .... Mireli, Gypsies
"Christmas Is Everyone's Holiday" .... Company
"The Sum of a Man" .... Mireli, Paul
"As Long As We Have Us" .... Madame Calcet, Suzy, Evelyne
"A Clean Start" .... Armand
"Something Called Love" .... Armand
Finale .... Armand, Company

New York Gilbert and Sullivan Players production of **The Pirates of Penzance** (12). Revival of the operetta with libretto by William S. Gilbert; music by Arthur Sullivan. Albert Bergeret artistic director, at City Center. Opened January 7, 2005. (Closed January 23, 2005)

Major-General Stanley .... Hal Linden	Sergeant of Police .... Keith Jurosko
Pirate King .... Ross David Crutchlow	Mabel .... Laurelyn Watson
Frederic .... Andrew MacPhail	Ruth .... Angela Smith

Directed by Mr. Bergeret; choreography, Bill Fabris; scenery, Lou Anne Gilleland; costumes, Gail J. Wofford; lighting, Sally Small; production stage manager, Jan Holland; press, Cromarty and Company, Peter Cromarty.

Presented in two parts.

An unwilling young pirate renounces his apprenticeship only to discover that duty binds him to the ways of the brigand. First presentation of record was given in New York at the Fifth Avenue Theatre (12/31/1879). It was the fifth collaboration by Messrs. Gilbert and Sullivan and their only work to have its premiere in this country.

Brooklyn Academy of Music presentation of the **Theatre Royal Bath** production of **As You Like It** (14). Revival of the play by William Shakespeare. Alan H. Fishman chairman of the board, Karen Brooks Hopkins president, Joseph V. Melillo executive producer, at the BAM Harvey Theater. Opened January 18, 2005. (Closed January 30, 2005)

Orlando .... Dan Stevens	Duke Frederick;
Adam; Corin .... David Barnaby	Banished Duke .... James Laurenson
Oliver .... Freddie Stevenson	Amiens .... Freddie Stevenson
Dennis .... Ronald Fernee	Jaques .... Philip Voss
Charles; William .... James Crossley	First Lord;
Celia .... Rebecca Callard	Jaques de Boys .... Kevin Collins
Rosalind .... Rebecca Hall	Second Lord .... Nyasha Fredrick Hatendi
Touchstone .... Michael Siberry	Silvius .... David Birkin
Le Beau;	Audrey .... Janet Greaves
Sir Oliver Martext .... Robin Browne	Phoebe .... Charlotte Parry

Directed by Peter Hall; scenery and costumes, John Gunter; lighting, Peter Mumford; sound, Gregory Clarke; music, Mick Sands; production stage manager, John McNamara; press, Sandy Sawotka, Fatima Kafele, Eva Chien, Tamara McCaw, Jennifer Lam.

Presented in two parts.

Noble women in disguise, a ruler unjustly deposed and the attractions of romance in a pastoral setting. Registered with the Stationers' Company—a booksellers's guild—in 1600 as a text not to be published, *As You Like It* is believed to have been presented first in the Globe's initial autumn season of 1599. The first presentation of record, under the title of *Love in a Forest*, came at the hand of adapter Charles Johnson in 1723 at the Drury Lane Theatre. The first presentation of record in this country was given at the John Street Theatre (7/14/1786).

Belfast Blues (96). By Geraldine Hughes. Produced by Anjelica Huston and The Culture Project, in association with That's Us Productions. Allan Buchman artistic director, at 45 Bleecker. Opened January 20, 2005. (Closed April 24, 2005)

Performed by Ms. Hughes.

Directed by Carol Kane; scenery and lighting, Jonathan Christman; sound, Jonathan Snipes; press, Origlio Public Relations; Philip Carrubba.

Presented without intermission.

Stories of the bleak lives led by Catholics in the Northern Ireland of the past generation. First presentation of record was given by the Virtual Theatre Project at Los Angeles's Black Dahlia Theatre (1/18–4/27/2003) followed by a tour of the UK and a stand in Chicago before the New York run.

Tale of "troubles": Geraldine Hughes in Belfast Blues. *Photo: Jonathan Christman*

*Thom Pain (based on nothing) (137). Solo performance piece by Will Eno. Produced by Daryl Roth and Bob Boyett at the DR2 Theatre. Opened February 1, 2005.

Performed by James Urbaniak.

Directed by Hal Brooks; scenery, David Korins; lighting, Mark Barton; production stage manager, Tom Taylor; press, Pete Sanders Group, Pete Sanders.

Presented without intermission.

Musings on a life of quiet desperation. First presentation of record was given in a workshop at London's Soho Theatre (3/10/2004) before a run at the Edinburgh Fringe Festival (8/5–30/2004).

Second Stage Theatre production of **The 25th Annual Putnam County Spelling Bee** (48). Musical with book by Rachel Sheinkin; music and lyrics by William Finn; conceived by Rebecca Feldman. Carole Rothman artistic director, Timothy J. McClimon executive director, at the Second Stage Theatre. Opened February 7, 2005. (Closed March 20, 2005)

Mitch Mahoney .... Derrick Baskin	Olive Ostrovsky .... Celia Keenan-Bolger
Gramercy Park .... Deborah S. Craig	Tripp Barrington ....Jose Llana
Leaf Coneybear .... Jesse Tyler Ferguson	Douglas Panch .... Jay Reiss
William Barfee .... Dan Fogler	Logan Schwarzen-
Rona Janet .... Lisa Howard	grubeniere .... Sarah Saltzberg

Orchestra: Vadim Feichtner conductor, piano; Carmel Dean assistant conductor, synthesizer; Amy Raiske cello; Richard Heckman reeds; Glenn Rhian drums.

Understudies: Messrs. Fogler, Ferguson, Baskin, Reiss, Llana—Willis White; Mses. Keenan-Bolger, Craig, Howard, Saltzberg—Lisa Yuen.

Directed by James Lapine; choreography, Dan Knechtges; scenery, Beowulf Boritt; costumes, Jennifer Caprio; lighting, Natasha Katz; sound, Dan Moses Schreier; wigs and hair, Marty Kopulsky;

orchestrations, Michael Starobin; vocal arrangements, Mr. Dean; music direction, Mr. Feichtner; casting, Tara Rubin; production stage manager, Andrea "Spook" Testani; stage manager, Kelly Hance; press, Richard Kornberg and Associates, Richard Kornberg, Tom D'Ambrosio.

Presented without intermission.

A young group of social misfits sing and spell their ways through a contest. This production transferred to Broadway's Circle in the Square Theatre (5/2/2005; 33 performances as of 5/31/2005). See Plays Produced on Broadway section of this volume for details. A 2002 version produced by The Farm, an improvisational theater group, went by the title *C-R-E-P-U-S-C-U-L-E*. Under the current title, the first presentation of record was given at Barrington Stage Company, Sheffield, Massachusetts (7/7/2004). See the Directory of New United States Productions section of this volume for details.

New York City Center Encores! presentation of **A Tree Grows in Brooklyn** (5). Concert version of the musical with book by George Abbott and Betty Smith; music by Arthur Schwartz; lyrics by Dorothy Fields; adapted by David Ives; based on the novel by Ms. Smith. Jack Viertel artistic director, Rob Fisher music director, at City Center. Opened February 10, 2005. (Closed February 13, 2005)

Johnny Nolan	Jason Danieley	Petey	Jeffrey Schecter
Katie	Sally Murphy	Swanswine	Jeff Brooks
Cissy	Emily Skinner	Aloysius	James Clow
Harry	John Ellison Conlee	Mae	Beth McVey
Hildy	Nancy Anderson	Della	Jennifer Hope Wills
Willie	Mark Ledbetter	Francie Nolan	Katherine Faye Barry
Allie	Sean Palmer		

Ensemble: Sean Attebury, Heather Ayers, Jordan Cable, Caitlin Carter, Carson Church, Joseph Dellger, Susan Derry, Sarah Jane Everman, Thom Graham, William B. Hubert II, Lorin Latarro, Jess Le Protto, Krisha Marcano, Julianna Rose Mauriello, Karyn Overstreet, Larry Raiken, Gordon Stanley, John Wilkerson, Laurie Williamson, Tony Yazbeck.

Directed by Gary Griffin; choreography, Sergio Trujillo; scenery, John Lee Beatty; costumes, Carrie Robbins; lighting, Ken Billington; sound, Tom Morse; orchestrations, Joe Glover and Robert Russell Bennett; music direction, Mr. Fisher; music coordination, Seymour Red Press; production stage manager, Rachel S. McCutchen.

Presented in two parts.

Musical adaptation that centers on a troubled marriage, its effect on a couple's young daughter, and a rogue aunt who calls all of her boyfriends "Harry." First presentation of record was given at the Alvin Theatre (4/19–12/8/1951; 267 performances).

Musical numbers included: "Growing Pains," "He Had Refinement," "I'll Buy You a Star," "I'm Like a New Broom," "Is That My Prince?," "Look Who's Dancing," "Love Is the Reason," "Make the Man Love Me," "Mine 'til Monday," "That's How It Goes."

Classic Stage Company presentation of the **Worth Street Theater Company** production of **Happy Days** (16). Revival of the play by Samuel Beckett. Brian Kulick artistic director, Jessica R. Jenen executive director, in association with Carol R. Fineman, Vern T. Calhoun and Jeff Cohen, at the East 13th Street Theatre. Opened February 15, 2005. (Closed February 27, 2005)

Winnie	Lea DeLaria	Willie	David Greenspan

Directed by Mr. Cohen; scenery, David P. Gordon; costumes, Kim Gill; lighting, Scott Bolman; sound, Jill BC DuBoff; production stage manager, Michal V. Mendelson; press, Ms. Fineman.

Presented in two parts.

A woman buried in the earth to her waist carries on, with the dirt rising, because she cannot do otherwise. First presentation of record was given at the Cherry Lane Theatre in a production directed by Alan Schneider (9/17/1961). Walter Kerr famously began his review in *The New York Herald Tribune*, "Well, happy days are gone again" (9/18/1961).

We're Still Hot! (96). Musical with book and lyrics by JJ McColl; music by Ms. McColl and Rueben Gurr. Produced by Entertainment Events Inc. and Waxman Williams Entertainment with Robert Dragotta, in association with Scott Prisand, Marcia Roberts, Danny Seraphine at the Theater at St. Luke's. Opened February 15, 2005. (Closed May 8, 2005)

Kate	Deborah Jean Templin	Marnie	Deirdre Kingsbury
Cynthia	Marnee Hollis	Zsu Zsu	Jane Seaman

Directed by Sue Wolf; scenery, Takeshi Kata; costumes, Philip Heckman; lighting, Gregory Cohen; sound, Drew Levy; musical direction, Alan J. Plado; production stage manager, Aubrey Shavonn; press, David Gersten and Associates.

Presented in two parts.

Four women of a certain age tell stories and sing about midlife. First presentation of record was given at Vancouver's Firehall Arts Center under the title *Menopositive! The Musical* (4/1998).

*Picon Pie (118). Play with music by Rose Leiman Goldemberg. Produced by Merriewold Enterprises, Edmund Gaynes and Nancy Bianconi at the Lamb's Theatre. Opened February 17, 2005.

Molly Picon	June Gable	Jacob "Yonkel" Kalich	Stuart Zagnit

Musicians: Steven Sterner piano; Margot Leverett clarinet; Kenny Kosek violin.

Directed by Pamela Hall; scenery, Matthew Maraffi; costumes, Laura Frecon; lighting, Graham Kindred; musical arrangements, Carl Danielsen; music direction, Mr. Sterner; production stage manager, Gregory Fletcher; press, David Gersten and Associates.

Presented in two parts.

Celebration of the life and career of a star of the Yiddish theater and Broadway stage. First presentation of record was given in California at Santa Monica Playhouse (4/6–12/15/2002). The current production is a transfer from Off Off Broadway at the DR2 (7/15/2004). Barbara Minkus played the title role in the Santa Monica production and from the New York opening until Ms. Gable assumed the role (11/22/2004).

Brooklyn Academy of Music presentation **The End of the Moon** (12). Solo performance piece by Laurie Anderson. Alan H. Fishman chairman of the board, Karen Brooks Hopkins president, Joseph V. Melillo executive producer, at the BAM Harvey Theater. Opened February 22, 2005. (Closed March 6, 2005)

Performed by Ms. Anderson

Lighting, Jennifer Tipton; sound, Jody Elff; press, Sandy Sawotka, Fatima Kafele, Eva Chien, Tamara McCaw, Jennifer Lam.

Presented without intermission.

Exploration of Ms. Anderson's tenure as NASA's first artist-in-residence. First presentation of record was given at MASS MoCA, an arts institution in North Adams, Massachusetts (9/13–9/14/2004; 2 performances).

Shockheaded Peter (112). Revival of the musical with book by Julian Bleach, Anthony Cairns, Julian Crouch, Graeme Gilmour, Tamzin Griffin, Jo Pocock, Phelim McDermott, Michael Morris, Martyn Jacques, Adrian Huge, Adrian Stout; music and lyrics by Mr. Jacques; based on *Struwwelpeter* by Heinrich Hoffmann. Produced by Dan Markley, Alan J. Schuster, Pomegranate Arts, Shockheaded Media, Harriet Newman Leve, Sonny Everett, Michael Skipper, True Love Productions, Dede Harris/Morton Swinsky, at the Little Shubert Theatre. Opened February 22, 2005. (Closed May 29, 2005)

Performed by Messrs. Bleach, Cairns, Gilmour, Huge, Jacques, Stout, Ms. Griffin, Rebekah Wild.

Directed by Messrs. McDermott and Crouch; scenery, Messrs. Crouch and Gilmour; costumes, Kevin Pollard; lighting, Jon Linstrum; sound, Mic Pool and Ronald Higham; music direction, Mr.

Jacques; music supervision, Shawn Gough; associate producers, Ian Osbourne, Cheryl Wiesenfeld, Michael McCarthy, Alisa E. Regas; executive producers, Linda Brumbach, Michael Morris, Christine Gettins; production stage manager, Elizabeth Burgess; press, Richard Kornberg and Associates.

Presented without intermission.

Musical staging of the gruesome 19th century children's book. First presentation of record was given at the West Yorkshire Playhouse, Leeds, UK (3/27–4/18/1998). First presentation of record in this country was given at the Wexner Center for the Arts, Columbus, Ohio (9/22–9/26/1999). First New York presentation of record was given at the New Victory Theater (10/14–10/31/1999).

Irish Repertory Theatre production of **Endgame** (53). Revival of the play by Samuel Beckett. Charlotte Moore artistic director, Ciarán O'Reilly producing director, at the Irish Repertory Theatre. Opened February 24, 2005. (Closed April 10, 2005)

Hamm	Tony Roberts	Nagg	Alvin Epstein
Clov	Adam Heller	Nell	Kathryn Grody

Directed by Ms. Moore; scenery, Hugh Landwehr; costumes, Linda Fisher; lighting; Clifton Taylor; production stage manager, Pam Brusoski; stage manager, Andrea Sarubbi; press, Shirley Herz Associates.

Presented without intermission.

Human existence in a void without hope. First presentation of record was given in French under the title *Fin de partie* at the Royal Court Theatre sponsored by the English Stage Company (4/3/1957; 6 performances). First New York presentation of record was given Off Broadway at the Cherry Lane Theatre in a production directed by Alan Schneider with Mr. Epstein in the role of Clov (1/28–4/20/1958; 96 performances).

Roundabout Theatre Company production of **McReele** (77). By Stephen Belber. Todd Haimes artistic director, Ellen Richard managing director, Julia C. Levy executive

Guilty or not? Michael O'Keefe and Anthony Mackie in McReele. *Photo: Joan Marcus*

director, in the Laura Pels Theatre at the Harold and Miriam Steinberg Center for Theatre. Opened February 24, 2005. (Closed May 1, 2005)

Darius McReele .... Anthony Mackie	Jim Cragen;		
Rick Dayne .... Michael O'Keefe	Donald Smathers;		
Katya .... Jodi Long	Gerry Phillips .... Henry Strozier		
Opal .... Portia			

Understudies: Mr. Mackie—Avery Glymph; Messrs. O'Keefe, Strozier—Ken Marks; Ms. Long—Jolly Abraham; Ms. Portia—Bianca LaVerne Jones.

Directed by Doug Hughes; scenery, Neil Patel, costumes, Paul Tazewell; lighting, Michael R. Chybowski; sound and music, David Van Tieghem; casting, Mele Nagler; production stage manager, Jay Adler; stage manager, Carrie Meconis; press, Boneau/Bryan-Brown, Adrian Bryan-Brown, Joe Perrotta, Matt Polk, Jessica Johnson.

Time: Now. Place: Delaware. Presented in two parts.

A convicted man is exonerated and becomes a celebrated political candidate who may have a dark secret.

Playwrights Horizons production of **On the Mountain** (22). By Christopher Shinn. Tim Sanford artistic director, Leslie Marcus managing director, William Russo general manager, in the Mainstage Theater. Opened February 24, 2005. (Closed March 13, 2005)

Sarah .... Amy Ryan	Jaime .... Alison Pill
Carrick .... Ebon Moss-Bachrach	Phil .... James Lloyd Reynolds

Directed by Jo Bonney; scenery, Neil Patel; costumes, Mimi O'Donnell; lighting, David Weiner; sound and music, John Gromada; casting, James Calleri and Alaine Alldaffer; production stage manager, Judith Schoenfeld; press, The Publicity Office, Bob Fennell, Marc Thibodeau, Michael S. Borowski.

Time: Summer 2003. Place: Portland, Oregon. Presented without intermission.

A dead rock star's long-lost song brings together a woman, her rebellious teenage daughter and a young man who may have ulterior motives. First presentation of record was given at South Coast Repertory, Costa Mesa, California (1/8–1/23/2005).

The Public Theater presentation of **The Controversy of Valladolid** (17). By Jean-Claude Carrière; translated by Richard Nelson. George C. Wolfe producer, Mara Manus executive director, in the Newman Theater. Opened February 27, 2005. (Closed March 13, 2005)

Sepulveda .... Steven Skybell	Superior of Monastery .... Herb Foster
Bartolome de las Casas .... Gerry Bamman	The Colonist .... Ron Moreno
The Pope's Legate .... Josef Sommer	

Directed by David Jones; scenery, Klara Zieglerova; costumes, Ilona Somogyi; lighting, Mark McCullough; sound, Sten Severson; fight direction, B.H. Barry; casting, Jordan Thaler and Heidi Griffiths; production stage manager, James Latus; press, Arlene Kriv, Elizabeth Wehrle.

Presented without intermission.

A papal tribunal debates the colonial project as it works toward a determination regarding the humanity of native peoples. First presentation of record was given on French television under the title *La Controverse de Valladolid* (1992) before a theatrical production at Théâtre de l'Atelier, Paris (1/20/1999).

*Altar Boyz (105). Transfer of the Off Off Broadway musical with book by Kevin Del Aguila; music and lyrics by Gary Adler and Michael Patrick Walker; conceived by Marc Kessler and Ken Davenport. Produced by Mr. Davenport and Robyn Goodman, in association with Walt Grossman, Ruth Hendel, Sharon Karmazin, Matt Murphy, Mark Shacket, at Dodger Stages. Opened March 1, 2005.

Chasing legends: Ebon Moss-Bachrach and Amy Ryan in On the Mountain. *Photo: Joan Marcus*

Matthew	Scott Porter	Juan	Ryan Duncan
Mark	Tyler Maynard	Abraham	David Josefsberg
Luke	Andy Karl	Voice of G.O.D.	Shadoe Stevens

Understudies: Kevin Kern, Daniel Torres.

Orchestra: Lynne Shankel conductor, keyboard; Matt Gallagher keyboard; David Matos guitar; Clayton Craddock drums.

Directed by Stafford Arima; choreography, Christopher Gattelli; scenery, Anna Louizos; costumes, Gail Brassard; lighting, Natasha Katz; sound, Simon Matthews; hair, Josh Marquette; orchestrations, Doug Katsaros, Ms. Shankel; vocal arrangements, Mr. Adler, Mr. Walker; musical direction and dance music, Ms. Shankel; associate producer, Stephen Kocis; casting, David Caparelliotis; production stage manager, Pat Sosnow; press, David Gersten and Associates, David Gersten, David Pringle.

Presented without intermission.

A male group of singers, "boy band" in the vernacular, exploit the rising tide of American Christianity. First presentation of record was given during the New York Musical Theatre Festival at the 47th Street Theatre (9/16–9/26/2004).

MUSICAL NUMBERS

"We Are The Altar Boyz"
"Rhythm in Me"
"Church Rulez"
"The Calling"
"The Miracle Song"
"Everybody Fits"

"Something About You"
"Body, Mind and Soul"
"La Vida Eternal"
"Epiphany"
"Number 918"
Finale: "I Believe"

Atlantic Theater Company production of **Romance** (72). By David Mamet. Neil Pepe artistic director, Andrew D. Hamingson managing director, at the Atlantic Theater Company. Opened March 1, 2005. (Closed May 1, 2005)

The Prosecutor .... Bob Balaban	The Judge .... Larry Bryggman
The Defendant .... Steven Goldstein	The Bailiff .... Steven Hawley
The Defense	Bernard .... Keith Nobbs
Attorney .... Christopher Evan Welch	The Doctor .... Jim Frangione

Directed by Neil Pepe; scenery, Robert Brill; costumes, Sarah Edwards; lighting, James F. Ingalls; sound, Obadiah Eaves; fight direction, Rick Sordelet; casting, Bernard Telsey Casting; production stage manager, Matthew Silver; press, Boneau/Bryan-Brown, Chris Boneau, Susanne Tighe, Joe Perrotta.

Time: The present. Place: A courtroom. Presented in two parts.

An overmedicated jurist runs a courtroom stirred by anti-Semitic comments, accusations of fraud, revelations of closeted sexuality and the quest for global peace. A 2004–05 *Best Plays* choice (see essay by Robert Vorlicky in this volume).

The Public Theater presentation of the **Labyrinth Theater Company** production of **The Last Days of Judas Iscariot** (39). By Stephen Adly Guirgis. George C. Wolfe producer, Mara Manus executive director, in Martinson Hall. Opened March 2, 2005. (Closed April 3, 2005)

Satan .... Eric Bogosian	Sigmund Freud;
Henrietta Iscariot .... Maggie Burke	St. Thomas; Soldier 1 .... Adrian Martinez
Fabiana Aziza	Pontius Pilate;
Cunningham .... Elizabeth Canavan	Uncle Pino ... Stephen McKinley Henderson
Gloria; Mother Teresa .... Liza Colón-Zayas	Matthias of Galilee;
Judge;	St. Peter; Soldier 2 .... Craig "Mums" Grant
Caiaphas the Elder;	Jesus of Nazareth .... John Ortiz
St. Matthew .... Jeffrey DeMunn	Judas Iscariot .... Sam Rockwell
Loretta;	Saint Monica;
Mary Magdalene;	Soldier 3 .... Elizabeth Rodriguez
Sister Glenna .... Yetta Gottesman	Butch Honeywell .... Kohl Sudduth
Bailiff;	Yusef El-Fayoumy .... Yul Vázquez
Simon the Zealot;	
Ensemble .... Salvatore Inzerillo	

Directed by Philip Seymour Hoffman; scenery, Andromache Chalfant; costumes, Mimi O'Donnell; lighting, Japhy Weideman; sound, Darron L. West; fight direction, Rick Sordelet; casting, Jordan Thaler and Heidi Griffiths; production stage manager, Monica Moore; press, Arlene Kriv, Elizabeth Wehrle.

Presented in two parts.

Courtroom drama weighs the guilt of Judas and argues for justice leavened with mercy. Part of a series of collaborations between the Public Theater and the Labyrinth Theater Company (Philip Seymour Hoffman, John Ortiz artistic directors).

*Woman Before a Glass (94). Solo performance piece by Lanie Robertson. Produced by Susan Quint Gallin, Mary Lu Roffe, Debra Black, Maria Cozzi and Morton Swinsky, at the Promenade Theatre. Opened March 10, 2005.

Peggy Guggenheim .... Mercedes Ruehl

Understudy: Patricia Hodges.

Directed by Casey Childs; scenery, Thomas Lynch; costumes, Willa Kim; lighting, Phil Monat; sound, David Van Tieghem; associate producer, Judith Katz; production stage manager, Renee Lutz; press, Barlow-Hartman Public Relations, John Barlow, Carol R. Fineman, Leslie Baden.

Presented without intermission.

Wealthy American tastemaker tells tales of her escapades in and out of the boudoir. Commissioned by Primary Stages (Casey Childs executive producer, Andrew Leynse artistic

In justice: Steven Goldstein, Christopher Evan Welch, Steven Hawley, Larry Bryggman, Keith Nobbs, Jim Frangione and Bob Balaban in Romance. *Photo: Gerry Goodstein*

director). First presentation of record was given as a staged reading at the John Drew Theater in East Hampton, New York (6/12/2004).

*Orson's Shadow (90). By Austin Pendleton; conceived by Judith Auberjonois. Produced by Planetearth Partners and Scott Morfee at the Barrow Street Theatre. Opened March 13, 2005.

Ken	Tracy Letts	Larry	John Judd
Sean	Ian Westerfer	Joan	Susan Bennett
Orson	Jeff Still	Vivien	Lee Roy Rogers

Directed by David Cromer; scenery, Takeshi Kata; costumes, Theresa Squire; lighting, Tyler Micoleau; sound, Jonah Lawrence; production stage manager, Richard A. Hodge; press, The Karpel Group, Bridget Klapinski, Billy Zavelson.

Time: February–April 1960. Place: Gaiety Theatre, Dublin; Royal Court Theare, London. Presented in two parts.

Orson Welles and Laurence Olivier collaborate on a London production of Eugene Ionesco's *Rhinoceros*, at the suggestion of critic Kenneth Tynan, with Olivier's present and future wives—Vivien Leigh and Joan Plowright—adding to the drama. First presentation of record was given at the Garage Theatre by Steppenwolf Theatre Company in Chicago (1/16–3/6/2000).

Brooklyn Academy of Music presentation of **Play Without Words** (21). By Matthew Bourne; music by Terry Davies; based on *The Servant* by Robin Maugham; inspired by the 1963 film by Joseph Losey; by special arrangement with Studio Canal. Alan H. Fishman chairman of the board, Karen Brooks Hopkins president, Joseph V. Melillo executive producer, in association with Center Theatre Group, at the BAM Harvey Theater. Opened March 15, 2005. (Closed April 3, 2005)

Anthony .... Sam Archer, Ewan Wardrop,
                                    Richard Winsor
Glenda .... Michela Meazza, Anjali Mehra,
                                    Emily Piercy
Prentice .... Scott Ambler, Steve Kirkham,
                                    Eddie Nixon

Sheila .... Maxine Fone,
                                    Valentina Formenti
Speight .... Eddie Nixon,
                                    Alan Vincent,
                                    Ewan Wardrop

Musicians: Bill Ellison, Todd Groves, Craig Johnson, Gregory Landes.

Directed and choreographed by Mr. Bourne; scenery and costumes, Lez Brotherston; lighting, Paule Constable; sound, Christopher Shutt; music direction, Michael Haslam; production stage manager, Dougie Wilson; press, Sandy Sawotka, Fatima Kafele, Eva Chien, Tamara McCaw, Jennifer Lam.

Presented in two parts.

Decline and decadence in 1960s London as told through Mr. Bourne's unique form of dance-theater. First presentation of record was given at London's National Theatre (8/20–9/14/2002).

Lincoln Center Theater production of **Dessa Rose** (80). Musical with book and lyrics by Lynn Ahrens; music by Stephen Flaherty: based on the novel by Sherley Ann Williams. André Bishop artistic director, Bernard Gersten executive producer, at the Mitzi E. Newhouse Theater. Opened March 21, 2005. (Closed May 29, 2005)

Dessa Rose .... LaChanze
Ruth .... Rachel York
Rose; others .... Tina Fabrique
Ruth's mother;
    others .... Rebecca Eichenberger
Dorcas; others .... Kecia Lewis
Kaine; others .... Eric Jordan Young

Sheriff Hughes; others .... David Hess
Adam Nehemiah .... Michael Hayden
Robert Steele; others .... William Parry
Nathan .... Norm Lewis
Harker; others .... James Stovall
Field Hand; others .... Soara-Joye Ross

Directed and choreographed by Graciela Daniele; scenery, Loy Arcenas; costumes, Toni-Leslie James; lighting, Jules Fisher and Peggy Eisenhauer; sound, Scott Lehrer; orchestrations, William David Brohn, Christopher Jahnke; vocal arrangements, Mr. Flaherty; music direction, David Holcenberg; casting, Cindy Tolan; production stage manager, Arturo E. Porazzi; press, Philip Rinaldi Publicity, Barbara Carroll.

Presented in two parts.

Musical concerning two women who struggle with issues surrounding slavery in the antebellum South.

New York Theatre Workshop production of **Eyewitness Blues** (24). By Mildred Ruiz and Steven Sapp; music by Antoine Drye, Carlos Pimentel and Paul Jonathan Thompson. James C. Nicola artistic director, Lynn Moffat managing director, at the New York Theatre Workshop. Opened March 21, 2005. (Closed April 10, 2005)

Muse .... Ms. Ruiz
Junior .... Mr. Sapp

Directed by Talvin Wilks; choreography, Jaime Coronado and Adesola Osakalumi; scenery, Narelle Sissons; costumes, Emilio Sosa; lighting, Heather Carson; sound, Darron L. West and Bray Poor; production stage manager, Antonia Gianino; press, Richard Kornberg and Associates, Richard Kornberg, Don Summa.

Presented without intermission.

Story of a musician's life told in vignettes, music and poetry. First presentation of record was given at Dance Theatre Workshop (2/14/2003).

The Public Theater production of **This Is How It Goes** (33) By Neil LaBute. George C. Wolfe producer; Mara Manus executive director, in the Anspacher Theater. Opened March 27, 2005. (Closed April 24, 2005)

Belinda .... Amanda Peet
Man .... Ben Stiller

Cody .... Jeffrey Wright

Directed by Mr. Wolfe; scenery, Riccardo Hernández; costumes, Sandra Hernandez; lighting, David Weiner; sound, Fitz Patton; fight direction, Luis Perez; projections, Batwin and Robin Productions; associate producers, Peter DuBois and Steven Tabakin; casting, Jordan Thaler and Heidi Griffiths; production stage manager, Rick Steiger; press, Arlene Kriv, Elizabeth Wehrle.

Presented without intermission.

An interracial love triangle traces the contours of American attitudes toward race.

Manhattan Theatre Club production of **Moonlight and Magnolias** (48). By Ron Hutchinson. Lynne Meadow artistic director, Barry Grove executive producer, at City Center Stage I. Opened March 29, 2005. (Closed May 8, 2005)

Ben Hecht	Matthew Arkin	David O. Selznick	Douglas Sills
Victor Fleming	David Rasche	Miss Poppenghul	Margo Skinner

Directed by Ms. Meadow; scenery, Santo Loquasto; costumes, Jane Greenwood; lighting, Rui Rita; sound, Obadiah Eaves; fight direction, Rick Sordelet; casting, Nancy Piccione and David Caparelliotis; production stage manager, Diane DiVita; press, Boneau/Bryan-Brown, Chris Boneau, Jim Byk, Aaron Meier.

Presented in two parts.

Movie mogul obsessed with making *Gone With the Wind* keeps a director and writer in his office until the three of them produce a workable script. First presentation of record was given at Chicago's Goodman Theatre (5/25–6/20/2004).

New York City Center Encores! presentation of **Purlie** (5). Concert version of the musical with book by Ossie Davis, Philip Rose and Peter Udell; music by Gary Geld; lyrics by Mr. Udell; adapted by David Ives; based on *Purlie Victorious* by Mr. Davis. Jack Viertel artistic director, Rob Fisher music director, at City Center. Opened March 31, 2005. (Closed April 3, 2005)

Purlie Victorious Judson	Blair Underwood	Gitlow Judson	Doug E. Doug
Church Soloist	Carol Dennis	Charlie Cotchipee	Christopher Duva
Lutiebelle Gussie		Idella Landy	Lynda Gravátt
Mae Jenkins	Anika Noni Rose	Ol' Cap'n Cotchipee	John Cullum
Missy Judson	Lillias White		

Ensemble: Christine Clemmons, Mamie Duncan-Gibbs, Duane Martin Foster, Danielle Lee Greaves, James Harkness, Derric Harris, Kathleen Murphy Jackson, Trent Armand Kendall, Monroe Kent III, C. Mingo Long, Krisha Marcano, Christopher L. Morgan, Darrell Grand Moultrie, April Nixon, Monica Patton, Stacey Sargeant, Carolyn Saxon, Levensky Smith, Cornelius White, Lisa Nicole Wilkerson, Kenny Redell Williams, Laurie Williamson.

Directed by Sheldon Epps; choreography, Ken Roberson; scenery, John Lee Beatty; costumes, Paul Tazewell; lighting, Ken Billington; sound, Scott Lehrer; orchestrations, Garry Sherman and Luther Henderson; music direction, Linda Twine; music coordination, Seymour Red Press; production stage manager, Tripp Phillips; press, Barlow-Hartman Public Relations, John Barlow, Rick Miramontez, Jon Dimond.

Presented in two parts.

A "new-fangled preacher man" comes to town aiming to right the wrongs of the Old South in this musical version of Mr. Davis's comic play. This Encores! concert was dedicated to the memory of Mr. Davis, who died February 4, 2005, at the age of 87. His play, *Purlie Victorious*, on which the musical is based, was first presented at the Cort Theatre (9/28/1961–5/12/1962; 261 performances). The cast included Mr. Davis, Ruby Dee, Helen Martin, Alan Alda and Godfrey M. Cambridge. After nearly two months at the Cort, it transferred to the Longacre Theatre for the final six months of the run. First presentation of record of the musical version was given at the Broadway Theatre (3/15/1970–11/6/1971; 688 performances). During the run of that first production, the musical transferred to the Winter Garden Theatre and to the ANTA Playhouse. *Purlie* received 1970 Tony Awards for best musical, actor (Cleavon Little), featured actress (Melba Moore), choreography (Louis Johnson) and direction (Philip Rose). The musical's cast also included Linda Hopkins, Novella Nelson and Sherman Hemsley. A revival in 1972 at the Billy Rose Theatre,

Art v. politics: Jill Eikenberry and Dennis Boutsikaris in A Picasso. *Photo: Joan Marcus*

with Robert Guillaume in the title role, was withdrawn after 14 performances (12/27/1972–1/7/1973).

Musical number include: "Walk Him Up the Stairs," "New Fangled Preacher," "Skinnin' a Cat," "Purlie," "The Harder They Fall," Charlie's Songs," "Big Fish, Little Fish," "I Got Love," "Great White Father," "Skinnin' a Cat" (Reprise), "Down Home," "First Thing Monday Mornin'," "He Can Do It," "The Harder They Fall" (Reprise), "The World Is Comin' to a Start." "Walk Him Up the Stairs" (Reprise).

Manhattan Theatre Club production of **A Picasso** (48). By Jeffrey Hatcher. Lynne Meadow artistic director, Barry Grove executive producer, in association with the Theatre Guild, at City Center Stage II. Opened April 19, 2004. (Closed May 29, 2005)

Pablo Picasso .... Dennis Boutsikaris   Miss Fischer .... Jill Eikenberry

Understudies: Mr. Boutsikaris—Stephen Rowe; Ms. Eikenberry—Elizabeth Norment.

Directed by John Tillinger; scenery, Allen Moyer; costumes, Jane Greenwood; lighting, Duane Schuler; sound, Scott Killian; casting, Nancy Piccione and David Caparelliotis; production stage manager, Barclay Stiff; stage manager, David H. Lurie; press, Boneau/Bryan-Brown, Chris Boneau, Jim Byk, Aaron Meier, Erika Creagh.

Time: October 1941. Place: A vault in Paris. Presented without intermission.

An attractive Nazi art critic confronts Pablo Picasso over the political content of his work. First presentation of record was given by the Philadelphia Theatre Company in a reading directed by Mr. Tillinger (11/2/2002).

Second Stage Theatre production of **Privilege** (28). By Paul Weitz. Carole Rothman artistic director, Timothy J. McClimon executive director, at the Second Stage Theatre. Opened April 25, 2005. (Closed May 18, 2005)

Charlie	Conor Donovan	Ted	Bob Saget
Erla	Florencia Lozano	Porter	Harry Zittel
Anna	Carolyn McCormick		

Directed by Peter Askin; scenery Thomas Lynch; costumes, Jeff Mahshie; lighting, Jeff Croiter; sound and music, Lewis Flinn; casting, Tara Rubin Casting; production stage manager, Michael McGoff; stage manager, Gerald Cosgrove; press, Richard Kornberg and Associates, Richard Kornberg, Tom D'Ambrosio.

Presented in two parts.

The children of wealthy parents are displaced and emotionally dislocated when the father is convicted of committing white-collar crimes.

*Beast on the Moon (40). By Richard Kalinoski. Produced by David Grillo and Matt Salinger at Century Center for the Performing Arts. Opened April 27, 2005.

Gentleman	Louis Zorich	Seta	Lena Georgas
Aram	Omar Metwally	Vincent	Matthew Borish

Directed by Larry Moss; scenery, Neil Patel; costumes, Anita Yavich; lighting, David Lander; sound, Peter Fitzgerald; production stage manager, Fredric H. Orner; press, Keith Sherman and Associates, Brett Oberman.

Presented in two parts.

Survivors of the Armenian genocide settle in Milwaukee to begin life anew, but the husband's ways remain fixed in the Old World past. First presentation of record was given by Actors Theatre of Louisville at the Humana Festival of New American Plays (3/1–3/8/1995). The author was honored for this play in 1996 by the American Theatre Critics Association with the M. Elizabeth Osborn Award, which is presented to a emerging playwright.

*New York Theatre Workshop production of **Score** (25). Solo performance piece by Jocelyn Clarke, in association with the SITI Company; based on the writings of Leonard Bernstein. James C. Nicola artistic director, Lynn Moffat managing director, at the New York Theatre Workshop. Opened May 1, 2005.

Leonard Bernstein .... Tom Nelis

Directed by Anne Bogart; scenery, Neil Patel; costumes, James Schuette; lighting, Christopher Akerlind; sound, Darron L. West; production stage managers, Elizabeth Moreau, Elizabeth Kegley; press, Richard Kornberg and Associates, Richard Kornberg, Don Summa.

Presented without intermission.

The multifaceted genius of Leonard Bernstein. First presentation of record was given by Actors Theatre of Louisville at the Humana Festival of New American Plays (3/21–4/7/2002).

*York Theatre Company production of **Captain Louie** (25). Musical with book by Anthony Stein; music and lyrics by Stephen Schwartz; based on *The Trip* by Ezra Jack Keats. James Morgan producing artistic director, in association with Meridee Stein, Pam Koslow, Kurt Peterson, at the Theatre at St. Peter's. Opened May 8, 2005.

Ziggy	Brandon Michael Arrington	Roberta; Mouse	Kelsey Fatebene
Archie	Alexio Barboza	Amy; Broom	Sara Kapner
Louie	Jimmy Dieffenbach	Julio	Ronny Mercedes

Ensemble: Jodie Bentley, Sarah Stiles, Mark Whitten.

Musicians: Edward Barnes keyboards; Zachary Redler percussion.

Directed by Meridee Stein; choreography, Joshua Bergasse; scenery, Jeff Subik; costumes, Elizabeth Flauto; lighting, Annmarie Duggan; multimedia, Joshua White; music direction, Mr. Barnes; production stage manager, Samone B. Weissman; press, Jonathan Slaff and Associates.

Presented without intermission.

Family-oriented musical based on a 1978 picture book that celebrated an imaginative life. First presentation of record was given by New York's First All Children's Theatre with the same creative team (12/2–12/4/1983).

Parent trap: Natalia Zvereva and Dianne Wiest in Memory House. *Photo: Joan Marcus*

New York City Center Encores! presentation of **The Apple Tree** (5). Concert version of the musical with book, music and lyrics by Sheldon Harnick and Jerry Bock; based on stories by Mark Twain, Frank R. Stockton, Jules Feiffer; additional book material by Jerome Coopersmith. Jack Viertel artistic director, Rob Fisher music director, at City Center. Opened May 12, 2005. (Closed May 15, 2005)

Eve; Princess Barbara;
  Ella; Passionella .... Kristin Chenoweth
Adam; Captain Sanjar;
  Flip;
The Prince Charming .... Malcolm Gets

Snake; Balladeer;
  Narrator .... Michael Cerveris
King Arik; Mr. Fallible;
  Producer .... Daniel Marcus
Voice of God .... James Earl Jones

Ensemble: Tony Capone, Julie Craig, Nikki Renee Daniels, Emily Rabon Hall, Ian Knauer, Jessica Kostival, Darren Lee, Krisha Marcano, Cindy Marchionda, Michele Ragusa, Devin Richards, Andre Ward, Christopher Windom, Tony Yazbeck.

Directed by Gary Griffin; choreography, Andy Blankenbuehler; scenery, John Lee Beatty; costumes, Jess Goldstein; lighting, Ken Billington; sound, Scott Lehrer; orchestrations, Eddie Sauter; music direction, Mr. Fisher; concert adaptation, David Ives; music coordinator, Seymour Red Press; production stage manager, Peter Hanson; press, Barlow-Hartman Public Relations, John Barlow, Rick Miramontez, Jon Dimond.

Presented in two parts.

Three musical tales centered on love and temptation. First presentation of record was given at Broadway's Shubert Theatre (10/18/1966–11/25/1967; 463 performances). Barbara Harris received the 1967 Tony Award for best actress in a musical, her co-stars included Alan Alda and Larry Blyden.

Musical numbers include: "Here in Eden," "Eve," "The Apple Tree (Forbidden Fruit)," "It's a Fish," "Go to Sleep Whatever You Are," "What Makes Me Love Him," "I'll Tell You a Truth," "Make Way," "I've Got What You Want," "Tiger, Tiger," "Oh, to Be a Movie Star," "Gorgeous," "(Who, Who, Who, Who) Who Is She?," "Wealth," "You Are Not Real."

Playwrights Horizons production of **Memory House** (16). By Kathleen Tolan. Tim Sanford artistic director, Leslie Marcus managing director, William Russo general manager, in the Mainstage Theater. Opened May 17, 2005. (Closed May 29, 2005)

Maggie .... Dianne Wiest   Katia .... Natalia Zvereva
    Directed by David Esbjornson; scenery, Loy Arcenas; costumes, Elizabeth Hope Clancy; lighting, Jane Cox; sound, Jill BC DuBoff; casting, James Calleri and Alaine Alldaffer; production stage manager, James Latus; press, The Publicity Office, Bob Fennell, Marc Thibodeau, Michael S. Borowski.
    Time: New Year's Eve. Place: A Soho loft. Presented without intermission.
    A story of mother-daughter conflict in which the daughter is a Russian adoptee who nurses anger toward her adoptive mother. First presentation of record was given by Actors Theatre of Louisville at the Humana Festival of New American Plays (2/27–4/9/2005).

*Trolls (15). Musical with book and lyrics by Bill Dyer; music by Dick DeBenedictis. Produced by DBD Productions, in association with Edmund Gaynes and Pamela Hall, at Actors Playhouse. Opened May 19, 2005.

Terry .... Mark Baker   Boomie .... Dale Radunz
Blane .... Bram Heidinger   Michael .... James Van Treuren
Juan .... Albert Insinnia   Phillip .... Christian Whelan
Jo................................... Barry McNabb   Myrna .... Brynn Neal
    Directed by Pamela Hall; choreography, John Hoshko, scenery, Matthew Maraffi; costumes, Karl A. Ruckdeschel; lighting, Graham Kindred; music direction, Carl Danielsen.
    Time: 1998. Place: West Hollywood.
    There is life (and hope) after age 40 for gay men.

*New York Theatre Workshop production of **Songs From an Unmade Bed** (4). Solo musical performance piece with lyrics by Mark Campbell; music by Debra Barsha,

Teen scene: James McMenamin and Olivia Oguma in BFE. *Photo: T. Charles Erickson*

Mark Bennett, Peter Foley, Jenny Giering, Peter Golub, Jake Heggie, Stephen Hoffman, Lance Horne, Gihieh Lee, Steve Marzullo, Brendan Milburn, Chris Miller, Greg Pliska, Duncan Sheik, Kim D. Sherman, Jeffrey Stock, Joseph Thalken. James C. Nicola artistic director, Lynn Moffat managing director. Opened May 24, 2005.

Performed by Michael Winther.

Directed by David Schweizer; scenery, Neil Patel; costumes, David Zinn; lighting, Brian H. Scott; sound, Michael Creason; music direction, Kimberly Grigsby; production stage manager, Elizabeth Miller; press, Richard Kornberg and Associates, Don Summa.

Presented without intermission.

Gay love and loss in the big city.

*Playwrights Horizons production of **BFE** (1). By Julia Cho. Tim Sanford artistic director, Leslie Marcus managing director, William Russo general manager, in association with Long Wharf Theatre, in the Peter Jay Sharp Theater. Opened May 31, 2005.

Panny	Olivia Oguma	Hugo	James McMenamin
Lefty	James Saito	Nancy	Kel Martin
Isabel	Kate Rigg	Jack	Jeremy Hollingworth
Hae-Yoon	Sue Jean Kim	Man	Scott Hudson
Evvie	Karen Kandel		

Directed by Gordon Edelstein; scenery, Takeshi Kata; costumes, Jayde Chabot; lighting, Paul Whitaker; sound, Andre Pluess and Ben Sussman; production stage manager, Linda Marvel; press, The Publicity Office, Bob Fennell, Marc Thibodeau, Michael S. Borowski.

Presented without intermission.

An Asian-American teenage girl struggles with her developing identity in a nowhere town. First presentation of record was given in a reading at Seattle Repertory Theatre under the title *BFE (Bum Fuck Egypt)* (6/4/2003).

CAST REPLACEMENTS
AND TOURING COMPANIES

○ ○ ○ ○ ○

Compiled by Paul Hardt

THE FOLLOWING IS a list of the major cast replacements of record in productions that opened during the current and in previous seasons, and other New York shows that were on a first-class tour in 2004–05.

The name of each major role is listed in *italics* beneath the title of the play in the first column. In the second column directly opposite appears the name of the actor who created the role in the original New York production (whose opening date appears in *italics* at the top of the column). Indented immediately beneath the original actor's name are the names of subsequent New York replacements—with the date of replacement when available.

The third column gives information about first-class touring companies. When there is more than one roadshow company, #1, #2, etc., appear before the name of the performer who created the role in each company (and the city and date of each company's first performance appears in *italics* at the top of the column). Subsequent replacements are also listed beneath names in the same manner as the New York companies, with dates when available.

AIDA

New York 3/23/00
Closed 9/5/04

Aida
Heather Headley
　Maya Days 9/13/01
　Simone 1/29/02
　Saycon Sengbloh 6/16/03
　Toni Braxton 6/30/03
　Michelle Williams 11/18/03
　Deborah Cox 2/17/04

Radames
Adam Pascal
　Richard H. Blake 6/16/03
　Will Chase 6/30/03
　Adam Pascal 6/23/04

Amneris
Sherie René Scott
　Taylor Dayne
　Idina Menzel 9/13/01
　Felicia Finley 1/29/02

                              Mandy Gonzales 6/30/03
                              Lisa Brescia

Mereb   Damian Perkins
                              Delisco
                              Eric LaJuan Summers 2/17/04

Zoser   John Hickok
                              Donnie Kehr
                              Micky Dolenz 1/6/04

AVENUE Q

                              New York 7/31/03

Princeton; Rod   John Tartaglia
                              Barrett Foa 2/1/05

Brian   Jordan Gelber

Kate Monster; Lucy   Stephanie D'Abruzzo

Nicky; Trekkie   Rick Lyon

Christmas Eve   Ann Harada
                              Ann Sanders 10/26/04
                              Ann Harada 1/25/05

Gary Coleman   Natalie Venetia Belcon

BEAUTY AND THE BEAST

                              New York 4/18/94

Beast   Terrence Mann
                              Jeff McCarthy
                              Chuck Wagner
                              James Barbour
                              Steve Blanchard
                              Jeff McCarthy 2/17/04
                              Steve Blanchard 4/13/04

Belle   Susan Egan
                              Sarah Uriarte Berry
                              Christianne Tisdale
                              Kerry Butler
                              Deborah Gibson
                              Kim Huber
                              Toni Braxton
                              Andrea McArdle
                              Sarah Litzsinger
                              Jamie-Lynn Sigler
                              Sarah Litzsinger 2/11/03
                              Megan McGinnis 4/15/03
                              Christy Carlson Romano 2/17/04
                              Brooke Tansley 9/14/04

Lefou   Kenny Raskin
                              Harrison Beal
                              Jamie Torcellini
                              Jeffrey Schecter
                              Jay Brian Winnick 11/12/99
                              Gerard McIsaac

	Brad Aspel
	Steve Lavner
	Aldrin Gonzalez
Gaston	Burke Moses
	Marc Kudisch
	Steve Blanchard
	Patrick Ryan Sullivan
	Christopher Sieber
	Chris Hoch 12/10/02
	Grant Norman
Maurice	Tom Bosley
	MacIntyre Dixon
	Tom Bosley
	Kurt Knudson
	Timothy Jerome
	JB Adams 11/12/99
	Jamie Ross
Cogsworth	Heath Lamberts
	Peter Bartlett
	Robert Gibby Brand
	John Christopher Jones
	Jeff Brooks 11/12/99
Lumiere	Gary Beach
	Lee Roy Reams
	Patrick Quinn
	Gary Beach
	Meshach Taylor
	Patrick Page
	Paul Schoeffler
	Patrick Page
	Bryan Batt
	Rob Lorey 5/7/02
	David DeVries
	Peter Flynn
Babette	Stacey Logan
	Pamela Winslow
	Leslie Castay
	Pam Klinger
	Louisa Kendrick
	Pam Klinger
Mrs. Potts	Beth Fowler
	Cass Morgan
	Beth Fowler
	Barbara Marineau 11/12/99
	Beth Fowler
	Cass Morgan
	Alma Cuervo 2/17/04

BUG

New York 2/29/04
Closed 1/30/05

Agnes	Shannon Cochran
	Kate Buddeke 8/31/04
Peter	Michael Shannon

	Paul Sparks 6/03/04 Jonno Roberts
RC	Amy Landecker Dee Pelletier 4/27/04 Helen Coxe
Goss	Michael Cullen
Dr. Sweet	Reed Birney Allyn Burrows 4/24/04 Michael Canavan 6/08/04 Troy West 8/31/04

CHICAGO

	New York 11/14/96	*Washington, DC 6/10/03*
Roxie Hart	Ann Reinking Marilu Henner Karen Ziemba Belle Calaway Charlotte d'Amboise Sandy Duncan 8/12/99 Belle Calaway 1/18/00 Charlotte d'Amboise 3/24/00 Belle Calaway Nana Visitor Petra Nielsen 10/8/01 Nana Visitor 11/19/01 Belle Calaway 1/13/02 Denise Van Outen 3/18/02 Belle Calaway 4/22/02 Amy Spanger 8/6/02 Belle Calaway Tracy Shayne 4/15/03 Melanie Griffith 7/11/03 Charlotte d'Amboise 10/7/03 Bianca Marroquin 12/15/03 Gretchen Mol 1/5/04 Charlotte d'Amboise 3/1/04 Tracy Shayne Charlotte d'Amboise	Bianca Marroquin Paige Davis Bianca Marroquin
Velma Kelly	Bebe Neuwirth Nancy Hess Ute Lemper Bebe Neuwirth Ruthie Henshall 5/25/99 Mamie Duncan-Gibbs 10/26/99 Bebe Neuwirth 1/18/00 Donna Marie Asbury 3/23/00 Sharon Lawrence 4/11/00 Vicki Lewis Jasmine Guy Bebe Neuwirth Donna Marie Asbury Deidre Goodwin Vicki Lewis Deidre Goodwin 6/29/01	Brenda Braxton Reva Rice 12/30/03 Terra C. MacLeod

Anna Montanaro 7/9/01
Deidre Goodwin 9/14/01
Donna Marie Asbury
Roxane Carrasco 1/13/02
Deidre Goodwin 3/18/02
Stephanie Pope
Roxane Carrasco
Caroline O'Connor 11/8/02
Brenda Braxton 3/3/03
Deidre Goodwin 6/24/03
Reva Rice 10/7/03
Brenda Braxton 1/1/04
Pia Dowes 4/8/04
Brenda Braxton 5/16/04
Terra C. MacLeod 7/27/04
Donna Marie Asbury 2/14/05
Brenda Braxton 2/21/05

Billy Flynn

James Naughton
Gregory Jbara
Hinton Battle
Alan Thicke
Michael Berresse
Brent Barrett
Robert Urich 1/11/00
Clarke Peters 2/1/00
Brent Barrett 2/15/00
Chuck Cooper
Brent Barrett 7/2/01
Chuck Cooper 8/27/01
George Hamilton 11/12/01
Eric Jordan Young 1/18/02
Ron Raines 3/26/02
George Hamilton 5/21/02
Michael C. Hall 8/8/02
Destan Owens
Taye Diggs
Billy Zane 11/8/02
Kevin Richardson 1/20/03
Clarke Peters
Gregory Harrison
Brent Barrett 6/2/03
Patrick Swayze 12/15/03
James Naughton 01/05/04
Norm Lewis 2/2/04
Christopher Sieber 3/23/04
Tom Wopat 5/16/04
Christopher Seiber 6/17/04
Marti Pellow 8/3/04
Wayne Brady 9/7/04
Tom Wopat 12/7/04
Brent Barrett 1/4/05

Gregory Harrison
Patrick Swayze 12/30/03
Tom Wopat 1/27/04
Gregory Harrison

Amos Hart

Joel Grey
Ernie Sabella
Tom McGowan
P.J. Benjamin
Ernie Sabella 11/23/99
P.J. Benjamin

Ray Bokhour
P.J. Benjamin
Kevin Carolyn

	Tom McGowan	
	P.J. Benjamin	
	Ray Bokhour 7/30/01	
	P.J. Benjamin 8/13/01	
	Rob Bartlett	
	P.J. Benjamin 3/3/03	
	Ray Bokhour	

Matron	Marcia Lewis	Roz Ryan
	Roz Ryan	Marcia Lewis 8/4/03
	Marcia Lewis	Carol Woods 9/23/03
	Roz Ryan	Roz Ryan
	Marcia Lewis	Carol Woods
	Roz Ryan	Patti LaBelle
	Marcia Lewis	Carol Woods
	Jennifer Holliday 6/18/01	
	Marcia Lewis 8/27/01	
	Roz Ryan 11/16/01	
	Michele Pawk 1/14/02	
	Alix Korey 3/4/02	
	B.J. Crosby 3/3/03	
	Angie Stone 4/15/03	
	Camille Saviola 6/10/03	
	Debbie Gravitte 12/15/03	
	Roz Ryan 3/15/04	
	Carol Woods	
	Roz Ryan	
	Anne L. Nathan 9/13/04	
	Carol Woods 1/31/05	
	Anne L. Nathan 2/21/05	
	Mary Testa	

Mary Sunshine	D. Sabella	R. Bean
	J. Loeffelholz	
	R. Bean	
	A. Saunders	
	J. Maldonado	
	R. Bean	
	A. Saunders 1/2/02	
	R. Bean 1/14/02	
	M. Agnes	
	D. Sabella 3/24/03	
	D. Sabella 3/24/03	
	R. Bean 5/17/04	
	R. Lowe	

FAT PIG

New York 12/15/04
Closed 2/26/05

Helen	Ashlie Atkinson
Tom	Jeremy Piven
	Steven Pasquale 1/5/05
Jeannie	Keri Russell
	Jessica Capshaw 1/17/05
Carter	Andrew McCarthy

FIDDLER ON THE ROOF

New York 2/26/04

Tevye	Alfred Molina
	Harvey Fierstein 1/4/05
Golde	Randy Graff
	Andrea Martin 1/4/05
Yente	Nancy Opel
Tzeitel	Sally Murphy
Hodel	Laura Michelle Kelly
	Laura Shoop 6/11/04
Chava	Tricia Paoluccio
Motel	John Cariani
	Peter Matthew Smith 3/15/05
	Michael Therriault
Perchik	Robert Petkoff
	Paul Anthony Stewart 2/15/05
Fyedka	David Ayers
	Patrick Heusinger 1/4/05

42ND STREET

	New York 5/2/01 *Closed 1/2/05*	*Kansas City 8/4/02*
Peggy Sawyer	Kate Levering Meredith Patterson Kate Levering 8/30/02 Nadine Isenegger	Catherine Wreford Shannon O'Bryan
Julian Marsh	Michael Cumpsty Michael Dantuono Tom Wopat 7/21/02 Patrick Ryan Sullivan Patrick Cassidy 5/7/04	Patrick Ryan Sullivan Darren Kelly
Billy Lawler	David Elder	Robert Spring
Dorothy Brock	Christine Ebersole Beth Leavel 6/9/02 Shirley Jones 5/7/04 Blair Ross 8/10/04	Blair Ross Marcy McGuigan

HAIRSPRAY

	New York 8/15/02	*Baltimore 9/17/03*
Tracy Turnblad	Marissa Jaret Winokur Kathy Brier 8/12/03 Carly Jibson 5/4/04	Carly Jibson Keala Settle 4/13/04
Edna Turnblad	Harvey Fierstein Michael McKean 5/4/04 Bruce Vilanch	Bruce Vilanch John Pinette
Wilbur Turnblad	Dick Latessa Peter Scolari Todd Susman	Todd Susman Stephen DeRosa

Amber Von Tussle	Laura Bell Bundy Tracy Jai Edwards 7/14/03 Jordan Ballard	Jordan Ballard Worth Williams
Velma Von Tussle	Linda Hart Barbara Walsh 7/14/03	Susan Cella Susan Henley
Link Larkin	Matthew Morrison Richard H. Blake 1/13/04	Austin Miller Serge Kushnier
Motormouth Maybelle	Mary Bond Davis	Charlotte Crossley
Seaweed	Corey Reynolds Chester Gregory II 7/14/03	Terron Brooks Alan Mingo Jr.
Penny Pingleton	Kerry Butler Jennifer Gambatese 6/15/04 Brooke Tansley 4/11/04 Jennifer Gambatese 6/15/04 Tracy Miller	Sandra DeNise Chandra Lee Schwartz
Corny Collins	Clarke Thorell Jonathan Dokuchitz 1/13/04	Troy Britton Johnson Paul McQuillan
Little Inez	Danelle Eugenia Wilson Aja Maria Johnson 7/19/03 Nia Imani Soyemi	Kianna Underwood Kahliah Fatima Rivers

I LOVE YOU, YOU'RE PERFECT, NOW CHANGE

Man #1	Jordan Leeds Danny Burstein 10/01/96 Adam Grupper 8/22/97 Gary Imhoff 2/09/98 Adam Grupper 4/01/98 Jordan Leeds 3/17/99 Bob Walton 10/27/00 Jordan Leeds 1/30/01 Darrin Baker 1/29/02 Danny Burstein 4/12/02 Jordan Leeds 6/03/02
Man #2	Robert Roznowski Kevin Pariseau 5/25/98 Adam Hunter 4/20/01 Sean Arbuckle 9/23/02 Frank Baiocchi 2/17/03 Colin Stokes 10/10/03
Woman #1	Jennifer Simard Erin Leigh Peck 5/25/98 Kelly Anne Clark 1/10/00 Andrea Chamberlain 3/13/00 Lori Hammel 11/04/00 Andrea Chamberlain 1/29/01 Amanda Watkins 8/24/01 Karyn Quackenbush 1/02/02 Marissa Burgoyne 8/09/02 Andrea Chamberlain 12/17/02 Karyn Quackenbush 2/17/03 Sandy Rustin 6/13/03 Andrea Chamberlain 11/19/04

Woman #2	Melissa Weil
	Cheryl Stern 2/16/98
	Mylinda Hull 9/17/00
	Melissa Weil 2/09/01
	Evy O'Rourke 3/13/01
	Marylee Graffeo 6/11/01
	Cheryl Stern 1/18/02
	Marylee Graffeo 3/11/02
	Janet Metz 4/26/02
	Anne Bobby 12/17/02
	Janet Metz 3/03/03
	Anne Bobby 5/23/05

THE LION KING

	New York 11/13/97	*#1 Gazelle Company*
		#2 Cheetah Company
Rafiki	Tsidii Le Loka	#1 Futhi Mhlongo
	Thuli Dumakude 11/11/98	Phindile
	Sheila Gibbs	#2 Thandazile A. Soni
	Nomvula Dlamini	Gugwana Dlamini
	Tshidi Manye	
Mufasa	Samuel E. Wright	#1 Alton Fitzgerald White
	Alton Fitzgerald White	Thomas Corey Robinson
		#2 Rufus Bonds Jr.
Sarabi	Gina Breedlove	#1 Jean Michelle Grier
	Meena T. Jahi 8/4/98	Lashanda Reese-Fletcher
	Denise Marie Williams	#2 Marvette Williams
	Meena T. Jahi	
	Robyn Payne	
	Jean Michelle Grier	
Zazu	Geoff Hoyle	#1 Jeffrey Binder
	Bill Bowers 10/21/98	Mark Cameron Pow
	Robert Dorfman	#2 Derek Hasenstab
	Tony Freeman	
	Adam Stein	
	Jeffrey Binder	
Scar	John Vickery	#1 Patrick Page
	Tom Hewitt 10/21/98	Dan Donohue
	Derek Smith	#2 Larry Yando
	Patrick Page	
	Derek Smith	
Banzai	Stanley Wayne Mathis	#1 James Brown-Orleans
	Keith Bennett 9/30/98	#2 Melvin Abston
	Leonard Joseph	
	Curtiss I'Cook	
	Rodrick Covington	
	Benjamin Sterling Cannon	
Shenzi	Tracy Nicole Chapman	#1 Jacquelyn Renae Hodges
	Vanessa S. Jones	Kimberly Hebert Gregory
	Lana Gordon	#2 Shaullanda Lacombe
	Marlayna Sims	
	Bonita J. Hamilton	
Ed	Kevin Cahoon	#1 Wayne Pyle
	Jeff Skowron 10/21/98	#2 Brian Sills

	Jeff Gurner Timothy Gulan Thom Christopher Warren Enrique Segura	Robbie Swift

Timon	Max Casella
	Danny Rutigliano 6/16/98
	John E. Brady
	Danny Rutigliano
		#1 John Plumpis
		#2 Benjamin Clost
		    Adam Hunter
		    Damian Baldet

Pumbaa	Tom Alan Robbins	#1 Ben Lipitz #2 Bob Amaral Phil Fiorini

Simba	Jason Raize
	Christopher Jackson
	Josh Tower
		#1 Alan Mingo Jr.
		    S.J. Hannah
		#2 Brandon Victor Dixon
		    Brandon Louis
		    Wallace Smith

Nala	Heather Headley
	Mary Randle 7/7/98
	Heather Headley 12/8/98
	Bashirrah Creswell
	Sharon L. Young
	Rene Elise Goldsberry
	Kissy Simmons
		#1 Kissy Simmons
		    Lisa Nicole Wilkerson
		    Adrienne Muller
		#2 Adia Ginneh Dobbins
		    Ta'rea Campbell

LITTLE SHOP OF HORRORS

	New York *Closed 8/22/04*	*Los Angeles* *Opened 8/29/04*
Seymour	Hunter Foster Joey Falcone 6/22/04	Anthony Rapp Jonathan Rayson
Audrey	Kerry Butler Jessica-Snow Wilson 6/22/04	Tari Kelly
Mr. Mushnik	Rob Bartlett	Lenny Wolpe Ray De Mattis Lenny Wolpe
Orin, et al.	Douglas Sills Robert Evan 6/19/04	James Moye

MAMMA MIA!

	New York 10/18/01	*#1 US Tour* *#2 2nd Tour* *#3 Las Vegas*
Donna Sheridan	Louise Pitre Dee Hoty 10/22/03	#1 Dee Hoty #2 Monique Lund #3 Tina Walsh
Sophie Sheridan	Tina Maddigan Jenny Fellner 10/22/03	#1 Chilina Kennedy #2 Kristie Marsden #3 Jill Paice
Tanya	Karen Mason Jeanine Morick Tamara Bernier	#1 Cynthia Sophiea #2 Ellen Harvey #3 Karole Foreman
Rosie	Judy Kaye Harriett D. Foy	#1 Rosalyn Rahn Kerins #2 Robin Baxter

		#3 Jennifer Perry
Sky	Joe Machota	#1 P.J. Griffith
	Aaron Staton	#2 Chris Bolan
		#3 Victor Wallace
Sam Carmichael	David W. Keeley	#1 Gary Lynch
	John Hillner	#2 Don Noble
	David W. Keeley	#3 Nick Cokas
	John Hillner	
Harry Bright	Dean Nolen	#1 Michael DeVries
	Richard Binsley	#2 James Kall
	Michael Winther	#3 Michael Piontek
Bill Austin	Ken Marks	#1 Craig Bennett
	Adam LeFevre	#2 Pearce Bunting
		#3 Mark Leydorf

MODERN ORTHODOX

	New York 11/11/04
	Closed 5/8/05
Ben Jacobson	Craig Bierko
	J. Anthony Crane
	Hunter Foster 4/12/05
Hershel Klein	Jason Biggs
	John Cariani 3/15/05
Hannah Ziggelstein	Molly Ringwald
	Gretchen Egolf
	Sarah Chalke 4/12/05
Rachel Feinberger	Jenn Harris

MOVIN' OUT

	New York 10/24/02	*Detroit 1/26/04*
Brenda	Elizabeth Parkinson	Holly Cruikshank
	Nancy Lemenager 5/8/04	Laurie Kanyok
	Elizabeth Parkinson	
Eddie	John Selya	Ron Todorowski
		Brendan King
Tony	Keith Roberts	David Gomez
	Ian Carney	Corbin Popp
	Keith Roberts	
	Desmond Richardson	
James	Benjamin G. Bowman	Matthew Dibble
	Kurt Froman	
Judy	Ashley Tuttle	Julieta Gros
	Mabel Modrono	
Vocalist	Michael Cavanaugh	Matt Wilson
		Darren Holden

A NUMBER

	New York 11/26/04
	Closed 2/13/05
Salter	Sam Shepard
	Arliss Howard 1/18/05
Michael	Dallas Roberts

THE PHANTOM OF THE OPERA

	New York 13/26/88	*National Tour*
The Phantom	Michael Crawford	Franc D'Ambrosio
	Thomas James O'Leary	Brad Little
	Hugh Panaro 2/1/99	Ted Keegan
	Howard McGillin 8/23/99	Brad Little
	Brad Little	Ted Keegan
	Howard McGillin	Brad Little
	Hugh Panaro 4/14/03	Gary Mauer
	Howard McGillin 12/22/03	
	Hugh Panaro 1/5/04	
Christine Daaé	Sarah Brightman	Tracy Shane
	Sandra Joseph 1/29/98	Kimilee Bryant
	Adrienne McEwan 8/2/99	Amy Jo Arrington
	Sarah Pfisterer 1/17/00	Rebecca Pitcher
	Sandra Joseph 10/30/00	Kathy Voytko
	Sarah Pfisterer 8/6/01	Julie Hanson
	Elizabeth Southard 3/25/02	Rebecca Pitcher
	Lisa Vroman 4/22/02	Lisa Vroman
	Sandra Joseph 6/10/03	Rebecca Pitcher
Christine Daaé (alt.)	Patti Cohenour	Tamra Hayden
	Adrienne McEwan	Marie Danvers
	Sarah Pfisterer	Megan Starr-Levitt
	Adrienne McEwan	Marni Raab
	Lisa Vroman 10/30/00	Elizabeth Southard
	Adrienne McEwan 7/9/01	
	Julie Hanson 9/20/03	
Raoul	Steve Barton	Ciaran Sheehan
	Gary Mauer 4/19/99	Jason Pebworth 1/29/97
	Jim Weitzer 4/23/01	Jim Weitzer
	Michael Shawn Lewis 11/2/01	Jason Pebworth 7/22/98
	John Cudia 4/7/03	Richard Todd Adams 3/31/99
	Jim Weitzer 10/3/03	Jim Weitzer 1/12/00
	John Cudia 12/21/03	John Cudia
	Tim Martin Gleason 5/27/05	Tim Martin Gleason

THE PRODUCERS

	New York 4/19/01	*#1 Max Company*
		#2 Leo Company
Max Bialystock	Nathan Lane	#1 Lewis J. Stadlen
	Henry Goodman 3/19/02	Jason Alexander 4/21/03
	Brad Oscar 4/16/02	Lewis J. Stadlen 1/6/04
	Lewis J. Stadlen	#2 Bob Amaral
	Fred Applegate 10/7/03	
	Nathan Lane 12/31/03	
	Brad Oscar 4/6/04	
	Richard Kind 1/11/05	
Leo Bloom	Matthew Broderick	#1 Don Stephenson
	Steven Weber 3/19/02	Martin Short 4/21/03
	Roger Bart 12/17/02	Alan Ruck 1/6/04
	Don Stephenson 5/20/03	#2 Andy Taylor
	Matthew Broderick 12/31/03	
	Roger Bart 4/6/04	
	Hunter Foster 6/13/04	
	Alan Ruck 1/11/05	

Ulla	Cady Huffman Sarah Cornell 8/5/03 Angie L. Schworer 11/4/03	#1 Angie L. Schworer Charley Izabella King 1/6/04 #2 Ida Leigh Curtis

Roger De Bris	Gary Beach
	John Treacy Egan
	Gary Beach 10/7/03
	Jonathan Freeman 8/31/04
		#1 Lee Roy Reams
		   Gary Beach
		   Lee Roy Reams 1/6/04
		#2 Stuart Marland

Carmen Ghia	Roger Bart
	Sam Harris 7/2/02
	Brad Musgrove 12/17/02
	Brooks Ashmanskas 8/31/04
		#1 Jeff Hyslop
		   Michael Paternostro
		   Josh Prince
		   Harry Bouvy
		#2 Rich Affanato

Franz Liebkind	Brad Oscar John Treacy Egan Peter Samuel John Treacy Egan	#1 Bill Nolte Fred Applegate #2 Bill Nolte

RENT

New York 4/29/96

Roger Davis	Adam Pascal Norbert Leo Butz Richard H. Blake (alt.) Manley Pope 6/1/02 Sebastian Arcelus 12/30/02 Ryan Link 9/8/03 Jeremy Kushnier 11/14/03 Carey Shields 1/18/05
Mark Cohen	Anthony Rapp Jim Poulos Trey Ellett 5/15/00 Matt Caplan 6/1/02 Joey Fatone 8/5/02 Matt Caplan 12/23/02 Drew Lachey 9/10/04 Matt Caplan 3/14/04
Tom Collins	Jesse L. Martin Michael McElroy Rufus Bonds Jr. 9/7/99 Alan Mingo Jr. 4/10/00 Mark Leroy Jackson 1/15/01 Mark Richard Ford 2/3/02 Destan Owens 8/16/04 Mark Richard Ford 12/20/04
Benjamin Coffin III	Taye Diggs Jacques C. Smith Stu James 3/13/00 D'Monroe Stu James 11/29/04 D'Monroe
Joanne Jefferson	Fredi Walker Gwen Stewart Alia León Kenna J. Ramsey Danielle Lee Greaves 10/4/99

Natalie Venetia Belcon 10/2/00
Myiia Watson-Davis 6/1/02
Merle Dandridge 10/28/02
Kenna J. Ramsey 3/03/03
Merle Dandridge

Angel Schunard   Wilson Jermaine Heredia
Wilson Cruz
Shaun Earl
Jose Llana
Jai Rodriguez
Andy Señor 1/31/00
Jai Rodriguez 3/10/02
Andy Señor 2/17/03
Jai Rodriguez 7/05/04
Andy Señor 7/19/04
Jai Rodriguez 8/2/04
Justin Johnson 8/16/04
Andy Señor 3/15/04

Mimi Marquez   Daphne Rubin-Vega
Marcy Harriell 4/5/97
Krysten Cummings
Maya Days
Loraine Velez 2/28/00
Karmine Alers 6/1/02
Krystal L. Washington 5/15/03
Melanie Brown 4/19/04
Krystal L. Washington 8/23/04

Maureen Johnson   Idina Menzel
Sherie René Scott
Kristen Lee Kelly
Tamara Podemski
Cristina Fadale 10/4/99
Maggie Benjamin 6/1/02
Cristina Fadale 10/28/02
Maggie Benjamin
Melanie Brown
Maggie Benjamin 4/19/04
Kelly Karbacz 7/19/04
Maggie Benjamin

SLY FOX

New York
Closed 8/29/04

Foxwell Sly   Richard Dreyfuss
Richard Kind 8/17/04

Able   Eric Stoltz
Bronson Pinchot 8/17/04

Mrs. Truckle   Elizabeth Berkley
Rachel York 8/17/04

Mr. Truckle   Bob Dishy

Miss Fancy   Rachel York
Carol Kane 8/17/04

Jethro Crouch   René Auberjonois
Richard Libertini

| *Police Chief* | Peter Scolari |
| | Larry Storch 8/03/04 |

THOROUGHLY MODERN MILLIE

	New York 4/18/02	*Kansas City 6/15/03*
	Closed 6/20/04	*Closed 5/8/05*
Millie	Sutton Foster	Darcie Roberts
	Susan Egan 2/16/04	Laura Schutter
Jimmy	Gavin Creel	Matt Cavenaugh
	Christian Borle 4/29/03	Joey Sorge 1/12/04
		Brian McElroy
Mrs. Meers	Harriet Harris	Hollis Resnik
	Delta Burke 2/26/03	Pamela Hamill
	Terry Burrell 2/16/04	
	Dixie Carter 2/23/04	
Trevor Grayson	Marc Kudisch	Sean Krill
	Christopher Sieber 1/28/03	John Ganun
	Kevin Earley 4/29/03	
Muzzy	Sheryl Lee Ralph	Pamela Isaacs
	Leslie Uggams 4/22/03	Stephanie Pope
Dorothy Brown	Angela Christian	Diana Kaarina
	Emily Rozek 6/11/04	Anne Warren
	Jessica Grové 6/15/04	
Miss Flannery	Anne L. Nathan	Janelle A. Robinson
	Liz McCartney 3/1/04	Robyn Payne

TWELVE ANGRY MEN

	New York 10/1/04
	Closed 4/03/05
Juror #1	Mark Blum
Juror #2	Kevin Geer
Juror #3	Philip Bosco
	Robert Foxworth 2/1/05
Juror #4	James Rebhorn
Juror #5	Michael Mastro
Juror #6	Robert Clohessy
Juror #7	John Pankow
Juror #8	Boyd Gaines
Juror #9	Tom Aldredge
Juror #10	Peter Friedman
Juror #11	Larry Bryggman
	Byron Jennings 2/1/05
Juror #12	Adam Trese
Guard	Matte Osian

WICKED

	New York 10/30/03
Glinda	Kristin Chenoweth
	Jennifer Laura Thompson 7/20/04
	Megan Hilty 5/31/05

Elphaba	Idina Menzel
	Eden Espinosa 6/15/04
	Idina Menzel 7/6/04
	Shoshana Bean 1/11/05
Wizard of Oz	Joel Grey
	George Hearn 7/20/04
Madame Morrible	Carole Shelley
	Rue McClanahan 5/31/05
Fiyero	Norbert Leo Butz 12/21/04
	Taye Diggs 1/18/05
	Norbert Leo Butz 1/20/05
	Joey McIntyre 7/20/04
	David Ayers 1/11/05
Boq	Christopher Fitzgerald
	Randy Harrison 6/22/04
	Christopher Fitzgerald 7/27/04
	Robb Sapp 1/4/05
	Jeffrey Kuhn 1/11/05
Dr. Dillamond	William Youmans

WONDERFUL TOWN

New York 11/23/03
Closed 1/30/05

Ruth Sherwood	Donna Murphy
	Linda Mugleston 7/26/04
	Brooke Shields 9/28/04
Eileen Sherwood	Jennifer Westfeldt
	Jennifer Hope Wills 9/28/04
Chick Clark	Michael McGrath
	Ray Wills
Helen	Nancy Anderson
	Kate Baldwin

FIRST-CLASS NATIONAL TOURS

BIG RIVER

San Francisco 6/11/04

Huck	Tyrone Giordano
Jim	Michael McElroy
	Jerald E. Soloman
	David Aaron Demane
Mark Twain	Daniel Jenkins
	Adam Monley

EVITA

Boston 11/02/04

Eva Peron	Kathy Voytko
Juan Peron	Philip Hernandez

Che	Bradley Dean
Mistress	Kate Manning
Magaldi	Gabriel Burrafato

THE GRADUATE

San Francisco 8/9/03

Mrs. Robinson	Jerry Hall
	Linda Gray 11/11/03
	Lorraine Bracco 1/6/04
	Kelly McGillis 3/16/04
	Morgan Fairchild 10/29/04
Benjamin Braddock	Ryder Strong
	Jonathan C. Kaplan 11/11/03
	Nate Corddry 10/29/04
Elaine Robinson	Devon Sorvari
	Winslow Corbett 10/29/04
Mr. Braddock	William Hill
Mrs. Braddock	Kate Skinner
	Corinna May
Mr. Robinson	Dennis Parlato

JESUS CHRIST SUPERSTAR

La Mirada, CA 11/11/02
Closed 1/30/05 Denver

Jesus	Sebastian Bach
	Eric Kunze
Judas	Carl Anderson
	Lawrence Clayton
Mary Magdalene	Natalie Toro
Pontius Pilate	Stephen Breithaupt
	Raymond Patterson 9/27/04
Caiaphas	Lawson Skala
Herod	Peter Kevoian
	Barry Dennen
	Daniel Guzman 9/27/04
Simon	Todd Fournier
Peter	James Clow
	Johnny Hawkins
	Brett Schindele 12/15/04

THE KING AND I

Pittsburgh 6/15/04

Anna	Sandy Duncan
	Stefanie Powers 1/5/05
King	Martin Vidnovic
	Ronobir Lahiri 1/5/05
Tuptim	Luz Lor
	Michelle Liu Coughlin

| *Lun Tha* | Martin Sola |
| *Lady Tiang* | Catherine MiEun Choi |

LES MISÉRABLES
Atlanta 9/9/03

Jean Valjean	Randal Keith
Javert	James Clow
	Joseph Mahowald
	Stephen Tewksbury
	Robert Hunt
Fantine	Tonya Dixon
	Joan Almedilla
Eponine	Ma-Anne Dionisio
	Melissa Lyons
Cosette	Amanda Huddleston
	Leslie Henstock
Marius	Josh Young
	Adam Jacobs
Enjolras	John-Andrew Clark
	Michael Halling
Thénardier	Michael Kostroff
	David McDonald
	David Benoit
	Norman Large
Madame Thénardier	Cindy Benson
	Jennifer Butt

OFF THE RECORD
Cleveland 11/09/04

Diane	Emily Skinner
	Kaitlin Hopkins 1/5/05
Julian	Brian Sutherland
Kristen	Ashley Brown
Nick	Andrew Samonsky

PETER PAN
San Diego 10/12/04

Peter Pan	Cathy Rigby
Captain Hook;	
Mr. Darling	Howard McGillin
Mrs. Darling	Tracy Lore
Wendy	Elisa Sagardia
Tiger Lily	Dana Solimando
	Lauren Masiello 3/15/05

THE SEASON OFF
OFF BROADWAY

THE SEASON OFF OFF BROADWAY

○ ○ ○ ○ ○   *By John Istel*   ○ ○ ○ ○ ○

O NE NIGHT IN the winter of 2004, I found myself sitting on risers in a converted garage while an intrepid theater troupe spouted snippets of quotations by French intellectual Guy Debord, gargled them down with quarts of Budweiser, and romped on a Rube Goldberg-like set in cowboy/girl attire (sometimes unbuttoned and unzipped), lampooning America's pop culture infatuation with the Wild West. *Radiohole Is Still My Name* was a quintessential Off Off Broadway show. It's just a lot farther "off": you have to cross the East River to get to this space. Nevertheless, Radiohole's small-budget spectacle at the Collapsable Hole, a converted garage in Williamsburg, indeed lies a few blocks from Broadway—Brooklyn's version—a dowdy avenue that runs from the river's edge into the borough's heart.

The OOB spirit of experimentation lives on in many venues around New York City—but more often, these days, risk-taking theater manifests itself farther from downtown Manhattan. Of course, neither physical distance nor geography ever really defined OOB in its infancy during the 1960s and 1970s—and some historians argue that the seeds for OOB's "risky" ventures extend even to the art theater movement of the World War I era—the work in those years was united by proximity at storied venues like Caffe Cino, Theater Genesis, or Judson Memorial Church. In a May 6, 2005, piece for *The Village Voice*, Obie Award founder Jerry Tallmer wrote about the early days of Off Off Broadway:

> Everything was within walking distance, especially everything that was exciting in theater, meaning the downtown theater. At worst, you might have to take a bus to get to the Emanuel Brotherhood on 6th Street, almost at the East River, where somebody named Joseph Papp had brought together a bunch of young unknown actors, *American* actors—J.D. Cannon, Roscoe Lee Browne, Colleen Dewhurst, et al.—in vivid, virile stagings of scary stuff like Shakespeare's *Titus Andronicus* and Middleton and Rowley's *The Changeling*, in black slacks, white shirts, and for the girls, prom dresses.

And even so, all this activity wasn't physically too far away from American theater's commercial Main Stem—it just was aesthetically very far out.

As if I needed proof that OOB's soul had oozed away from downtown Manhattan, at Radiohole's show, I see a young woman scribbling next to me, who, when asked if she was reviewing the show, responded: "No," in heavily accented English, "I am doing research on American experimental theater for my doctoral thesis. My friends said this is where I should come."

Here is the next generation of theater on the margins, the new spirit of OOB. Indeed, this young ensemble is clearly part son of Sam (Shepard), part offspring of godfather Richard Foreman and soul mom Elizabeth LeCompte (Wooster Group). In Williamsburg alone, there are nearly 10 OOB theaters, though none of the directors would refer to their spaces in such a way, and they're still rarely listed in those event sections of newspapers and magazines. In the season under review, you could find wonderfully head-spinning OOB productions in converted bathhouses and office buildings in Brooklyn, in a chocolate factory in Queens, in the reviving South Bronx and quickly gentrifying Harlem.

Director and playwright Charles Randolph-Wright, one of a handful of theater professionals asked to highlight the best moments in the 2004-05 OOB season, remembers Tony Award nominee Andre DeShields's shattering turn in *Caligula* at the audacious and accomplished Classical Theatre of Harlem. "It was a performance of total abandon that left one's mouth agape," Randolph-Wright said. Every major critic agreed. The Drama Desk, in fact, awarded the theater an achievement award, along with the Flea Theater, down at the other end of Manhattan. But *Variety*'s rave review of *Caligula* encapsulates all that one expects from an OOB show: "Savage and beautiful, the play tears through conventions—of the theater, of morality, of history—to unleash a vicious new view of the world."

Sometimes, it seems, there aren't enough "vicious new views" at OOB theaters. Due to economics, so much of the vast OOB scene seems like an extension of Broadway's commercial impulses—to mount well-made (or at least well-meaning) plays infused with irony; cute and very producable musicals that seem to pant for commercial transfer; and solo shows once the domain of outré comics such as Lenny Bruce or avant-garde performers such as the late Spalding Gray or Karen Finley. In fact, the commercialization of the confessional monologue, decked out with a bit of striptease to enliven the lurid, self-flagellating tales, may have been epitomized by Steven Fales's *Confessions of a Mormon Boy*. It began as an award-winning hit of the 2004 Fringe Festival, an endeavor totally infused with OOB spirit, which then toured to Chicago and San Francisco before an Off Broadway run planned for the 2005–06 season. *Mormon Boy* fits the model of many solo shows: repression, confession, celebration. The road from experimental outposts like the East Village's P.S. 122 to a commercial run on or Off Broadway has become short indeed. As our colleague Mel Gussow wrote here last year, "The line between Off Off Broadway and the so-called commercial theater has become blurred."

So what is an OOB production? Writers and editors often are at a loss to define OOB, except in economic terms: the section that follows this essay contains listings of "professional theater in New York that is covered

---

The spirit of experimentation lives on in many venues around New York City.

---

by neither Broadway nor full Off Broadway contracts." David A. Crespy's history of the movement, *Off Off Broadway Explosion* (Watson-Guptill, 2003) defines an OOB production in the 1960s as "a play or workshop staged in a small space anywhere in Manhattan, where the actors receive minimal or no pay." If the "Manhattan" and "small space" designations no longer apply as artists have found vast lofts and industrial buildings in outer boroughs, then what's left again, is the economics, the "minimal or no pay" part. Yet, again, there are exceptions. The Brooklyn Academy of Music's Next Wave Festival mounts large spectacles and productions in houses with either hundreds or thousands of seats. The pay may be "minimal" but it is union scale, at the least.

As the *Village Voice* critic and theater editor Ross Wetzsteon used to point out, the term "Off Off Broadway" is a troubling double negative. Defining what you are by what you are not can't help but be a losing proposition: OOB is not Broadway; not even Off Broadway. And defining what it actually *is* often only brings forth more negatives: not-for-profit and non-commercial. The longtime Obie Award chairman would have been positive about one development: the Obies turned 50 this season.

The Spirit Lives

IT IS EASY to argue that no other company in New York, if not the United States, has so influenced experimental theater in the last two decades as the Wooster Group. Surely it's coincidence that the Wooster Group returned to its Soho home base, the Performing Garage, with *Poor Theater*—which first premiered in the 2003–04 season and generated controversy over the contested use of critic Margaret Croyden's voice and image in part of a video. (Croyden's voice and image ultimately were replaced by an actor's.) The production's title encapsulates the economic state of many of the Wooster Group's theater colleagues while paying homage to the seminal 1960s influence of visionary Polish director Jerzy Grotowski, whose book *Towards a Poor Theatre* made his case for an unadorned, ensemble-centered aesthetic. Subtitled *A Series of Simulcra*, the production was an *über*-work with five actors—including Kate Valk, one of this country's finest performers—reenacting a trip to Poland and then re-creating one of the Polish Laboratory Theatre's most famous pieces, *Akropolis,* a gritty comment on World War II concentration camps. The Wooster Group always explores performance vernacular from various sources (hula dance, blackface, pornography), and usually marries it to an adaptation that not only deconstructs a classic, but shatters it—before re-constructing it. As in past productions, *Poor Theater* used technology as a mirror and model, but was focused on the Wooster Group's own process more than about reformulating a classic (*The Crucible, The Emperor Jones*). The second simulacrum was a similar autopsy of performance: this time an homage to choreographer William Forsythe who brought Ballett Frankfurt to world prominence before disbanding the company in 2004. Considering the influence of Grotowski's work on so many OOB artists since his company's visit to Washington Square Methodist Church in 1969, perhaps no production so encapsulated the past, present and future spirit of OOB as this one.

The past was well represented this season in the persons of the three "R's" of theatrical adventurousness who shaped the downtown OOB scene in the 1960s are still producing—Robert Wilson, Richard Foreman and Richard Schechner. They worked familiar haunts. Back at the Brooklyn Academy of Music's Opera House, Wilson's most remarkable trait—his ability to convince all manner of accomplished musical artists to work with him (Philip Glass, David Byrne, Tom Waits)—continued as he enjoined Bernice Johnson Reagon, the founder and longtime leader of the African-American a capella group Sweet Honey in the Rock, to collaborate on his staging of Flaubert's *The Temptation of St. Anthony.* The result, most critics agreed, was one of the most populist and accessible Wilson productions ever—although still dominated by his trademark abstractions of movement and narrative—all set in an austere but brilliantly composed setting. Downtown actor and writer Carl Hancock Rux won over audiences in the title role. Jon Pareles in *The New York Times* drew a comparison to another luminous figure in the

OOB experimental scene that began at BAM: "As in the Lee Breuer-Bob Telson adaptation of the Oedipus tragedy, *The Gospel at Colonus*, African-American music cuts through the abstractions. True to its roots, it unites mind, body and spirit." (In another felicitous coincidence, Breuer and Telson's award-winning resetting of Sophocles's second play in the Theban trilogy, *Oedipus at Colonus*, was revived Off Broadway—in a limited commercial run at the Apollo Theatre in Harlem in the fall of 2004, as part of a "20th Anniversary Tour." Charles S. Dutton played the narrator-preacher role originated at the Brooklyn Academy of Music in 1983 by Morgan Freeman before the 1988 Broadway run.)

Back downtown, Richard Schechner continued to produce at La MaMa with his East Coast Artists company. This season, he directed *YokastaS Redux,* a continuation of the group's exploration of the character of Oedipus's mother. Romanian playwright Saviana Stanescu created four title characters at different points in the Queen's life. Richard Foreman, never one to use classics when his own helter-skelter writings will do, was up to his old shenanigans at the Ontological Theater at Saint Mark's Church. He billed his annual offering, *The Gods Are Pounding My Head! (AKA Lumberjack Messiah)* as his last stage effort before moving onto film and performance projects. In the show, two woodsmen, Frenchie (T. Ryder Smith) and Dutch (Jay Smith), whack away at the stage, each amplified chop reverberating over the audience, threatening, it seems, to end the world. Foreman's twinkly mischievousness takes on a darker melancholia here, not unusual given the state of the world.

Political Plays

PERHAPS THE GREATEST theatrical spectacle of the 2004–05 New York season took place mere blocks from Broadway: the Republican National Convention in August. It was surreal and fantastical, although lacking in drama except for what was created by protestors and the New York City police who did an overzealous job of arresting them. Nevertheless, the convention—and the ensuing national election in November—provided enough inspirational fodder for an unusual glut of political theater around town.

One of the highlights of this genre had to be *George and Martha*, by the infamous symbol of all things OOB: Karen Finley, and performance art colleague Neal Medlyn. Indeed, the two-character satire takes place in a hotel room during the Republican convention. The characters? Not the Washingtons, nor the quarreling couple from *Who's Afraid of Virginia Woolf?*

Instead, Finley and Medlyn embodied President Bush and Martha Stewart. "Their inner turmoil gives us a glimpse to our own neurotic needs," explained Finley. "*George and Martha* gives a symbolic meaning to pathological destruction and behavior." Presented by Collective: Unconscious and P.S. 122, the production received lukewarm reviews—perhaps the real-life drama in the lives of Bush and Stewart proved too hard to compete with.

Even Off Broadway producers got into the act. *Newsical,* a topical musical revue, written by Rick Crom and directed by Donna Drake, included a sketch called "Martha Stewart the Musical" amid the other tidbits of satire that brought to mind another entertaining Stewart—Jon. The Associated Press called the show, which opened Upstairs at Studio 54 in October 2004 and ran for seven months, "*The Daily Show* set to music." Elsewhere Off Broadway, another famously politicized Martha—Mitchell—ghostwalked onstage this season at the Public Theater in John Jeter's bioplay *Dirty Tricks.* The production starred stage treasure Judith Ivey as the eccentric, poison-lipped political wife whom Richard Nixon credited with starting the Watergate scandal. She regaled the audience with her idiosyncratic charms while telling stories into a tape recorder, ostensibly for Mike Wallace. But most of the political commentary was historical and less trenchant, especially in a time that needed contemporary connections to be made.

Svejk, a new adaptation of Jaroslav Hasek's 1923 satiric novel *The Good Soldier Svejk,* arrived courtesy of Theatre for a New Audience, the venerable outfit that gave Julie Taymor her start, among many other accomplishments. Critic Elyse Sommer called it "the year's canniest antiwar play." Starring Stephen Spinella as *Svejk* (rhymes with "cake"), a madcap clown of a soldier, gleefully romping amid the carnage of war (think Georg Büchner's *Woyzeck* on drugs), it flew under most critics' radar screens. After many years of drifting through various venues—most recently for several seasons at the Lucille Lortel Theatre on Christopher Street, and subsequently at the Duke on 42nd Street for this season—TFANA has planned to build a Frank Gehry co-designed theater in Brooklyn, across the street from BAM.

A couple of documentary plays made an impact this season. The documentary form is political by definition: writers craft and edit transcripts, letters, interviews, proceedings, and other material to focus audiences' attention on an issue or topic. The claim of "verbatim" text imbues these plays with the authority of objectivity, the truth of "facts"—although this claim has been deconstructed and interrogated using the same "objective" techniques in the work of Anne Bogart, Charles L. Mee and others. But alternative-theater history has long been home to some of the best examples of the genre, from Martin Duberman's *In White America* (1963) and Emily Mann's *Still Life* (1981) to Moisés Kaufman's *The Laramie Project* (2000). Following the 2003–04 success of *The Exonerated,* the most pointed political commentary of the 2004–05 season arrived Off Broadway, via England, in the form of the documentary play *Guantánamo: Honor Bound to Defend Freedom* (see Charles Wright's essay in this volume). Based on verbatim transcripts and letters from detainees, the play offered a harrowing indictment of the way the US (and its allies) were prosecuting prisoners from the war in Afghanistan and Iraq. Few could miss the significance of the timing of its opening: as Republicans were turning Madison Square Garden into their own security fortress (or detention center). As George Orwell might concur, the most insidious detention occurs where citizens imprison themselves.

A more traditional documentary play was Michael Murphy's *Sin (A Cardinal Deposed)* produced by the New Group. As in one of the 2004–05 Best Plays, *Doubt, a Parable* (see Jeremy McCarter's essay in this volume), the general topic was the Catholic Church's involvement in child molestation. Unlike John Patrick Shanley's play, however, any doubt about the New England Cardinal Bernard Law's complicity in covering up charges of child abuse by priests under his jurisdiction is erased as we watch a deposition unfold. Letters from parents, parishioners and priests are also read, but the primary focus of the play is on Law's role. In John Cullum's acclaimed performance, we saw an arrogant, unshakable man of God start to crumble before the evidence.

Classical Revivals

ONE OF THE most interesting revivals of the season was also one of the more political. Using Euripides, Brecht or Shakespeare to make contemporary corollaries is nothing new, but the Women's Project, whose work is sociopolitical by its nature and mission, produced an intriguing event this season: The Antigone Project. Five playwrights—Chiori Miyagawa, Tanya Barfield, Karen Hartman, Lynn Nottage and Caridad Svich—used Sophocles's *Antigone* as inspiration for new plays of 10 to 20 minutes in length. The production shared an ensemble of actors but had widely different takes on the central character and her dilemma of whether to follow state law or a higher law. While Hartman's *Hang Ten* took place on a surfer beach, with Antigone and Ismene arguing over their incestuous family while eyeing the guys, Nottage's *A Stone's Throw* is about a woman condemned to death by stoning, obviously inspired by recent events in Nigeria.

If OOB's origins were in postwar downtown New York bohemia, hand in hand with bebop and abstract expressionism, then its theater artists have always been in a double opposition: to any new play that smacks of mass appeal, boulevard comedy or star vehicle but also to humdrum "standard" revivals of classics. Of course, these days all of the above can be found in one 99-seat house or another on most any given weekend. The Pearl Theatre Company (where you can always find the estimable Joanne Camp) and Jean Cocteau Repertory (which continues to undergo growing pains following the departure of longtime ensemble members who formed the Phoenix Theatre Ensemble) are two veteran devotees of respectful revivals. Pearl's production of George Bernard Shaw's rarely produced early effort, *Widowers' Houses*, was an example.

Sometimes the best way to address a new social or political reality is through a revival of an old play. There were several revivals—renewals, really—that stood out during the 2004–05 season. Many artists and critics were enraptured by director Ivo van Hove's *Hedda Gabler* (it won four Obie Awards). Two artistic directors—Playwrights Horizons's Tim Sanford and Classic Stage Company's new leader Brian Kulick—both singled it out as a personal highlight of the season. Another example of the blurred lines of distinction between Off Broadway and OOB—it met the criteria for inclusion in the Plays Produced Off Broadway section of this volume—the initial impact of the production at New York Theatre Workshop was felt upon entering the auditorium. The room was a box of glaring asylum-white sheetrock covering the walls. The stage, stripped of ornament, was inhabited by a piano. Jan Versweyveld's design created dramatic tension before a line of Ibsen was spoken and earned the designer Obie and Lortel awards. The contemporary setting allowed the characters' emotional lives to seethe, smolder and boil over. For Elizabeth Marvel, one of New York theater's most accomplished actors, her work in the title role was a fitting achievement.

Kulick also singled out another Theatre for a New Audience production as a personal pick. "Karin Coonrod's production of *Coriolanus* was one of my favorites," he said. Yet most critics, including Charles Isherwood in *The New York Times*, found the director's approach and the acting underwhelming. The actors were costumed in uniformly gray—slightly contemporary, almost corporate—clothing. The set featured towering walls on which grafitti was written along with the act and scene numbers. The fine Roberta Maxwell played Volumnia, a major role that can steal the play—but she didn't. As Martin Harries put it in *The Village Voice*, Maxwell "never enjoys her character's voluptuous delectation in carnage."

Director Doug Hughes, who himself was awarded an Obie for sustained achievement, picked an unusual revival as a top season choice. "I was a fan of Anne Bogart's adaptation of a German medieval allegorical poem, at Classic Stage Company," he said. "It was beautiful, sublime." Based on a 14th century work by Johannes von Saaz—never before seen on a US stage—*Death and the Ploughman* was treated respectfully but unenthusiastically by mainstream critics such as those from the *Times* and *Newsday*, but was panned by the *Voice*. It featured many of the regulars in Bogart's SITI Company: Ellen Lauren, another of this country's acting treasures, who filled the same space at the end of the 2001–02 season in *Room,* a meditation on Virginia Woolf, played the Ploughman's wife whose passing inspires her husband (played by Will Bond) to confront the figure of Death (Stephen Webber). Piers is increasingly maddened by the unfair state of the world that has such pain in it, but Death doesn't back down, as seen here in Irish playwright Michael West's translation:

> DEATH: Behold the bears and the lions in the wilderness;
> the horses, valiant and proud; the men, forever skillful,
> surprising and wise. Behold all these creatures of the
> earth. How intelligent they are! How beautiful! How
> strong! How Alive! . . . They will all die.

The scenery and costumes, by James Schuette, were subtly spectacular. Aided by the award-winning sound designs of Darron L. West, Bogart's Viewpoints-infused direction created a "dance of death" that was one of the more life-affirming experiences OOB.

One of the critical highlights of the season was a visiting production from Chicago by way of England: *Rose Rage* produced at the Duke on 42nd Street. This five-plus hour adaptation by director Edward Hall and collaborator Roger Warren of Shakespeare's *Henry VI* trilogy—with an all-male cast of 12—may have been the season's most bloody revival of the Bard. Set in a slaughterhouse befitting its origin in Chicago, actors when not in a scene would lean against the abattoir walls and sharpen knives and cleavers, creating a percussive soundtrack to the human butchery onstage. If that wasn't enough to ratchet up the tension in the truncated and condensed script, symbolizing the destructive forces of the internecine Wars of the Roses, animal organs were splattered and cabbage heads shredded whenever another character met its violent end. Considering Hall's own company, Propeller, had recently made its inspired New York debut at BAM in the spring of 2004 with *A Midsummer Night's Dream,* the director's ability to wield similar magic with the Chicago Shakespeare Theater cast makes both accomplishments all the more impressive.

But you don't have to go to BAM to find fascinating revivals in the borough of Brooklyn. One of the more notable productions of the season occurred when an intrepid ensemble, named Working Mutt Productions (many not long graduated from the North Carolina School of the Arts), staged *Hamlet* in a former opera-house basement in a Bedford-Stuyvesant building that was converted into apartments. The audience was led from scene to scene, surrounded by all of the junk and detritus stored as the building awaits renovation. The environment allows some evocative scenes; as when the audience encounters the gravediggers sitting on a pile of bricks. The most striking scene occurred when Claudius is sitting on an old crumbling staircase praying and Hamlet enters stealthily behind him to deliver his "Now may I do it pat" speech.

Such site-specific productions aren't new, of course; the much-missed En Garde Arts brought audiences to all corners of Manhattan (crumbling piers, the meatpacking district, the original Lower East Side amphitheater where Joe Papp once produced Shakespeare in his earliest days). But the meatpacking district is one example of a neighborhood that's been transformed, gentrified and lost its allure, which explains why so much of the work like Working Mutt's has moved into the outer boroughs. Another example occurred this season at Long Island City's Chocolate Factory. Attendees of artistic director Brian Rogers's revival of Christopher Marlowe's *Dr. Faustus and the Seven Deadly Sins* began outside, on 49th Avenue, as a character listed as the "Vagrant" offers a prologue before a gate slides open and the audience is led onto an old staircase to meet the "Doctor." The spirits of the deadly sins grab at your ankles as you then ascend into the theater—where again you have no place to sit. Such a sense of dislocation allows new insights into material that is centuries old, and the experience has become a rare one in traditional Manhattan OOB haunts.

The Play's the Thing

OFF OFF BROADWAY since its inception more than 40 years ago has always been an incubator for new playwrights, and most amateur historians can tick off the most famous: Sam Shepard, Terrence McNally, Lanford Wilson, Amiri Baraka (LeRoi Jones), Ed Bullins, Maria Irene Fornes. As a member of the newest generation to find her work produced OOB, playwright Sarah Ruhl (an ATCA/Steinberg honoree) found inspiration in some of the most notable productions of plays by women writers of the previous generation. "The most exciting group of plays for me was Paula Vogel's year at Signature Theatre Company," she said. "Les Waters's haunting production of *Hot 'n'*

Throbbing (a play that I find to be more relevant now than ever), and Mark Brokaw's elegant painful production of *The Baltimore Waltz* (one of my favorite plays for the ages) were highlights of the season for me." Despite Ruhl's enthusiasm, *Hot 'n' Throbbing* was closed two weeks early after receiving less than generous reviews from the mainstream press. It was, nonetheless, chosen as a Best Play.

Ruhl also agreed with the *Best Plays* editorial board—and most drama critics—in pointing to Caryl Churchill's boundary-blurring Off Broadway play, *A Number,* as produced by New York Theatre Workshop as one of the most important events of the season (see Robert Hurwitt's essay in this volume). "It was a play that I leaned over the balcony for," Ruhl recalls, "so very moved to hear one playwright [Sam Shepard] speaking another playwright's words, and breathless to see what Churchill would do with language and form in every moment-to-moment incarnation."

Tim Sanford, artistic director of Playwrights Horizons, relished the chance to select and praise a few of his best OOB dramatists and their plays. He was particularly enamored of *Pyretown* by John Belluso, which was produced by the Keen Company and remarkable for its central performance by Deirdre O'Connell as a single mother on welfare with three kids. "Since this production," Sanford noted, "the waves of praise for actress Didi O'Connell have been cresting." Another choice was *Orange Flower Water,* by Craig Wright, directed by Carolyn Cantor who leads the Edge Theatre Company with her husband, set designer David Korins. "It was a really brave production," Sanford said, "brilliantly acted, with a great scenic environment—sublime."

Sanford's other favorite plays—not including those at his own theater—included Best Play *After Ashley* by Gina Gionfriddo at the Vineyard Theatre (see Elizabeth Maupin's essay in this volume). "There are many great things about this beautifully directed piece by Terry Kinney, especially the intelligence and intensity of the characters played by Kieran Culkin and Anna Paquin, but do not underestimate Tim Hopper's unsung contribution to the piece. He always made me care." Sanford added another OOB play: *Inky* by Rinne Groff at the Women's Project, directed by artistic director Loretta Greco.

Centrifugal Forces

THESE REFLECTIONS ON the nature of Off Off Broadway were sparked by perusing the astounding array of listings offered in this reference book under that heading. As any writer would, I tried to discern trends and new directions. But it has become increasingly clear that the diaspora of OOB theater is akin to an aesthetic Big Bang: over the last 40 years, the original intensity of the artists working OOB in a small, 20-block radius has exploded, sending adventurous actors, artists, and playwrights not only into the outer boroughs, but across the country. Unfortunately, that makes critics' jobs longer and harder as they must often forsake covering the newest troupes springing up farther and farther from their outlet's offices—or spend a lot more time on the subway, in a cab or flying to see work around the country. The huge growth and dispersion of all this artistry makes it increasingly difficult for young theater ensembles to attract attention from the press. Complete artistic freedom sometimes happens in critical isolation. Such a reality would seem to suggest that theater critics' role in discovering new ensembles or innovative productions and explaining that work has become more vital—even as space for theater reviews declines, at least in print.

The most important antidote to this physical dispersion is the flowering of theater festivals, most notably the New York Fringe Festival. For a few weeks every summer, the intensity of physical proximation conjures that original OOB artistic soul as the festival converges in lower Manhattan. The Fringe Festival's success has encouraged others such as Arielle Tepper's Summer Play Festival (SPF) and the Tribeca Theater Festival, which presented original short plays by the likes of Jon Robin Baitz, Douglas Carter Beane, David Henry Hwang, Neil LaBute, Warren Leight, Kenneth Lonergan, Frank Pugliese, Paul Rudnick and Wendy Wasserstein. In the end, given the economic forces that force emerging artists to migrate away from Manhattan, these festivals serve as rejuvenating annual events, energizing the aesthetic force and artistic spirit once quaintly contained in a compact geography known as Off Off Broadway.

PLAYS PRODUCED OFF OFF BROADWAY
AND ADDITIONAL NYC PRESENTATIONS
○ ○ ○ ○ ○
Compiled by Vivian Cary Jenkins

BELOW IS A broad sampling of 2004–05 Off Off Broadway productions in New York. There is no definitive "Off Off Broadway" area or qualification. To try to define or regiment it would be untrue to its fluid, often exploratory purpose. This listing of hundreds of works produced by scores of OOB groups is as inclusive as reliable sources allow. This section pertains to professional theater in New York that is covered by neither Broadway nor full Off Broadway contracts.

The more active and established producing groups are identified in **bold face type**, in alphabetical order, with artistic policies and the names of its leaders given whenever possible. Each group's 2004–05 schedule, with emphasis on new plays, is listed with play titles in CAPITAL LETTERS. Often these are works-in-progress with changing scripts, casts and directors, sometimes without an engagement of record (but an opening or early performance date is included when available).

Many of these Off Off Broadway groups have long since outgrown a merely experimental status and offer programs that are the equal—and in many cases the superior—of anything in the New York theater. These listings include special contractual arrangements such as the showcase code, letters of agreement (allowing for longer runs and higher admission prices than usual) and, closer to the edge of commercial theater, so-called "mini-contracts." In the list below, available data has been compiled from press representatives, company managers and publications of record.

A large selection of developing groups and other shows that made appearances Off Off Broadway during the season under review appears under the "Miscellaneous" heading at the end of this listing. Festival listings include samples of the schedules offered and are often limited to the title and author of the work listed to allow for the inclusion of more works.

Amas Musical Theatre. Dedicated to bringing people of all races, creeds, colors and national origins together through the performing arts. Donna Trinkoff producing director.

> LONE STAR LOVE. Musical with book by John L. Haber; music and lyrics by Jack Herrick; based on *The Merry Wives of Windsor* by William Shakespeare. December 8, 2004. Directed by Michael Bogdanov; choreography, Randy Skinner; scenery, Derek McLane; costumes, Jane Greenwood; lighting, Jeff Croiter; sound, Matt Krauss. With Jay O. Sanders, Stacia

Love blooms: Clarke Thorell and Julie Tolivar in the Amas Musical Theatre production of John L. Haber and Jack Herrick's Lone Star Love. *Photo: Joan Marcus*

Fernandez, Beth Leavel, Gary Sandy, Dan Sharkey, Clarke Thorell, Kevin Bernard, Shane Braddock, Peter Connelly, Harriett D. Foy, Asmeret Ghebremichael, Stacey Harris, Drew McVety, Nick Sullivan, Julie Tolivar, Brandon Williams, Dana Zihlman, Emily Mikesell, David Longworth, and the Red Clay Ramblers (Clay Buckner, Chris Frank, Mr. Herrick).

Atlantic Theater Company. Produces new plays and reinterpretations of classics that speak in a contemporary voice on issues reflecting today's society. Neil Pepe artistic director.

THE BALD SOPRANO and THE LESSON by Eugene Ionesco; translated by Tina Howe. September 19, 2004. Directed by Carl Forsman; scenery, Loy Arcenas; costumes, Theresa Squire; lighting, Josh Bradford; sound, Obadiah Eaves. *The Bald Soprano* with John Ellison Conlee, Michael Countryman, Maggie Kiley, Seana Kofoed, Maggie Lacey, Jan Maxwell, Robert Stanton. *The Lesson* with Maggie Kiley, Christa Scott-Reed, Steven Skybell.

Brooklyn Academy of Music Next Wave Festival. Since 1983, this annual festival has presented hundreds of cutting-edge events, including dozens of world premieres. With its focus on leading international artists, it is one of the world's largest and most prestigious festivals of contemporary performing arts. Alan H. Fishman chairman of the board; Karen Brooks Hopkins president; Joseph V. Melillo executive producer.

OTHELLO. By William Shakespeare. October 5, 2004. Directed by Declan Donnellan; choreography, Jane Gibson; scenery and costumes, Nick Omerod; lighting, Judith Greenwood; music, Catherine Jayes. With Nonso Anozie, Kirsty Besterman, Matthew Douglas, Michael Gardiner, Jaye Griffiths, David Hobbs, Ryan Kiggell, Caroline Martin, Jonny Phillips. Presented in association with Cheek by Jowl and Théâtre du Nord.

THE DYBBUK. Based on texts by Szymon Ansky and Hanna Krall; translated by Awiszaj Hadari. October 13, 2004. Directed by Krzysztof Warlikowski; scenery, Malgorzata Szczesniak;

lighting, Felice Ross; music, Pawel Mykietyn. With Stanislawa Celinska, Magdalena Cielecka, Renate Jett, Maria Maj, Orna Porat, Andrzej Chyra, Marek Kalita, Zygmunt Malanowicz. Presented in association with TR Warszawa and Wroclawski Teatr Wspolczesny.

THE TEMPTATION OF ST. ANTHONY. Music-theater production with book and music by Bernice Johnson Reagon; based on the novel by Gustav Flaubert. October 19, 2004. Direction, scenery and lighting by Robert Wilson; costumes, Geoffrey Holder; sound, Peter Cerone; music direction, Ms. Reagon. With Carl Hancock Rux, Helga Davis, Marcelle Lashley, Charles Williams, Christalyn Wright, Ms. Reagon.

A PASSAGE TO INDIA. By E.M. Forster; adapted by Martin Sherman. November 2, 2004. Directed by Nancy Meckler; scenery and costumes, Niki Turner; lighting, Chris Davey; music, Peter Salem. With Antony Bunsee, Alex Caan, Maxwell Hutcheon, Ranjit Krishnamma, Rina Mahoney, Chris Nayak, William Osborne, Gary Pillai, Simon Scardifield, Susan Tracy, Fennela Woolgar. Presented in association with Shared Experience and Nottingham Playhouse.

NORA (A DOLL'S HOUSE). By Henrik Ibsen; November 9, 2004.Directed by Thomas Ostermeier; scenery, Jan Pappelbaum; costumes, Almut Eppinger; lighting, Erich Schneider; music, Lars Eidinger. With Jörg Hartmann, Anne Tismer, Lars Eidinger, Jenny Schily, Kay Bartholomäus Schulze, Milena Bühring, Constantin Fischer, Robin Meisner, Agnes Lampkin, Enrico Stolzenburg. Presented in association with Schaubühne am Lehniner Platz, Berlin.

FAUST/HOW I ROSE. By John Jesurun. November 16, 2004. Directed by Martin Acosta; scenery and video, Mr. Jesurun; costumes, Martin Lopez; lighting, Matias Gorlero; sound, Joaquin Lopez. With Ari Brickman, Mónica Dionne, Guillermina Campuzano, Carolina Politti, Manuel Dominguez, Emilio Savinni.

THE CHAIRS. By Eugene Ionesco; translated by Michael Feingold. December 1, 2004. Directed and choreographed by David Gordon; lighting, Jennifer Tipton; music, Michael Gordon. With Valda Setterfield, Mr. Gordon, Karen Graham, Guillermo Resto, Wendy Sutter. Presented in association with Pick Up Performance Company.

And Howe: Maggie Kiley and Steven Skybell in the Atlantic Theater Company production of Eugene Ionesco's The Lesson. *Photo: Carol Rosegg*

ISABELLA'S ROOM. By Jan Lauwers. December 14, 2004. Direction, scenery and lighting by Mr. Lauwers; costumes, Lot Lemm; sound, Dré Schneider; music, Hans Petter Dahl and Maarten Seghers. With Viviane De Muynck, Mr. Dahl, Julien Faure, Tijen Lawton, Anneke Bonnema, Benoit Gob. Presented in association with Needcompany, Belgium.

Classic Stage Company. Reinventing and revitalizing the classics for contemporary audiences. Brian Kulick artistic director, Jessica R. Jenen executive director.

DEATH AND THE PLOUGHMAN. By Johannes von Saaz; translated by Michael West. November 10, 2004. Directed by Anne Bogart; scenery and costumes, James Schuette; lighting, Brian H. Scott; sound, Darron L. West. With Will Bond, Ellen Lauren, Stephen Webber. Presented in association with SITI Company.

THREE SISTERS. By Anton Chekhov; translated by Paul Schmidt. January 5, 2005. Directed by Pavol Liska; scenery, Jian Jung; costumes, Anka Lupes; lighting, Tim Cryan; sound, Kristin Worral. With Amanda Boekelheide, Marc Dale, Anne Gridley, Rebecca Henderson, Karen Koontz, Walker Lewis, Fletcher Liegerot, Luis Moreno, Zachary Oberzan, Mario Quesda. Presented in association with Nature Theater of Oklahoma.

THE FALSE SERVANT. By Pierre Marivaux; translated by Kathleen Tolan. April 10, 2005. Directed by Brian Kulick; scenery and costumes, Mark Wendland; lighting, Kevin Adams. With Martha Plimpton, Bill Buell, Jesse Pennington, Paul Lazar, Tina Benko, Jerry Matz.

KASIMIR AND KAROLINE. By Ödön von Horváth. April 20, 2005. Directed by Pavol Liska; scenery, Jian Jung; costumes, Hillary Moore and Jocelyn Worrall; lighting, Tim Cryan; sound, Kristina Worrall. With Zalman Abramchik, Laura Butler, Elliotte Crowell, James Ferguson, Robert Johanson, Fletcher Liegerot, Caitlin McDonough-Thayer, Jo Moskow, Zachary Oberzan, Carla Tassara. Presented in association with Nature Theater of Oklahoma.

Drama Dept. A collective of theater artists who create new works and revive neglected classics. Douglas Carter Beane artistic director, Michael S. Rosenberg.

THE DOWNTOWN PLAYS. October 21–31, 2004. Directed by John Rando; scenery, Alexander Dodge; costumes, Gregory Gale; lighting, Kirk Bookman; sound, Kai Harada.

PRIDE AND JOY. By Paul Rudnick. With Jackie Hoffman.

HE MEANING HIM. By Douglas Carter Beane. With Josh Hamilton, Julie White.

TRUE TO YOU. By Kenneth Lonergan. With J. Smith-Cameron, Mr. Hamilton.

HAPPY FOR YOU. By Warren Leight.

PSYCHE IN LOVE. By Wendy Wasserstein. With Peter Jacobson.

MY BEAUTIFUL GODDAMN CITY. By Jon Robin Baitz. With Maria Tucci, Ms. White.

TRYING TO FIND CHINATOWN. By David Henry Hwang. With Joel de la Fuente, Ross Gibby.

UNION SQUARE. By Neil LaBute. With Mr. Hamilton.

LATE NIGHT, EARLY MORNING. By Frank Pugliese. With Chris Messina, Marilyn Torres.

Ensemble Studio Theatre. Membership organization of playwrights, actors, directors and designers dedicated to supporting individual theater artists and developing new works. Projects range from readings to fully staged productions. Curt Dempster artistic director.

Season included:
CHOPPER. By Leah Ryan. February 26, 2005. Directed by Ed Cheetham; scenery, Christina Aprea; costumes, Emma Britton; lighting, Dave Starr. With Jen Albano, Jason Kaminsky, Paul Megna, Christiane Szabo. Presented in association with Wildfire Productions.

LUMINESCENCE DATING. By Carey Perloff. April 21, 2005. Directed by Will Pomerantz; scenery, Troy C. Hourie; costumes, Devon Painter; lighting, Gregg MacPherson; sound, Lindsay Jones. With Betsy Aidem, Ato Essandoh, Judith Roberts, John Wojda.

MARATHON 2005. (SERIES A). May 25–June 11, 2005.

MADAGASCAR. By John Guare. Directed by Will Pomerantz. With Remy Auberjonois, Amy Love.

THE AIRPORT PLAY. By Alexandra Gersten-Vassilaros. Directed by Shirley Kaplan. With Ann Talman, Edward A. Hajj, Brady Ovson.

MR. MORTON WAITS FOR HIS BUS. By Warren Leight. Directed by Andrew McCarthy. With Donald Symington, Ean Sheehy.

THE GREAT PRETENDERS. By Leslie Lyles. Directed by Billy Hopkins. With Amy Irving, Bruce MacVittie, Foss Curtis, J.J. Kandel, Haskell King.

The Flea Theater. Formed to present distinctive, cutting-edge work that raises the standards of Off Off Broadway. Jim Simpson artistic director, Carol Ostrow producing director.

THE VOMIT TALK OF GHOSTS. By Kevin Oakes. June 23, 2004. Directed by Jay Scheib; scenery and costumes, Oana Boetz-Ban; lighting, Benjamin C. Tevelow; sound, Leah Gelpe. With Meghan Carroll, Katy Downing, Charles Kornegay, Kevin T. Moore, Dan O'Brien, Sayra Player.

THE WANDERER. By Dmitry Lipkin. July 11, 2004. Directed by Adam Melnick; scenery, Nathan Heverin; costumes, Natasha Landau; lighting, Doug Filomena; sound, Ann Warren. With Amelia Campbell, Larry Block, Brian Gottesman, Irma St. Paule, Matthew Dellapina, Seth Kanor, Stan Lachow, Chris Kipiniak.

KATE CRACKERNUTS. By Sheila Callaghan. July 29, 2004. Directed by Hayley Finn; scenery, Cavanagh Holland; costumes, Melissa Schlachtmeyer; lighting, Dana Sterling; sound and music, Sophocles Papavasilopoulos. With Blake Barlowe, Ross Beschler, Zina Camblin, Nicol Cole, Alex Dawson, Kevin Dedes, Aaron Fili, Flannery Foster, Gene Gallerano, Parrish Hurley, Aly Mawji, Stacey Melich, Mollye Mirowitz, Summer Shirey, Andi Shrem, Sara Stewart, Sakurako Sugihara, Meredith Toole.

MRS. FARNSWORTH. Revival of the play by A.R. Gurney. September 29, 2004. Directed by Jim Simpson; scenery, Kyle Chepulis; costumes, Claudia Brown; lighting, Brian Aldous. With Leslie Lyles, Gerry Bamman, Danny Burstein, Kate Benson, Fernando Gambaroni, Tarajia Morell.

A HEARTBEAT TO BAGHDAD. By Glyn O'Malley. October 31, 2004. Directed by Jim Simpson; scenery and lighting, Kyle Chepulis; costumes, Melissa Schlachtmeyer; sound, Jeremy Wilson. With Gloria Reuben, Phyllis Somerville, Christian Baskous, Steven Rishard, Kristin Stewart Chase, Joanie Ellen, Gordon Holmes, Joe Holt, Jace McLean, David Marcus, Alfredo Narciso, Irene Walsh.

SUMMA DRAMATICA. By Lee Breuer. February 20, 2005. Directed by Mr. Breuer; sound, Eamonn Farrell. With Sri Moo Parahamsa, Ruth Maleczech, Clove Galilee. Presented in association with Mabou Mines.

JABU. Musical by Elizabeth Swados. February 26, 2005. Directed by Ms. Swados; scenery, Sue Rees; costumes, Melissa Schlachtmeyer; lighting, Garin Marschall. With Nicola Barber, Stephanie Braun, Paula Ehrenberg, Michael Francis, Meredith Holzman, Parrish Hurley, Nicolas Job, Derrick Karg, Jamie King, Danielle Levanas, Taylor Mac, Emily Mattheson, Kevin T. Moore, John Pizzolato, Ana Valle, Hondo Weiss-Richmond, Matt Wells, Matt Wilson.

MARGO VEIL. By Len Jenkin. March 24, 2005. Directed by Mr. Jenkin; scenery, Sue Rees; costumes, Michelle R. Phillips; lighting, Andrew Hill; sound, John Kilgore. With Heather Christian, Aaron Fili, Benjamin Fine, Michael Grenham, David Marcus, Lauren McCord, Julie Shavers, Lisa Sauber.

SCREEN PLAY. By A.R. Gurney. May 27, 2005. Directed by Jim Simpson; costumes, Melissa Schlachtmeyer; lighting, Joe Novak; sound, Greg Duffin. With Derrick Edwards, John Fico, Meredith Holzman, Drew Hildebrand, Kevin T. Moore, Brian Morvant, Raushanah Simmons.

WORK. By Charlotte Meehan. May 28, 2005. Directed by Jim Simpson; costumes, Melissa Schlachtmeyer; lighting, Joe Novak; sound, Greg Duffin. With Adeel Akhtar, Nicola Barber, Michael Diskint, Parrish Hurley, Audrey Lynn Weston, Kerry-Jane Wilson.

Intar. Identifies, develops and presents the talents of gifted Hispanic-American artists. Eduardo Machado artistic director.

WITH WHAT ASS DOES THE COCKROACH SIT? Solo performance piece by Carmelita Tropicana. November 16, 2004. Directed by David Schweizer. With Ms. Tropicana.

BLUES FOR A GRAY SUN. Solo performance piece by Nilaja Sun. November 17, 2004. Directed by Louis Moreno. With Ms. Sun.

LOBSTER FACE. By Magdalena Gomez. December 17, 2004. Directed by Daniel Jaquez; scenery, Susan Zeeman-Rogers; costumes, Ruth Pongstaphone and Sarah Maiorino; lighting, Yael Lubetzy; sound and music, Jane Shaw. With David Anguelo, Yetta Gottesman, Jezabel Montero, Gerardo Rodriguez, Liam Torres, Peggy Trecker, Haleh Aleghari.

HISPANIC PLAYWRIGHTS IN RESIDENCE LABORATORY . January 31–February 21, 2005.

ALWAYS IN MY HEART. By Oscar Colon. January 31, 2005. Directed by Susana Tubert.

THE CUBAN JOAN OF ARC. By Lorenzo Mans. February 7, 2005. Directed by Bernice Rohret.

TELLING TALES. By Migdalia Cruz. February 14, 2005. Directed by Candido Tirado.

MODERN LADIES OF GUANABACOA. By Eduardo Machado. February 21, 2005. Directed by Jorge Cacheiro.

Irish Repertory Theatre. Brings works by Irish and Irish-American playwrights to a wider audience and develops new works focusing on a variety of cultural experiences. Charlotte Moore artistic director, Ciarán O'Reilly producing director.

AFTER THE BALL. By Noël Coward; based on *Lady Windermere's Fan* by Oscar Wilde; additional material by Barry Day. December 16, 2004. Direction and scenery, Tony Walton; choreography, Lisa Shriver; lighting, Brian Nason; music direction, Mark Hartman. With Kristin Huxhold, Mary Illes; Paul Carlin, David Staller, Collette Simmons, Greg Mills, Kathleen Widdoes, Josh Grisetti, Drew Eshelman, Elizabeth Inghram.

SHE STOOPS TO CONQUER. By Oliver Goldsmith. May 12, 2005. Directed by Charlotte Moore; scenery, James Morgan; costumes, Linda Fisher; lighting, Mary Jo Dondlinger. With Remak Ramsey, Patricia O'Connell, Tim Smallwood, Danielle Ferland, Jennifer Bryan, Tommy Schrider, Donald Grody, Brian Hutchison, Lucas Caleb Rooney.

Jean Cocteau Repertory. Dedicated to nurturing a permanent resident acting company and developing a diverse audience through a rotating repertory. David Fuller producing artistic director.

DAMES AT SEA. Musical with book and lyrics by George Haimsohn and Robin Miller; music by Jim Wise. September 3, 2004. Directed by David Fuller; choreography, Barbara Brandt; scenery, Roman Tatarowicz; costumes, Joanne Haas; lighting, Giles Hogya. With Campbell Bridges, Judith Jarosz, Andy Meyers, Chrysten Peddie, Joey Stocks, Kathleen White.

ROMEO AND JULIET. By William Shakespeare. October 8, 2004. Directed by Rod McLucas; scenery and costumes, Michael McKowen; lighting, David Kniep. With Danaher Dempsey, Seth Duerr, Kate Holland, Kristina Klebe, David Ledoux, Anna Zostrow.

PYGMALION. By George Bernard Shaw. December 12, 2004. Directed by Rose Burnett Bonczek; scenery, Michael Carnahan; costumes, Viviane Galloway; lighting, David Kniep. With Sarah Jeanne Asselin, Danaher Dempsey, Ramona Floyd, Angus Hepburn, Kate Holland, Melanie Hopkins, Lynn Marie Macy, Marlene May, Tim Morton, Jay Nickerson, Mickey Ryan.

INTRIGUE AND LOVE. By Friedrich von Schiller; translated and adapted by Lynn Marie Macy. February 20, 2005. Directed by David Fuller; scenery, Michael Carnahan; costumes, Sean Sullivan; sound, Charles Berigan. With Sarah Jeanne Asselin, Natalie Ballesteros, Angus Hepburn, Amanda Jones, David Ledoux, Lynn Marie Macy, Jay Nickerson, Ralph Petrarca, Mickey Ryan, Chad A. Suitts.

THE MAIDS. By Jean Genet; translated by Bernard Frechtman. April 17, 2005. Directed by Ernest Johns; scenery, Roman Tatarowicz; costumes, Nicole Frachiseur; lighting, Richard Dunham. With Natalie Ballesteros, Kate Holland, Amanda Jones.

Labyrinth Theater Company. Provides artists from diverse backgrounds an opportunity to work. A multicultural collective producing new plays that reflect diverse voices in the New York City community. Philip Seymour Hoffman, John Ortiz artistic directors.

SAILOR'S SONG. By John Patrick Shanley. November 7, 2004. Directed by Chris McGarry; choreography, Barry McNabb; costumes, Mimi O'Donnell; lighting, Beverly Emmons; sound, Elizabeth Rhodes. With Katie Nehra, Melissa Paladino, Danny Mastrogiorgio, Stephen Payne, Alexis Croucher.

LOOKING FOR MR. BRADY. Solo performance by Rebecca Cohen. October 31, 2004. Directed by Marieke Gaboury; costumes, Mimi O'Donnell; lighting, Sarah Sidman. With Ms. Cohen.

La MaMa Experimental Theatre Club (ETC). A workshop for experimental theater of all kinds. Ellen Stewart founder and director.

Season included:
BLIND NESS: THE IRRESISTIBLE LIGHT OF ENCOUNTER. By Ping Chong and Michael Rohd. June 18, 2004. Directed by Mr. Chong in collaboration with Bobby Bermea, Jeff Randall, M. Burke Walker; scenery, lighting and projections, Randy Ward; costumes, Stefani Mar; sound, Stephen Zapytowski. With Messrs. Bermea, Randall, Rohd, Walker.

THE INTERLUDE. By Kim Ima. October 7, 2004. Directed by Ms. Ima; scenery, Gian Marco Lo Forte; costumes, Melissa Schlachtmeyer; sound, Stefano Zazzera. With Ms. Ima, Glenn Cruz, Lindy Jamil Gomez, Yoshiro Kono, Sarah Hayon, Sam Hurlbut, Yoshiro Kono, Katie Takahashi, Tristan Roque, Sora Suzuki.

A JAPANESE DAUGHTER REMEMBERS AMERICAN CONCENTRATION CAMPS IN IDAHO. By Kim Ima. October 7, 2004. Directed by Ms. Ima; scenery, Gian Marco Lo Forte; costumes, Melissa Schlachtmeyer; lighting, Adam Larson; sound, Stefano Zazzera. With Ms. Kim, Katie Takahashi, Glenn Cruz, Lindy Jamil Gomez, Yoshiro Kono, Sarah Hayon, Sam Hurlbut.

BROKE. By Vishakan Jeyakmar. October 21, 2004. Directed by Abigail Marateck; scenery, Tania Bijlani; lighting, Jeff McCrum; sound, Ezekiel Kendrick. With Paul Coughlan, Ian Eaton, Amol Shah, Sekou Campbell.

THE UNPOSSESSED. By Stacy Klein; based on *The Adventures of Don Quixote* by Cervantes. October 28, 2004. Directed by Ms. Klein; lighting, Mary Louise Geiger; music, Justin Handley. With Carlos Uriona, Matthew Glassman, Mr. Handley, Joanna Wichowska, Hayley Brown, Richard Newman.

SEA CHANGE and ARCTIC CIRCLE. By Beth Skinner. October 28, 2004. Directed by Ms. Skinner; scenery, Jun Maeda and WindRose Morris; costumes, Heidi Henderson; lighting, Paul Clay; music, Edward Herbst. With Mari Andrejco, Sara Bragdon, Mr. Herbst.

BOKAN, THE BAD HEARTED. By Federico Restrepo; music by Elizabeth Swados. December 3, 2004. With Mr. Restrepo, Carolyn Cryer, Kate Duyn, Denise Greber, Dennis Guzman, Aaron Haskell, Tom Lee, Chris Mehmed, Eugene the Poogene, Ollie Rasini, Abigail Rasminsky, Shigeko Suga, Maggie Thom, Jennifer Bruno, Golnaz Fakhimi, Amanda Miller.

THE PATHOLOGICAL PASSION OF THE CHRIST. By Dario D'Ambrosi. December 9, 2004. Directed by Mr. D'Ambrosi. With Arthur Adair, Brian Glover, Peter Case, Shawneeka Woodward, D'arcy Drollinger, Alex Plat, Jonathan Slaff.

MAMILLIUS. By Sheldon Deckelbaum; adapted from *The Winter's Tale* by William Shakespeare. December 30, 2004. Directed by Mr. Deckelbaum; choreography, MaryBeth Cavanaugh; scenery, Sandra Goldmark; costumes, Camille Assaf; lighting, Hilary Manners. With Diane Ciesla, Dan Cordle, Adriean Delaney, Deb Heinig, Meg Howrey, Reginald Metcalf.

Personality plus: Ashlie Atkinson and Jeremy Piven in the MCC Theater production of Neil LaBute's Fat Pig. *Photo: Joan Marcus*

BELIZE. By Paul Zimet. January 6, 2005. Directed by Mr. Zimet; choreography, Stefa Zawerucha; scenery, Nic Ularu; costumes, Kiki Smith; lighting, Carol Mullins; sound, Tim Schellenbaum; music, Ellen Maddow. With Liz Albertson, William Badgett, Kwesi Ifatola Camara, Eisa Davis, David Greenspan, John Keating, Ms. Maddow, Audrey Pernell, Randolph Curtis Rand, Steven Rattazzi, Tina Shepard, Vivian Warfield, Connie Winston.

THE BITTERNESS OF THE MERINGUE. By Jorge Kuri; translated by Edith Luna. January 20, 2005. Directed by Raine Bode; scenery, Ms. Bode and Antonio Cerezo. With Mr. Cerezo, Nicky Paraiso, Siho Ellsmore, John Benoit, Sasha Painter.

BUTTER MELTS AWAY MY LETTERS. By Gian Marco Lo Forte. February 10, 2005. Directed by Mr. Lo Forte; choreography, Stephanie Rafferty; costumes, Denise Greber; sound, Stefano Zazzera. With Valois Mickens, Julia Martin, Chris Wild, Allison Hiroto, Chris Mehmed, Marissa Lichwick.

YOKASTAS REDUX. By Richard Schechner and Saviana Stanescu. February 17, 2005. Direction and scenery by Mr. Schechner; costumes, Oana Boetz-Ban; lighting, Lucrecia Briceno. With Daphne Gaines, Rachel Bowditch, Phyllis Johnson, Jennifer Lim, Sarah Kozinn, Christopher Logan Healy.

KOLIADA: TWELVE DISHES. By Serhiy Zhadan. March 4, 2005. Directed by Virlana Tkacz, in collaboration with Mr. Zhadan; scenery, costumes and lighting, Watoku Ueno. With Andrew Colteaux, Olenka Denysenko, Siho Ellsmore, Allison Hiroto, Olga Shuhan, Vira Slywotzky, Meredith Wright.

IPHIGENIA. By Euripides; adapted by Theodora Skipitares. March 17, 2005. Directed by Ms. Skipitares; with Chris Maresca, Nicky Paraiso, Alissa Mello, Amanda Villalobos, John Benoit, Carolyn Goelzer, Sonja Perryman.

ROSARIES AND VODKA. By Daniel Haben Clark. March 24, 2005. Directed by Mr. Clark. With Kat Jameson, Joe De Feo, Aliza Hedges, Brendan Burke, Eugene Solfanelli, Melissa Nearman, Jorge Rios, Marjorie Conn, Chris Kelly.

UP! UP! AND MORE UP! By Chris Tanner, Brandon Olson and Lance Cruce. April 14, 2005. Directed by Julie Atlas; scenery, Steven Hammel and Garry Hayes; costumes, Becky Hubbert. With Robert Appleton, Mr. Cruce, Benjamin Marcantoni, Mr. Olson, Armen Ra, Mr. Tanner.

PERSEUS. By Ellen Stewart; translated by Marina Kotzamani. April 29, 2005. Directed by Ms. Stewart; choreography, Renouard Gee; costumes, Camille Assaf; lighting, Carol Mullins; sound, Tim Schellenbaum; music, Ms. Assaf, Elizabeth Swados, Michael Sirotta, Heather Paauwe, Yukio Tsuji, Carlos Valdez. With Arthur Adair, Raine Bode, Peter Case, Cary Gant, Renouard Gee, Phillip Gerba, Denise Greber, Allison Hiroto, Kim Ima, Marjorie Jean, Onni Johnson, Juliana Lau, Gian Marco Lo Forte, Benjamin Marcantoni, Valois Mickens, Kazuma G. Motomura, JT Netterville, Prisca Ouya, Federico Restrepo, Yasmine Soiffer, Chris Wild, Meredith Wright, Kat Yew.

A CASE OF MURDER. By Robert Montgomery. May 5, 2005. Directed by Benno Haenel; scenery, Dennis Leder; lighting, Deborah Constantine; music direction, Jeremy Fenn-Smith. With Brian McCormack, Nic Tyler, Judy Jerome, Rich Hollman, Brian W. Seibert, Maggie Low, Rachel Valdati, Dean Goldman.

DRESS SUITS TO HIRE. By Holly Hughes. May 19, 2005. Directed by Lois Weaver; choreography, Stormy Brandenberger; costumes, Susan Young; sound, Vivian Stoll. With Ms. Weaver, Peggy Shaw.

Lincoln Center Festival 2004. An annual international summer arts festival offering classic and contemporary work.

WAR AND PEACE. By Leo Tolstoy; adapted by Piotr Fomenko. July 6, 2004. Directed by Mr. Fomenko. With Andrei Kazakov, Ilia Lyubimov, Polina Kutepova, Madeleine Djabrailova, Ksenia Kutepova, Galina Tyunina.

EGYPTIAN NIGHTS. By Piotr Fomenko; adapted from works by Alexander Pushkin and Valery Bryusov. July 6, 2004. Directed by Mr. Fomenko. With Ilia Lyubimov, Polina Kutepova.

FORBIDDEN CHRISTMAS, OR THE DOCTOR AND THE PATIENT. By Rezo Gabriadze; translation by Ryan McKittrick and Julia Smeliansky. July 9, 2004. Directed by Mr. Gabriadze; choreography, Luis Perez; scenery and costumes, Mr. Gabriadze; lighting, Jennifer Tipton; sound, David Meschter. With Mikhail Baryshnikov, Jon DeVries, Mr. Perez, Pilar Witherspoon, Yvonne Woods.

NATSUMATSURI NANIWA KAGAMI. By Senryu Namiki. July 17, 2004. Directed by Kushida Kazuyoshi; scenery, Yuichiro Kanai; costumes, Kumiko Arai; lighting, Shigeo Saito; sound, Nobuya Iida. With Kankuro Nakamura V, Senjaku Nakamura, Hashinosuke Nakamura, Yajuro Bando, Kamezo Kataoka, Shichinosuke Nakamura, Muneo Nakamura, Takashi Sasano, Kamenojo Nakamura, Kannojo Nakamura, Shinobu Nakamura.

THE SLAVE and SHOSHA. By Isaac Bashevis Singer; adapted by Yevgeny Arye and Yelena Laskina. July 20–25, 2004. Directed by Mr. Arye; choreography by Yehezkiel Lazarov; scenery, Mr. Arye and Michael Kramenko; costumes, Rakefet Levy; lighting, Avi-Yona Bueno; sound by Michael Vaisburd. With Israel Demidov, Yevgenya Dodina, Natalia Voytulevich-Manor, Mr. Lazarov, Miki Leon, Klim Kamenko, Boris Achanov, Nelli Gosheva, Michal Weinberg.

THE ELEPHANT VANISHES. By Haruki Murakami; adapted by Simon McBurney. July 23, 2004. Directed by Mr. McBurney; scenery, Michael Levine; costumes, Christina Cunningham; lighting, Paul Anderson; sound, Christopher Shutt. With Mitsuru Fukikoshi, Atsuko Takaizumi, Yuko Miyamoto, Keitoku Takata, Ryoko Tateishi, Kentaro Mizuki, Yasuyo Mochizuki, Masaaki Yato.

MCC Theater. Dedicated to the promotion of emerging writers, actors, directors and theatrical designers. Robert LuPone and Bernard Telsey artistic directors, William Cantler associate artistic director.

LAST EASTER. By Bryony Lavery. October 7, 2004. Directed by Doug Hughes; scenery, Hugh Landwehr; costumes, Catherine Zuber; lighting, Clifton Taylor; sound and music, Fabian Obispo. With Jeffrey Carlson, Clea Lewis, Veanne Cox, Florencia Lozano, Jeffrey Scott Green.

FAT PIG. By Neil LaBute. December 15, 2004. Directed by Jo Bonney; scenery, Louisa Thompson; costumes, Mimi O'Donnell; lighting, Matt Frey; sound and music, Robert Kaplowitz; fight direction, Rick Sordelet. With Ashlie Atkinson, Andrew McCarthy, Jeremy Piven, Keri Russell.

WHAT OF THE NIGHT. By Jane Alexander, Noreen Tomassi, Birgitta Trommler; based on the work of Djuna Barnes. April 6, 2005. Directed by Ms. Trommier; scenery, Rob Odorisio; costumes, Ann Roth; lighting, Beverly Emmons; sound, Fabian Obispo.

Mint Theater Company. Committed to reinvigorating worthy but neglected plays. Jonathan Bank artistic director.

ECHOES OF THE WAR. Two one-act plays by J.M. Barrie. *The New Word* and *The Old Lady Shows Her Medals.* July 18, 2004. Directed by Eleanor Reissa; scenery, Vicki R. Davis; costumes, Debra Stein; lighting, Traci Klainer; sound, Bruce Ellman. With Frances Sternhagen, Richard Easton, Gareth Saxe, Aaron Krohn, Katherine McGrath, Pat Nesbit, Mary Ellen Ashley, Anne-Marie Cusson, Jenny Strassberg.

THE LONELY WAY. By Arthur Schnitzler; translated by Margaret Schaefer and Jonathan Bank. February 13, 2005. Directed by Mr. Bank; scenery, Vicki R. Davis; costumes, Henry Shaffer; lighting, Ben Stanton; sound, Jane Shaw. With Eric Alperin, Lisa Bostnar, Ronald Guttman, Jordan Lage, Bennett Leak, George Morfogen, Sherry Skinner, Constance Tarbox, John Leonard Thompson.

New Dramatists. An organization devoted to playwrights. Members may use the facilities for projects ranging from private readings of their material to public scripts-in-hand readings. Listed below are readings open to the public during the season under review. Todd London artistic director, Joel K. Ruark executive director.

Season included:

New Playwright Welcome. September 13, 2004. DURANGO. By Julia Cho. Directed by Victor Maog. With Tim Kang, Ron Nakahara, Aaron Yoo. THE MUSEUM PLAY. By Jordan Harrison. With Noah Bean, Carla Harting, Suli Holum, Trey Lyford. TOUGH TITTY. By Oni Faida Lampley. Directed by Seret Scott. With Rhonda Ross, Keith Randolph Smith. PRACTICING. By Rinne Groff. With Carla Harting, Jason Pugatch, Chris Wells. BIRD IN THE HAND. By Jorge Ignacio Cortiñas. With Vanessa Aspillaga, Sarah Ruhl, Rafael Sardina. SKINNED. By Zakiyyah Alexander. Directed by Jackson Gay. With Edward A. Hajj, Marin Ireland, Frank Liotti, Bill Thompson. THE CLEAN HOUSE. By Sarah Ruhl. With Zakiyyah Alexander, Julia Cho, Jorge Ignacio Cortiñas, Rinne Groff, Jordan Harrison, Oni Faida Lampley. MILLENNIUM 7. September 21, 2004. By Edgar Nkosi White. Directed by Dana Manno. With Billie Allen, Larry Block, John-Andrew Morrison, Alice Spivak, Mary Vivian.

THE BARBARA BARONDESS MACLEAN FESTIVAL. MY FIRST RADICAL. October 4, 2004. By Rogelio Martinez. Directed by Michael Sexton. With Carlo Alban, Chris De Oni, Mario Mendez, Halley Wegryn Gross, Frank Wood, Buzz Bovshow. MALAYA. October 5, 2004. By Chay Yew. With Tim Kang, Sophia Skiles, Wai Ching Ho, Ben Wang, Mia Katigbak, Simon Kendall, Melissa Bowen. MOOT THE MESSENGER. October 7, 2004. By Kia Corthron. Directed by Tim Bond. With Tamilla Woodard, Mike Hodge, J. Kyle Manzay, Laura Heisler, Brenda Thomas, Jonathan Hogan, Maulik Pancholy, Elizabeth Bunch. VIPER. October 7, 2004. By Stephanie Fleischmann. Directed by Debbie Saivetz. With Laura Esterman, Peggy Scott, Jayne Houdyshell, Vanessa Aspillaga, Sarah Lord, Christopher Lentz. OUT OF BODY. October 8, 2004. By Neena Beber. Directed by Lynn Thomson. With Vanessa Aspillaga, Keith Randolph Smith, Michael Chernus, Joanna P. Adler, Melinda Wade, Frank Wood, Marissa Copeland, Mary Fogarty.

A BODY OF WATER. October 16, 2004 By Lee Blessing. Directed by Ethan McSweeny. With Jayne Atkinson, Jon DeVries, Carrie Preston.

SICK. November 1, 2004. By Zakiyyah Alexander. Directed by Glynis Rigsby. With April Yvette Thompson, Dominic Taylor, Stephanie Bast, Noah Bean, Marissa Copeland.

RED BESSIE. November 9, 2004. By Jack Gilhooley and Daniel Czitrom. Directed by Mr. Gilhooley. With Charlotte Northeast, Damon Bonetti.

HONOUR IN MOLLOY, OR THE ANIMAL I ONCE WAS. November 15, 2004. By Honour Kane. Directed by David Grimm. With Ms. Kane, Eisa Davis, Aedin Moloney, Donna Villella.

OPUS. December 2, 2004. By Michael Hollinger. With Jon Krupp, Richard Topol, Keith Randolph Smith, Jason Manuel Olazábal, Quincy Tyler Bernstine.

PLAYTIME. KILLING THE BOSS. December 16, 2004. By Catherine Filloux. Directed by Kay Matschullat. With Laura Flanagan, Aaron Yoo, John Daggett, Chris Wells, Keith Randolph Smith, Mercedes Herrero, Matthew Lewis. WRECKAGE. December 16, 2004. By Caridad Svich. Directed by Stefan Novinski. With Alfredo Narciso, Aaron Yoo, Florencia Lozano, Keith Randolph Smith, Chris Wells, William Reid. MAREA. December 17, 2004. By Alejandro Morales. Directed by Debbie Saivetz. With Zabryna Guevara, Polly Lee, Maggie Bofill, Mercedes Herrero. MARY PEABODY IN CUBA. December 17, 2004. By Anne Garcia-Romero. Directed by Seret Scott. With Maggie Bofill, Jennifer Gibbs, Joaquin Torres, Edmond Genest, Tessa Auberjonois, Kate Wetherhead.

POINTS OF DEPARTURE. January 10, 2005. By Michael John Garcés. Directed by Sturgis Warner. With Gilbert Cruz, Chaz Mena, Doris Difarnecio, Mateo Gomez, Zabryna Guevara, Opal Alladin, Gerardo Rodriguez.

TOUCH. February 11, 2005. By Carrie Nutt. Directed by Lynn Thomson. With Susan O'Connor, Lanna Joffrey, LeeAnne Hutchison, Matthew DeCapua, Eric Altheide, Jeff Biehl.

ROBINSON AWAKE. March 14, 2005. By Barbara Wiechmann. With T. Ryder Smith.

WHITE BUFFALO. April 15, 2005. By Don Zolidis; music by DeArmand Williams. Directed by Victor Maog. With Lynn McCollough, Michael Countryman, Elizabeth Bunch, David Medina, Ron Riley, Gil Silverbird, Sami Sargent, Shirley Rumierk, Freedome Bradley.

THE WEB. April 18, 2005. By Michael John Garcés. With Paolo Andino, Michael Chernus, Richard Petrocelli, Jordan Lage, Phyllis Johanson, Matthew Maguire, Lourdes Martin, Andres Munar.

I KNOW YOU'RE THE ONE. April 19, 2005. By Mary Gallagher. Directed by Mary B. Robinson. With David Deblinger, Maggie Siff, Brad Malow, Maggie Burke, Charles Goforth, Socorro Santiago.

MAREA. April 25, 2005. By Alejandro Morales. Directed by Debbie Saivetz. With Mercedes Herrero, Polly Lee, Zabryna Guevara, Maggie Bofill, Meg Allan.

FUBAR. May 5, 2005. By Karl Gajdusek. Directed by Larissa Kokernot. With Lisa Velten, Andrew William Smith, Katie Sigismund, Alex Cranmer, Peter Macon, Lila Rose Kaplan.

KISSING FIDEL. May 23, 2005. By Eduardo Machado. Directed by Michael John Garcés. With Ed Vassallo, Lazaro Perez, Karen Kondazian, Judith Delgado, Andres Munar, Jason Lopez.

IN THE EYE OF HEAVEN. May 31, 2005. By Harding Lemay. Directed by Lynn Thomson. With Eloise Watt, Mary Alice McGuire, Camille Troy, Judith Barcroft, Neil Martin, Lino Delcore, Monro M. Bonnell, David Cole Wheeler, Christopher Lentz.

New Federal Theatre. Dedicated to integrating minorities into the mainstream of American theater through the training of artists and the presentation of plays by minorities and women. Woodie King Jr. producing director.

WAITIN' 2 END HELL. By William A. Parker. June 30, 2004. Directed by Woodie King Jr.; scenery, Roger Predmore; costumes, Stephanie Rafferty; lighting, Antoinette Tynes; sound, Anthony Dixon. With Marcus Naylor, Trish McCall, Thyais Walsh, O.L. Duke, Elica Funatsu, Ron Scott, Eric McLendon.

SWEET SONGS OF THE SOUL. Solo performance piece by Melba Moore. April 3, 2005. Directed by Rhonda Passion Hansome; scenery and lighting, Antoinette Tynes; sound, Sean O'Halloran. With Ms. Moore.

The New Group. Provides an artistic home for fresh acting, writing and design talent. Committed to cultivating a young and diverse theatergoing audience. Scott Elliott artistic director, Geoffrey Rich executive director.

SIN (A CARDINAL DEPOSED). By Michael Murphy. October 26, 2004. Directed by Carl Forsman; scenery, Nathan Heverin; costumes, Theresa Squire; lighting, Josh Bradford; sound, Samuel Doerr. With John Cullum, Dan Daily, Cynthia Darlow, Thomas Jay Ryan, Pablo T. Schreiber, John Leonard Thompson.

A LIKELY STORY. Solo performance by David Cale. December 1, 2004. Directed by Tamara Jenkins. With Mr. Cale.

HURLYBURLY. By David Rabe. January 27, 2005. Directed by Scott Elliott; scenery, Derek McLane; costumes, Jeff Mahshie; lighting, Jason Lyons; sound, Ken Travis. With Bobby Cannavale, Josh Hamilton, Ethan Hawke, Catherine Kellner, Parker Posey, Wallace Shawn, Halley Wegryn Gross.

CRITICAL DARLING. By Barry Levey. February 20, 2005. Directed by Ian Morgan; scenery, Peter R. Feuchtwanger; costumes, Deirdre Wegner; lighting, S. Ryan Schmidt; sound, Matt Sherwin. With Elizabeth Hess, Mark Jacoby, Daniel London, Andrew Polk.

TERRORISM. By the Presnyakov Brothers; translated by Sasha Dugdale. May 23, 2005. Directed by Will Frears; scenery, David Korins; costumes, Sarah Beers; lighting, Marcus Doshi; sound, Bart Fasbender. With Adam Alexi-Malle, Alex Draper, Laura Esterman, Anna George, Darren Goldstein, Daniel Oreskes, Elizabeth Marvel, Lola Pashalinski, R.E. Rodgers. Presented in association with the Play Company.

Pan Asian Repertory Theatre. Creates opportunities for Asian-American artists to perform under the highest professional standards while promoting plays by and about Asians and Asian Americans. Tisa Chang founding artistic director.

MOM, DAD, I'M LIVING WITH A WHITE GIRL. By Marty Chan. October 13, 2004. Directed by Ron Nakahara; scenery, Eric Lowell Renschler; costumes, Carol Pelletier; lighting, James F. Primm II; percussion, Shigeko Suga; fight direction, Michael G. Chin. With Pun Bandhu, Bea Soong, Mary Kickel, Henry Yuk, Shigeko Suga.

CHINA DOLL. By Elizabeth Wong. April 13, 2005. Directed by Tisa Chang; scenery, Kaori Akazawa; costumes, Carol Pelletier; lighting, James F. Primm II; sound, Michael Mittelsdorf. With Rosanna Ma, Jamie Cummings, Jackson Ning, Michael Scott, Ruth Zhang, Sandy York, Robert Wedig, Peter Von Berg.

Performance Space 122 (P.S. 122). Exists to give artists of a wide range of experience a chance to develop work and find an audience. Vallejo Gantner artistic director.

Season included:

US. Solo performance piece by Tim Miller. September 9, 2004. With Mr. Miller.

NOBODY'S LUNCH. By Steven Cosson; music and lyrics by Michael Friedman. September 24, 2004. Directed by Mr. Cosson; choreography, Karinne Keithley; scenery, Andromache Chalfant; costumes, Sarah Beers; lighting Marcus Doshi; sound, Shane Rettig; dramaturgy, Jim Lewis. With Damian Baldet, Daoud Heidami, Christina Kirk, Alix Lambert, Caitlin Miller, KJ Sanchez, Baron Vaughn, Andy Boroson.

APHRODISIAC. By Rob Handel. January 9, 2005. Directed by Ken Rus Schmoll; scenery, Sue Rees; costumes, Michelle R. Phillips; lighting, Garin Marschall; sound, Bray Poor. With Jennifer Dundas, Thomas Jay Ryan, Alison Weller.

PULLMAN, WA. By Young Jean Lee. March 10, 2005. Directed by Ms. Lee; lighting, Eric Dyer. With Thomas Bradshaw, Pete Simpson, Tory Vasquez.

GORILLA MAN. By Kyle Jarrow. March 10, 2005. Directed by Habib Azar; choreography, Julia Hart; scenery, Timothy R. Mackabee; costumes, Sky Switser; lighting, Ben Fox. With Stephanie Bast, Mr. Jarrow, Nell Mooney, Burl Moseley, Perry Silver, Matt Walton, Jason Fuchs.

THE MAMMY PROJECT. Solo performance piece by Joan Evans and Michelle Matlock. April 14, 2005. Directed by Kim Moore. With Ms. Matlock.

SERVANT OF TWO MASTERS. By Carlo Goldoni; adapted by Holly Golden. March 7, 2005. Directed by Ms. Golden; scenery, Reuben Saunders; costumes, Jessica Gaffney; sound,

Ryan Streber. With Amanda Brown, Dennis Fox, Karl Gregory, Khris Lewin, John Pieza, Mr. Saunders, Dara Seitzman, Leigh Williams, Justin Yorio.

ALL STORIES ARE FICTION. March 12, 2005. Solo performance piece by Mike Daisey. Directed by Jean-Michele Gregory; with Mr. Daisey.

THERE GOES THE NEIGHBORHOOD. Solo performance piece by Mari Brown. May 12, 2005. Directed by Ms. Brown and David Travis; lighting, Alistair Wandesforde-Smith; sound, Eric DeArmon. With Deanna Pacelli.

UNCLE JIMMY'S DIRTY BASEMENT. By James Godwin, Peter Baird, Paul Braucher, Tom Burnett, Ceili Clemens, Jennifer A. Cooper, Matt Hausmann, Andrew Innes, Tom Kazumplik, Tim Lagasse, John Pavlik, Leigh Secrest, Martin Small, Russ Tucker, David Yearwood. May 19, 2005. A collective rock-and-roll production with live actors and puppets.

Primary Stages. Dedicated to new American plays. Casey Childs executive producer, Andrew Leynse artistic director.

THE DAY EMILY MARRIED. By Horton Foote. August 5, 2004. Directed by Michael Wilson; scenery, Jeff Cowie; costumes, David C. Woolard; lighting, Rui Rita; sound, Andre Pluess. With Estelle Parsons, James Colby, Hallie Foote, William Biff McGuire, Teri Keane, Delores Mitchell, Pamela Payton-Wright.

STRING OF PEARLS. By Michele Lowe. September 28, 2004. Directed by Eric Simonson; scenery, Loy Arcenas; costumes, David Zinn; lighting, D.M. Wood; sound, Lindsay Jones. With Antoinette LaVecchia, Ellen McLaughlin, Mary Testa, Sharon Washington.

SABINA. By Willy Holtzman. February 2, 2005. Directed by Ethan McSweeny; scenery, Mark Wendland; costumes, Michael Sharpe; lighting, Jane Cox; sound, Robert Kaplowitz. With Marin Ireland, Victor Slezak, Adam Stein, Peter Strauss, Batya MacAdam-Somer. Presented in association with Rising Light Productions.

Full bloom: Katherine Helmond, Bernard Corbett, Carlin Glynn and Joyce Van Patten in the Signature Theatre Company production of Paula Vogel's The Oldest Profession. *Photo: Carol Rosegg*

Voulez-vous? Jeremy Webb and Kristen Johnston in the Signature Theatre Company production of Paula Vogel's The Baltimore Waltz. *Photo: Joan Marcus*

GOING TO ST. IVES. By Lee Blessing. March 29, 2005. Directed by Maria Mileaf; scenery, Neil Patel; costumes, Ann Hould-Ward; lighting, David Lander. With Vivienne Benesch, L. Scott Caldwell.

The Public Theater. Schedule of special projects, in addition to its regular Off Broadway productions. George C. Wolfe producer, Oskar Eustis artistic director, Mara Manus executive director.

NEW WORKS NOW! FESTIVAL OF NEW PLAY READINGS.

MEASURE FOR PLEASURE. By David Grimm. June 7, 2004.

GHETTO SUPERSTAR. Solo performance by Billy Porter. March 6, 2005. Directed by Brad Rouse; costumes, Miguel Angel Huidor; lighting, Chad McArver. With Mr. Porter.

J.A.P. CHRONICLES. Solo performance piece by Isabel Rose. May 18, 2005. Directed by Carl Andress. With Ms. Rose.

Signature Theatre Company. Dedicated to the exploration of a playwright's body of work over the course of a single season. James Houghton artistic director.

THE OLDEST PROFESSION. By Paula Vogel. September 26, 2004. Directed by David Esbjornson; choreography, Lisa Shriver; scenery, Narelle Sissons; costumes, Elizabeth Hope Clancy; lighting, James Vermeulen; sound, Darron L. West. With Marylouise Burke, Carlin Glynn, Katherine Helmond, Priscilla Lopez, Joyce Van Patten.

THE BALTIMORE WALTZ. By Paula Vogel. December 5, 2004. Directed by Mark Brokaw; scenery, Neil Patel; costumes, Michael Krass; lighting, Mark McCullough; sound, David Van Tieghem and Jill BC DuBoff; music, Mr. Van Tieghem; projections, Jan Hartley. With David Marshall Grant, Kristen Johnston, Jeremy Webb.

HOT 'N' THROBBING. By Paula Vogel. March 28, 2005. Directed by Les Waters; choreography, David Neumann; scenery, Mark Wendland; costumes, Ilona Somogyi; lighting, Robert Wierzel;

sound, Darron L. West. With Lisa Emery, Suli Holum, Elias Koteas, Tom Nelis, Matthew Stadelmann, Rebecca Wisocky. A 2004–05 *Best Plays* choice (see essay by David Savran in this volume).

Soho Repertory Theatre. Dedicated to new and cutting edge US playwrights. Daniel Aukin artistic director, Alexandra Conley executive director.

FRANKENSTEIN. By Mary Shelley; adapted by Joshua Carleback, with additional text by Jason Lindner; additional source material from Fyodor Dostoyevsky's *Crime and Punishment*. December 11, 2004. Directed by Mr. Carleback; scenery, Marisa Frantz, costumes, Theresa Squire; lighting, James Japhy Weideman; sound, Jeff Lorenz; music, Jacob Lawson. With Richard Crawford, Carine Montbertrand, Adrienne Kapstein, Mr. Lindner, Tami Stronach, Joshua Koehn, Robert Ross Parker, Damian Baldet. Presented in association with the Flying Machine.

EVERYTHING WILL BE DIFFERENT. By Mark Schultz. April 9. 2005. Directed by Daniel Aukin; scenery, Kip Marsh; costumes, Kim Gill; lighting, Jane Cox; sound, Shane Rettig. With Naomi Aborn, Laura Heisler, Geoffrey Nauffts, Reynaldo Valentin, Jason Jurman, Christopher McCann. Presented in association with True Love Productions.

Theater for the New City. Developmental theater and experimental works. Crystal Field executive director.

DUBYA AND THE GANG OF SEVEN. Musical with book by Leon Katz; music by Clifford J. Tasner; lyrics by Mr. Katz. August 30, 2004. Directed by Jed Allen Harris; music director, Jon Rosen. With Mr. Rosen, Keith Arthur Bolden, Jim Brigman, Ian Christiansen, Jason Howard, Miles Johnson, Aaron Kaburick, Jennifer Kidwell, Tracey Conyer Lee, Nick Newell, Michael J. Miller, Ann Rooney, Esther Triggs, Nicholas Webber.

FOUL SHOTS. By Raymond J. Barry. September 9, 2004. Directed by Thomas Draper. With Mr. Barry, Joseph Culp.

THE CLAIMING RACE. By Robert Glaudini. September 18, 2004. Directed by Brian Roff; scenery, Kelly Hanson; costumes, Mimi O'Donnell; lighting, Josh Epstein; sound, Brooks Williams. With Gerry Becker, Chris McKinney, Lola Glaudini.

THE SUN SHALL RISE. By Cao Yu; adapted by Joanna Chan. October 1, 2004. Directed by Ms. Chan; scenery, Chris Jones; lighting, Dana Sterling. With YiLing Li, Shaung Deng, John Wu, Sam Song, Kevin Fang, Jo Mei, Fang YuLin, Vivian Chiu, Ling King Yuen, Cathy Liu, Lu Yu, Yu JianHuai. Presented in association with Yangtze Repertory Theatre of America.

THE SECRET AGENT. By Joseph Conrad; adapted by David Willinger. November 18, 2004. Directed by Mr.Willinger; scenery, Shiho Kondo; costumes, Stacey Hanes; lighting, Nripal Adhikary, sound, Ithai Benjamin. With Primy Rivera, Sana Haque, Mike Amurata, Steve Greenstein, Michael Andrews, Susham Bedi, Clayton Campbell, Robert Hieger, Jorge Merced, Raj Pannu, Eric Vetter, Ruth Sullivan.

PIECEWORK. By Robyn Burland. November 20, 2005. Directed by George Ferencz; scenery, Tom Lee; costumes, Sally Lesser; sound, Tim Schellenbaum. With Alexander Alioto, Jamie Ansley, Felipe Bonilla, Charles Britt, Nell Gwynn, Allison Hiroto, Jennifer Mann, Juliet O'Brien, Micki Paley, Heather Rogers, Julie Rosier, Chriztopher Zaborowski.

THE AXIS OF EVIL VAUDEVILLE REVUE. Musical with book by Martin Bard; music by Arthur Abrams; lyrics by Mr. Bard. January 14, 2005. Directed by Mr. Bard; choreography, Merete Muenter; scenery, Anne Goetz; lighting, Dylan Vok. With Pat Dixon, Carson Hinners, Tom Martin, Chanel Mobley, Courtney Everette, Kyle Minshew, Quinn Murphy, Adam Purvis.

FINDING CLAIRE. By Kim Merrill. February 3, 2005. Directed by Susan Einhorn; scenery, Ursula Belden; costumes, Kim Cook; lighting, Michael Lincoln. With Deirdre Madigan, Helen Gallagher, Shana Dowdeswell, Geneva Carr.

THE BALLAD OF BAXTER STREET. By Barbara Kahn. February 24, 2005. Directed by Ms. Kahn; scenery, Mark Marcante; costumes, Dolores DeCrisanti; lighting, Jon D. Andreadakis; music by Nicola Barber. With Stephanie Abbinanti, Jocelyn Adams, Evan Bass, Sansan Fibri, Andi Hogan, Robert Marlowe, Dan McVey, Collette Porteous, Kelsey Robinson, Sean Seibert, Taniya Sen, Meave Shelton.

WAITING: A TRILOGY. By Paulanne Simmons. February 24, 2005. Directed by Ted Thompson; scenery, James Greco; lighting, Carrie Yacono; sound, Dave Nolan Audio. With Pierre O'Farrell, Stephanie Lynn Hakun, Deborah Paulter, Joe Salgo, Patrick Toon.

ORANGE FLOWER WATER. By Craig Wright. March 27, 2005. Directed by Carolyn Cantor; scenery, David Korins; costumes, Jenny Mannis; lighting, Ben Stanton; sound, Eric Shim. With Arija Bareikis, Pamela J. Gray, Jason Butler Harner, Paul Sparks. Presented in association with Edge Theatre Company.

RIDING THE BULL. By August Schulenberg. April 28, 2005. Directed by Kelly O'Donnell; scenery, Jason Paradine; sound, Matt Given; music, Gary Keenan. With Will Ditterline, Liz Dailey.

Theatre for a New Audience. Founded in 1979, the company helps develop the performance of Shakespeare and other works of classic drama. Jeffrey Horowitz founding artistic director.

SVEJK. By Colin Teevan; based on *The Good Soldier Svejk* by Jaroslav Hasek; music by Lenny Pickett; lyrics by Mr. Teevan. November 14, 2004. Directed by Dalia Ibelhauptaite; scenery, Gideon Davey; costumes, Anita Yavich; lighting, Mimi Jordan Sherin; sound, Robert Kaplowitz; fight direction, B.H. Barry. With Stephen Spinella, Max Casella, Jo Flores Chase, David Deblinger, Juliana Francis, Michael Gotch, Ken Jennings, Paul Lazar, Peter McRobbie, Mark Mineart, Chip Persons, Richard Poe, Ryan Shively.

CORIOLANUS. By William Shakespeare. February 17, 2004. Directed by Karin Coonrod; scenery, John Conklin; costumes, Anita Yavich; lighting, Scott Zielinski; sound, Ben Neill; fight direction, J. Steven White. With Christian Camargo, Jonathan Fried, Ezra Knight, Roberta Maxwell, Anne Louise Zachry, Teagle F. Bougere, Michael Ray Escamilla, Patrice Johnson, Matthew Maher, Simeon Moore, Michael Rogers, Charles Tuthill.

SOULS OF NAPLES. By Eduardo De Filippo; translated by Michael Feingold. April 14, 2005. Directed by Roman Paska; scenery and costumes, Donna Zakowska; lighting, Stephen Strawbridge; sound, Richard Martinez; music, John T. La Barbera; puppets, Mr. Paska. With John Turturro, Felix Blaska, Bill Bowers, Max Casella, Didi Conn, Juan Carlos Hernandez, Rocco Sisto, Aida Turturro, Francesca Vannucci.

Vineyard Theatre. Chamber theater dedicated to the development of new plays and musicals, music-theater collaborations and innovative revivals. Douglas Aibel artistic director.

PEOPLE ARE WRONG! Musical with book, music and lyrics by Julia Greenberg and Robin Goldwasser. November 4, 2004. Directed by David Herskovits; choreography, Jody Ripplinger; scenery, G.W. Mercier, costumes, Mattie Ullrich; lighting, Lenore Doxsee; sound, Brian Speiser; music direction, Jeremy Chatzky and Joe McGinty. With Chris Anderson, Ms. Goldwasser; Connie Petruk, Todd Almond, Tricia Scotti, John Flansburgh, Erin Hill, David Driver, Maggie Moore, Dan Miller, John Spurney, Clem Waldmann, Mr. Chatzky, Mr. McGinty. Presented in association with Target Margin Theater.

AFTER ASHLEY. By Gina Gionfriddo. February 28, 2005. Directed by Terry Kinney; scenery, Neil Patel; costumes, Laura Bauer; lighting, David Lander; sound and music, Michael Bodeen and Rob Milburn. With Kieran Culkin, Anna Paquin, Tim Hopper, Grant Shaud, Dana Eskelson, Mark Rosenthal. A 2004–05 *Best Plays* choice (see essay by Elizabeth Maupin in this volume).

THE ARGUMENT. By Alexandra Gersten-Vassilaros. May 25, 2005. Directed by Maria Mileaf; scenery, Neil Patel; costumes, Katherine Roth; lighting, David Lander; sound and music, Obadiah Eaves. With Melissa Leo, John Rothman, Jay O. Sanders.

Women's Project. Nurtures, develops and produces plays written and directed by women. Loretta Greco producing artistic director, Julia Miles founding artistic director, Julie Crosby managing director.

THE ANTIGONE PROJECT. October 13–November 7, 2004. Adaptations of the play by Sophocles; scenery, Rachel Hauck; costumes, Elizabeth Hope Clancy; lighting, Sarah Sidman; sound and music, Robert Kaplowitz; projections, Nick Schwartz-Hall.

HANG TEN. By Karen Hartman. Directed by Anne Kauffman. With Angel Desai, Jeanine Seralles, DeSean Terry.

MEDALLION. By Tanya Barfield. Directed by Dana Iris Harrel. With Joey Collins, April Yvette Thompson, Angel Desai, Jeanine Seralles.

ANTIGONE ARKHE. By Caridad Svich, directed by Annie Dorsen. With Jeanine Seralles, Joey Collins, April Yvette Thompson.

A STONE'S THROW. By Lynn Nottage. Directed by Liesl Tommy. With Tracie Thoms, DeSean Terry, April Yvette Thompson, Joey Collins, Angel Desai, Jeanine Seralles.

RED AGAIN. By Chiori Miyagawa. Directed by Barbara Rubin. With Angel Desai, Joey Collins, Tracie Thoms.

BEST OF BOTH WORLDS. Musical with book by Randy Weiner, Diane Paulus; music by Diedre Murray; lyrics by Ms. Weiner; adapted from William Shakespeare's *The Winter's Tale.* December 12, 2004. Directed by Ms. Paulus; choreography, Maria Torres; scenery, Mark Wendland; costumes, Gabriel Berry; lighting, Kevin Adams. With Jeanette Bayardelle, Ronnell Bey, William Scott Davison, Shaun Hoggs, Charles R. King Jr., Griffin Mathews, Kenita R. Miller, Richard E. Waits. Presented in association with Music-Theatre Group.

INKY. By Rinne Groff. March 13, 2005. Directed by Loretta Greco; scenery, Robert Brill; costumes, Valerie Marcus Ramshur; lighting, Sarah Sidman; sound and music, Robert Kaplowitz. With Jessi Campbell, Marianne Hagan, Jason Pugatch, Elizabeth Schweitzer.

The Wooster Group. Ensemble of artists collaborating on the development and production of theatre pieces that respond to the evolving culture. Elizabeth LeCompte director.

POOR THEATER. By the Wooster Group; based on the works of Jerzy Grotowski, William Forsythe and Max Ernst. November 10, 2004. Directed by Elizabeth LeCompte; scenery, Ruud van den Akker and Jim Findlay; lighting Jennifer Tipton; sound, Geoff Abbas and John Collins; video J. Reid Farrington, Ken Kobland and Christopher Kondek. With Ari Fliakos, Sheena See, Scott Shepherd, Kate Valk.

HOUSE/LIGHTS. By the Wooster Group; based on *Doctor Faustus Lights the Lights* by Gertrude Stein. February 5, 2005. Directed by Elizabeth LeCompte; scenery, Jim Findlay; costumes, Elizabeth Jenyon; lighting, Jennifer Tipton; sound, James "J.J." Johnson and John Collins; music, Hans Peter Kuhn and John Lurie; video, Philip Bussmann. With Kate Valk, Suzzy Roche, Roy Faudree, Ari Fliakos, Tanya Selvaratnam, Helen Eve Pickett, Sheena See, John Collins.

York Theatre Company. Dedicated to the development of small-scale musicals, to the rediscovery of underappreciated musicals from the past and to serving the community through educational initiatives. James Morgan artistic director.

LINGOLAND. Musical with book by Kenward Elmslie; music by Claibe Richardson, Jack Beeson, Stephen Dolginoff, William Elliott, Mr. Elmslie, Marvin Fisher, Andrew Gerle, Doug Katsaros, Thomas Pasatierie, Ned Rorem, Joshua Rosenblum, Steven Taylor. February 23, 2005. Direction and scenery, James Morgan; costumes, Suzy Benzinger; lighting, Mary Jo Dondlinger. With Mr. Elmslie, Jane Bodle, Jason Dula, Jeanne Lehman, Steve Routman, Lauren Shealy.

MUSICALS IN MUFTI. April 1–17, 2005.

GOD BLESS YOU, MR. ROSEWATER. Musical with book by Howard Ashman; music by Alan Menken; lyrics by Mr. Ashman; additional lyrics by Dennis Green; based on the novel by Kurt Vonnegut. April 1, 2005. Directed by Sheryl Kaller; music direction, Fred Lassen. With Anastasia Barzee, John Ellison Conlee, Wally Dunn, Dann Fink, Howard Kaye, Beth Leavel, Anthony Newfield, Patti Perkins, David Pittu, J. Robert Spencer, Jamison Stern, Amanda Watkins, Lee Zarrett.

JAMAICA. Musical with book by E.Y. Harburg and Fred Saidy; music by Harold Arlen; lyrics by Mr. Harburg; book adapted by Jeff Hochhauser. April 8, 2005. Directed by Harold Scott; music direction, Jack Lee. With Monica Patton, Terri White, Jim Weaver, Glenn Turner, Nikki Walker, Ricky Smith, Korey Jackson, David Staller, Q. Smith, J.D. Webster, Ty Robinson, Sergia Anderson.

DARLING OF THE DAY. Musical with book by Nunnally Johnson; music by Jule Styne; lyrics by E.Y. Harburg; revised by Erik Haagensen. April 15, 2005. Directed by Michael Montel; music direction, Andrew Gerle. With Beth Fowler, Rebecca Luker, Simon Jones, Stephen Mo Hanan.

THRILL ME. Musical with book, music and lyrics by Stephen Dolginoff. May 26, 2005. Directed by Michael Rupert; scenery, James Morgan; costumes, Jennifer Paar; lighting, Thom Weaver. With Matt Bauer, Doug Kreeger, Stephen Bogardus, John McMartin, Michael Rupert.

MISCELLANEOUS

In the listing of 2004–05 Off Off Broadway productions below, the names of the producing groups, theater venues or festivals appear in CAPITAL LETTERS and the titles of the works in *italics*.

ABINGDON THEATRE COMPANY. *Touch the Names* by Randal Myler and Chic Street. July 4, 2004. Directed by Mr. Myler; with Kristin Stewart Chase, Matthew Cowles, Catherine Curtin, Zabryna Guevara, Jing He, T.J. Kenneally, Carolyn McCormick, Ray Anthony Thomas, Myk Watford, Charles Weldon, "Mississippi" Charles Bevel. *God's Daughter* by Barton Bishop. October 27, 2004. Directed by Alex Dmitriev; with Peter Brouwer, Anne DuPont, Jim Ireland, Susanne Marley. *Hemingway* by Laurence Luckinbill. December 3, 2004. Directed by Benjamin Luckinbill; with Laurence Luckinbill. *Texas Homos* by Jan Buttram. February 2, 2005. Directed by Melvin Bernhardt; with Richard Bekins, Reed Birney, Michael Busillo, Karen Culp, David Van Pelt. *Sunday on the Rocks* by Theresa Rebeck. February 23, 2005. Directed by Kitt Lavoie; with Zoë Frazer, Jane Pfitsch, Stephanie Roche, Lana Faye Taradash.

ABINGDON THEATRE COMPLEX. *Peace* by Aristophanes; adapted by Julie Fei-Fan Balzer. October 20, 2004. Direct by Ms. Balzer; with Nicola Barber, Zack Calhoon, Don Circle Jr., Michelle Lane, Leigh Williams. *Ashes* by ML Kinney. October 20, 2004. Directed by Julie Fei-Fan Balzer; with Nicole duFresne, Carolyn McDermott. *The Owl and the Pussycat* by Bill Manhoff. February 9, 2005. Directed by Zina Jasper; with Patrick Christiano, Chantal Georges. *Caz Dies Alone* by Robert Davenport. March 16, 2005. With Andrew Cassese, Anna Cody, Laura Flanagan; Lawrence Jansen, Tricia McAlpin. *Someone Who'll Watch Over Me* by Frank McGuinness. May 26, 2005. Directed by Orlando Pabotoy; with Damian Buzzerio, Laurence Lowry, Rob Cameron.

ACCESS THEATER. *The Americans* by Matthew Freeman. November 4, 2004. Directed by Gary Shrader; with Kyle Ancowitz, Mr. Freeman, Vince Gatton. *The Golden Age* by A.R. Gurney. With Laura Baldasare, Alison Wright, Rod Cassavale. *Sex and Hunger* by Kyoung H. Park. January 14, 2005. Directed by Catherine Miller; with Chantal Bushelle, Nicholas Gray, Hana Moon, Ron Moreno, Asher Rapkin, Matthew Rini, Sammy Tunis. *The Furies* by Elise McCredie and Trudy Hellier. February 4, 2005. With Maria Theodorakis. *The Information She Carried* by David L. Williams. March 25, 2005. Directed by Carolyn Malone; with Breanna Pine, Christine Carroll, Christopher Drescher, Judson Jones, Christa Kimlicko Jones, Matthew Morgan. *The Dying Goldfish* by James Comtois. May 5, 2005. Directed by Pete Boisvert; with Ree Davis, Jeremy Goren, Sabrina Howells, Leslie E. Hughes, Cat Johnson, Ed Knauer, Marc Landers, John McCausland, Patrick Shearer, Elizabeth Stewart.

THE ACTING COMPANY. *The Turn of the Screw* by Henry James; adapted by Jeffrey Hatcher. Directed by Davis McCallum; with Glenn Peters, Aysan Celik.

THE ACTORS COMPANY THEATRE (TACT). *Flare Path* by Terence Rattigan. October 16, 2004. Directed by Simon Jones; with Jamie Bennett, Jack Koenig, Geoffrey Malloy, Margaret Nichols, James Prendergast, Kathleen Doyle, Darrie Lawrence, Scott Schafer, Graeme Malcolm. *The Firebugs* by Max Frisch; translated by Michael Bullock. November 20, 2004. Directed by Scott Alan Evans;

with Sean Arbuckle, Nora Chester, Francesca DiMauro, Kyle Fabel, Kelly Hutchinson, Simon Jones, Greg McFadden, Scott Schafer, Jim Holdridge, Joel Hurt Jones, Jefferson Slinkard. *Zack* by Harold Brighouse. January 22, 2005. Directed by Victor Pappas; with Mary Bacon, Nora Chester, Richard Ferrone, Rachel Fowler, Sam Gregory, Margaret Nichols, James Prendergast, Gregory Salata, Scott Schafer. *Home* by David Storey. March 12, 2005. Directed by Scott Alan Evans; with Cynthia Darlow, Cynthia Harris, Simon Jones, Larry Keith, Ron McClary. *R.U.R.* by Karel Capek. April 30, 2005. Directed by Scott Alan Evans; with Nora Chester, Kelly Hutchinson, James Murtaugh, Gregory Salata, Scott Schafer, Ashley West, Tony Aylward, Rob Breckenridge, Chris Kipiniak, Josh Renfree, Victor Slezak.

THE ACTORS STUDIO DRAMA SCHOOL THEATRE. *The God of Hell* by Sam Shepard. November 16, 2004. Directed by Lou Jacob; with Randy Quaid, Tim Roth, J. Smith-Cameron, Frank Wood.

AMERICAN THEATRE OF ACTORS. *Entertaining Mr. Sloane* by Joe Orton. September 3, 2004. Directed by Jonathan Silver; with Stephen Weston, Caroline Langford, Sean Dill, Steve Pesola. *Contracts* by Justin Deabler. October 29, 2004. Directed by Ari Kreigh. *Irrationals*. Musical with book by John Marans; music by Edward Thomas; lyrics by Mr. Marans. November 10, 2004. Directed by Martin Platt; with Brandon Michael Arrington, Meredith Kaye Clark, Cicily Daniels, J.D. Goldblatt, Rodney Hicks, Trisha Jeffrey, Nia Jervier, Matt Mundy, Marcus Neville, Greg Pierce, Pearl Sun. *Election Day*. Musical with book by Alex Goldberg; music by Joel Stein; lyrics by Messrs. Goldberg and Stein. January 19, 2005. Directed by Laurie Sales; with Jonathan C. Kaplan, Michele Ragusa, Jeremy Ellison-Gladstone, Ian Kahn, Robert Scott Denny, Shane Desmond, Jennifer J. Katz, Rick Kiley, Alison Mahoney, Meghan McGeary, Jane C. Pejtersen, Tom Richter, Bones Rodriguez, Monica Yudovich. *Fiddlin' 'n' Burnin'* by Paul Buzinski. March 9, 2005. Directed by Merry Beamer; with Alex Goldberg, Allan Hasnas, Jackie Jenkins, Paul Kawecki, Mark Kinch, Teri Monahan, Ellen Reif, David Silberger, Kymm Zuckert. *Wonder Comes on the Seventh Day* by Barry Primus. May 7, 2005. Directed by Mr. Primus; with Tali Friedman, Jeremy Lawrence, Lucille Patton, Barbara Spiegel, Charles Stransky, Rod Sedgwick.

AQUILA THEATRE COMPANY. *Agamemnon*. Concert performance of the opera by Sergey Taneyev; libretto by A. Wekstern; based on the play by Aeschylus, as translated by Peter Meineck. June 16, 2004. Conducted by Peter Tiboris; with Nina Terentieva, Stefan Szkafarowsky, Angela Brown, Peter Lightfoot, Mark Risinger, Olympia Dukakis, Louis Zorich. *The Man Who Would Be King*, adaptation by Peter Meineck from a story by Rudyard Kipling. July 13, 2004. Directed by Robert Richmond; with Louis Butelli, Anthony Cochrane and Richard Willis. *A Very Naughty Greek Play* by Peter Meineck; based on *The Wasps* by Aristophanes. March 5, 2005. Directed by Robert Richmond; with Mr. Richmond, Alex Webb, Richard Willis, Anthony Cochrane.

ARCLIGHT THEATRE. *The Seagull 2288* by A. Marine. Directed by Mr. Marine; with Jill Larson, James Hallett. *Impossible Marriage* by Beth Henley. March 3, 2005. Directed by Deana Morenoff; with Wendi Black, Paul Firestone, Oona Flaherty, Armand Gabriel, Andrew Lincoln, Neil Potter, Barbara J. Spence. *Do Not Go Gentle* by Leon Pownall. April 25, 2005. Directed by Mr. Pownall; with Geraint Wyn Davies.

ARS NOVA. *Vices* by Everett Bradley, Susan Draus, Michael Heitzman, Ilene Reid. September 12, 2004. Directed by Ms. Draus; with Mr. Bradley, James Dybas, Stacia Fernandez, Alexander Gemignani, Mr. Heitzman, Ms. Reid. *Star of Mine* by Gary Sunshine. November 8, 2004. Directed by Trip Cullman; with Michael Chernus, Peter Frechette, Jason Butler Harner, Jonno Roberts, Miriam Shor, Matt Wilkas.

ATLANTIC 453. *Get What You Need* by Jessica Goldberg. June 2, 2004. Directed by Will Frears; with Jenny Bacon, Alex Draper, Josh Hamilton, Lois Smith. *Arrangements* by Ken Weitzman. January 12, 2005. Directed by Christian Parker; with Chrisopher Duva, Katy Grenfell, Stephen Kunken, Julia Murney, Ben Walker.

AXIS THEATRE COMPANY. *Seven in One Blow, or The Brave Little Kid* by the Brothers Grimm; conceived by the Axis Company. December 3, 2004. Directed by Randy Sharp; with Wren Arthur, Brian Barnhart, David Crabb, George Demas, Laurie Kilmartin, Sue Ann Molinell, Edgar Oliver, Marc Palmieri, Abigail Savage, Jim Sterling. *Not Yet Diagnosed (Nervous)* by the Axis Company. April 9, 2005. Directed by Randy Sharp; with Brian Barnhart, David Crabb, George Demas, Marc Palmieri, Margo Passalaqua, Jim Sterling, Ian Tooley.

BANK STREET THEATRE. *Bright Day* by Tom Ellis. August 5, 2004. Directed by Philip Cruise; with Mr. Cruise, Edward Miller, Christopher Lee, Jonny Spanish, Jeanine Bartel, Sara Klingebiel, Sarah K. Lippmann, Kate Sandberg, Eli Ganias, Gerry Vermillion, Joe Salgo, Jack McGowan, Liz Patek, Vance Clemente, Laurena Barros. *The Talk of the Town*. Musical with book, music and lyrics by Ginny Redington and Tom Dawes. October 28, 2004. Directed by Dan Wackerman; with Jeffrey Biering, Donna Coney Island, Rob Seitelman, Caroline McMahon, Chris Weikel, Kellie Drinkhahn, Aaron Kaburick, Matthew Tweardy. *The Top Ten People of the Millennium* by Alec Duffy. January 13, 2005. Directed by Mr. Duffy; with Arthur Aulisi, Barnaby Carpenter, Eugene Rohrer, David Schreiner, Amy Laird Webb.

THE BARROW GROUP (TBG). *Girl Talk* by Kellie Overbey. November 4, 2004. Directed by Carrie Preston; with Marcia DeBonis, Fiona Gallagher, Liz Morton. *Birth Story* by Hilary Baack. February 4, 2005. Directed by Alex P. Baack; with Ms. Baack. *Pentecost* by David Edgar. February 28, 2005. Directed by Seth Barrish; with Oksana Lada, Marc Aden Grey, Stephen Singer, Alysia Reiner, Gene Farber, Yuri Astakhov, Monique Gabriela Curnen, Eliza Foss, Peter Vouras, Jacob Garrett White, Patrick Ssenjovu, Melania Livitsky, Gregory Korostishevsky, Mousa Kraish, Andres Peterson, Katrin Redfern, Anjali Bhimani, Jessica Avellone, Yevgeniy Dekhtyar.

BARROW STREET. *Eat the Taste* by Greg Kotis. October 4, 2004. Directed by John Clancy; with Mr. Kotis, Mark Hollmann, Bill Coelius, Gibson Frazier, Paul Urcioli, Eva van Dok.

BELT THEATER. *Too Much Light Makes the Baby Go Blind* by Greg Allen. February 4, 2005. Directed by Mr. Allen; with Desiree Burch, Regie Cabico, Michael Cyril Creighton, Chris Dippel, Molly Flynn, Lindsay Brandon Hunter, Sarah Levy, Rob Neill, Justin Tolley, Katrina Toshiko. *This or That* by Fred Kahl and Julie Atlas Muz. February 4, 2005. With Mr. Kahl, Ms. Muz.

BLUE HERON ARTS CENTER. *Corporate Rock* by William Bennett. July 12, 2004. Directed by Timothy Haskell; with Travis York, Dorian Missick, Natalia Hernandez, Charles Jang, Gerry Sheridan, Jamie Benge, Aaron Haskell, Kellie Arens, Nick Arens. *I Love Paris* by Doug Field. July 26, 2004. Directed by Timothy Haskell; with Kevin Shinick. *Farm Boys* by Dean Gray and Amy Fox; based on a book by Will Fellows. September 23, 2004. Directed by Jim Pelegano; with David Drake, Joan Grant, Craig Jorczak, Jim Madden, Thomas James O'Leary. *Robeson* by Miriam Jensen Hendrix. April 15, 2005. Directed by Keith Oncale; with Ezra Knight, W. Emory Rose, Korey Jackson, John Marino, Roy Bacon, Vince Phillip, Ty Robinson, Abena Koomson, Ronald Wyche, Bruce Kronenberg, Robert Lydiard, Dathan B. Williams, Annmarie Benedict, Stacey Robinson. *There's the Story* by Timothy McCracken. May 6, 2005. Directed by Christopher Grabowski; with Sean Dougherty, Tara Falk, Mr. McCracken.

BOOMERANG THEATRE COMPANY. *You'll Have Had Your Hole* by Irving Welsh. August 13, 2004. Directed by Francis Kuzler; with Mac Brydon, Zack Calhoon, Thea McCartan, Ian Pfister. *Beyond the Horizon* by Eugene O'Neill. September 8, 2005. Directed by Cailin Heffernan; with Emma Devine, John C. Fitzmaurice, Margaret A. Flanagan, Justin G. Krauss, Jennifer Larkin, Dolores McDougal, Peter Morr, Peter O'Connor, Ron Sanborn. *Burning the Old Man* by Kelly McAllister. September 10, 2004. Directed by Tim Errickson; with Brett Christiansen, Philip Emeott, John C. Fitzmaurice, Christine Goodman, Timothy McCracken, Sara Thigpen. *Patience* by Jason Sherman. September 15, 2004. Directed by Amy Henault; with Peter Bisgaier, Larry Giantonio, Jenn Marie Jones, Peter Picard, Dawn Sobczak, Christine Verlany.

CAP 21 THEATER. *The Independent*. Musical with book by Steven Scott Smith, music by Steven Schoenberg, lyrics by Mr. Smith. October 11, 2003. Directed by Phil Reno. *Hypochrondriac: A Love Story* by Tony DiMurro. November 22, 2004. *Becoming Ingrid* by Liza Lentini. December 6, 2004. *Six of One*. Musical with book by Scott Burkell; music by Paul Loesel; lyrics by Mr. Burkell. May 16, 2005. Directed by Frank Ventura; with Leslie Becker, Danyelle Bossardet, Zachary Halley, Guy Lemonnier, Tia Speros.

CASTILLO THEATRE. *Stealin' Home* by Fred Newman. October 8, 2004. Directed by Mr. Newman; with Garrett Lee Hendricks, Andy Parker, Donisha Brown. *Nothing Really Happens* by Fred Newman. October 15, 2004. Directed by Mr. Newman; with Judith Malina, Madelyn Chapman, Mary Round, David Nackman, Lindsey White, Kenneth Hughes, Anthony Bagnetto, Roger Grunwald, Leonard Chetkin, Rosemary Quinn, Donald Rizzo, Jason Troy Van Pelt, Judith Caporale, Arthur Rubin, Gwen Hagerty, Amy Hoerler, Amy Beth Sherman, Vinz Feller. *Robin Hood: A Political Romance* by Dan Friedman. February 25, 2005. Directed by Mr. Friedman; with Michael Alcide, Donique Banks,

Darnelle Cadet, Franceli Chapman, Natasha Danielian, Vanessa Emmanuel, Devon Ewalt, Peter Graham, Mary Holder, Antonie Joyce, Angela Lamouth, Katie McClenahan, Jade Mulvan, Armando Newbold, Alethea Rivera, Zenobia Shroff, Serge Velez. *Revising Germany* by Fred Newman. March 11, 2005. Directed by Gabrielle Kurlander; with Jeff Aron, Madelyn Chapman, Belinda Fevrier, Maggie Gouldin, Roger Grunwald, Ellen Korner, Mary Round, Cathy Rose Salit, Vicky Wallace, Lindsey White.

CHASHAMA. *Sleeping in Tomorrow* by Duncan Pflaster. October 19, 2004. Directed by Clara Barton Green; with Lauren Adler, Sue Berch, Elizabeth Boskey, Wael Haggiagi, Dawn Pollock Jones, Paul Martin Kovic, Ehud Segev, Jason Specland, Sami Zetts. *Titus X: The Musical*. Musical by Shawn Northrip. November 5, 2004. Directed by Peter Sanfilippo; with Amanda Bond, Bat Parnas, Joe Pendelski, Ben Pryor, Peter Schuyler, T-Boy. *A Matter of Choice* by Chad Beckim. March 24, 2005. Directed by John Gould Rubin; with Chris Chalk, Sharon Freedman, Sarah Hayon, Molly Pearson, Maduka Steady, Jeremy Strong, John Summerour. *Good Fences Make Good Neighbors* by Adam Klasfeld. April 14, 2005. Directed by Sherri Kronfeld; with Donna Abraham, Nick Choksi, Michael De Nola, Michelle Dingoor, Mark Lane. *She Who Burns* by R.M. Philippi. May 6, 2005. Directed by Ms. Philippi; with Aaron Beall, Vera Beren, Joyia Bradley, Mi Sun Choi, Corey Corey, Ryan Farley, Evan Laurence, Marty McDonough, Maggie Steele, Michael Tomlinson.

CHERRY LANE THEATRE. *Miss Julie* by August Strindberg; translated by Truda Stockenström. June 22, 2004. Directed by Scott Schwartz; with Mimi Bilinski, Michael Aronov, Opal Alladin. *Five Bottles in a Six Pack* by Renita Martin. October 26, 2004. Directed by Laurie Carlos; with Ms. Martin, Jane Wange. MENTOR PROJECT 2005. January 17-31, 2005. *The Grille Room* by Sam Forman; mentored by Michael Weller. *Morbidity and Mortality* by Courtney Baron; mentored by David Auburn. *Huck and Holden* by Rajiv Joseph; mentored by Theresa Rebeck. *Slag Heap* by Anton Dudley. April 13, 2005. Directed by Michael Morris; with Brienin Bryant, Alexander Flores, Vincent Kartheiser, Polly Lee, Maggie Moore, Janelle Anne Robinson.

CLASSICAL THEATRE OF HARLEM. *Macbeth* by William Shakespeare. July 16, 2004. Directed by Alfred Preisser; with Ty Jones, Roslyn Ruff, Arthur French. *Ain't Supposed to Die a Natural Death*. Musical with book, music and lyrics by Melvin Van Peebles. October 1, 2004. Directed by Alfred Preisser; with Carmen Baika, Ralph Carter, Shamika Cotton, Neil Dawson, D. Rubin Green, Rashad Ernesto Greene, Tracy Jack, Ty Jones, J. Kyle Manzay, Yusef Miller, Lizan Mitchell, Simone Moore, Nyambi Nyambi, Ron Simons, Glenn Turner, Althea Vyfhuis, Robyn Landiss Walker, Kendra Ware. *The Cherry Orchard* by Anton Chekhov; adapted by Christopher McElroen. February 3, 2005. Directed by Mr. McElroen; with Earle Hyman, Wendell Pierce, Vinie Burrows, Petronia Paley, Darian Dauchan, Carolyn Ratteray, Chandra Thomas, J. Kyle Manzay, George Hosmer. *Caligula* by Alfred Preisser and Randy Weiner. April 1, 2005. Directed by Mr. Preisser; with Andre De Shields, Jeanine T. Abraham, Cecilia Aderonke, Tory Andrus, Carmen Barika, Donisha Brown, Noshir Dalal, George Gallagher, Zainab Jah, Adam Kern, Angela Lewis, Galway McCullough, Paul J. Medford, John-Andrew Morrison, Channie Waites.

CLUBBED THUMB. SUMMERWORKS FESTIVAL 2004. June 2–26, 2004. *Of A White Christmas* by Rinne Groff. Directed by Trip Cullman. *Crumble (Lay Me Down, Justin Timberlake)* by Sheila Callaghan. Directed by Katie Pearl. *Those Who Can, Do* by Brighde Mullins. Directed by Maria Mileaf. SUMMERWORKS FESTIVAL 2005. May 4–28, 2005. *100 Aspects of the Moon* by Ethan Lipton. Directed by Emma Griffin. *Madame Killer* by Honour Kane. Directed by Wier Harman. *Dearest Eugenia Haggis* by Ann Marie Healy. Directed by Melissa Kievman.

COLLECTIVE: UNCONSCIOUS. *George and Martha* by Karen Finley. September 17, 2004. Directed by Ms. Finley; with Ms. Finley, Neal Medlyn. *Serenade* and *Philosopher Fox* by Slawomir Mrozek. February 3, 2005. Directed by Paul Bargetto; with Heather Benton, Michelle Guthrie, Ray Kaim, Troy Lavallee, Ray Wasik. *Couplets* by Mike Bencivenga. May 7, 2005. Directed by Mr. Bencivenga; with Stephen Aloi, Julie Hera, Jay Aubrey Jones, Suzanne Levinson, John McDermott, Misha Pogul, Talia Rubel.

CONNELLY THEATRE. *Push Up 1–3* by Roland Schimmelpfennig; translated by Melanie Dreyer. September 20, 2004. Directed by Cynthia Dillon; with Ken Bolden, Cate Brewer, Chris Campbell, Steven Hess, Leo Kittay, Thea McCartan, Tashya Valdevit. *Edward II* by Christopher Marlowe; adapted by Rebecca Patterson. October 9, 2004. Directed by Ms. Patterson; with Lauren Jill Ahrold, E.J. An, Virginia Baeta, Marwa Bernstein, Jennifer Boggs, Zainab Jah, Marsha Jelleff, Kittson O'Neill, Beverley Prentice, Erin Roe, Gisele Richardson.

THE DIRECTORS COMPANY. *Tales From the Saltmines* by Mary Lathrop. September 13, 2004. Directed by Michael Parva; with Kaitlin Hopkins. *Tales of Tinseltown*. Musical with book and lyrics by Michael Colby; music by Paul Katz. December 6, 2004. Directed by Barry Ivan; with Kate Baldwin, Montego Glover, Eddie Korbich, Leslie Kritzer, Jonathan Rayson, Ryan Silverman, Jennifer Smith, Tony Yazbeck. *Murder in the First* by Dan Gordon. April 7, 2005. Directed by Michael Parva; with Jeremy Bobb, Dan Patrick Brady, Laurie Ann Bulman, Suzie Cho, James Ecklund, James Michael Farrell, Mark Goldbaum, Daren Kelly, Mike Lim, Allen McCullough, Thomas Ryan, Stelio Savante, William Severs, Gene Silvers, John Stanisci.

DUKE ON 42ND STREET. *Rose Rage* by Edward Hall and Roger Warren; adaptation of *Henry VI* by William Shakespeare. September 17, 2004. Directed by Mr. Hall; with Richard W. Clothier, Jason Denuszek, Will Dickerson, Joe Forbrich, Sean Fortunato, Chris Genebach, Carman Lacivita, Fletcher McTaggart, Mark L. Montgomery, Scott Parkinson, Jay Whittaker, Bruce A. Young.

EMERGING ARTISTS THEATRE COMPANY. *The Gay Naked Play* by David Bell. June 3, 2004. Directed by Christopher Borg and Jason Bowcutt; with Mr. Borg, Jessica Calvello, Brett Douglas, Desmond Dutcher, Wayne Henry, Gregory Marcel, Ellen Reilly, Michael Silva, Christopher Yustin, Daniel Nardicio. EATFEST. March 29–April 17, 2005. *Foreign Bodies* by Andrew Biss. Directed by Dylan McCullough; with Laura Fois, Kurt Kingsley. *Asteroid Belt* by Lauren Feldman. Directed by Caden Hethorn; with Valerie David, Rachel Eve Moses, Sam Sagenkahn. *Invisible* by Marc Castle. Directed by Mark Finley; with Ryan Berit, Neil W. Garguilo, Jack Garrity, William Reinking. *A Watched Pot* by Kevin Drzakowski. Directed by Tom Wojtunik; with Ashley Green, Rebecca Hoodwin, J. Michael Zally, Nick Ruggeri. *Man on Dog* by Ry Herman. Directed by Deb Guston; with Richard Busser, Desmond Dutcher, Erin Hadley, Aimee Howard, Peter Levine. *Roast Beef and the Rare Kiss* by Gregory Fletcher. Directed by Troy Miller; with Patrick Arnheim, Matt Boethin, Lavette Gleis, Danae Hanson. *The Child* by Kerri Kochanski. Directed by Steven McElroy; with Michael Cleeff, Leecia Manning. *Twelve Rounds* by Sheldon Senek. Directed by Nick Micozzi; with Matt Boethin, Danae Hanson, Jason Hare, Stacy Mayer.

59E59. *The Booth Variations* by Todd Cerveris and Caridad Svich; conceived by Mr. Cerveris, Nick Philippou and Ms. Svich. August 8, 2004. Directed by Mr. Philippou; with Mr. Cerveris, Michael Cerveris, Josh Mann, Lila Donnolo. *Sakharam Binder* by Vijay Tendulkar; translated by Kumud Mehta and Shanta Gokhale. October 30, 2004. Directed by Maria Mileaf; with Adam Alexi-Malle, Sarita Choudhury, Anna George, Sanjiv Jhaveri, Bernard White. *A Tale of a Tiger* by Dario Fo; adapted by Ami Dayan. November 23, 2004. Directed by Mr. Dayan; with Mr. Dayan. *1984* by George Orwell; adapted by Alan Lyddiard. January 12, 2005. Directed by Joe Tantalo; with Gregory Konow, Randy Falcon, Julie E. Fitzpatrick, Mike Roche, David Bartlett, Sarah Cook, Sarah Matthay, Julie Torsiello, Katherine Boynton. *A Clockwork Orange* by Anthony Burgess. January 19, 2005. Directed by Joe Tantalo; with Randy Falcon, Gregory Konow, Julie E. Fitzpatrick, David MacNiven, Mike Roche, Jace McLean, David Bartlett, Sarah Cook, Sarah Matthay, Dana Tyler, Katherine Boynton, Rocco Turso. *Taxi to Jannah* by Mark Sickman. February 8, 2005. Directed by Donald Douglass; with Regina Bartkoff, Amir Darvish, Christopher Diaz, Amir Khafagy, Jacob C. Mirer, Remy K. Selma, Natasha Williams. *The God Botherers* by Richard Bean. February 26, 2005. Directed by David Travis; with Heidi Armbruster, Michael Warner, Kola Ogundiran, Tinashe Kajese. *A Little Rebellion Now* by Lisa Voss. March 4, 2005. Directed by Susanna Harris; with Lionel Gentle, Joan Green, Suzette Gunn, Garrett Lee Hendricks, Siobhan Parisi, Dan Renkin, Jessenia Rivas, Margot White, Derek T. Bell. *The Germans in Paris* by Jonathan Leaf. March 11, 2005. Directed by Jose Zayas; with Kevin Kelly, Ali Marsh, Jennifer Don, Corey Moosa, Brian Louis Hoffman, Henry Caplan, Bruce Barton, Paul Siemens, Monica West.

45 BLEECKER. *Night Sings Its Songs* by John Fosse; translated by Sarah Cameron Sunde. June 7, 2004. Directed Ms. Sunde, with Louis Cancelmi, Anna Guttormsgaard, Diane Ciesla, Peter Davies, George Hannah. REVELATION READINGS. September 13–October 18, 2004. Schedule included: *Fortinbras* by Lee Blessing. September 13, 2004. Directed by Jesse Berger; with Paul Rudd, Dallas Roberts, Daniel Breaker. *The Roman Actor* by Phillip Massinger. Directed by Kay Matschullat; with Richard Thomas. *Women Beware Women* by Thomas Middleton. Directed by Paul Mullins. *The Knight of the Burning Pestle* by Francis Beaumont. Directed by Christopher Bayes; with Daniel Breaker. *Don Jonny* by Anton Dudley and Jonathan Spottiswoode. Directed by Jesse Berger; with Steve Ratazzi, Tracie Thoms. *Ragozine, or the Second-Best Bed Trick* by Michael Feingold. THE DEMOCRACY PROJECT. September 14, 2004–October 2, 2004. *Sullivan Travels Again* by Nicole

Burdette. *Lip Service* by Jerome Hairston. *How We Get to Where We're Going* by Theresa Rebeck. *The Dying City* by Christopher Shinn. *Patriot, Schmatriot* by Louise Rozett. *To Be Human* by Stephen Belber. *Reagan in Hell* by Lee Blessing. *Samsara* by Juana Kennedy. *Medieval Scene* by Kenneth Lonergan. *Kandor* by Tom Fontana. *Fear Network News* by Warren Leight. *The Conductor* by Eduardo Machado. *Hecuba* by Euripides; translated by William Arrowsmith. October 10, 2004. Directed by Alex Lippard; with Kristin Linklater, Lucas Blondheim, Janna Gjesdal, Starla Bedford, Phyllis Johnson, Dale Soules, Kathleen Turco-Lyon, Heather Tom, Curzon Dobell, Scott Casper, Craig Myers, Matthew R. Wilson, Helmar Augustus Cooper, Mike Genovese, Christopher McCann, James Gabriel Gilbert, Matthew Reid Seife, Ching Valdes-Aran, Allison Leyton-Brown, Kaveh Nabatian. *Fefu and Her Friends* by Maria Irene Fornes. December 2, 2004. Directed by Krissy Smith; with Nikki Alikakos, Elizabeth Howard, Margarita Martinez, Sameerah Luqman-Harris, Courtney Reynolds, Sasha Cucciniello, Nicola Riske, Kiki Allgeier. *The Shooting Stage* by Michael Lewis Maclennan. February 27, 2005. Directed by John Pinckard; with Chris Durham, Hunter Gilmore, Ben Masur, Noah Peters, Robin Taylor. *The Trial of K* by Franz Kafka. March 30, 2005. Directed by Joy Leonard and Chris Nichols; with Margaret O'Sullivan, Clinton Powell, Tina West Chavous, Aubrey Hardwick, Ten Hannan, Joy Lynn Alegarbes, Ginger Legon, M.A. Makowski. *Index to Idioms* by Deb Margolin. April 3, 2005. Directed by Merri Milwe; with Ms. Margolin. *The Beauty Inside* by Catherine Filloux. April 19, 2005. Directed by Kay Matschullat; with Jennifer Gibbs, Tatiana Gomberg, Edward A. Hajj, A-men Rasheed, Michelle Rios.

FOUNDRY THEATRE. *K.I. From "Crime"* by Daniil Gink; adapted from Fyodor Dostoyevsky's *Crime and Punishment.* January 10, 2005. Directed by Kama Ginkas; with Oksana Mysina, Elizabeth Boiko, Bridget Clark, Eugene Vovk.

14TH STREET Y THEATER. *Voting for Godot* by Cliff Hahn. August 28, 2004. Directed by Mr. Hahn; with Neil Levine, Marshall York, Mina Kim, Fred Rueck, Ken Simon, Bashir Solebo. *Hazard County* by Allison Moore. October 10, 2004. Directed by Blake Lawrence; with Alice Barden, Stephen Bienskie, John Grady, Jeanne Hime, Kate VanDevender. *Wuthering High* by Karen Grenke, Christina Nicosia, Jonathan Van Gieson, David Vining. February 14, 2005. Directed by Mr. Vining; with Stephen Blackwell, Bryn Boice, John Grace, Ms. Grenke, Ginna Hoben, Andrew Hurley, Meghan Love, Christina Nicosia, Timothy Shaw, Rachel Speicher, Mr. Van Gieson, Dov Weinstein. *Snake in the Fridge* by Brad Fraser. April 14, 2005. Directed by Blake Lawrence; with Angela Ai, Susan O'Connor, Mimi Bilinski, Sarah K. Lippmann, Kevin Hogan, Matthew J. Nichols, Patrick Fellows, Gabriel Grilli, Christian Michael Felix.

GREENWICH STREET THEATRE. THIRD ANNUAL HALLOWEEN FESTIVAL. October 7–31, 2004. Schedule included: *The Lizards* by Alan Bowne. Directed by Scott Amen. *Eternity: Time Without End* by Duncan Pflaster. Directed by Mr. Pflaster. *Sin Times Seven* by Daniel Haben Clark. Directed by Mr. Clark. *Radioactive Republicans and Dancing Democrats* by Elias Stimac. Directed by Mr. Stimac; with Susan Bucci, Rodney E. Reyes, Jasmine Bermudez, Nancy Pagan, Elizabeth Anne Wood, Glory Sims Bowen, Caroline Samaan, Ali Baynes, Jonathan Weirich, Richard Renner, Liz Lord, Christine Seisler, Lynn Compton, Joanna Hughes, Carl Owens, Tami Gebhardt, Nirene DiNardo. *Laura Cleans House* by Ed Valentine. Directed by Peter Bloch. *Mapplethorpe's Flowers* by Gregory Fletcher. Directed by Judith Partelow. *Dirty Works* by Jamie Linley. January 23, 2005. Directed by Kevin Kittle; with Micky Campbell, Martin Ewens, Martin Hiller, Polly Lee, Mr. Linley, Aidan Redmond, Christine Rendel, Louise Traynor, Victor Villar-Hauser. *Tales of the Lost Formicans* by Constance Congdon. March 3, 2005. Directed by Sharon Fogarty; with Rhonda Harrington, Terri Mintz, Bill Weeden, Ed Varley, Claude Deering, Michael Dermansky, Wanda O'Connell. *Women of Manhattan* by John Patrick Shanley. March 17, 2005. Directed by Peggy Lewis; with Victor Barbella, Tiki Barber, Leah Blesoff, Sandra Cordero, Erin Quinn Purcell.

HB PLAYWRIGHTS THEATRE. THE WEDDING PLAYS. June 8–27, 2004. Schedule included: *Green Sappho Rising* by Cusi Cram. Directed by Brad Rouse. *Waukegan Wedding* by Adam Kraar. Directed by Brad Rouse. *Wedding Picture* by Quincy Long. Directed by Kathleen Dimmick. *Hope* by Julie McKee. Directed by Margo Cohn. *One Hand, One Heart* by Lisa-Marie Radano. Directed by Nela Wagman. *The Lovely Just So* by Susan Sandler. Directed by Gus Kaikkonen. *John's Dad* by Joe Sutton. Directed by Paul Weidner. *Married Before* by Laura Shaine Cunningham. Directed by Susan Einhorn. *Our Son's Wedding* by Donna de Matteo. Directed by Amy Wright. *Marriage à Trois* by Catherine Filloux. Directed by David Letwin. *The Wedding Play* by Alexandra Gersten-Vassilaros. Directed by Amy Wright. *Little Monsters* by Jocelyn Meinhardt. Directed by Andy Goldberg.

What You Can't Hear by Daniel Reitz. Directed by Jules Ochoa. *Venice in Vegas* by James Ryan. Directed by Mr. Ryan. *Just the Two of Us* by Tug Yourgrau. Directed by Susan Einhorn. *The Habitation of Dragons* by Horton Foote. December 4, 2004. Directed by William Carden; with David Adams, Pierce Green, Tim Hopper, Kahan James, John Juback, Richard Mawe, Jim McGurn, Carol Morley, Rochelle Oliver, Jess Osuna, Kathleen Peirce, Amanda Plant, Lorca Simons, Victor Slezak, Adam Stern, Mark Thornton.

HERE ARTS CENTER. QUEER @ HERE FESTIVAL. June 15–26, 2004. Schedule included: *Cardiac Arrest or Venus on a Half Clam* by Taylor Mac. *In Heat: An Amusing Evening of Discomforting Essays* by Lisa Haas. *Naked and Famous* by Andy Horowitz. *High/Limbo/High* by A. Rey Pamatmat. *Hijack's First Show in New York* by Kristin Van Loon and Arwen Wilder. *Descendants of Freedom* by Andre Lancaster. *Honey Toes Makes a Scene* by Amy Jo Goddard. *Eager Martyrs* by Matt Jensen. *The Good Enemy* by Jesse Phillips-Fein. *Two Works From Dark Earth* by Ariel Goldberger. *Civil Woman* by Jenni Werner. *Rush's Dream* by Julian Mulvey. June 17, 2004. Directed by Alexandra Farkas; with Chris Breyer, Baz Snider, Richard Mawe, John Michalski, Chris Briggs, Michael Poignand, Margaret Ritchie, Matt Walton, Rob Yamall. THE AMERICAN LIVING ROOM FESTIVAL. July 22– September 5, 2004. Schedule included: *Foreign* by Dario Tangelson. *Mrs. Sweetney* by Robert Saietta. *Moloch and Other Demons* by Jason Grote. *The Nostalgic Recollections of Raymond Boggs* by Emily Witt. *And I Love You* by Sarah Kozinn. *Unpublished Research* by Diego Pardo. *Kawaisoo (The Pity of Things)* by Jason Grote. *I'm in Love With the President* by Rick Fiori. *Border* by Zohar Tzur. *The Feeling of a Beard* by Ksenia Dragunskaya. *Post Oedipus* by Steven Gridley. *The Female Terrorism Project* by Ken Urban. *Democracy in America: Part One* by Annie Dorsen. *Dark River: The Diary of a Nobody* by Kevin Lawler. *Safe* by Babak Ebrahimian. *Girlstory* by Ellen Hagan and Lisa Ascalon. *Brave Smiles . . . Another Lesbian Tragedy* by the Five Lesbian Brothers. November 12, 2004. Directed by Jason S. Little; with Leah Bonvissuto, Christina Hackim, Nicole Hayes, Victoria Healy, Maggie Neuwald. *Hanjo* by Yukio Mishima. November 24, 2004. Directed by Kameron Steele; with Ivana Catanese, Nathan Guisinger, Anilu Pardo. *Suspicious Package* by Brian Parks. November 24, 2004. Directed by Paul Urcioli; with David Calvitto, Christopher Carley, Leslie Farrell, Jody Lambert, Jona Tuck. *From: A Masque in Seven Inventions* by Connie Beckley. December 3, 2004. Directed by Ms. Beckley; with Frederick Neumann, Rob Schwimmer. *The Three Ecstasies* by Suzy Khimm. December 5, 2004. Directed by Emma Rika; with Desiree Burch, Asia Dillon, Eliisa Frazier, Madeleine Maby, Tim Mullaney, Christopher Myers. *Conquest of the Universe* by Charles Ludlam. December 9, 2004. Directed by Emma Griffin; with Matthew Maher, Maria Striar, Gibson Fraizer, Bryan Salfi, Clayton Dean Smith, Rachel Shukert, Suzi Takahashi, Chris Wells. CULTURE MART. January 5–16, 2005. Schedule included: *Zong* by Kim Mayhom. *Radio Wonderland* by Joshua Fried. *The Littlewood Project* by Mallory Catlett. *Freefall* by Lynn Brown and Lynn Marie Ruse. *A Seemingly Unified Spectacle* by Kate Brehm. *Alice in Wonderland* by Lewis Carroll; adapted by Lake Simons and John Dyer. *Rest/Less* by Thalia Field and Jamie Jewett. *Café Antarsia* by Ruth Margraff. *Disposable Men* by James Scruggs. February 3, 2005. Directed by Kristin Marting; with Mr. Scruggs. *Nita and Zita* by Lisa D'Amour. January 27, 2005. Directed by Ms. D'Amour; with Katie Pearl, Kathy Randels. *The Confessions of Punch and Judy* by Tannis Kowalchuck and Ker Wells. February 8, 2005. Directed by Raymond Bobgan; with Ms. Towalchuck, Mr. Wells. *All Wear Bowlers* by Trey Lyford and Geoff Sobelle. February 17, 2004. Directed by Aleksandra Wolska; with Messrs. Lyford and Sobelle.

HYPOTHETICAL THEATRE COMPANY. *The Action Against Sol Schumann* by Jeffrey Sweet. June 19, 2004. Directed by Julie Feinberg; with Tandy Cronyn, Douglas Dickerman, Kim Donovan, Catherine Lynn Dowling, Margaret A. Flanagan, Bruce Mohat, Susan O'Connor, Postell Pringle, Jerry Rockwood, Herbert Rubens, Nathan M. White.

THE INDEPENDENT THEATER. *Hearts Beating Faster* by Ralph Pape. August 22, 2004. Directed by Ken Marini; with Heidi Karlsen, Annabel LaLonde, Amy McKenzie, Dave Rosenberg, Stewart J. Zully. *Fall of the House of Usher* by Edgar Allan Poe; adapted by Steven Berkoff. October 21, 2004. Directed by Gabriel Shanks; with Frank Blocker, Shannon Maddox, Janice Herndon.

INTAR 53. *Eyes of the Heart* by Catherine Filloux. October 12, 2004. Directed by Kay Matschullat; with Mia Katigbak, Nadia Bowers, Alexis Camins, James Saito, Virginia Wing, Eunice Wong.

IRISH ARTS. *Women on the Verge* by Marie Jones. September 30, 2004. Directed by Lynne Taylor-Corbett; with Joan Slavin, Kelly Taylor, Tom Souhrada. *Frankie* by Daniel Roberts. April 3, 2005. Directed by Alex Lippard; with Andrea Gallo, Davis Hall, Aaron Muñoz, Kristina Klebe, Anthony

Patellis. *Howie the Rookie* by Mark O'Rowe. May 18, 2005. Directed by Nancy Malone; with John O'Callaghan, Mark Byrne.

JOHN HOUSEMAN THEATRE. *Pandora's Box: A Vaudeville.* Musical with book by Robert Lawson; music, Henry Akona; lyrics, Mr. Lawson. October 27, 2004. Directed by Mr. Akona; with Krista Berry, Jonathan Farmer, Corey Michener, Meredith Nicholaev, Nick Marcotti, Allegra Gilfenbaum, DJ Potter, Nadia Taalbi, Maria Torti, Erik White, Liz Wisan, Sadie Rose Zavgren. *Mud* by Maria Irene Fornes. February 24, 3005. Directed by James Mishook; with Haley Channing, James Gash, Adrian Roman. *The Home for Lost Boys* by Craig J. Weiner. March 5, 2005. Directed by Renee Blinkwold; with Cameron Cash, Lexy Fridell, Gary Littman, John Michalski, Jonathan Monk. *Lazer Vaudeville.* March 9, 2005. Directed by Carter Brown; with Mr. Brown, Cindy Marvell, Nicholas Flair. *Audience, Unveiling, Protest* by Vaclav Havel. March 23, 2005. Directed by Jesse Edward Rosbrow; with Gregg David Shorr, Mike Durell, David Abeles, Lyndsay Becker, Isaac Scranton.

JOHN MONTGOMERY THEATRE Company. *The Collard Green: Contributions by Cornbread Divas* by Ernie McClintock; adapted by Indira Etwaroo. January 6, 2005. Directed by Ms. Etwaroo; with Tamela Aldridge, Ms. Etwaroo, Tamara Xavier.

KEEN COMPANY. *Pullman Car Hiawatha* by Thornton Wilder. June 24, 2004. Directed by Henry Wishcamper; with Jonathan Hogan, Susan Pellegrino, Dan Cordle, Jocelyn Rose, Martin Carey, Maria Dizzia, Christa Scott-Reed, Glenn Pannell, Ann Dowd, Shane McRae, Peter Russo, Jimonn Cole, Ryan Ward, John Patrick, Michael Warner, Pi Smith, Wilbur Edwin Henry, Christopher Keough, Melodie Sisk, Laura Plouffe, Kristen Bedard, Lael Logan, David Standish, DJ Mifflin. *The Happy Journey to Trenton and Camden* by Thornton Wilder. June 24, 2004. Directed by Carl Forsman. Jonathan Hogan, Ann Dowd, Ryan Ward, Wilbur Edwin Henry, Laura Plouffe, Lael Logan. *The Hasty Heart* by John Patrick. November 26, 2004. Directed by Jonathan Silverstein; with Keith Nobbs, Stephen Bradbury, Chris Chalk, Emily Donahoe, Lucas Hall, Chris Hutchison, Anthony Manna, Brian Sgambati, Paul Swinnerton. *Pyretown* by John Belluso. January 29, 2005. Directed by Carl Forsman; with Deirdre O'Connell, Christopher Thornton. *Outward Bound* by Sutton Vane. April 16, 2005. Directed by Robert Kalfin; with Joe Delafield, Drew Eliot, Laura Esterman, Wilbur Edwin Henry, Susan Pellegrino, Michael Pemberton, Clayton Dean Smith.

KIRK THEATRE. *Paradise* by Glyn O'Malley. March 12, 2005. Directed by Mr. O'Malley; with Sanaz Alexander, Janine Barris, Vaneik Echeverria, Arian Moayed, Carmen Roman. *Absolutely Fascinating.* April 11, 2005. Directed by Russell Churney; with Adele Anderson, Dillie Keane, Liza Pulman.

KRAINE THEATER. *Hopscotch: The New York Sex Comedy* by Wendy R. Williams. October 6, 2004. Directed by Ms. Williams; with Brianna Leigh Hansen, Doug Hurley, Jonas Graham, Diedre Kilgore, Josh McLane, Jeffrey Perkins, Rachel Plotkin, Rachael Roberts. *The Secret Narrative of the Phone Book* by Gordon Cox. February 7, 2005. Directed by Suzanne Agins; with Bill Dawes, Natalie Gold, Brandon Miller, John C. Vennema. *Golden Age* by Roberto Aguirre-Sacasa. April 1, 2005. Directed by Claire Lundberg; with Cameron Cash, Michael Chernus, Patch Darragh, Sarah Elliott, Greg Felden, Christopher J. Hanke, Christopher Kromer, Tami Mansfield, Charles F. Wagner IV.

LARK PLAY DEVELOPMENT CENTER. Schedule included: *Merchant on Venice* by Shishir Kurup. September 17, 2004. Directed by Tracy Young; with Amir Arison, Purva Bedi, Vedant Gokhale, Sajiv Jahveri, Tony Javed, Rizwan Manji, Alfredo Narciso, Sunita Param, Ami Shukla, Bernard White, Sam Younis. *Where's Annie?* by Eric Henry Sanders. November 11, 2004. Directed by Steven Williford; with Mary Bacon, Mary Carver, Alan Oppenheimer. *Clean Alternatives* by Brian Dykstra. November 17, 2004. Directed by Margarett Perry; with Matthew Boston, Mr. Dykstra, Kathryn Foster. *Welcome to Arroyo's* by Kristoffer Diaz. January 28, 2005. Directed by Margarett Perry; with Utkarsh Ambudkar, Victoria Cartagena, Hillel Meltzer, Andres Munar, Brandon Scott, Sheila Tapia. *Apple Cove* by Lynn Rosen. March 9, 2005. Directed by Giovanna Sardelli; with Paul Carlin, Erin Gann, Erica Schroeder, Marguerite Stimpson, C.J. Wilson.

LEFRAK GYMNASIUM. *Tierno Bokar* by Amadou Hampate Ba; adapted by Marie-Hélène Estienne. March 30, 2005. Directed by Peter Brook; with Habib Dembélé, Rachid Djaidani, Djénéba Kone, Sotigui Kouyaté, Tony Mpoudja, Bruce Myers, Abdou Ouologuem, Héléne Patarot, Dorcy Rugamba, Pitcho Womba Konga.

LION THEATRE. *Rockaway Boulevard* by Richard Vetere. October 20 2004. Directed by Charles Messina. *Twelfth Night* by William Shakespeare. November 4, 2004. Directed by Beverly Bullock; with David Blatt, Geoffrey Dawe, Gregg Dubner, Marc Greece, Kristen Hammer, Peter Herrick,

Gretchen Howe, Jonathan J. Lidz, Katherine Kelly Lidz, John Montague, Benjamin Rishworth, Simon Peter Shea, Nicholas Stannard, Debra Zane. *The Winter's Tale* by William Shakespeare. March 18, 2005. Directed by Beverly Bullock; with David Blatt, Carrie-Ann Brown, Lisa Came, Geoffrey Dawe, Jon Dean, Sri Gordon, Kristen Hammer, Catherine Hennessey, Peter Herrick, Gretchen Howe, Tyler Ashby Jones, Jonathan J. Lidz, Katherine Kelly Lidz, Patricia McNamara, Matt Mercer, Jeff Riebe, Benjamin Rishworth, Joanie Schumacher, Nicholas Stannard, Kaleb Szabo, Hannah Wolfe. *A Midsummer Night's Dream* by William Shakespeare. March 19, 2005. Directed by Beverly Bullock; with David Blatt, Carrie-Ann Brown, Geoffrey Dawe, Jon Dean, Sri Gordon, Kristen Hammer, Catherine Hennessey, Peter Herrick, Gretchen Howe, Tyler Ashby Jones, Jonathan J. Lidz, Katherine Kelly Lidz, Patricia McNamara, Matt Mercer, John Montgomery, Jeff Riebe, Benjamin Rishworth, Joanie Schumacher, Nicholas Stannard, Kaleb Szabo, Lisa Came, Hannah Wolfe. *Pith!* by Stewart Lemoine. April 6, 2005. Directed by Mr. Lemoine; with Jeff Haslam, Davina Stewart, Leona Brausen.

MANHATTAN ENSEMBLE THEATER. *The Lower Depths* by Maxim Gorky; adapted by Eric Parness. June 4, 2004. Directed by Mr. Parness; with Christopher Burris, Kristin Stewart Chase, Al Choy, Sean Dill, Loris Diran, Ledger Free, Nicole Godino, Emily Laochua, Aaron Lisman, Patrick Melville, Annette Previti, Stu Richel, Martin Treat, Stewart Walker, James T. Ware, Gameela Wright, Maxwell Zener. *Time to Burn* by Charles L. Mee. June 4, 2004. Directed by Leland Patton; with Christopher Burris, Sean Dill, Tran T. Thuc Hanh, Emily Laochua, Aaron Lisman, Patrick Melville, Ian Pfister, Annette Previti, Lou Tally, Elisa Terrazas, Martha Tompoulidou, James T. Ware, Gameela Wright, Maxwell Zener, Evan Zes. *The Greeks* by John Barton and Kenneth Cavander. July 9, 2004. Directed by Kaipo Schwab; with Eric Anderson, David Anzuelo, Peejay Bodoy, Sandi Carroll, Daniella Chiminelli, Tina Chow, Corinne Colon, Johanna Cox, Claro De Los Reyes, Andrew Eisenman, Esra Gaffin, Kristen Harlow, Lizzie Henney, Patrick Henney, Karl Herlinger, Susan Hyon, Matthew Johnson, Qurrat Kadwani, Liliane Klein, Evan Lai, Robyn Levine, Jamil Mangan, Sevrin Anne Mason, Gregg Mozgala, Tim Mullaney, Jenny Neale, Rachel Neuman, Mariana Newhard, Patrick Noonan, Jocelyn O'Neill, Kathleen O'Neill, Orlando Pabotoy, Jennifer Robinson, Benjamin Sands, Gillian Sheffler, Marybeth Warley, Inga Wilson, Keo Woolford, Aaron Yoo.

MANHATTAN THEATRE SOURCE. *Arcadia* by Tom Stoppard. December 1, 2004. Directed by David Epstein; with Christine Albright, Maggie Bell, Avery Clark, Adam Devine. *Woyzeck* by Georg Büchner; adapted by Andrew Frank. January 6, 2005. Directed by Mr. Frank; with McCready Baker, Daryl Boling, Lou Carbonneau, Max Davis, Jason Howard, Fiona Jones, Mac Rogers, Teddy Sears, Nancy Sirianni, Ben Thomas, Jennifer Thomas, Kim Vasilakis, Lex Woutas. *The Workroom* by Jean-Claude Grumberg; translated by Daniel A. Stein with Sara O'Connor. February 19, 2005. Directed by Moni Yakim; with Kristen Cerelli, Max Damashek, Charles E. Gerber, Rick Gifford, John Grimball, Emily Gunyou, Anna Guttormsgaard, Jody R. Hegarty, Carla Matero, Jill Van Note, Kevin Orton. *The Rite of the Serpent Skirt* by Dan Pulick. March 31, 2005. Directed by Glynis Rigsby; with Erin Walls, Christina Fanizzi, Deanna Companion, Kristen Fiorella, Tijuana Ricks, Daryl Boling. *7 Blowjobs* by Mac Wellman. April 21, 2005. Directed by Steven Gillenwater. *Machinal* by Sophie Treadwell. May 26, 2005. Directed by Morgan Anne Zipf; with Molly Pope, Jake Alexander, Drew Kulow, Richard Lovejoy, Dan McEllroy, Brian Nemiroff, Chinasa Ogbuagu, Ruth Ann Phimister, Karina Richardson, Alondra Salinas, Jordan Smith. *Tiny Dynamite* by Richard Lovejoy. May 28, 2005. Directed by Brad Raimondo; with Anne Carlisle, Brad Heikes, Racheline Maltese, Kent Meister, Megan Kingery, Max Seide.

MA-YI THEATRE Company. *Savage Acts* by Kia Corthron, Jorge Ignacio Cortiñas, Han Ong and Sung Rno. October 10, 2004. Directed by Ralph B. Peña; with Jeanine T. Abraham, Jesse Bernstein, Ron Domingo, Piter Marek, Orlando Pabotoy, Sophia Skiles, Aaron Yoo. *Sides: The Fear Is Real* by Sekiya Billman, Cindy Cheung, Paul H. Juhn, Peter Kim, Hoon Lee, Mr. Miyagi, and Rodney To. April 7, 2005. Directed by Anne Kauffman; with Ms. Billman, Jane Cho, Mr. Juhn, Mr. Kim, Mr. Lee, Eileen Rivera, Jonathan Salkin, Mr. To.

MCGINN/CAZALE THEATRE. NEW PLAYS UPTOWN. June 21–August 21, 2004. *The Mystery Plays* by Roberto Aguirre-Sacasa. Directed by Connie Grappo; with Gavin Creel, Scott Ferrara, Leslie Lyles, Mark Margolis, Heather Mazur, Peter Stadlen. *Triple Happiness* by Brooke Berman. Directed by Michael John Garcés; with Betsy Aidem, Mark Blum, Marin Ireland, Keith Nobbs, Jesse J. Perez, Ally Sheedy. *Dear Vienna* by Catherine Allen. November 8, 2004. Directed by Julie Hamberg; with Ross Beschler, Tug Coker, Jessi Gotta, Judith Hawking, G.R. Johnson, Ron McClary.

MELTING POT THEATRE COMPANY. *Flight* by Garth Wingfield. May 16, 2005. Directed by Nick Corley; with Gregg Edelman, Kerry O'Malley, Brian d'Arcy James, Andrew Polk, Rex Young, Victoria Mack.

METROPOLITAN PLAYHOUSE. *The Devil's Disciple* by George Bernard Shaw. November 11, 2004. Directed by Yvonne Opffer Conybeare; with Alex Roe, George Taylor, Ian Gould, Laura Livingston, Michael Hardart, Mike Durkin, Nicholas Waterfall, Peter Judd, Shana Dowdeswell, Susannah Mackintosh. EAST VILLAGE CHRONICLES. January 20–February 13, 2005. *Commedia Della Poca Italia* by Anthony P. Pennino. Directed by Derek Jamison; with Aaron Muñoz, Rob Pedini, Melanie Rey. *Floating Home* by Adrian Rodriguez. Directed by Derek Jamison; with Alberto Bonilla, Aaron Muñoz, Scott Phillips. *Ukrainian Blues* by Saviana Stanescu. Directed by Derek Jamison; with Melanie Rey, Barbara J. Spence. *Kaddish* by Anthony P. Pennino. Directed by Jude Domski; with Rob Pedini. *The Gate* by Renée Flemings. Directed by Jude Domski; with Cherita A. Armstrong, Michael Colby Jones, Kwaku Driskell, Scott Phillips. *The Pigeon Tree* by Gino DiIorio. Directed by Jude Domski; with Cherita A. Armstrong, Arthur Acuña, Scott Phillips. *Bike Wreck* by Qui Nguyen. Directed by Jude Domski; with Michael Colby Jones, Kwaku Driskell, Arthur Acuña. *Missouri Legend* by E.B. Ginty. March 11, 2005. Directed by Yvonne Opffer Conybeare; with Alex Roe, Jenni Tooley, Mike Durkin, Melody Bates, Marc Donovan, Lance Olds, Peter Loureiro, Teresa Kelsey, Putnam Smith. *Children's Crusader* by Anthony P. Pennino. April 29, 2005. Directed by Alex Roe; with Melanie Rey, Kathryn Barnhardt, Jeff Farber, Sidney Fortner, Erik Gratton, Ellen Seltz, Christopher Wakefield, Jonas Amadeus Barranca.

MIDTOWN INTERNATIONAL THEATER FESTIVAL. July 12–August 1, 2004. Schedule included: *CaribBeing* by Tessa Martin. Directed by Bill Van Horn. *Copito* by Blake Cass. Directed by Adam Brilliant. *A Cosmic Mishap in an Accidental Universe in America* by Aaron Petrovich. Directed by Shana Lee. *Cul de Sac Rock* by Jeffrey Marshek. Directed by Darren Katz. *Dead Woman Home* by May Nazareno. Directed by Teresa Thuman. *Do You Have Anything Closer?* by Lawrence Paone and Matthew Aibel. Directed by Mr. Aibel. *Ed the Fourth* by Joe Hartin. Directed by Nancy Larsen. *Fortune* by Jesse Schmitt. Directed by Mr. Schmitt. *Great White American Teeth* by Fiona Walsh. Directed by Virginia Scott. *Hearing Voices (Speaking in Tongues)* by Michael Mack. Directed by Manny Frenz. *In Spite of Myself* by Antoinette LaVecchia. Directed by Ludovica Villar-Hauser. *Insomnia*. Musical with book, music and lyrics by Charles Bloom. Directed by Allison Bergman. *Mind the Gap* by Tom Grady. Directed by Keith Oncale. *A Musical Journey With the Music of Brel, Weill, Aznavour, and Blau* by Bob Ost. Directed by Mr. Ost. *My Life in the Trenches* by Jill Dalton. Directed by Jack McCullough. *Time and the Beast* by Marina Shron. Directed by Daniela Varon. *On the Couch with Nora Armani* by Nora Armani. Directed by François Kergourlay. *Safety in Numbers* by Jan Rudd. Directed by Rod Menzies. *A Shining Love*. Musical with book by Greg Senf; music by Jeremy Rosen and Richard Sussman; lyrics by Mr. Senf. Directed by George Reily. *Sometimes Over the Summer* by Andrea Kolb. Directed by Kathleen Brant. *Southern Gothic Novel* by Frank Blocker. Directed by Gabriel Shanks. *The Baby Monitor* by Jude Albert. Directed by Marc-Anthony Thomas. *The Subject Was Roses* by Frank D. Gilroy. Directed by John Capo. *That Men Do* by Adam Perkins. Directed by Mr. Perkins. *Toasted* by Elisa DeCarlo. Directed by Roger Danforth. *Unaccustomed to My Name* by Marta Rainer. Directed by Angela Peterson. *Woman of Flowers (Blodeuwedd)* by Saunders Lewis. Directed by Ludovica Villar-Hauser.

MINT SPACE. *The First (And Last) Musical on Mars* by George Zarr. September 13, 2004. Directed by Mr. Zarr; with Paul Amodeo, Alissa Hunnicutt, Christina D'Orta, Barbara Rosenblat, Gary Kiffel, Miles Phillips, Steven Wenslawski, Nicole Kempskie, Sandy York, Kimberly McNeese, Elyse Locurto. *When Aunt Daphne Went Nude* by Miriam Jensen Hendrix. October 17, 2004. Directed by Keith Oncale; with Roy Bacon, Scott Ferrara, Tarah Flanagan, Patricia Hodges, J.C. Hoyt, Lucille Patton, Josh Shirley, Jane Titus. *The Penetration Play* by Winter Miller. November 22, 2005. Directed by Josh Hecht; with Mia Barron, Kathryn Grody, Mandy Siegfried.

NATIONAL ASIAN-AMERICAN THEATRE COMPANY (NAATCO). *Antigone* by Sophocles; translated by Brendan Kennelly. July 28, 2004. Directed by Jean Randich; with Mia Katigbak, Arthur Acuña, Alexis Camins, Cindy Cheung, Siho Ellsmore, Emi Fujinami Jones, Tim Kang, Orville Mendoza, Nicky Paraiso, Fausto Pineda, James Shubert, Eunice Wong. *Ivanov* by Anton Chekhov; translated by Paul Schmidt. May 23, 2005. Directed by Jonathan Bank; with Michi Barall, Joel de la Fuente, Mel Duane Gionson, Keiko Green, Deepti Gupta, Mia Katigbak, Daniel Dae Kim, C.S. Lee, Orville Mendoza, Stephen Park, Rochelle Tillman, Virginia Wing.

NEW GEORGES. MANFEST. September 12–25, 2004. Repertory schedule included: *Still Waters*. Musical with book and lyrics by Sonya Sobieski; music by Jana Zielonka. Directed by Daniella Topol. *Manilova* by Alice Tuan. Directed by Alyse Rothman. *Again and Against* by Betty Shamieh. Directed by Meredith McDonough. *Stu and Ray* by Trista Baldwin. Directed by Shoshana Gold. *Devil Must Be Deep* by Kirsten Greenidge. Directed by Jessica Bauman. *Hell and Back* by Sheri Wilner. Directed by Brook Brod. With Gabriel Fazio, John Ficarra, Samuel R. Gates, Benton Greene, Nina Hellman, J. Elaine Marcos, April Mathis, Hana Moon, Matt Neely, Orlando Pabotoy, Abby Royle.

NEW YORK INTERNATIONAL FRINGE FESTIVAL. August 14–21, 2004. Schedule included: *Africa and Plumbridge* by Sue Carey, Karena Mendoza, Carson Grace Becker and Jim Brochu. Directed by Mr. Brochu; with Eric Anthony, Charissa Armon, Jane Brewer, Rachel Cerrone, Chipper Cooke, Sharyon Culberson, Janeece Aisha Freeman, Richard White, Jim Meade, Folin Ponce DeLeon, Susan Powell, Jasmine Randle, Gerald Richardson, Giselle Vaughn Ruecking, Monique Whittington. *Haven* by Sara Kahn. Directed by Padraic Lillis; with Ms. Kahn. *Barrymore's Body* by Jeff Tabnick. Directed by Mr. Tabnick; with Christian Baskous, Dan Truman, Gregory Steinbruner. *Confessions of a Mormon Boy*. Solo performance piece by Steven Fales. Directed by Jack Hofsiss; with Mr. Fales. *Simple Thoughts* by Langston Hughes; adapted by James Vesce. Directed by Mr. Vesce; with Calvin Thompson, Lamont Bryant, J. Morong. *Scarlet Sees the Light* by Nathan Parker. Directed by Ted Sod; with Carlina Salemi. *Moonchild* by Maureen FitzGerald. Directed by Alex Lippard; with Heather Tom, Jonathan Cantor, Mardie Millit, Andrew Shulman, Abby Wathen. *The Cosmic Calamities of Henry Noodle*. Musical with book, music and lyrics by Tim McCanna. Directed by Stephen Tomac; with Ken Kleiber, Meara McIntyre, Stephanie Sine, Matt Wilson. *Jonestown: The Musical*. Musical with book by Brian Stillman; music by Larry Lees; lyrics by Messrs. Stillman and Lee. Directed by Karen Azenberg; with Maria Schaffel, Matt Cavenaugh, Robert Creighton, Howard Emanuel, Ronica Reddick, Eadie Scott, Rebecca Sherman, Dustin Sullivan, Joe Pace, Chad Hudson.

NEW YORK MUSICAL THEATRE FESTIVAL. September 13–October 3, 2004. Schedule included: *Altar Boyz*. Musical with book by Kevin Del Aguila; music and lyrics by Gary Adler and Michael Patrick Walker; conceived by Marc Kessler and Ken Davenport. Directed by Stafford Arima; with Cheyenne Jackson, David Josefsberg, Ryan Duncan, Andy Karl, Tyler Maynard. *The Blue Flower*. Musical with book by Ruth Bauer and Jim Bauer; music and lyrics by Mr. Bauer. Directed by Will Pomerantz; with Meghan McGeary, Andrew Dawson, Marc Geller, Todd Alan Johnson, Jamie LaVerdiere, Clayton Dean Smith, Jean Arbeuter. *Caligula: An Ancient Glam Epic*. Musical with book, music and lyrics by Eric Svejcar. Directed by Michael Unger; with Euan Morton, Denise Summerford, Gilles Chiasson, Brooke Sunny Moriber, Jeb Brown, Sebastian Arcelus, Bradford W. Anderson, Meredith Kaye Clark, Daniel Cochran, Desmond Confoy, Izetta Fang, Brian M. Golub, Alan H. Greene, Moeisha McGill, Michael Minarik, Mary Mossberg, Jeffrey Pufahl, Jody Reynard, Heather Tepe, Shorey Walker. *Ducks and Lovers*. Musical with book by Peter Gootkind and Marni Goltsman; music and lyrics by Mr. Gootkind; based on the play by Murray Schisgal. Directed by Dan Foster; with Chad Kimball, Jessica-Snow Wilson, Charlotte Cohn, Buddy Crutchfield, Lorinda Lisitza, Larry Picard, Phyllis Somerville, Mary Stout, Stephen Tewksbury, Tom Souhrada, Bruce Winant, Chris Yates, Stuart Zagnit. *Emma*. Musical with book, music and lyrics by Stephen Karam. Directed by Patricia Birch; with Karl Kenzler, Marty Thomas, Michael Longoria, Leslie Kritzer, Blair Ross, Michelle Dawson, Colin Hanlon, Tim Jerome, Robyn Kramer, Chad Ackerman, Nick Collins, Rebecca Bellingham, Sarah Coogan, Kristen Bell, Nick Austin, Emily Whyte. *Enchanted Cottage*. Musical with book by Thomas Edward West; music by Kim Oler; lyrics by Alison Hubbard; based on the play by Arthur Wing Pinero. Directed by Peter Flynn; with Willy Falk, Andrea Burns, Barbara Marineau, Joe Kolinski, Annie Golden, Steve Routman, Rose McGuire, Rex Hayes, Jeff Brooks. *Far From the Madding Crowd*. Musical with book and lyrics by Barbara Campbell; music by Gary Schocker; adapted from the work of Thomas Hardy. Directed by Jamibeth Margolis; with Kate Fisher, Richard Todd Adams, D.B. Bonds, William Broderick, Rena Strober, Mark Campbell, Liz Donathan, Linda Pierson Huff, Daniel Johnson, Jayne Ackley Lynch, Lisa Morris, Edward Prostak, Jonathan Root, Tamara Spiewak, Bruce Warren, Darryl Winslow. *Fringical!: A Fringical!!* Musical with book by Sam Forman and Thomas Kail; music by Eli Bolin; lyrics by Mr. Forman. Directed by Mr. Kail; with Patch Darragh, Jessica-Snow Wilson, Anne Jacoby, Patrick Heusinger, Ryan Vaughn. *The Great American Trailer Park Musical*. Musical with book by Betsy Kelso; music and lyrics by David Nehls. Directed by Ms. Kelso; with Robin Baxter, Carter Calvert, Jenn Colella, Marya Grandy, Amanda Ryan Paige, Geoffrey Scheer, Dan Sharkey. *A Hundred Years Into the*

Heart. Musical with book by Richard Vetere; music by Jeffrey Lodin; lyrics by William Squier. Directed by Brett Bernardini; with Charma Bonanno, David Bonanno, Jonathan Todd Ross, Mark Lotito, Barbara Marineau. *Like You Like It.* Musical with book and lyrics by Sammy Buck; music by Daniel S. Acquisto. Directed by Jen Bender; with Michele Ragusa, Joshua Park, Rebecca Bellingham, Jason Blaine, Ayler Evan, Colby Foytik, Charlie Mechling, Michael Messer, Jonathan Monk, Tara Sands, Stephanie Schweitzer, Charly Seamon, Joanna Young, Monica Yudovich. *The Man Who Would Be King.* Musical with book and lyrics by DJ Salisbury; music by Neil Berg. Directed by Paul Dobie; with Tony Lawson, Paul Anthony Stewart, Don Richard, Mandy Bruno. *[title of show].* Musical with book by Hunter Bell; music and lyrics by Jeff Bowen. Directed by Michael Berresse; with Messrs. Bell and Bowen, Susan Blackwell, Heidi Blickenstaff, Larry Pressgrove. *Tusk.* Musical with book by Steven Billing, Norman Rea and Steven Yuhasz; music by Bryon Sommers, David Salih and Craig Strang; lyrics by Messrs. Rea and Billing. Directed by Mr. Yuhasz; with Ashley Arnold, Sandra Bargman, Marnie Baumer, Charles Bergell, Darryl E. Calmese Jr., Stacey Haughton, Val Moranto, Will Perez, Heidi Stallings, Chris Vasquez, Paul Robert Verhoest Jr., Billy Wheelan. *The Woman Upstairs.* Musical with book by Kait Kerrigan; music and lyrics by Brian Lowdermilk. Directed by Ms. Kerrigan; with Alison Fraser, Kate Shindle, Deb Heinig, Aaron Ramey.

NUYORICAN POETS CAFÉ. *Spider Holes* by Frederick Stroppel. January 13, 2005. Directed by Mr. Stroppel; with Kevin Kash, Cindy Keiter, Joanna Keylock, Heather Male, Peter Plano. *Runt* by Michael Phillip Edwards. March 3, 2005. Directed by Kimberly Elise; with Mr. Edwards. *Miles Davis* by Jacqueline Wade. April 21, 2005. Directed by Arthur French; with Gene Hughes.

OHIO THEATRE. ICE FACTORY 2004. July 7–August 14, 2004. Schedule included: *Expense of Spirit* by Josh Fox. Directed by Mr. Fox. *The Making of Eugene Doe* by Susan Mosakowski. Directed by Ms. Mosakowski. *The Franklin Thesis* by Les Freres Corbusier. *Fatboy* by John Clancy. Directed by Mr. Clancy. *Doctor Tedrow's Last Breath* by Matthew Earnest. Directed by Mr. Earnest. *Tannhauser (The Play)* by Joseph Gallo. *Secret Bridesmaids' Business* by Elizabeth Coleman. September 7, 2004. Directed by Gary Schwartz; with Tamara Lovatt-Smith, Deb Crisford, Jen Apostolou, Emily Vacchiano, Victoria Roberts, Jeremy Waters. *The John Wayne Principle* by Tony McNamara. September 8, 2004. Directed by Rosemary Andress; with James M. Larmer, Jay Riedl, Guy Mandic, Raphael Fetta, Kathryn Alexander, Jessamyn Blakeslee. *Hell Meets Henry Halfway* by Adriano Shaplin; based on *The Possessed* by Witold Gombrowicz. November 3, 2004. Directed by Dan Rothenberg; with Gabriel Quinn Bauriedel, Emmanuelle Delpech-Ramey, Sarah Sanford, Geoff Sobelle, James Sugg, Dito van Reigersberg. *Innocents* by Rachel Dickstein; adapted from *The House of Mirth* by Edith Wharton. January 10, 2005. Directed by Ms. Dickstein; with Andy Paris, Margot Ebling, LeeAnne Hutchison, Nicole Halmos, Paula McGonagle, Grant Neale, Christopher Oden, Jill A. Samuels. *Boozy: The Life, Death, and Subsequent Vilification of Le Corbusier and, More Importantly, Robert Moses* by Adam Scully; conceived by Juliet Chia, David Evans Morris, Alex Timbers. February 15, 2005. Directed by Mr. Timbers; with Jacob Grigolia-Rosenbaum, Nina Hellman, Daniel Larlham, Ryan Karels, John Summerour, Keith Price, Simon Feil, Ian Oldaker, Virginia Callaway, Matthew DeVriendt, Shareefah Hamilton, Scott Hoffer, Leslie Klug, Brian McTaminey, Elizabeth Meriwether, Max Miner, Mary C. Wilson. *Monopoly!* by Mike Daisey. February 18, 2005. Directed by Jean-Michele Gregory; with Mr. Daisey. *Faust in Love* by Douglas Langworthy. March 23, 2005. Directed by David Herskovits; with David Greenspan, George Hannah, Eunice Wong, Nicole Halmos, Wayne Alon Scott, Kendra Ware.

ONTOLOGICAL-HYSTERIC THEATRE. BLUEPRINT SERIES. July 23–August 4, 2004. Schedule included: *Abraham (A Shot in the Head)* by Sam Hunter. Directed by Mr. Hunter; with Jeffrey Maxwell, Elizabeth Neptune, Patrick Carlyle. *Crochet: I Dream Ballet* by Beth Kurkjian. Directed by Ms. Kurkjian; with Wendy Luker, Beth Manspeizer, Kristen Pratt, Beth Portnoy. *A Child Is Being Beaten* by Keith Mayerson. Directed by Mr. Mayerson; with Sumner Hatch, Elizabeth Meriwether, Alice Barrett Mitchell, Bruce Kronenberg, Steven Rattazzi. *The Gods Are Pounding My Head! (AKA Lumberjack Messiah)* by Richard Foreman. January 18, 2005. Directed by Mr. Foreman; with Jay Smith, T. Ryder Smith, Charlotta Mohlin.

PEARL THEATRE COMPANY. *The Imaginary Invalid* by Molière; translated by Earle Edgerton. October 10, 2004. Directed by Eleanor Holdridge; with Joanne Camp, Dominic Cuskern, Robert Hock, Sean McNall, Christopher Moore, Allison Nichols, Carol Schultz. *Marriage* by Nikolai Gogol; translated by Milton Ehre and Fruma Gottschalk. November 21, 2004. Directed by Jesse Berger; with Joanne Camp, Dominic Cuskern, Robert Hock, Sean McNall, Christopher Moore, Carol Schultz,

John Robert Tillotson, Allison Nichols, Jo Anne Tolassi, Tom Wells. *The House of Bernarda Alba* by Federico Garcia Lorca; translated by Caridad Svich. January 16, 2005. Directed by Shepard Sobel; with Robin Leslie Brown, Joanne Camp, Carol Schultz, Ifeoma Sesiana Amobi, Elena Araoz, Marjorie Johnson, Carmen de Lavallade, Melissa Maxwell, Emily Mostyn-Brown, Allison Nichols, Fulvia Vergel, Eunice Wong. *I Have Been Here Before* by J.B. Priestley. February 27, 2005. Directed by Gus Kaikkonen; with Rachel Botchan, Robin Leslie Brown, Dominic Cuskern, Dan Daily, Sean McNall, Edward Seamon. *Widowers' Houses* George Bernard Shaw. April 10, 2005. Directed by J.R. Sullivan; with Ryland Blackinton, Rachel Botchan, Robin Leslie Brown, Dominic Cuskern, Dan Daily, Edward Griffin, Sean McNall, Edward Seamon.

PHIL BOSAKOWSKI THEATRE. *The Vampires* by Harry Kondoleon. June 5, 2004. Directed by Patrick Diamond; with Keith Anderson, Sean Breault, Amanda Fekety, Robyn Ganeles, Elissa Lash, Jason Woodruff. *The Lepers of Baile Baiste* by Ronan Noone. September 13, 2004. Directed by David Sullivan; with Dara Coleman, Ciaran Crawford, Charles Stransky, Kevin Hagan, Jeffrey M. Bender, David Ian Lee, Michael Shelle, Zac Springer. *Communion* by Aidan Mathews. January 7, 2005. Directed by M. Burke Walker; with James Kennedy, John Seidman, Barbara Sims, Colin Lane, Ean Sheehy, Jessica Dickey. *The Frankenstein Summer* by Catherine Bush. February 13, 2005. Directed by Marc Geller; with Mr. Geller, Tracey Gilbert, Brad Malow, Brendan McMahon, Bill Roulet, Abby Royle.

PHOENIX THEATRE ENSEMBLE. *The Trial* by Franz Kafka; adapted by Andre Gide and Jean-Louis Barrault; translated by Joseph Katz and Leon Katz. December 17, 2004. Directed by Eve Adamson; with John Lenartz, Craig Smith, Elise Stone, Jason Crowl, Angela Madden, Michael Surabian, Jason O'Connell, Douglas McKeown, Antonio Edwards Suarez, Carolyn Ratteray, Karen Case Cook, Dan Snow, Jolie Garrett, Matt Neely. PLAY IN A PUB. April 4, 2005. *A Perfect Analysis Given by a Parrot* by Tennessee Williams. Directed by Jonathan Silverstein; with Mara Stephens, Michele Tauber, Brian Costello, Jolie Garrett, Robert Ierardi. *Can Can* by Romulus Linney. Directed by Mr. Linney; with Kelli Holsopple, Robert Ierardi, Erin Espelie, Libby Hughes.

PRAXIS THEATRE PROJECT. *The Fastest Woman Alive* by Karen Sunde. June 3, 2004. Directed by Joel Froomkin, with Janet Dunson, Kellie Johnson, Tom Pavey, Michael Sinnott, Jake Speck.

THE PRODUCERS CLUB. *Those the River Keeps* by David Rabe. October 14, 2004. Directed by Simcha Borenstein; with Quentin Barber, Jessica Clough, Carlo Fiorletta, Monica Gaydos. *Fade Out, or the Imperfections of a Man* by V. Stephen Bauer. November 21, 2004. Directed by Anthony DiDio; with Mr. Bauer. *Chicken Delight* by John Glines. December 7, 2004. Directed by Dave McCracken; with Gil Bar-Sela, Dale Church, August Costa, Michael Eisenbrown, Bill Hanson, Christian Irizarry, David Perlman. *Shift Change* by Ben Carlin. February 4, 2005. Directed by Shawn Rozsa; with Chet Carlin, Eric Petersen. *Jackie "Moms" Mabley and Her Ladies* by Clarice Taylor. March 2, 2005. With Ms. Taylor. *Girls* by Mitchell Malnati. April 7, 2005. Directed by Maura Smith; with Sarah Bell, Stephanie Bush, Kelley Curran, Jordan Kamp, Christina Lind, John McClellan, Brian Murphy.

PROSPECT THEATER COMPANY. *Taxi Cabaret*. Musical with book, music and lyrics by Peter Mills; conceived by Cara Reichel. September 21, 2004. Directed by Ms. Reichel; with Sebastian Arcelus, Alison Cimmet, Leon Ash Evans, Amy Justman, Jason Mills, Simone Zamore. *The Pursuit of Persephone*. Musical with book by Cara Reichel and Peter Mills; music and lyrics by Mr. Mills. April 30, 2005. Directed by Ms. Reichel; with David Abeles, William Brock, Cheryl Dowling, Chris Fuller, Matt Gibson, Piper Goodeve, Jessica Grové, Dennis Holland, Julie Lachance, Maclain Looper, Jaye Maynard, Shannon McShane, Brandon Parish, Dominic Roberts, Melissa Robinette, Benjamin Sands, Paul A. Schaefer, Robby Sharpe, Courter Simmons, Daniel Yates.

RATTLESTICK PLAYWRIGHTS THEATER. *Boise* by David Folwell. June 14, 2004. Directed by Rob Bundy; with Chris Burns, Geneva Carr, Alex Kilgore, Tasha Lawrence, Matt Pepper. *Medea in Jerusalem* by Roger Kirby; based on Euripides. August 9, 2004. Directed by Steven Little; with Rebecca Wisocky, Jennifer McCabe, Jason Kaufman, Miller Lade, Ariel Shafir. *Finer Noble Gases* by Adam Rapp. September 20, 2004. Directed by Michael John Garcés; with Connor Barrett, Robert Beitzel, Michael Chernus, Ray Rizzo, Paul Sparks, Curtis Flynn. *God Hates the Irish: The Battle of Armless Johnny* by Sean Cunningham. March 31, 2005. Directed by Will Frears; with Lisa Altomare, Remy Auberjonois, Anne Bobby, Anna Camp, James A. Stephens, William Thompson. *Miss Julie* by August Strindberg; adapted by Craig Lucas. May 19, 2005. Directed by Anders Cato; with Marin Hinkle, Reg Rogers, Julia Gibson.

THE RED ROOM. *The Room/La Habitacion* by Bárbara Colio. August 17, 2004 Directed by Marissa Béjar; with Rafael Childress, Elena Adames, Susan Stewart, Mark G. Cisneros. *Curious Woodman and Snowman* by Bob Powers. December 9, 2004. Directed by Mr. Powers; with Johnny Fido, Erin Foley, Jaimie Greenberg, Deb Rabbai. *The Great One-Man Commedia Epic* by Matthew R. Wilson. February 8, 2005. Directed by Mr. Wilson; with Mr. Wilson. *Keanu Reeves Saves the Universe* by Rob Reese. April 15, 2005. Directed by Mr. Reese; with Jamie Ansley, Natalie Beran, Marcus Bonnee, Shane Breaux, Nitra Gutierrez, Elizabeth Kennedy, Dave McKeel, Jodi Skeris, Rodney Umble, Amelia Zirin-Brown. *Bite* by Suzanne Bachner. April 21, 2005. Directed by Rick Vorndran; with Robert Brown, Jennifer Gill, Theresa Goering, Amy Overman, Jason Plowman, Jason Unfried, Theresa Unfried.

ST. ANN'S WAREHOUSE. *Good Samaritans* by Richard Maxwell. October 6, 2004. Directed by Mr. Maxwell; with Rosemary Allen, Kevin Hurley, Catherine McRae. *4:48 Psychosis* by Sarah Kane. October 26, 2004. Directed by James Macdonald; with Jason Hughes, Marin Ireland, Jo McInnes. *Risk Everything* by George F. Walker. November 10, 2004. Directed by Grzegorz Jarzyna; with Aleksandra Konieczna. UNDER THE RADAR. January 7–10, 2005. Schedule included: *Word Becomes Flesh* by Marc Bamuthi Joseph. *Accidental Nostalgia* by Cynthia Hopkins. Directed by Ms. Hopkins; with Ms. Hopkins, Jim Findlay, Jeff Sugg. *¡Cantinflas!* by Herbert Sigüenza. Directed by Max Ferrá; with Mr. Sigüenza. *Gone Missing* by the Civilians. Directed by Steven Cosson; music by Michael Friedman; with Damian Baldet, Michael Esper, Jennifer R. Morris, Mark Saturno, Alison Weller, Colleen Werthmann.

SAMUEL BECKETT THEATRE. *Oswald's Backyard*. By Leslie Bramm. October 12, 2004. Directed by Scott R.C. Levy; with Drake Andrew, Elizabeth A. Bell, Joshua P. Garland, Douglas Gowland, Mikki Jordan, Matt Mullin. *Learning Curve* by Rogelio Martinez. February 10, 2005. Directed by Michael Sexton; with Chadwick Boseman, Mike Hodge, Graeme Malcolm, John McAdams, Natalia Payne, Demond Robertson, Daniel Talbott.

SANFORD MEISNER Theatre. *All-Male Importance of Being Earnest*. Adaptation of the play by Oscar Wilde. August 16, 2004. Directed by Hugh Hysell; with Adam Beckworth, Lee Blair, Gary Hilborn, John Kudan, Joe LaRue, Jerry Marsini, Ricky Oliver, Kila Packett, William Reinking. *Samuel the Fourth* by Maria Ferrari. October 19, 2004. Directed by Jesse Geiger; with Anthony Bagnetto, Patrick Blumer, Allison Crain, Amos Crawley, Chad Kessler, Larry "Rock" Kolber, Eli Kranski. *Loose Knit* by Theresa Rebeck. January 19, 2005. Directed by Kevin Molesworth; with Matthieu Cornillon, Valerie Donaldson, Don Fowler, Helen Kim, Hannah Mason, Gia Rhodes, Madeline Virbasius-Walsh. SIN. March 25–April 2, 2005. Schedule included: *The Company Kept* by Daria Polatin. Directed by Dan Fields; with Matthew G. Rashid, Jeff Biehl, Lia Aprile. *The Blasphemy Tree* by TC Higgins. Directed by John Ruocco; with Randy Redd, Peter Michael Marino. *Envy* by Hettienne Park. Directed by John Ruocco; with SuEllen Estey, Mikki Jordan. *Removing the Head* by Josh Ben Friedman. Directed by Dan Fields; with Rob Devaney, Greg Derelian. *Danny's Line* by James Scruggs. Directed by John Ruocco; with Jeffery Thompson. *Sate* by Damin Luaiye. Directed by Dan Fields; with Katie Barrett, Deepa Purohit, John Eckland. *Good Help* by Ellen Shanman. Directed by Dan Fields; with Jessica Arinella, Matthew G. Rashid, Philip Kain. *Slappy's Sliding Scale* by Louise Rozett. Directed by John Ruocco; with Joffre Myers, Mary Faber. *Abandonment* by Kate Atkinson; adapted by Kit Thacker. April 12, 2005. Directed by Mr. Thacker; with Veronica Cruz, Lisa De Mont, Ali Marsh, James Martinez, Linda Marie Larson, Eric Singer, Sarah Megan Thomas.

78TH STREET THEATRE LAB. *Straight on 'til Morning* by Trish Harnetiaux. September 10, 2004. Directed by Jude Domski; with David Carson, Maurice Edwards, Edward Furs, Jason Griffin, Corey Stieb, Kate Turnbull, Michael Colby Jones. *Kenneth–What Is the Frequency?* by Paul Allman. October 24, 2004. Directed by Eric Nightengale; with Lawrence E. Bull, Stephanie Dodd, Phillip Douglas, Adam Erdossy, Toby Wherry. *The Last Christmas of Ebenezer Scrooge* by Marvin Kaye. November 26, 2004. With Stacey Jenson, H. Clark Kee, Anne Pasquale, Nancy Temple, Marvin Kaye. *Oranges Like the Sun* by Judylee Vivier. January 22, 2005. Directed by Tom Bullard; with Ms. Vivier. *Uncle Vanya* by Anton Chekhov; translated by Arnold Shvetsov. February 25, 2005. Directed by Mr. Shvetsov; with Peter Von Berg, Aleks Shaklin, Barbara Hammond, Natia Dune, Emily Mitchell, Ruth Miller, H. Clark Kee, Richard Sterne, Michael Huber. *How Light Is Spent* by Joshua Feldman. May 12, 2005. Directed by Sheila Dvorak; with Michael Ellison, Frank Favia, Emily Lodish, Sarah Northmore, Paco Tolson.

SOHO PLAYHOUSE. *Carnival Knowledge* by Todd Robbins. August 17, 2004. Directed by Kirsten Sanderson; with Mr. Robbins, Shannon Morrow, Jennifer Miller. *Dog Sees God* by Bert V. Royal. September 8, 2004. Directed by Susan W. Lovell; with Michael Gladis, Bridget Barkan, Karen Diconcetto, Tate Ellington, Daniel Franzese, Jay Sullivan, Melissa Picarello, Stelianie Tekmitchov. *Orgasms: The Play* by Dan Israely. April 21, 2005. Directed by Mr. Israely; with Kimmie Fadem, Michael J. Scarpelli Jr., Ed Asner.

THE STORM THEATRE. *The Shoemakers Holiday* by Thomas Dekker. February 3, 2005. Directed by Peter Dobbins; with Jason Adams, Brad Coolidge, Amanda Cronk, Ashton Crosby, Paul Jackel, Hugh Brandon Kelly, Kelleigh Miller, Julia Motyka, Kevin Prowse, Jose Sanchez, Joshua Vasquez, Gabriel Vaughan, Travis Walters. *Twelfth Night* by William Shakespeare. May 20, 2005. Directed by Peter Dobbins; with Emanuele Ancorini, Marc Cajigao, Gregory Couba, Michael Daly, Robyn Haynes, Jamil Mena, Benita Robledo, Jose Sanchez, Miguel Sierra, Matthew Simon, Heather Spore, Julia Tobey, Joshua Vasquez.

STUDIO DANTE. *Ponies* by Mike Batistick. October 14, 2004. Directed by Nick Sandow; with Michael Imperioli, Babs Olusanmokun, Tonye Patano, John Ventimiglia. *Late Fragment* by Francine Volpe. February 9, 2005. Directed by Michael Imperioli; with Julianna Margulies, Michael Rispoli, Will Janowitz, Ken Forman, James McCaffrey. *Henry Flamethrowa* by John Belluso. May 11, 2005. Directed by Nick Sandow; with Tim Daly, Yvonne Woods, Jake M. Smith.

SUMMER PLAY FESTIVAL (SPF). July 5–August 1, 2004. Schedule included: *The Dew Point* by Neena Beber. *Sam and Lucy* by Brooke Berman. *It's Only Life* by John Bucchino. *Honor and the River* by Anton Dudley. *Wet* by Liz Duffy Adams. *Earthquake Chica* by Anne Garcia-Romero. *Kitty Kitty Kitty* by Noah Haidle. *Kid Simple* by Jordan Harrison. *Anatomy 1968* by Karen Hartman. *Pin* by Heather Lynn MacDonald. *Arrivals and Departures* by Rogelio Martinez. *Colorado* by Peter Sinn Nachtrieb. *Stealing Sweets and Punching People* by Phil Porter. *El Paso Blue* by Octavio Solis. *Prozak and the Platypus* by Elise Thoron and Jill Sobule. *Mayhem* by Kelly Stuart. *Sweetness* by Gary Sunshine. *Spin Moves* by Ken Weitzman.

THEATER BY THE BLIND. *Dial M For Murder* by Frederick Knott. June 6, 2004. Directed by Ike Schambelan, with George Ashiotis, J.M. McDonough, Pamela Sabaugh, Xen Theo, Nicholas Viselli.

THEATRE AT ST. CLEMENT'S. *The Mistress Cycle*. Musical by Jenny Giering and Beth Blatt. November 15, 2004. Directed by Joe Calarco; with Rebecca Luker, Mary Bond Davis, Julia Murney, Stephanie Bast. *Clara's Christmas Dream* by Alexander Dumas; adapted by E. Thomalen. November 24, 2004. Directed by Bruce Merrill. *Counsellor-at-Law* by Elmer Rice. January 30, 2005. Directed by Dan Wackerman; with John Rubinstein, D. Michael Berkowitz, Mary Carver, Nat Chandler, Corinne Fitamant, Beth Glover, Nell Gwynn, Steven Hack, Jane Lanier, David Lavine, Mark Light-Orr, Lanie MacEwan, Sal Mistretta, Robert O'Gorman, Ginger Rich, Justin Riordan, Tara Sands, Brian N. Taylor, Ashley West. *The Capital Mall* by Eric Jaimes. May 13, 2005. Directed by Mr. Jaimes; with Michael Briatico, Lee Cavellier, Lindsay Drew, Todd Evans, Max Ferguson, Molly Karlin, Thom O'Hanlon, Sheena Marie Ortiz, Patricia Sanz, Eric Sisco, Rachel Soll, Katie Vagnino.

THEATRE FOUR. *My Big Gay Italian Wedding* by Anthony Wilkinson. June 11, 2004. Directed by Peter Rapanaro; with James Getzlaff, Mr. Wilkinson, Concetta Maria Aliotta, JC Alvarez, Jon Vincent Blake, Barry Brisco, Lorenzo Cambriello, Michael Ciriaco, Meridith Cullen, Brett Douglas, Laura Gaspari, Joe Grimaldi, Nate Johnson, Randi Kaplan, Lisa Liaromatis, Carla-Marie Mercun, Amanda Minker, Maria Nazzaro, Guy Olivieri, Rocco Parente, Anthony Raymond, Julie Scalione, Joe Scanio.

THEATRE 3. *Another Life?* Musical with book, music and lyrics by Jeffrey Todd Fernandez. June 27, 2004. Direction and choreography by David Robertson; with Stephen Amato, Michele Bloom, Ryan Brunton, Esther Cohn, Duquincy Cooks, Kim Crawford, Greg Louis, Carlos Knauth, Jon Mantes, Lindsay Packard, Nuno Sousa, Elysa Tirrell, Jill Tirrell. *Acharnians* by Aristophanes; adapted by Liat Ron; translated by Douglass Parker. October 7, 2004. Directed by Gregory Simmons; with Amos Crawley, Rene Collins, Dustin Olson, Heather Lamb, Marty McDonough, Richard Kohn, Ward Nixon, Youssif Eid, Kevin Whittinghill, Jason Munt, Hong Chau, J. Enrique Rivas, Yoko Hyun. *Sex and Other Matters* directed by Cheryl Paley. March 18, 2005. With Kim Arzillo, Kenton Cummings, Cory Gibson, John Henke, Loreslee Hernandez, Jenna Louie, Robert Moreira, Owen Panettieri, Dream Parker, Julia Pisetsky, Amanda Schill, Mario Thelemaque, Crystal Quallo, Amanda Gloria Valdes, Ryland Shelton, Electra Yao. *Monica! The Musical*. Musical with book and lyrics by Daniel J. Blau and Tracie Potochnik; music by Adam Blau. May 20, 2005. Directed by Casey

Hushion; with Christine DiGiallonardo, Megan Lawrence, Duke LaFoon, Eric Sommers, Roz Beauty Davis, Natalie Joy Johnson, Ron DeStefano.

29TH STREET REP. *Hiding Behind Comets* by Brian Dykstra. February 17, 2005. Directed by David Mogentale; with Moira MacDonald, Amber Gallery, Robert Mollohan, Dan Moran.

URBAN STAGES. *Comfort Women.* By Chungmi Kim. October 28, 2004. Directed by Frances Hill; with Tina Chen, Jade Wu, Jo Yang, Haerry Kim, Ji-young Kim.

VITAL THEATRE COMPANY. *Croatoan* by Ross Maxwell. September 13, 2004. Directed by Aimée Hayes; with Sara Barnett, Chad Beckim, Sekou Campbell, Brennan Roberts, Alyssa Siemon. *Laura's Bush* by Jane Martin. October 11, 2004. With Laura Lebleu, Hilda Guttormsen, Jane Aquilina. *Dear Vienna* by Catherine Allen. November 8, 2004. Directed by Julie Hamberg; with Ross Beschler, Tug Coker, Jessi Gotta, Judith Hawking, G.R. Johnson, Ron McClary. NEW WORKS FESTIVAL. December 2–19, 2004. Schedule included: *Jupiter* by Scott C. Smith. Directed by Andrew Sheppard. *Stress Test* by Patt Pfeiffer. Directed by Mahayana Landowne. *Death Comes for the Therapist* by Laura Owen. Directed by Jason Chimonides. *Local Potatoes* by Norman Kline. Directed by Mr. Kline. *Driving School of America* by Daniel Brenner. Directed by Joanna Lukes. *Defacing Michael Jackson* by Aurin Squire. Directed by Denyse Owens. *Mina* by Kyoung H. Park. Directed by C.S. Lee. *True Love Story of My Parents* by Elizabeth Meriwether. Directed by Shira Milikowsky. *Never Never Land* by Laura Rohrman. Directed by Habib Azar. *#9* by Chisa Hutchinson. Directed by Christopher Kloko. *Coyotes* by Catherine Gillet. Directed by Emily Tetzlaff. *Falling* by William Bordon. Directd by Aimée Hayes. *Juice* by Jane Shepard. Directed by Ms. Shepard. *Suspense* by Ian Finley. Directed by David Hilder. *Jesus Hates You* by Robert Shaffron. Directed by Paul Adams. *Overhead* by Kellie Overbey. Directed by Linda Ames Key. VITAL SIGNS. January 27–February 5, 2005. Schedule included: *Spanky* by Mark Loewenstern. Directed by Karen Sommers. *The Mechanicals* by Ross Maxwell. Directed by Frank Pisco. *Al and Audrey* by Norman Kline. Directed by David Hilder. *Miami Connection* by Stephen Bittrich. Directed by Greg Thorson. *The Way, the Truth, the Life* by Stephen Bittrich. Directed by Hamilton Clancy. *Angels and Trauma* by Kara Hartig. Directed by Mary Kate Burke. *Shakin' the Mess Outta Misery* by Shay Youngblood. February 10, 2005. Directed by Stephen Sunderlin; with Johnnie Mae, Kimberly Penwah, Donisha Brown, Kimberly Hebert Gregory, Erika Myers, Nysheva-Starr, Renee Threatte. *Death Party* by John Pastore. April 14, 2005. Directed by Marc Eardley; with Nick Amick, Danny Clayborne, Steve Devito, Taylor Girard, Luciana Magnoli, Albert Sanchez Jr., Zac Springer, Hilary Thompson.

WALKERSPACE. *Diary of a Chambermaid.* Based on the novel by Octave Mirbeau; adapted by Adrian Giurgea. July 26, 2004. Directed by Mr. Giurgea; with Lael Logan, Patrick McNulty, Atosa Babaoff, Brooke Delaney, Antonia Fairchild, Ryan Farley, Jeff Galfer, Christopher Oden, Allison Schubert, Finnerty Steeves. *Ondine* by Jean Giraudoux; translated by Roger Gellert. September 11, 2004. Directed by Jill A. Samuels; with Rhonda S. Musak, Tim Spanjer, Anne Bates, Bill Berg, Brina Bishop, Liza Bryn, Michael Crane, Gregory Dubin, Tiffany Hodges, Adrian Jevicki, Meghan Jones, Ryan Justesen, Richard Pait, David Pixley, David F. Slone. *A Man's Best Friend* by Jeffrey M. Jones. February 25, 2005. Directed by Katherine Owens; with Tom Lenaghen, Bruce DuBose.

WEBSTER HALL. *The Awesome 80s Prom* by Ken Davenport. September 10, 2004. Directed by Mr. Davenport; with Sheila Berezan, Anne Bobby, Nicole Cicchella, Stephen Guarino, Jeff Hiller, Emily McNamara, Troy Metcalf, Jenna Pace, Brian Peterson, Jessica West Regan, Kathy Searle, Noah Weisberg, Brandon Williams, Simon Wong, Fletcher Young.

WHERE EAGLES DARE THEATRE. *Inside Cherry Pitz* by Cyndi Freeman. November 16, 2004. Directed by Cheryl King; with Ms. Freeman. *The Mermaid* by Mark Finley. May 5, 2005. Directed by Barry Childs; with Paul Caiola, Gail Dennison, Nathan Johnson, Rachel Eve Moses, Karen Stanion, Derek Staranowski, Joe Tuttle.

WHITE BIRD PRODUCTIONS. *Neverland: The World of Games.* Developed by White Bird Productions; based on *Peter Pan.* October 15, 2004. Directed by Kathryn Dickinson; with April Mathis, Lorrie Harrison, Cindy Hanson, T. Scott Lilly, Julie Rapoport, Stephanie Bok, Victor Caneva.

WINGS THEATRE COMPANY. *Pulling the Lever* by Sanjit De Silva and Deepa Purohit. October 28, 2004. Directed by Rod Bowen; with Catherine Jhung, Don Nahaku, Lethia Nall, Matt Pendergast, A-men Rasheed, Antonio G. Del Rosario, Tijuana Ricks, Debargo Sanyal, Ragini Shah, Sam Younis. *Looking4sex* by Jonathan Kronenberger. November 12, 2004. Directed by Mr. Kronenberger; with Jason Alan Griffin, Robert Maisonett, Brian Patacca, Dan Salyer, Andrew Shoffner, Brad Thomason,

Phoenix Walker, Karen Stanion. *They All Knew*. Musical with book, music and lyrics by Robert Mitchell. December 20, 2004. Directed by Judith Fredericks; with Adam MacDonald, David Tillistrand, Valerie Issembert, Susan Kokot Stokes, Elizabeth Cherry, Annie Ramsey, Stephan Stubbins, Michael McIntosh, Charles Statham. *Fools in Love* by Sarah Rosenberg and Louis Reyes Cardenas; adapted from the work of William Shakespeare. March 10, 2005. Directed by Ms. Rosenberg and Mr. Cardenas; with Annelise Abrams, Amelia Campbell, Mr. Cardenas, Laura Cloutier, Margaret Curry, Joseph DeSantis, Anthony Galluccio, Simon Galon, Mike Gomez, Frank Kelly, Tom Falborn, Ryan Knowles, Andy Langton, Nova Mejia, Deborah Paulter, Jacqueline Raposo, Anthony Raymond, Matt Schuneman, Taylor Stockdale, Erika Villalba, Brandy Wykes. *The Three Musketeers* by Clint Jefferies and Paul L. Johnson. April 15, 2005. Directed by Jeffery Corrick; with Ryan Boda, Steven Cabral, David Velarde, David Weitzer, David Macaluso, Pamela Brumley, Kim Reed, Nigel Columbus, Adrienne Couvillion, Alexander Elisa, David Garry, Christopher Gleason, Josh Grisetti, Lynne Henderson, Nalina Mann, Tim Ott, Fausto Pineda, Stephen Raman, Stephen Smith, Elisa Winter.

WORKSHOP THEATER COMPANY. *LOL* by Tony Sportiello. September 10, 2004. Directed by Jerry Less; with C.K. Allen, Jed Dickinson, Lori Faiella, Richard Kent Green, Kathy Gail MacGowan, Anne Richardson, Nicole Taylor. *When It Rains* by Rahti Gorfien. September 21, 2004. Directed by Thomas Cote; with Blayne Perry, David Pincus, Laksh Singh, Emily Zacharias. *Pierre and Marie* by Ron Clark; based on the play *Les Palmes de M. Schultz* by Jean-Noel Fenwick. October 21, 2004. Directed by Christopher Bellis; with Teri Black, Michael Edmund, Martha Lopez Gilpin, Michael Gilpin, John Quilty. *Rattlesnake* by Fred Pezzuli. December 2, 2004. Directed by Elysa Marden; with Jim Bray, Christopher Burke, Canan Erguder, Jake Robards, Ellen Saland, Ben Sumrall, Brittney Venable. *Foreign Affairs* by Rich Orloff. January 7, 2005. Directed by Holli Harms; with Richard Kent Green, Gary Mink, Laurie Ann Orr, Gerrianne Raphael, Kim Reed, Greg Skura, Baz Snider. *The Forever Waltz* by Glyn Maxwell. March 12, 2005. Directed by Elysa Marden; with Barry Jay Abramowitz, Jennifer Kathryn Marshall, Joshua Spafford. *Radium* by Alex S. DeFazio. March 24, 2005. Directed by Jody P. Person; with Bobby Abid, Nathaniel Claridad, Jon Deliz, Thay Floyd, Dustyn Gulledge, Elizabeth Sugarman. *Incredible Sex* by Rich Orloff. May 1, 2005. Directed by Jeffrey C. Wolf; with Julie Ferrell, Deborah Green, Traci Hovel, Jason Liebman, William McCall, Peter R. Thewes.

ZIPPER THEATER. *Lypsinka: The Passion of the Crawford*. May 5, 2005. Directed by Kevin Malony; with Steve Cuiffo, John Epperson.

THE SEASON AROUND
THE UNITED STATES

AMERICAN THEATRE CRITICS/STEINBERG NEW PLAY AWARD AND CITATIONS

○ ○ ○ ○ ○

A DIRECTORY OF NEW UNITED STATES PRODUCTIONS

THE AMERICAN THEATRE CRITICS ASSOCIATION (ATCA) is the organization of drama critics in all media throughout the United States. One of the group's stated purposes is "To increase public awareness of the theater as a national resource." To this end, ATCA has annually cited outstanding new plays produced around the US, which were excerpted in our series beginning with the 1976–77 volume. As we continue our policy of celebrating playwrights and playwriting in *Best Plays*, we offer essays on the recipients of the 2005 American Theatre Critics/Steinberg New Play Award and Citations. The ATCA/Steinberg New Play Award of $15,000 was awarded to Craig Lucas for his play *Singing Forest*. ATCA/Steinberg New Play Citations were given to Gina Gionfriddo for *After Ashley*—which was also named a Best Play following its Off Off Broadway run—Sarah Ruhl for *The Clean House*. Citation honorees receive prizes of $5,000 each.

The ATCA awards are funded by the Harold and Mimi Steinberg Charitable Trust, which supports theater throughout the United States with its charitable giving. The ATCA/Steinberg New Play Award and Citations are given in a ceremony at Actors Theatre of Louisville. Essays in the next section—by Misha Berson (*The Seattle Times*) and Michele Volansky (Washington College)—celebrate the ATCA/Steinberg Citation honorees. An essay by Elizabeth Maupin on *After Ashley* appears in The Best Plays of 2004–2005 section of this volume.

ATCA's 12th annual M. Elizabeth Osborn Award for a new playwright was voted to J.T. Rogers for *Madagascar*, which was produced in 2004 by the Salt Lake Acting Company in Salt Lake City, Utah.

The process of selecting these outstanding plays is as follows: any American Theatre Critics Association member may nominate the first full professional production of a finished play (not a reading or an airing as a play-in-progress) that premieres outside New York City during the calendar year under consideration.

Nominated 2004 scripts were studied and discussed by the New Plays Committee chaired by Elizabeth Maupin (*The Orlando Sentinel*). The committee included ATCA members Jonathan Abarbanel (freelance, Chicago), Misha Berson (*The Seattle Times*), Jackie Demaline (*The Cincinnati Enquirer*), Michael Elkin (*Jewish Exponent,* Philadelphia), Bill Gale (Theatre New England), Barbara Gross (freelance, Rockville, Maryland), George Hatza (*Reading Eagle*), Claudia W. Harris (freelance, Orem, Utah), Bill Hirschman (*South Florida Sun-Sentinel*, Dick Kerekes (freelance, Jacksonville, Florida), Kevin Nance (*Chicago Sun-Times*) and Andy Propst (American Theater Web).

Committee members made their choices on the basis of script rather than production. If the timing of nominations and openings prevents some works from being considered in any given year, they may be eligible for consideration the following year if they haven't since moved to New York City.

2005 ATCA/Steinberg New Play Award

SINGING FOREST

By Craig Lucas

○ ○ ○ ○ ○

Essay by Misha Berson

OLIVER: But, mother, don't you think we all have a fascist inside us? Isn't that part of what Freud taught us?

LOË: I am not discussing Freud with you. But yes, I do . . . we mustn't fool ourselves: Analysis is helpless in the face of this beast . . . It's like trying to use an electron microscope to comb your hair—wasn't designed for it. You and everyone who is young enough, and even those who aren't, are designed for it, together.

IN CRAIG LUCAS'S *Singing Forest*, the twisted family tree of the Lear-like matriarch Loë Rieman, branches into the terrors of fascism and the flowering of psychic insight, the toxicity of guilt and betrayal, and the yearning for forgiveness and reconciliation. But the play's central theme is how refusal to confront truth can poison generations, and entire societies.

The play weaves a complex story of an Austrian immigrant psychoanalyst and her estranged offspring. By turns it is a door-slamming sex farce, a dysfunctional family saga and a Holocaust tragedy, swerving between breathless screwball comedy and a lamentation of unbearable loss.

The first two productions—at Seattle's Intiman Theatre and New Haven's Long Wharf Theatre—of *Singing Forest* struck some reviewers as too cluttered and confusing in its ambitions. But most recognized the unique and far-reaching nature of Lucas's vision. As *New Haven Register* drama critic E. Minor Kyle put it, the play grapples with "the threat and reality of fascism and self-perception in a fashion that is alternately haunting and farcical, and personal and political."

Act I of the play, "Beyond the Pleasure Principle" (named, as are the two other acts, after a major theoretical text by Freud) is set in New York in 2000, and introduces a frayed circle of people connected by blood, sex and coincidence.

Freudian "family": Laurence Ballard, Jay Goede, Kristin Flanders, Daniel Eric Gold, Malte Frid-Nielsen, Anne Scurria in Craig Lucas's Singing Forest *at Intiman Theatre Company. Photo: Chris Bennion*

We first meet Loë Rieman, a vigorous and formidable octogenarian, at an Alcoholics Anonymous meeting, riffing on the 9th step of the 12-Step recovery program, "making amends":

> LOË: This is your story: You lose your entire family through an act of your own. . . . your own. You flee to America with two small children, twins, Oliver and Bertha—you arrange a new life for them, try to make some form of redress—amends. To spare them from the horror you witness.

Soon, in parallel scenes, Loë's offspring enter the picture: the gay psychoanalyst Oliver, the wealthy widow Bertha and Bertha's son Jules—whose inheritance from his Arab mogul father has made him one of the richest (and most reclusive) men in the world.

IN MULTI-LAYERED scenes, which often divide the stage into several locales at once, we learn that none of Loë's relations are on speaking terms with each other. But as the play's farcical plot spins a web of suspicion, masquerades, secrets and lies, the fragmented clan reconnects. Also entangled in the web are Gray, a handsome, adrift actor Jules hires as his therapy "stand-in," Gray's pregnant girlfriend Beth, Oliver's therapist-ex-boyfriend Shar and current lover, Laszlo. The last is a barista at a Manhattan Starbucks where, naturally, all paths criss-cross.

While the intricate sexual and therapeutic relationships among these people ramp up the screwball comedy quotient in *Singing Forest*, the play also more somberly revisits Loë's agonizing past in wartime Austria.

The elderly Loë's reclamation of that past begins when she tells her AA friend Bill that Sigmund Freud was her analyst and mentor in Vienna in the 1930s. She goes on to rail at the intellectual and historical blindness of her adopted country:

Refusal to confront truth can poison generations and entire societies.

> LOË: Everything here has been ruined by haste; no one has time to contemplate, examine: "It's history! Forget it. You're thinking too much." Einstein, Socrates, they think too much[. . . .] Anyone you meet, anywhere, try asking, "What do you suppose might constitute a civilized bearing in regard to the individual, the ego, in relation to our responsibility to others?" They'll stab you to death.

But Loë has denied her own history, hiding essential truths from her children, including the identity of their father. Now they are neurotics who—in a jumble of phone and live conversations—complain bitterly about her, and perpetuate the family dysfunction.

It is, paradoxically, the intimacy Loë develops toward the end of Act I with the young actor Gray that cracks open her vault of secrets. Through a quirky phone-sex-and-psychoanalysis service she has created, Loë forges a disembodied but profound bond with Gray, partly maternal and partly erotic, as he faces his own fears of impending parenthood. (Loë's symbolically apropos phone-sex handle is Cassandra, after the Greek bearer of hard truths that are destined never to be believed.) She advises Gray to "stand in the dark" with his child, even when faced with "questions you can't answer," and to "never believe the things that everyone agrees on."

The first act ends as the elder Loë is suddenly flooded with memories of Vienna. She looks on as a much younger version of herself appears in an early 1930s flashback, in the family home in Austria. Loë's elder brother Walter is telling her that, because of Loë's severe anxiety and fainting spells, their father has asked the illustrious Sigmund Freud to pay a house call.

In Act II ("Civilization and Its Discontents"), the action hopscotches more frenetically between 2000 comedy and 1930s drama. From now on, the actors (except the woman playing the older Loë) juggle two roles, changing identities quickly between overlapping New York and Vienna scenes.

As the scene opens, Loë confides her terrors to the kindly Dr. Freud. She fears the Nazis will occupy Austria, and brutalize Jews and gays (including her brother, Walter, and his lover Simon). But Freud interprets her fears as neurotic symptoms:

> FREUD: And who does Hitler stand for? Supreme leader of the. . . . Fatherland? Perhaps? We can do nothing here in this room about what is happening across national boundaries but we can do something about irrational fears.

He also insists (as did the real Dr. Freud, in the early 1930s), that Germany would never annex Austria, and that Austrians "are not inclined to German brutality."

Ghostly presence: Anne Scurria and Kristin Flanders in Craig Lucas's Singing Forest *at Intiman Theatre Company. Photo: Chris Bennion*

BACK IN MODERN-DAY New York, a pastiche of scenes reveal that the hermitic Jules has been "outed" by the press. Shar has also become, unknowingly, a new phone-sex client of Loë's. Her son, Oliver, finally reveals to Laszlo what little he knows of his family's Viennese past. He shows his lover a photo of his late Uncle Walter, noting he "died in the camps. And this is his lover, Simon, another golden boy, apparently. I think sometimes maybe . . . [Mother] loved them more than us. . . ."

As the farcical pot comes to a boil, the play's focus shifts to Loë's Staten Island home, where all the New York characters, in turn, converge—in a Freudian version of the Marx Brothers' stateroom scene, in *A Night at the Opera.*

Oliver turns up first, after years of trying to find his elusive mother. She greets him angrily:

> LOË: Spiteful, selfish, self-aggrandizing, greedy, solipsistic—narrow, punishing, recriminatory—
> OLIVER: Mother, mother please, stop, hello, it's Oliver your son, your family, your flesh and blood, MOTHER SHUT UP! Yes, I'm all those things, what are you?

Eventually Shar and Gray, Bertha, Beth, Bill and Laszlo turn up too, in search of a lover or relative. As the door-slamming comic frenzy peaks, Loë's mind jolts back again to her Austrian past.

We are transported to 1938 Vienna. Germany is invading Austria, and Nazi agents are forcing their way into the Rieman family home. Act II ends with the image (a memory? a nightmare?) of Loë cowering before the SS men.

In Act III ("Analysis Terminable and Interminable"), the ordeal Loë and others endured at the hands of the Nazis dominates. Simultaneously, we see her friends and family hearing about these events for the first time, in the Staten Island gathering circa 2000. Occasionally, the modern characters comment, Greek chorus-style, on the terrible past events as they unfold.

It is again 1938. And as the Nazis march into Vienna, the Riemans host a small goodbye party for the still-jovial Freud, who is finally fleeing Austria for England with his family. As the assembled friends toast his departure, young Loë (now a trained analyst) voices her hope that psychotherapy will be a weapon against "unexamined sadism and cruelty." She also asks Freud to prescribe her brother and Simon a deadly dose of the sleeping drug Veronal, but he counters:

> FREUD: Why should we kill ourselves? Simply because they would like us to?

Suddenly the Gestapo agent Gerhardt Zeitzler arrives to arrest Simon and Walter on charges of "public indecency"—though in a quieter, less violent manner than presaged at the end of Act II. In a skein of numerous short scenes, Loë visits Zeitzler's office repeatedly, bribing him to find her brother and father (who has also been detained). Gerhardt strings her along, promising to help. But later he jails Loë also, for "safekeeping."

Several years pass, as Gerhardt accepts Loë's bribes while keeping her as his sex slave. At one juncture, a benumbed, sorrowful Loë sings a poignantly ironic song by Gustav Mahler, "*Ich bin der Welt abhanden gekommen* (I have lost track of the world)." Learning Mahler was a Viennese Jew, the Gestapo officer responds:

> GERHARDT: I will tell you something. The Viennese behave toward the Jews in ways I could never have imagined. It took the Germans a very long time to accept what needed to be done. Here, such enthusiasm right away.

Toward the end of the war, the Red Army advances on Vienna, and Gerhardt brings Loë back to her deserted family home. She pliantly offers him the deed to the house, but when he turns his back she coolly cuts his throat.

AS YOUNG LOË flees Vienna, the older Loë voices her guilt about deserting her missing loved ones. We next see young Loë visiting friends near Paris, in 1945. She is pregnant by Gerhardt and expecting twins. Asked if the Nazi had raped her, she responds:

> LOË: Who was it who said, "God made everything out of nothing, but the nothing shows through"?

But when urged to have an abortion, Loë vows to keep her babies:

> LOË: Whatever is inside me is all I intend to carry, and you musn't waste another breath or tactic to take it from me, because all, all suffering and sacrifice and genius lost, all the promise and costs, the wages paid, the needless kindnesses [. . .] now nestled here, taken seed . . . in my soil; and I intend to guard it all and to give it pride of place, and that is what I will give our world[. . . .]

At this point, the elder and younger Loë in unison bitterly announce that her murdered father was Jewish, but hid his ethnicity (even from his own children) so he could assimilate and prosper in Vienna.

The focus returns exclusively to the 2000 gathering in Loë's flat. Loë reveals Walter and Simon were likely killed by ravenous dogs the Nazis unleashed on them. While Bertha and Oliver try to absorb their mother's

Haunting grounds: Anne Scurria in Craig Lucas's Singing Forest *at Intiman Theatre Company. Photo: Chris Bennion*

shocking revelations, Loë's "surrogate" children, Gray and Beth, are deeply moved and assure her that she isn't to blame for these cruel deaths.

Singing Forest closes with a chorus of seriocomic apologies, circling round to the amends foreshadowed in the play's first scene. Children ask parents for forgiveness and vice versa, lovers and ex-lovers reconcile, wine is poured, and there is a choral mantra on the expression: "Okay," with Loë giving the last affirmation. The play closes with a bittersweet sense of new beginnings, and new life rising from the ashes of past horrors, as Mahler's plaintive "*Ich bin der Welt abhanden gekommen*" is heard once more.

2005 ATCA/Steinberg New Play Citation

THE CLEAN HOUSE

By Sarah Ruhl

○ ○ ○ ○ ○

Essay by Michele Volansky

> MATILDE: The perfect joke makes you forget about your life. The perfect joke makes you remember your life. The perfect joke is stupid when you write it down. The perfect joke was not made up by one person. It passed through the air and you caught it. A perfect joke is somewhere between an angel and a fart.

*T*HE CLEAN HOUSE opens with a joke told entirely in Portuguese by Matilde, a Brazilian maid who, we come to learn, doesn't so much want to clean as she wants to mourn her parents, the funniest people in Brazil. She would also like to continue to study humor, jokes, as she did in her native country. Her grieving process is interrupted by her job as a maid in the home of Lane, an overworked doctor and her surgeon husband, Charles. Into this mix, add Lane's sister Virginia who, conveniently, loves to clean. We later meet Ana, the woman with whom Charles falls in love "to the point of invention."

An early exchange between Virginia and Matilde gives the audience emotional insight into these characters while revealing just how pointed (and funny) Sarah Ruhl's writing can be:

> VIRGINIA: Lane didn't describe you accurately. How old are you?
>
> MATILDE: Young enough that my skin is still good.
> Old enough that I am starting to think: is my skin still good?
> Does that answer your question?
>
> VIRGINIA: Yes. You're twenty-seven.
>
> (*Matilde nods.*)
>
> MATILDE: You're good.
>
> VIRGINIA: Thank you.

The two concoct a plan that allows Virginia the satisfaction of cleaning Lane's house, leaving Matilde time to come up with the perfect joke. It is a unique, mutually beneficial opportunity for two women in search of an elusive "something" to make their lives whole once again.

Reluctant duster: Zilah Mendoza in Sarah Ruhl's The Clean House *at Yale Repertory Theatre. Photo: Joan Marcus*

RUHL HAS BEEN widely celebrated for *Clean House*, with awards that include the prestigious Susan Smith Blackburn prize and a citation from the American Theatre Critics Association in its Steinberg New Play Award competition. These honors place the young playwright in the excellent company of such theatrical luminaries as Paula Vogel, Wendy Wasserstein, Marie Irene Fornes, August Wilson, Craig Wright and Arthur Miller. *Clean House* is not, however, an easy play, nor does it seem to be finished. Questions about what Ruhl wants to say linger: The play is marked by odd shifts of language and emotion—and it is difficult to discern just whose story the play tells.

Sarah Ruhl's *The Clean House* has been called "charming," "whimsical," "poignant" and, even, "loony." While all of these words aptly describe the play, there is also something unsettling about it, something that moves it away from whimsy or frivolity and toward social criticism. In meeting Lane, we find a character who is very much a reflection of contemporary culture. There is a certain familiarity about this woman trying to keep everything together: her pristine white house, her ailing patients, her own heart and soul. Despite the fact that there is a great deal of high-minded talk in the play about the plight of those who make minimum wage, Lane is certainly not in the mold of Barbara Ehrenreich. She's angry that her cleaning lady won't clean the house: "*I've* been cleaning my house! I'm sorry but I did not go to medical school to clean my own home." We can feel her pain, but does one actually articulate such feelings?

Ruhl, in discussing the play, suggested that the idea for it sprang from a cocktail-party conversation among a group of doctors. As the conversation evolved, the playwright found herself growing increasingly uncomfortable. This is not, however, a run-of-the-mill play about domestic work. Nor is it a rigorous examination of how we live in the global economy today, with others (sometimes from other lands) raising our children, cleaning our houses

Ruhl suggested that the idea sprang from a cocktail-party conversation.

(almost always from other lands) or fixing our troubled computers. While we can certainly understand Lane's frustration with Matilde, we also yearn for Matilde's happiness. Add Virginia's and Ana's plights into the mix and things are suddenly far more complicated than they seem—or perhaps even than Ruhl intended.

The playwright presents women in the context of their relationships to one another, to their work and to the men in their lives. As it often does, class rears its ugly head. We learn fairly quickly that Lane is at the top of this ladder, while Matilde and, to a certain extent, Ana, are most assuredly below. This hierarchy is disrupted when the housekeeper stops cleaning, a married (male) doctor falls in love with a sick woman from Argentina and the audience is left to wonder for whom they should be rooting.

We all know, in this era of political-correctness, how we are supposed to think and feel about class issues, but, as presented in the play, we are unsure. The play features an always-shifting tone, from linear realism to what can only be described as "magic realism." Some critics found it difficult to classify and label such flux, observing that the play, while containing many positive attributes, might be a bit of a mystery to some audience members. There is a sense, as the play moves forward, that we are on unsteady emotional ground. Do we laugh? Do we cry? Why does Lane agree to take Ana into her home? What are we to make of the seeming-ineptitude (or lack of the big picture) in the character of Charles, who, instead of sitting by Ana's side, journeys to Alaska:

LANE: He's not crazy. It's a yew tree. Y-E-W. *(Spelling it out)* A Pacific yew tree. The bark was made into Taxol in 1967. The compound prevents microtubule from decomposing. Cancer cells become so clogged with microtubules that they are slower to grow and divide.[…]

MATILDE: He wants to plant it in the middle of Ana's courtyard. So she can smell the tree, while she's on her balcony.

VIRGINIA: That's beautiful.

LANE: It's not beautiful, Virginia. There is a woman dying, alone, while Charles chops down a fucking tree. How heroic.

Ruhl navigates the language of the play with the same boldness that is reflected in the play's emotional shifts and questions. It is lyrical and poetic, yet also grounded deeply in the specific worlds of medicine, sibling rivalry and international relations. On one page, she will write about the act of forgiveness:

They sit, looking at the fish.
They breathe.
Lane forgives Ana.
Lane taps on the glass bowl.
The fish wiggles around.

Passing time: Zilah Mendoza, Elizabeth Norment and Laurie Kennedy in Sarah Ruhl's The Clean House *at Yale Repertory Theatre. Photo: Joan Marcus*

She then smoothly switches gears to give us:

> LANE: So.
> Are you happy there? At the other house?
>
> MATILDE: Yes.
>
> LANE: What's her house like?
>
> MATILDE: It's little. She has a balcony that overlooks the sea.
>
> LANE: What's her furniture like?
>
> MATILDE: A table from one place—a chair from another place. It doesn't go together.
> But it's nice.
>
> LANE: What does she cook?
>
> MATILDE: I am not a spy!
>
> LANE: I'm sorry.

WE MOVE AND swirl through the many layers of story in this play, until we then come to the sisters. Ruhl offers Lane and Virginia the chance to rehash and potentially rehabilitate their long-simmering sibling rivalry. No Stella and Blanche, these two. Instead, we get two sisters full of longing for love, for meaning and, most importantly, for a connection to each other. Longing runs through the entire play, but Ruhl brings it all into focus in the evolution of Lane and Virginia. Indeed, Virginia's elegiac recitation of her life touches her sister:

> VIRGINIA: I wake up in the morning, and I wish that I could sleep through the whole day because it is too painful, but there I am, I'm awake. So I get out of bed, I make eggs for my husband. I throw the eggshells in the disposal. I listen to the sound of delicate eggshells being ground by an indelicate machine. I clean the sink. I sweep the floor. I wipe coffee grounds from the counter.
>
> I might have done something with my life. I might have been a scholar. I might have described one particular ruin with the cold-blooded poetry of which only a first-rate scholar is capable. Why didn't I? [. . .] I wanted something—big. I didn't know how to ask for it.

So we are left with the women—Matilde, Virginia, Lane and Ana—all struggling to make sense of the odd new domesticity that has befallen them. Ruhl's gifts as a writer shine when she allows Virginia and Lane to come to an understanding about their roles in each other's lives, when Ana dies a death that is at once peaceful and jarring, and when Matilde, finally, finds her perfect joke.

A DIRECTORY OF NEW UNITED STATES PRODUCTIONS

○ ○ ○ ○ ○

Compiled by Rue E. Canvin

THIS LISTING INCLUDES professional productions that opened during the June 1, 2004–May 31, 2005 season. Its focus is on new plays—and other productions of note—by a variety of resident companies around the United States. Production information listed here in alphabetical order, by state, was supplied by the 76 producing organizations included. Resident theaters producing new plays and operating under contracts with Actors' Equity Association were queried for this comprehensive directory. Active US theater companies not included in this list may not have presented new (or newly revised) scripts during the year under review or had not responded to our query by July 1, 2005. Productions listed below are world premieres, US premieres, regional premieres, substantial revisions or otherwise worthy of note. Relatively new plays that have received widespread production—such as Nilo Cruz's Pulitzer Prize-winning *Anna in the Tropics*, which was produced in at least a dozen diverse theaters—are not listed here due to space and other considerations. Theaters in the US are encouraged to submit proposed listings of new works and new adaptations, in addition to the premieres indicated above, to the editor of *The Best Plays Theater Yearbook* series.

ALABAMA

Alabama Shakespeare Theatre, Montgomery

Kent Thompson producing artistic director, Alan Harrison managing director

Southern Writers' Festival of New Plays. June 4–6, 2004.
PURE CONFIDENCE. By Carlyle Brown. Direction, Clinton Turner Davis; sound, Reid Rejsa; dramaturgy, Tanya Palmer; stage management, Tanya J. Searle and Kat Dunham.

Simon Cato	Robert Barry Fleming	Auctioneer; Reporter	Antony Hagopian
Col. Wiley Johnson	Philip Pleasants	Mattie Johnson	Greta Lambert
George Dewitt	Sam Gregory	Caroline	Kelly Taffe

THE PATRON SAINT OF PEANUTS. By Keith Josef Adkins. Direction, Kent Thompson; dramaturgy, Susan Willis; stage management, Mark D. Leslie.

George Carver	Rodney Hicks	Christian Schweitzer	Joe Kolbow
James Carver	Jeremy Alan Richards	Booker T. Washington	Aaron Cabell

313

Felix Payne .... Spencer Scott Barros   Lucy Seymour .... Margo Moorer
    Ensemble: Rodney Clark, Frederick Snyder, Sonja Lanzener.

SUSPENDED IN AMBER. By Janece Shaffer. Direction, Bruce K. Sevy; dramaturgy, Jennifer Hebblethwaite; stage management, Jenny Watkins.

Beth .... Kathleen McCall   Ben .... Michael Bakkensen
Lillian .... Libby George   Manny .... Paul Hebron
Ilene .... Jennifer Hunt   Lane Overstreet .... Mary Proctor

HAZARD COUNTY. By Allison Moore. Direction, Richard Caliban; dramaturgy, Lenora Inez Brown; stage management, Sara Lee Howell.

Ruth .... Amy Tribbey   Quinn; others .... Chris Mixon
Camille .... Suzanne Curtis   Quinton; others .... Julia Watt
Blake .... Harry Carnahan

Southern Writer's Project of New Plays. February 4–6, 2005.

THE DREAMS OF SARAH BREEDLOVE. By Regina Taylor. February 4, 2005 (world premiere). Direction, Ms. Taylor; choreography, Hope Clarke; scenery, Troy C. Hourie; costumes, Linda Cho; lighting, D.M. Wood; sound, Don Tindall; music, Daryl Waters; dramaturgy, Susan Willis, stage management, Sara Lee Howell.

Sarah .... Greta Oglesby   Freeman B. Ransom .... K. Todd Freeman
Lelia .... Karen Aldridge   Mae .... Lakeisha Woodard
C.J. Walker .... Keith Randolph Smith   Nola .... Carol Mitchell-Leon
    Time: 1904-1919. Place: St. Louis, Indiana, New York.

TREASURE ISLAND. Adaptation by Eric Schmiedl from the novel by Robert Louis Stevenson. February 4, 2005. Direction, Greta Lambert; stage management, Shannon S. Denvil.
    Performed by James Denvil, Larnelle Foster, Jonathan Gibson, Lauren Hendler, Chris Qualls, Mike Rhyne, Christian Rummel, Shannon Warrick.

SANCTIFIED. By Javon Johnson. February 4, 2005. Direction, Rajendra Ramoon Maharaj; dramaturgy, Lenora Inez Brown; music, Ron Metcalf; stage management, Mark D. Leslie.
    Performed by Clare Bathé, Glenn Gordon, Bryan Jones, Chris Morgan, Alexis Phillips, Cleo Pizana, Wayne Pretlow, Norrisa Pearson, Roxanne Reese, Fred Strothers, Kellie Turner.

THE PARTY'S OVER. By Alexander Crompton. February 5, 2005. Direction, Bruce K. Sevy; stage management, Colleen Williams.
    Performed by Lauren Bloom, Meghan Lisi, Doug Rossi, Craig Pattison, Anthony Stockard, Eboni Witcher.

JESUS HATES ME. By Wayne Lemon. February 5, 2005. Direction, Bruce K. Sevy; stage management, Kimberly J. First, dramaturgy, Carlyle Brown.
    Performed by Robert Barry Fleming, Kathleen McCall, Craig Pattison, Doug Rossi, Christian Rummel, Julia Watt.

FOUR SPIRITS. By Sena Jeter Naslund and Elaine W. Hughes. Based on the novel by Ms. Naslund. February 5, 2005. Direction, Susan Willis; dramaturgy, Eric Schmiedl; stage management, Sara Lee Howell.
    Performed by Karen Aldridge, Aaron Cabell, Quinton Cockrell, James Denvil, Ruth Eglsaer, Larnelle Foster, Jonathan Gibson, Betty Hart, Lauren Hendler, Jennifer Hunt, Chris Mixon, Greta Oglesby, Keith Randolph Smith, Anthony Stockard, Eric Ware, Robert Jazz Williams, Lakeisha Woodard.

THE SLEEPING GIRL. By Suzanne Bradbeer. February 6, 2005. Direction, Olivia Honegger; stage management, Tanya J. Searle; dramaturgy, Melissa Hardy.
    Performed by Lauren Bloom, Tim Gittings, Greta Lambert, Dan McCleary, Shannon Warrick, Eboni Witcher.

ARIZONA

Arizona Theatre Company, Tucson

David Ira Goldstein artistic director, Jessica L. Andrews managing director

FOR BETTER OR WORSE. By Georges Feydeau; translated and adapted by Geoff Hoyle. January 21, 2005 (world premiere). Direction, David Ira Goldstein; scenery, Kent Dorsey; costumes, David Kay Mickelsen; lighting, York Kennedy, sound, Brian Jerome Peterson; composer, Fitz Patton. stage management, Robyn Lambert. Presented in association with the Berkeley Repertory Theatre.

Bastien Follavoine	Geoff Hoyle	M. de Champrinet	Richard Trujillo
Julie Follavoine	Sharon Lockwood	Rose	Amy Resnick
Clémence	Amy Resnick	Adhéume Chouilloux	Jarion Monroe
Mme. de Champrinet	Lynnda Ferguson	Toto	Roman Cratty-Lewis

Time: Before the Great War. Place: Paris.

ARKANSAS

Arkansas Repertory Theatre, Little Rock

Robert Hupp producing artistic director, Michael McCurdy general manager

THE SLEEPER. By Catherine Butterfield. October 14, 2004 (world premiere). Direction, Brad Mooy; costumes, Robert A. Pittenridge; lighting, Andrew Meyers; sound, M. Jason Pruzin; stage management, Christine Lomaka.

Gretchen	Amy Tribbey	Ensemble	Maggie Marshall
Bill	Christopher Cass		David Rhodes
Vivien	Clarinda Ross		Matt Walker
Matthew	Gino Anthony Pesi		

Time: March–May, 2002. Place: California.

CALIFORNIA

American Conservatory Theater, San Francisco

Carey Perloff artistic director, Heather Kitchen managing director

THE GOOD BODY. By Eve Ensler. June 24, 2004 (world premiere). Direction, Peter Askin; costumes, Susan Hilferty; scenery, Robert Brill; sound, David Van Tieghem; lights, Kevin Adams; projections, Wendall K. Harrington.

Performed by Ms. Ensler.

THE BLACK RIDER: THE CASTING OF THE MAGIC BULLETS. Musical with text by William S. Burroughs; music and lyrics, Tom Waits. September 25, 2004. Direction, Robert Wilson; scenery and lighting, Mr Wilson; costumes, Frida Parmeggiani; sound, Nicholaj Aarup; arrangements, Greg Cohen; orchestrations, Ben Clausen; dramaturgy, Wolfgang Wiens.

Performed by Sona Cervena, Marianne Faithfull, Mark McGrath, Janet Henfrey, Mary Margaret O'Hara, Robert Parsons, Nigel Richards, Dean Robinson, Gabriella Santinelli, Richard Strange, Monika Tahal, Jake Thornton, Jack Willis.

Musical numbers included: "Overture (Lucky Day)," "Black Box Theme," "The Black Rider," "But He's Not Wilhelm," "November," "Carnival," "That's the Way," "The Briar and the Rose," "Just the Right Bullets," "Chase the Clouds Away," "Flash Pan Hunter," "In the Morning," "George Schmid," "T'aint No Sin," "I'll Shoot the Moon," "Gospel Train," "Lucky Day," "Last Rose of Summer."

WELL. By Lisa Kron. February 16, 2005. Direction, Leigh Silverman; scenery, Allen Moyer; costumes, Miranda Hoffman, lighting, Christopher Akerlind, sound, Garth Hemphill.

Performed by Ms. Kron, Saidah Arrika Ekulona, Jayne Houdyshell, Joel Van Liew, Welker White, A-men Rasheed.

THE GAMESTER. By Freyda Thomas; based on *Le Joueur* by Jean-Francois Regnard; January 12, 2005. Direction, Ron Lagomarsino; scenery, Kate Edmunds; costumes, Beaver Bauer; lighting, Nancy Schertler; sound, Garth Hemphill; production stage management; Kimberly Mark Webb.

Valère .... Lorenzo Pisoni	Mme. Argante .... Rene Augesen
Angelique .... Margot White	Dorante .... Ron Campbell
Hector .... Gregory Wallace	Marquis de Fauxpas .... Anthony Fusco
Thomas .... Steve Irish	Betty .... Lianne Marie Dobbs
Mme. Securite .... Joan Mankin	Croupier .... Andy Murray
Mme. Preferee .... Stacy Ross	Ensemble .... Nancy Carlin, Gregory Crane

Presented in two parts.

HILDA. By Marie Ndiaye; translated by Erika Rundle. February 1, 2005. Direction, Carey Perloff; scenery, Donald Eastman; costumes, David F. Draper; sound, Cliff Caruthers; lighting, Nancy Shertler; music, David Lang, dramaturgy, Paul Walsh. Presented in association with Laura Pels Productions.

Mrs. Lemarchand .... Ellen Karas	Corinne .... Lauren Grace
Frank .... Marco Barricelli	

Presented without intermission.

LILIES. By Michel Marc Bouchard; translated by Linda Gaboriau. March 11, 2005. Direction, Serge Denoncourt; scenery and lighting, Alexander V. Nichols; costumes, Cassandra Carpenter; stage management, Karen Runk. Presented in association with Theatre Rhinoceros, San Francisco.

Simon Doucet (1912) .... Steven Strobel	Timothée; Simon (1952) .... Steve Irish
Vallier de Tilly .... Clayton B. Hodges	Baron de Hüe .... Will Huddleston
Fr. Saint-Michel .... Andrew Fonda Jackson	Lydie-Anne de Rozier .... Kevin Crook
Jean Bilodeau .... Andy Butterfield	Baroness de Hüe .... Kraig Kehrer
Marie-Laure de Tilly .... Gregory Wallace	Bishop Jean Bilodeau .... Tim Hendrixson

Time: 1952. Place: A prison in Québec. Presented without intermission.

FEMALE TRANSPORT. By Steve Gooch. March 8, 2005. Direction, Anne Kauffman; scenery and lighting, Alexander V. Nichols; costumes, Callie Floor; sound, Jake Rodriguez; stage management, Ember Cook.

Winnie .... Colleen Harris	Charlotte .... Sarayu Rao
Madge .... Anna Moore	Tommy .... Jomar Tagatac
Nance .... Gwynne Flanagan	Sarge .... Steven Anthony Jones
Pitty .... Alexandra Wilson	The Captain .... Reid Morgan
Sarah .... Allison Jean White	The Surgeon .... Peter Allen Stone

Time: 1807. Place: Aboard the Sydney Cove, a convict ship headed from London to Botany Bay, New South Wales, Australia.

Presented without intermission.

THE VOYSEY INHERITANCE. By Harley Granville Barker; adapted by David Mamet. March 23, 2005 (world premiere). Direction, Carey Perloff; scenery, Ralph Funicello; costumes, Deborah M. Dryden; lighting, Russell H. Champa; sound, Garth Hemphill. Presented in association with Kansas City Repertory Theatre.

Edward Voysey	Anthony Fusco	Hugh Voysey	Stephen Caffrey
Alice	Rene Augesen	Ethel	Lauren Grace
Edward's Father	Ken Ruta	Peacey; Trenchard	Mark Robbins
Mrs. Voysey	Barbara Oliver	George Booth	Neal Johnson
Edward's Brother	Andy Murray	Honor	Cheryl Weaver

Berkeley Repertory Theatre
Tony Taccone artistic director, Susan Medak managing director

THE SECRET IN THE WINGS. By Mary Zimmerman. September 8, 2004. Direction, Ms. Zimmerman; scenery, Daniel Ostling, costumes, Mara Blumenfeld; lighting, T.J. Gerckens; sound, Andre Pluess and Ben Sussman; stage management, Cynthia Cahill. Presented in association with Seattle Repertory Theatre, McCarter Theatre and Lookingglass Theatre Company.

Performed by Mark Alhadeff, Christopher Donahue, Laura Eason, Anne Fogarty, Raymond Fox, David Kersnar, Louise Lamson, Erik Lochtefeld, Tiffany Scott.

EURYDICE. By Sarah Ruhl. October 20, 2004 (world premiere). Direction, Les Waters, scenery, Scott Bradley; costumes, Meg Neville; lighting, Russell H. Champa; sound, Bray Poor; stage management, Michael Suenkel.

Eurydice	Maria Dizzia	Chorus of Stones	
Orpheus	Daniel Talbott	Little Stone	T. Edward Webster
Eurydice's Father	Charles Shaw Robinson	Big Stone	Ramiz Monsef
Nasty Interesting Man;		Loud Stone	Aimée Guillot
Lord of the Underworld	Mark Zeisler		

Presented without intermission.

FETES DE LA NUIT. By Charles L. Mee. February 2, 2005 (world premiere). Direction, Les Waters; scenery, Annie Smart; costumes, Christal Weatherly; lighting, Alexander V. Nichols; sound, Jake Rodriguez; dramaturgy, Amy Utstein; stage management, Michael Suenkel.

Henry	Dileep Rao	Sumiko	Michi Barall
Yvette	Maria Dizzia	Catherine	Lorri Holt
Lartique	James Carpenter	George	Danny Scheie
Barbesco	Joseph Kamal	Roland	Ramiz Monsef
Jean Francois	Bruce McKenzie	Ensemble	Corinne Blum, Sally Clawson,
Nanette	Maria Elena Ramirez		Joe Mandragona, Jeffery Lynn McCann

Presented in two parts.

THE PEOPLE'S TEMPLE. By Leigh Fondakowski with Greg Pierotti, Stephen Wangh and Margo Hall. April 20, 2005 (world premiere). Direction, Ms. Fondakowski; scenery, Sarah Lambert; costumes, Gabriel Berry; lighting, Betsy Adams; sound, Jake Rodriguez; music direction, Miche Braden; dramaturgy, Kelli Simpkins; stage management, Michael Suenkel. Presented in association with Z Space Studio.

Hyacinth Thrash	Miche Braden	Phil Tracy	Bob Ernst
Elsie Bell	Velina Brown	Zipporah Edwards	Margo Hall
Tim Carter	James Carpenter	Liz Forman Schwartz	Lauren Klein
Jim Jones Jr.	Colman Domingo	Jack Beam	John McAdams

Garry Lambrev .... Greg Pierotti   Juanita Bogue .... Kelli Simpkins
Meredith Reese .... Barbara Pitts   Hue Fortson .... Adam Wade
    Presented in two parts.

Center Theatre Group, Los Angeles
Gordon Davidson founding artistic director, Charles Dillingham managing director

NOTHING BUT THE TRUTH. By John Kani. September 26, 2004. Direction, Janice Honeyman; scenery and costumes, Sarah Roberts; lighting, Mannie Manim; production stage management, James T. McDermott; in the Mark Taper Forum.

Sipho Makhaya .... John Kani   Disa MacKay .... Esmeralda Bihl
Thando Makhaya .... Warona Seane
    Presented without intermission.

A PERFECT WEDDING. By Charles L. Mee. November 7, 2004 (world premiere). Direction, Gordon Davidson and Yehuda Hyman; choreography, Christine Kellogg; scenery, Donna Marquet; costumes, Christal Weatherly; lighting, D. Martyn Bookwalter, music and sound, Karl Fredrik Lundeberg; dramaturgy, Pier Carlo Talenti; production stage management, David S. Franklin; in the Kirk Douglas Theatre.

Edmund .... Tony Abatemarco   Vikram .... Brian George
Dieter .... Jim Anzide   Bob .... Katherine Griffith
Father Thane .... Julian Barnes   Djamila .... Veralyn Jones
Ariel .... Melody Butiu   Meridee .... Ruth Livier
Francois .... Mark Capri   James .... Leo Marks
Heiner .... Jon David Casey   Karl .... Raymond O'Connor
Tessa .... Jennifer Elise Cox   Jonathan .... Jason Peck
Julian .... Wilson Cruz   Willy .... Dileep Rao
Amadou .... Harry Dillon   Maria .... Cristine Rose
Isaac .... John Fleck   Frank .... James Sutorius
    Time: June. Place: Martha's Vineyard. Presented in two parts.

CAROLINE, OR CHANGE. Musical with book and lyrics by Tony Kushner; music by Jeanine Tesori. November 14, 2004. Direction, George C. Wolfe, choreography, Hope Clarke; scenery, Riccardo Hernández; costumes, Paul Tazewell; lighting, Jules Fisher and Peggy Eisenhauer; sound, Jon Weston; music direction, Kimberly Grigsby; production stage management, Rick Steiger. Presented in asssociation with Carole Shorenstein Hays, in the Ahmanson Theatre.

Caroline Thibodeaux .... Tonya Pinkins   Rose Stopnik Gellman .... Veanne Cox
The Washing Machine .... Capathia Jenkins   Stuart Gellman .... David Costabile
The Radio .... Tracy Nicole Chapman,   Dotty Moffett .... Paula Newsome
            Marva Hicks, Kenna J. Ramsey   The Moon .... Aisha de Haas
Noah Gellman .... Sy Adamowsky,   The Bus .... Michael A. Shepperd
            Benjamin Platt (alt.)   Emmie Thibodeaux .... Anika Noni Rose
The Dryer .... Michael A. Shepperd   Jackie Thibodeaux .... Leon G. Thomas III
Grandma Gellman .... Alice Playten   Joe Thibodeaux .... Corwin Tuggles
Grandpa Gellman .... Reathel Bean   Mr. Stopnick .... Larry Keith
    Musical numbers included: "Washer/Dryer," "Cabbage," "Long Distance," "Moon Change," "Duets," "The Bleach Cup," "Ironing," "The Chanukah Party," "The Twenty Dollar Bill," "Aftermath," "Lot's Wife," "How Long Has This Been Going On?"
    Time. November–December 1963. Place: Lake Charles, Louisiana. Presented in two parts.

THE PARIS LETTER. By Jon Robin Baitz. December 12, 2004 (world premiere). Direction, Michael Morris; scenery, Michael Brown; costumes, Alex Jaeger; lighting, Christopher

Akerlind, sound, Adam Phalen; music, Nathan Wang; dramaturgy, John Glore; production stage managment, Lisa J. Snodgrass; in the Kirk Douglas Theatre.

Burt Sarris;	Sandy Sonenberg;
Young Anton .... Neil Patrick Harris	Dr. Moritz Schiffman .... Ron Rifkin
Anton Kilgallen .... Lawrence Pressman	Katie Arlen;
Sam Arlen; Young Sandy .... Josh Radnor	Lillian Sonenberg .... Patricia Wettig

Time: 1962–2002. Place: Locations in New York City and Paris. Presented in three parts.

FLIGHT. By Charlayne Woodard. January 22, 2005 (world premiere). Direction, Robert Egan, choreography, Otis Sallid; scenery and costumes, Myung Hee Cho; lighting, Geoff Korf; sound, Adam Phalen; music, Karl Fredrik Lundeberg; dramaturgy, John Glore; production stage management, Michelle Blair; in the Kirk Douglas Theatre.

Mercy .... Chastity Dotson	Percussionist .... Ameenah Kaplan
Nate ....Frank Faucette	Ezra .... Meshach Taylor
Alma .... Julanne Chidi Hill	Oh Beah .... Myra Lucretia Taylor

Time: 1858. Place: A plantation near Savannah, Georgia.

THE GOAT, OR WHO IS SYLVIA? By Edward Albee. February 6, 2005. Direction, Warner Shook, scenery, Michael Olich, costumes, Frances Kenny; lighting, Mary Louise Geiger; sound, Jon Gottlieb; production stage management, Mary Michele Miner; in the Mark Taper Forum.

Stevie .... Cynthia Mace	Ross .... James Eckhouse
Martin .... Brian Kerwin	Billy .... Patrick J. Adams

AS YOU LIKE IT. By William Shakespeare. February 7, 2005. Direction, Peter Hall; scenery and costumes, John Gunter; lighting and projections, Peter Mumford; sound, Gregory Clarke; music, Mick Sands; production stage management, John McNamara. Presented in association with Theatre Royal Bath/Peter Hall Company, in the Ahmanson Theatre.

Orlando .... Dan Stevens	Forest Lord 1 .... Kevin Collins
Adam .... David Barnaby	Forest Lord 2 .... Nyasha Fredrick Hatendi
Oliver; Amiens .... Freddie Stevenson	Corin .... David Barnaby
Dennis .... Ronald Fernee	Silvius .... David Birkin
Charles .... James Crossley	Audrey .... Janet Greaves
Celia.. Rebecca Callard	Sir Oliver Mar-Text .... Robin Browne
Rosalind .... Rebecca Hall	Phoebe .... Charlotte Parry
Touchstone .... Michael Siberry	William .... James Crossley
Le Beau .... Robin Browne	Second Gentleman .... Gráinne Gillis
Frederick; Duke .... James Laurenson	Jaques .... Kevin Collins
Jaques (Frederick) .... Philip Voss	

Court Lords: David Birkin, Robin Browne, Kevin Collins, James Crossley, Ronald Fernee, Gráinne Gillis, Janet Greaves, Nyasha Fredrick Hatendi, Madeleine Hutchins, Mitchell Mullen, Charlotte Parry.

Forest Lords: David Birkin, Robin Browne, Kevin Collins, James Crossley, Ronald Fernee, Gráinne Gillis, Janet Greaves, Nyasha Fredrick Hatendi, Madeleine Hutchins, Mitchell Mullen, Charlotte Parry.

THE VERY PERSISTENT GAPPERS OF FRIP. Musical with book and lyrics by Doug Cooney; music by David O; based on the book by George Saunders. March 5, 2005 (world premiere). Direction, Corey Madden; choreography, Mary Ann Kellogg; scenery, Keith Mitchell; costumes, Audrey Fisher; lighting, Shaun Fillion; sound, John Zalewski, music direction, Mr. O; puppets, Alice Dinnean Vernon; production stage management, Winnie Y. Lok; in the Kirk Douglas Theatre.

Bea Romo .... Sonja Alarr
Sid Ronsen .... Tom Beyer
Gilbert Romo .... Lena Gwendolyn Hill
    Presented without intermission.

Dad .... Hubert Hodgin
Capable ....Jamey Hood
Robert Romo .... Olivia Killingsworth

PLAY WITHOUT WORDS. By Matthew Bourne; inspired by Joseph Losey's film, based on *The Servant* by Robin Maugham. April 11, 2005. Direction and choreography, Mr. Bourne; scenery and costumes by Lez Brotherston; lighting, Paule Constable; sound, Christopher Shutt; music, Terry Davies. Presented in association with the Brooklyn Academy of Music, in the Ahmanson Theatre.

Anthony .... Sam Archer,
                                    Ewan Wardrop,
                                    Richard Winsor
Glenda................................... Michela Meazza,
                                    Anjali Mehra,
                                    Emily Piercy
Prentice .... Scott Ambler,
                                    Steve Kirkham,
                                    Eddie Nixon

Sheila .... Maxine Fone,
                                    Valentina Formenti
Speight .... Eddie Nixon,
                                    Alan Vincent,
                                    Ewan Wardrop
Alternates .... Madelaine Brennan,
                                    Darren Ellis,
                                    Neil Penlington

Time:1965. Place: In and around Anthony's new house in Chelsea, London. Presented in two parts.

ELECTRICIDAD. By Luis Alfaro; based on Sophocles's *Electra*. April 14, 2005. Direction, Lisa Peterson; scenery, Rachel Hauck; costumes, Christopher Acebo; lighting, Geoff Korf; sound and music, Paul James Pendergast; fight direction, Steve Rankin; dramaturgy, John Glore, production stage management, James T. McDermott; in the Mark Taper Forum.

La Carmen................................... Denise Blasor
La Connie............................ Catalina Maynard
La Cuca .... Wilma Bonet
Electricidad .... Zilah Mendoza

Abuela .... Alma Martinez
Ifigenia .... Elisa Bocanegra
Clemincia .... Bertila Damas
Orestes ....Justin Huen

A DISTANT SHORE. By Chay Yew. May 1, 2005 (world premiere). Direction, Robert Egan; scenery and costumes, Myung Hee Cho; lighting, Rand Ryan; sound and music, Karl Fredrik Lundeberg; production stage management, Katie Ailinger; in the Kirk Douglas Theatre.

Alan .... Daniel Blinkoff
Afrah; Mina .... Esther K. Chae
Patricia .... Maria Cina
Wardin .... Emily Kuroda

Sulaiman .... Nelson Mashita
Zul .... Eric D. Steinberg
Salman .... Tamlyn Tomita

Time: 1920s; 2004. Place: A Southeast Asian colonial city. Presented in two parts.

East West Players, Los Angeles

Tim Dang producing artistic director, Bill Rauch artistic director

MIXED MESSAGES. By Cherylene Lee. September 15, 2004 (world premiere). Direction, Jon Lawrence Rivera; scenery, John Binkley; costumes, Marya Krakowiak; lighting, Gerry Gregory Linsangan; sound, John Zalewski; stage management, Robert Fromer.

Dad .... Walter Beery
Councilman .... Miguel Najera
Mom .... Natsuko Ohama
    Presented in two parts.

Wai .... Mia Riverton
Lawyer .... Lisa Tharps
Jake .... Luis Villalta

AS VISHNU DREAMS. By Shishir Kurup. November 10, 2004 (world premiere). Direction, Juliette Carrillo; choreography, Naila Azad; scenery, Christopher Acebo; costumes, Ivy Chou; lighting, Geoff Korf and Jessica Trundy; songs, Mr. Kurup, sound and music, Chris Webb; additional music, Paul Livingstone; puppets, Lynn Jeffries; dramaturgy, Scott Horstein, stage management, Anna Gelle Gilbert. Presented in association with Cornerstone Theater Company.

Vahu	Naila Azad	Valmiki	Natch Narasimhan
Rama	Sunkrish Bala	Reporter	Uma Nithipalan
Musician	Pial Hossain	Hanuman	Francis Reyes
Indra	Peter Howard	Tara	Ritu Marwah Portugal
Musician	Peter Jacobson	Vali	Berkeley Sanjay
Dancer	Sri Kesava	Sita	Meena Serendib
Ravana	Sean T. Krishnan	Reporter	Seema Shastri
Shurpanaka	Meena Kumari	Head Puppeteer	Piyush Ved
Mondodari	Page Leong	Sugriva	Ogie Zulueta
Lakshman	René Millán		

Presented in two parts.

PROOF. By David Auburn. February 2, 2005. Direction, Heidi Helen Davis; scenery, Victoria Petrovich; costumes, Dori Quan; lighting, Jose Lopez; sound, Bob Bresnik; stage management, Robert Fromer.

Catherine	Kimiko Gelman	Robert	Dom Magwili
Hal	David J. Lee	Claire	Joanne Takahashi

Presented in two parts.

IMELDA. Musical with book by Sachi Oyama; music by Nathan Wang; lyrics by Aaron Coleman. May 11, 2005 (world premiere). Direction, Tim Dang; choreography, Reggie Lee; scenery and projections, Victoria Petrovich; costumes, Ivy Chou; lighting, Jerry M. Sonnenberg; sound and music direction, Mr. Wang; stage management, Robert Fromer.

Dovey Beams	Rinabeth Apostol	Peasant mother	Golda Inquito
Mother	Louise Marie Cornillez	Assassin	Marc Macalintal
Mayor	Evan D'Angeles	Muse	Blythe Matsui
Imelda Marcos	Liza Del Mundo	Corazon Aquino	Myra Cris Ocenar
Peasant Daughter	M.J. Deocariza	Ferdinand Marcos	Giovanni Ortega
Benigno Aquino	Antoine Reynaldo Diel	Peasant Father	Michael C. Palma
Muse	Ramona DuBarry	Muse	Annie Katsura Rollins
Announcer	Bryan Geli		

Musical numbers included: "The Origins of the Philippines," "Forever Part of You," "3,000 Pairs of Shoes," "1952 Transition," "Dreaming of a Dance," "See What I See," "Maharlika," "1954 Transition," "The Education of Imelda," "East West," "A Beautiful Place," "1971 Transition," "Like God," "Martial Law . . . with a Smile," "Anak Ko (Lullaby)," "If I Had Raised the Butterfly," "Imeldific," "Flight Back to the Philippines," "Myself, My Heart," "People Power," "1986 Transition," "Montage Finale."

Presented in two parts.

Geffen Playhouse, Los Angeles
Randall Arney artistic director

PAINT YOUR WAGON. Musical with book and lyrics by Alan Jay Lerner; music, Frederick Loewe; book revised by David Rambo. December 1, 2004. Direction, Gilbert Cates; choreography, Kay Cole; scenery and lighting, Daniel Ionazzi; costumes, David Kay Mickelsen; sound, Philip G. Allen; music direction, Steve Orich; production stage management, Grayson Meritt.

Ben Rumson .... Tom Wilson	Ah-Wah .... Ian Shen
Jennifer Rumson .... Jessica Rush	Miwok .... Daniel Lujan
Ulysses Wilson .... David Jennings	Julio Valveras .... Alex Mendoza
Wilmer Wagner .... Morgan Rusler	Kwai Fa .... Janelle Dote
"Bull" Bullnack .... Rob Kahn	Lupita .... Tracy Powell
Salem Strauss .... Steven Hack	Lily Smith .... Sharon Lawrence
Jake Whippany .... Robert Alan Clink	Father Ignacio .... Joe J. Garcia
Cherry Jourdel .... Erika Amato	John Woodling .... Andy Umberger
Preacher .... Harry S. Murphy	

Musical numbers included: "Wand'rin' Star," "I'm on My Way," "Rumson Town," "What's Goin' on Here?," "I Talk to the Trees," "How Can I Wait?," "I Still See Elisa," "There's a Coach Comin' In," "In Between," "Carino Mio," "Whoop-Ti-Ay!," "I'm on My Way"/"Wandrin' Star," "Another Autumn," "My Little Girl," "Mormon Trio," "The Strike," "My Last Love," "They Call the Wind Maria."

Presented in two parts.

La Jolla Playhouse

Des McAnuff artistic director, interim managing director Debby Buchholz

SUITCASE, OR THOSE THAT RESEMBLE FLIES FROM A DISTANCE. By Melissa James Gibson, July 11, 2004. Direction, Daniel Aukin; scenery, Louisa Thompson; costumes, Maiko Matsushima; lighting, Matt Frey; sound, Shane Rettig; music, Michael Friedman; stage management, Dana Victoria Anderson. Presented in association with Soho Repertory Theatre and True Love Productions.

Sallie .... Christina Kirk	Karl .... Jonathan M. Woodward
Lyle .... Thomas Jay Ryan	Jen .... Colleen Werthmann

Presented without intermission.

Page to Stage Workshop. July 27–August 15, 2004.

PARIS COMMUNE. By Steven Cosson and Michael Friedman. July 27, 2004. Direction, Mr. Cosson; choreography, Jean Isaacs; scenery, Kevin Judge; costumes, Emily Pepper; lighting, Jennifer Setlow; sound, Walter Trarbach.

Mignon .... Aysan Celik	Milliner; others .... Katie Sigismund
Bakery Owner; others .... Brad Fleischer	Baker; others .... Brian Slaten
Opera Singer .... Stacey Fraser	Priest; others .... Andrew William Smith
Père Duchene .... Bruce McKenzie	Baker's Mother; others .... Dale Soules
Militiaman; others .... Geno Monteiro	Schoolteacher; others .... Lisa Velten

Time: May 21, 1871. Place: A hall in the Tulieries Palace in Paris. Presented in two parts.

THE LOVE OF THREE ORANGES. By Nona Ciobanu; translated from Romanian by Mihnea Mircan; American adaptation by James Magruder; from a scenario by Carlo Gozzi. September 19, 2004. Direction, Ms. Ciobanu; scenery and costumes, Iulian Baltatescu and Ms. Ciobanu; lighting and music, Mr. Baltatescu; dramaturgy, Shirley Fishman. Presented in association with Toaca Cultural Foundation.

Truffaldino .... John Altieri	Clarice; others .... Carmen Gill
Ninetta; others .... Pascale Armand	Leandro; others .... Owiso Odera
Girl 1; others .... Colette Beauvais	Tartaglia .... Jim Parsons
Smeraldina; others .... Tina Benko	Silvio; others .... Time Winters
Pantalone; others .... Donald Corren	

Presented without intermission.

JERSEY BOYS. Musical with book by Marshall Brickman and Rick Elice; music by Bob Gaudio; lyrics by Bob Crewe; based on the story of Frankie Valli and the Four Seasons. October 17, 2004 (world premiere). Direction, Des McAnuff; choreography, Sergio

Trujillo; scenery, Klara Zieglerova; costumes, Jess Goldstein; lighting, Howell Binkley; sound, Steve Canyon Kennedy; music direction, Ron Melrose; orchestrator, Steve Orich; fight direction, Steve Rankin; dramaturgy, Allison Horsley; production stage management, Richard Hester.

Girl Singer; others	Sara Avery	Frankie Valli	David Noroña
Garl Singer; others	Marisa Echeverria	Yanni; others	Leslie Odom Jr.
Cop; others	Steve Gouveia	Hank	Joe Payne
Bob Crewe; others	Peter Gregus	Bob Gaudio	Daniel Reichard
Tommy DeVito	Christian Hoff	Judge; others	Sean Smith
Gyp De Carlo; others	Donnie Kehr	Nick Massi	J. Robert Spencer
Girl Singer; others	Jennifer Naimo	Swing	Joy Yandell
Swing	Dominic Nolfi		

Musical numbers included: "Ces Soirées-La" ("Oh What a Night"), "Silhouettes," "You're the Apple of My Eye," "I Can't Give You Anything But Love," "Earth Angel," "A Sunday Kind of Love," "My Mother's Eyes," "I Go Ape," "Short Shorts," " I'm In the Mood for Love/Moody's Mood for Love," "Cry for Me," "An Angel Cried," "I Still Care," "Trance," "Sherry," "Big Girls Don't Cry," "Walk Like a Man," "December, 1963" ("Oh What a Night"), "My Boyfriend's Back," "My Eyes Adored You," "Dawn, Go Away," "Big Man in Town," "Beggin'," "Stay," "Let's Hang On," "Opus 17" ("Don't You Worry 'Bout Me"), "Bye Bye Baby," "C'mon Marianne," "Can't Take My Eyes Off of You," "Working My Way Back to You," "Fallen Angel," "Rag Doll," "Who Loves You?"

Presented in two parts.

PRIVATE FITTINGS. By Georges Feydeau; translated and adapted by Des McAnuff. February 27, 2005 (world premiere). Direction, Mr. McAnuff; scenery, Neil Patel; costumes, Paul Tazewell; lighting, Howell Binkley; sound, Walter Trarbach; music, Michael Friedman; dramaturgy, Allison Horsley; stage management, Nevin Hedley.

Suzanne	Jessica Boevers	Yvonne	Stana Katic
Rosa	Lucia Brawley	Conan	Chris Kipiniak
Eric	Kyle Fabel	Harriet	Joan van Ark
Drew	Chris Hoch	Steve	Eric Wippo

Time: Early morning; one hour later; the following day. Place: Eric and Yvonne's house; Drew's rental property. Presented in two parts.

Lamb's Players Theatre, Coronado
Robert Smyth producing artistic director

METAMORPHOSES. By Mary Zimmerman; adapted from Ovid. April 8, 2005. Direction, Robert Smyth; scenery, Mr. Smyth and Nathan Peirson; costumes, Jeanne Reith; lighting, Mr. Peirson; music by Deborah Gilmour Smyth; stage management, Maria Mangiavellano.

Performed by Nick Cordileone, David Cochran Heath, Colleen Kollar, Paul Maley, Nate Parde, Chrissy Reynolds Vögele, Ms. Smyth, Tom Stephenson, Greg Thompson, Ayla Yarkut.

Magic Theatre, San Francisco
Chris Smith artistic director, David Gluck managing director

THE OPPOSITE OF SEX. Musical with book by Robert Jess Roth and Douglas J. Cohen; music and lyrics by Mr. Cohen; based on the screenplay by Don Roos. October 2, 2004 (world premiere). Direction, Mr. Roth; scenery, Derek McLane; costumes, Patricia Field; lighting, Norm Schwab; sound, Jonathan Deans and Daryl Frame; music direction, Brad Haak; fight direction, Rick Sordelet; production stage management, Dick Daley.

Dedee Truitt	Kerry Butler	Randy, others	Ian Scott McGregor
Bobette, others	Donna Vivino	Jason Bock	Joe Mandragona

Bill Truitt .... John Bolton   Lucia Dalury .... Karen Ziemba
Matt Matteo .... David Burtka   Carl Tippett ....Jeff McCarthy

Musical numbers included: "I've Got News for You, "Rub a Little Lotion," "It Just Happened," "A Normal Life," "Blessing in Disguise," "I Think You Know What I Want," "LA," "Destiny," "You Are Going Back to Indiana," "I'd Sooner Die," "Dead Ex-Lover," "Rightful Name," "Lucia," "Not Tom," "Labor of Love," "Look for Me First," "The Opposite of Sex."

Presented in two parts.

THE RIGHT KIND OF PEOPLE. By Charles Grodin. November 20, 2004 (world premiere). Direction, Chris Smith, scenery, Annie Smart; costumes, Fumiko Bielefeldt; lighting, Russell H. Champa; sound, Norman Kern; stage management, Rosie Goldman.

Frank Rashman .... Ken Ruta   Bill Hayes................................... Clive Worsley
Tom Rashman.......................... Robert Parsons   Betty Butler ....Frances Lee McCain
Jack Carmichael .... Jarion Monroe   Claire Wilson .... Carrie Paff
Doug Bernstein .... Eric Siegel   Craig Hutto .... Tom Blair
Coles Lange .... Will Marchetti   Bruce Delson............................... Fred Burrell

Presented without intermission.

THE SWEETEST SWING IN BASEBALL. By Rebecca Gilman. January 29, 2005. Direction, Amy Glazer; scenery, J.B. Wilson; costumes, Maggie Whitaker; lighting, Kurt Landisman; sound, Don Seaver; stage management, Sabrina Kniffin.

Dana .... Barbara Pitts   Rhonda; Dr. Gilbert .... Velina Brown
Roy; Gary ....Michael Ray Wisely   Brian; Michael ....Joseph Parks
Erica; Dr. Stanton .... Anne Darragh

Presented in two parts.

A RECKONING. By Wesley Moore. March 5, 2005. Direction, Richard Seyd; scenery, John Iacovelli; costumes, Maggie Moran; lighting, York Kennedy; sound, Bill Williams; stage management, Donna Rose Fletcher.

Irene ....Jennifer Tighe   Spencer .... Kevin Tighe

Presented without intermission.

THE RULES OF CHARITY. By John Belluso. April 30, 2005. Direction, Chris Smith, scenery, Kris Stone; costumes, Callie Floor; lighting, Chris Studley; sound, Chuck McGee II; production stage management, Leslie Grisdale.

Loretta .... Arwen Anderson   Paz .... Sally Clawson
Monty .... Warren David Keith   Horace .... Gabriel Marin
LH .... Andrew Hurteau

Presented in two parts.

THE BLACK EYED. By Betty Shamieh. May 14, 2005. Direction, Jessica Heidt, scenery, Kris Stone, costumes, Callie Floor; lighting, Chris Studley; sound, D. Schultz; stage management, Leslie Grisdale.

Aiesha ....Nora El Samahy   Taman .... Bridgette Loriaux
Delilah .... Sofia Ahmad   Architect .... Atosa Babaoff

3F, 4F. By Victor Lodato. May 28, 2005. Direction, Pam MacKinnon; scenery, Andrea Bechert; costumes, Tod Roehrman; lighting, Jim Cave; sound, Bill Williams; production stage management, Nicole Dickerson.

Myrna .... Wanda McCaddon   Kurt ....Ian Scott McGregor
Alfred...................................... Edward Sarafian   Khula .... Cassie Beck
Murph ....Daniel Talbott

Marin Theatre Company, Mill Valley
Lee Sankowich artistic director

FORTUNE. By Deborah Zoe Laufer. January 19, 2005 (world premiere). Direction, Lee Sankowich; scenery, Steven Coleman; costumes, Cassandra Carpenter; lighting, Jaymi Lee Smith; sound, Norman Kern; production stage management, Janet Cates.

Jeremy	Darren Bridgett	Maude	Julia Brothers

The Old Globe, San Diego
Jack O'Brien artistic director, Louis Spisto executive director

FICTION. By Steven Dietz. September 30, 2004. Direction, Richard Seer; scenery, Robin Sanford Roberts; costumes, Charlotte Devaux; lighting, Trevor Norton; sound, Paul Peterson; stage management, Diana Moser.

Linda Waterman	Nancy Williamson	Abby Drake	Rachel Fowler
Michael Waterman	Kurt Rhoads		

Time: The present and before. Place: Various American cities and Paris. Presented in two parts.

DIRTY ROTTEN SCOUNDRELS. Musical with book by Jeffrey Lane; music and lyrics, David Yazbek; based on the film by Dale Launer, Stanley Shapiro and Paul Henning. September 22, 2004 (world premiere). Direction, Jack O'Brien; choreography, Jerry Mitchell; scenery, David Rockwell; costumes, Gregg Barnes; lighting, Kenneth Posner; sound, Acme Sound Partners; music direction, Ted Sperling, stage management, Michael Brunner. Presented in association with Dirty Rotten Producers, LLC in association with MGM On Stage.

Andre Thibault	Gregory Jbara	Freddy Benson	Norbert Leo Butz
Lawrence Jameson	John Lithgow	Jolene Oakes	Sara Gettelfinger
Muriel Eubanks	Joanna Gleason	Christine Colgate	Sherie René Scott

Ensemble: Timothy J. Alex, Andrew Asnes, Roxane Barlow, Rachel deBenedet, Joe Cassidy, Julie Connors, Laura Marie Duncan, Sally Mae Dunn, Rick Faugno, Tom Galantich, Jason Gillman, Amy Heggins, Grasan Kingsberry, Rachelle Rak, Tony Yazbeck.

Musical numbers included: "Give Them What They Want," "What Was a Woman to Do," "Great Big Stuff," "Chimp in a Suit," "Oklahoma?," "All About Ruprecht," "Here I Am," "Nothing Is Too Wonderful to Be True," "The Miracle," "Ruffhousin' mit Shüffhausen," "Like Zis, Like Zat," "The More We Dance," "Love Is My Legs," "Love Sneaks In," "Above the Waist," "The Soap," "Dirty Rotten."

Presented in two parts.

I JUST DROPPED BY TO SEE THE MAN. By Stephen Jeffreys. February 10, 2005. Direction, Seret Scott; scenery, Robert Morgan; costumes, Charlotte Devaux; lighting, Peter Maradudin; sound, Paul Peterson; stage management, Tracy Skoczelas.

Jesse	Henry Afro-Bradley	Della	Tracey A. Leigh
Karl	Manoel Feliciano		

HIMSELF AND NORA. Musical with book and lyrics by Sheila Walsh; music and lyrics, Jonathan Brielle. March 16, 2005 (world premiere). Directors, Jeff Calhoun and Joseph Hardy; choreography, Mr. Calhoun; scenery and costumes, Tobin Ost; lighting, Michael Gilliam; sound, Jon Weston; music direction, Jana Zielonka; stage management, Leila Knox.

James Joyce	Matt Bogart	Woman	Kathy Santen
Man #2	David Edwards	Nora Barnacle	Kate Shindle
Man #1	Frank Mastrone		

Musical numbers included: "Himself," "Kiss," "Compatriots," "River Liffey," "Stand Fast," "Let's Have a Drink," "What Better Thing," "All Expenses Paid," "I Say Yes!" "The Grand Himself," "The Children of Mister Joyce," "Lucky," "Always . . . in Love," ""How They Swoon," "Touch Kiss."

Time: 1882–1941. Place: Dublin; Trieste; Paris; Zurich. Presented in two parts.

South Coast Repertory, Costa Mesa
David Emmes producing artistic director, Martin Benson artistic director

BROOKLYN BOY. By Donald Margulies. September 11, 2004 (world premiere). Direction, Daniel Sullivan; scenery, Ralph Funicello; costumes, Jess Goldstein; lighting, Chris Parry; sound, Michael Roth; dramaturgy, Jerry Patch; stage management, Scott Harrison. Presented in association with Manhattan Theatre Club.

Eric Weiss	Adam Arkin	Alison	Ari Graynor
Manny Weiss	Allan Miller	Melanie Fine	Mimi Lieber
Ira Zimmer	Arye Gross	Tyler Shaw	Kevin Isola
Nina	Dana Reeve		

Time: The present. Place: Brooklyn; Manhattan; Los Angeles. Presented in two parts.

ON THE MOUNTAIN. By Christopher Shinn. January 8, 2005 (world premiere). Direction, Mark Rucker; scenery, Donna Marquet; costumes, Melanie Watnick; lighting, Rand Ryan; sound, Aram Arslanian; dramaturgy, Jerry Patch, stage management, Randall K. Lum.

Jaime	Daisy Eagan	Carrick	Nathan Baesel
Sarah	Susannah Schulman	Phil	Matt Roth

Time: Summer 2003. Place: A small but well-kept home in Portland, Oregon. Presented without intermission.

THE CLEAN HOUSE. By Sarah Ruhl. January 29, 2005. Direction, Kate Whoriskey; choreography, Randy Duncan; scenery, Rachel Hauck; costumes, Joyce Kim Lee; lighting, Scott Zielinski; sound, Rob Milburn and Michael Bodeen; dramaturgy, Jennifer Kiger; stage management, Jamie A. Tucker.

Matilde	Adriana Sevan	A Man; Charles	Timothy Landfield
Lane	Mary Beth Fisher	A Woman; Ana	Ivonne Coll
Virginia	Mary Lou Rosato		

Time: The present. Place: A metaphysical Connecticut. Presented in two parts.

PRINCESS MARJORIE. By Noah Haidle. March 12, 2005 (world premiere). Direction, David Chambers; scenery, Darcy Scanlin; costumes, Angela Balogh Calin; lighting, Peter Maradudin; dramaturgy, Jerry Patch; stage management, Randall K. Lum.

Harper	Michael Gladis	Steven; others	John Vickery
Charlie	Nathan Baesel	Marjorie	Khrystyne Haje

Presented in two parts.

A NAKED GIRL ON THE APPIAN WAY. By Richard Greenberg. April 8, 2005 (world premiere). Direction, Mark Rucker; scenery, Tony Fanning; costumes, Joyce Kim Lee; lighting, Peter Maradudin; sound, Steven Cahill; dramaturgy, Jerry Patch; stage management, Scott Harrison.

Bess	Linda Gehringer	Jeffrey	John de Lancie

Sadie .... Ann Guilbert
Elaine .... Mary Joy
Juliet .... Dawn-Lyen Gardner
Thad .... Terrence Riordan
Billy .... James Yaegashi

Time: The present. Place: A beautiful house in the Hamptons. Presented in two parts.

VESUVIUS. By Lucinda Coxon. April 30, 2005 (world premiere). Direction, David Emmes; scenery, Christopher Barreca; costumes, Nephelie Andonyadis; lighting, Tom Ruzika, sound, Lindsay Jones; dramaturgy, Jennifer Kiger, stage management, Randall K. Lum.

The Woman .... Natacha Roi
The Man .... Tony Ward
Miguel .... Bobby Plasencia
Dr. Paul .... David Paul Francis
The Girl .... Jennifer Hinds

Time: The present; the past. Place: London; Naples.

8th Pacific Playwrights Festival. May 6–8, 2005.
TOUGH TITTY. By Oni Faida Lampley. Direction, Mark Rucker; dramaturgy, Jerry Patch.
     Performed by John Cothran Jr., Nike Doukas, Saidah Arrika Ekulona, Juanita Jennings, Tracey A. Leigh; Allan Miller, Elaine Tse.
BOSSA NOVA. By Kirsten Greenidge. Direction, Casey Stangl; dramaturgy, Lenora Inez Brown.
     Performed by Alexandra Gaines, Dawn-Lyen Gardner, Angela Goethals, Christina Haag, Ella Joyce, Ben Livingston, Jennifer Leigh Warren.
THE FURTHER ADVENTURES OF HEDDA GABLER. By Jeff Whitty. Direction, Bill Rauch; dramaturgy, Jennifer Kiger.
     Performed by Jonathan Del Arco, Patrick Kerr, Hamish Linklater, Joan MacIntosh, Alec Mapa, Susannah Schulman, Kimberly Scott, Bahni Turpin.
RABBIT HOLE. By David Lindsay-Abaire. Direction, Carolyn Cantor; dramaturgy, John Glore.
     Performed by Ann Gunn, Kevin Kilner, Lynn Milgrim, Sara Rafferty, Phillip C. Vaden.
RIDICULOUS FRAUD. By Beth Henley. Direction, Sharon Ott; dramaturgy, Janice Paran.
     Performed by Nathan Baesel, Emily Bergl, Colette Kilroy, Matt Letscher, Cerris Morgan-Moyer; Randy Oglesby, Jeremy Shamos, Jimmie Ray Weeks.

Theatre Rhinoceros, San Francisco
John Fisher artistic director, John Simpson managing director

BEAUTIFUL CHILD. By Nicky Silver. March 31, 2005. Direction, John Dixon; scenery, Erik Flatmo; costumes, Floriana Alessandria; lighting, Dave Robertson; sound, Michael Davison; stage management, Jennifer Garagliano.

Isaac .... Matt Weimer
Harry .... Donald Currie
Delia .... Libby O'Connell
Nan .... Adrienne Krug
Elizabeth Hilton .... Ann Lawler

Time: Now. Place: Harry and Nan's home. Presented in two parts.

TheatreWorks, Mountain View
Robert Kelley artistic director, John Simpson managing director

A LITTLE PRINCESS. Musical with book and lyrics by Brian Crawley; music by Andrew Lippa; based on Frances Hodgson Barnett's novel. August 28, 2004 (world premiere). Direction, Susan H. Schulman; choreography, Andy Blankenbuehler; scenery, Heidi

Ettinger; costumes, Catherine Zuber; lighting, Paul Gallo; sound, Brian Ronan; music direction, Joel Fram; dramaturgy, Vickie Rozell.

Umbrella Man	Jesse Nager	Miss Minchin	Kimberly King
Djembe Drummer	Dennis Stowe	Lavinia	Lyndsay Faye
Sara Crewe	Mackenzie Mauzy	Ermengarde	Courtney Stokes
Native Woman	Dawn K. Burroughs	Lottie	Lizzi Jones
African Man	Ralph William Boone	Becky	Remy Zaken
Aljana	C. Kelly Wright	Jessie	Hayley Steele
Pasko	Casey Ford Alexander	Nora	Sophie Tamiko Oda
Head-Man	Levensky Smith	Jane	Catherine Smith
Captain Crew	Will Chase	Queen Victoria	Lianne Marie Dobbs
Organ Grinder	Brian Herndon	Mr. Skipwith; others	Noel Anthony
Miss Amelia	Molly Bell		

African Dancers: Maia Evwaraye-Griffin, Asmeret Ghebremichael, Carmichael Blankenship, Jesse Nager, Levensky Smith, Dennis Stowe.

Time: 1838–39. Place: West Africa; London. Presented in two parts.

SHAKESPEARE IN HOLLYWOOD. By Ken Ludwig. January 22, 2005. Direction, Robert Kelley; scenery, Andrea Bechert; costumes, Fumiko Bielefeldt; lighting, Steven B. Mannshardt; sound, Cliff Caruthers.

Puck	Rebecca Dines	Lydia	Lucy Owen
Oberon	Don Carrier	Will Hayes	William Todd Tressler
Max Reinhardt	Gerry Hiken	Joe E. Brown	Robb Bauer
Louella Parsons	Suzanne Grodner	Olivia	Lisa Anne Morrison
James Cagney	Noel Wood	Jack Warner	Gary S. Martinez
Dick Powell	Craig W. Marker	Ensemble	Emily Duarte-Rosenthal,
Daryl	Joseph J. Parks		Elias Escobedo, Megan Smith

COLORADO

Curious Theatre Company, Denver
Chip Walton artistic director

PARIS ON THE PLATTE: THE REMARKABLE REIGN OF ROBERT SPEER. By Joan Holden. March 12, 2005 (world premiere). Direction, Chip Walton; scenery, Michael R. Duran; costumes, Ann Piano; lighting, Shannon McKinney; sound, Matthew Morgan; dramaturgy, Bonnie Metzgar, stage management; Lisa Boehm.

Mattie Silks; others	Dee Covington	Virginia; Val	Kendra Crain McGovern
Mayor Speer; Irish Cop	Tupper Cullum	Kate Speer; others	Megan Meek
Piano Man	David Dunbar	Delores; others	Jada Roberts
Ben Lindsey; others	Christopher Leo	Election clerk; others	Erik Sandvold

Presented in two parts.

Denver Center Theatre Company
Donovan Marley artistic director, Kent Thompson artistic director,
Barbara E. Sellars producing director

A SELFISH SACRIFICE. By Charles F. (OyamO) Gordon. An adaptation of *A Doll House* by Henrik Ibsen. January 27, 2005 (world premiere). Direction, Israel Hicks; scenery,

Michael Brown; costumes, David Kay Mickelsen; lighting, Charles R. MacLeod; sound, Matthew C. Swartz; stage management, Lyle Raper.

Ammajean	Gwen Harris	Samuel Armstrong	Harvy Blanks
Akumma Bobagunwa	Kim Staunton	Obadele Rhineheart	Charles Weldon
Delivery Boy	Vincent Nappo	Nana Nwadialu	Marlene Warfield
Amb. Bobagunwa	Terrence Riggins	Mamadou	Tyrone Mack Jr.
Balogun	Michael Cherrie	Ayo	Gabrielle Martin
Ijeudo Chidike	Veralyn Jones	Lya	Lya Bridges-Farrow

Time: The present. Place: The home of the Nigerian Ambassador to the United Nations, NYC. Presented in two parts.

A LOVELY SUNDAY FOR CREVE COEUR. By Tennessee Williams. January 20, 2005. Direction, Laird Williamson; scenery, Andrew V. Yelusich and Lisa M. Orzolek; costumes, David Kay Mickelsen; lighting, Kevin Cloughley; sound, David Dodson.

Dorothea	Caitlin O'Connell	Helena	Carol Halstead
Bodey	Kathleen M. Brady	Miss Gluck	Robynn Rodriguez

Time: June, the mid-1930's. Place: An efficiency apartment in St. Louis. Presented in two parts.

Germinal Stage, Denver
Ed Baierlein director, Sallie Diamond associate producer

HEARTS TO GOD. By Jim Lillie. November 12, 2004 (world premiere). Direction and scenery, Ed Baierlein; costumes, Sallie Diamond; lighting and sound, Mr. Baierlein; production stage management, Linda A. Barner.

Mildred	Jenny MacDonald	Elder Henry	Stephen R. Kramer
Sister Harriet	Margaret Amateis Casart	Isaac	Tad Baierlein
Marie	Kristina Denise Pitt	Offstage Voice	Ed Baierlein

Presented two parts.

CONNECTICUT

Eugene O'Neill Theater Center, Waterford
Richard Kuranda producing director, Amy Sullivan executive director

Playwrights Conference. July 16–31, 2004.
DARK YELLOW. By Julia Jordan.
AFTERDARK. By Kara Manning.
TRANSFERENCE. By Wayne Peter Liebman.
ERIN GO BRAGH-LESS. By John Shea.
SLAY THE DRAGON. By Victor Lodato.
THE ELECTRIC CENTURY. By Andrew Case.
AS REAPER IN SUMMER GRAIN. By Keith Byron Kirk.
BLIND MOUTH SINGING. By Jorge Ignacio Cortiñas.
THE FRUGAL REPAST. By Ron Hirsen.
LIVING ROOM IN AFRICA. By Bathsheba Doran.

Directors: Melvin Bernhardt, Daniel Goldstein, Joe Grifasi, Josh Hecht, Melissa Kievman, Gene Lasko, Bill Partlan, Oz Scott.

Featured artists: Katie Barrett, Rob Campbell, Elizabeth Canavan, Kevin Carroll, Michael Chernus, Caroline Stefanie Clay, Michael Countryman, Patch Darragh, Ramon de Ocampo, Matthew Del Negro, MacIntyre Dixon, Angelina Fiordellisi, Rita Gardner, Kevin Geer, Meg Gibson, Yetta Gottesman, Chris Grant, Pamela J. Gray, Ronan Greenwood, Brad Heberlee, Addie Johnson, Bill Kennedy, James Knight, Polly Lee, Victor Lodato, Katie Lowes, Florencia Lozano, Derek Lucci, Charlotte Madere, Anthony Manna, Will Manning, Tim McGeever, Nancy McNulty, Deirdre O'Connell, Charles Parnell, Melinda Peinado, Keith Reddin, Christopher Michael Rivera, Niki Sarich-Rising, Samantha Soule, Vassi Spanos, Daniel Talbott, Ann Talman, Joseph Urla, Tamilla Woodard, Jeff Woodman.

Goodspeed Musicals, East Haddam
Michael P. Price executive director, Sue Frost associate producer

WHERE'S CHARLEY? Musical with book by George Abbott; music and lyrics by Frank Loesser; based on Brandon Thomas's *Charley's Aunt*. August 11, 2004. Direction, Tony Walton; choreography, Lisa Shriver; scenery, Mr. Walton and Kelly Hanson; costumes, Mr. Walton and Martha Bromelmeier; lighting, Richard Pilbrow; music direction, Michael O'Flaherty; production stage management, Donna Cooper Hilton.

Charley Wykeham	Noah Racey	Francis Chesney	Paul Carlin
Jack Chesney	Greg Mills	Donna Lucia	Mary Illes
Kitty Verdun	Kristin Huxhold	Brassett	Drew Eshelman
Amy Spettigue	Nili Bassman	Wilkinson	Jeff Williams
Mr. Spettigue	Ron Lee Savin		

Ensemble: Evan Bryant, Callie Carter, Christian Delcroix, Jennifer Evans, Elizabeth Inghram, Josh Grisetti, Michael D. Jablonski, Dayla Perkins, Amber Stone, Jeff Williams.

Musical numbers included: "The Years Before Us," "A Tune for Humming," "Better Get Out of Here," "Don't Introduce Me to That Angel," "The New Ashmolean Marching Society and Students' Conservatory Band," "My Darling, My Darling," "Make a Miracle," "Serenade With Asides," "Lovelier Than Ever," "The Woman In His Room," "Where's Charley?," "I Wish I Didn't Love You So," "Once In Love with Amy," "Pernambuco," "Why Fight the Feeling," "Hyacinth," "He Can Waltz," "Red Rose Cotillion."

Presented in two parts.

MACK AND MABEL. Musical with book by Michael Stewart; music and lyrics by Jerry Herman; book revision by Francine Pascal. October 27, 2004. Direction, Arthur Allan Seidelman; choreography, Dan Siretta; scenery and costumes, Eduardo Sicangco; lighting, Kirk Bookman; music direction, Michael O'Flaherty; production stage management, Donna Cooper Hilton.

Mack Sennett	Scott Waara	Ella	Jessica Anderson
Mabel Normand	Christiane Noll	Bauman	Gus Corrado
Lottie Ames	Donna McKechnie	Kessel	Steve Pudenz
Fatty Arbuckle	Robert Machray	William D. Taylor	Gary Lindemann
Frank	Zachary Halley		

Ensemble: Bobby Clark, Tim Foster, Merritt Tyler Hawkins, Shannon Kline, Julia Krohn, Stephanie Janette Meade, Missy Morrison, Danea Lee Polise, Elizabeth Polito, Amanda Rose, Karen Sieber, Dana Winkle.

Musical numbers included: "Movies Were Movies," "Look What Happened to Mabel," "Big Time," "I Won't Send Roses," "I Wanna Make the World Laugh," "Mack and Mabel," "Wherever He Ain't," "Hundreds of Girls," "When Mabel Comes in the Room," "Hit 'em on the Head," "Every Time a Kop Falls Down," "Time Heals Everything," "Tap Your Troubles Away," "I Promise You a Happy Ending."

SEVEN BRIDES FOR SEVEN BROTHERS. Musical with book by Lawrence Kasha and David S. Landay; music by Johnny Mercer and Gene De Paul; additional songs by Al

Kasha and Joel Hirschhorn; based on the MGM film and "The Sobbin' Women" by Stephen Vincent Benét. May 8, 2005. Direction, Greg Ganakas; choreography, Patti Colombo; scenery, Russell Metheny; costumes, Gregory Gale; lighting, Michael Lincoln; music direction, Michael O'Flaherty; fight direction, David DeBesse; orchestrations, Michael Morris; production stage management, Donna Cooper Hilton.

Adam	Burke Moses	Zeke	Drew DiStefano
Milly	Jacquelyn Piro	Carl	Shane Rhoades
Caleb	Kevin Bernard	Matt	Trevor Illingworth
Ephraim	Karl Warden	Joel	Drew Franklin
Daniel	David Tankersley	Jeb	Ryan Jackson
Benjamin	Jim T. Ruttman	Luke	Matt Baker
Frank	Eric Sciotto	Preacher Bixby	David Barron
Gideon	Brian Hissong	Mrs. Hoallum	Emily Mikesell
Dorcas	Mahri Relin	Joe Sanders	Spiff Wiegand
Ruth	Liz Pearce	Mrs. Bixby	Anna McNeely
Sarah	Heather Janneck	Henry Perkins	Tom Flagg
Liza	Kristen Dawn Calgaro	Swings	Ryan Ghysels,
Martha	Sara Hart		Christina Hedrick
Alice	Sarah Jane Everman		

Musical numbers included: "Bless Your Beautiful Hide," "Wonderful, Wonderful Day," "I Married Seven Brothers," "Goin' Courtin'," "The Challenge Dance," "Love Never Goes Away," "Sobbin' Women," "Where Were You?," "We Gotta Make It Through the Winter," "Lonesome Polecat," "Spring, Spring, Spring," "Glad That You Were Born," "Wedding Celebration."

Time: 1850. Place: Oregon Territory. Presented in two parts.

Hartford Stage
Michael Wilson artistic director, Jim Ireland managing director

THE BAY AT NICE. By David Hare. October 14, 2004. Direction, Michael Wilson; scenery, Tony Straiges; costumes, Willa Kim; lighting, Rui Rita; sound, John Gromada.

Sophia	Angelica Torn	Peter Linitsky	Peter Mahoney
Assistant Curator	Corey Brill	Valentina Nrovka	Estelle Parsons

BRAND:NEW Festival of New Works. October 24–31, 2004.

STUFF HAPPENS. By David Hare. Direction, Michael Wilson.

ONLY WE WHO GUARD THE MYSTERY SHALL BE UNHAPPY. By Tony Kushner. Direction, Oskar Eustis.

THE LEARNED LADIES OF PARK AVENUE. By David Grimm; translated and adapted from Molière's *Les Femmes Savantes*. Direction, Michael Wilson.

THE DREAMS OF SARAH BREEDLOVE. By Regina Taylor. Direction, Ms. Taylor.

FLOYD AND CLEA UNDER THE WESTERN SKY. By David Cale and Jonathan Kreisberg. Direction, Michael Wilson.

ON THE MARCH TO THE SEA. By Gore Vidal. Direction, Warner Shook.

12 VOLT HEART. By Jeremy B. Cohen and Michael Elyanow. Direction, Mr. Cohen.

SPLITTING INFINITY. By Jamie Pachino. Direction, Will Pomerantz.

THE COOK. By Eduardo Machado February 24, 2005. Direction, Michael John Garcés; scenery, Adam Stockhausen; costumes, Elizabeth Hope Clancy; lighting. Ben Stanton; sound, David Margolin Lawson.

Gladys	Zabryna Guevara	Carlos	Felix Solis

Julio .... Che Ayenda
Elena .... Joselin Reyes

Adria; Lourdes .... Monica Perez-Brandes

OTHELLO. By William Shakespeare. April 13, 2005. Direction, Karin Coonrod; scenery, Efren Delgadillo Jr.; costumes, Ellen McCartney; lighting, Justin Townsend; sound, Annalise Albright.

Othello .... Firdous Bamji
Desdemona .... Danielle Skraastad
Iago .... David Patrick Kelly
Emilia .... Gordana Rashovich
Brabantio .... Nafe Katter
Roderigo .... Simeon Moore

Bianca .... Molly Ward
Cassio .... Christopher Michael Rivera
Duke .... Michael Rogers
Montano .... Scott Barrow
Ludovico .... Ezra Barnes

Long Wharf Theatre, New Haven

Gordon Edelstein artistic director, Michael Stotts managing director

SINGING FOREST. By Craig Lucas. January 5, 2005. Direction, Bartlett Sher; scenery, John McDermott; costumes, Elizabeth Caitlin Ward; lighting, Stephen Strawbridge; sound, Peter John Still; dramaturgy, Beatrice Basso and Oskar Eustis; production stage management, Linda Marvel. Presented in association with Intiman Theatre, Seattle. (See Intiman listing for additional details.)

Loë Rieman .... Robin Bartlett
Jules Ahmad; Simon .... Mark H. Dodd
Beth Adler; Young Loë .... Kristin Flanders
Bill; Freud .... Ben Hammer
Laszlos; Gerhardt .... Roderick Hill

Gray Korankyi; Walter .... Hamish Linklater
Bertha Ahmad; Marie .... Kristine Nielsen
Shar Unger; Max .... Henry Stram
Oliver; Martin .... John Vickery

Time: 2000; 1933–38; spring 1945. Place: New York City; Vienna; a forest outside of Paris. Presented in three parts.

RAG AND BONE. By Noah Haidle. February 6, 2005 (world premiere). Direction, Tina Landau; scenery, G.W. Mercier; costumes, Candice Donnelly; lighting, Scott Zielinski; sound, John Gromada; dramaturgy, Beatrice Basso; production stage management, Lori Lundquist.

Jeff .... Ian Brennan
George .... Justin Hagan
The Customer .... Carolyn Baeumler
The Poet .... David Sims Bishins

The Hooker .... Annie Golden
T-Bone .... Frederick Owens
The Millionaire .... Tom Riis Farrell

Presented in two parts.

THE ROMANCE OF MAGNO RUBIO. By Lonnie Carter; Tagalog text by Ralph B. Peña; based on the short story by Carlos Bulosan. March 18, 2005. Direction and scenery, Loy Arcenas; costumes, Myung Hee Cho; lighting, James Vermeulen; sound, Fabian Obispo; production stage manager, April Kline.

Nick .... Arthur Acuña
Prudencio .... Ron Domingo
Magno .... Jojo Gonzalez

Atoy .... Narciso Lobo
Claro .... Orville Mendoza

Time: 1930s and beyond. Place: A bunkhouse for migrant workers, California.

BFE. By Julia Cho. April 20, 2005 (world premiere). Direction, Gordon Edelstein; scenery, Takeshi Kata; costumes, Jayde Chabot; lighting, Paul Whitaker; sound, Andre Pluess; dramaturgy, Beatrice Basso; production stage management, Linda Marvel. Presented in association with Playwrights Horizons, New York City.

Panny	Olivia Oguma	Evvie	Karen Kandel
Isabel	Kate Rigg	Hugo	James McMenamin
Lefty	James Saito	Jack	Jeremy Hollingworth
Nancy	Kel Martin	Man	Scott Hudson
Hae-Yoon	Sue Jean Kim		

TRAVESTIES. By Tom Stoppard. May 11, 2005. Direction, Gregory Boyd; choreography, Marlo Hunter; scenery, Neil Patel; costumes, Judith Dolan; lighting, Rui Rita; sound, John Gromada; dramaturgy, Beatrice Basso; production stage management, Alan Fox.

Henry Carr	Sam Waterston	Nadya	Isabel Keating
Tristan Tzara	Tom Hewitt	Gwendolyn	Cheryl Lynn Bowers
James Joyce	Don Stephenson	Cecily	Maggie Lacey
Lenin	Gregor Paslawsky	Bennett	Graeme Malcolm

Backstage crew: Ryan Barry, Megan Gaffney, Christi Pidskalny, Shelara Pullen, Tom Simonetti, Matthew Wrather.

Presented in two parts.

Yale Repertory Theatre, New Haven
James Bundy artistic director, Victoria Nolan managing director

THE CLEAN HOUSE. By Sarah Ruhl. September 23, 2004 (world premiere). Direction, Bill Rauch; scenery, Christopher Acebo; costumes, Shigeru Yaji; lighting, Geoff Korf; sound, Andre Pluess; dramaturgy, Rachel Rusch; production stage management, James Mountcastle.

A Woman, Ana	Franca M. Barchiesi	Matilde	Zilah Mendoza
A Man; Charles	Tom Bloom	Lane	Elizabeth Norment
Virginia	Laurie Kennedy		

Time: The present. Place: A metaphysical Connecticut. Presented in two parts.

Shocking news: Zilah Mendoza and Laurie Kennedy in Sarah Ruhl's The Clean House *at Yale Repertory Theatre. Photo: Joan Marcus*

Jenny v. Jenny: Seema Sueko and Keiko Yamamoto in Rolin Jones's The Intelligent Design of Jenny Chow *at Yale Repertory Theatre. Photo: T. Charles Erickson*

THE INTELLIGENT DESIGN OF JENNY CHOW. By Rolin Jones. October 28, 2004. Direction, Jackson Gay; scenery, Lee Savage; costumes, Chloe Chapin; lighting, Miriam Nilofa Crowe; sound, Hillary Charnas; fight direction, Peter Katona; dramaturgy, Christine Mok; stage management, Marion Friedman.

Jennifer Marcus	Seema Sueko	Todd; Boy	Carson Elrod
Adele; Mrs. Zhang	Janet Zarish	Preston	Remy Auberjonois
Mr. Marcus; Zhang	Ken Marks	Jenny Chow	Keiko Yamamoto

Time: The present. Place: A second-floor bedroom in Calabasas, California. Presented in two parts.

RADIO GOLF. By August Wilson. April 28, 2005 (world premiere). Direction, Timothy Douglas; scenery, David Gallo; costumes, Susan Hilferty; lighting, Donald Holder; sound, Vincent Olivieri; dramaturgy, Todd Kreidler; stage management, Narda E. Alcorn.

Harmond Wilks .... Richard Brooks
Elder Joseph Barlow .... Anthony Chisholm
Sterling Johnson .... John Earl Jelks
Mame Wilks .... Michele Shay
Roosevelt Hicks .... James A. Williams

Time: 1997. Place : The Hill District, Pittsburgh. Presented in two parts.

DELAWARE

Delaware Theatre Company, Wilmington
Anne Marie Cammarto producing director

PARTNERS. By Allan Katz. September 22, 2004 (world premiere). Direction, Zane Busby; scenery, Nick Embree; costumes, Millie B. Hiibel; lighting and sound, Shannon Zura; stage management, Djuana M. Strauch. Presented in association with Ostar Enterprises.

Tony DeLuca	Rich Duva	Jack	Vyto Ruginis
Cynthia	Jennifer Flynn	Louie	Bill Saluga
Norm	Alan Rosenberg	Mrs. Epstein	Eve Sigall

Presented in two parts.

DISTRICT OF COLUMBIA

Arena Stage, Washington
Molly Smith artistic director, Stephen Richard executive director

INTIMATIONS FOR SAXOPHONE. By Sophie Treadwell, adapted by Michael Kinghorn. January 27, 2005 (world premiere). Direction, Anne Bogart; choreography, Barney O'Hanlon; scenery, Neil Patel; costumes, James Schuette; lighting, Christopher Akerlind;

Cycle complete: Richard Brooks and Anthony Chisholm in August Wilson's Radio Golf *at Yale Repertory Theatre. Photo: Carol Rosegg*

sound, Darron L. West; dramaturgy, Michael Kinghorn, stage management, Elizabeth Moreau. Presented in association with SITI Company.

French Maid	Akiko Aizawa	Stanislos	Marcus Kyd
Texas	Shawn Fagan	Maid	Susan Lynskey
Chicago	Gian-Murray Gianino	Kartner	Christopher McCann
Lily	Karron Graves	Gilly	Barney O'Hanlon
Mrs. Lethe	Susan Hightower	Millie	Makela Spielman

Presented in two parts.

Downstairs Readings

LEWIS AND CLARK REACH THE EUPHRATES. By Robert Schenkkan. October 29, 2004. Direction, Molly Smith.

CRITICAL DARLING. By Barry Levey. October 30, 2004. Direction, Wendy C. Goldberg.

THE AS IF BODY LOOP. By Ken Weitzman. April 15, 2005. Direction, Rebecca Taichman.

THE SWEETEST SWING IN BASEBALL. By Rebecca Gilman. April 16, 2005. Direction, Wendy C. Goldberg.

UNDISCOVERED GENIUS OF THE CONCRETE JUNGLE. April 18, 2005. By Psalmayene 24. Direction, Wendy C. Goldberg.

The Kennedy Center, Washington
Eric Schaeffer artistic director, Max Woodward producer

CAT ON A HOT TIN ROOF. By Tennessee Williams. June 17, 2004. Direction, Mark Lamos; scenery, John Lee Beatty; costumes, Jane Greenwood; lighting, Howell Binkley; sound, John Gromada; production stage management, Elaine M. Randolph.

Margaret	Mary Stuart Masterson	Trixie	Erin Elizabeth Wall
Brick	Jeremy Davidson	Dixie	Caitlin Redding
Mae	Emily Skinner	Big Daddy	George Grizzard
Big Mama	Dana Ivey	Gooper	T. Scott Cunningham
Sookey	Aakhu TuahNera Freeman	Reverend Tooker	Harry A. Winter
Sonny	Nathan Pratt	Doctor Baugh	Brian Reddy
Polly	Lexi Haddad	Lacey	Jeorge Watson
Buster	M. Justin Hancock		

Presented in three parts.

THE GLASS MENAGERIE. By Tennessee Williams. July 22, 2004. Direction, Gregory Mosher; scenery, John Lee Beatty; costumes, Jane Greenwood; lighting, Aaron Copp; sound, John Gromada; production stage management, Elaine M. Randolph.

Tom Wingfield	Jason Butler Harner	Laura Wingfield	Jennifer Dundas
Amanda Wingfield	Sally Field	Gentleman Caller	Corey Brill

Presented in two parts.

ON GOLDEN POND. By Ernest Thompson. October 2, 2004. Direction, Leonard Foglia; scenery, Ray Klausen; costumes, Jane Greenwood; lighting, Brian Nason; sound, Dan Moses Schreier. Presented in association with Jeffrey Finn and Soupbone Prods.

Norman Thayer Jr.	James Earl Jones	Chelsea Thayer Wayne	Linda Powell
Ethel Thayer	Leslie Uggams	Billy Ray	Alexander Mitchell
Charlie Martin	Craig Bockhorn	Bill Ray	Peter Francis James

Presented in two parts.

MISTER ROBERTS. By Thomas Heggen and Joshua Logan. March 17, 2005. Direction, Robert Longbottom; scenery, Andrew Jackness; costumes, Suzy Benzinger; lighting, Ken Billington, sound, John Gromada; fight direction, Brad Waller; production stage management, Elaine M. Randolph.

Wiley	Field Blauvelt	Doc	Stephen Kunken
Dolan	Clinton Brandhagen	Patrol Officer	Robert Michael McClure
Stefanowski	Jeff Cusimano	Military Policeman	Thomas Nunan
The Captain	Frank Deal	Lindstrom	Kip Pierson
Lt. (JG) Roberts	Michael Dempsey	Medic	Michael Vitaly Sazonov
Mannion	Ted Feldman	Dowdy	Todd Scofield
Ensign Pulver	Hunter Foster	Seaman	Stephen Thomas
Schlemmer	Andrew Honeycutt	Seaman	Jacob Michael Thornhill
Lt. Ann Girard	Beth Hylton	Insigna	Timothy Warmen
Payne	David Johnson	Reber	Peter Wylie
Gerhart	Nehal Joshi	Chief Johnson	Jim Zidar

Presented in two parts.

The Shakespeare Theatre, Washington
Michael Kahn artistic director, Nicholas T. Goldsborough managing director

LORENZACCIO. By Alfred de Musset; translated and adapted by John Strand. January 23, 2005. Direction, Michael Kahn; scenery, Ming Cho Lee; costumes, Murrell Horton; lighting, Howell Binkley; sound, Scott Killian; fight direction, Brad Waller; stage management, M. William Shiner.

Lorenzo de Medici	Jeffrey Carlson	Countess Cibo	Chandler Vinton
Alessandro de Medici	Robert Cuccioli	Salviati; Nicolini	Bernard Burak Sheredy
Count Cibo; Ruccellio	Ralph Cosham	Mafeo	Tyler Pierce
Louisa Strozzi	Colleen Delany	Gabriella	Kim Stauffer
Marie de Medici	Tana Hicken	Young Cibo	Austin Riggs
Sofia	Kate Kiley	Agnolo	Sebastian Rodriguez
Valori	Floyd King	Tebaldéo	Aubrey Deeker
Piero Strozzi	Pedro Pascal	Bindo	J. Fred Shiffman
Catherine de Medici	Marni Penning	Rolle	John Livingstone Rolle
Cardinal Cibo	Michael Rudko	Scoron	David B. Heuvelman
Paolo	David Sabin	Cosimo de Medici	Sean Brennan
Philip Strozzi	Ted van Griethuysen	Young Cibo	Austin Riggs

Ensemble: Randolph Adams, Sean Brennan, David B. Heuvelman, Teresa Lim, Gamal Palmer; John Livingstone Rolle, Kim Stauffer, Patrick C. Tansor, Jonathan Wiener, Derek Wilson.

ReDiscovery Series. December 6, 2004–February 7, 2005

THE DOG IN THE MANGER. By Lope de Vega. December 6, 2004. Translated by David Johnston. Direction, David Muse.

Performed by Ryan Artzberger, Ralph Cosham, Colleen Delany, Ted Feldman, Glenn Fleshler, Hugh Nees, Gamal Palmer, Jesse J. Perez, Angela Pierce, Tyler Pierce, John Livingstone Rolle, Michelle Shupe, Kim Stauffer, Erik Steele, Ted van Griethuysen, Chandler Vinton, Jonathan Wiener, Derek Wilson.

A BUSY DAY. By Fanny Burney. Direction, David Muse. February 7, 2005.

Performed by Daniel Breaker, Helen Carey, Ralph Cosham, Colleen Delany, Aubrey Deeker, Kip Pierson, Susan Lynskey, Hugh Nees, Nancy Robinette, Samantha Soule, Michael Tolaydo, Tymberlee Chanel, Jonathan Wiener, Derek Wilson.

THE BEAUX STRATAGEM. By George Farquhar; adapted by Thornton Wilder and Ken Ludwig. Direction, David Muse. May 2, 2005.

Performed by Daniel Breaker, Nathaniel Claridad, Andrew Long, Jennifer Mendenhall, Hugh Nees, Ian Merrill Peakes, Nancy Robinette, David Sabin, Jeanine Serralles, Jenna Sokolowski, Anne Stone, Michael Tolaydo, Derek Wilson, Gregory Woodward.

The Studio Theatre, Washington

Joy Zinoman founding artistic director, Keith Alan Baker managing director

BLACK MILK. By Vassily Sigarev; translated by Sasha Dugdale. January 9, 2005. Direction, Serge Seiden; scenery and lighting, Michael Phillippi; costumes, Alex Jaeger; sound, Gil Thompson.

Lyovchik	Matthew Montelongo	Mishanya	Tobin Atkinson
Shura	Holly Twyford	Old Drunk	Bob Barr
Ticket Clerk	Anne Stone	Antie Pasha	Elizabeth Stripe
Petrovna	June Hansen		

Ensemble: Marynell Hinton, Morgan Peter Brown, Jeff Wisnlewski, Tina Renay Fulp, Carol Arthur.

Presented in two parts.

AFTERPLAY. By Brian Friel. March 13, 2005. Direction, Joy Zinoman; scenery, Debra Booth; costumes, Devon Painter; lighting, Michael Giannitti.

Sonya Serebriakova	Nancy Robinette	Andrey Prozorov	Edward Gero

Presented in two parts.

Theater J, Washington

Ari Roth artistic director, Jeannette Buck associate producer

THE TATTOOED GIRL. By Joyce Carol Oates. February 3, 2005 (world premiere). Direction, John Vreeke; scenery, Dan Conway; costumes, Sue Chiang; lighting, Colin K. Bills.

Alma Busch	Michelle Shupe	Dmitri Meate	Christopher Browne
Joshua Seigl	Michael Russotto	Jeremy Essler	Karl Miller
Jetimah Seigl	Cam Magee		

Presented in two parts.

Woolly Mammoth Theatre, Washington

Howard Shalwitz artistic director, Kevin Moore managing director

THE RADIANT ABYSS. By Angus MacLachlan. June 15, 2004 (world premiere). Direction, Lou Jacob; scenery, James Kronzer; costumes, Anne Kennedy; lighting, Daniel MacLean Wagner; sound, Ryan Rumery; fight direction, Paul Galigar; dramaturgy, Mary Resing; production stage management, Annica Graham. Presented in association with A.S.K. Theater Projects New Plays/New Ways program.

Erin Skidmore	Janis Dardaris	Ina	Dana Acheson
Steve Enloe	Jeremy Beazlie		

Time: The present. Place: Winston-Salem, North Carolina. Presented in two parts.

LENNY AND LOU. By Ian Cohen. August 23, 2004 (world premiere). Direction, Tom Prewitt; scenery, Anne Gibson; costumes, Debra Kim Sivigny; lighting, Adam Magazine, sound, Michael Kraskin; fight direction, John Gurski; dramaturgy, Jessica Burgess; production stage management, Elizabeth Wiesner.

Lenny Feinstein .... Howard Shalwitz
Lou Feinstein .... Michael Russotto
Fran Feinstein .... Nancy Robinette

Julie Riggio .... Jennifer Mendenhall
Sabrina DeChamp .... Erika Rose

Presented in two parts.

GRACE. By Craig Wright. October 31, 2004 (world premiere). Direction, Michael John Garcés; scenery, James Kronzer; costumes, Debra Kim Sivigny; lighting, Lisa L. Ogonowski; sound, Neil McFadden; dramaturgy, Mary Resing; production stage management, Taryn Colberg.

Karl .... Michael Willis
Steve .... David Fendig

Sara .... Jennifer Mendenhall
Sam .... Paul Morella

Time: The present. Place: Two identical condos on the Florida shore. Presented without intermission.

BIG DEATH AND LITTLE DEATH. By Mickey Birnbaum. May 10, 2005 (world premiere). Direction, Howard Shalwitz; scenery and costumes, Elena Zlotescu; lighting, Colin K. Bills; sound, Neil McFadden; dramaturgy, Mary Resing; production stage management, Colleen Martin.

Kristi .... Kimberly Gilbert
Gary .... Mark J. Sullivan
Farley .... Scott McCormick
Anita .... Maia DeSanti

Harley .... Andrew Wassenich
Dad .... Paul Morella
Uncle Jerry .... Michael Willis
Mom .... Marni Penning

Time: October 1992 and June 1991. Place: A suburb of Los Angeles.

FLORIDA

Coconut Grove Playhouse, Coral Gables
Arnold Mittelman producing artistic director

HOAGY: THE HOAGY CARMICHAEL MUSICAL. Musical with book by Bruce Dettman and William C. Trichon; music by Mr. Carmichael; lyrics by Mr. Carmichael, Johnny Mercer, Frank Loesser, Mitchell Parish and others. November 5, 2004. Direction and choreography, Walter Painter; scenery, David Mitchell; costumes, Ellis Tillman; lighting, David F. Segal; sound, Steve Shapiro; production stage management, Naomi Littman.

Hoagy Carmichael .... Billy Philadelphia
B.J. .... B.J. Crosby

Joanna .... Joanna Louise
Bob .... Bob Gaynor

Musical numbers included: "Moon Country," "New Orleans," "Heart and Soul," "Reggie's Rag," "Two Sleepy People," "I'm A Cranky Old Yank," "Stardust," "Thanksgivin'," "Men With Wings," "The Nearness of You," "Can't Get Indiana Off My Mind," "Memphis in June," "Rockin' Chair," "Riverboat Shuffle," "Small Fry," "Sing Me a Swing Song (And Let Me Dance)," "Washboard Blues," "Lazy Bones," "Huggin' and Chalkin'," "Lazy River," "Georgia on My Mind," "I Get Along Without You Very Well (Except Sometimes)," "In the Cool, Cool, Cool, Of The Evening," "Hong Kong Blues," "Ain't There Anyone Here for Love?," "Ole Buttermilk Sky," "Skylark," "Baltimore Oriole."

Presented in two parts.

CRUSH THE INFAMOUS THING: THE ADVENTURES OF THE HOLLYWOOD FOUR. By Tina Benko and Gabrielle Reznek and Sam Turich. December 3, 2004 (world premiere). Direction, Carl Andress; scenery, Michael Anania; costumes, Gregory Gale; lighting, Kirk Bookman; sound, Fitz Patton; production stage management, Naomi Littman. Presented in association with Randall L. Wreghitt and Fox Theatricals.

Persimmon Montgomery .... Ms. Benko   Meryl Lombardy .... Ms. Reznek
Kent Grattan .... Mr. Turich   Tommy Tompkins .... Tim McGeever
    Time: The mid-1930s. Place: Hollywood and environs. Presented in two parts.

REAL MEN. Revue with music and lyrics by Charles Strouse. January 7, 2005 (world premiere). Direction, Jeffrey B. Moss; choreography, Barbara Siman; scenery, James Noone; costumes, Ellis Tillman; lighting, Kirk Bookman; sound, Steve Shapiro; music direction, Denes Van Parys; production stage management, Naomi Littman.

    Performed by Jordan Bennett, David Brummel, Michael Rupert, M. Sappington.

    Musical numbers included: "Home," "The Day My Wife Got Sick," "Emily," "Living Alone," "One Love," "Things," "Nothing," "Man of the World," "Where Are You Now, Baby?," "Chatting," "Trapped," "You Never Know," "Do It," "My Son, My Son," "Home Movie," "At the Diner," "What Am I Going to Do Without You?," "I Don't Want to Grow Old," "Train," "Sailing," "Can't Stop Dancing,"

ANN AND DEBBIE. By Lionel Goldstein. March 19, 2005 (world premiere). Direction, Robert Kalfin; scenery, Steve Lambert; costumes, Ellis Tillman; lighting, David Goodman; sound, Steve Shapiro.

Ann .... Elizabeth Ashley   Debbie .... Lucie Arnaz

New Theatre, Coral Gables
Rafael de Acha artistic director, Eileen Suarez managing director

2004–2005 Season of Play Readings.

DAY OF RECKONING. By Melody Cooper. July 28, 2004. Direction, James S. Randolph.
    Performed by Lucy Parsons, Albert Parsons, Albert Parsons Jr., Lulu Parsons.

YEMAYA'S BELLY. By Quiara Alegria Hudes. August 4, 2004. Direction, Ricky J. Martinez.
    Performed by Carlos Alleto, Alex Cordova, Evelyn Perez, Kevin Perez, Cecilia Isis Torres, Tara Vodihn.

UNREASONABLE DOUBT. By Michael McKeever. August 18, 2004. Direction, Stuart Meltzer.
    Performed by Kimberly Daniel, Ursula Freundlich, Joe Kimble, Amy London, Gordon McConnell, Michael McKeever.

THE JOURNEY THROUGH THE FIRE. By Lawrence Bullock. September 28, 2004. Direction, Lisa Morgan-Hulse.
    Performed by Irene Adjan, Jeffrey Bower, Kimberly Daniel, David Kwiat, Jacqueline Laggy, Michael McKeever, Marjorie O'Neill-Butler, Wayne Robinson.

SECRET THINGS. By Elaine Romero. October 12, 2004. Direction, Javier Siut.
    Performed by Jorge Almeyda, Patricia Azan, Aurora Castellanos, Ramon Gonzales-Cuevas, Nicholas Richberg.

THE WOMAN FROM THE SEA. By Spence Porter. October 20, 2004. Direction, Barbara Sloan.
    Performed by David Alt, Keith Cassidy, Ursula Freundlich, Michael Ives, Sandra Ives, Larry Jurrist, Lisa LaGrande, Chris Vicchiollo.

DEAR PRESIDENT: LETTERS TO THE PRESIDENT. By Marcus Woollen. October 27, 2004. Direction, Geoffrey Tangeman.
    Performed by Rafael de Acha, Stephen S. Neal, Barbara Sloan, Tara Vodihn.

A HEARTBEAT TO BAGHDAD. By Glyn O'Malley. November 3, 2004. Direction, Stephen S. Neal.
    Performed by Kay Brady, Keith Cassidy, Dave Corey; Heather Gallagher, Patty Gardner, Teddy Harrell, Autumn Horne, Sandra Ives, Paul Lasa, Robert Strain, Nicholas Richberg.

THE BEAUTY INSIDE. By Catherine Filloux. December 8, 2004. Direction, Barbara Lowery.

Performed by Avi Hoffman, Devrim Inan, Ricky J. Martinez.

THE CONTEST. By Shirley Lauro. January 18, 2005. Direction, Avi Hoffman.

Performed by Linda Bernhard, Kay Brady, Bridget Connors, Dave Corey, Terry Francois, Zoe Galitz, Chloe Golden, Avi Hoffman, Lindsay Savin.

MAN MEASURES MAN. By David Robson. January 26, 2005. Direction, Desmond Gallant.

Performed by John Bixler, Carole Courtland, Paul Lasa, Jenny Levine, Euriamis Losada, Stephen S. Neal.

THE FINAL TOUR. By Doug Cooney. February 9, 2005. Direction, Tara Vodihn.

Performed by Kay Brady, Malinda Farrington, David Kwiat, Euriamis Losada, Bill Schwartz.

LINCOLNESQUE. By John Strand. February 28, 2005. Direction, Tara Vodihn.

Performed by Keith Cassidy, Jenny Levine, Bruce Miller, Stephen S. Neal.

SPLITTING INFINITY. By Jamie Pachino. April 27, 2005. Direction, Ricky J. Martinez.

Performed by Lauren Feldman, Gail Garrison, Avi Hoffman, Craig Kaul, Sally Levin, Dean Swann.

WAIT AND SEE. By Michael McKeever. September 10, 2004 (world premiere). Direction, Barbara Lowery, scenery, Mr. McKeever; lighting, Pedro A. Remirez; sound, Ozzie Quintana; production stage management, Joseph M. NeSmith.

Sister Felicity	Bridget Connors	Dr. Elliott	Barry Tarallo
Andy Starr	Nicholas Richberg	Council Chairman	Bill Schwartz

Presented without intermission.

BARRIO HOLLYWOOD. By Elaine Romero. October 15, 2004 (world premiere). Direction, Rafael de Acha; scenery, Michael McKeever; lighting, Pedro A. Remirez, sound, Ozzie Quintana; production stage management, Joseph M. NeSmith.

Alex Moreno	Euriamis Losada	Ama	Marta Velasco
Graciela Moreno	Beatriz Montañez	Michael	John Baldwin

Time: 1999. Place: Mexico; Arizona. Presented in two parts.

CLARENCE DARROW'S LAST TRIAL. By Shirley Lauro. January 22, 2005 (world premiere). Direction, Rafael de Acha; scenery, Rich Simone; costumes, Estela Vrancovich; lighting, Michael Foster; sound, M. Anthony Reimer; production stage management, Joseph M. NeSmith.

Clarence Darrow	John Felix	Theodora Ramsey	Jenny Levine
Ruby Darrow	Susan Dempsey	Naniloa Whitefield Chan	Tara Vodihn
Mrs. Montegu	Angie Radosh	Dr. David Stein	William Schwartz
Lt. John Ramsey	John Bixler	Reporter; Tommy Lou	Ricky J. Martinez

Time: The 1930s and onwards. Place: United States; territory of Hawaii. Presented in two parts.

GEORGIA

Alliance Theatre Company, Atlanta
Susan V. Booth artistic director

THE COLOR PURPLE. Musical with book by Marsha Norman; music and lyrics by Brenda Russell; Allee Willis and Stephen Bray; based on the novel by Alice Walker and the Warner Brothers/Amblin Entertainment film. September 17, 2004 (world premiere).

Direction, Gary Griffin; choreography, Ken Roberson; scenery, John Lee Beatty; costumes, Paul Tazewell; lighting, Brian MacDevitt; sound, Jon Weston; music direction, Linda Twine; orchestrations, Jonathan Tunick; production stage management, Joel Rosen.

The Mayor	Barry Anbinder	Rev. Avery	Don Mayo
Ensemble	Philip Michael Baskerville	Young Celie	Tatiana McConnico
Young Nettie	Khadijah Davis	Pa	JC Montgomery
Harpo	Brandon Victor Dixon	Adam	Darrell Grand Moultrie
Corrinne	Anika Ellis	Young Harpo	Desi Raines
Miss Millie	Shannon Eubanks	Olivia	Stacey Sargeant
Sofia	Felicia P. Fields	Nettie	Saycon Sengbloh
Buster	James Harkness	Tashi	Debra M. Walton
Doris	Kimberly Ann Harris	Sofia's Child	Marah Elizabeth Williams
Celie	LaChanze	Bartender	Kenny Redell Williams
Mister	Kingsley Leggs	Jarene	Maia Nkenge Wilson
Shug Avery	Adriane Lenox	Darlene	Virginia Ann Woodruff
Squeak	Krisha A. Marcano		

Musical numbers included: "Walkin' Home/Move On Up," "Huckleberry Pie," "I Really Want That Girl," "That Fine Mister," "She Be Mine," "Bring My Nettie Back," "Dear God, Sofia!," "A Tree Named Sofia," "Hell No!," "Brown Betty," "Shug Avery Comin' To Town," "Hussy That Ain't Too Fussy," "Dear God, Shug Avery!," "Too Beautiful For Words," "Push Da Button," "Uh-Oh," "What About Love?," "Dear Celie," "Africa," "Olinka Exodus," "The Color Purple," "A Church Ladies' Easter," "I'm Free," "In Miss Celie's Pants," "Let Her Grace Lift Me Up," "Is There Anything I Can Do For You?," "A Church Ladies' 4th of July."

DAY OF THE KINGS. By Daphne Greaves. January 26, 2005 (world premiere). Direction, Susan V. Booth; scenery, Scott Bradley; costumes, Mariann S. Verheyen; lighting, Ken Yunker; sound, Lindsey Jones; dramaturgy, Megan Monaghan.

Atalaya Nunez	Romi Dias	Esteban	Theroun Patterson
Dr. Faber	Katie Firth	Cecilia	Crystal Porter
Diego de la Hoya	Sandro Isaack	Don Alarico	Maurice Ralston
Hector Nunez	Triney Sandoval	Hector Nunez	Triney Sandoval
Blanca Nunez	Maria Parra		

THE HEART IS A LONELY HUNTER. By Rebecca Gilman; adapted from the novel by Carson McCullers. March 30, 2005 (world premiere). Direction, Doug Hughes; scenery, Neil Patel; costumes, Catherine Zuber; lighting, Michael R. Chybowski; sound, David Van Tieghem; projections, Jan Hartley; production stage management, Kate McDoniel. Presented in association with the Acting Company, New York.

Singer	Henry Stram	Jake Blount	Andrew Weems
Mick Kelly	Julie Jesneck	Antonapoulos	John Sierros
Dr. Copeland	Ron Cephas Jones	Mr. Kelly	David de Vries
Portia	Roslyn Ruff	Willie	Jimonn Cole
Biff Brannon	Randall Newsome	Harry	Adam Green

Presented in two parts.

ILLINOIS

Chicago Shakespeare Theater
Barbara Gaines artistic director, Criss Henderson executive director

KABUKI LADY MACBETH. By Karen Sunde; based on the Scottish play by William Shakespeare. March 11, 2005 (world premiere). Direction, Shozo Sato; scenery, Katherine Ross; lighting, Michael Rourke; sound, Lindsay Jones.

Lady Macbeth .... Barbara Robertson	Witch .... Laura T. Fisher,
Macbeth .... Michael F. Goldberg	George Keating, Elizabeth Laidlaw
Koken .... Ben Dickie, Jesse GrothOlson,	Lady-in-Waiting .... Peggy Roeder
Gregor Mortis; Elizabeth Tanner	Macduff .... Anthony Starke
Key Player .... Gregor Mortis	

The Goodman Theatre, Chicago

Robert Falls artistic director, Roche Schulfer executive director

ELECTRICIDAD. By Luis Alfaro. June 29, 2004 (world premiere). Direction, Henry Godinez; choreography, Wilfredo Rivera; scenery, Riccardo Hernández; costumes, Christopher Acebo; lighting, Christopher Akerlind; sound, Ray Nardelli and Joshua Horvath; dramaturgy, Rick DesRochers.

Electricidad .... Cecilia Suárez	A Vecina .... Sandra Delgado
Ifigenia .... Charin Alvarez	Clemencia .... Sandra Marquez
Orestes .... Maximino Arciniega Jr.	A Vecina .... Tanya Saracho
Abuela .... Ivonne Coll	A Vecina .... Marisabel Suarez
A Vecina .... Laura E. Crotte	Nino .... Edward Torres

FINISHING THE PICTURE. By Arthur Miller. October 5, 2004 (world premiere). Direction, Robert Falls; scenery, Thomas Lynch; costumes, Martin Pakledinaz; lighting, Michael Phillippi; sound, Richard Woodbury; production stage management, Joseph Drummond.

Phillip Ochsner .... Stacy Keach	Flora Fassinger .... Linda Lavin
Edna Meyers .... Frances Fisher	Terry Case .... Scott Glenn
Kitty .... Heather Prete	Paul .... Matthew Modine
Derek Clemson .... Harris Yulin	Jerome Fassinger .... Stephen Lang
Presented in two parts	

MARIELA IN THE DESERT. By Karen Zacarias. February 8, 2005 (world premiere). Direction, Henry Godinez; scenery and projections, John Boesche; costumes, Jacqueline Firkins; lighting, Robert Christen; sound, Andre Pluess and Ben Sussman.

Mariela .... Sandra Marquez	Oliva .... Laura E. Crotte
Jose .... Ricardo Gutierrez	Blanca .... Sandra Delgado
Carlos .... Eric Lloyd Ambriz	Adam .... Mark Ulrich

New Stages Series. March 22–26, 2005.

MY BUDDY BILL. By Rick Cleveland. Direction, Bill Payne. March 22, 2005.

A CHANGE IN THE WEATHER. By Ron Hutchinson. Direction, Steve Scott. March 23, 2005.

THE FRUGAL REPAST. By Ron Hirsen. Direction, Joe Grifasi. March 24, 2005.

SWEET WATER TASTE. By Gloria Bond Clunie. Direction, Mignon McPherson Nance. March 25, 2005.

ELLIOT: A SOLDIER'S FUGUE. By Quiara Alegria Hudes. Direction, Ann Filmer. March 26, 2005.

FLOYD AND CLEA UNDER THE WESTERN SKY. Musical with book and lyrics by David Cale; music by Jonathan Kreisberg and Mr. Cale. April 19, 2005 (world premiere). Direction, Michael Wilson; scenery, Jeff Cowie; costumes, David C. Woolard; lighting, Rui Rita; sound, Andre Pluess.

Floyd Duffner .... David Cale	Clea Johnson .... Faryl Millet
Musicians: Malcolm Ruhl, Dylan Schiavone, John Spiegel.	

SILK. By Mary Zimmerman; adapted from the novel by Alessandro Baricco. May 3, 2005 (world premiere). Direction, Ms. Zimmerman; scenery, Scott Bradley; costumes, Mara Blumenfeld; lighting, T.J. Gerckens; music and sound, Andre Pluess and Ben Sussman; production stage management, Joseph Drummond.

Hervé Joncour .... Ryan Artzberger	Servant .... Denice Lee
Hélène .... Colleen Delany	Hara Kei .... Tohoru Masamune
The Mayor .... Joe Dempsey	Woman in Japan .... Elaine Yuko Qualter
Narrator .... Christopher Donahue	Madame Blanche .... Lisa Tejero
Baldabiou .... Glenn Fleshler	The Boy .... Philip White
Hara Kei's Servant .... Andre Ing	

Time: 1860–74. Place: France; Japan.

Lookingglass Theatre Company, Chicago
David Catlin artistic director, Jacqueline Russell executive director

1984. By George Orwell; adapted by Andrew White. October 16, 2004 (world premiere). Direction, Mr. White; scenery, Geoffrey M. Curley; costumes, Mara Blumenfeld, lighting, Chris Binder; sound, Joshua Horvath and Andre Pluess; production stage management, Sara Gmitter.

Parsons .... Jason Ball	Tillotson .... Lawrence Grimm
Winston .... Thomas J. Cox	Julia .... Jenn SavaRyan
Ampleforth .... Lawrence E. DiStasi	Syme .... Lisa Tejero
O'Brien .... Anthony Fleming III	Charrington .... Gary Wingert

Presented without intermission.

LOOKINGGLASS ALICE. By David Catlin; adapted from the work of Lewis Carroll. February 12, 2005 (world premiere). Direction, Mr. Catlin; choreography, Sylvia Hernandez-DiStasi; scenery, Daniel Ostling; costumes, Mara Blumenfeld, lighting, Chris Binder; sound, Andre Pluess and Ben Sussman; production stage management, Sara Gmitter. Presented in association with the Actors Gymnasium.

White Knight .... Lawrence E. DiStasi	Red Queen .... Tony Hernandez
Cheshire Cat .... Anthony Fleming III	Alice .... Lauren Hirte
Mad Hatter .... Doug Hara	

Northlight Theatre, Skokie
BJ Jones artistic director, Phil Santora managing director

CAT FEET. By Monte Merrick. October 13, 2004 (world premiere). Direction, BJ Jones; scenery, Matthew York; lighting, Joseph Appelt; costumes, Frances Maggio; sound, Andre Pluess and Ben Sussman; dramaturgy, Rosanna Forrest; production stage management, Laura D. Glenn.

Julia Elliot .... Rengin Altay	Rocco Baldecchi .... Keith Kupferer
Molly Johnson .... Julie Ganey	Cara Elliot .... Mary Ann Thebus

Steppenwolf Theatre Company, Chicago
Martha Lavey artistic director, David Hawkanson executive director

ONE ARM. By Moisés Kaufman; adapted from the work of Tennessee Williams. December 4, 2004. Direction, Mr. Kaufman; scenery, Derek McLane; costumes, Janice Pytel; lighting,

Mike Baldassari; sound, Andre Pluess and Ben Sussman; dramaturgy, Eric Rosen and Laura Newman; stage management, Anjali Bidani. Presented in association with About Face Theatre and Tectonic Theater Project.

Ollie	Reynaldo Rosales	Divinity student	Steve Key
Narrator	John McAdams	Nurse	Sandra Marquez
Willie	Jason Denuszek	Woman on Yacht	Shané Williams
Kewpie	Michael Stahl-David	Woman on Steamer	Kelli Simpkins
Lester	Joe Van Slyke	Ensemble	Marilyn Bielby,
Yachtsman	David Parkes		Josh Bywater, Eltony Williams

Presented in two parts.

PACIFIC. By Andrew Case. February 17, 2005. Direction, Molly Regan; scenery, John Dalton; costumes, Christine Pascual; lighting, J.R. Lederle; sound, Victoria DeIorio; fight direction, Jeffrey Baumgartner; dramaturgy, Edward Sobel; stage management; Michelle Medvin.

Susan	Rebecca Spence	Andersen	Brian Hamman
Robert	James Krag		

Time: A few years ago. Place: A town on the seacoast between Los Angeles and San Diego.

THE BLUEST EYE. By Toni Morrison; adapted by Lydia Diamond. March 3, 2005 (world premiere). Direction, Hallie Gordon; choreography, Ann Boyd; scenery, Stephanie Nelson; costumes, Alison Heryer; lighting, J.R. Lederle; sound, Victoria DeIorio; dramaturgy, Lenora Inez Brown; stage management, Deb Styer.

Claudia	Libya V. Pugh	Mrs. Breedlove	Chavez Ravine
Frieda; Darlene	Monifa M. Days	Soaphead Church	Sati Word
Pecola Breedlove	Alana Arenas	Cholly	Phillip Edward VanLear
Mama	TaRon Patton	Maureen Peal	Noelle Hardy

Time: 1940–41. Place: Lorain, Ohio.

LOST LAND. By Stephen Jeffreys. April 10, 2005 (world premiere). Direction, Terry Johnson; choreography, Rachel Rockwell; scenery, James Schuette; costumes, John Malkovich; lighting, Scott Zielinski; sound, Rob Milburn and Michael Bodeen; fight direction, Robin H. McFarquhar; dramaturgy, Edward Sobel; stage management, Malcolm Ewen.

Kristóf	John Malkovich	Ilona	Martha Lavey
Tamás	Ian Barford	Miklós	Yasen Peyankov
Anna	Katrina Lenk		

Ensemble: Katherine R. Foster, Max Grilly, Isabel Guzmán-Barrrón, Christopher LaBove.

Time: October 1918; June 1919. Place: A medieval castle in Northern Hungary. Presented in two parts.

RED LIGHT WINTER. By Adam Rapp. May 30, 2005 (world premiere). Direction, Mr. Rapp; scenery, Todd Rosenthal; costumes, Michelle Tesdall; lighting, Keith Parham; sound, Andre Pluess and Ben Sussman; stage management, Kerry Epstein.

Matt	Christopher Denham	Christina	Lisa Joyce
Davis	Gary Wilmes		

Time: The present. Place: Amsterdam's Red Light District; New York's East Village.

Victory Gardens Theater, Chicago
Dennis Zacek artistic director, Marcelle McVay managing director

THE ROMANCE OF MAGNO RUBIO. By Lonnie Carter; Tagalog text by Ralph B. Peña; based on the short story by Carlos Bulosan. June 7, 2004. Direction and scenery, Loy

Arcenas, costumes, Christine Pascual; lighting, Todd Hensley; music, Fabian Obispo; sound, Andre Pluess and Ben Sussman; production stage management, Ellyn Costello.

Prudencio	Bernardo Bernardo	Clarabelle	Narciso Lobo
Nick	Joseph Anthony Foronda	Magno Rubio	Rodney To
Claro	Frederick Garcia		

Time: 1930s and beyond. Place: A bunkhouse for migrant workers in California.

THE FAMILY GOLD. By Annie Reiner. September 20, 2004 (world premiere). Direction, Dennis Zacek; scenery, Mary Griswold; costumes, Michelle Tesdall; lighting, Jaymi Lee Smith; sound, Joe Cerqua; production stage management, Tina M. Jach.

Ruth	Roslyn Alexander	Luis	Tony Sancho
Ted	Harold Gould	Mrs. Gilheany	Mary Seibel
Dory	Julia Neary		

Time: The present. Place: Brooklyn. Presented in two parts.

PYRETOWN. By John Belluso. October 13, 2004. Direction, Tim Farrell; scenery, costumes and lighting, Samuel C. Ball; sound, Joe Huppert; production stage management, Richard Lundy.

Rebecca Adler	Melissa Carlson Joseph	Harry Weston	Aaron Roman Weiner
Louise Josephson	Elaine Rivkin		

Time: The present. Place: A small industrial New England town. Presented in two parts.

HANGING FIRE. By Claudia Allen. November 15, 2004 (world premiere). Direction, Sandy Shinner; scenery, John C. Stark; costumes, Carol J. Blanchard; lighting, Rita Pietraszek; sound, Andrew Hopson; production stage management, Tina M. Jach.

Young Lillian	Bethanny Alexander	Deb	Meg Thalken
Young Ruth	Mattie Hawkinson	Calvin	Mick Weber
Donny Fletcher	Les Hinderyckx	Lillian	Ann Whitney
Ruth	Rachel Stephens		

Time: 1940–2000. Place: Small town in Michigan. Presented in two parts.

SHOES. By Gloria Bond Clunie. January 24, 2005 (world premiere). Direction, Andrea J. Dymond; scenery, Rick Paul; costumes, Judith Lundberg; lighting, Charles Cooper; sound, Ms. Dymond; music direction, Vernon Clark; dramaturgy, Charles Smith; production stage management, Ellyn Costello.

Spook	Denise M. Chapman	Choir; Miss Brame	Ora B. Nance
Choir; Reverend	Tory O. Davis	Choir	Wynter Spears
John	Kenn E. Head	Carol	Linara Washington
Cephus	Warren Jackson	Grandma; Miz Lottie	Jacqueline Williams
Roberta	Ora Jones		

Time: 1957–63. Place: Birmingham, Alabama and Almost Heaven. Presented in two parts.

BERLIN '45. By Jeffrey Sweet. March 28, 2005 (world premiere). Direction, Calvin MacLean; choreography, Mark Goldweber; scenery, Jack Magaw; costumes, Judith Lundberg; lighting, Julie Mack; sound, Andre Pluess and Ben Sussman.

Second Doubling Actor	Chris Cantelmi	First Doubling Actor	Gary Houston
Second Doubling Actress	Melissa Carlson	First Doubling Actress	Deborah Leydig
Ilse	Tandy Cronyn	Gregor	Roderick Peeples

Presented in two parts.

KENTUCKY

Actors Theatre of Louisville
Marc Masterson artistic director, Alexander Speer executive director

29th Annual Humana Festival of New American Plays. February 27–April 9, 2005.

HAZARD COUNTY. By Allison Moore. February 27, 2005. Direction, Chris Coleman; scenery, Paul Owen; costumes, Catherine F. Norgren; lighting, Deb Sullivan; sound, Matt Callahan; music, Juggernaut Jug Band, dramaturgy, Julie Felise Dubiner, stage management, Nancy Pitterman. Presented in association with the National New Play Network.

Ruth	Chelsey Rives	Camille	Elizabeth Meadows Rouse
Quinn	Jesse Hooker	Blake	Sean Dougherty
Quintin	Mary Bacon		

Time: The present. Place: A very small town in southwestern Kentucky and the spaces between New York and California. Presented in two parts.

A NERVOUS SMILE. By John Belluso. March 5, 2005. Direction, David Esbjornson; scenery, Paul Owen; costumes, Junghyun Georgia Lee; lighting, Deb Sullivan; sound, Jill BC DuBoff; dramaturgy, Adrien-Alice Hansel; stage management, Heather Fields.

Brian	Sean Haberle	Nic	Mhari Sandoval
Eileen	Maureen Mueller	Blanka	Dale Soules

Time: The present. Place: Brian and Eileen's Upper West Side apartment in Manhattan.

THE SHAKER CHAIR. By Adam Bock. March 10, 2005. Direction, Marc Masterson; scenery, Paul Owen; costumes, Catherine F. Norgren; lighting, Mary Louise Geiger; sound, Matt Callahan; dramaturgy, Adrien-Alice Hansel; production stage management, Paul Mills Holmes.

Marion	Kathleen Butler	Tom	Andy Prosky
Jean	Geraldine Librandi	Lou	Brie Eley
Dolly	Sarah Peterson	Frank	Larry John Meyers

Presented in two parts.

MOOT THE MESSENGER. By Kia Corthron. March 12, 2005. Direction, Marion McClinton, scenery, Paul Owen; costumes, Junghyun Georgia Lee; lighting, Deb Sullivan; sound, Jill BC DuBoff; dramaturgy, Tanya Palmer, stage management, Brady Ellen Poole.

Briar	Tamilla Woodard	Harmon; Mel	Bob Ari
Pappy	Cortez Nance Jr.	Hamid; Prisoner	Sami Metwasi
Tax	Erik LaRay Harvey	Mary; Pat; Amy	Anna Bullard
Louise	Chelsey Rives	Soldiers	Ian Frank, Ira Hill,
Mamma; Vaughn	Brenda Thomas		Emily Hyberger, Chris Powers

Presented in two parts.

PURE CONFIDENCE. By Carlyle Brown. March 19, 2005. Direction, Clinton Turner Davis, scenery, Paul Owen; costumes, Lorraine Venberg; lighting, Mary Louise Geiger; sound, Matt Callahan; dramaturgy, Tanya Palmer; stage management, Debra Anne Freeman.

Simon Cato	Gavin Lawrence	Auctioneer; Reporter	Andy Prosky
Dewitt; Clerk	Larry John Meyers	Caroline	Kelly Taffe
Colonel Wiley Johnson	William McNulty	Mattie Johnson	Jane Welch

Presented in two parts.

2005
Humana Festival
10-Minute Plays

Top to Bottom: Jane Welch, Jesse Hooker, Mary Bacon in Dream of Jeannie-by-the-Door; *Megan Goodchild, Deanna McGovern in* Goody Fucking Two Shoes; *Sarah Peterson, William McNulty in* Johannes, Pyotr and Marge. *Photos: Harlan Taylor*

MEMORY HOUSE. By Kathleen Tolan. March 23, 2005. Direction, Sandy Shinner; scenery, Paul Owen; costumes, Lorraine Venberg; lighting, Deb Sullivan; sound, Lindsay Jones; dramaturgy, Julie Felise Dubiner; stage management, Bethany Ford.

Maggie .... Taylor Miller   Katia .... Cassandra Bissell
     Time: New Year's Eve. Place: New York City.

UNCLE SAM'S SATIRIC SPECTACULAR: ON DEMOCRACY AND OTHER FICTIONS, FEATURING PATRIOTISM ACTS AND BLUE SONGS FROM A RED STATE. By Greg Allen, Sheila Callaghan, Bridget Carpenter, Eric Coble, Richard Dresser, Michael Friedman, Hilly Hicks. March 25–April 3, 2005. Direction, Wendy McClellan; scenery, Paul Owen; costumes, John P. White; lighting, Nick Dent; sound, Benjamin Marcum; dramaturgy, Adrien-Alice Hansel; stage management, Abigail Wright.
    Performed by Mark Bovino, Anna Bullard, Becky Chong, Joseph Curnutte, Joanna Edie, Brie Eley, Ian Frank, Kirstin Rebekah Franklin, Megan Goodchild, Ira Hill, Emily Hyberger, Andrew Jessop, C.J. LaRoche, Jeff Lepine, Deanna McGovern, Devin McKnight, Melissa Ortiz, Sarah Parker, Chris Powers, Carolyn Michelle Smith, Matthew Summersgill, Alexander V. Thompson.

Ten-Minute Plays. April 2–3, 2005.
JOHANNES, PYOTR AND MARGE. By Jeffrey Essmann. Direction, Sturgis Warner; scenery, Paul Owen; costumes, Kevin Thacker and John P. White; lighting, Paul Werner; sound, Benjamin Marcum; dramaturgy, Mervin P. Antonio; production stage management, Paul Mills Holmes.

Brahms .... William McNulty   Marge .... Sarah Peterson
Tchaikovsky .... Andy Prosky

Bedtime story: Mary Bacon, Chelsey Rives and Jesse Hooker in Allison Moore's Hazard County *during the 2005 Humana Festival of New American Plays. Photo: Harlan Taylor*

LONG DREAM IN SUMMER. By Saïd Sayrafiezadeh. Direction, Sturgis Warner; scenery, Paul Owen; costumes, Kevin Thacker and John P. White; lighting, Paul Werner; sound, Benjamin Marcum; dramaturgy, Mervin P. Antonio; production stage management, Paul Mills Holmes.

A Soldier	Joseph Curnutte	Alexander Cartwright	Larry John Meyers
His Mother	Geraldine Librandi	Time	Gavin Lawrence

Time: June 19, 1846. Place: Elysian Fields in Hoboken, New Jersey.

GOODY FUCKING TWO SHOES. By Jennifer Maisel. Direction, Wendy McClellan; scenery, Paul Owen; costumes, Kevin Thacker and John P. White; lighting, Paul Werner; sound, Benjamin Marcum; dramaturgy, Mervin P. Antonio; production stage management, Paul Mills Holmes.

Abigail	Deanna McGovern	Man's Voice	Sean Dougherty
Bet	Megan Goodchild		

DREAM OF JEANNIE-BY-THE-DOOR. By David Valdes Greenwood. Direction, Steve Moulds; scenery, Paul Owen; costumes, Kevin Thacker and John P. White; lighting, Paul Werner; sound, Benjamin Marcum; dramaturgy, Mervin P. Antonio; production stage management, Paul Mills Holmes.

Wilma	Jane Welch	Gary	Jesse Hooker
Bonnie	Mary Bacon		

MARYLAND

Center Stage, Baltimore
Irene Lewis artistic director, Michael Ross managing director

ELMINA'S KITCHEN. By Kwame Kwei-Armah. January 5, 2005. Direction, Marion McClinton; scenery, Neil Patel; costumes, David Burdick; lighting, Michelle Habeck; sound, Shane Rettig; fight direction, David Leong; stage management, Debra Acquavella.

Digger	Thomas Jefferson Byrd	Deli	Curtis McClarin
Anastasia	Yvette Ganier	Baygee	Ernest Perry Jr.
Ashley	LeRoy McClain	Clifton	Sullivan Walker

Time: Today. Place: Elmina's Kitchen: Hackney, London. Presented in two parts.

First Look. February 21–March 24, 2005

THE MOONLIGHT ROOM. By Tristine Skyler. February 21, 2005. Direction, Madeleine Oldham.

Performed by Doug Brown, Kimberly Gilbert, Marcus Kyd, Kate Levy, Mark J. Sullivan.

HAZARD COUNTY. By Allison Moore. March 7, 2005. Direction, Gavin Witt.

Performed by Aubrey Deeker, Susan Lynskey, Jennifer Mendenhall, Paul Nicholas, Kirsten Wyatt.

HELP WANTED: A PERSONAL SEARCH FOR MEANINGFUL EMPLOYMENT AT THE START OF THE 21ST CENTURY. By Josh Lefkowitz. March 21, 2005.

Performed by Mr. Lefkowitz.

AMERICAMISFIT. By Dan Dietz. March 23, 2005. Direction, Trip Cullman.

Performed by Brent Werzner, Harris Doran, Rick Hammerly, Laurence O'Dwyer, Stephen F. Schmidt, Kimberly Gilbert, Rana Kay, Miriam Lior Ganz, Phillip D. Owen.

Round House Theatre, Silver Springs
Jerry Whiddon producing artistic director, Ira Hillman managing director

COLUMBINUS. By P.J. Paparelli, Stephen Karam and Sean McNall. March 7, 2005 (world premiere). Direction by Mr. Paparelli; scenery, Tony Cisek; costumes, Denise Umland; lighting, Dan Covey; sound, Martin Desjardins; projections, JJ Kaczynski. Presented in association with Perseverance Theatre and the United States Theatre Project.

Performed by Anne Bowles, Daniel Frith, Jeanne Dillon, James Flanagan, Gene Gillette, Karl Miller, Ekatrina Oleksa, Will Rogers.

Presented in two parts.

MASSACHUSETTS

American Repertory Theatre, Cambridge
Robert Woodruff artistic director, Robert J. Orchard executive director

THE MISER. By Molière; adapted by David Ball. June 19, 2004. Direction, Dominique Serrand; scenery, Riccardo Hernández; costumes, Sonya Berlovitz; lighting, Marcus Dilliard; sound, David Remedios; dramaturgy, Ryan McKittrick and Barbara Whitney; stage management, Thomas Kauffman. Presented in association with Theatre de la Jeune Lune, Minneapolis, and Actors Theatre of Louisville.

Harpagon	Steven Epp	Frosine	Karen MacDonald
Cléante	Stephen Cartmell	Master Jacques	Remo Airaldi
Elise; Dame Claude	Sara Agnew	La Flèche	Nathan Keepers
Valère	Will LeBow	Servants	Peter Cambor, Jodi Dick,
Mariane	Natalie Moore		Paul DiMilla, Jane Elliott
Anselme; Master Simon	Bern Budd		

THE PROVOK'D WIFE. By John Vanbrugh. December 4, 2004. Direction, Mark Wing-Davey; scenery, Marina Draghici; costumes, Gabriel Berry; lighting, Jennifer Tipton; music and sound, David Remedios; fight direction, Doug Elkins; dramaturgy, Kirsten Bowen and Ryan McKittrick; production stage management, Chris De Camillis.

Sir John Brute	Bill Camp	Justice of the Peace	Jeremy Geidt
Lady Brute	Kate Forbes	Colonel Bully	Thomas Derrah
Constant	Peter Rini	Lord Rake	Jorge Rubio
Heartfree	Adam Dannheisser	Watch	Peter Cambor
Constable	Remo Airaldi	Tailor	Mickey Solis
Bellinda	Deborah Knox Meschan	Cornet	Shawtane Monroe Bowen
Lady Fanciful	Effie Johnson	Pipe	Julia Benn
Mademoiselle	Karen MacDonald	Lovewell	Jeremy Geidt

Presented in two parts.

THE FAR SIDE OF THE MOON. By Robert Lepage with Peder Bjurman. February 4, 2005. Direction, Mr. Lepage; costumes, Marie-Chantale Vaillancourt; music, Laurie Anderson; puppets, Pierre Robitaille and Sylvie Courbron.

Performed by Yves Jacques.

OLLY'S PRISON. By Edward Bond. April 7, 2005. Direction, Robert Woodruff; scenery and costumes, David Zinn; lighting, Christopher Akerlind; sound, David Remedios; fight direction, Doug Elkins; production stage management, Anne King.

Mike	Bill Camp	Oliver	Mickey Solis
Sheila	Zofia Goszcznska	Guards	Shawtane Monroe Bowen,
Vera	Angela Reed		Jason Christopher Brown,
Frank	David Wilson Barnes		Sam Chase
Barry	Thomas Derrah	Prisoners	Alejandro Simoes,
Smiler	Peter Dylan Richards		Amara Sridstava
Ellen	Karen MacDonald	Lucy's Mother	Zuzanna Szadkowsku

Barrington Stage Company, Sheffield

Julianne Boyd artistic director, Mitch Weiss managing director

THE GOD COMMITTEE. By Mark St. Germain, July 25, 2004 (world premiere). Direction, David Saint; scenery, Eric Renschler; costumes, David Murin; lighting, Christopher J. Bailey; sound, Randy Hansen; production stage management, C. Renee Alexander.

Nella Redwood	Michele Shay	Dr.Ann Ross	Amy Van Nostrand
Dr. Alex Gorman	Armand Schultz	Dr. Jack Klee	David Rasche
Dr. Keira Banks	Kelly Hutchinson	Dominick Piero	Ron Orbach
Fr. Charles Dunbar	Gerritt Graham		

   Time: Present. Place: St. Patrick's Hospital, NYC. Presented in two parts.

THE 25TH ANNUAL PUTNAM COUNTY SPELLING BEE. Musical with book by Rachel Sheinkin; music and lyrics by William Finn; conceived by Rebecca Feldman. July 7, 2004 (world premiere). Direction, Michael Unger and Ms. Feldman; choreography, Dan Knechtges; scenery, Beowulf Boritt; costumes, Jen Caprio; lighting, Tyler Micoleau; sound, Randy Hansen; music direction, Vadim Feichtner; production stage management, Angela DeGregoria.

Gramercy	Deborah S. Craig	Olive	Celia Keenan-Bolger
Mitch	Derrick Baskin	Douglas Panch	Jay Reiss
Leaf	Jesse Tyler Ferguson	Logan	Sarah Saltzberg
William	Dan Fogler	Tripp	Robb Sapp
Rona Janet	Lisa Howard		

   Musical numbers included: "25th Annual Putnam County Spelling Bee," "My Friend the Dictionary," "Pandemonium," "I'm Not That Smart," "Magic Foot," "Serenity Prayer," "Finalists," "I Don't Remember Anything At All," "My Unfortunate Erection," "Why I Love Spelling," "Woe Is Me," "I Speak Six Languages," "The I Love You Song," "I Always Come in Second."

Berkshire Theatre Festival, Stockbridge

Kate Macguire executive director

SIDDHARTHA. By Herman Hesse; adapted by Eric Hill. July 7, 2004 (world premiere). Direction, Mr. Hill; scenery, Yoshi Tanokura; costumes, Marija Djordjevic; lighting, Carleton Coffrin; sound, Nathan Leigh; stage management, Mary Costello.

Carl Jung; others	Jereme Anglin	Govinda	John Lysaght
Siddhartha's Father; Freud	Chris Bolden	Young Hesse	Michael McComiskey
Shakti	Erin Gorski	Sarasvati; Nurse	Jill Michael
Siddhartha's Son	Alexander Hill	Hesse	Andrew Michael Neiman
Vasuveda	Joe Jung	Kamaswami	Brian Sell
Siddhartha; Ka	Brad Kilgore	Lakshmi; Kamala	Isadora Wolfe
Presented in two parts.			

EUGENE'S HOME. By Kathy Levin Shapiro. August 4, 2004 (world premiere). Direction, Scott Schwartz; scenery, Beowulf Boritt; costumes, Junghyun Georgia Lee; lighting, Mr.

Schwartz and Adam Scott Howarth; sound, Scott Killian; production dramaturgy, James Magruder; stage management, Mona El-Khatib.

Eugene .... Arnie Burton   Talie .... Kelly McAndrew
Nurse; others .... Kathleen Doyle
    Time: One week in 1998. Setting: A Baltimore hospital room. Presented in two parts.

Huntington Theatre Company, Boston
Nicholas Martin artistic director

SONIA FLEW. By Melinda Lopez. October 13, 2004 (world premiere). Direction, Nicholas Martin; scenery, Adam Stockhausen; costumes, Kristin Glans; lighting, Frances Aronson; sound, Drew Levy; production stage management, David H. Lurie.

Sonia; Marta .... Carmen Roman   Jen; Young Sonia .... Amelia Alvarez
Daniel; Tito .... Jeremiah Kissel   Sam; Orfeo .... Will LeBow
Zak; José .... Ivan Quintanilla   Nina; Pilar .... Zabryna Guevara
    Time: 2001; 1961. Place: Minneapolis; Havana. Presented in two parts.

THE RIVALS. By Richard Brinsley Sheridan. January 15, 2005. Direction, Nicholas Martin; scenery, Alexander Dodge; costumes, Michael Krass; lighting, Dennis Parichy; sound, Jerry Yager; production stage management, Stephen M. Kaus.

Fag .... Dennis Staroselsky   Jack Absolute .... Scott Ferrara
Thomas .... Nathaniel McIntyre   Faulkand .... Gareth Saxe
Lydia Languish .... Cheryl Lynn Bowers   Bob Acres .... Brian Hutchison
Lucy .... Helen McElwain   Errand Boy .... Edward Tournier
Julia Melville .... Mia Barron   Sir Lucius O'Trigger .... Rod McLachlan
Mrs. Malaprop .... Mary Louise Wilson   David .... Eric Anderson
Sir Anthony Absolute .... Will LeBow
    Ensemble: Bill Barclay, Daniel Berger-Jones, Jessica Grant, Murisa Harba, Patrick Lynch, Max Rosenak.
    Presented in two parts.

Williamstown Theatre Festival
Roger Rees artistic director, Deborah Fehr managing director

THE WATER'S EDGE. By Theresa Rebeck. July 1, 2004 (world premiere). Direction, Will Frears; scenery, Thomas Lynch; costumes, Junghyun Georgia Lee; lighting, Frances Aronson; sound, David Wallingford; stage management, Matthew Silver.

Helen .... Kate Burton   Erica .... Gretchen Cleevely
Richard .... Michael Gaston   Lucy .... Fiona Gallagher
Nate .... Austin Lysy
    Presented in two parts.

Williamstown Theatre Festival New Play Readings. July 2–August 6, 2004.
PASS YOU BY. By Liz Flahive. Direction, Evan Cabnet.
EPITAPH. By Ethan Sandler and Adrian Wenner. Direction, Betsy Thomas.
RESURRECTION BLUES. By Arthur Miller. Direction, Will Pomerantz.
ARRANGEMENTS. By Ken Weitzman. Direction, Suzanne Agins.
JAMES AND ANNIE. By Warren Leight. Direction, Jack Hofsiss.
THIRD. By Wendy Wasserstein. Direction, Michael Bavakiva.

RODNEY'S WIFE. By Richard Nelson. July 15, 2004 (world premiere). Direction, Mr. Nelson; scenery and costumes, Susan Hilferty; lighting, David Weiner; sound, Scott Lehrer; stage management, Leslie C. Lyter.

Rodney	David Strathairn	Lee	Susan May Pratt
Fay	Haviland Morris	Henry	John Rothman
Eva	Maryann Plunkett	Ted	Thomas Sadoski

Time: 1962. Place: The kitchen and living room of a small villa on the outskirts of Rome.

Presented without intermission.

R SHOMON. Musical by Michael John LaChiusa; adapted from the stories of Ryunosuke Akutagawa; translated by Takashi Kojima. July 29, 2004 (world premiere). Direction, Ted Sperling; choreography, Jonathan Butterell; scenery, Thomas Lynch; costumes, Susan Hilferty; lighting, Christopher Akerlind; sound, Acme Sound Partners; music direction, Brad Haak; stage management, Barclay Stiff.

Kesa; others	Audra McDonald	Husband; CPA	Tom Wopat
Janitor; Priest	Henry Stram	Medium; Aunt	Mary Testa
Morito; others	Michael C. Hall		

R shomon musical numbers included: "Kesa," "The Janitor's Statement, " "The Thief's Statement," "She Looked at Me," "See What I Wanna See," "Big Money," "You'll Go Away With Me," "Best Not to Get Involved," "The Wife's Statement," "Louie," "The Medium's Statement," "The Husband's Statement," "No More," "Simple," "Light in the East," "Morito."

Time: 1951. Place: A police interrogation room and a clearing in Central Park, New York.

Gloryday musical numbers included: "Last Year," "The Greatest Practical Joke," "First Message," "Central Park," "Second Message," "Coffee," "Gloryday," "Curiosity," "Prayer," "Third Message/ Feed the Lions," "There Will Be a Miracle," "Rising Up."

Time: The present or near future. Place: Central Park, New York.

DEDICATION OR THE STUFF OF DREAMS. By Terrence McNally. August 19, 2004 (world premiere). Direction, Scott Ellis; scenery, Anna Louizos; costumes, William Ivey Long; lighting, Kenneth Posner; sound, Eileen Tague; stage management, Matthew Silver.

Lou Nuncle	Boyd Gaines	Arnold Chalk	Larry Pine
Jessie	Debra Monk	Annabelle Willard	Marian Seldes
Ida Head	Kellie Overbey	Edward	R.E. Rodgers
Toby Cassidy	Darren Pettie		

Time: Now. Place: A theater. Presented in two parts.

MICHIGAN

Purple Rose Theatre, Chelsea

Guy Sanville artistic director, Jeff Daniels executive director

DUCK HUNTER SHOOTS ANGEL. By Mitch Albom. July 2, 2004 (world premiere). Direction, Guy Sanville; scenery, Steven Klein; costumes, Christianne Myers; lighting, Reid G. Johnson; sound, Quintessa Gallinat; fight direction, David Woolley; stage management, Michelle DiDomenico.

Phil	Randolph Fitzgerald	Duwell	Joseph Albright
Sandy	James Krag	Lenny	Wallace Bridges
The Voice	Grant R. Krause	Woman	Jenny McKnight
Lester	Ryan Carlson	Kansas	Molly Jessica Cloud
Duane	Wayne David Parker		

NORMA AND WANDA. By Jeff Daniels. January 28, 2005 (world premiere). Direction, Guy Sanville; scenery, Daniel C. Walker; costumes, Christianne Myers; lighting, Dana White; sound, Quintessa Gallinat; fight direction, David Woolley; stage management, Amy Hickman.

Norma Randolph .... Michelle Mountain   Paulie Perkins .... Grant R. Krause
Wanda Dembrowski .... Sandra Birch   Mel Randolph .... Jim Porterfield
Mary Sue Thornberry .... Terry Heck   A Local Man .... Chris Korte

MINNESOTA

The Guthrie Theater, Minneapolis
Joe Dowling artistic director, Thomas C. Proehl managing director

4:48 PSYCHOSIS. By Sarah Kane. October 14, 2004. Direction, James Macdonald; scenery, Jeremy Herbert; costumes, Iona Kenrick; lighting, Heidi Riley; sound, Paul Arditti. Presented in association with David Eden Productions, Baryshnikov Dance Foundation, the Royal Court Theatre and the Playwrights' Center.
    Performed by Jason Hughes, Marin Ireland, Jo McInnes.

Beautiful dreamer: Marian Seldes in Terrence McNally's Dedication or the Stuff of Dreams *at Williamstown Theatre Festival. Photo: Richard Feldman*

THE SEX HABITS OF AMERICAN WOMEN. By Julie Marie Myatt. November 3, 2004. Direction, Michael Bigelow Dixon; scenery, Victor A. Becker; costumes, Marcia Dixcy Jory; lighting, Matthew Reinert; sound, Paul A. Estby; dramaturgy, Amy Wegener; stage management, Michaella K. McCoy.

1950		2004	
Agnes Tittels	Tana Hicken	Joy	Sally Wingert
Dr. Fritz Tittels	Richard Ooms	Dan	Ron Menzel
Daisy Tittels	Charity Jones	Katie	Hadija Steen-Omari
Ruby Lawrence	Melissa Anne Murphy		
Edgar Green	Kris L. Nelson		
Waiter	Jason Clusman		

Time: 1950; 2004. Place: New York City; Joy's house. Presented in two parts.

OEDIPUS. By Ellen McLaughlin; based on Sophocles's *Oedipus Rex*. January 21, 2005. Direction, Lisa Peterson; scenery, Riccardo Hernández; costumes, David Zinn; lighting, Christopher Akerlind; sound, Scott W. Edwards; dramaturgy, Carla Steen; stage management, Chris A. Code.

Oedipus	Peter Macon	Messenger	Tom Bloom
Creon	Stephen Yoakam	Shepherd	Richard S. Iglewski
Tiresias	Sandra Shipley	Boy	Dylan Frederick; Ryan McCartan
Jocasta	Isabell Monk O'Connor		

Chorus of Citizens: Barbara Bryne, Benny S. Cannon, Wayne A. Evenson, Emil Herrera, Richard Ooms, Regina Marie Williams.

Presented without intermission.

Penumbra Theatre Company, St. Paul
Lou Bellamy artistic director, Stewart Widdess managing director

SLIPPERY WHEN WET. By S.H. Murakoshi. February 4, 2005. Direction, Ching Valdes-Aran; scenery, Ms. Valdes-Aran and Jason Allyn-Schwerin; costumes, Sheryl Paulson-Price; lighting, Mark Dougherty; production stage management, Ronald Alois Schultz.

Helen	Katrina Toshiko	Musician	Marc Anderson
Rakim	DeSean Terry		

Time: A place in time. Presented without intermission.

MISSOURI

Kansas City Repertory Theatre
Peter Altman producing artistic director

I HAVE BEFORE ME A REMARKABLE DOCUMENT GIVEN TO ME BY A YOUNG LADY FROM RWANDA. By Sonja Linden. April 2, 2005. Direction, Michael Bloom; scenery, Michael B. Raiford; costumes, Whitney Locher; lighting, Victor En Yu Tan; sound, Lindsay Jones; production stage management, Lori Lundquist.

Juliette	Kenya Brome	Simon	Paul DeBoy

NEW JERSEY

Centenary Stage Company, Hackettstown
Carl Wallnau producing director, Catherine Rust associate producer

SISTER WEEK. By Heather McCutchen. February 25, 2005 (world premiere). Direction, Margo Whitcomb; scenery, Will Rothfuss; costumes, Julia Sharp; lighting, Ed Matthews; stage management, Rafi Levavy.

Sally	Carolyn Popp	June	Becky Engborg
Mary Martha	Betty Hudson	Kitty	MaryEthel Schmidt
May	Maria Brodeur	Jay Jay	Jack Moran

Time: Present. Place: Sally and Jay's old house in Macon, Georgia.

Women Playwrights Series. April 13–27, 2005
THE POETRY OF PIZZA. By Deborah Brevoort.
OTMA. By Kate Moira Ryan.
LITTLE OLD LADY. By Darrah Cloud.

George Street Playhouse, New Brunswick
David Saint artistic director, Mitchell Krieger managing director

HALLELUJAH, BABY! Musical with book by Arthur Laurents; music by Jule Styne; lyrics by Betty Comden and Adolph Green; additional lyrics, Amanda Green. October 8, 2004. Direction, Mr. Laurents; choreography, Hope Clarke; scenery and projections, Jerome Sirlin; costumes, Theoni V. Aldredge; lighting, David Lander; sound, Shannon Slaton; music direction, David Alan Bunn, production stage management, Thomas Clewell. Presented in association with Arena Stage, Washington, D.C.

Georgina	Suzzanne Douglas	Harvey	Stephen Zinnato
Tip	Randy Donaldson	Mary; others	Laurie Gamache
Tap	Gerry McIntyre	Hutchinson; others	Todd Cerveris
Momma	Ann Duquesnay	Chloe; Maid	Crystal Noelle
Clem	Curtiss I'Cook		

Musical numbers included : "Hallelujah, Baby!," "Back in the Kitchen," "My Own Morning," "When the Weather's Better," "Feet, Do Yo Stuff," "You're Welcome," "Smile, Smile," "Double, Double," "Same Boat," "Being Good," "Talking to Yourself," "Not Mine," "I Don't Know Where She Got It," "Now's the Time."

Presented in two parts.

CELADINE. By Charles Evered. November 19, 2004 (world premiere). Direction, David Saint; scenery, Michael Anania; costumes, David Murin; lighting, Joe Saint; sound, Christopher J. Bailey; production stage management, Mona El-Khatib.

Mary	Leslie Lyles	Jeffrey	Bob Eigenbrod
Elliot	Matt Pepper	Rowley	Michael Countryman
Celadine	Amy Irving		

Time: 1670's. Place: Teale Coffee House, London. Presented in two parts.

ADDRESS UNKNOWN. By Kathrine Kressman Taylor. March 18, 2005. Direction, Frank Dunlop; scenery, James Youmans; costumes, Jim Stewart; lighting, Scott Davis; sound, Christopher J. Bailey; production stage management, Christine Catti.

Max Eisenstein .... Sam Freed   Martin Schulse .... Mark La Mura
Time: November 1932–March 1934. Place: Office of a San Francisco art gallery; a country mansion near Munich, Germany. Presented without intermission.

McCarter Theatre, Princeton
Emily Mann artistic director, Jeffrey Woodward managing director

LAST OF THE BOYS. By Steven Dietz. September 26, 2004 (world premiere). Direction, Emily Mann; scenery, Eugene Lee; costumes, David Murin; lighting, Jeff Croiter; sound, Rob Milburn and Michael Bodeen; dramaturgy, Janice Paran; production stage management, Cheryl Mintz.

Jeeter .... Tom Wopat   Young Soldier .... Steven Boyer
Ben .... Joseph Siravo   Lorraine .... Deborah Hedwall
Salyer .... Jenny Bacon
Time: The present. Place: An abandoned trailer park somewhere in the Great Central Valley of California. Presented in two parts.

POLK COUNTY. By Zora Neale Hurston and Dorothy Waring; adapted by Kyle Donnelly and Cathy Madison; music by Chic Street Man. October 15, 2004. Direction, Ms. Donnelly; choreography, Dianne McIntyre; scenery, Thomas Lynch; costumes, Michael Krass; lighting, Allen Lee Hughes; sound, Karin Graybash; music direction, Mr. Man; production stage management, Alison Coe. Presented in association with Berkeley Repertory Theatre, California.

Quarters Boss .... Eric L. Abrams   Lonnie .... Kevin Jackson
Few Clothes .... "Mississippi" Charles Bevel   Box Car .... Marc Damon Johnson
Sop-the-Bottom .... Carl Cofield   Do Dirty .... Michael Keck
My Honey .... Clinton Derricks-Carroll   Maudella .... Aliza Kennerly
Stew Beef .... Doug Eskew   Big Sweet .... Kecia Lewis
Dicey Long .... Perri Gaffney   Nunkie .... Rudy Roberson
Ella Wall .... Deidre Goodwin   Preacher .... Bill Sims Jr.
Laura B .... Gabrielle Goyette   Leafy Lee .... Tiffany Thompson
Bunch .... Lynda Gravátt
Time: 1930s. Place: A lumber camp in Polk County, Florida. Presented in two parts.

Readings. October 28, 2004–February 10, 2005.

ANTIGONE. By Sophocles; adapted by Emily Mann. October 28, 2004. Direction, Daniel Fish.
Performed by Jenny Bacon, David Chandler, Beth Dixon, Jason Butler Harner, Daphne Rubin-Vega, Michael Rudko, John Seitz, Haynes Thigpen.

THE BELLS. By Theresa Rebeck. November 1, 2004. Direction, Emily Mann.
Performed by Jeffrey DeMunn, Fiona Gallagher, Marin Ireland, Christopher Innvar, Hoon Lee, Michael McCarty, John Douglas Thompson.

RIDICULOUS FRAUD. By Beth Henley. December 1, 2004. Direction, Lisa Peterson.
Performed by Michael Countryman, Jeffrey DeMunn, Barbara Garrick, Heather Goldenhersh, Daniel London, Reg Rogers, Ali Marsh Weller, Frederick Weller.

LIVING ROOM IN AFRICA. By Bathsheba Doran. December 6, 2004. Direction, Emily Mann.
Performed by Guy Boyd; Brienin Bryant, Jason Butler Harner, Marin Ireland, Charles Parnell, Jeremy Webb.

MISS WITHERSPOON. By Christopher Durang. February 7, 2005. Direction, Emily Mann.
Performed by Caroline Stefanie Clay, Randy Danson, Mahira Kakkar, Jeremy Shamos, Anne O'Sullivan.

THE PEOPLE NEXT DOOR. By Henry Adam. February 10, 2005.
Performed by Airrion Doss, Marylouise Burke, Anthony Ruivivar, Lee Sellers.

THE BELLS. By Theresa Rebeck. March 25, 2005 (world premiere). Direction, Emily Mann; scenery, Eugene Lee; costumes, Jennifer von Mayrhauser; lighting, Frances Aronson; sound, Darron L. West.

Xiu Fie	Pun Bandhu	Annette	Marin Ireland
Jim	Paul Butler	Mathias	Ted Marcoux
Sally	Fiona Gallagher	Charlie	Michael McCarty
Baptiste	Christopher Innvar		

Paper Mill Playhouse, Millburn
Michael Gennaro president, Diane Claussen managing director

HAROLD AND MAUDE. Musical with book and lyrics by Tom Jones; music by Joseph Thalken; based on the film by Colin Higgins. January 9, 2005 (world premiere). Direction and choreography, Mark S. Hoebee; scenery, Rob Odorisio; costumes, Miguel Angel Huidor; lighting, Paul Szczepanski; sound, Randy Hansen; music direction, David Loud; production stage management, Gail P. Luna. Presented in association with James Cass Rogers and Edward and Mildred Lewis.

Maude	Estelle Parsons	Priest; Dr. Sigmoid; others	Danny Burstein
Harold	Eric Millegan	Maria; others	Donna Lynne Champlin
Mrs. Chasen	Donna English		

Musical numbers included: "Harold's Theme," "Self, Self, Self," "Woe," "The Cosmic Dance," "Where Do You Go?," "Flush It Out!," "The Road Less Traveled," "Two Sides of a River," "Quartet," "The Real Thing," "Maude's Waltz," "Song in My Pocket," "Montezuma," "Calm," "Harold and Maude," "The Chance to Sing."

Time: Before the end of the last millennium. Place: Suburban America.

Shakespeare Theatre of New Jersey, Madison
Bonnie J. Monte artistic director, Stephen Klein managing director

A VERY OLD MAN WITH ENORMOUS WINGS. By Nilo Cruz; adapted from the short story by Gabriel García Márquez. June 26, 2004. Direction, Bonnie J. Monte; scenery, Carrie Mossman; costumes, Regina García; lighting, Steven Rosen; sound, Steven L. Beckel; music direction, Kris Kukul; dramaturgy, Kerri Allen; production stage management, Lisa Jean Lewis.

Old Man	Gregory Mitchell	Juan Jose; Agracelio	Jaime Román Tirelli
Pelayo	Mark Elliot Wilson	Crying Woman; Worker #1	Selenis Leyva
Fefé	Danielle Larracuente	Showman; Mountain Man	Alfredo Narciso
Momó	Robin De Jesús	Spider Woman; Worker #2	Jessica Pimentel
Elisanda	Saundra Santiago	Girl With a Box of Prayers	Magaly Roig
Man With Panama Hat;		Selim Al Din	Michael Earle
Don Galante	Emilio Delgado	Worker #3; Townsperson	Mary Floyd
Justina; Bonafacia	Yolande Bavan	Townsperson	Drew Valins

Time: Back in the time that got lost in a hundred years. Place: A small town close to the Caribbean Sea. Presented without intermission.

ILLYRIA. Musical with book, music and lyrics by Peter Mills; adapted by Mr. Mills and Cara Reichel from William Shakespeare's *Twelfth Night*. December 4, 2004. Direction, Paul Mullins; choreography, Becky Timms; scenery, Michael Schweikardt; costumes,

Kim Gill; lighting, Shelly Sabel; music direction, F. Wade Russo, production stage management, Brenda J. Lillie.

Feste .... Joel Blum
Duke Orsina .... Steve Wilson
Lady Olivia .... Maria Couch
Toby Belch .... T. Doyle Leverett
Malvolio .... Ames Adamson
Viola .... Elena Shaddow
Maria .... Kristie Dale Sanders

Sebastian .... Chris Peluso
Andrew Aguecheek .... Benjamin Eakeley
Antonio .... Darren Matthias
Orsino's servants .... Howard Emanuel,
Peter Maris
Olivia's servants .... Susanne Houston,
Justine Williams

Musical numbers included: "The Shipwreck," "Any in Illyria," "How These Things Start," "Silly Little Syllogisms," "Olivia," "Cakes and Ale," "Patience," "The Man Is Mine," "We Men," "The Love Letter," "Undone," "Save One," "Malvolio's Tango," "Whoever You Are," "The Duel," "The Lunatic," "The Lady Must Be Mad," "Second Act Finale."

NORTH CAROLINA

Reynolds Theater, Durham
Zannie Giraud Voss producing director

LITTLE WOMEN. Musical with book by Allan Knee; music by Jason Howland; lyrics by Mindi Dickstein; based on the novel *Little Women* by Louisa May Alcott. October 15, 2004 (world premiere). Direction, Susan H. Schulman; choreography, Michael Lichtefeld; scenery, Derek McLane; costumes, Catherine Zuber; sound, Peter Hylenski; music direction, Andrew Wilder. Presented in association with Randall L. Wreghitt, Dani Davis, Ken Gentry, Chase Mishkin, Ruben Brache, Lisa Vioni.

Jo .... Sutton Foster
Professor Bhaer .... John Hickok
Amy .... Amy McAlexander
Meg .... Jenny Powers
Beth .... Megan McGinnis

Marmee .... Maureen McGovern
Mr. Laurence .... Robert Stattel
Laurie .... Danny Gurwin
Aunt March; Mrs. Kirk .... Janet Carroll
John Brooke .... Jim Weitzer

Musical numbers included: "An Operatic Tragedy (Parts One and Two)," "Better," "Here Alone," "Could You?," "I'd Be Delighted," "Take a Chance on Me," "Beyond This Tiny Room," "Off to Massachusetts," "I'll Love You Anyway," "More Than I Am," "Astonishing," "The Weekly Volcano Press," "How I Am," "Some Things Are Meant to Be," "The Most Amazing Thing," "Days of Plenty," "The Fire Within Me," "Small Umbrella in the Rain."

Time: 1863; 1865; 1866. Place: Concord, Massachusetts and New York City.

ON THE MARCH TO THE SEA. By Gore Vidal. February 25, 2005. Direction, Warner Shook; production stage management, Matthew Farrell.

Stage Directions .... Kenneth Strong
Mrs. Blair .... Michael Learned
Minna Hinks .... Isabel Keating
Mr. John Hinks .... Harris Yulin
Colonel Sutcliffe .... Charles Durning
Amelia Blair .... Cheryl Chamblee

Aaron Hinks .... David Turner
Mr. Grayson .... Richard Easton
Grayson Hinks .... Corey Brill
Union Capt.; Union Sgt. .... John Feltch
Colonel Thayer .... Chris Noth

Time: October 1863; November 1864. Place: John Hinks's house, Waynesville, Georgia.

OHIO

Cincinnati Playhouse in the Park

Edward Stern producing artistic director, Buzz Ward executive director

LEAP. By John Yearley. February 17, 2005 (world premiere). Direction, Melia Bensussen; scenery, Judy Gailen; costumes, Claudia Stephens; lighting, Jeff Croiter; sound, David Remedios; stage management, Suann Pollock.

Man	Greg McFadden	Martin	Edmond Genest
Natalie; Wendy	Annie Meisels	Luther	Jeff Skowron
Grace	Jeanine Serralles	Jude	Anthony Marble

Time: September 11–12, 2001. Place: New York City and Long Island. Presented in two parts.

Cleveland Play House

Michael Bloom artistic director, Dean R. Gladden managing director,
Seth Gordon director of new play development

LEADING LADIES. By Ken Ludwig. September 10, 2004 (world premiere). Direction, Mr. Ludwig; choreography, Michael Tapley; scenery, Neil Patel; costumes, Judith Dolan; lighting, David Weiner; sound, John Gromada; stage management, Terry Cranshaw. Presented in association with Alley Theatre, Houston, Texas.

Leo	Brent Barrett	Duncan	Mark Jacoby
Jack	Christopher Duva	Florence	Jane Connell
Meg	Erin Dilly	Doc	Dan Lauria
Audrey	Lacey Kohl	Butch	Tim McGeever

Time: 1995. Place: Shrewsbury, Pennsylvania. Presented in two parts.

The Next Stage Festival of New Plays. October 29–November 20 2004.

PAPER ARMOR. By Eisa Davis. October 29, 2004. Direction, Leah C. Gardiner.

Performed by Donna Duplantier, Margaret Ford-Taylor, Seth Gilliam, Lisa Renee Pitts, Lelund Durond Thompson.

ENEMIES: A LOVE STORY. October 30, 2004. By Sarah Schulman; adapted from the novel by Isaac Bashevis Singer. Direction, Seth Gordon.

Performed by Mia Barron, David Greenspan, Joel Hammer, Bruce MacVittie, Joshua John McKay, Dorothy Silver, Sara Surrey, Colleen Werthmann.

SEX, DEATH AND THE BEACH BABY. November 6, 2004. By Kim Merrill. Direction, Maria Mileaf.

Performed by Rob Campbell, Shelley Delaney, Samuel Holloway, Polly Lee, Casey Spindler, Jack Willis.

WOMEN IN FLAMES. By Tina Howe. November 7, 2004. Direction, Mark Nelson.

Performed by Liza Colón-Zayas, Elizabeth A. Davis, Linda Gehringer, Paul Hecht, Kimberly King, Steve McCue, Jason Michael Miller, Christopher Mowod.

THICKER THAN WATER. By Eleanor Reissa. November 12, 2004. Direction, Paul Moser.

Performed by Liza Colón-Zayas, Tim Jerome, RaSheryl McCreary, Marc Moritz, Reuben Silver, Bailey Varness.

ONE WEEK TO LIVE. By Eric Coble. November 13, 2004. Direction, Seth Gordon.

Performed by Catherine Albers, Elizabeth A. Davis, Nicole Hedges, Samuel Holloway, Todd S. Krispinsky, Jason Michael Miller, Elizabeth A. Townsend.

PECAN TAN. By Tanya Barfield. November 19, 2004. Direction, Kate Whoriskey.
Performed by Daniel Breaker, Sterling K. Brown, Elizabeth A. Davis, Margaret Ford-Taylor, Tracie Thomas, Bailey Varness.

SWANN. By Sandra Perlman. November 20, 2004. Direction, Mark Alan Gordon.
Performed by Beth Dixon, Joel Hammer, Nicole Hedges, Joshua John McKay, Lelund Durond Thompson.

RESTORING THE SUN. By Joe Sutton. March 22, 2005 (world premiere). Direction, Connie Grappo; scenery, James Youmans; costumes, Michael Krass; lighting, Jack Mehler; sound designer, James C. Swonger; stage management, Corrie E. Purdum.

Parker Stevens........................... Joseph Adams
Arthur Dewindt .... Stephen Bradbury
Len Spitzer .... Daniel Cantor
Laura Scott .... Keira Naughton
Otto Boltzmann........................ Geddeth Smith

Presented in two parts.

OREGON

Oregon Shakespeare Festival, Ashland
Libby Appel artistic director, Paul Nicholson executive director

HENRY VI, PARTS TWO AND THREE: HENRY AND MARGARET. By William Shakespeare; adapted by Scott Kaiser. June 19, 2004. Directors, Libby Appel and Mr. Kaiser; scenery, William Bloodgood; costumes, Deborah M. Dryden; lighting, Robert Peterson; fight direction, John Sipes; dramaturgy, Barry Kraft; stage management, Susan L. McMillan.

The House of Lancaster (The Red Rose)
King Henry VI ....Cristofer Jean
Queen Margaret .... Robin Goodrin Nordli
Edw., Prince of Wales ......Juan Rivera LeBron

The King's Uncles
Cardinal Beaufort .... Richard Farrell
Humphrey .... Mark Murphey
Eleanor .... Demetra Pittman
Earl of Suffolk .... Jeff Cummings
Duke of Somerset .... Christopher DuVal
Duke of Buckingham .... Robert Sicular
Old Clifford .... Brad Whitmore
Young Clifford .... Mirron E. Willis
Earl of Northumberland .... Robert Sicular

The House of York (The White Rose)
Duke of York ....William Langan

Sons of York (as children)
Edward .... Miles Nerenberg
George .... Ian Greenberg
Richard .... Kyle Barnes

Sons of York
Edward, later Edward IV .... Ray Porter
George .... Gregory Linington
Richard .... James Newcomb
Rutland .... Kyle Barnes
Earl of Salisbury .... Clive Rosengren
Earl of Warwick .... Armando Durán
Lady Grey .... Tyler Layton
Tutor to Rutland...................... Richard Farrell

Other English
John Hume ....Brad Whitmore
Margery Jourdain .... Sarah Rutan
Nurse ....Charisse Loriaux
Father ....Clive Rosengren
A son .... Christopher DuVal
Humfrey .... Mirron E. Willis

The French
King Louis XI ....Mark Murphey
Lady Bona ....Charisse Loriaux

Ensemble: Matthew Brown, Jeff Davis, Kyle Haden, Juan Rivera LeBron, Charisse Loriaux, Matt McTighe, Clive Rosengren, Sarah Rutan, Brad Whitmore, Mirron E. Willis.
Presented in two parts.

OEDIPUS COMPLEX. By Frank Galati; based on Sophocles's *Oedipus Rex* and the life and writing of Sigmund Freud. July 31, 2004 (world premiere). Direction, Mr. Galati;

scenery, James Schuette; costumes, Mara Blumenfeld; lighting, Michael R. Chybowski; sound, Todd Barton; fight direction, John Sipes; dramaturgy, Douglas Langworthy; stage management, Gwen Turos.

Sigmund Freud; Teiresias .... William Langan	Corinthian; Ensemble .... Kenneth Albers
Wilhelm Fliess; Chorus ..... Gregory Linington	Shepherd; Ensemble .... Michael J. Hume
Oedipus .... Jonathan Haugen	Nurses; Ensemble .... Dee Maaske,
Amalia Freud; Jocasta ...... Judith-Marie Bergan	Linda K. Morris
Creon; Ensemble .... Armando Durán	

Children of Jocasta and Oedipus: Alexander Barnes, Kyle Barnes, Natasha Barnes, Alicia Rendall. Chorus and Ensemble: Dane Bowman, Leith Burke, Jeff Cummings, Richard Farrell, Robert Vincent Frank, Nell Geisslinger, Cristofer Jean, John Tufts, Brad Whitmore.

Presented without intermission.

BY THE WATER OF BABYLON. By Robert Schenkkan. February 27, 2005 (world premiere). Direction, Bill Rauch; choreography, Janis Rosenthal; scenery, Michael Ganio; costumes, Denise Damico; lighting, James F. Ingalls; sound, Jeremy J. Lee; fight direction, John Sipes; dramaturgy, Lue Morgan Douthit; stage management, Jeremy Eisen.

Catherine .... Catherine E. Coulson	Arturo .... Armando Durán

Presented in two parts.

NAPOLI MILIONARIA! By Eduardo De Filippo; translated by Linda Alper and Beatrice Basso. April 23, 2005. Direction, Libby Appel, scenery, Michael Dempsey; costumes, Robert Morgan; lighting, Robert Peterson; music, Irwin Appel; dramaturgy, Ms. Basso; fight direction, John Sipes; stage management, Jeremy Eisen.

Gennaro .... Richard Elmore	Miezo Prevete .... Brad Whitmore
Amalia .... Linda Alper	Pascalino;Doctor .... John Pribyl
Amedeo .... Juan Rivera LeBron	Ciappa .... Tony DeBruno
Maria Rosaria .... Heather Robison	Federico .... Jason McBeath
Errico Settebellezze .... Armando Durán	Donna Peppenella .... Catherine E. Coulson
Peppe the Jack .... Shad Willingham	Margherita .... Laura Morache
Ricardo Spasiano .... Richard Howard	Teresa .... Sarah Rutan
Adelaide .... Judith-Marie Bergan	Wine Mine; Guard .... Matt McTighe
Assunta .... Terri McMahon	

Time: World War II. Place: Naples, Italy. Presented in two parts.

PENNSYLVANIA

City Theatre, Pittsburgh
Tracy Brigden, artistic director

OUTLYING ISLANDS. By David Greig. October 13, 2004. Direction, Tracy Brigden; scenery, Tony Ferrieri; lighting, Rand Ryan; costumes, Michael McAleer; sound, Elizabeth Atkinson.

Robert .... Lea Coco	Kirk .... Peter Haig
John .... Michael McMillian	Ellen .... Robin Abramson

Philadelphia Theatre Company
Sara Garonzik producing artistic director, Ada Coppock general manager

TRUMBO: RED, WHITE AND BLACKLISTED. By Christopher Trumbo. October 13, 2004. Direction, Peter Askin; scenery, Loy Arenas; costumes, Janus Stefanowicz; lighting, Jeff Croiter; sound, John Gromada; stage management, Rachel R. Bush.

Dalton Trumbo .... Bill Irwin   Christopher Trumbo .... William Zielinski
    Presented without intermission.

Stages: Festival of New Plays. October 25–November 8, 2004.

LOST HERO. By Peter Mattaliano. Direction, Robert Hedley.
    Performed by Michael Friel, Joe Guzman, John Lumia, Tom McCarthy, Christy Parker, Buck Schirner, Steven Smith, John Zak.

DONNA MORELLI. By Gina Barnett. Direction, Mary B. Robinson.
    Performed by Nick Cregor, Nicole D'Amico, Dylan Dawson, David Ingram, Wi-Moto Nyoka.

SALLY'S PORCH. By Russell Davis. Direction, Paul Meshejian.
    Performed by Tobias Segal, David Strathairn, Janet Zarish.

Pittsburgh Public Theater
Ted Pappas artistic director

Public Exposure: New Play Reading Series. October 18, 2004–February 7, 2005

SAFE HOUSE. By Lydia Stryk. Direction, Ted Pappas.
    Performed by Ms. Stryk, Deirdre Madigan, Doug Mertz, Helena Ruoti.

NEXT YEAR IN MANHATTAN. By Ellen Melaver. Direction, Kyle W. Brenton.
    Performed by Ms. Melaver, Jarrod Fry, Dan Krell, Rebecca Harris, Ingrid Sonnichsen.

THE ICE BREAKER. By David Rambo. Direction, Ted Pappas.
    Performed by Mr. Rambo, Tom Atkins, Elena Passarello.

HAND, FOOT, ARM AND FACE. By Mat Smart. Direction, Kyle W. Brenton.
    Performed by Mr. Smart, Everett Bradley, Tressa Glover, Ethan Hova, Amy Landis, Q. Smith.

INCUBUS. By James Hindman. Direction, Ted Pappas.
    Performed by Mr. Hindman, Melanie Julian, Dan Krell, Deirdre Madigan, Michael McKenzie, Drew Weinstein.

THE WHIM OF EVENTS. By Eric Burns. Direction, Kyle W. Brenton.
    Performed by Mr. Burns, Jeffrey Howell, Larry John Meyers, Chance Muehleck, Sam Nicotero, Mary Rawson.

CALLING APHRODITE. By Velina Hasu Houston. Direction, Pamela Berlin.
    Performed by Ms. Houston, Carla Bianco, Martin Rayner, Julyana Soelistyo, Eunice Wong.

THE BIRD SANCTUARY. By Frank McGuinness. April 22, 2005. Direction, Kent Paul; scenery, Michael Schweikardt; costumes, Nanzi Adzima; lighting, Phil Monat; sound, Zach Moore; dramaturgy, Kyle W. Brenton, production stage management, Fred Noel.

Eleanor .... Elizabeth Franz   Tina .... Diane Ciesla
Marianne .... Hayley Mills   Stephen .... David Turner
Robert .... Martin Rayner

Prince Music Theater, Philadelphia
Marjorie Samoff producing artistic director

GEMINI: THE MUSICAL. Musical with book by Albert Innaurato; music by Charles Gilbert; lyrics by Messrs. Innaurato and Gilbert. October 16, 2004 (world premiere). Direction, Douglas C. Wager; choreography, Nancy Berman Kantra; scenery, Tobin Ost; costumes, André D. Harrington; lighting, Troy Martin O'Shia; sound, Nick Kourtides, music direction, Eric Ebbenga; production stage management, Scott P. McNulty.

Francis .... Barry James   Fran .... Robert Picardo

Maria	Anne DeSalvo	Randy	Jeremiah B. Downes
Bunny	Linda Hart	Herschel	Todd Buonopane
Judith	Jillian Louis	Lucille	Anne De Salvo

Musical numbers included : "Lo Cantero Per Te," "Avanti!," "Happy Birthday, Francis," "The Hunk Who's Got the Funk," "The Boy I Thought I Knew," "Time for an Aria (Intermezzo)," "Welcome to My Life," "Women, Wonderful Women," "Trolley," "Strut, Bunny, Strut," "Concrete," "Francis's Nightmare," "Not Your Typical Fairy Tale," "I'm Gonna Jump," "Someday You'll Turn Into Me," "Tu Padre E Per Sempre," "It's Been A Long, Long Time," "Let's Find Out," "Judith's Mad Scene," "Here's to You," "Francis, My Son," "Francis's Final Moments," "Finale Ultimo."

Time: June 1973. Place: The Geminiani and Weinberger backyard, South Philadelphia.

CHASING NICOLETTE. Musical with book and lyrics by Peter Kellogg; music by David Friedman; based on the fable "Aucassin and Nicolette." December 11, 2004 (world premiere). Direction, Ethan McSweeny; choreography, Karma Camp; scenery, Neil Patel; costumes, Constance Hoffman; lighting, Howell Binkley; sound, Nick Kourtides; music direction, Robert K. Mikulski; fight direction, Rick Sordelet; production stage management, Lori Aghazarian.

Mostansir; King of Carthage	Kingsley Leggs	Lord Montescue	Dale Radunz
Nicolette	Jasika Nicole Pruitt	Valere	Bronson Pinchot
Nemur	Kevin R. Free	Count de Valence	Richard White
Count de Beauclaire	Bill Buell	Gwendolyn	Rebecca Bellingham
Aucassin	Davis Duffield	Mother Superior	Mary Martello

Servants, Monks and Nuns: Shauntee Blow, Susan Fowler, David Alan Heayn, Melissa Kolcynski, J.J. Orgera, Valerie June Shaffer, Jay Wahl.

Musical numbers included: "Modern Times," "Nicolette," "Now and Forever," "You Have to Lie," "I'm Not Upset," "Nothing in Common," "Agnus Dei," "Romance," Sword Against Sword," "I Was Raised in a Convent," "You're Always on My Mind," "Do What You Will," "Sing to Her," "There Once Was a Man," "Stranger and Stranger," "Do Nothing," "If You Were in Love."

Time: 1224. Place: Provence; Carthage.

Wilma Theater, Philadelphia

Blanka Zizka and Jiri Zizka artistic directors, Lynn Landis managing director

RAW BOYS. By Dael Orlandersmith. March 12, 2005. Direction, Blanka Zizka; scenery, Klara Zieglerova; costumes, Anita Yavich; lighting, Russell H. Champa; sound, Elliot Sharp; fight direction, J. Alex Cordaro; production stage management, Patreshettarlini Adams.

Billy	Jamie Harris	William	James Gale
Shane	John Keating	Neruda	Mateo Gomez
Rose	Nancy Boykin	Altagracia	January LaVoy

TEXAS

Dallas Theater Center

Richard Hamburger artistic director, Mark Hadley managing director

BAD DATES. By Theresa Rebeck. January 5, 2005. Direction, John Benjamin Hickey; scenery, Derek McLane; costumes, Mattie Ullrich; lighting, Frances Aronson; sound, Bruce Ellman, stage management, David H. Lurie.

Haley Walker .... Julie White
Time: The present. Place: New York City. Presented without intermission.

THE VIOLET HOUR. By Richard Greenberg. February 23, 2005. Direction, David Kennedy; scenery, Leiko Fuseya; costumes, Katherine Hampton Noland; lighting, Matthew Richards; sound, Bruce Richardson; stage management, Linda Harris.

John Pace Seavering	Matthew Floyd Miller	Rosamund Plinth	Jessica D. Turner
Denis McCleary	Chris Henry Coffey	Gidger	Matthew Boston
Jessie Brewster	Christen Simon		

Time: April 1919. Place: John Pace Seavering's office in a Manhattan Tower. Presented in two parts.

Kitchen Dog Theater, Dallas

Dan Day artistic director, Tina Parker adminstrative director

Staged Readings. June 2–June 27, 2004.

A LINE IN THE SAND. By Adina Taubman. June 2, 2004. Direction, Benjamin Lutz.

HAZARD COUNTY. By Allison Moore. June 6, 2004. Direction, Tina Parker.

JAPANESE DEATH POEM. By D.T. Arcieri. June 13, 2004. Direction, Stephen Tobolowsky.

TRANSFERENCE. By Wayne Peter Liebman. June 20, 2004. Direction, Jonathan Taylor.

THAT SLUT! By Toni Press-Coffman. June 23, 2004. Direction, Vicki Cheatwood.

WAIT! By Julie Jensen. June 27, 2004. Direction, Jonathan Taylor.

JESUS HOPPED THE "A" TRAIN. By Stephen Adly Guirgis. October 2, 2004. Direction, Dan Day; scenery, Jake Maudlin; costumes, Tina Parker; lighting, Russell Dyer; sound, Mr. Maudlin and Michael Turner.

Angel Cruz	Sean T. Perez	D' Amico	Aaron Roberts
Valdez	Christopher Carlos	Mary Jane Hanrahan	Karen Parrish
Lucius Jenkins	Michael Turner		

Time: The present. Place: Riker's Island, New York City. Presented in two parts.

CIRCUMFERENCE OF A SQUIRREL. By John Walch. November 19, 2004. Direction, Tina Parker; scenery, Mary Wynn Allen; lighting, Jeff Stover; sound, Jonathan Taylor; stage management, Ruth Stephenson.

Chester .... David Goodwin
Presented without intermission.

THE DEAD MONKEY. By Nick Darke. February 11, 2005. Direction, Aaron Ginsburg; scenery, Paul Eric Pape; costumes, Christina Vela; lighting, Russell Dyer; sound, John Flores and Mark Ridlen; fight direction, Bill Lengfelder; stage management, Ruth Stephenson.

Vet	Christopher Carlos	Hank	Wm. Paul Williams
Dolores	Tina Parker		

Presented without intermission.

Rude Mechanicals, Austin

Madge Darlington, Lana Lesley, Kirk Lynn, Sarah Richardson, Shawn Sides artistic directors

CHERRYWOOD. By Kirk Lynn. October 22, 2004 (world premiere). Direction, Shawn Sides; scenery, Leilah Stewart; costumes, Laura Cannon; lighting, Brian H. Scott; sound, Robert S. Fisher; production stage management, José Angel Hernández.

Performed by Mr. Fisher, Thomas Graves, Joey Hood, Jodi Jinks, Lana Lesley, Ellie McBride, Robert Pierson, Aron Taylor, Carlos Treviño.

StageWest, Fort Worth
Jerry Russell managing director, Jim Covault associate director

VOICE OF GOOD HOPE. By Kristine Thatcher. October 29, 2004. Direction, Jim Covault; scenery, Stage Works; sound, Dana Schultes; production stage management, Peggy Kruger-O'Brien.

Barbara Jordan	Natalie Wilson King	John Ed Patten	Tyrone King
Nancy Earl	Judy Keith	Robert Strauss	Matthew Stephen Tompkins
Karen Woodruff	Dana Schultes	Julie Dunn	Eleanor T. Threatt
Heart	Whitney Smith		

CHERRY DOCS. By David Gow. February 11, 2005. Direction, Jim Covault; scenery, Nelson Robinson; lighting, Michael O'Brien; sound, Adam Schwartz; production stage management, Peggy Kruger-O'Brien.

Danny	Paul Taylor	Mike	Justin Flowers

[SIC]. By Melissa James Gibson. May 26, 2005. Direction, Jerry Russell; scenery, Nelson Robinson; costumes, Jim Covault and Peggy Kruger-O'Brien; lighting, Michael O'Brien; sound, Amanda L. West.

Theo	David M. Dixon	Man; Delivery Person	Justin Flowers
Babette	Trisha Miller Smith	Woman; Mrs. Jorgenson	Amanda L. West
Frank	Jakie Cabe	Dr. Greenspan	Peggy Kruger-O'Brien

Time: Now-ish. Place: A prewar apartment building. Presented in two parts.

VIRGINIA

Signature Theatre, Arlington
Eric Schaeffer artistic director, Ronnie Gunderson producing director

ONE RED FLOWER. Musical with book and lyrics by Paris Barclay; adapted from *Dear America: Letters From Vietnam*, edited by Bernard Edelman. August 22, 2004 (world premiere). Direction, Eric Schaeffer; scenery, Eric Grims; costumes, Jenn Miller; lighting, Chris Lee; sound, Tony Angelini; music direction, Jon Kabfleisch; production stage management, Jess W. Speaker III. Presented in association with Dee Gee Theatricals and Barlove Productions.

Alan Chisholm	Kurt Boehm	Marion Johnson	Josh Lefkowitz
George McDuffy	Joshua Davis	"Spanky" Bridges	Stephen Gregory Smith
Rutherford	Clifton A. Duncan	Eleanor Bridges	Florence Lacey
Michael Sandberg	Charles Hagerty		

Musical numbers included: Prologue, "Free/Glossary," "Paper Soldier," "Mud and Blood and Water," "The Land of Make Believe," "All I Need Is You," "Time Heals," "If You Are Able," "I Don't Understand This War," "4:16 a.m," "Saigon Tea," "No More Good-Byes," "Lament (Mother)," "My Own Dream," "(There Will Still Be) Christmas," "Mrs. Rutherford (I Don't Understand This War)," "Debby," "One Red Flower," "The Kid Is Coming Home."

THE HIGHEST YELLOW. Musical with book by John Strand; music and lyrics by Michael John LaChiusa. November 7, 2004 (world premiere). Direction, Eric Schaeffer; scenery, Walt Spangler; costumes, Anne Kennedy; lighting, Daniel MacLean Wagner; sound, Tony Angelini; music direction, Jon Kabfleisch; production stage management, Ronnie Gunderson.

Dr. Felix Rey .... Jason Danieley
Vincent van Gogh .... Marc Kudisch
Rachel .... Judy Kuhn
Patient One .... Donna Migliaccio

Patient Two .... Stephen Gregory Smith
Patient Three .... R. Scott Thompson
Dr. Urpar .... Harry A. Winter

Musical numbers included: "Somewhere: Paris," "Such Sad, Lost Souls," "Doctor Rey's Patient #1," "The Highest Yellow," "Doctor Rey's Patient #2," "Have You Ever Loved?," "His Heart," "Doctor Rey's Patient #3," "To Make The Light, Lighter," "The Mistral Wind," "Intermezzo: The Madam's Song," "You," "Doctor Rey's Patient #4," "Dark and Light," "Rachel's Room," "Doctor Rey's Patient #5," "Portrait of Doctor Rey," "Rachel's Letter."

FALLEN FROM PROUST. By Norman Allen. January 16, 2005 (world premiere). Direction, Will Pomerantz; scenery, James Kronzer; costumes, Jenn Miller; lighting, Jason H. Thompson; sound, Brendon Vierra; production stage management, Jess W. Speaker III.
Performed by Damon Boggess, Daniel Firth, Michael Glenn, Hope Lambert.

WASHINGTON

ACT Theatre, Seattle
Kurt Beattie artistic director, Susan Trapnell managing director

ALKI. By Eric Overmyer; adapted from Henrik Ibsen's *Peer Gynt*. June 4, 2004. Direction, Kurt Beattie; choreography, Wade Madsen; scenery, Scott Weldin; costumes, Deb Trout; lighting, Geoff Korf; sound, Dominic CodyKramers; projection designers, Mr. Weldin and Martin Christoffel; stage management, Jeffrey K. Hanson.

John Johnson .... Justin Alley
Woman in Green .... Suzanne Bouchard
Remedios .... Julie Briskman
Alberta .... Deborah Fialkow
Sally .... Mary Jane Gibson
Preacher Rowe .... Ray Gonzales
Smitty .... Douglas Moening
Presented in two parts.

Bad Otter .... Todd Jefferson Moore
Hannah Gynt .... Marianne Owen
Mysterious Stranger .... David Pichette
Ugly Boy .... Jonah Von Spreecken
King of the Haints .... Michael Winters
Peer Gynt .... R. Hamilton Wright

GOOD BOYS. By Jane Martin. September 30, 2004. Direction; Jon Jory; scenery, Carey Wong; costumes, Marcia Dixcy Jory; lighting, Greg Sullivan; sound, Chris R. Walker; fight direction, Geoffrey Alm; stage management, Anne Kearson.

Thomas Thurman ...... Thomas Jefferson Byrd
James Erskine .... Jeffrey Hayenga
Marcus Thurman .... Dennis Mosley
Presented without intermission.

Michael Scott .... Ethan Erskine
Corin Thurman .... Adam Western

FICTION. By Steven Dietz. October 28, 2004. Direction, Mr. Dietz; scenery, Scott Weldin; costumes, Carolyn Keim; lighting, Rick Paulsen; sound, Eric Chappelle; stage management, Jeffrey K. Hanson.

Linda Waterman .... Suzanne Bouchard
Abby Drake .... Emily Cedergreen
Presented in two parts.

Michael Waterman .... John Procaccino

Book-It Repertory Theatre, Seattle
Jane Jones and Myra Platt artistic directors, Sharon Burke managing director

REBECCA. By Rachel Atkins; adapted from a novel by Daphne du Maurier. February 25, 2005. Direction, Jane Jones; scenery, Craig B. Wollam; costumes, Ron Erickson;

lighting, Patti West and Jennifer Yaros; dramaturgy, Lenore Bensinger; production stage management, Miller Freeman.

Maxim DeWinter	David Quicksall	Frank Crawley	Laurence Hughes
Mrs. DeWinter	Annette Toutonghi	Captain Julyan	Frank Lawler
Rebecca	Janet Haley	Jack Favell	Andrew Litzky
Mrs. Danvers	Amy Thone	Frith, Tabb, Dr. Baker	Dennis Kleinsmith

Ensemble: Jenny Adams, Kjerstine Anderson, Lauren Herrick, Lauren Leigh Merritt, Hilary Pickles, Sam Wykes.

Musicians: Paul Beck, Makaela Pollock.

Intiman Theatre, Seattle
Bartlett Sher artistic director, Laura Penn managing director

SINGING FOREST. By Craig Lucas. July 30, 2004 (world premiere). Direction, Bartlett Sher, scenery, John McDermott; costumes, Elizabeth Caitlin Ward, lighting, Stephen Strawbridge; sound, Stephen LeGrand; dramaturgy, Oskar Eustis; stage management, Wendiana Walker. Presented in association with Long Wharf Theatre, New Haven, Connecticut. (See Long Wharf listing for additional details.)

New York, 2000		*Vienna, 1930s*	
Loë Rieman	Anne Scurria	Sigmund Freud	Laurence Ballard
Gray	Daniel Eric Gold	Walter Rieman	Daniel Eric Gold
Dr. Shar Unger	John Procaccino	Young Loë	Kristin Flanders
Bill	Laurence Ballard	Martin Rieman	David Garrison
Dr. Oliver Pfaff	David Garrison	Marie Bonaparte	Jeanne Paulsen
Laszlo	Malte Frid-Nielsen	Simon Hirsch	Jay Goede
Beth	Kristin Flanders	Dr. Max Schur	John Procaccino
Bertha Ahmad	Jeanne Paulsen	Gerhardt Zeitzler	Malte Frid-Nielsen
Jules Ahmad	Jay Goede	Ensemble	Barry Cogswell,
Therapist	Laurence Ballard		Andrew J. Peterson

Time: 2000; 1933–1938; spring 1945. Place: New York City; Vienna; a forest outside of Paris. Presented in three parts.

OUR TOWN. By Thornton Wilder. October 13, 2004. Direction, Bartlett Sher; scenery and lighting, Christopher Akerlind; costumes, Elizabeth Caitlin Ward; sound, Peter John Still; stage management, Wendiana Walker.

Stage Manager	Tom Skerritt	Man; Baseball Player	Andrew J. Peterson
Dr. Gibbs	Laurence Ballard	Lady in the Box	Patti Cohenour
Joe Crowell	Max Piscioneri	Simon Stimson	Larry Paulsen
Howie Newsome	Earl Alexander	Lady in the Choir	Alyssa Keene
Mrs. Gibbs	Lisa Li	Mrs. Soames	Josephine Howell
Mrs. Webb	Jeanne Paulsen	Constable Warren	Erwin Thomas
George Gibbs	Joaquin Torres	Si Crowell	Lukas Shadair
Rebecca Gibbs	Ella Mora	Baseball Player; Sam Craig	Justin Emeka
Wally Webb	Dominique Duncan	Baseball Player	Jarvis Antonio Green
Emily Webb	Celia Keenan-Bolger	Man in the Town	Vincent Balestri
Professor Willard	Jose J. Gonzales	Joe Stoddard	Philip Davidson
Mr. Webb	Allen Gilmore	Man in the Town	Vincent Balestri
Woman	Kelly Mak		

Time: The years before World War I. Place: Grover's Corners, New Hampshire. Presented in three parts.

Seattle Repertory Theatre

Sharon Ott artistic director, Benjamin Moore managing director

8th Annual Women Playwrights Festival. April 13–16, 2005.
SIRIUS RISING. By Gwendolyn Schwinke. April 13, 2005. Direction, Sharon Ott; dramaturgy, Carrie Ryan.
THE AERODYNAMICS OF ACCIDENT. By Deborah Isobel Stein. April 14, 2005. Direction, Adam Greenfield; dramaturgy, Christine Sumption.
COURTING VAMPIRES. By Laura Schellhardt. April 15, 2005. Direction, Sharon Ott; dramaturgy, Carrie Ryan.
HARDBALL. By Victoria Stewart. April 16, 2005. Direction, Jerry Manning; dramaturgy, Christine Sumption.

WISCONSIN

Milwaukee Repertory Theater

Joseph Hanreddy artistic director, Timothy J. Shields managing director

THE UNDERPANTS. By Carl Sternheim; adapted by Steve Martin. January 30, 2005. Direction, Risa Brainin; scenery, Geoffrey M. Curley; costumes, Devon Painter; lighting, Michael Klaers; sound, Lindsay Jones; dramaturgy, Paul Kosidowski; stage management, Kelly O'Rourke.

Klinglehoff	Jim Baker	Benjamin Cohen	Ross Lehman
Louise Maske	Deborah Staples	Theo Maske	Steve Pickering
Frank Versati	Dougfred Miller	King	Ryan Schabach
Gertrude Deuter	Carole Healey		

   Time: March 1910. Place: Dusseldorf. Presented in two parts.

YES. NO. (MAYBE SO . . .). By Luigi Pirandello; adapted by Joseph Hanreddy. January 21, 2005 (world premiere). Direction, Mr. Hanreddy; choreography, Ed Burgess; scenery, Michael Frenkel; costumes, Susan E. Mickey; lighting, Thomas C. Hase; sound, Barry G. Funderburg; dramaturgy, Paul Kosidowski and Patricia Gaborik; stage management, Judy Berdan.

Lamberto Laudisi	Torrey Hanson	Governor	James Pickering
Assemblyman Agazzi	Peter Silbert	Police Comm.	Jonathan Gillard Daly
Amelia	Laura Gordon	Signor Ponza	Mark Corkins
Dina	Emily Trask	Signora Ponza	Lanise Antoine Shelley
Signor Sirelli	William Dick	Signora Frola	Rose Pickering
Signora Sirelli	Jenny Wanasek	Neighborhood couple	Collin Geraghty,
Signora Cini	Leslie Brott		Jen Tuttle
Maddalena	Sienna Harris		

   Citizens of the Town: Kay Allmand, Marjorie Armstrong, Eddie Collins, Jackson Doran, Seth Patterson, Steven Piechocki, Fábio Pires, Pamela Vogel, Anthony Wills Jr.

   Time: 1915. Place: Valdana, Italy. Presented in two parts.

BACH AT LEIPZIG. By Itamar Moses. March 4, 2005. Direction, Pam MacKinnon; choreography, Ed Burgess; scenery, Vicki R. Davis; costumes, Mathew J. Lefebvre; lighting, Thomas C. Hase; sound, Jorge Cousineau; fight direction, Lee E. Ernst; dramaturgy, Paul Kosidowski; stage management, Richelle Harrington.

Georg Balthasar Schott ....Lee E. Ernst
Johann Friedrich Fasch ....Torrey Hanson
Georg Friedrich Kaufman ......James Pickering
Greatest Organist ....Collin Geraghty

Johann M. Steindorf ....Gerard Neugent
Johann C. Graupner ....Jonathan Smoots
Georg Lenck ....Brian Vaughn

Time: 1772; later, 1750. Place: The Thomaskirche, Leipzig, Germany. Presented in two parts.

FACTS AND
FIGURES

LONG RUNS ON BROADWAY

○ ○ ○ ○ ○

THE FOLLOWING SHOWS have run 500 or more continuous performances in a single production, usually the first, not including previews or extra non-profit performances, allowing for vacation layoffs and special one-booking engagements, but not including return engagements after a show has gone on tour. In all cases, the numbers were obtained directly from the show's production offices. Where there are title similarities, the production is identified as follows: (p) straight play version, (m) musical version, (r) revival, (tr) transfer.

THROUGH MAY 31, 2005

PLAYS MARKED WITH ASTERISK WERE STILL PLAYING JUNE 1, 2005

Plays	Performances
Cats	7,485
*The Phantom of the Opera	7,231
Les Misérables	6,680
A Chorus Line	6,137
Oh! Calcutta! (r)	5,959
*Beauty and the Beast	4,560
Miss Saigon	4,097
*Rent	3,787
*Chicago (m)(r)	3,555
42nd Street	3,486
Grease	3,388
Fiddler on the Roof	3,242
Life With Father	3,224
*The Lion King	3,185
Tobacco Road	3,182
Hello, Dolly!	2,844
My Fair Lady	2,717
Annie	2,377
Cabaret (r)	2,377
Man of La Mancha	2,328
Abie's Irish Rose	2,327
Oklahoma!	2,212
Smokey Joe's Cafe	2,036
Pippin	1,944
South Pacific	1,925
The Magic Show	1,920
Aida	1,852
Deathtrap	1,793
Gemini	1,788
Harvey	1,775
Dancin'	1,774
La Cage aux Folles	1,761
Hair	1,750

Plays	Performances
The Producers	1,711
The Wiz	1,672
Born Yesterday	1,642
The Best Little Whorehouse in Texas	1,639
Crazy for You	1,622
Ain't Misbehavin'	1,604
Mary, Mary	1,572
Evita	1,567
The Voice of the Turtle	1,557
Jekyll & Hyde	1,543
Barefoot in the Park	1,530
Brighton Beach Memoirs	1,530
42nd Street (r)	1,524
Dreamgirls	1,522
*Mamma Mia!	1,519
Mame (m)	1,508
Grease (r)	1,503
Same Time, Next Year	1,453
Arsenic and Old Lace	1,444
The Sound of Music	1,443
Me and My Girl	1,420
How to Succeed in Business Without Really Trying	1,417
Hellzapoppin'	1,404
The Music Man	1,375
Funny Girl	1,348
Mummenschanz	1,326
Angel Street	1,295
Lightnin'	1,291
Promises, Promises	1,281
The King and I	1,246
Cactus Flower	1,234
Sleuth	1,222

375

Plays	Performances
Torch Song Trilogy	1,222
1776	1,217
Equus	1,209
Sugar Babies	1,208
Guys and Dolls	1,200
Amadeus	1,181
Cabaret	1,165
*Hairspray	1,160
Mister Roberts	1,157
Annie Get Your Gun	1,147
Guys and Dolls (r)	1,144
The Seven Year Itch	1,141
Bring in 'da Noise, Bring in 'da Funk	1,130
Butterflies Are Free	1,128
Pins and Needles	1,108
Plaza Suite	1,097
Fosse	1,092
They're Playing Our Song	1,082
*Movin' Out	1,081
Grand Hotel (m)	1,077
Kiss Me, Kate	1,070
Don't Bother Me, I Can't Cope	1,065
The Pajama Game	1,063
Shenandoah	1,050
Annie Get Your Gun (r)	1,046
The Teahouse of the August Moon	1,027
Damn Yankees	1,019
Contact	1,010
Never Too Late	1,007
Big River	1,005
The Will Rogers Follies	983
Any Wednesday	982
Sunset Boulevard	977
Urinetown	965
A Funny Thing Happened on the Way to the Forum	964
The Odd Couple	964
Anna Lucasta	957
Kiss and Tell	956
Show Boat (r)	949
Dracula (r)	925
Bells Are Ringing	924
The Moon Is Blue	924
Beatlemania	920
Proof	917
The Elephant Man	916
Kiss of the Spider Woman	906
Thoroughly Modern Millie	903
Luv	901
The Who's Tommy	900
Chicago (m)	898
Applause	896
Can-Can	892
Carousel	890
I'm Not Rappaport	890
Hats Off to Ice	889
Fanny	888

Plays	Performances
Children of a Lesser God	887
Follow the Girls	882
Kiss Me, Kate (m)(r)	881
City of Angels	878
Camelot	873
I Love My Wife	872
The Bat	867
My Sister Eileen	864
No, No, Nanette (r)	861
Ragtime	861
Song of Norway	860
Chapter Two	857
A Streetcar Named Desire	855
Barnum	854
Comedy in Music	849
Raisin	847
Blood Brothers	839
You Can't Take It With You	837
La Plume de Ma Tante	835
Three Men on a Horse	835
The Subject Was Roses	832
Black and Blue	824
The King and I (r)	807
Inherit the Wind	806
Anything Goes (r)	804
Titanic	804
No Time for Sergeants	796
Fiorello!	795
Where's Charley?	792
The Ladder	789
Forty Carats	780
Lost in Yonkers	780
The Prisoner of Second Avenue	780
M. Butterfly	777
The Tale of the Allergist's Wife	777
Oliver!	774
The Pirates of Penzance (1980 r)	772
The Full Monty	770
Woman of the Year	770
My One and Only	767
Sophisticated Ladies	767
Bubbling Brown Sugar	766
*Avenue Q	765
Into the Woods	765
State of the Union	765
Starlight Express	761
The First Year	760
Broadway Bound	756
You Know I Can't Hear You When the Water's Running	755
Two for the Seesaw	750
Joseph and the Amazing Technicolor Dreamcoat (r)	747
Death of a Salesman	742
For Colored Girls . . .	742
Sons o' Fun	742
Candide (m, r)	740

Plays	Performances	Plays	Performances
The Real Thing	566	The Red Mill (r)	531
Happy Birthday	564	Rumors	531
Look Homeward, Angel	564	A Raisin in the Sun	530
Morning's at Seven (r)	564	Godspell (tr)	527
The Glass Menagerie	563	Fences	526
I Do! I Do!	560	The Solid Gold Cadillac	526
Wonderful Town	559	Biloxi Blues	524
The Last Night of Ballyhoo	557	Irma La Douce	524
Rose Marie	557	The Boomerang	522
Strictly Dishonorable	557	Follies	521
Sweeney Todd	557	Rosalinda	521
The Great White Hope	556	The Best Man	520
A Majority of One	556	Chauve-Souris	520
The Sisters Rosensweig	556	Blackbirds of 1928	518
Sunrise at Campobello	556	The Gin Game	517
Toys in the Attic	556	Side Man	517
Jamaica	555	Sunny	517
Stop the World—I Want to Get Off	555	Victoria Regina	517
Florodora	553	Fifth of July	511
Noises Off	553	Half a Sixpence	511
Ziegfeld Follies (1943)	553	The Vagabond King	511
Dial "M" for Murder	552	The New Moon	509
Good News	551	The World of Suzie Wong	508
Peter Pan (r)	551	The Rothschilds	507
How to Succeed in Business		On Your Toes (r)	505
Without Really Trying (r)	548	Sugar	505
Let's Face It	547	Shuffle Along	504
Milk and Honey	543	Up in Central Park	504
Within the Law	541	Carmen Jones	503
Pal Joey (r)	540	Saturday Night Fever	502
The Sound of Music (r)	540	The Member of the Wedding	501
What Makes Sammy Run?	540	Panama Hattie	501
The Sunshine Boys	538	Personal Appearance	501
What a Life	538	Bird in Hand	500
Crimes of the Heart	535	Room Service	500
Damn Yankees (r)	533	Sailor, Beware!	500
The Unsinkable Molly Brown	532	Tomorrow the World	500

LONG RUNS OFF BROADWAY

Plays	Performances	Plays	Performances
The Fantasticks	17,162	Vampire Lesbians of Sodom	2,024
*Perfect Crime	7,458	Jacques Brel	1,847
*Tubes	7,004	Forever Plaid	1,811
Tony 'n' Tina's Wedding	4,914	Vanities	1,785
*Stomp	4,724	You're a Good Man, Charlie Brown	1,597
Nunsense	3,672	The Blacks	1,408
*I Love You, You're Perfect,		The Vagina Monologues	1,381
Now Change	3,672	One Mo' Time	1,372
The Threepenny Opera	2,611	Grandma Sylvia's Funeral	1,360
De La Guarda	2,473	*Menopause: The Musical	1,336
Forbidden Broadway 1982–87	2,332	*The Donkey Show	1,329±
*Naked Boys Singing!	2,244	Let My People Come	1,327
Little Shop of Horrors	2,209	Late Nite Catechism	1,268
Godspell	2,124	Driving Miss Daisy	1,195

Plays	Performances
The Hot l Baltimore	1,166
I'm Getting My Act Together and Taking It on the Road	1,165
Little Mary Sunshine	1,143
Steel Magnolias	1,126
El Grande de Coca-Cola	1,114
The Proposition	1,109
Our Sinatra	1,096
Beau Jest	1,069
Tamara	1,036
One Flew Over the Cuckoo's Nest (r)	1,025
The Boys in the Band	1,000
Fool for Love	1,000
Other People's Money	990
Forbidden Broadway: 20th Anniversary Celebration	983
Cloud 9	971
Secrets Every Smart Traveler Should Know	953
Sister Mary Ignatius Explains It All for You & The Actor's Nightmare	947
Your Own Thing	933
Curley McDimple	931
Leave It to Jane (r)	928
Hedwig and the Angry Inch	857
Forbidden Broadway Strikes Back	850
When Pigs Fly	840
The Mad Show	871
Scrambled Feet	831
The Effect of Gamma Rays on Man-in-the-Moon Marigolds	819
Over the River and Through the Woods	800
A View From the Bridge (r)	780
The Boy Friend (r)	763
True West	762
Forbidden Broadway Cleans Up Its Act!	754
Isn't It Romantic	733
Dime a Dozen	728
The Pocket Watch	725
The Connection	722
The Passion of Dracula	714
Love, Janis	713
Adaptation & Next	707
Oh! Calcutta!	704
Scuba Duba	692

Plays	Performances
The Foreigner	686
The Knack	685
Fully Committed	675
The Club	674
The Balcony	672
Penn & Teller	666
Dinner With Friends	654
America Hurrah	634
Oil City Symphony	626
The Countess	618
The Exonerated	608
Hogan's Goat	607
Beehive	600
Criss Angel Mindfreak	600
The Trojan Women	600
The Syringa Tree	586
The Dining Room	583
Krapp's Last Tape & The Zoo Story	582
Three Tall Women	582
The Dumbwaiter & The Collection	578
Forbidden Broadway 1990	576
Dames at Sea	575
The Crucible (r)	571
The Iceman Cometh (r)	565
Forbidden Broadway 2001: A Spoof Odyssey	552
The Hostage (r)	545
Wit	545
What's a Nice Country Like You Doing in a State Like This?	543
Forbidden Broadway 1988	534
Gross Indecency: The Three Trials of Oscar Wilde	534
Frankie and Johnny in the Clair de Lune	533
Six Characters in Search of an Author (r)	529
All in the Timing	526
Oleanna	513
*Cookin'	513
Making Porn	511
The Dirtiest Show in Town	509
Happy Ending & Day of Absence	504
Greater Tuna	501
A Shayna Maidel	501
The Boys From Syracuse (r)	500

± Total unverified at press time

NEW YORK DRAMA CRITICS' CIRCLE
1935–1936 TO 2004–2005

○ ○ ○ ○ ○

L ISTED BELOW ARE the New York Drama Critics' Circle Awards from 1935–1936 through 2004–2005 classified as follows: (1) Best American Play, (2) Best Foreign Play, (3) Best Musical, (4) Best, Regardless of Category (this category was established by new voting rules in 1962–63 and did not exist prior to that year).

1935–36 (1) *Winterset*
1936–37 (1) *High Tor*
1937–38 (1) *Of Mice and Men*, (2) *Shadow and Substance*
1938–39 (1) No award, (2) *The White Steed*
1939–40 (1) *The Time of Your Life*
1940–41 (1) *Watch on the Rhine*, (2) *The Corn Is Green*
1941–42 (1) No award, (2) *Blithe Spirit*
1942–43 (1) *The Patriots*
1943–44 (2) *Jacobowsky and the Colonel*
1944–45 (1) *The Glass Menagerie*
1945–46 (3) *Carousel*
1946–47 (1) *All My Sons*, (2) *No Exit*, (3) *Brigadoon*
1947–48 (1) *A Streetcar Named Desire*, (2) *The Winslow Boy*
1948–49 (1) *Death of a Salesman*, (2) *The Madwoman of Chaillot*, (3) *South Pacific*
1949–50 (1) *The Member of the Wedding*, (2) *The Cocktail Party*, (3) *The Consul*
1950–51 (1) *Darkness at Noon*, (2) *The Lady's Not for Burning*, (3) *Guys and Dolls*
1951–52 (1) *I Am a Camera*, (2) *Venus Observed*, (3) *Pal Joey* (Special citation to *Don Juan in Hell*)
1952–53 (1) *Picnic*, (2) *The Love of Four Colonels*, (3) *Wonderful Town*
1953–54 (1) *The Teahouse of the August Moon*, (2) *Ondine*, (3) *The Golden Apple*
1954–55 (1) *Cat on a Hot Tin Roof*, (2) *Witness for the Prosecution*, (3) *The Saint of Bleecker Street*
1955–56 (1) *The Diary of Anne Frank*, (2) *Tiger at the Gates*, (3) *My Fair Lady*
1956–57 (1) *Long Day's Journey Into Night*, (2) *The Waltz of the Toreadors*, (3) *The Most Happy Fella*
1957–58 (1) *Look Homeward, Angel*, (2) *Look Back in Anger*, (3) *The Music Man*

1958–59 (1) *A Raisin in the Sun*, (2) *The Visit*, (3) *La Plume de Ma Tante*
1959–60 (1) *Toys in the Attic*, (2) *Five Finger Exercise*, (3) *Fiorello!*
1960–61 (1) *All the Way Home*, (2) *A Taste of Honey*, (3) *Carnival*
1961–62 (1) *The Night of the Iguana*, (2) *A Man for All Seasons*, (3) *How to Succeed in Business Without Really Trying*
1962–63 (4) *Who's Afraid of Virginia Woolf?* (Special citation to *Beyond the Fringe*)
1963–64 (4) *Luther*, (3) *Hello, Dolly!* (Special citation to *The Trojan Women*)
1964–65 (4) *The Subject Was Roses*, (3) *Fiddler on the Roof*
1965–66 (4) *The Persecution and Assassination of Marat as Performed by the Inmates of the Asylum of Charenton Under the Direction of the Marquis de Sade*, (3) *Man of La Mancha*
1966–67 (4) *The Homecoming*, (3) *Cabaret*
1967–68 (4) *Rosencrantz and Guildenstern Are Dead*, (3) *Your Own Thing*
1968–69 (4) *The Great White Hope*, (3) *1776*
1969–70 (4) *Borstal Boy*, (1) *The Effect of Gamma Rays on Man-in-the-Moon Marigolds*, (3) *Company*
1970–71 (4) *Home*, (1) *The House of Blue Leaves*, (3) *Follies*
1971–72 (4) *That Championship Season*, (2) *The Screens* (3) *Two Gentlemen of Verona* (Special citations to *Sticks and Bones* and *Old Times*)
1972–73 (4) *The Changing Room*, (1) *The Hot l Baltimore*, (3) *A Little Night Music*
1973–74 (4) *The Contractor*, (1) *Short Eyes*, (3) *Candide*
1974–75 (4) *Equus* (1) *The Taking of Miss Janie*, (3) *A Chorus Line*

381

1975–76 (4) *Travesties*, (1) *Streamers*, (3) *Pacific Overtures*

1976–77 (4) *Otherwise Engaged*, (1) *American Buffalo*, (3) *Annie*

1977–78 (4) *Da*, (3) *Ain't Misbehavin'*

1978–79 (4) *The Elephant Man*, (3) *Sweeney Todd, the Demon Barber of Fleet Street*

1979–80 (4) *Talley's Folly*, (2) *Betrayal*, (3) *Evita* (Special citation to Peter Brook's Le Centre International de Créations Théâtrales for its repertory)

1980–81 (4) *A Lesson From Aloes*, (1) *Crimes of the Heart* (Special citations to *Lena Horne: The Lady and Her Music* and the New York Shakespeare Festival production of *The Pirates of Penzance*)

1981–82 (4) *The Life & Adventures of Nicholas Nickleby*, (1) *A Soldier's Play*

1982–83 (4) *Brighton Beach Memoirs*, (2) *Plenty*, (3) *Little Shop of Horrors* (Special citation to Young Playwrights Festival)

1983–84 (4) *The Real Thing*, (1) *Glengarry Glen Ross*, (3) *Sunday in the Park With George* (Special citation to Samuel Beckett for the body of his work)

1984–85 (4) *Ma Rainey's Black Bottom*

1985–86 (4) *A Lie of the Mind*, (2) *Benefactors* (Special citation to *The Search for Signs of Intelligent Life in the Universe*)

1986–87 (4) *Fences*, (2) *Les Liaisons Dangereuses*, (3) *Les Misérables*

1987–88 (4) *Joe Turner's Come and Gone*, (2) *The Road to Mecca*, (3) *Into the Woods*

1988–89 (4) *The Heidi Chronicles*, (2) *Aristocrats* (Special citation to Bill Irwin for *Largely New York*)

1989–90 (4) *The Piano Lesson*, (2) *Privates on Parade*, (3) *City of Angels*

1990–91 (4) *Six Degrees of Separation*, (2) *Our Country's Good*, (3) *The Will Rogers Follies* (Special citation to Eileen Atkins for her portrayal of Virginia Woolf in *A Room of One's Own*)

1991–92 (4) *Dancing at Lughnasa*, (1) *Two Trains Running*

1992–93 (4) *Angels in America: Millennium Approaches*, (2) *Someone Who'll Watch Over Me*, (3) *Kiss of the Spider Woman*

1993–94 (4) *Three Tall Women* (Special citation to Anna Deavere Smith for her unique contribution to theatrical form)

1994–95 (4) *Arcadia*, (1) *Love! Valour! Compassion!* (Special citation to Signature Theatre Company for outstanding artistic achievement)

1995–96 (4) *Seven Guitars*, (2) *Molly Sweeney*, (3) *Rent*

1996–97 (4) *How I Learned to Drive*, (2) *Skylight*, (3) *Violet* (Special citation to *Chicago*)

1997–98 (4) *Art*, (1) *Pride's Crossing*, (3) *The Lion King* (Special citation to the revival production of *Cabaret*)

1998–99 (4) *Wit*, (3) *Parade*, (2) *Closer* (Special citation to David Hare for his contributions to the 1998–99 theater season: *Amy's View*, *Via Dolorosa* and *The Blue Room*)

1999–00 (4) *Jitney*, (3) *James Joyce's The Dead*, (2) *Copenhagen*

2000–01 (4) *The Invention of Love*, (1) *Proof*, (3) *The Producers*

2001–02 (4) *Edward Albee's The Goat, or Who is Sylvia?* (Special citation to Elaine Stritch for *Elaine Stritch at Liberty*)

2002–03 (4) *Take Me Out*, (2) *Talking Heads*, (3) *Hairspray*

2003–04 (4) *Intimate Apparel* (Special citation to Barbara Cook for her contribution to the musical theater)

2004–05 (4) *Doubt, a Parable*, (2) *The Pillowman*

NEW YORK DRAMA CRITICS' CIRCLE VOTING 2004–2005

Michael Sommers (*The Star-Ledger*), President

AT ITS MAY 11, 2005 meeting the New York Drama Critics' Circle declined to honor any musicals of the 2004–05 season. The group voted a best-play award to John Patrick Shanley's *Doubt, a Parable* in an overwhelming (and unusual) first-ballot victory. Martin McDonagh's *The Pillowman* was later chosen best foreign play.

Of the 21 members of the Circle, only Frank Scheck of *The Hollywood Reporter* voted via absentee ballot. The voting for best play was tallied as follows: *Doubt, a Parable* 17 (David Cote, *Time Out New York*; Gordon Cox, *Newsday*; Michael Feingold, *The Village Voice*; Robert Feldberg, *The Bergen Record*; Adam Feldman, *Time Out New York*; Howard Kissel, *Daily News*; Michael Kuchwara, The Associated Press; Jacques le Sourd, Gannett/*The Journal News*; Ken Mandelbaum, Broadway.com; Jeremy McCarter, *The New York Sun*; David Rooney, *Variety*; Frank Scheck, *The Hollywood Reporter*; David Sheward, *Back Stage*; John Simon, *New York*; Michael Sommers, *The Star-Ledger*/Newhouse Newspapers; Terry Teachout, *The Wall Street Journal*; Linda Winer, *Newsday*), *The Pillowman* 4 (Elysa Gardner, *USA Today*; John Heilpern, *The New York Observer*; Richard Zoglin, *Time*), *Democracy* 1 (Clive Barnes, *New York Post*).

In the voting for best foreign play, three contenders emerged: *The Pillowman*, Michael Frayn's *Democracy* and Caryl Churchill's *A Number*. *The Pillowman* won easily with 14 of 20 votes cast (Michael Feingold abstained). The voting for best foreign play was tallied as follows: *The Pillowman* 14 (David Cote, *Time Out New York*; Gordon Cox, *Newsday*; Robert Feldberg, *The Bergen Record*; Adam Feldman, *Time Out New York*; Elysa Gardner, *USA Today*; John Heilpern, *The New York Observer*; Michael Kuchwara, The Associated Press; Jacques le Sourd, Gannett/*The Journal News*; Ken Mandelbaum, Broadway.com; Frank Scheck, *The Hollywood Reporter*; David Sheward, *Back Stage*; Terry Teachout, *The Wall Street Journal*; Linda Winer, *Newsday*; Richard Zoglin, *Time*), *Democracy* 3 (Clive Barnes, *New York Post*; Howard Kissel, *Daily News*; John Simon, *New York*), *A Number* 3 (Jeremy McCarter, *The New York Sun*; David Rooney, *Variety*; Michael Sommers, *The Star-Ledger*/Newhouse Newspapers).

Honorees received their accolades at an Algonquin cocktail party May 24, 2005.

PULITZER PRIZE WINNERS
1916–1917 TO 2004–2005

1916–17   No award
1917–18   *Why Marry?* by Jesse Lynch Williams
1918–19   No award
1919–20   *Beyond the Horizon* by Eugene O'Neill
1920–21   *Miss Lulu Bett* by Zona Gale
1921–22   *Anna Christie* by Eugene O'Neill
1922–23   *Icebound* by Owen Davis
1923–24   *Hell-Bent fer Heaven* by Hatcher Hughes
1924–25   *They Knew What They Wanted* by Sidney Howard
1925–26   *Craig's Wife* by George Kelly
1926–27   *In Abraham's Bosom* by Paul Green
1927–28   *Strange Interlude* by Eugene O'Neill
1928–29   *Street Scene* by Elmer Rice
1929–30   *The Green Pastures* by Marc Connelly
1930–31   *Alison's House* by Susan Glaspell
1931–32   *Of Thee I Sing* by George S. Kaufman, Morrie Ryskind, Ira and George Gershwin
1932–33   *Both Your Houses* by Maxwell Anderson
1933–34   *Men in White* by Sidney Kingsley
1934–35   *The Old Maid* by Zoe Akins
1935–36   *Idiot's Delight* by Robert E. Sherwood
1936–37   *You Can't Take It With You* by Moss Hart and George S. Kaufman
1937–38   *Our Town* by Thornton Wilder
1938–39   *Abe Lincoln in Illinois* by Robert E. Sherwood
1939–40   *The Time of Your Life* by William Saroyan
1940–41   *There Shall Be No Night* by Robert E. Sherwood
1941–42   No award
1942–43   *The Skin of Our Teeth* by Thornton Wilder
1943–44   No award
1944–45   *Harvey* by Mary Chase
1945–46   *State of the Union* by Howard Lindsay and Russel Crouse
1946–47   No award
1947–48   *A Streetcar Named Desire* by Tennessee Williams
1948–49   *Death of a Salesman* by Arthur Miller
1949–50   *South Pacific* by Richard Rodgers, Oscar Hammerstein II and Joshua Logan
1950–51   No award
1951–52   *The Shrike* by Joseph Kramm
1952–53   *Picnic* by William Inge

1953–54   *The Teahouse of the August Moon* by John Patrick
1954–55   *Cat on a Hot Tin Roof* by Tennessee Williams
1955–56   *The Diary of Anne Frank* by Frances Goodrich and Albert Hackett
1956–57   *Long Day's Journey Into Night* by Eugene O'Neill
1957–58   *Look Homeward, Angel* by Ketti Frings
1958–59   *J.B.* by Archibald MacLeish
1959–60   *Fiorello!* by Jerome Weidman, George Abbott, Sheldon Harnick and Jerry Bock
1960–61   *All the Way Home* by Tad Mosel
1961–62   *How to Succeed in Business Without Really Trying* by Abe Burrows, Willie Gilbert, Jack Weinstock and Frank Loesser
1962–63   No award
1963–64   No award
1964–65   *The Subject Was Roses* by Frank D. Gilroy
1965–66   No award
1966–67   *A Delicate Balance* by Edward Albee
1967–68   No award
1968–69   *The Great White Hope* by Howard Sackler
1969–70   *No Place To Be Somebody* by Charles Gordone
1970–71   *The Effect of Gamma Rays on Man-in-the-Moon Marigolds* by Paul Zindel
1971–72   No award
1972–73   *That Championship Season* by Jason Miller
1973–74   No award
1974–75   *Seascape* by Edward Albee
1975–76   *A Chorus Line* by Michael Bennett, James Kirkwood, Nicholas Dante, Marvin Hamlisch and Edward Kleban
1976–77   *The Shadow Box* by Michael Cristofer
1977–78   *The Gin Game* by D.L. Coburn
1978–79   *Buried Child* by Sam Shepard
1979–80   *Talley's Folly* by Lanford Wilson
1980–81   *Crimes of the Heart* by Beth Henley
1981–82   *A Soldier's Play* by Charles Fuller
1982–83   *'night, Mother* by Marsha Norman
1983–84   *Glengarry Glen Ross* by David Mamet
1984–85   *Sunday in the Park With George* by James Lapine and Stephen Sondheim
1985–86   No award

1986–87 *Fences* by August Wilson
1987–88 *Driving Miss Daisy* by Alfred Uhry
1988–89 *The Heidi Chronicles* by Wendy Wasserstein
1989–90 *The Piano Lesson* by August Wilson
1990–91 *Lost in Yonkers* by Neil Simon
1991–92 *The Kentucky Cycle* by Robert Schenkkan
1992–93 *Angels in America: Millennium Approaches* by Tony Kushner
1993–94 *Three Tall Women* by Edward Albee
1994–95 *The Young Man From Atlanta* by Horton Foote

1995–96 *Rent* by Jonathan Larson
1996–97 No award
1997–98 *How I Learned to Drive* by Paula Vogel
1998–99 *Wit* by Margaret Edson
1999–00 *Dinner With Friends* by Donald Margulies
2000–01 *Proof* by David Auburn
2001–02 *Topdog/Underdog* by Suzan-Lori Parks
2002–03 *Anna in the Tropics* by Nilo Cruz
2003–04 *I Am My Own Wife* by Doug Wright
2004–05 *Doubt, a Parable* by John Patrick Shanley

2005 TONY AWARDS

○ ○ ○ ○ ○

THE AMERICAN THEATRE WING'S 59th annual Tony Awards, named for Antoinette Perry, are presented in recognition of distinguished achievement in the Broadway theater. The League of American Theatres and Producers (Jed Bernstein, president) and the American Theatre Wing (Sondra Gilman, chairman; Doug Leeds, president; Howard Sherman, executive director) present these awards, founded by the Wing in 1947. Legitimate theater productions opening in 40 eligible Broadway theaters during the present Tony season—May 6, 2004 to May 5, 2005—were considered by the Tony Awards Nominating Committee (appointed by the Tony Awards Administration Committee) for the awards in 25 competitive categories. The 2004–2005 Nominating Committee consisted of Victoria Bailey, Ira Bernstein, Susan Birkenhead, Stephen Bogardus, Edward Burbridge, Ben Cameron, Schulyer G. Chapin, Kirsten Childs, Jacqueline Davis, Merle Debuskey, Edgar Dobie, Mercedes Ellington, Nancy Ford, Julie Hughes, David Henry Hwang, David Lindsay-Abaire, Jon Nakagawa, Enid Nemy, Peter Neufeld, Bill Schelble, Marc Shaiman, William Tynan, Jac Venza.

The Tony Awards are voted from the list of nominees by members of the theater and journalism professions: the governing boards of the five theater artists' organizations (Actors' Equity Association, the Dramatists' Guild, the Society of Stage Directors and Choreographers, United Scenic Artists and the Casting Society of America), members of the designated first night theater press, the board of directors of the American Theatre Wing and the membership of the League of American Theatres and Producers. Because of fluctuation in these groups, the size of the Tony electorate varies from year to year. For the 2004–2005 season there were 758 qualified Tony voters.

The 2004–2005 nominees follow, with winners in each category listed in **bold face type**.

PLAY (award goes to both author and producer). *Democracy* by Michael Frayn, produced by Boyett Ostar Productions, Nederlander Presentations, Inc., Jean Doumanian, Stephanie P. McClelland, Arielle Tepper, Amy Nederlander, Eric Falkenstein, Roy Furman. **Doubt, a Parable** by **John Patrick Shanley**, produced by **Carole Shorenstein Hays, MTC Productions, Inc., Lynne Meadow, Barry Grove, Roger Berlind, Scott Rudin**. *Gem of the Ocean* by August Wilson, produced by Carole Shorenstein Hays, Jujamcyn Theaters. *The Pillowman* by Martin McDonagh, produced by Boyett Ostar Productions, Robert Fox, Arielle Tepper, Stephanie P. McClelland, Debra Black, Dede Harris/Morton Swinsky, Roy Furman/Jon Avnet, Joyce Schweickert, The National Theatre of Great Britain.

MUSICAL (award goes to the producer). *Dirty Rotten Scoundrels* produced by Marty Bell, David Brown, Aldo Scrofani, Roy Furman, Dede Harris, Amanda Lipitz, Greg Smith, Ruth Hendel, Chase Mishkin, Barry and Susan Tatelman, Debra Black, Sharon Karmazin, Joyce Schweickert, Bernie Abrams/Michael Speyer, Barbara Whitman, Weissberger Theater Group/Jay Harris, Cheryl Wiesenfeld/Jean Cheever, Clear Channel Entertainment, Harvey Weinstein, MGM On Stage/Darcie Denkert and Dean Stolber. *The Light in the Piazza* produced by Lincoln Center Theater, André Bishop, Bernard Gersten. **Monty Python's Spamalot** produced by **Boyett Ostar Productions, The Shubert Organization, Arielle Tepper, Stephanie P. McClelland/Lawrence Horowitz, Elan V. McAllister/Allan S. Gordon, Independent Presenters Network, Roy Furman, GRS Associates, Jam Theatricals, TGA Entertainment, Clear Channel Entertainment**. *The 25th Annual Putnam County Spelling Bee* produced by David Stone, James L. Nederlander, Barbara Whitman, Patrick Catullo, Barrington Stage Company, Second Stage Theatre.

BOOK OF A MUSICAL. Jeffrey Lane for *Dirty Rotten Scoundrels*, Craig Lucas for *The Light in the Piazza*, Eric Idle for *Monty Python's Spamalot*, **Rachel Sheinkin** for **The 25th Annual Putnam County Spelling Bee**.

ORIGINAL SCORE (music and/or lyrics). David Yazbek (music and lyrics) for *Dirty Rotten Scoundrels*. **Adam Guettel** (music and lyrics) for **The Light in the Piazza**. John Du Prez (music) and Eric Idle (music and lyrics) for *Monty Python's Spamalot*. William Finn (music and lyrics) for *The 25th Annual Putnam County Spelling Bee*.

REVIVAL OF A PLAY (award goes to the producer). *Who's Afraid of Virginia Woolf?* produced by Elizabeth Ireland McCann, Daryl Roth, Terry Allen Kramer, Scott Rudin, Roger Berlind, James L. Nederlander, Nick Simunek, Joey Parnes. **Glengarry Glen Ross** produced by **Jeffrey Richards, Jerry Frankel, Jam Theatricals, Boyett Ostar Productions, Ronald Frankel, Philip Lacerte, Stephanie P. McClelland/CJM Productions, Barry Weisbord, Zendog Productions, Herbert Goldsmith Productions, Roundabout Theatre Company, Todd Haimes, Ellen Richard, Julia C. Levy**. *On Golden Pond* produced by Jeffrey Finn, Arlene Scanlan, Stuart Thompson. *Twelve Angry Men* produced by Roundabout Theatre Company, Todd Haimes, Ellen Richard, Julia C. Levy.

REVIVAL OF A MUSICAL (award goes to the producer). **La Cage aux Folles** produced by **James L. Nederlander, Clear Channel Entertainment, Kenneth Greenblatt, Terry Allen Kramer, Martin Richards**. *Pacific Overtures* produced by Roundabout Theatre Company, Todd Haimes, Ellen Richard, Julia C. Levy, Gorgeous Entertainment. *Sweet Charity* produced by Barry and Fran Weissler, Clear Channel Entertainment, Edwin W. Schloss.

SPECIAL THEATRICAL EVENT (award goes to the producer). **Billy Crystal: 700 Sundays** produced by **Janice Crystal, Larry Magid, Face Productions**. *Dame Edna: Back With a Vengeance!* produced by Creative Battery, Harley Medcalf and Boxjellyfish LLC. *Laugh Whore* produced by Showtime Networks. *Whoopi: The 20th Anniversary Show* produced by Mike Nichols, Hal Luftig, Leonard Soloway, Steven M. Levy, Tom Leonardis, Eric Falkenstein, Amy Nederlander.

PERFORMANCE BY A LEADING ACTOR IN A PLAY. Philip Bosco in *Twelve Angry Men*, Billy Crudup in *The Pillowman*, **Bill Irwin** in *Who's Afraid of Virginia Woolf?*, James Earl Jones in *On Golden Pond*, Brían F. O'Byrne in *Doubt, a Parable*.

PERFORMANCE BY A LEADING ACTRESS IN A PLAY. **Cherry Jones** in *Doubt, a Parable*, Laura Linney in *Sight Unseen*, Mary-Louise Parker in *Reckless*, Phylicia Rashad in *Gem of the Ocean*, Kathleen Turner in *Who's Afraid of Virginia Woolf?*

PERFORMANCE BY A LEADING ACTOR IN A MUSICAL. Hank Azaria in *Monty Python's Spamalot*, Gary Beach in *La Cage aux Folles*, **Norbert Leo Butz** in *Dirty Rotten Scoundrels*, Tim Curry in *Monty Python's Spamalot*, John Lithgow in *Dirty Rotten Scoundrels*.

PERFORMANCE BY A LEADING ACTRESS IN A MUSICAL. Christina Applegate in *Sweet Charity*, **Victoria Clark** in *The Light in the Piazza*, Erin Dilly in *Chitty Chitty Bang Bang*, Sutton Foster in *Little Women*, Sherie René Scott in *Dirty Rotten Scoundrels*.

PERFORMANCE BY A FEATURED ACTOR IN A PLAY. Alan Alda in *Glengarry Glen Ross*, Gordon Clapp in *Glengarry Glen Ross*, David Harbour in *Who's Afraid of Virginia Woolf?*, **Liev Schreiber** in *Glengarry Glen Ross*, Michael Stuhlbarg in *The Pillowman*.

PERFORMANCE BY A FEATURED ACTRESS IN A PLAY. Mireille Enos in *Who's Afraid of Virginia Woolf?*, Heather Goldenhersh in *Doubt, a Parable*, Dana Ivey in *The Rivals*, **Adriane Lenox** in *Doubt, a Parable*, Amy Ryan in *A Streetcar Named Desire*.

PERFORMANCE BY A FEATURED ACTOR IN A MUSICAL. **Dan Fogler** in *The 25th Annual Putnam County Spelling Bee*, Marc Kudisch in *Chitty Chitty Bang Bang*, Michael McGrath in *Monty Python's Spamalot*, Matthew Morrison in *The Light in the Piazza*, Christopher Sieber in *Monty Python's Spamalot*.

PERFORMANCE BY A FEATURED ACTRESS IN A MUSICAL. Joanna Gleason in *Dirty Rotten Scoundrels*, Celia Keenan-Bolger in *The 25th Annual Putnam County Spelling Bee*, Jan Maxwell in *Chitty Chitty Bang Bang*, Kelli O'Hara in *The Light in the Piazza*, **Sara Ramirez** in *Monty Python's Spamalot*.

SCENIC DESIGN OF A PLAY. John Lee Beatty for *Doubt, a Parable*, David Gallo for *Gem of the Ocean*, Santo Loquasto for *Glengarry Glen Ross*, **Scott Pask** for *The Pillowman*.

SCENIC DESIGN OF A MUSICAL. Tim Hatley for *Monty Python's Spamalot*, Rumi Matsui for *Pacific Overtures*, Anthony Ward for *Chitty Chitty Bang Bang*, **Michael Yeargan** for *The Light in the Piazza*.

COSTUME DESIGN OF A PLAY. **Jess Goldstein** for *The Rivals*, Jane Greenwood for *Who's Afraid of Virginia Woolf?*, William Ivey Long for *A Streetcar Named Desire*, Constanza Romero for *Gem of the Ocean*.

COSTUME DESIGN OF A MUSICAL. Tim Hatley for *Monty Python's Spamalot*, Junko Koshino for *Pacific Overtures*, William Ivey Long for *La Cage aux Folles*, **Catherine Zuber** for *The Light in the Piazza*.

LIGHTING DESIGN OF A PLAY. Pat Collins for *Doubt, a Parable*, Donald Holder for *Gem of the Ocean*, Donald Holder for *A Streetcar Named Desire*, **Brian MacDevitt** for *The Pillowman*.

LIGHTING DESIGN OF A MUSICAL. **Christopher Akerlind** for *The Light in the Piazza*, Mark Henderson for *Chitty Chitty Bang Bang*, Kenneth Posner for *Dirty Rotten Scoundrels*, Hugh Vanstone for *Monty Python's Spamalot*.

DIRECTION OF A PLAY. John Crowley for *The Pillowman*, Scott Ellis for *Twelve Angry Men*, **Doug Hughes** for *Doubt, a Parable*, Joe Mantello for *Glengarry Glen Ross*.

DIRECTION OF A MUSICAL. James Lapine for *The 25th Annual Putnam County Spelling Bee*, **Mike Nichols** for *Monty Python's Spamalot*, Jack O'Brien for *Dirty Rotten Scoundrels*, Bartlett Sher for *The Light in the Piazza*.

CHOREOGRAPHY. Wayne Cilento for *Sweet Charity*, Jerry Mitchell for *Dirty Rotten Scoundrels*, **Jerry Mitchell** for *La Cage aux Folles*, Casey Nicholaw for *Monty Python's Spamalot*.

ORCHESTRATIONS. Larry Hochman for *Monty Python's Spamalot*. **Ted Sperling**, **Adam Guettel** and **Bruce Coughlin** for *The Light in the Piazza*. Jonathan Tunick for *Pacific Overtures*. Harold Wheeler for *Dirty Rotten Scoundrels*.

LIFETIME ACHIEVEMENT. **Edward Albee**.

REGIONAL THEATRE TONY AWARD. **Theatre de la Jeune Lune**, Minneapolis, Minnesota.

TONY AWARD WINNERS, 1947–2005

L ISTED BELOW ARE the Antoinette Perry (Tony) Award winners in the catgories of Best Play and Best Musical from the time these awards were established in 1947 until the present.

1947—No play or musical award
1948—*Mister Roberts*; no musical award
1949—*Death of a Salesman*; *Kiss Me, Kate*
1950—*The Cocktail Party*; *South Pacific*
1951—*The Rose Tattoo*; *Guys and Dolls*
1952—*The Fourposter*; *The King and I*
1953—*The Crucible*; *Wonderful Town*
1954—*The Teahouse of the August Moon*; *Kismet*
1955—*The Desperate Hours*; *The Pajama Game*
1956—*The Diary of Anne Frank*; *Damn Yankees*
1957—*Long Day's Journey Into Night*; *My Fair Lady*
1958—*Sunrise at Campobello*; *The Music Man*
1959—*J.B.*; *Redhead*
1960—*The Miracle Worker*; *Fiorello!* and *The Sound of Music* (tie)
1961—*Becket*; *Bye Bye Birdie*
1962—*A Man for All Seasons*; *How to Succeed in Business Without Really Trying*
1963—*Who's Afraid of Virginia Woolf?*; *A Funny Thing Happened on the Way to the Forum*
1964—*Luther*; *Hello, Dolly!*
1965—*The Subject Was Roses*; *Fiddler on the Roof*
1966—*The Persecution and Assassination of Marat as Performed by the Inmates of the Asylum of Charenton Under the Direction of the Marquis de Sade*; *Man of La Mancha*
1967—*The Homecoming*; *Cabaret*

1968—*Rosencrantz and Guildenstern Are Dead*; *Hallelujah, Baby!*
1969—*The Great White Hope*; *1776*
1970—*Borstal Boy*; *Applause*
1971—*Sleuth*; *Company*
1972—*Sticks and Bones*; *Two Gentlemen of Verona*
1973—*That Championship Season*; *A Little Night Music*
1974—*The River Niger*; *Raisin*
1975—*Equus*; *The Wiz*
1976—*Travesties*; *A Chorus Line*
1977—*The Shadow Box*; *Annie*
1978—*Da*; *Ain't Misbehavin'*
1979—*The Elephant Man*; *Sweeney Todd, the Demon Barber of Fleet Street*
1980—*Children of a Lesser God*; *Evita*
1981—*Amadeus*; *42nd Street*
1982—*The Life & Adventures of Nicholas Nickleby*; *Nine*
1983—*Torch Song Trilogy*; *Cats*
1984—*The Real Thing*; *La Cage aux Folles*
1985—*Biloxi Blues*; *Big River*
1986—*I'm Not Rappaport*; *The Mystery of Edwin Drood*
1987—*Fences*; *Les Misérables*
1988—*M. Butterfly*; *The Phantom of the Opera*
1989—*The Heidi Chronicles*; *Jerome Robbins' Broadway*
1990—*The Grapes of Wrath*; *City of Angels*

1991—*Lost in Yonkers*; *The Will Rogers Follies*
1992—*Dancing at Lughnasa*; *Crazy for You*
1993—*Angels in America, Part I: Millennium Approaches*; *Kiss of the Spider Woman*
1994—*Angels in America, Part II: Perestroika*; *Passion*
1995—*Love! Valour! Compassion!*; *Sunset Boulevard*
1996—*Master Class*; *Rent*
1997—*The Last Night of Ballyhoo*; *Titanic*

1998—*Art*; *The Lion King*
1999—*Side Man*; *Fosse*
2000—*Copenhagen*; *Contact*
2001—*Proof*; *The Producers*
2002—*The Goat, or Who is Sylvia*; *Thoroughly Modern Millie*
2003—*Take Me Out*; *Hairspray*
2004—*I Am My Own Wife*; *Avenue Q*
2005—*Doubt, a Parable*; *Monty Python's Spamalot*

2005 LUCILLE LORTEL AWARDS

○ ○ ○ ○ ○

THE LUCILLE LORTEL AWARDS for outstanding Off Broadway achievement were established in 1985 by a resolution of the League of Off Broadway Theatres and Producers, which administers them and has presented them annually since 1986. Eligible for the 20th annual awards in 2005 were all Off Broadway productions that opened between April 1, 2004 and March 31, 2005.

PLAY. ***Doubt, a Parable*** by John Patrick Shanley.

MUSICAL. ***The 25th Annual Putnam County Spelling Bee***. Book by Rachel Sheinkin, music and lyrics by William Finn.

SOLO SHOW. ***Nine Parts of Desire*** by Heather Raffo, starring Ms. Raffo.

REVIVAL. ***Counsellor-at-Law*** by Elmer Rice, produced by Peccadillo Theater Company.

ACTOR. **John Rubinstein** in *Counsellor-at-Law*.

ACTRESS. **Cherry Jones** in *Doubt, a Parable*.

FEATURED ACTOR. **Dan Fogler** in *The 25th Annual Putnam County Spelling Bee*.

FEATURED ACTRESS (tie). **Jenn Harris** in *Modern Orthodox*; **Adriane Lenox** in *Doubt, a Parable*; **Parker Posey** in *Hurlyburly*.

DIRECTION. **Doug Hughes** for *Doubt, a Parable*.

CHOREOGRAPHY. **Christopher Gattelli** for *Altar Boyz*.

SCENERY. **Derek McLane** for *Intimate Apparel*.

COSTUMES. **Catherine Zuber** for *Intimate Apparel*.

LIGHTING. **David Weiner** for *Rodney's Wife*.

SOUND. **Obadiah Eaves** for *Nine Parts of Desire*.

BODY OF WORK. **Irish Repertory Theatre**.

EDITH OLIVER AWARD. **Frances Sternhagen**.

LORTEL AWARD WINNERS 1986–2005

L ISTED BELOW ARE the Lucille Lortel Award winners in the categories of Outstanding Play and Outstanding Musical from the time these awards were established until the present.

1986—*Woza Africa!*; no musical award
1987—*The Common Pursuit*; no musical award
1988—No play or musical award
1989—*The Cocktail Hour*; no musical award
1990—No play or musical award
1991—*Aristocrats*; *Falsettoland*
1992—*Lips Together, Teeth Apart*; *And the World Goes 'Round*
1993—*The Destiny of Me*; *Forbidden Broadway*
1994—*Three Tall Women*; *Wings*
1995—*Camping With Henry & Tom*; *Jelly Roll!*
1996—*Molly Sweeney*; *Floyd Collins*

1997—*How I Learned to Drive*; *Violet*
1998—*Gross Indecency*, and *The Beauty Queen of Leenane* (tie); no musical award
1999—*Wit*; no musical award
2000—*Dinner With Friends*; *James Joyce's The Dead*
2001—*Proof*; *Bat Boy: The Musical*
2002—*Metamorphoses*; *Urinetown*
2003—*Take Me Out*; *Avenue Q*
2004—*Bug*; *Caroline, or Change*
2005—*Doubt, a Parable*; *The 25th Annual Putnam County Spelling Bee*

AMERICAN THEATRE CRITICS/STEINBERG NEW PLAY AWARDS AND CITATIONS

○ ○ ○ ○ ○

INCLUDING PRINCIPAL CITATIONS AND NEW PLAY AWARD WINNERS, 1977–2005

B EGINNING WITH THE season of 1976–77, the American Theatre Critics Association (ATCA) has cited one or more outstanding new plays in United States theater. The principal honorees have been included in *The Best Plays Theater Yearbook* since the first year. In 1986 the ATCA New Play Award was given for the first time, along with a $1,000 prize. The award and citations were renamed the **American Theatre Critics/Steinberg New Play Award and Citations** in 2000 (see essays on the 2005 ATCA/Steinberg honorees in the Season Around the United States section of this volume). The award dates were renumbered beginning with the 2000–2001 volume to correctly reflect the year in which ATCA conferred the honor.

New Play Citations (1977–1985)

1977—*And the Soul Shall Dance* by Wakako Yamauchi
1978—*Getting Out* by Marsha Norman
1979—*Loose Ends* by Michael Weller
1980—*Custer* by Robert E. Ingham
1981—*Chekhov in Yalta* by John Driver and Jeffrey Haddow
1982—*Talking With* by Jane Martin
1983—*Closely Related* by Bruce MacDonald
1984—*Wasted* by Fred Gamel
1985—*Scheherazade* by Marisha Chamberlain

New Play Award (1986–1999)

1986—*Fences* by August Wilson
1987—*A Walk in the Woods* by Lee Blessing
1988—*Heathen Valley* by Romulus Linney
1989—*The Piano Lesson* by August Wilson
1990—*2* by Romulus Linney
1991—*Two Trains Running* by August Wilson
1992—*Could I Have This Dance?* by Doug Haverty
1993—*Children of Paradise: Shooting a Dream* by Steven Epp, Felicity Jones,
        Dominique Serrand and Paul Walsh
1994—*Keely and Du* by Jane Martin
1995—*The Nanjing Race* by Reggie Cheong-Leen
1996—*Amazing Grace* by Michael Cristofer
1997—*Jack and Jill* by Jane Martin
1998—*The Cider House Rules, Part II* by Peter Parnell
1999—*Book of Days* by Lanford Wilson.

ATCA/Steinberg New Play Award and Citations

2000—*Oo-Bla-Dee* by Regina Taylor
        Citation: *Compleat Female Stage Beauty* by Jeffrey Hatcher
        Citation: *Syncopation* by Allan Knee
2001—*Anton in Show Business* by Jane Martin
        Citation: *Big Love* by Charles L. Mee
        Citation: *King Hedley II* by August Wilson
2002—*The Carpetbagger's Children* by Horton Foote
        Citation: *The Action Against Sol Schumann* by Jeffrey Sweet
        Citation: *Joe and Betty* by Murray Mednick
2003—*Anna in the Tropics* by Nilo Cruz
        Citation: *Recent Tragic Events* by Craig Wright
        Citation: *Resurrection Blues* by Arthur Miller
2004—*Intimate Apparel* by Lynn Nottage
        Citation: *Gem of the Ocean* by August Wilson
        Citation: *The Love Song of J. Robert Oppenheimer* by Carson Kreitzer
2005—*Singing Forest* by Craig Lucas
        Citation: *After Ashley* by Gina Gionfriddo
        Citation: *The Clean House* by Sarah Ruhl

ADDITIONAL PRIZES AND AWARDS 2004–2005

THE FOLLOWING IS a list of major awards for achievement in the theater this season. The names of honorees appear in **bold type**.

2003–2004 GEORGE JEAN NATHAN AWARD. For dramatic criticism. **Trey Graham**.

24TH ANNUAL WILLIAM INGE THEATRE FESTIVAL AWARD. For distinguished achievement in American theater. **Tina Howe**. Otis Guernsey New Voices Award: **Lynne Kaufman**.

2005 M. ELIZABETH OSBORN AWARD. Presented by the American Theatre Critics Association to an emerging playwright. **J.T. Rogers** for *Madagascar*.

27TH ANNUAL KENNEDY CENTER HONORS. For distinguished achievement by individuals who have made significant contributions to American culture through the arts. **Warren Beatty**, **Ossie Davis** and **Ruby Dee**, **Elton John**, **Joan Sutherland**, **John Williams**.

8TH ANNUAL KENNEDY CENTER–MARK TWAIN PRIZE. For American humor. **Steve Martin**.

2004 NATIONAL MEDALS OF THE ARTS. For individuals and organizations who have made outstanding contributions to the excellence, growth, support and availability of the arts in the United States, selected by the President from nominees presented by the National Endowment. **Andrew W. Mellon Foundation**, **Ray Bradbury**, **Carlisle Floyd**, **Frederick Hart** (deceased), **Anthony Hecht** (deceased), **John Ruthven**, **Vincent Scully**, **Twyla Tharp**.

2005 DRAMATISTS GUILD AWARDS. Elizabeth Hull–Kate Warriner Award to the playwright whose work deals with social, political or religious mores of the time, selected by the Dramatists Guild Council. **John Patrick Shanley** for *Doubt, a Parable*. Frederick Loewe Award for

Dramatic Composition: **Charles Strouse**. Flora Roberts Award: **Michael John LaChiusa**. Lifetime Achievement: **Stephen Sondheim**.

2005 HENRY HEWES DESIGN AWARDS (formerly American Theatre Wing Design Awards). For design originating in the US, selected by a committee comprising Jeffrey Eric Jenkins (chairman), Tish Dace, Michael Feingold, Glenda Frank, Mario Fratti, Randy Gener, Henry Hewes and Joan Ungaro. Scenic design: **Michael Yeargan** for *The Light in the Piazza*. Costume design: **William Ivey Long** for *La Cage aux Folles*. Lighting design: **Christopher Akerlind** for *The Light in the Piazza*. Notable effects: **Basil Twist** for the production design of *Symphonie Fantastique*; **Darron L. West** for the sound design of *Hot 'n' Throbbing*.

27TH ANNUAL SUSAN SMITH BLACKBURN PRIZE. For women who have written works of outstanding quality for the English-speaking theater. **Gurpreet Kaur Bhatti** for *Behzti (Dishonour)*. Special commendations: **Chloe Moss** for *How Love Is Spelt*; **Heather Raffo** for *Nine Parts of Desire*.

2004 GEORGE FREEDLEY MEMORIAL AWARD. For the best book about live theater published in the United States the previous year. ***Striptease: The Untold History of the Girlie Show*** by **Rachel Shteir**. Special jury prize: ***Broadway Musicals: The 101 Greatest Shows of All Time*** by **Ken Bloom** and **Frank Vlastnik**.

24th ANNUAL ASTAIRE AWARDS. For excellence in dance and choreography, administered by the Theatre Development Fund and selected by a committee comprising Douglas Watt (chairman), Clive Barnes, Howard Kissel, Michael Kuchwara, Donald McDonagh, Richard Philp, Charles

L. Reinhart and Linda Winer. Special award: **Charlotte d'Amboise**. Male dancer: **Norbert Leo Butz** in *Dirty Rotten Scoundrels*.

60TH ANNUAL CLARENCE DERWENT AWARDS. Given to a female and a male performer by Actors' Equity Association based on New York work that demonstrates promise. **Ari Graynor** and **Christian Borle**.

2005 RICHARD RODGERS AWARDS. For staged readings of musicals in nonprofit theaters, administered by the American Academy of Arts and Letters and selected by a jury including Stephen Sondheim (chairman), Lynn Ahrens, Jack Beeson, Sheldon Harnick, and Richard Maltby Jr., Jeanine Tesori and John Weidman. *Bringers* by **Dave Hudson** and **Paul Libman**. *Broadcast* by Nathan Christensen and Scott Murphy; *Red* by **Brian Lowdermilk** and **Marcus Stevens**.

71st ANNUAL DRAMA LEAGUE AWARDS. For distinguished achievement in the American theater. Play: *Doubt, a Parable*. Musical: *Dirty Rotten Scoundrels*. Revival of a play: *Twelve Angry Men*. Revival of a musical: *La Cage aux Folles*. Performance: **Norbert Leo Butz** in *Dirty Rotten Scoundrels*. Julia Hansen Award for excellence in directing: **Mike Nichols**. Achievement in Musical Theatre: **BMI Musical Theatre Workshop**. Unique contribution to theater: **Billy Rose Theatre Collection** of the New York Public Library at Lincoln Center.

2005 GEORGE OPPENHEIMER AWARD. To the best new American playwright, presented by *Newsday*. **Mark Schultz** for *Everything Will Be Different*.

2005 NEW DRAMATISTS LIFETIME ACHIEVEMENT AWARD. To an individual who has made an outstanding artistic contribution to the American theater. **George C. Wolfe**.

2005 *THEATRE WORLD* AWARDS. For outstanding debut performers in Broadway or Off Broadway theater during the

2004–2005 season, selected by a committee including Peter Filichia, Harry Haun, Ben Hodges, Frank Scheck, Matthew Murray, Michael Sommers, Douglas Watt, John Willis, and Linda Winer. **Christina Applegate** for *Sweet Charity*, **Ashlie Atkinson** for *Fat Pig*, **Hank Azaria** for *Monty Python's Spamalot*, **Gordon Clapp** for *Glengarry Glen Ross*, **Conor Donovan** for *Privilege*, **Dan Fogler** for *The 25th Annual Putnam County Spelling Bee*, **Heather Goldenhersh** for *Doubt, a Parable*, **Carla Gugino** for *After the Fall*, **Jenn Harris** for *Modern Orthodox*, **Cheyenne Jackson** for *All Shook Up*, **Celia Keenan-Bolger** for *The 25th Annual Putnam County Spelling Bee*, **Tyler Maynard** for *Altar Boyz*.

50TH ANNUAL DRAMA DESK AWARDS. For outstanding achievement in the 2004–2005 season, voted by an association of New York drama reporters, editors and critics from nominations made by a committee. New play: *Doubt, a Parable*. New musical: *Monty Python's Spamalot*. Revival of a play: *Twelve Angry Men*. Revival of a musical: *La Cage aux Folles*. Revue: *Forbidden Broadway: Special Victims Unit*. Book of a musical: **Rachel Sheinkin** for *The 25th Annual Putnam County Spelling Bee*. Music: **Adam Guettel** for *The Light in the Piazza*. Lyrics: **Eric Idle** for *Monty Python's Spamalot*. Actor in a play: **Brían F. O'Byrne** in *Doubt, a Parable*. Actress in a play: **Cherry Jones** in *Doubt, a Parable*. Featured actor in a play: **Michael Stuhlbarg** in *The Pillowman*. Featured actress in a play: **Adriane Lenox** in *Doubt, a Parable*. Actor in a musical: **Norbert Leo Butz** in *Dirty Rotten Scoundrels*. Actress in a musical: **Victoria Clark** in *The Light in the Piazza*. Featured actor in a musical: **Denis O'Hare** in *Sweet Charity*. Featured actress in a musical: **Jan Maxwell** in *Chitty Chitty Bang Bang*. Solo performance: **Billy Crystal** in *Billy Crystal: 700 Sundays*. Director of a play: **Doug Hughes** for *Doubt, a Parable*. Director of a musical: **James Lapine** for *The 25th Annual Putnam County Spelling Bee*. Choreography: **Jerry Mitchell** for *La Cage aux Folles*. Orchestrations: **Ted Sperling**,

Adam Guettel and Bruce Coughlin for *The Light in the Piazza*. Set design of a play: **Santo Loquasto** for *Glengarry Glen Ross*. Set design of a musical: **Michael Yeargan** for *The Light in the Piazza*. Costume design: **Tim Hatley** for *Monty Python's Spamalot*. Lighting design: **Christopher Akerlind** for *The Light in the Piazza*. Sound design: **Paul Arditti** for *The Pillowman*. Unique Theatrical Experience: **Slava's Snowshow**. Career achievement: **Julie Harris**. Ensemble performance: The casts of *Glengarry Glen Ross* and *The 25th Annual Putnam County Spelling Bee*. Special awards: **Keen Company** and **The Public Theater**.

55TH ANNUAL OUTER CRITICS' CIRCLE AWARDS. For outstanding achievement in the 2004–2005 season, voted by critics on out-of-town periodicals and media. Broadway play: ***Doubt, a Parable***. Off-Broadway play (tie): ***Fat Pig*** and ***Going to St. Ives***. Revival of a play: ***Twelve Angry Men***. Actor in a play: **Brían F. O'Byrne** in *Doubt, a Parable*. Actress in a play: **Cherry Jones** in *Doubt, a Parable*. Featured actor in a play: **Jeff Goldblum** in *The Pillowman*. Featured actress in a play: **Amy Ryan** in *A Streetcar Named Desire*. Director of a play: **Doug Hughes** for *Doubt, a Parable*. Broadway musical: ***Monty Python's Spamalot***. Off-Broadway musical: ***Altar Boyz***. Revival of a musical: ***La Cage aux Folles***. Actor in a musical: **Norbert Leo Butz** in *Dirty Rotten Scoundrels*. Actress in a musical: **Victoria Clark** in *The Light in the Piazza*. Featured actor in a musical: **Dan Fogler** in *The 25th Annual Putnam County Spelling Bee*. Featured actress in a musical: **Sara Ramirez** in *Monty Python's Spamalot*. Director of a musical: **Mike Nichols** for *Monty Python's Spamalot*. Choreography: **Jerry Mitchell** for *La Cage aux Folles*. Scenic design: **Anthony Ward** for *Chitty Chitty Bang Bang*. Costume design: **Tim Hatley** for *Monty Python's Spamalot*. Lighting design: **Christopher Akerlind** for *The Light in the Piazza*. Solo performance: **Billy Crystal** in *Billy Crystal: 700 Sundays*. John Gassner Playwriting Award: **Ron Hutchinson** for *Moonlight and Magnolias*. Special award: **Marjorie Gunner**.

50TH ANNUAL *VILLAGE VOICE* OBIE AWARDS. For outstanding achievement in Off and Off Off Broadway theater. Performance: **Jeremy Shamos** in *Engaged*; **Elizabeth Marvel** in *Hedda Gabler*; **Jason Butler Harner** in *Hedda Gabler*; **Rosemary Allen** in *Good Samaritans*; **Cherry Jones** in *Doubt, a Parable*; **Larry Bryggman** in *Romance*; **Kieran Culkin** in *After Ashley*; **Mercedes Ruehl** in *Woman Before a Glass*; **LaChanze** in *Dessa Rose*; **Deirdre O'Connell** for sustained excellence; **Vivienne Benesch** in *Going to St. Ives*; **L. Scott Caldwell** in *Going to St. Ives*. Direction: **Dan Wackerman** for *Counsellor-at-Law*; **Ivo van Hove** for *Hedda Gabler*; **Doug Hughes** for sustained excellence. Playwriting: **Christopher Shinn** for *Where Do We Live*; **John Patrick Shanley** for *Doubt, a Parable*; **Caryl Churchill** for *A Number*; **Lynn Nottage** for *Fabulation or, the Re-Education of Undine*. Design: **John Lee Beatty** for *Engaged* (scenery); **Rui Rita** for *Engaged* (lighting); **Aural Fixation** for *Engaged* (sound); **Catherine Zuber** for *Engaged* (costumes); **Thomas Lynch** for *Woman Before a Glass* (scenery); **Phil Monat** for *Woman Before a Glass* (lighting); **David Van Tieghem** for *Woman Before a Glass* (sound); **Willa Kim** for *Woman Before a Glass* (costumes); **Jan Versweyveld** for *Hedda Gabler* (scenery).

Special Citations: **The Imagine Festival of Arts, Issues and Ideas**; ***Hell Meets Henry Halfway***; ***Sin (A Cardinal Deposed)***. Ross Wetzsteon Award: **New Dramatists**. Sustained Achievement: **John Guare**. Grants: **13P**; **Epic Theatre Company**; **Little Theater at Tonic**. Distinguished emerging playwright: **Gina Gionfriddo**.

15TH ANNUAL CONNECTICUT CRITICS' CIRCLE AWARDS. For outstanding achievement in Connecticut theater during the 2004–2005 season. Production of a play: **Yale Repertory Theatre** for *The Intelligent Design of Jenny Chow*. Production of a musical: **Goodspeed Musicals** for *Seven Brides for Seven*

Brothers. Actress in a play: **Alyssa Bresnahan** in *A Moon for the Misbegotten*. Actor in a play: **Tom Hewitt** in *Travesties*. Actress in a musical (tie): **Christiane Noll** in *Mack and Mabel*; **Jacquelyn Piro** in *Seven Brides for Seven Brothers*. Actor in a musical: **Noah Racey** in *Where's Charley?* Direction of a play: **Gregory Boyd** for *Travesties*. Direction of a musical: **Julie Arenal** for *Hair*. Choreography: **Patti Colombo** for *Seven Brides for Seven Brothers*. Set design: **Lee Savage** for *The Intelligent Design of Jenny Chow*. Lighting design: **Jennifer Tipton** for *A Moon for the Misbegotten*. Costume design: **Linda Fisher** for *The School for Husbands*. Sound design: **Hillary Charnas** for *The Intelligent Design of Jenny Chow*. Ensemble performance: **Mark A. Bailey, J. Cameron Barnett, Jeff Scot Carey, Emily Drennan, Karin Hendricks, Lauren Hooper, Matthew Hydzik, Liza Marie Johnston, Jumanne Langston, Daniel C. Levine, Pat McRoberts, Dana Mierlak, Dennis Moench, Lauren Moss, Kenny Moten, Andrea Rae, Stephanie St. Hilaire** and **Nirayl Wilcox** in *Hair*.

Roadshow: **Hartford Stage** for *My Fair Lady*. Debut award: **Dan McCabe** in *Kimberly Akimbo*. Tom Killen Memorial Award: **Michael Wilson**, artistic director of Hartford Stage. Special award: **Joanne Woodward**.

23rd ANNUAL ELLIOT NORTON AWARDS. For outstanding contribution to the theater in Boston, voted by a Boston Theater Critics Association Selection Committee comprising Terry Byrne, Carolyn Clay, Iris Fanger, Joyce Kulhawik, Jon Lehman, Bill Marx, Ed Siegel and Caldwell Titcomb. Sustained Excellence: **Oskar Eustis**. Productions—Visiting company: *The Far Side of the Moon* produced by Ex Machina, Quebec at the American Repertory Theatre; Large resident company: *The Miser* produced by American Repertory Theatre; Small resident company: *The Sanctuary Lamp* produced by Súgán Theatre Company; Local fringe company: *Blue/Orange* produced by Zeitgeist Stage Company.

Solo performance: **Pamela Gien** in *The Syringa Tree*, American Repertory Theatre. New script: *Sonia Flew* by **Melinda Lopez**, American Repertory Theatre. Actor—Large company: **John Kelly** in *Dido, Queen of Carthage*, American Repertory Theatre. Actor—Small company: **Benjamin Evett** in *Permanent Collection* and *Quills*, New Repertory Theatre; and *Richard III*, Actors' Shakespeare Project. Actress—Large company: **Phylicia Rashad** in *Gem of the Ocean*, Huntington Theatre Company. Actress—Small company: **Andrea C. Ross** in *A Little Night Music*, Lyric Stage Company of Boston; *The Sound of Music* and *Ramona Quimby*, Wheelock Family Theatre. Director—Large company: **Kent Gash** for *Topdog/Underdog*, Trinity Repertory Company and New Repertory Theatre. Director—Small company: **Adam Zahler** for *Permanent Collection*, New Repertory Theatre. Scene design—Large company: **Adam Stockhausen** for *Sonia Flew* and *36 Views*, Huntington Theatre Company. Scene design—Small company: **Richard Chambers** for *The Glider*, Boston Playwrights' Theatre. Special citations: **Shear Madness**; **City Stage Company**. Guest of Honor: **Elaine Stritch**.

21ST ANNUAL HELEN HAYES AWARDS. In recognition of excellence in Washington, D.C., theater, presented by the Washington Theatre Awards Society.

Resident productions—Play: *Cyrano* produced by The Shakespeare Theatre. Musical (tie): *Allegro* produced by Signature Theatre (Virginia); *Señor Discretion Himself* produced by Arena Stage. Lead actress, musical: **Bernardine Mitchell** in *Mahalia: A Gospel Musical*, MetroStage. Lead actor, musical: **Jason Danieley** in *The Highest Yellow*, Signature Theatre (Virginia). Lead actress, play: **Gin Hammond** in *The Syringa Tree*, The Studio Theatre. Lead actor, play: **Geraint Wyn Davies** in *Cyrano*, The Shakespeare Theatre. Supporting actress, musical: **Ann Duquesnay** in *Hallelujah, Baby!*, Arena Stage and George Street Playhouse. Supporting actor, musical: **David James** in *Godspell*, Toby's Dinner Theatre. Supporting actress, play: **Holly Twyford** in *The Two Gentlemen of Verona*, Folger Theatre. Supporting actor, play: **David Toney** in *Two Trains Running*, The African Continuum Theatre Company. Director, play (tie): **Michael Kahn** for *Cyrano*, The Shakespeare Theatre; Aaron Posner for *The Two Gentlemen of Verona*, Folger Theatre. Director, musical: **Eric Schaeffer** for *Allegro*, Signature Theatre (Virginia). Scenic design, play or musical (tie): **James Kronzer** for *The Diary of Anne Frank*, Round House Theatre; **James Noone** for *Cyrano*, The Shakespeare Theatre. Costume design, play or musical: **Gregg Barnes** for *Allegro*, Signature Theatre (Virginia). Lighting design, play or musical: **Daniel MacLean Wagner** for *The Diary of Anne Frank*, Round House Theatre. Sound design, play or musical: **Martin Desjardins** for *The Diary of Anne Frank*, Round House Theatre. Choreography: **Irina Tsikurishvili** for *The Master and Margarita*, Synetic-Classika Theatre. Musical direction: **Jon Kalbfleisch** for *The Highest Yellow*, Signature Theatre (Virginia).

Non-resident productions—Production: **The Producers** produced by The Kennedy Center. Lead actress: **Holly Cruikshank** in *Movin' Out*, The National Theatre. Lead actor: **Ron Todorowski** in *Movin' Out*, The National Theatre. Supporting performer: **Lee Roy Reams** in *The Producers*, The Kennedy Center.

Charles MacArthur Award for outstanding new play: *Melissa Arctic* by **Craig Wright**, Folger Theatre.

36TH ANNUAL JOSEPH JEFFERSON AWARDS. For achievement in Chicago theater during the 2003–2004 season, given by the Jefferson Awards Committee in 21 competitive categories. Twenty-five producing organizations were nominated for various awards; 9 different companies were honored. Chicago Shakespeare Theater topped all other companies by winning seven awards. The Goodman Theatre followed with five awards; About Face Theatre and Victory Gardens Theater were each thrice honored. The awards ceremony was held November 1, 2004 at the North Shore Center for the Performing Arts in Skokie, Illinois.

Resident productions—New work (non-competitive): *Free Man of Color* by **Charles Smith**, Victory Gardens Theater; *Trying* by **Joanna McClelland Glass**, Victory Gardens Theater. New Adaptation (non-competitive): *Winesburg, Ohio* by **Eric Rosen**, **Andre Pluess** and **Ben Sussman**, About Face Theatre. Play: *Rose Rage: Henry VI, Parts 1, 2 and 3* produced by Chicago Shakespeare Theater. Musical: *The Light in the Piazza* produced by The Goodman Theatre, in association with Intiman Theatre Company. Director, play: **Edward Hall** for *Rose Rage: Henry VI, Parts 1, 2 and 3*, Chicago Shakespeare Theater. Director, musical: **Gary Griffin** for *A Little Night Music*, Chicago Shakespeare Theater. Ensemble: *Rose Rage: Henry VI, Parts 1, 2 and 3*, Chicago Shakespeare Theater. Actor in a principal role, play: **Fritz Weaver** in *Trying*, Victory Gardens Theater. Actress in a principal role, play: **Rondi Reed** in *The Fall to Earth*, Steppenwolf Theatre Company. Actor in a supporting role, play: **Scott Parkinson** in *Rose Rage: Henry VI, Parts 1, 2 and 3*, Chicago Shakespeare Theater. Actress in a supporting role, play: **Deanna Dunagan** in *I Never Sang for My Father*, Steppenwolf Theatre Company. Actor in a principal role, musical: **Ross Lehman** in *A Man of No Importance*, Apple Tree Theatre. Actress in a principal role, musical: **Victoria Clark** in *The Light in the Piazza*, The Goodman Theatre, in association with Intiman Theatre Company. Actor in a supporting role, musical: **Jeff Dumas** in *Winesburg, Ohio*, About Face Theatre. Actress in a supporting role, musical: **Samantha Spiro** in *A Little Night Music*, Chicago Shakespeare Theater. Actor in a revue: **Eugene Fleming** in *Ain't Misbehavin'*, Marriott Theatre. Scenic design: **James Leonard Joy** for *The Taming of the Shrew*, Chicago Shakespeare Theater. Costume design: **Rachel Anne Healy** for *Lady Windermere's Fan*, Northlight Theatre. Lighting design: **Christopher Akerlind** for *The Light in the Piazza*, The Goodman Theatre, in association with Intiman Theatre Company. Sound design: **Ray Nardelli** and **Joshua Horvath** for *Electricidad*, The Goodman Theatre. Choreography: **Marc Robin** for *West Side Story*, Marriott Theatre. Original music: **Patricia Kane**, **Amy Warren** and **Andre Pluess** for *Pulp*, About Face Theatre. Musical direction: **Alan Johnson** for *The Sound of a Voice*, Court Theatre in association with American Repertory Theatre. Special achievement: **David Pleasant** for *Crowns* (percussion), The Goodman Theatre

32ND ANNUAL JOSEPH JEFFERSON CITATIONS WING AWARDS. For outstanding achievement in professional productions during the 2004–2005 season of Chicago area theaters not operating under union contracts. Production, play (tie): *A Streetcar Named Desire*, produced by Raven Theatre; *Equus*, produced by The Hypocrites; *This Happy Breed*, produced by TimeLine Theatre Company. Production, musical: *Parade*, produced by Bailiwick Repertory. Ensemble (tie): *Action Movie: The Play*, Defiant Theatre in association with Keith Geller and John York Noble; *Parade*, Bailiwick Repertory; *This Happy Breed*, TimeLine Theatre Company. Director, play (tie): **Nick Bowling** for *This Happy Breed*, TimeLine Theatre Company; **Sean Graney** for *Equus*, The Hypocrites; **Michael Menendian** for *A Streetcar Named Desire*, Raven Theatre. Director, musical or revue: **David Zak** for *Parade*, Bailiwick Repertory. New Work (tie): *The Upper Room* by **David Barr III**, Pegasus Players; *Arrangement for Two Violas* by **Susan Lieberman**, Visions and Voices Theatre Company. New adaptation: *Strong Poison* by **Frances Limoncelli**, Lifeline Theatre. Actress in a principal role, play (tie): **Michele DiMaso** in *Duet for One*, Stockyards Theatre Project; **Liz Fletcher** in *A Streetcar Named Desire*, Raven

Theatre; **Demetria Thomas** in *The Divine Order of Becoming*, MPAACT. Actress in a principal role, musical (tie): **Amy Arbizzani** in *Parade*, Bailiwick Repertory; **Sarah Swanson** in *Jane Eyre*, Circle Theatre; **Cassie Wooley** in *Merrily We Roll Along*, White Horse Theatre Company. Actor in a principal role, play (tie): **Geoff Button** in *Equus*, The Hypocrites; **Terry Hamilton** in *This Happy Breed*, TimeLine Theatre Company; **Mike Vieau** in *A Streetcar Named Desire*, Raven Theatre. Actor in a principal role, musical (tie): **Nicholas Foster** in *Parade*, Bailiwick Repertory; **Jon Steinhagen** in *The Mystery of Edwin Drood*, Circle Theatre. Actress in a supporting role, play: **Molly Brennan** in *Curse of the Crying Heart*, The House Theatre of Chicago. Actress in a supporting role, musical or revue (tie): **Yolanda Davis** in *Spoon River Anthology*, Theo Ubique Theatre Company in association with Michael James; **Darrelyn Marx** in *Jane Eyre*, Circle Theatre. Actor in a supporting role, play: **Terry Hamilton** in *Pravda*, TimeLine Theatre Company. Actor in a supporting role, musical (tie): **Sean Reid** in *Parade*, Bailiwick Repertory; **Joel Sutliffe** in *The Mystery of Edwin Drood*, Circle Theatre. Scenic design (tie): **Brian Sidney Bembridge** for *Inventing Van Gogh*, Bailiwick Repertory; **Michael Menendian** and **Leif Olsen** for *A Streetcar Named Desire*, Raven Theatre; **Joey Wade** for *Impossible Marriage*, Strawdog Theatre Company. Costume design (tie): **Nicole Rene Burchfield** for *This Happy Breed*, TimeLine Theatre Company; **Laurie LaMere Klapperich** for *Curse of the Crying Heart*, The House Theatre of Chicago; **Alison Siple** for *Leonce und Lena*, The Hypocrites. Lighting design: **Jared Moore** for *Inventing Van Gogh*, Bailiwick Repertory. Sound design (tie): **Andrew Hansen** for *Antigone*, Greasy Joan and Co.; **Gregor Mortis** for *Action Movie: The Play*, Defiant Theatre in association with Keith Geller and John York Noble. Choreography: **Tommy Rapley** for *Cave With Man*, The House Theatre of Chicago. Fight choreography (tie): **Joe Foust** and **Geoff Coates**, *Action*

Movie: The Play, Defiant Theatre in association with Keith Geller and John York Noble; **Matthew Hawkins** for *Curse of the Crying Heart*, The House Theatre of Chicago. Original incidental music (tie): **Andrew Hansen** for *This Happy Breed*, TimeLine Theatre Company; **Kevin O'Donnell** for *Cave With Man*, The House Theatre of Chicago. Musical direction (tie): **Alan Bukowiecki** for *Parade*, Bailiwick Repertory; **Nick Sula** for *Merrily We Roll Along*, White Horse Theatre Company.

THE THEATER HALL OF FAME

○ ○ ○ ○ ○

THE THEATER HALL OF FAME was created in 1971 to honor those who have made outstanding contributions to the American theater in a career spanning at least 25 years. Honorees are elected annually by members of the American Theatre Critics Association, members of the Theater Hall of Fame and theater historians. Names of those elected in 2004 and inducted January 24, 2005 appear in **_bold italics_**.

GEORGE ABBOTT

MAUDE ADAMS

VIOLA ADAMS

JACOB ADLER

STELLA ADLER

EDWARD ALBEE

THEONI V. ALDREDGE

IRA ALDRIDGE

JANE ALEXANDER

MARY ALICE

WINTHROP AMES

JUDITH ANDERSON

MAXWELL ANDERSON

ROBERT ANDERSON

JULIE ANDREWS

MARGARET ANGLIN

JEAN ANOUILH

HAROLD ARLEN

GEORGE ARLISS

BORIS ARONSON

ADELE ASTAIRE

FRED ASTAIRE

EILEEN ATKINS

BROOKS ATKINSON

LAUREN BACALL

PEARL BAILEY

GEORGE BALANCHINE

WILLIAM BALL

ANNE BANCROFT

TALLULAH BANKHEAD

RICHARD BARR

PHILIP BARRY

ETHEL BARRYMORE

JOHN BARRYMORE

LIONEL BARRYMORE

HOWARD BAY

NORA BAYES

JOHN LEE BEATTY

JULIAN BECK

SAMUEL BECKETT

BRIAN BEDFORD

S.N. BEHRMAN

NORMAN BEL GEDDES

DAVID BELASCO

MICHAEL BENNETT

RICHARD BENNETT

ROBERT RUSSELL BENNETT

ERIC BENTLEY

IRVING BERLIN

SARAH BERNHARDT

LEONARD BERNSTEIN

EARL BLACKWELL

KERMIT BLOOMGARDEN

JERRY BOCK

RAY BOLGER

EDWIN BOOTH

JUNIUS BRUTUS BOOTH

SHIRLEY BOOTH

PHILIP BOSCO

DION BOUCICAULT

ALICE BRADY

BERTOLT BRECHT

FANNIE BRICE

PETER BROOK

JOHN MASON BROWN

ROBERT BRUSTEIN

BILLIE BURKE

ABE BURROWS

RICHARD BURTON

MRS. PATRICK CAMPBELL

ZOE CALDWELL

EDDIE CANTOR

LEN CARIOU

MORRIS CARNOVSKY

MRS. LESLIE CARTER

GOWER CHAMPION

FRANK CHANFRAU

CAROL CHANNING

STOCKARD CHANNING

RUTH CHATTERTON

PADDY CHAYEFSKY

ANTON CHEKHOV

INA CLAIRE

BOBBY CLARK

HAROLD CLURMAN

LEE J. COBB

RICHARD L. COE

GEORGE M. COHAN

ALEXANDER H. COHEN

JACK COLE

CY COLEMAN

CONSTANCE COLLIER

ALVIN COLT

BETTY COMDEN

MARC CONNELLY

BARBARA COOK

EUGENE HOWARD

LESLIE HOWARD

SIDNEY HOWARD

WILLIE HOWARD

BARNARD HUGHES

HENRY HULL

JOSEPHINE HULL

WALTER HUSTON

EARLE HYMAN

HENRIK IBSEN

WILLIAM INGE

BERNARD B. JACOBS

ELSIE JANIS

JOSEPH JEFFERSON

AL JOLSON

JAMES EARL JONES

MARGO JONES

ROBERT EDMOND JONES

TOM JONES

JON JORY

RAUL JULIA

MADELINE KAHN

JOHN KANDER

GARSON KANIN

GEORGE S. KAUFMAN

DANNY KAYE

ELIA KAZAN

GENE KELLY

GEORGE KELLY

FANNY KEMBLE

JEROME KERN

WALTER KERR

MICHAEL KIDD

RICHARD KILEY

SIDNEY KINGSLEY

KEVIN KLINE

FLORENCE KLOTZ

JOSEPH WOOD KRUTCH

BERT LAHR

BURTON LANE

FRANK LANGELLA

LAWRENCE LANGNER

LILLIE LANGTRY

ANGELA LANSBURY

CHARLES LAUGHTON

ARTHUR LAURENTS

GERTRUDE LAWRENCE

JEROME LAWRENCE

EVA LE GALLIENNE

CANADA LEE

MING CHO LEE

ROBERT E. LEE

LOTTE LENYA

ALAN JAY LERNER

SAM LEVENE

ROBERT LEWIS

BEATRICE LILLIE

HOWARD LINDSAY

FRANK LOESSER

FREDERICK LOEWE

JOSHUA LOGAN

SANTO LOQUASTO

PAULINE LORD

LUCILLE LORTEL

ALFRED LUNT

CHARLES MACARTHUR

STEELE MACKAYE

JUDITH MALINA

DAVID MAMET

ROUBEN MAMOULIAN

RICHARD MANSFIELD

ROBERT B. MANTELL

FREDRIC MARCH

NANCY MARCHAND

JULIA MARLOWE

ERNEST H. MARTIN

MARY MARTIN

RAYMOND MASSEY

ELIZABETH IRELAND MCCANN

IAN MCKELLEN

SIOBHAN MCKENNA

TERRENCE MCNALLY

HELEN MENKEN

BURGESS MEREDITH

ETHEL MERMAN

DAVID MERRICK

JO MIELZINER

ARTHUR MILLER

MARILYN MILLER

LIZA MINNELLI

HELENA MODJESKA

FERENC MOLNAR

LOLA MONTEZ

VICTOR MOORE

ROBERT MORSE

ZERO MOSTEL

ANNA CORA MOWATT

PAUL MUNI

BRIAN MURRAY

THARON MUSSER

GEORGE JEAN NATHAN

MILDRED NATWICK

NAZIMOVA

PATRICIA NEAL

JAMES M. NEDERLANDER

MIKE NICHOLS

ELLIOT NORTON

SEAN O'CASEY

CLIFFORD ODETS

DONALD OENSLAGER

LAURENCE OLIVIER

EUGENE O'NEILL

JERRY ORBACH

GERALDINE PAGE

JOSEPH PAPP

ESTELLE PARSONS

OSGOOD PERKINS

BERNADETTE PETERS

MOLLY PICON

HAROLD PINTER

LUIGI PIRANDELLO

CHRISTOPHER PLUMMER

COLE PORTER

Robert Preston
Harold Prince
Jose Quintero
Ellis Rabb
John Raitt
Tony Randall
Michael Redgrave
Vanessa Redgrave
Ada Rehan
Elmer Rice
Lloyd Richards
Ralph Richardson
Chita Rivera
Jason Robards
Jerome Robbins
Paul Robeson
Richard Rodgers
Will Rogers
Sigmund Romberg
Harold Rome
Billy Rose
Lillian Russell
Donald Saddler
Gene Saks
Diana Sands
William Saroyan
Joseph Schildkraut
Harvey Schmidt
Alan Schneider
Gerald Schoenfeld
Arthur Schwartz
Maurice Schwartz
George C. Scott
Marian Seldes
Irene Sharaff

George Bernard Shaw
Sam Shepard
Robert E. Sherwood
J.J. Shubert
Lee Shubert
Herman Shumlin
Neil Simon
Lee Simonson
Edmund Simpson
Otis Skinner
Maggie Smith
Oliver Smith
Stephen Sondheim
E.H. Sothern
Kim Stanley
Jean Stapleton
Maureen Stapleton
Frances Sternhagen
Roger L. Stevens
Isabelle Stevenson
Ellen Stewart
Dorothy Stickney
Fred Stone
Peter Stone
Tom Stoppard
Lee Strasberg
August Strindberg
Elaine Stritch
Charles Strouse
Jule Styne
Margaret Sullavan
Arthur Sullivan
Jessica Tandy
Laurette Taylor
Ellen Terry

Cleon Throckmorton
Tommy Tune
Gwen Verdon
Robin Wagner
Nancy Walker
Eli Wallach
James Wallack
Lester Wallack
Tony Walton
Douglas Turner Ward
David Warfield
Ethel Waters
Clifton Webb
Joseph Weber
Margaret Webster
Kurt Weill
Orson Welles
Mae West
Robert Whitehead
Richard Wilbur
Oscar Wilde
Thornton Wilder
Bert Williams
Tennessee Williams
Lanford Wilson
P.G. Wodehouse
Peggy Wood
Alexander Woollcott
Irene Worth
Teresa Wright
Ed Wynn
Vincent Youmans
Stark Young
Florenz Ziegfeld
Patricia Zipprodt

THE THEATER HALL OF FAME
FOUNDERS AWARD

ESTABLISHED IN 1993 in honor of Earl Blackwell, James M. Nederlander, Gerard Oestreicher and Arnold Weissberger, The Theater Hall of Fame Founders Award is voted by the Hall's board of directors to an individual for his or her outstanding contribution to the theater.

1993 James M. Nederlander	1998 Edward Colton	2002 No Award
1994 Kitty Carlisle Hart	1999 No Award	2003 Price Berkley
1995 Harvey Sabinson	2000 Gerard Oestreicher	2004 No Award
1996 Henry Hewes	2000 Arnold Weissberger	
1997 Otis L. Guernsey Jr.	2001 Tom Dillon	

MARGO JONES
CITIZEN OF THE THEATER MEDAL

PRESENTED ANNUALLY TO a citizen of the theater who has made a lifetime commitment to theater in the United States and has demonstrated an understanding and affirmation of the craft of playwriting.

1961 Lucille Lortel	1970 Joseph Papp	1988 No Award
1962 Michael Ellis	1971 Zelda Fichandler	1989 Margaret Goheen
1963 Judith R. Marechal	1972 Jules Irving	1990 Richard Coe
George Savage	1973 Douglas Turner Ward	1991 Otis L. Guernsey Jr.
1964 Richard Barr,	1974 Paul Weidner	1992 Abbot Van Nostrand
Edward Albee	1975 Robert Kalfin	1993 Henry Hewes
Clinton Wilder	1976 Gordon Davidson	1994 Jane Alexander
Richard A. Duprey	1977 Marshall W. Mason	1995 Robert Whitehead
1965 Wynn Handman	1978 Jon Jory	1996 Al Hirschfeld
Marston Balch	1979 Ellen Stewart	1997 George C. White
1966 Jon Jory	1980 John Clark Donahue	1998 James Houghton
Arthur Ballet	1981 Lynne Meadow	1999 George Keathley
1967 Paul Baker	1982 Andre Bishop	2000 Eileen Heckart
George C. White	1983 Bill Bushnell	2001 Mel Gussow
1968 Davey Marlin-Jones	1984 Gregory Mosher	2002 Emilie S. Kilgore
1968 Ellen Stewart	1985 John Lion	2003 No Award
1969 Adrian Hall	1986 Lloyd Richards	2004 Christopher Durang
Edward Parone	1987 Gerald Chapman	Marsha Norman
1969 Gordon Davidson		

MUSICAL THEATRE HALL OF FAME

THIS ORGANIZATION WAS established at New York University on November 10, 1993.

HAROLD ARLEN

IRVING BERLIN

LEONARD BERNSTEIN

EUBIE BLAKE

ABE BURROWS

GEORGE M. COHAN

DOROTHY FIELDS

GEORGE GERSHWIN

IRA GERSHWIN

OSCAR HAMMERSTEIN II

E.Y. HARBURG

LARRY HART

JEROME KERN

BURTON LANE

ALAN JAY LERNER

FRANK LOESSER

FREDERICK LOEWE

COLE PORTER

ETHEL MERMAN

JEROME ROBBINS

RICHARD RODGERS

HAROLD ROME

2004–2005 NEW PUBLICATION OF PLAYS

○ ○ ○ ○ ○

Compiled by Rue E. Canvin

Anna in the Tropics. Nilo Cruz. Dramatists Play Service (acting ed.). $6.50

Autobahn: Short Plays Cycle. Neil LaBute. Faber and Faber (paper). $13

Bad Axe. P.J. Barry. Samuel French (acting ed.). $6.50

Barbra's Wedding. Daniel Stern. Samuel French (acting ed.). $6.50

Beard of Avon, The. Amy Freed. Samuel French (acting ed.). $6.50

Beautiful Bodies. Laura Shaine Cunningham. Broadway Play Publishing (paper). $12.95

Beautiful Child. Nicky Silver. Dramatists Play Service (acting ed.). $6.50

Behzti (Dishonour). Gurpreet Kaur Bhatti. Oberon (paper). $15.95

Bicycle Country, A. Nilo Cruz. Dramatists Play Service (acting ed.). $6.50

Blackbird. Adam Rapp. Broadway Play Publishing (paper). $12.95

Bluff. Jeffrey Sweet. Samuel French (acting ed.) $6.50

Bright Ideas. Eric Coble. Dramatists Play Service (acting ed.) $6.50

Brooklyn Boy. Donald Margulies. Theatre Communications Group (paper). $12.95

Caroline, or Change. Tony Kushner and Jeanine Tesori. Theatre Communications Group (paper). $13.95

Cavedweller. Kate Moira Ryan. Dramatists Play Service (acting ed.). $6.50

Cellophane. Mac Wellman. Performing Arts Journal (paper). $19.95

Contest, The. Shirley Lauro. Samuel French (acting ed.). $6.50

Continental Divide: Daughters of the Revolution and Mothers Against. David Edgar. Nick Hern (paper). $21.95

Cook, The. Eduardo Machado. Samuel French (acting ed.). $6.50

Dumb Show. Joe Penhall. Methuen (paper). $14.95

Each Day Dies With Sleep. Jose Rivera. Broadway Play Publishing (acting ed.). $7.95

Ears on a Beatle. Mark St. Germain. Samuel French (acting ed.) $6.50

East/West Quartet, The. Ping Chong. Theatre Communications Group (paper). $16.95

Ecstatic Bible, The. Howard Barker. Oberon (paper). $40

Exonerated, The. Jessica Blank and Erik Jensen. Dramatists Play Service. (acting ed.) $6.50

Fat Pig. Neil LaBute. Faber and Faber (paper). $13

Faustus: A Play. David Mamet. Random House (paper). $12

Festen. David Eldridge. Methuen (paper). $14.95

Flesh & Blood. Peter Gaitens. Dramatists Play Service (paper). $6.50

Frozen. Bryony Lavery. Dramatists Play Service (acting ed.). $6.50

Goat, or Who Is Sylvia?, The. Edward Albee. Overlook Press. $14.95

Good German, The. David Wiltse. Samuel French. (acting ed.) $6.25

Goodnight Children Everywhere and Other Plays. Richard Nelson. Theatre Communications Group (paper). $18.95

Guantanamo: Honor Bound to Defend Freedom. Victoria Brittain and Gillian Slovo. Oberon (paper). $14.95

Hannah and Martin. Kate Fodor. Dramatists Play Service (acting ed.). $6.50

Hollywood Arms. Carrie Hamilton and Carol Burnett. Dramatists Play Service (acting ed). $6.50

Homebody/Kabul (Revised Edition). Tony Kushner. Theater Communications Group (paper). $13.95

Hortensia and the Museum of Dreams. Nilo Cruz. Dramatists Play Service (acting ed.). $6.50

Kaufman and Co.: Broadway Comedies. George S. Kaufman et al. Ed. Laurence Maslon. Library of America (cloth). $35

Kenneth's First Play. Richard Nelson and Colin Chambers. Broadway Play Publishing (paper). $12.95

Long Christmas Ride Home, The. Paula Vogel. Theatre Communications Group. (paper) $12.95

Match. Stephen Belber. Dramatists Play Service (acting ed.) $6.50

Matt and Ben. Mindy Kaling and Brenda Withers. Overlook Press (cloth). $12.95

Men From the Boys, The. Mart Crowley. Samuel French. (acting ed.) $6.50

Meshugah. Emily Mann. Dramatists Play Service (acting ed.). $6.50

Mr. Charles, Currently of Palm Beach. Paul Rudnick. Dramatists Play Service (acting ed.). $6.50

Moonlight Room, The. Tristine Skyler. Dramatists Play Service (acting ed.). $6.50

Night Train to Bolina. Nilo Cruz. Dramatists Play Service (acting ed.). $6.50

Observe the Sons of Ulster Marching Towards the Somme. Frank McGuinness. Samuel French (acting ed.). $6.50

O'Conner Girls, The. Katie Forgette. Dramatists Play Service (acting ed.). $6.50

Orange Flower Water. Craig Wright. Dramatists Play Service (acting ed.). $6.50

Peter Pan: Peter and Wendy and Peter Pan in Kensington Gardens. J.M. Barrie. Penguin (paper). $9

Pillowman, The. Martin McDonagh. Faber and Faber (paper). $13

Play Yourself. Harry Kondoleon. Dramatists Play Service (acting ed.). $6.50

Plays: Volume 1. Richard Maxwell. Theatre Communications Group (paper). $16.95

Private Jokes, Public Places. Oren Safdie. Dramatists Play Service (acting ed.). $6.50

Recent Tragic Events. Craig Wright. Dramatists Play Service. (acting ed.) $6.50

Resident Alien. Stuart Spencer. Broadway Play Publishing (paper). $12.95

Retreat From Moscow, The. William Nicholson. Dramatists Play Service (acting ed.). $6.50

Revelations. Stephen Lowe. Methuen (paper). $15.95

Rose's Dilemma. Neil Simon. Samuel French (acting ed.). $6.50

Rounding Third. Richard Dresser. Dramatic Publishing (acting ed.). $6.50

Sea of Tranquility. Howard Korder. Dramatists Play Service (acting ed.). $6.50

Seven Rabbits on a Pole. John C. Picardi. Samuel French. (acting ed.) $6.50

[sic]. Melissa James Gibson. Dramatists Play Service (acting ed.). $6.50

Silent Laughter. Billy Van Zandt and Jane Milmore. Samuel French (acting ed.). $6.50

Sonnets for an Old Century. Jose Rivera. Broadway Play Publishing (acting ed.). $12.95

Stendhal Syndrome: Full Frontal Nudity and Prelude and Liebstod, The. Terrence McNally. Grove Press. (paper) $13

Stone Cold Dead Serious and Other Plays. Adam Rapp. Faber and Faber (paper). $16

Stonewall Jackson's House. Jonathan Reynolds. Broadway Play Publishing (paper). $12.95

Take Me Out. Richard Greenberg. Dramatists Play Service (acting ed.). $6.50

Ten Unknowns. Jon Robin Baitz. Grove Press (paper). $13

IN MEMORIAM
JUNE 2004–MAY 2005

○ ○ ○ ○ ○

PERFORMERS

Adams, Mason (86) – April 26, 2005
Albert, Eddie (99) – May 26, 2005
Allen, Dayton (85) – November 18, 2004
Bailey, David (71) – November 25, 2004
Bancroft, Anne (73) – June 6, 2005
Bangley, Jimmy (48) – December 10, 2004
Boyett, William (77) – December 29, 2004
Brand, Phoebe (96) – July 3, 2004
Brando, Marlon (80) – July 1, 2004
Branigan, Laura (47) – August 26, 2004
Choate, Tim (49) – September 25, 2004
Coates, Carolyn (77) – March 27, 2005
Davis, Ossie (87) – February 4, 2005
DeHuff, Nicole (30) – February 16, 2005
Dennis, Beverly (79) – January 20, 2005
Dillon, Tom (86) – March 14, 2005
Distel, Sacha (71) – July 22, 2004
D'Jola, Badja (56) – January 8, 2005
Dowling, Doris (81) – June 18, 2004
Eaton, Charles (94) – August 15, 2004
Elliott, Stephen (86) – May 21, 2005
Esmond, Carl (97) – December 4, 2004
Evers, Jason (83) – March 13, 2005
Fernandez, Jaime (67) – April 16, 2005
Fraser, Elizabeth (85) – May 5, 2005
Gades, Antonio (67) – July 20, 2004
Garner, Paul (95) – August 8, 2004
Gordon, Haskell (83) – January 8, 2005
Gorshin, Frank (71) – May 17, 2005
Guilmain, Ofelia (83) – January 14, 2005
Harris, Julius (81) – October 17, 2004
Hoffman, Jane (93) – July 26, 2004
Holley, Treva Y. (95) – October 6, 2004
Hussey, Ruth (93) – April 19, 2005
Jacobson, Max (89) – August 13, 2004
Karlan, Richard (85) – September 10, 2004
Keel, Howard (85) – November 7, 2004
Kemmer, Ed (84) – November 9, 2004
Lause, Hermann (66) – March 28, 2005
Louden, Michael (40) – September 4, 2004
Lupino, Richard (75) – February 9, 2005
Lux, Lillian (86) – June 11, 2005
Martin, Barney (82) – March 21, 2005

Manning, Ruth (84) – November 19, 2004
Maxwell, Frank (87) – August 4, 2004
Mayo, Virginia (84) – January 17, 2005
Mills, John (97) – May 23, 2005
Mitchell, Gregory (52) – November 11, 2004
Morris, Howard (85) – May 21, 2005
Murray, Leland (75) – November 26, 2004
O'Herlihy, Daniel (85) – February 17, 2005
Owens, Elizabeth (77) – March 8, 2005
Paretz, Susan (59) – August 27, 2004
Peterson, Ray (65) – January 25, 2005
Raitt, John (88) – February 20, 2005
Reggiani, Serge (82) – July 22, 2004
Roche, Eugene (75) – July 28, 2004
Rose, Norman (87) – November 12, 2004
Rowlands, Patsy (71) – January 22, 2005
Ryan, Peggy (80) – October 30, 2004
Sanford, Isabel (86) – July 9, 2004
Schell, Maria (79) – April 26, 2005
Skinner, Margo (55) – April 11, 2005
Smith, Archie (86) – June 9, 2004
Smith, Charles Rome (77) – August 16, 2004
Solov, Zachary (81) – November 6, 2004
Takla, Waguih (61) – November 12, 2004
Tebaldi, Renata (82) – December 19, 2004
Villeret, Jacques (53) – January 28, 2005
Walsh, Kay (90) – April 16, 2005
Warrick, Ruth (88) – January 15, 2005
Wayne, Steve (84) – September 5, 2004
Welch, Charles (83) – July 16, 2004
Woodthorpe, Peter (72) – August 13, 2004
Wray, Fay (96) – August 8, 2004
Wright, Teresa (86) – March 6, 2005

PRODUCERS, DIRECTORS, CHOREOGRAPHERS

Beakel, Walter (79) – June 15, 2004
Broca, Philippe de (71) – November 26, 2004
Buchanan, Larry (81) – December 2, 2004
Burkick, Richard (88) – March 17, 2005
Deguere, Philip (60) – January 24, 2005

Frankel, Gene (85) – April 20, 2005
Hill, Debra (54) – March 7, 2005
Lane, Sharyn (55) – March 7, 2005
Levy, Jacques (69) – September 30, 2004
Lewitzky, Bella (88) – July 16, 2004
Louden, Michael (40) – September 4, 2004
Madigan, Thomas (85) – July 8, 2004
Mordecai, Benjamin (60) – May 8, 2005
O'Neil, Louise Westergaard (67) – May 6, 2005
Parks, Hildy (78) – October 7, 2004
Patterson, John (64) – February 7, 2005
Pratt, Charles A. (81) – April 27, 2005
Ramos, Sergio (69) – June 2, 2004
Rodriguez, Ismael (86) – August 7, 2004
Simmons, Richard A. (80) – November 13, 2004
Skaggs, Jimmie F. (59) – June 6, 2004
Stix, John, (83) – October 2, 2004
Turner, Jerry (76) – September 2, 2004
White, Onna (83) – April 8, 2005

COMPOSERS, LYRICISTS, SONGWRITERS

Allen, Ralph G. (70) – September 9, 2004
Bernstein, Elmer (82) – August 18, 2004
Coleman, Cy (75) – November 19, 2004
Colombier, Michel (65) – November 14, 2004
Diamond, David (89) – June 13, 2005
Ebb, Fred (76) – September 11, 2004
Endsley, Melvin (70) – August 16, 2004
Gallagher, Dick (49) – January 20, 2005
Goldsmith, Jerry (75) – July 21, 2004
Harper, Wally (63) – October 8, 2004
Jolly, Pete (72) – November 6, 2004
Layton, Billy Jim (79) – October 30, 2004
Lewine, Richard (94) – May 19, 2005
Melcher, Terry (62) – November 20, 2004
Melle, Gil (72) – October 28, 2004
Mottola, Tony (86) – August 9, 2004
Raskin, David (92) – August 9, 2004
Velazquez, Consuela (88) - January 22, 2005

PLAYWRIGHTS

Allan, Ralph G. (70) – September 9, 2004
Barnes, Peter (73) – July 1, 2004
Chodorov, Jerome (93) – September 12, 2004

Clontz, Dennis (51) – June 14, 2004
Miller, Arthur (89) – February 10, 2005
Milner, Ron (68) – July 16, 2004

DESIGNERS

Deshields, Jack (81) – November 29, 2004
Koon, Charles (85) – November 11, 2004
Yelusich, Andrew (50) – October 28, 2004

MUSICIANS

Bunker, Larry (76) – March 8, 2005
Bushkin, Joe (87) – November 3, 2004
Carter, Joe (78) – March 2, 2005
Charles, Ray (73) – June 11, 2004
Denny, Martin (93) – March 2, 2005
Dryden, Spencer (66) – January 11, 2005
Griffiths, Eric (64) – January 29, 2005
Hester, Paul (46) – March 27, 2005
Jones, Russell T. (35) – November 13, 2004
Kane, Arthur (55) – July 13, 2004
Kenyatta, Robin (62) - October 26, 2004
Mottola, Tony (86) – August 9, 2004
Patten, Edward (66) – February 25, 2005
Quine, Robert (61) – May 31, 2004
Rittman, Trude (96) – February 22, 2005
Smith, Jimmy (76) – February 8, 2005
Waller, Charlie (69) – August 18, 2004
Williams, James (53) – July 20, 2004
York, William (85) – August 15, 2004

OTHERS

Binger, James H. (88) – November 3, 2004
Chairman of Jujamcyn Theaters
Carson, Johnny (79) – January 23, 2005
Late night television host of the "Tonight" show
Chaney, Frances (89) – November 23, 2004
Blacklisted Radio Star
Gussow, Mel (71) – April 29, 2005
Critic and champion of playwrights
Herscher, Sylvia (91) – December 29, 2004
Agent, general manager and producer
Kente, Gibson (73) – November 6, 2004
"Father of black theater" in South Africa
Patterson, Tom (84) – February 23, 2005
Founder of Canada's Stratford Festival
Zeisler, Peter (81) – January 16, 2005
Co-founder of Guthrie Theater

THE BEST PLAYS AND MAJOR PRIZEWINNERS
1894–2005

○ ○ ○ ○ ○

LISTED IN ALPHABETICAL order below are all works selected as Best Plays in previous volumes of the *Best Plays Theater Yearbook* series, except for the seasons of 1996–97 through 1999–2000. During those excluded seasons, *Best Plays* honored only major prizewinners and those who received special *Best Plays* citations. Opposite each title is given the volume in which the play is honored, its opening date and its total number of performances. Two separate opening-date and performance-number entries signify two separate engagements when the original production transferred. Plays marked with an asterisk (*) were still playing June 1, 2005 and their numbers of performances were figured through May 31, 2005. Adaptors and translators are indicated by (ad) and (tr), the symbols (b), (m) and (l) stand for the author of the book, music and lyrics in the case of musicals and (c) signifies the credit for the show's conception, (i) for its inspiration. Entries identified as 94–99, 99–09 and 09–19 are late–19th and early–20th century plays from one of the retrospective volumes. 94–95, 95–96, 96–97, 97–98, 98–99 and 99–00 are late–20th century plays.

PLAY	VOLUME	OPENED	PERFS
Abe Lincoln in Illinois—Robert E. Sherwood	38–39	Oct. 15, 1938	472
Abraham Lincoln—John Drinkwater	19–20	Dec. 15, 1919	193
Accent on Youth—Samson Raphaelson	34–35	Dec. 25, 1934	229
Adam and Eva—Guy Bolton, George Middleton	19–20	Sept. 13, 1919	312
Adaptation—Elaine May; and Next—Terrence McNally	68–69	Feb. 10, 1969	707
Affairs of State—Louis Verneuil	50–51	Sept. 25, 1950	610
After Ashley—Gina Gionfriddo	04–05	Feb. 28, 2005	35
After the Fall—Arthur Miller	63–64	Jan. 23, 1964	208
After the Rain—John Bowen	67–68	Oct. 9, 1967	64
After-Play—Anne Meara	94–95	Jan. 31, 1995	400
Agnes of God—John Pielmeier	81–82	Mar. 30, 1982	599
Ah, Wilderness!—Eugene O'Neill	33–34	Oct. 2, 1933	289
Ain't Supposed to Die a Natural Death—(b, m, l) Melvin Van Peebles	71–72	Oct. 20, 1971	325
Alien Corn—Sidney Howard	32–33	Feb. 20, 1933	98
Alison's House—Susan Glaspell	30–31	Dec. 1, 1930	41
All My Sons—Arthur Miller	46–47	Jan. 29, 1947	328
All in the Timing—David Ives	93–94	Feb. 17, 1994	526
All Over Town—Murray Schisgal	74–75	Dec. 29, 1974	233
All the Way Home—Tad Mosel, based on James Agee's novel *A Death in the Family*	60–61	Nov. 30, 1960	333
Allegro—(b, l) Oscar Hammerstein II, (m) Richard Rodgers	47–48	Oct. 10, 1947	315

CONTRIBUTORS TO *BEST PLAYS*

○ ○ ○ ○ ○

Misha Berson is the theater critic for *The Seattle Times*, a post she has held since 1992. She is a regular contributor to *American Theatre*, has taught at the University of Washington, San Francisco State University and the USC/Annenberg NEA Theatre Critics Institute. She is also a frequent commentator for public radio on KUOW-FM. Berson is the author of several books on theater including *The San Francisco Stage* and *Between Worlds: Contemporary Asian-American Plays*. She was a fellow in the National Arts Journalism Program at Columbia University.

Rue E. Canvin worked at the *New York Herald Tribune*, first as a secretary in the advertising department and then as an editorial assistant in the drama department for 15 years where she worked with the editors and the arts critics until the demise of the newspaper in 1966. She also worked at the *World Journal Tribune* until it closed in 1967. Canvin has served as an assistant editor of *The Best Plays Theater Yearbook* series since 1963. She has also transcribed taped interviews for the Dramatists Guild and Authors League.

Michael Feingold has worked in the theater for more than three decades as a translator, playwright, lyricist, director, dramaturg and literary manager. A graduate of Columbia University and the Yale School of Drama, he has translated more than 50 plays and operas. Feingold has held literary posts at the Yale Repertory Theatre, the Guthrie Theater and the American Repertory Theatre. He has been an O'Neill Conference playwright and is a "Usual Suspect" at New York Theatre Workshop. He is best known as the chief theater critic for *The Village Voice*, for which he received the George Jean Nathan Award. In 2001, he was named a senior fellow of the National Arts Journalism Program. He has taught dramatic literature, criticism and dramaturgy at Columbia, NYU and the O'Neill Critics Institute.

Paul Hardt of Stuart Howard Associates works in casting for theatre, television and film. His casting credits include the national tours of *The Who's Tommy*, *Leader of the Pack* and *Game Show*. Stuart Howard Associates cast *I Love You, You're Perfect, Now Change*, *On Golden Pond* starring James Earl Jones and Leslie Uggams, and the upcoming revival of *The Pajama Game* starring Harry Connick Jr.

Robert Hurwitt is the theater critic for the *San Francisco Chronicle*. He was the theater critic and arts editor for the *East Bay Express* from 1979 until 1992, when he became chief theater critic for the *San Francisco Examiner*, moving to the *Chronicle* in 2000. He was editor of the new-play anthology series *West Coast Plays*, volumes 15–22, and has been awarded the George Jean Nathan Award for Dramatic Criticism.

John Istel has edited and contributed to a variety of performing arts, general interest and reference publications over the last 20 years including *American Theatre*, *The Atlantic*, *Back Stage*, *Contemporary Playwrights*, *Elle*, *Mother Jones*, *Newsday*, *New York*, *Stagebill* and *The Village Voice*. He has taught at New York University, Medgar Evers College and currently teaches English at Manhattan Theatre Lab High School in Harlem, a New Visions school, which he helped create in partnership with Roundabout Theatre Company.

Jeffrey Eric Jenkins began editing *The Best Plays Theater Yearbook* series in 2001. Before joining *Best Plays* he served as theater critic, contributor and editor for a wide variety of publications. Since 1998, he has taught in the Department of Drama at New York University's Tisch School of the Arts. Jenkins has also taught at Carnegie Mellon University, the University of Washington, and SUNY–Stony Brook. He received degrees in drama and theater arts from Carnegie Mellon University and San Francisco State University, and he has directed more than two dozen productions in professional and educational theaters across the United States. Jenkins is a former chairman of the American Theatre Critics Association. He now serves on the American Theatre Wing's board of directors, for which he chairs the Henry Hewes Design Awards and the Wing's Grants and Scholarships Committee. He also serves on the executive committee of the Theater Hall of Fame.

Vivian Cary Jenkins spent more than twenty years as a healthcare executive and teacher before focusing on editorial work for *The Best Plays Theater Yearbook* series. Prior to her career in healthcare, she was a dancer and a Peace Corps volunteer in Honduras.

Chris Jones is a theater critic and columnist on the staff of the *Chicago Tribune*. For the past 20 years, he has covered Midwestern theater and pre-Broadway tryouts for *Variety*. His writing also has appeared in *American Theatre*, *The New York Times* and *The Los Angeles Times*, among many other publications.

Robert Kamp is the owner of I Can Do That Productions, Inc., a graphic design company in New York City. Prior to starting his own business, Kamp worked for several arts and entertainment publications including *Stagebill* and *City Guide Magazine*. Kamp designed the *Best Plays* logo, and has worked on the book's photos and graphic images since the 2000–2001 edition.

Elizabeth Maupin has been theater critic for *The Orlando Sentinel* since 1983. She graduated from Wellesley College in 1973 and received a master's in journalism at the University of California, Berkeley, in 1976. Maupin chaired the executive committee of the American Theatre Critics Association from 1996 to 1999 and is serving her third term on ATCA's executive committee. She also chairs the association's awards program for new plays. Maupin was a fellow at Columbia's National Arts Journalism Program in 1995–96 and was an O'Neill Critics Institute fellow at the Eugene O'Neill Theater Center in 1986. She is married to Jay Yellen, a professor of mathematics at Rollins College.

Jeremy McCarter is the chief theater critic of *New York* magazine. He previously served as chief theater critic of *The New York Sun*, and is a contributing editor of *The New Republic*. His writing has also appeared in *The New York Times*, *The Los Angeles Times*, *The Guardian* (UK), and other publications. In the theater, he has worked as an adapter, director, and dramaturg. He studied history at Harvard and lives in Brooklyn.

Christopher Rawson is drama critic and drama editor of the *Pittsburgh Post-Gazette*. Along with local reviews, features, news and columns, he also reviews regularly in New York, London and Canada. His love of theater is partly inherited from his father, actor Richard Hart, but he started professional life teaching English literature at the University of Pittsburgh, where he still teaches Shakespeare and critical writing. His BA is from Harvard and his PhD from the University of Washington. A former chairman of the American Theatre Critics Association, he is a member of the executive committee of the Theater Hall of Fame, managing the selection process with Henry Hewes.

David Savran is a specialist in 20th century American theater, popular culture, and social theory. He has written seven books, including *Breaking the Rules: The Wooster Group*; *Communists, Cowboys, and Queers*; and most recently, *A Queer Sort of Materialism: Recontextualizing American Theatre*. He has published two books of interviews with playwrights, *In Their Own Words* and *The Playwright's Voice*, and has served as a judge for the Obie Awards and the Lucille Lortel Awards. He is Vera Mowry Roberts Distinguished Professor of Theatre at the Graduate Center of the City University of New York.

Michele Volansky is Assistant Professor of Drama at Washington College. She has been dramaturg at Philadelphia Theatre Company, Steppenwolf Theatre Company and Actors Theatre of Louisville. Volansky has served as guest dramaturg for the Arden Theatre, South Coast Repertory, Atlantic Theater Company, Victory Gardens Theater, Next Theatre and others. She is the inaugural co-recipient of the Elliot Hayes Award for Dramaturgy and has worked on more than 100 new and established plays. Volansky is preparing a book on playwriting and collaboration with playwright Bruce Graham. She holds an MA in theater from Villanova University.

Robert Vorlicky is Associate Professor of Drama, Tisch School of the Arts, New York University. He is also Affiliate Faculty in the Department of English and the Center for Study of Gender and Sexuality at NYU. Vorlicky's books include *Act Like a Man: Challenging Masculinities in American Drama, Tony Kushner in Conversation, From Inner Worlds to Outer Space: The Multimedia Performances of Dan Kwong*. Past President of the American Theatre and Drama Society, Vorlicky is also co-editor with Una Chaudhuri of the Critical Performances series for the University of Michigan Press, an editorial board member of several journals, the author of numerous articles, anthologized essays, book and performance reviews, and he speaks both nationally and internationally on US drama and performance.

Charles Wright has been a contributor to five editions of *Best Plays Theater Yearbook*. A native of Tennessee and long-time resident of New York City, he holds degrees from Vanderbilt, Oxford, and the University of Pennsylvania. As a business affairs executive at A&E Television Networks for the past 11 years, Wright has been involved in hundreds of hours of nonfiction programming, including *The Farm: Angola, USA*, which received the 1998 Grand Jury Prize at Sundance and was nominated for an Academy Award as Best Documentary Feature the following year, such prime time series as *Intervention* and *Rollergirls*, and a new motion picture production initiative known as A&E IndieFilms.

Index

Play titles appear in bold. Asterisks (*) mark titles shortened for the index.
Page numbers in italic indicate essay citations.
Page numbers in bold italic indicate Broadway and Off Broadway listings.
Nouns or numbers in parentheses delineate different entities with similar names.